Ordnance Survey

STREET ATLAS Warwickshire

Contents

III *Key to map symbols*

IV-V *Key to map pages*

VI-VII *Route planning*

VIII *Administrative and post code boundaries*

1 *Street maps*

151 *Extra-large-scale map of Coventry town centre*

152 *Town maps of Banbury and Tamworth*

153 *Index of hospitals, industrial estates, railway stations, schools, shopping centres, street names and universities*

PHILIP'S

First edition published 1992
First colour edition published 1998 by

Ordnance Survey® and George Philip Ltd
Romsey Road
Maybush
Southampton
SO16 4GU

George Philip Ltd
a division of Octopus Publishing Group Ltd
Michelin House, 81 Fulham Road,
London SW3 6RB

ISBN 0-540-07560 4 (hardback)
ISBN 0-540-07561 2 (spiral)

To the best of the Publishers' knowledge, the information in this atlas was correct at the time of going to press. No responsibility can be accepted for any errors or their consequences.

The representation in this atlas of a road, track or path is no evidence of the existence of a right of way.

The mapping between pages 1 and 152 (inclusive) in this atlas is derived from Ordnance Survey® Large Scale and Landranger® mapping, and revised using OSCAR® and Land-Line® data.

Ordnance Survey, OSCAR, Land-line and Landranger are registered trade marks of Ordnance Survey, the national mapping agency of Great Britain.

Printed and bound in Spain by Cayfosa

Key to map symbols

22a **Motorway** (with junction number)

Primary route (dual carriageway and single)

A road (dual carriageway and single)

B road (dual carriageway and single)

Minor road (dual carriageway and single)

Other minor road

Road under construction

Pedestrianised area

DY7 **Post code boundaries**

County and Unitary Authority boundaries

Railway

Tramway, miniature railway

Rural track, private road or narrow road in urban area

Gate or obstruction to traffic (restrictions may not apply at all times or to all vehicles)

Path, bridleway, byway open to all traffic, road used as a public path

The representation in this atlas of a road, track or path is no evidence of the existence of a right of way

105 85 **Adjoining page indicators** (The colour of the arrow indicates the scale of the adjoining page – see scales below)

143 152 **The map areas within the pink/blue bands are shown at a larger scale on the page, indicated by the red/blue blocks and arrows**

Walsall **British Rail station**

Midland Metro

Metrolink station

Underground station

Docklands Light Railway station

Tyne and Wear Metro

Private railway station

Bus, coach station

Ambulance station

Coastguard station

Fire station

Police station

Accident and Emergency entrance to hospital

Hospital

Church, place of worship

Information centre (open all year)

P P&R **Parking, Park and Ride**

PO PO **Post Office**

Prim Sch **Important buildings, schools, colleges, universities and hospitals**

River Medway **Water name**

Stream

River or canal (minor and major)

Water

Tidal water

Woods

Houses

House **Non-Roman antiquity**

VILLA **Roman antiquity**

Acad	**Academy**	Ct	**Law Court**	PH	**Public House**
Crem	**Crematorium**	L Ctr	**Leisure Centre**	Recn Gd	**Recreation Ground**
Cemy	**Cemetery**	LC	**Level Crossing**	Resr	**Reservoir**
C Ctr	**Civic Centre**	Liby	**Library**	Ret Pk	**Retail Park**
CH	**Club House**	Mkt	**Market**	Sch	**School**
Coll	**College**	Meml	**Memorial**	Sh Ctr	**Shopping Centre**
Ent	**Enterprise**	Mon	**Monument**	TH	**Town Hall/House**
Ex H	**Exhibition Hall**	Mus	**Museum**	Trad Est	**Trading Estate**
Ind Est	**Industrial Estate**	Obsy	**Observatory**	Univ	**University**
Inst	**Institute**	Pal	**Royal Palace**	YH	**Youth Hostel**

■ The dark grey border on the inside edge of some pages indicates that the mapping does not continue onto the adjacent page

■ The small numbers around the edges of the maps identify the 1 kilometre National Grid lines

The scale of the maps is 5.52 cm to 1 km (3½ inches to 1 mile)

0 ¼ ½ ¾ 1 mile
0 250 m 500 m 750 m 1 kilometre

The scale of the maps on pages numbered in red is 11.04 cm to 1 km (7 inches to 1 mile)

0 220 yards 440 yards 660 yards ½ mile
0 125m 250m 375m ½ kilometre

The scale of the maps on pages numbered in green is 2.76 cm to 1 km (1¾ inches to 1 mile)

0 ¼ ½ ¾ 1 mile
0 250m 500m 750m 1 kilometre

Key to map pages

Page Scale

151 This page is at 7 inches to the mile

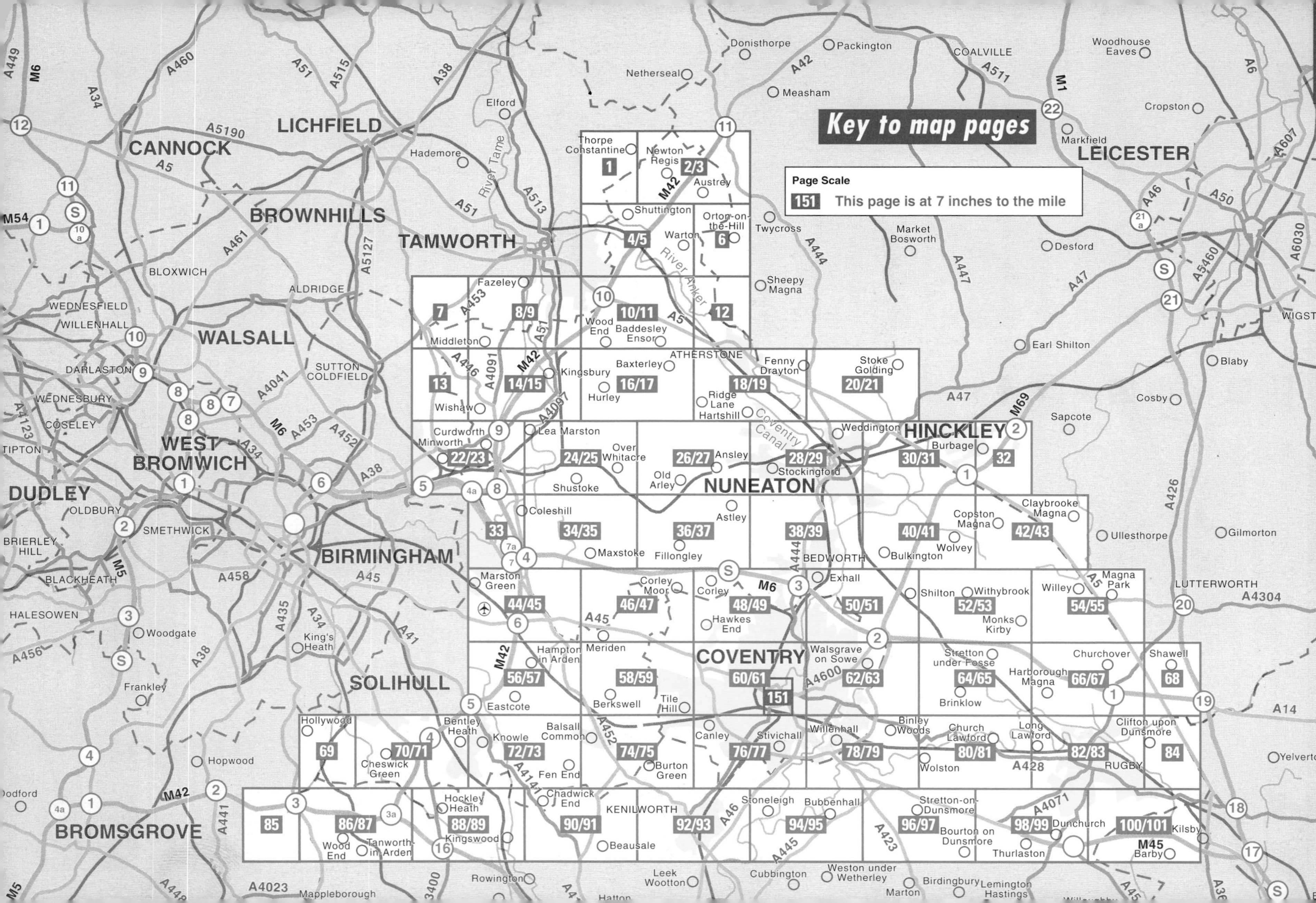

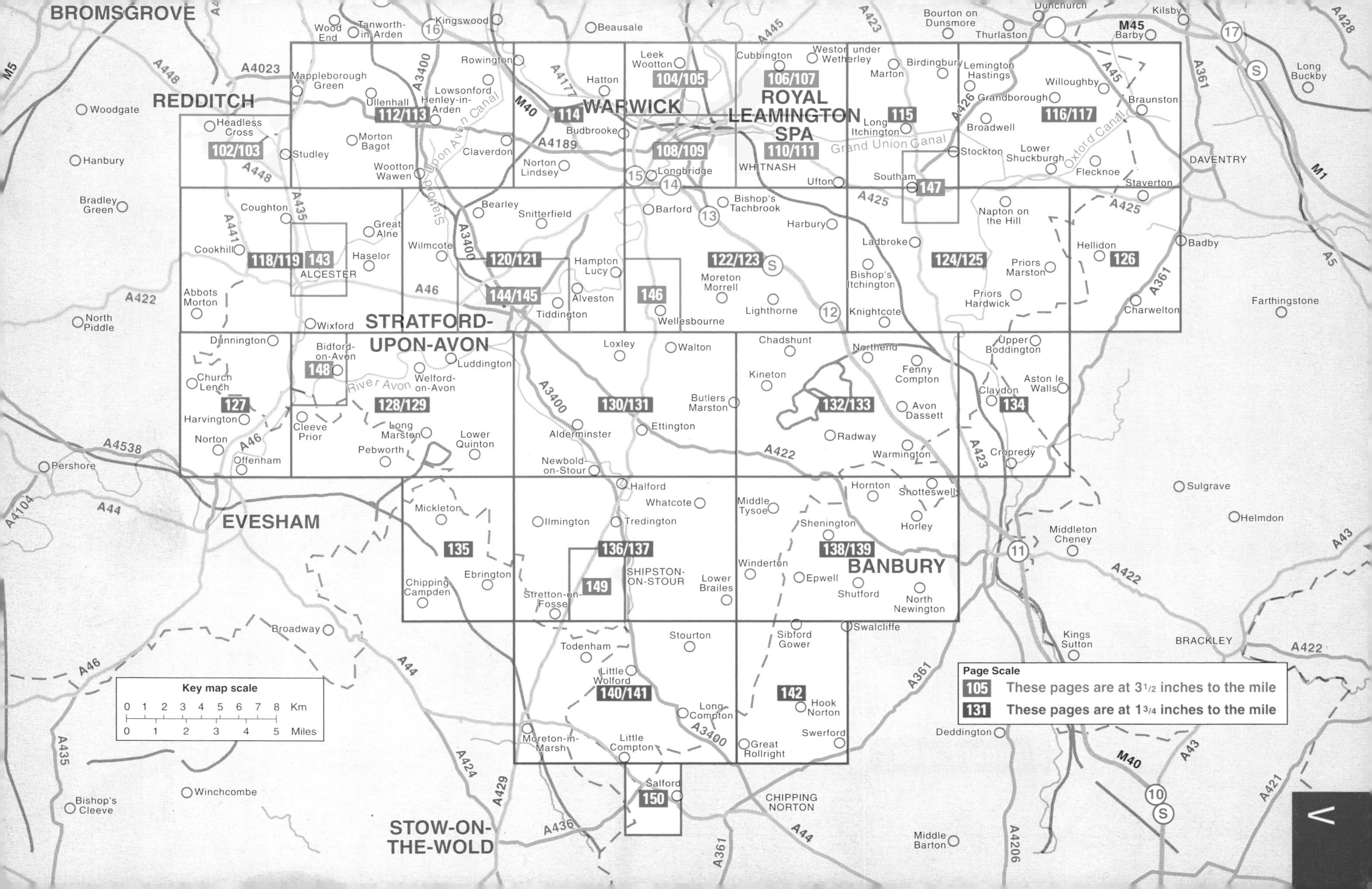
Page Scale
105 These pages are at 3 1/2 inches to the mile
131 These pages are at 1 3/4 inches to the mile
Key map scale
0 1 2 3 4 5 6 7 8 Km
0 1 2 3 4 5 Miles
BROMSGROVE
REDDITCH
WARWICK
ROYAL LEAMINGTON SPA
STRATFORD-UPON-AVON
EVESHAM
BANBURY
STOW-ON-THE-WOLD
DAVENTRY
BRACKLEY
CHIPPING NORTON
ALCESTER
WHITNASH
SHIPSTON-ON-STOUR
102/103
104/105
106/107
108/109
110/111
112/113
114
115
116/117
118/119
120/121
122/123
124/125
126
127
128/129
130/131
132/133
134
135
136/137
138/139
140/141
142
143
144/145
146
147
148
149
150
M1
M5
M40
M45
A5
A44
A45
A46
A361
A422
A423
A424
A425
A426
A428
A429
A435
A436
A441
A445
A448
A3400
A4023
A4104
A4177
A4189
A4206
A4421
A4538
Grand Union Canal
Oxford Canal
Stratford Upon Avon Canal
River Avon
Woodgate
Hanbury
Bradley Green
North Piddle
Pershore
Bishop's Cleeve
Winchcombe
Broadway
Headless Cross
Studley
Mappleborough Green
Wood End
Tanworth-in-Arden
Kingswood
Ullenhall
Morton Bagot
Henley-in-Arden
Lowsonford
Rowington
Wootton Wawen
Claverdon
Hatton
Budbrooke
Norton Lindsey
Beausale
Leek Wootton
Cubbington
Weston under Wetherley
Marton
Birdingbury
Long Itchington
Ufton
Longbridge
Bourton on Dunsmore
Thurlaston
Dunchurch
Barby
Kilsby
Long Buckby
Lemington Hastings
Grandborough
Willoughby
Braunston
Broadwell
Stockton
Lower Shuckburgh
Flecknoe
Southam
Staverton
Coughton
Cookhill
Abbots Morton
Great Alne
Haselor
Wixford
Wilmcote
Bearley
Snitterfield
Hampton Lucy
Alveston
Tiddington
Barford
Bishop's Tachbrook
Harbury
Moreton Morrell
Lighthorne
Wellesbourne
Ladbroke
Bishop's Itchington
Knightcote
Napton on the Hill
Priors Marston
Priors Hardwick
Hellidon
Badby
Charwelton
Farthingstone
Dunnington
Church Lench
Harvington
Norton
Offenham
Bidford-on-Avon
Cleeve Prior
Welford-on-Avon
Luddington
Long Marston
Pebworth
Lower Quinton
Loxley
Walton
Butlers Marston
Ettington
Alderminster
Newbold-on-Stour
Chadshunt
Kineton
Northend
Fenny Compton
Avon Dassett
Radway
Warmington
Upper Boddington
Aston le Walls
Claydon
Cropredy
Mickleton
Ebrington
Chipping Campden
Ilmington
Halford
Whatcote
Tredington
Stretton-on-Fosse
Lower Brailes
Middle Tysoe
Shenington
Winderton
Epwell
Shutford
Hornton
Shotteswell
Horley
North Newington
Middleton Cheney
Sulgrave
Helmdon
Kings Sutton
Swalcliffe
Todenham
Stourton
Little Wolford
Long Compton
Moreton-in-Marsh
Little Compton
Salford
Sibford Gower
Hook Norton
Swerford
Great Rollright
Deddington
Middle Barton
10
11
12
13
14
15
16
17
S

Route planning
CANNOCK
LICHFIELD
BROWNHILLS
TAMWORTH
BLOXWICH
ALDRIDGE
WALSALL
WILLENHALL
WEDNESFIELD
BILSTON
DARLASTON
WEDNESBURY
COSELEY
SUTTON COLDFIELD
WEST BROMWICH
OLDBURY
SMETHWICK
BLACKHEATH
BIRMINGHAM
SOLIHULL
BROMSGROVE
REDDITCH
ATHERSTONE
HINCKLEY
NUNEATON
BEDWORTH
COVENTRY
LUTTERWORTH
LEICESTER
WIGSTON

Route map scale
0 1 2 3 4 5 6 7 8 Km
0 1 2 3 4 5 Miles
DAVENTRY
BANBURY
BRACKLEY
BICESTER
ROYAL LEAMINGTON SPA
WARWICK
STRATFORD-UPON-AVON
CHIPPING NORTON
STOW-ON-THE-WOLD
EVESHAM
REDDITCH
CHELTENHAM
Chipping Campden
Moreton-in-Marsh
Winchcombe
Southam
Alcester
Pershore
Broadway
Henley-in-Arden
M40
M1
A46
A44
A429
A422
A423
A425
A435
A43
VALE OF EVESHAM
EDGE HILL

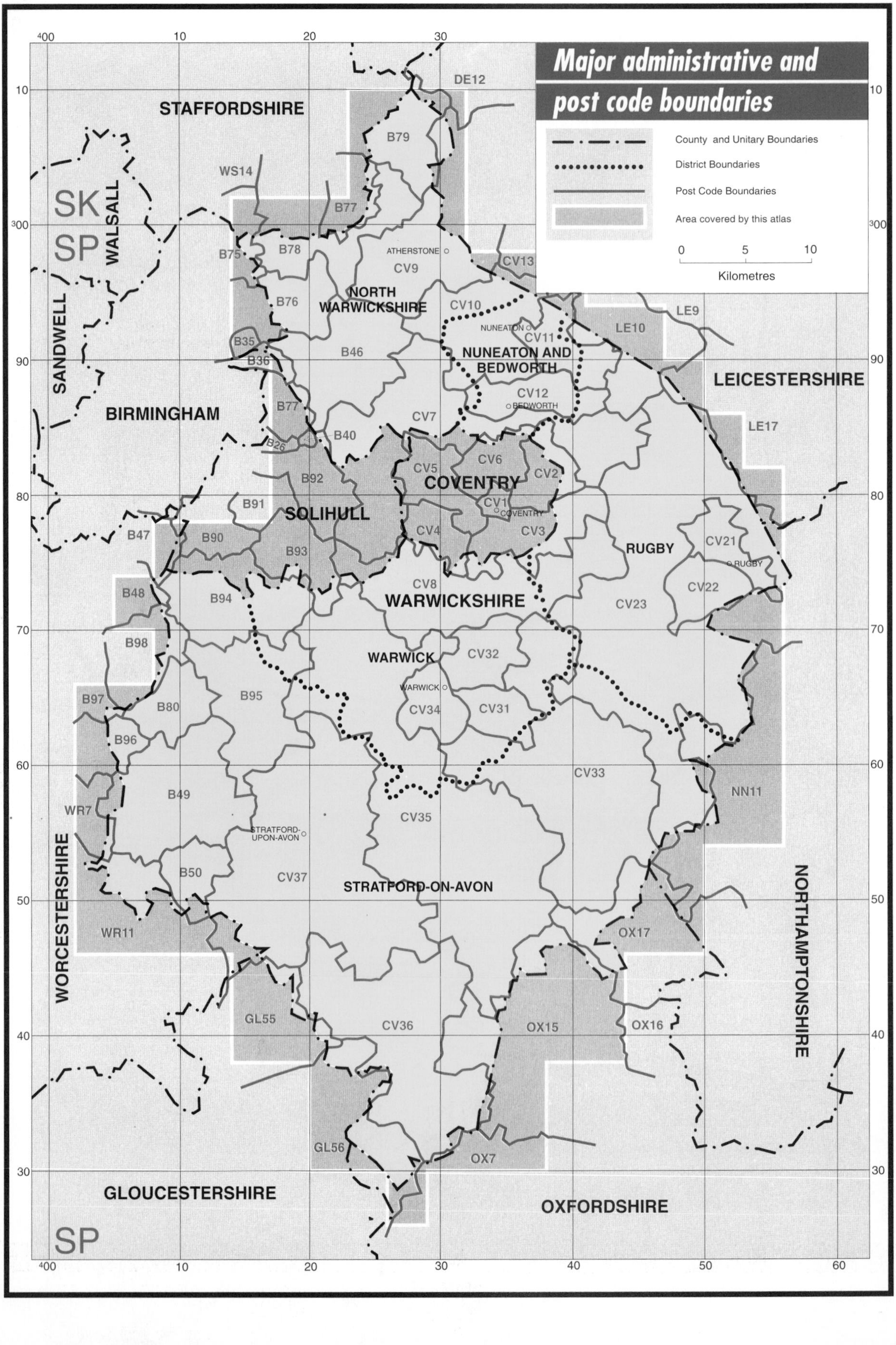
Major administrative and post code boundaries
County and Unitary Boundaries
District Boundaries
Post Code Boundaries
Area covered by this atlas
0 5 10
Kilometres
STAFFORDSHIRE
WALSALL
SANDWELL
BIRMINGHAM
SK
SP
NORTH WARWICKSHIRE
NUNEATON AND BEDWORTH
COVENTRY
SOLIHULL
WARWICKSHIRE
WARWICK
RUGBY
LEICESTERSHIRE
STRATFORD-ON-AVON
WORCESTERSHIRE
NORTHAMPTONSHIRE
GLOUCESTERSHIRE
OXFORDSHIRE
ATHERSTONE
NUNEATON
BEDWORTH
WARWICK
STRATFORD-UPON-AVON
DE12
B79
WS14
B77
B78
B75
B76
CV9
CV13
CV10
CV11
LE10
LE9
B35
B36
B46
CV12
LE17
B26
B40
CV7
CV6
CV5
CV2
B92
B91
CV1
CV3
CV4
B47
B90
B93
CV21
CV22
CV8
B48
B94
CV23
B98
CV32
B97
B80
B95
CV34
CV31
B96
CV33
NN11
B49
WR7
CV35
B50
CV37
WR11
OX17
GL55
CV36
OX15
OX16
GL56
OX7
SP
400
10
20
30
40
50
60
300

2

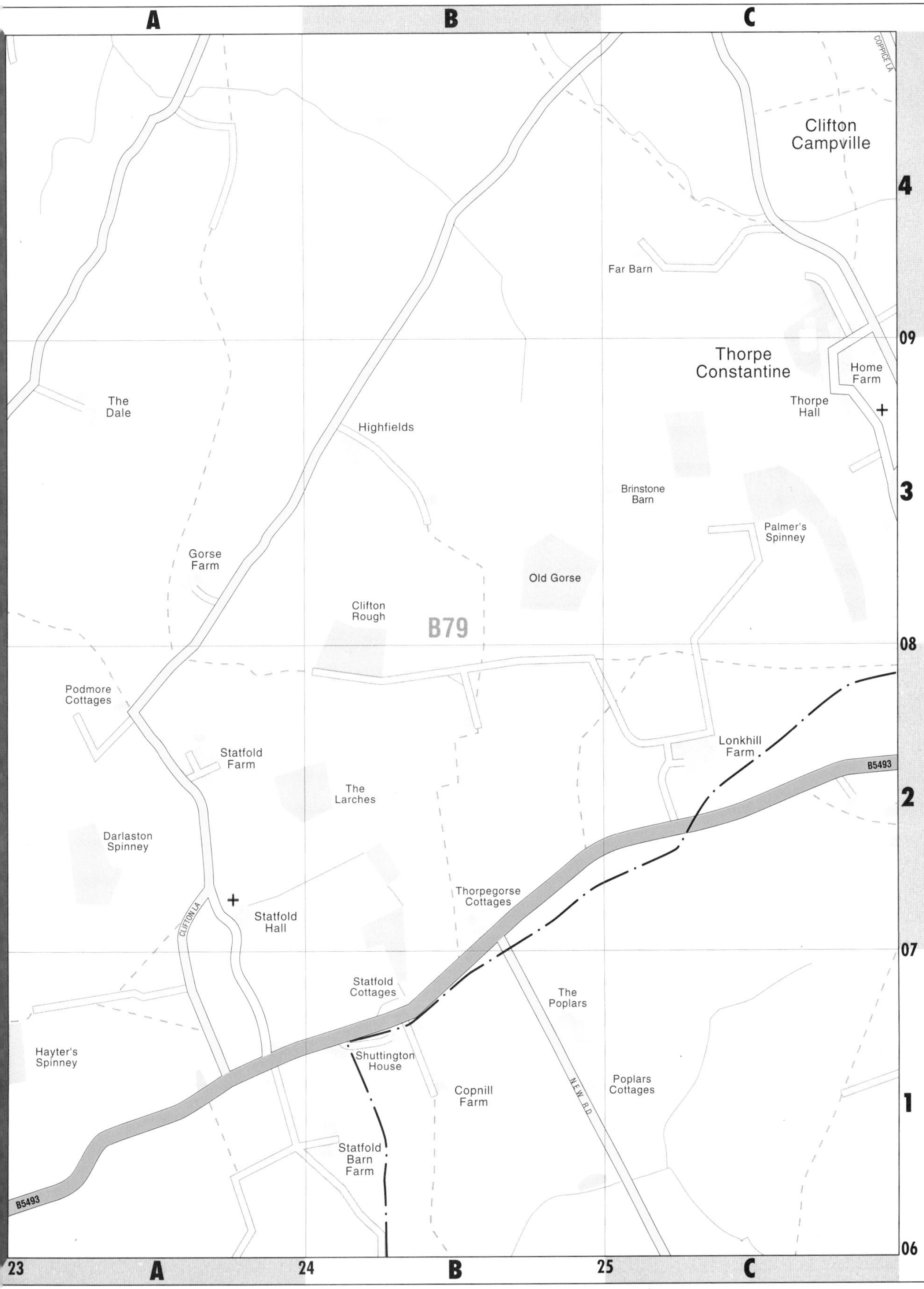
A
B
C
COPPICE LA
Clifton Campville
4
Far Barn
09
Thorpe Constantine
Home Farm
Thorpe Hall
The Dale
Highfields
3
Brinstone Barn
Palmer's Spinney
Gorse Farm
Old Gorse
Clifton Rough
B79
08
Podmore Cottages
Lonkhill Farm
Statfold Farm
B5493
The Larches
2
Darlaston Spinney
Thorpegorse Cottages
CLIFTON LA
Statfold Hall
07
Statfold Cottages
The Poplars
Hayter's Spinney
Shuttington House
Copnill Farm
Poplars Cottages
NEW RD
1
Statfold Barn Farm
B5493
06
23
A
24
B
25
C

4
2

1

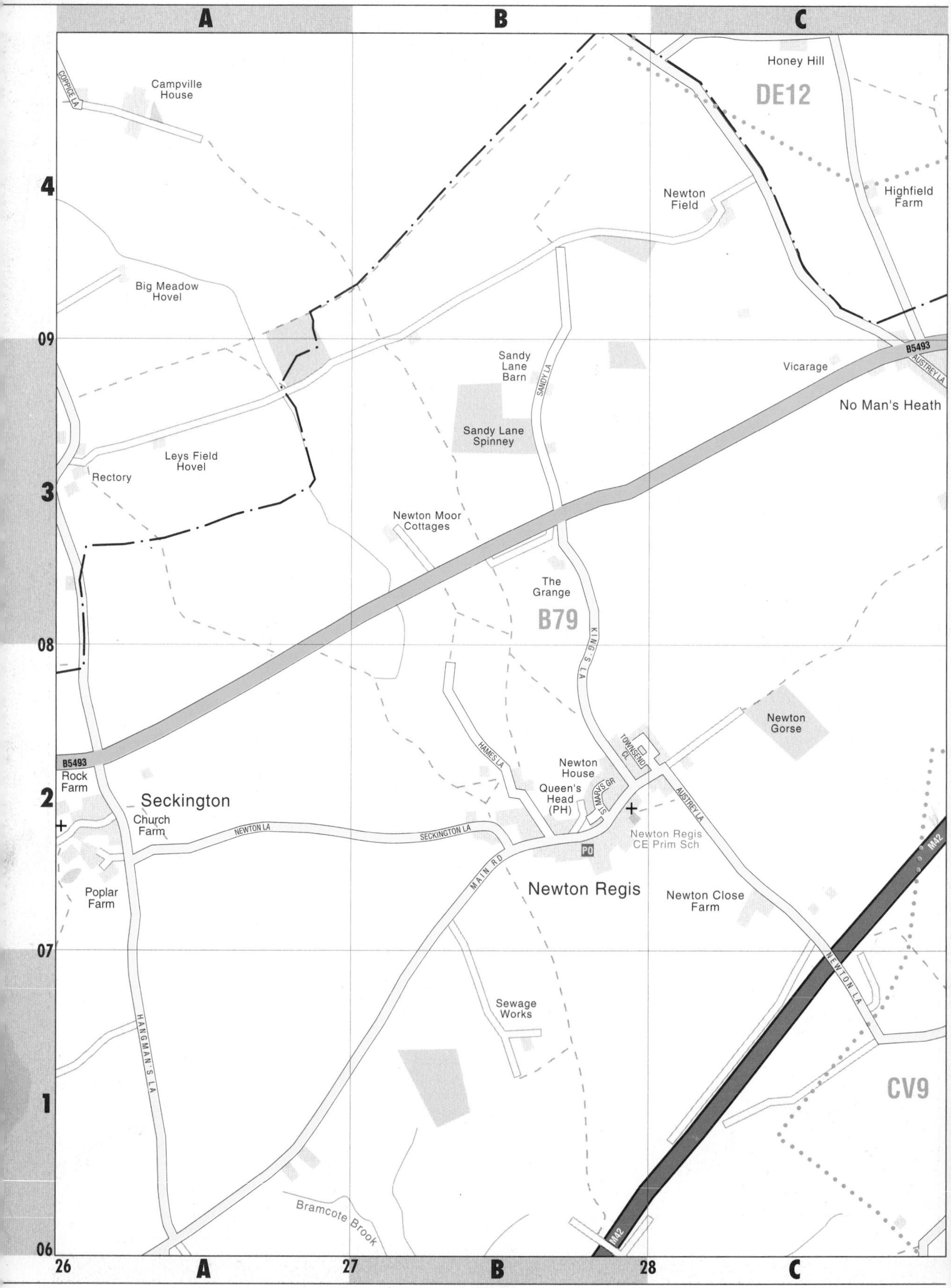
A
B
C
Campville House
COPPICE LA
Honey Hill
DE12
Newton Field
Highfield Farm
Big Meadow Hovel
Sandy Lane Barn
SANDY LA
B5493
AUSTREY LA
Vicarage
No Man's Heath
Sandy Lane Spinney
Leys Field Hovel
Rectory
Newton Moor Cottages
The Grange
B79
KING'S LA
Newton Gorse
TOWNSEND CL
HAMES LA
Newton House
Queen's Head (PH)
ST MARYS GR
AUSTREY LA
B5493
Rock Farm
Seckington
Church Farm
NEWTON LA
SECKINGTON LA
PO
Newton Regis CE Prim Sch
M42
MAIN RD
Newton Regis
Newton Close Farm
Poplar Farm
NEWTON LA
Sewage Works
HANGMAN'S LA
CV9
Bramcote Brook
M42
4
09
3
08
2
07
1
06
26
27
28

1
5

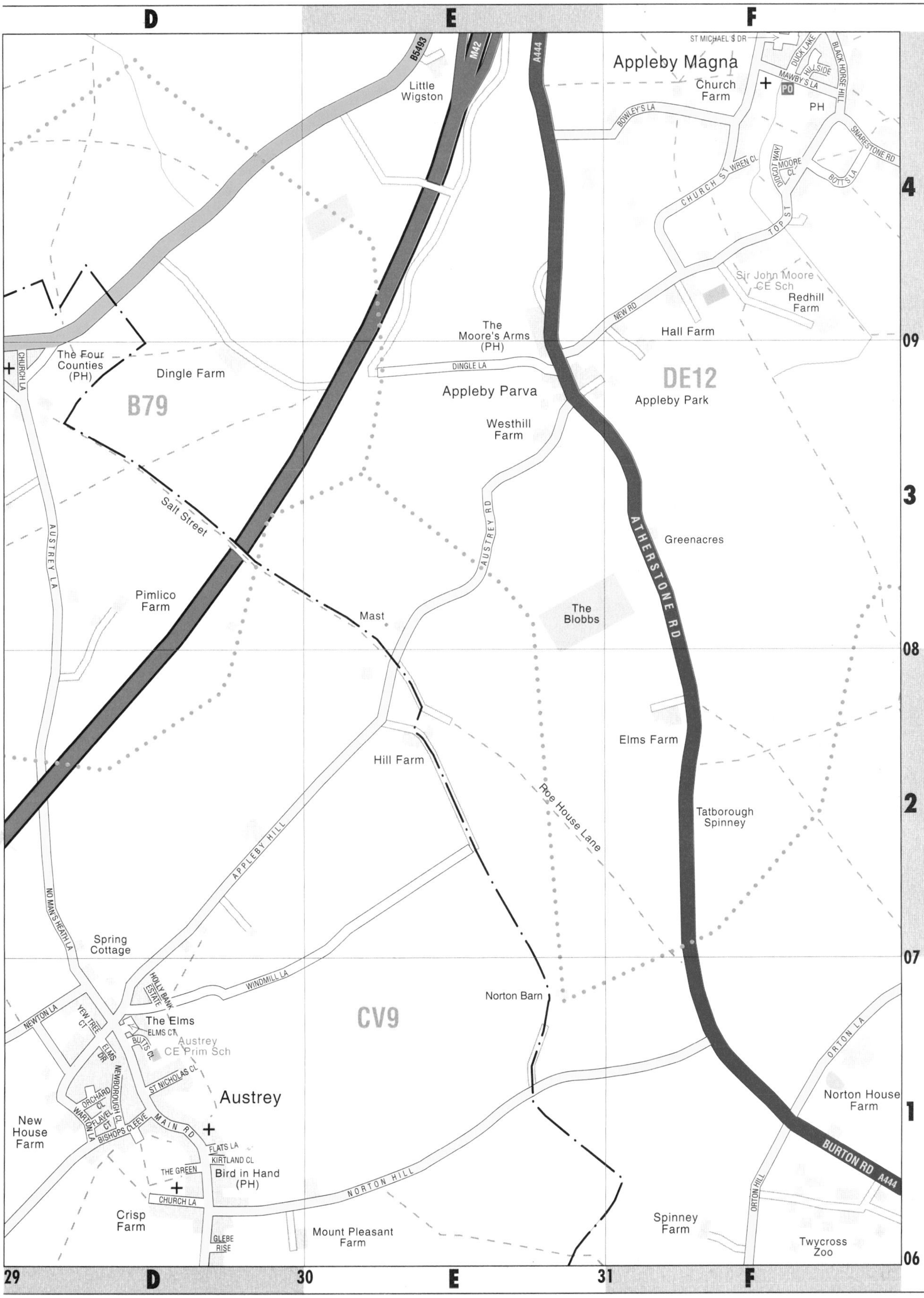
D
E
F
B5493
M42
A444
ST MICHAEL'S DR
Appleby Magna
Church Farm
DUCK LAKE
HILLSIDE
BLACK HORSE HILL
MAWBY'S LA
PO
PH
Little Wigston
BOWLEY'S LA
SNARESTONE RD
WREN CL
DIDCOT WAY
MOORE CL
BOTTS LA
CHURCH ST
TOP ST
Sir John Moore CE Sch
Redhill Farm
NEW RD
Hall Farm
The Moore's Arms (PH)
DINGLE LA
The Four Counties (PH)
CHURCH LA
Dingle Farm
B79
Appleby Parva
DE12
Appleby Park
Westhill Farm
Salt Street
AUSTREY LA
AUSTREY RD
ATHERSTONE RD
Greenacres
Pimlico Farm
Mast
The Blobbs
Elms Farm
Hill Farm
Roe House Lane
Tatborough Spinney
APPLEBY HILL
NO MAN'S HEATH LA
Spring Cottage
WINDMILL LA
HOLLY BANK ESTATE
Norton Barn
CV9
NEWTON LA
YEW TREE CT
The Elms
ELMS CT
BUTTS CL
Austrey CE Prim Sch
ELMS DR
NEWBOROUGH CL
ST NICHOLAS CL
ORCHARD CL
FLAVEL CT
WARTON LA
BISHOPS CLEEVE
MAIN RD
Austrey
ORTON LA
Norton House Farm
New House Farm
FLATS LA
KIRTLAND CL
THE GREEN
Bird in Hand (PH)
NORTON HILL
BURTON RD
A444
CHURCH LA
ORTON HILL
Crisp Farm
GLEBE RISE
Mount Pleasant Farm
Spinney Farm
Twycross Zoo
4
3
2
1
09
08
07
06
29
30
31

6

1

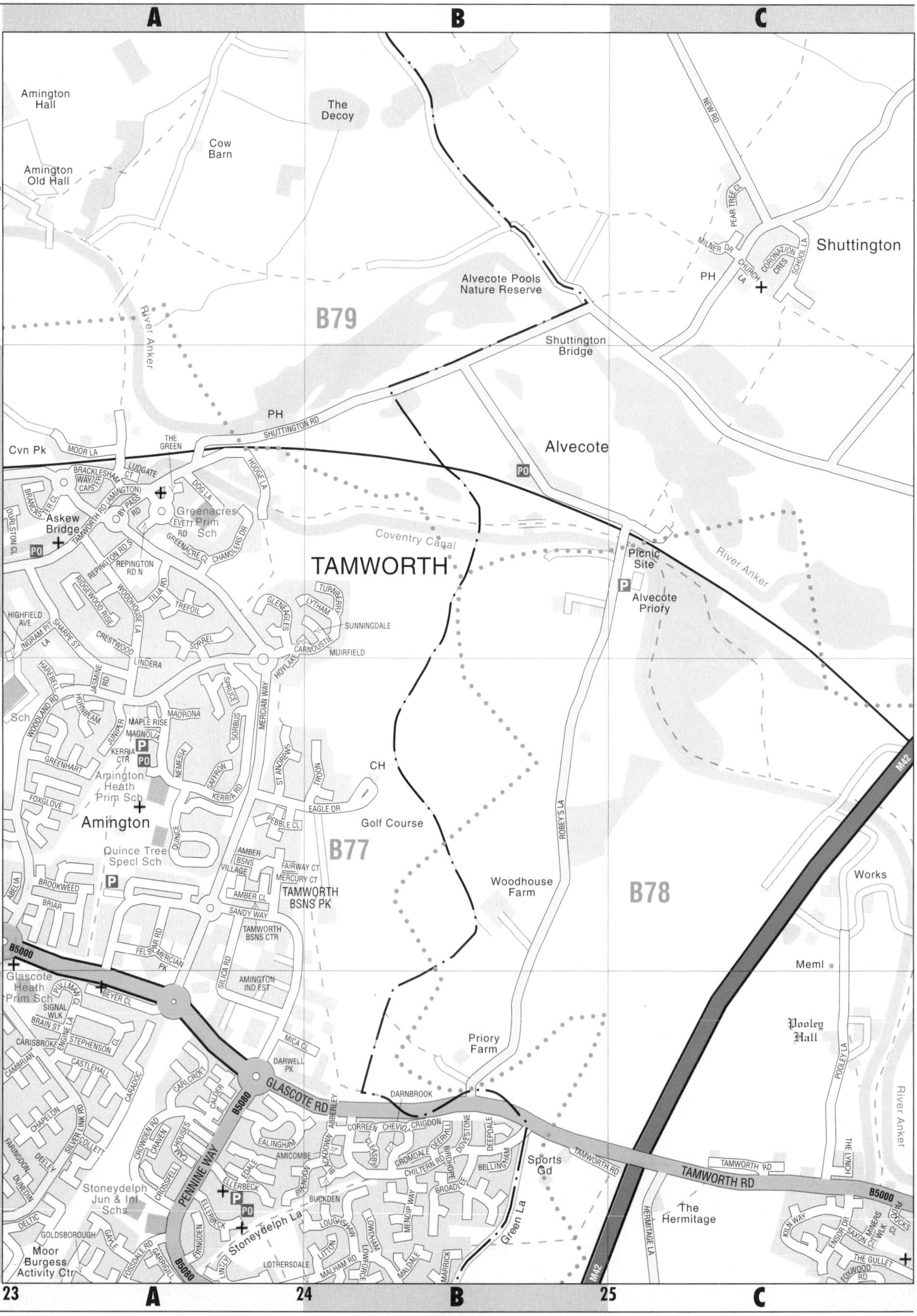
A
B
C
Amington Hall
The Decoy
Cow Barn
Amington Old Hall
Shuttington
Alvecote Pools Nature Reserve
B79
River Anker
Shuttington Bridge
PH
SHUTTINGTON RD
Cvn Pk
MOOR LA
THE GREEN
LUDGATE
Alvecote
PO
Askew Bridge
Greenacres Prim Sch
Coventry Canal
TAMWORTH
Picnic Site
Alvecote Priory
River Anker
SUNNINGDALE
MUIRFIELD
HOYLAKE
MERCIAN WAY
Sch
Amington Heath Prim Sch
Amington
CH
EAGLE DR
Golf Course
B77
Quince Tree Specl Sch
TAMWORTH BSNS PK
Woodhouse Farm
ROBEY'S LA
B78
M42
Works
B5000
Glascote Heath Prim Sch
Meml
Priory Farm
Pooley Hall
POOLEY LA
GLASCOTE RD
DARNBROOK
B5080
PENNINE WAY
Sports Gd
TAMWORTH RD
Stoneydelph Jun & Inf Schs
Stoneydelph La
Green La
The Hermitage
HERMITAGE LA
Moor Burgess Activity Ctr
THE GULLET
4
05
3
04
2
03
1
02
23
24
25

10

2
6

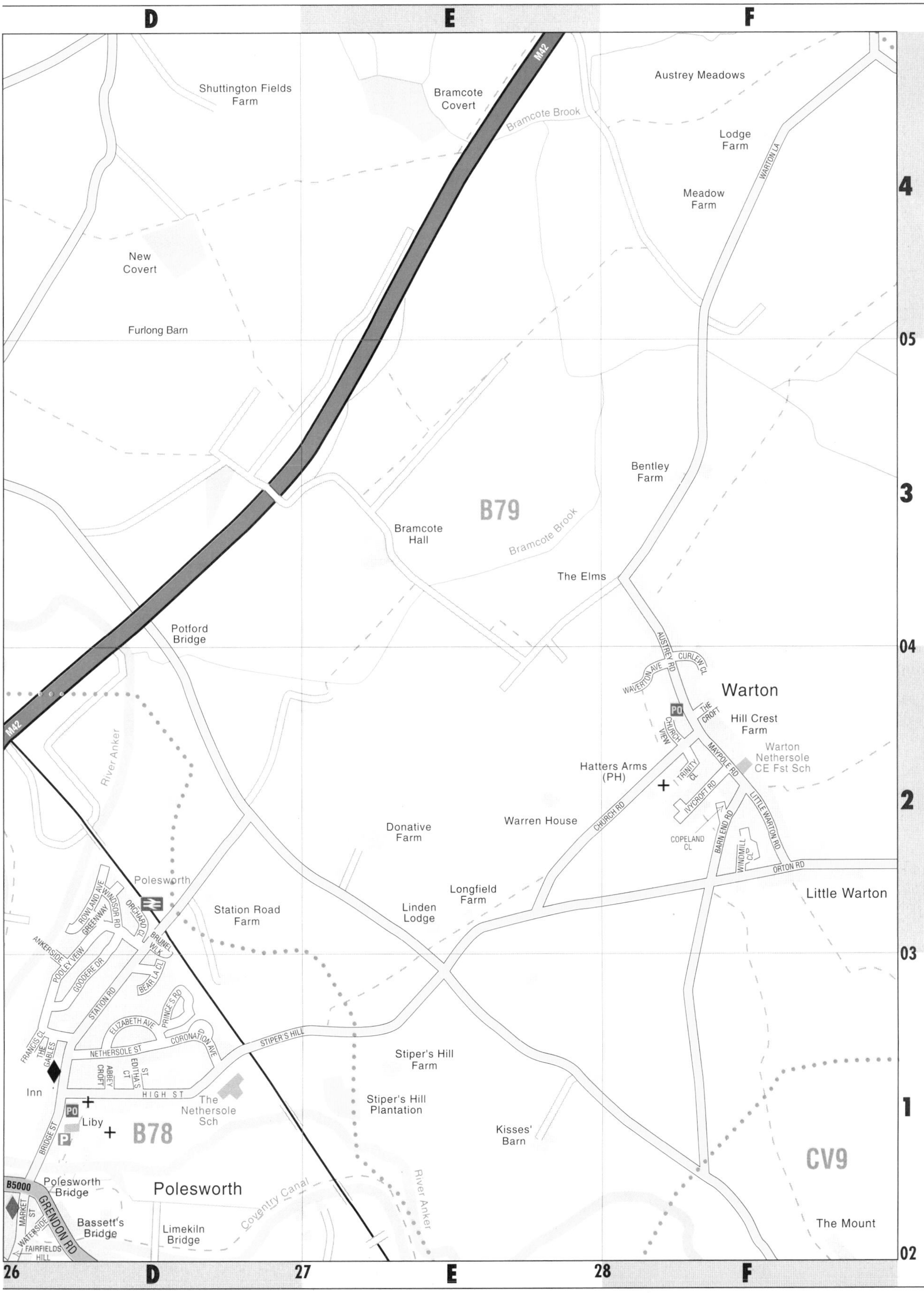
D
E
F
Shuttington Fields Farm
Bramcote Covert
Austrey Meadows
M42
Bramcote Brook
Lodge Farm
WARTON LA
Meadow Farm
4
New Covert
Furlong Barn
05
Bentley Farm
3
B79
Bramcote Hall
Bramcote Brook
The Elms
Potford Bridge
04
AUSTREY RD
CURLEW CL
WAVERTON AVE
Warton
PO
THE CROFT
CHURCH VIEW
Hill Crest Farm
Warton Nethersole CE Fst Sch
M42
River Anker
Hatters Arms (PH)
TRINITY CL
MAYPOLE RD
2
IVYCROFT RD
LITTLE WARTON RD
Warren House
CHURCH RD
Donative Farm
COPELAND CL
BARN END RD
WINDMILL CL
ORTON RD
Polesworth
Longfield Farm
Little Warton
ROWLAND AVE
WINDSOR RD
GREENWAY
ORCHARD CL
Station Road Farm
Linden Lodge
BRUNEL WLK
ANKERSIDE
POOLEY VIEW
GOODERE DR
BEAR LA CL
03
STATION RD
PRINCE'S RD
ELIZABETH AVE
CORONATION AVE
STIPER'S HILL
FRANCIS CL
THE GABLES
NETHERSOLE ST
Stiper's Hill Farm
ABBEY CROFT
EDITHA'S CT
ST
HIGH ST
Inn
The Nethersole Sch
Stiper's Hill Plantation
1
PO
Liby
B78
Kisses' Barn
BRIDGE ST
CV9
B5000
Polesworth Bridge
Polesworth
GRENDON RD
Coventry Canal
River Anker
MARKET ST
WATERSIDE
Bassett's Bridge
Limekiln Bridge
The Mount
FAIRFIELDS HILL
02
26
27
28

11
6

5
3

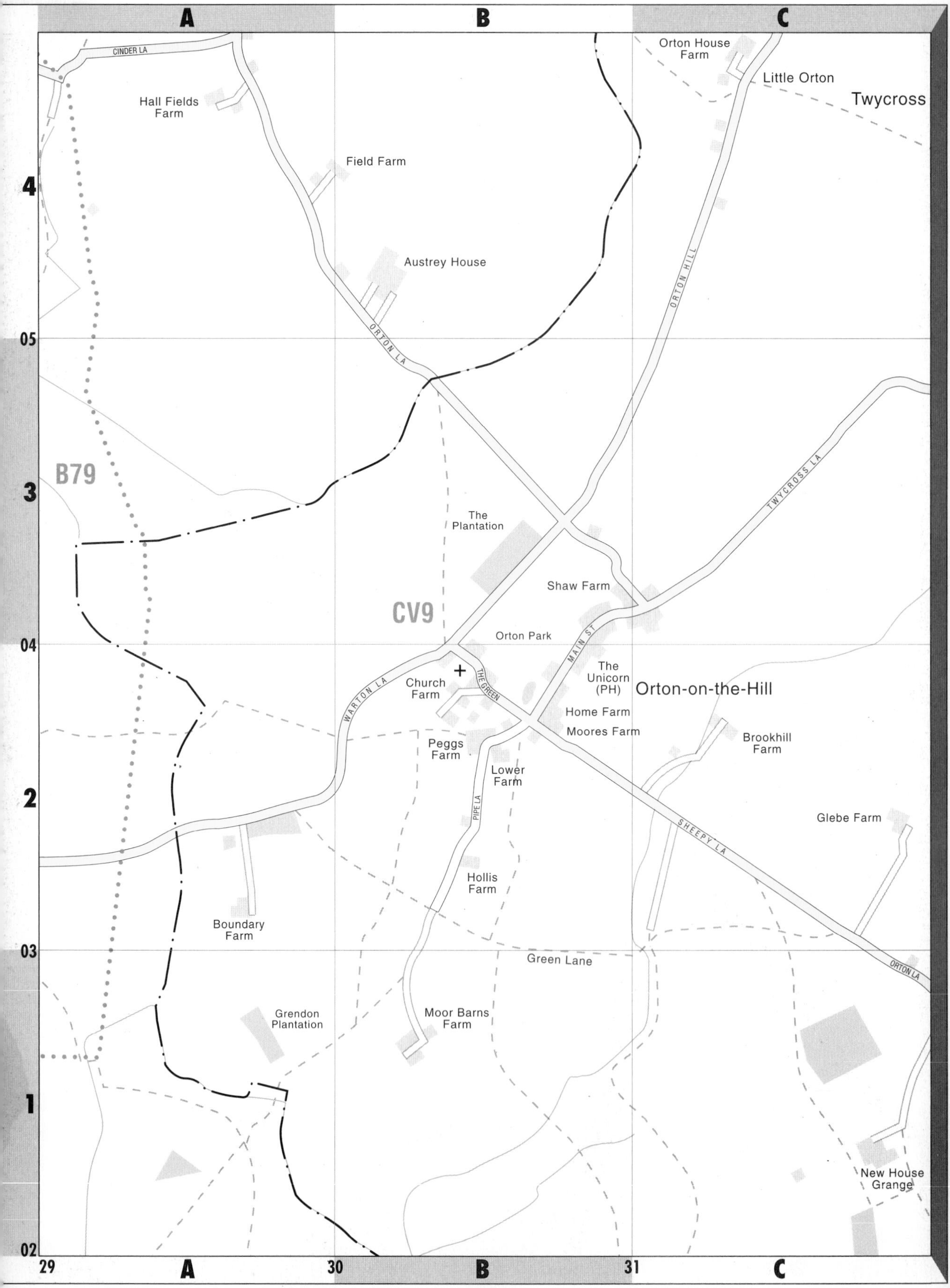
A
B
C
4
05
3
04
2
03
1
02
29
30
31
CINDER LA
Hall Fields Farm
Field Farm
Austrey House
ORTON LA
Orton House Farm
Little Orton
Twycross
ORTON HILL
B79
CV9
The Plantation
Shaw Farm
TWYCROSS LA
Orton Park
MAIN ST
The Unicorn (PH)
Orton-on-the-Hill
Church Farm
THE GREEN
WARTON LA
Home Farm
Moores Farm
Peggs Farm
Lower Farm
Brookhill Farm
PIPE LA
SHEEPY LA
Glebe Farm
Hollis Farm
Boundary Farm
Green Lane
ORTON LA
Grendon Plantation
Moor Barns Farm
New House Grange

5
12

D E F

Brockhurst Cottages

Weeford Park

Brock Hurst

Brockhurst Farm

Fordway Farm

Woodside Farm

Lower Bangley

4

Stockfields

WAGGONER'S LA

BROCKHURST LA

Hints Farm

Heart of England Way

01

Great Bangley Farm

A453

Brick Kiln Plantation

Three Parish Wood

Draytonlane End Farm

SUTTON RD

Canwell Hall

Bangley Hill

BANGLEY LA

DRAYTON LA

3

Home Farm

CANWELL DR

Nursery

CANWELL DR

Pithole Plantation

Meadow Farm

CRANEBROOK HILL

Shirral Coppice

Loddy Wood

00

CARROWAY HEAD HILL

A38

LONDON RD

B75

Carroway Head

Middle Park Plantation

Shirrall Hall

Heath Plantation

B4151

Carroway Head Farm

SHIRRALL DR

B78

2

Lamb Farm

SLADE RD

B4151

Shirrall Gorse

Trickley Coppice

Slade LA

Slade Farm

Collets Brook

A453

Bassett's Pole (PH)

A446

Trickley Coppice

99

FOX HILL RD

TAMWORTH RD

COLLETS BROOK

HILL LA

Trickley Coppice Farm

COPPICE LA

Collets Brook Farm

Woodlands

Parkwood House Farm

Fox Hill Farm

Sports Gd

Woodside Farm

TAMWORTH RD

Crem

A453

LONDON RD

Middleton Wood Farm

1

A38

A446

Woodlands Farm

98

14 D 15 E 16 F

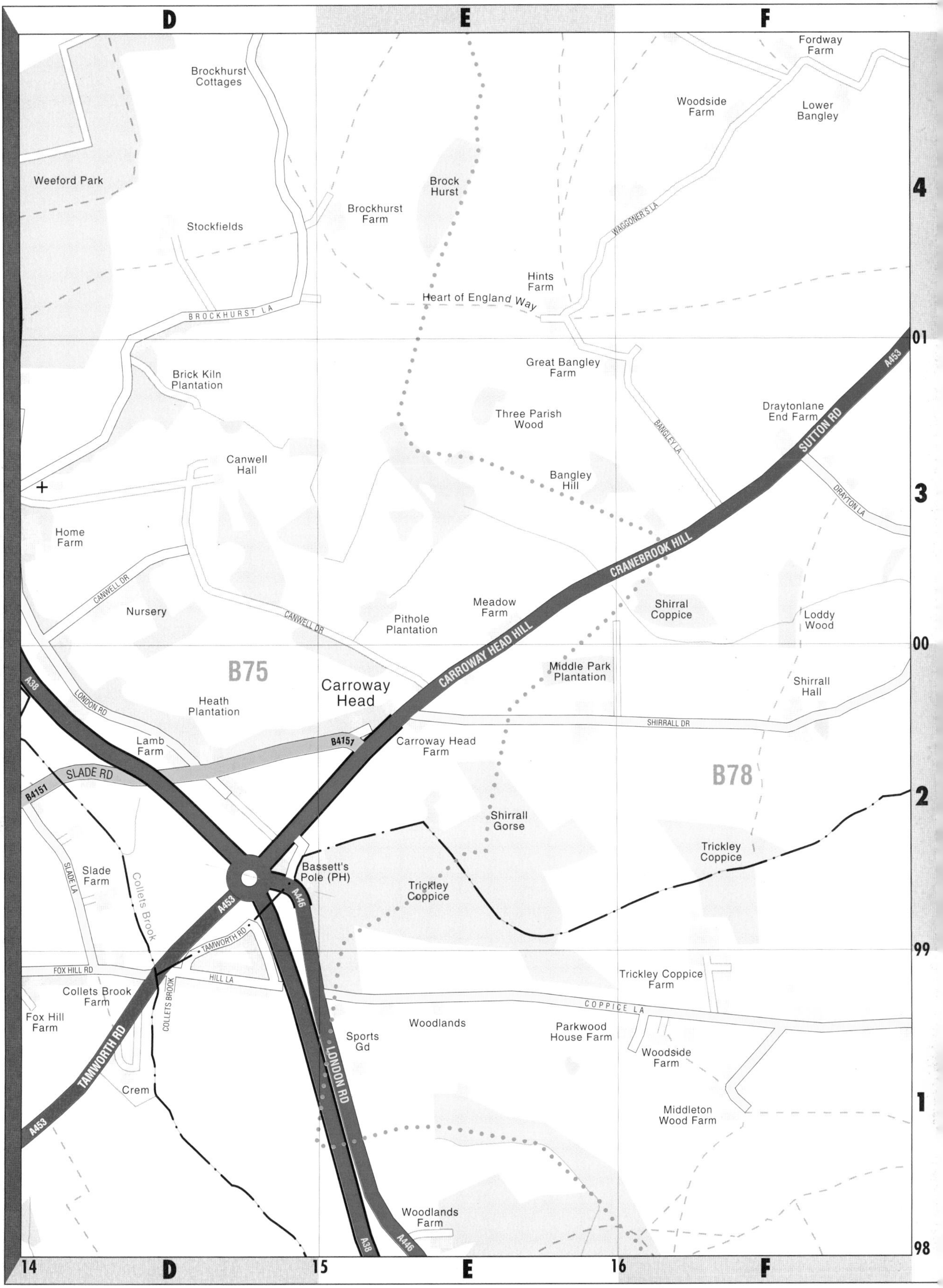

7

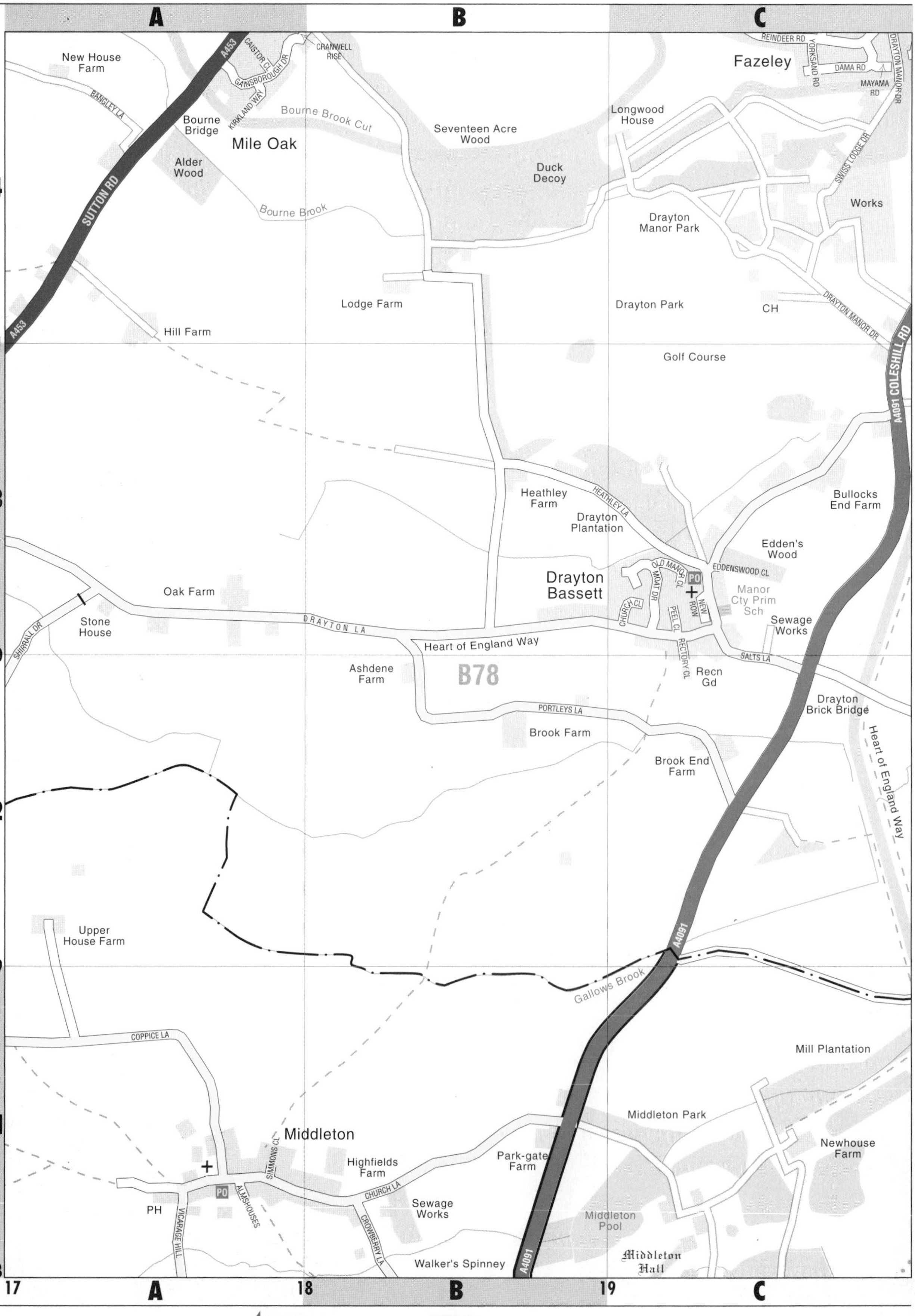
A
B
C
4
3
2
1
01
00
99
98
17
18
19
New House Farm
BANGLEY LA
A453
SUTTON RD
CAISTOR CL
GAINSBOROUGH DR
KIRKLAND WAY
CRANWELL RISE
Bourne Bridge
Mile Oak
Alder Wood
Bourne Brook Cut
Bourne Brook
Seventeen Acre Wood
Duck Decoy
Longwood House
Fazeley
REINDEER RD
YORKSAND RD
DAMA RD
MAYAMA RD
DRAYTON MANOR DR
SWISS LODGE DR
Works
Drayton Manor Park
Lodge Farm
Hill Farm
Drayton Park
CH
Golf Course
A4091 COLESHILL RD
Heathley Farm
HEATHLEY LA
Drayton Plantation
Bullocks End Farm
Edden's Wood
EDDENSWOOD CL
Drayton Bassett
OLD MANOR CL
MOAT DR
PO
CHURCH CL
PEEL CL
NEW ROW
Manor Cty Prim Sch
Sewage Works
Oak Farm
Stone House
SHIRRALL DR
DRAYTON LA
Heart of England Way
RECTORY CL
SALTS LA
Recn Gd
Ashdene Farm
B78
PORTLEYS LA
Drayton Brick Bridge
Brook Farm
Brook End Farm
Heart of England Way
Upper House Farm
A4091
Gallows Brook
COPPICE LA
Mill Plantation
Middleton Park
Newhouse Farm
Middleton
SIMMONS CL
Highfields Farm
Park-gate Farm
PH
PO
VICARAGE HILL
ALMSHOUSES
CHURCH LA
Sewage Works
CROWBERRY LA
Middleton Pool
Walker's Spinney
Middleton Hall
A4091

7

14

21 10

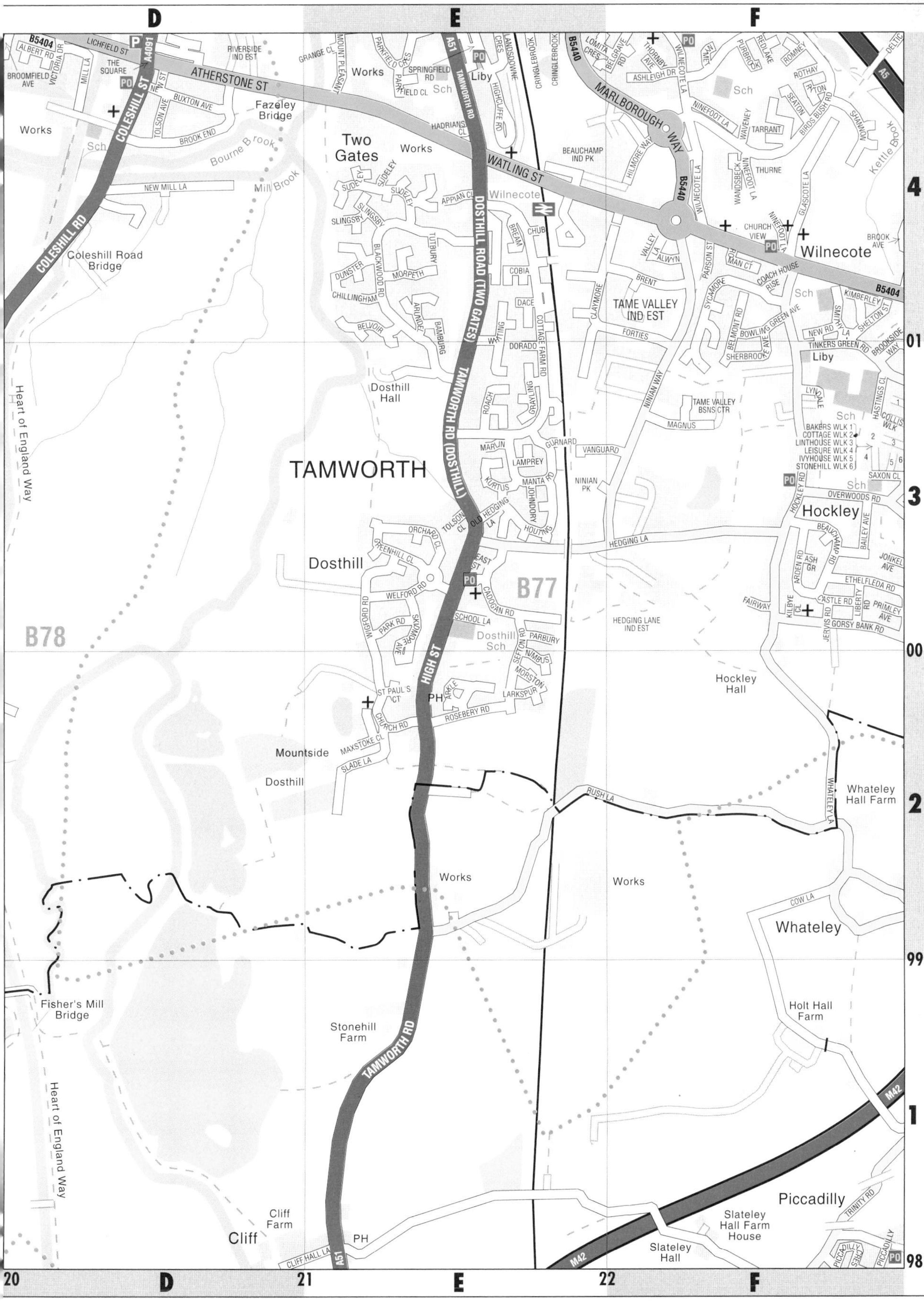
D
E
F
B5404
ALBERT RD
VICTORIA DR
BROOMFIELD AVE
MILL LA
LICHFIELD ST
THE SQUARE
A4091
COLESHILL ST
NEW ST
TOLSON AVE
BUXTON AVE
RIVERSIDE IND EST
ATHERSTONE ST
Fazeley Bridge
BROOK END
Works
Sch
Bourne Brook
Mill Brook
NEW MILL LA
COLESHILL RD
Coleshill Road Bridge
Heart of England Way
B78
GRANGE CL
MOUNT PLEASANT
PARKFIELD CRES
SPRINGFIELD RD
FIELD CL
Works
Two Gates
HADRIANS CL
A51
TAMWORTH RD
Liby
LANSDOWNE CRES
HIGHCLIFFE RD
CRINGLEBROOK
WATLING ST
APPIAN CL
Wilnecote
DOSTHILL ROAD (TWO GATES)
SUDELEY
SLINGSBY
TUTBURY
BLACKWOOD RD
DUNSTER
MORPETH
CHILLINGHAM
ARUNDEL
BELVOIR
BAMBURG
BREAM
CHUB
COBIA
DACE
WHITING
DORADO
COTTAGE FARM RD
ROACH
GRAYLING
Dosthill Hall
TAMWORTH RD (DOSTHILL)
TAMWORTH
MARLIN
GURNARD
LAMPREY
KURTUS
MANTA RD
JOHN DORY
HOUTING
OLD HEDGING LA
TOLSON CL
ORCHARD CL
GREENHILL CL
Dosthill
WELFORD RD
EAST ST
B77
CADOGAN RD
WIGFORD RD
PARK RD
SKIDMORE AVE
SCHOOL LA
Dosthill Sch
PARBURY
SEFTON RD
NIMBUS
MORSTON
LARKSPUR
ARKLE
HIGH ST
ST PAUL'S CT
PH
ROSEBERY RD
CHURCH RD
MAXSTOKE CL
SLADE LA
Mountside
Dosthill
Works
Stonehill Farm
TAMWORTH RD
Fisher's Mill Bridge
Cliff Farm
Cliff
CLIFF HALL LA
B5440
LOMITA CRES
BELGRAVE RD
THORNBY AVE
ASHLEIGH DR
WILNECOTE LA
PURBROOK
REDLAKE
ROMNEY
ROTHAY
SEATON
BIRDS BUSH RD
SHANNON
A5
Kettle Brook
MARLBOROUGH WAY
BEAUCHAMP IND PK
HILLMORE WAY
NINEFOOT LA
WAVENEY
TARRANT
WANDSBECK
THURNE
GLASCOTE LA
CHURCH VIEW
Wilnecote
BROOK AVE
VALLEY LA
ALWYN
PARSON ST
COACH HOUSE RISE
BRENT
CLAYMORE
TAME VALLEY IND EST
SYCAMORE
BELMONT RD
BOWLING GREEN AVE
SHERBROOKE AVE
FORTIES
NINIAN WAY
TAME VALLEY BSNS CTR
MAGNUS
KIMBERLEY
SMITH ST
SHELTON ST
NEW RD
TINKERS GREEN RD
BROOKSIDE WAY
Liby
LYNDALE
HASTINGS CL
COLLIS WLK
BAKERS WLK 1
COTTAGE WLK 2
LINTHOUSE WLK 3
LEISURE WLK 4
IVYHOUSE WLK 5
STONEHILL WLK 6
VANGUARD
NINIAN PK
SAXON CL
OVERWOODS RD
HOCKLEY RD
Hockley
BEAUCHAMP RD
BAILEY AVE
HEDGING LA
JONKEL AVE
ARDEN RD
ASH GR
ETHELFLEDA RD
FAIRWAY
KILBYE CL
CASTLE RD
LIBERTY RD
PRIMLEY AVE
JERVIS RD
GORSY BANK RD
HEDGING LANE IND EST
Hockley Hall
Whateley Hall Farm
WHATELEY LA
RUSH LA
Works
COW LA
Whateley
Holt Hall Farm
M42
Piccadilly
TRINITY RD
Slateley Hall Farm House
Slateley Hall
PICCADILLY CRES
PICCADILLY
PO
4
01
3
00
2
99
1
98
20
21
22

15 10

9
4

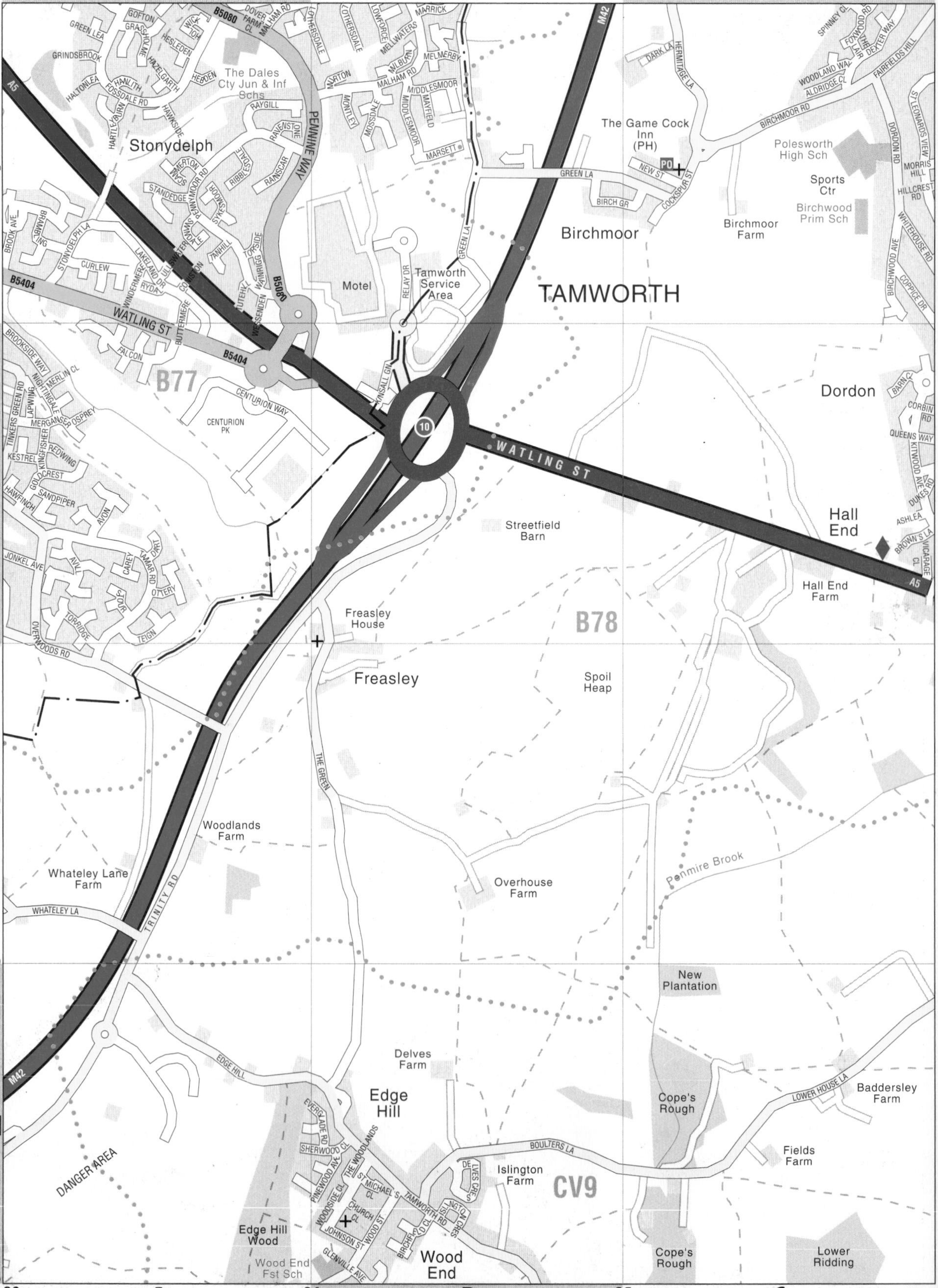
A
B
C
4
3
2
1
01
00
99
98
23
24
25
Stonydelph
The Dales
Cty Jun & Inf
Schs
PENNINE WAY
B5080
A5
B5404
WATLING ST
B77
CENTURION PK
CENTURION WAY
Motel
Tamworth
Service
Area
RELAY DR
GREEN LA
M42
10
TAMWORTH
The Game Cock
Inn
(PH)
PO
NEW ST
BIRCH GR
COCKSPUR ST
HERMITAGE LA
DARK LA
BIRCHMOOR RD
Birchmoor
Birchmoor
Farm
Polesworth
High Sch
Sports
Ctr
Birchwood
Prim Sch
DORDON RD
BIRCHWOOD AVE
Dordon
Hall
End
Hall End
Farm
Streetfield
Barn
Freasley
House
Freasley
B78
Spoil
Heap
THE GREEN
Woodlands
Farm
Whateley Lane
Farm
WHATELEY LA
TRINITY RD
Overhouse
Farm
Penmire Brook
New
Plantation
Delves
Farm
Edge
Hill
EDGE HILL
Cope's
Rough
LOWER HOUSE LA
Baddersley
Farm
Fields
Farm
BOULTERS LA
Islington
Farm
CV9
DANGER AREA
Edge Hill
Wood
Wood End
Fst Sch
Wood
End
TAMWORTH RD
Cope's
Rough
Lower
Ridding
OVERWOODS RD
JONKEL AVE
BROOKSIDE WAY
BROOK AVE
STONYDELPH LA
CURLEW
FALCON
BUTTERMERE
WINDERMERE
LAKESIDE DR
GRINDSBROOK
GREEN LEA
GOFTON
HALTONLEA
FOSSDALE RD
MALHAM RD
MIDDLESMOOR
MAYFIELD
MARSETT
MORTON
MONTLEY
LOTHERSDALE

9
16

5
12

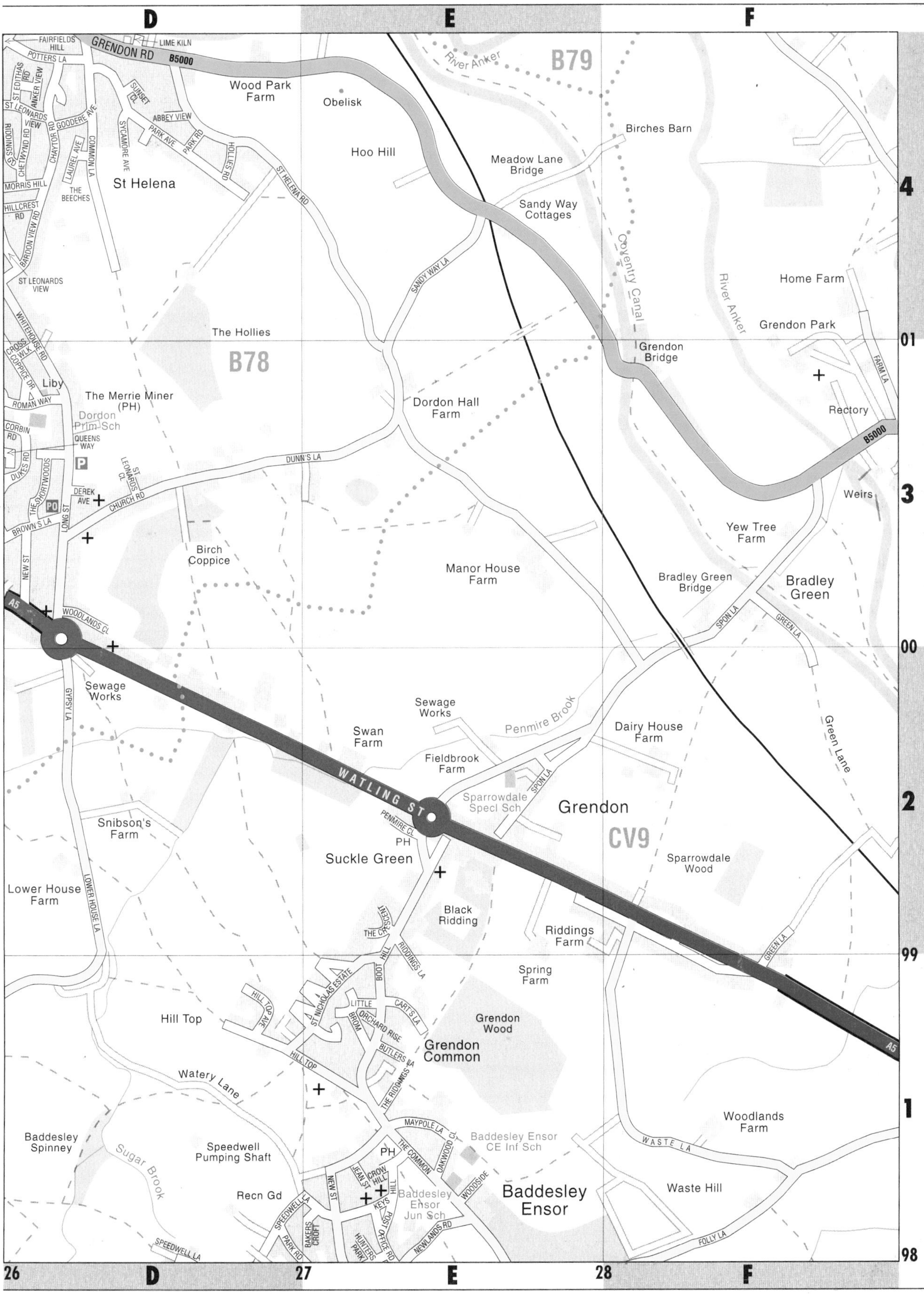
D
E
F
B79
B78
CV9
B5000
A5
4
3
2
1
01
00
99
98
26
27
28
GRENDON RD
FAIRFIELDS HILL
LIME KILN
POTTERS LA
Wood Park Farm
Obelisk
Hoo Hill
River Anker
Birches Barn
Meadow Lane Bridge
Sandy Way Cottages
St Helena
ST HELENA RD
SANDY WAY LA
Coventry Canal
Home Farm
Grendon Park
Grendon Bridge
The Hollies
Liby
The Merrie Miner (PH)
Dordon Prim Sch
Dordon Hall Farm
Rectory
FARM LA
DUNN'S LA
CHURCH RD
Weirs
Yew Tree Farm
Birch Coppice
Manor House Farm
Bradley Green Bridge
Bradley Green
SPON LA
GREEN LA
WOODLANDS CL
Sewage Works
GYPSY LA
Sewage Works
Swan Farm
Penmire Brook
Dairy House Farm
Green Lane
Fieldbrook Farm
Sparrowdale Specl Sch
Grendon
WATLING ST
PENMIRE CL
PH
Suckle Green
Snibson's Farm
Sparrowdale Wood
Lower House Farm
LOWER HOUSE LA
Black Ridding
Riddings Farm
THE CRESCENT
RIDDINGS LA
Spring Farm
Hill Top
HILL TOP AVE
ST NICHOLAS ESTATE
Grendon Wood
Grendon Common
Watery Lane
HILL TOP
Woodlands Farm
WASTE LA
Baddesley Spinney
Sugar Brook
Speedwell Pumping Shaft
PH
Baddesley Ensor CE Inf Sch
Baddesley Ensor
Waste Hill
Recn Gd
Baddesley Ensor Jun Sch
NEWLANDS RD
FOLLY LA
SPEEDWELL LA

17
12

11
6

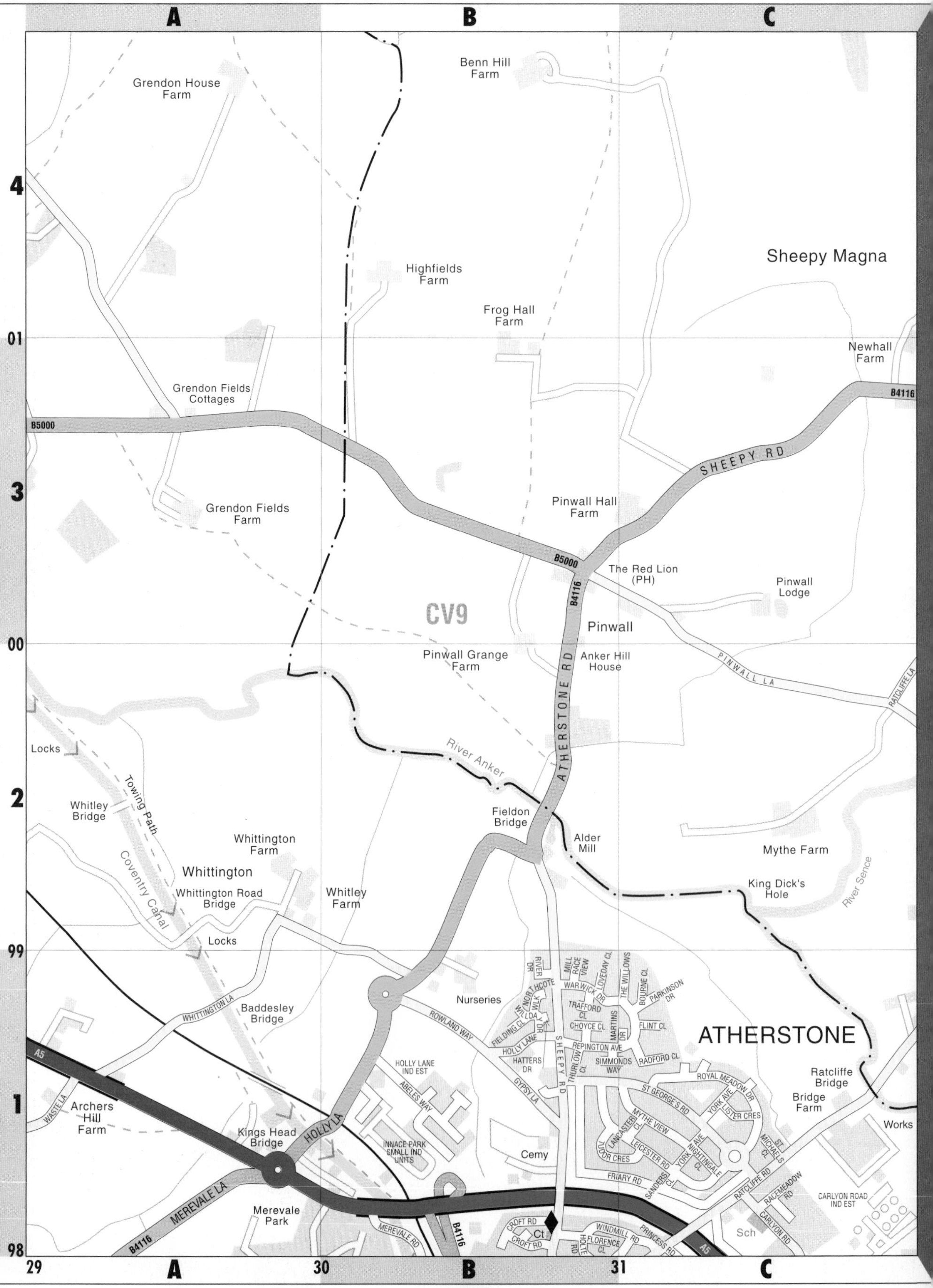
A
B
C
4
01
3
00
2
99
1
98
29
30
31
Benn Hill Farm
Grendon House Farm
Highfields Farm
Frog Hall Farm
Sheepy Magna
Newhall Farm
B4116
Grendon Fields Cottages
B5000
SHEEPY RD
Pinwall Hall Farm
Grendon Fields Farm
B5000
The Red Lion (PH)
Pinwall Lodge
B4116
CV9
Pinwall
Pinwall Grange Farm
Anker Hill House
PINWALL LA
RATCLIFFE LA
Locks
River Anker
ATHERSTONE RD
Towing Path
Whitley Bridge
Fieldon Bridge
Alder Mill
Whittington Farm
Mythe Farm
Coventry Canal
Whittington
Whittington Road Bridge
Whitley Farm
King Dick's Hole
River Sence
Locks
RIVER DR
MILL RACE VIEW
LOVEDAY CL
THE WILLOWS
BOURNE CL
PARKINSON DR
NORTHCOTE WALK
WARWICK DR
WILLDAY DR
TRAFFORD CL
MARTINS DR
Nurseries
FLINT CL
WHITTINGTON LA
Baddesley Bridge
ROWLAND WAY
FIELDING CL
CHOYCE CL
ATHERSTONE
HOLLY LANE
SHEEPY RD
REPINGTON AVE
HATTERS DR
THURLOW CL
SIMMONDS WAY
RADFORD CL
A5
HOLLY LANE IND EST
ROYAL MEADOW DR
Ratcliffe Bridge
ABELES WAY
ST GEORGE'S RD
YORK AVE
LISTER CRES
Bridge Farm
WASTE LA
Archers Hill Farm
GYPSY LA
MYTHE VIEW
LANCASTER CL
Works
Kings Head Bridge
HOLLY LA
INNAGE PARK SMALL IND UNITS
Cemy
TUDOR CRES
LEICESTER RD
YORK AVE
NIGHTINGALE CL
ST MICHAELS CL
FRIARY RD
SANDERS CL
RATCLIFFE RD
RACEMEADOW RD
MEREVALE LA
CARLYON ROAD IND EST
Merevale Park
B4116
CROFT RD
Ct
WINDMILL RD
PRINCESS RD
Sch
CARLYON RD
MEREVALE RD
CROFT RD
FLORENCE CL
HOLTE RD
B4116
A5

11
18

7
14

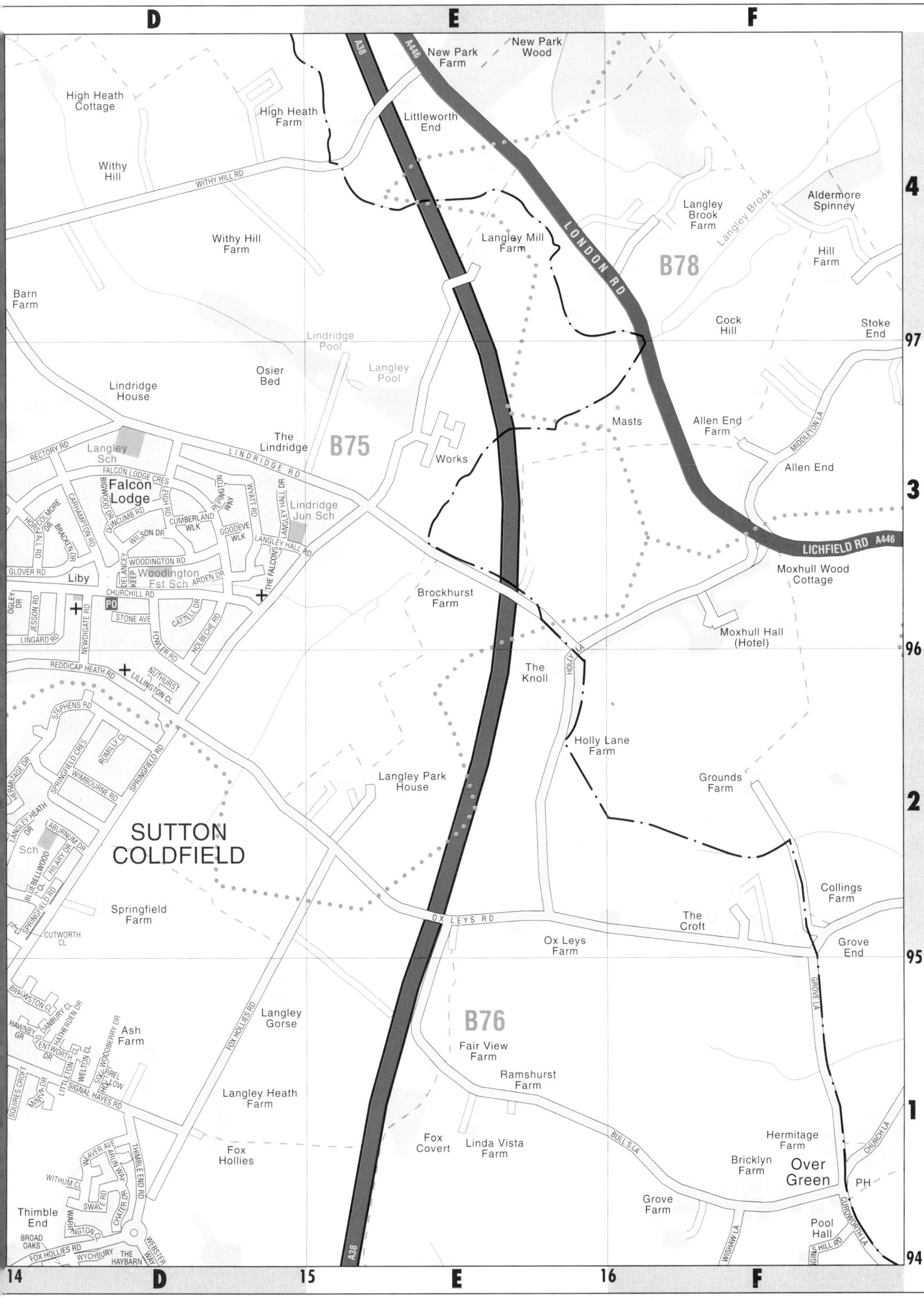
D
E
F
A38
A446
New Park Farm
New Park Wood
High Heath Cottage
High Heath Farm
Littleworth End
Withy Hill
WITHY HILL RD
Withy Hill Farm
Langley Mill Farm
LONDON RD
Langley Brook Farm
Langley Brook
Aldermore Spinney
Hill Farm
B78
Barn Farm
Cock Hill
Stoke End
Lindridge Pool
Langley Pool
Osier Bed
Lindridge House
Masts
Allen End Farm
MIDDLETON LA
Allen End
The Lindridge
B75
Works
RECTORY RD
Langley Sch
LINDRIDGE RD
FALCON LODGE CRES
Falcon Lodge
BIGWOOD DR
LEIGH RD
REPINGTON WAY
WYATT RD
LANGLEY HALL DR
Lindridge Jun Sch
COLMORE DR
HORSFALL RD
CARHAMPTON RD
BRACKEN DR
DUNCUMB RD
CUMBERLAND WLK
GOODEVE WLK
WILSON DR
LANGLEY HALL RD
LICHFIELD RD
Moxhull Wood Cottage
GLOVER RD
Liby
DELANCEY KEEP
WOODINGTON RD
Woodington Fst Sch
ARDEN DR
THE FALCONS
CHURCHILL RD
PO
Brockhurst Farm
OGLEY DR
JESSON RD
NEWDIGATE RD
STONE AVE
CATTELL DR
HOLBECHE RD
FOWLER RD
LINGARD RD
Moxhull Hall (Hotel)
HOLLY LA
REDDICAP HEATH RD
NUTHURST
LILLINGTON CL
The Knoll
STEPHENS RD
Holly Lane Farm
HERMITAGE DR
SPRINGFIELD CRES
ROMILLY CL
WIMBOURNE RD
SPRINGFIELD RD
Langley Park House
Grounds Farm
LANGLEY HEATH DR
LABURNUM DR
SUTTON COLDFIELD
Sch
BLUEBELLWOOD CL
HILARY DR
SPRINGFIELD RD
Collings Farm
Springfield Farm
OX LEYS RD
The Croft
CUTWORTH CL
Ox Leys Farm
Grove End
BRAWSTON CL
DANBURY CL
HATHERDEN DR
HAWNBY GR
ENTWORTH DR
ASH Farm
WOODBERRY DR
FOX HOLLIES RD
Langley Gorse
GROVE LA
B76
Fair View Farm
LITTLETON CL
WELTON CL
SQUIRREL HOLLOW
SIGNAL HAYES RD
Ramshurst Farm
SQUIRES CROFT
Langley Heath Farm
BULL'S LA
Hermitage Farm
CHURCH LA
Fox Hollies
Fox Covert
Linda Vista Farm
Bricklyn Farm
Over Green
PH
WEAVER AVE
ARUN WAY
THIMBLE END RD
WITHUM CL
SWALE RD
CHATER DR
Grove Farm
CURDWORTH LA
Thimble End
WISHAW LA
Pool Hall
HILL RD
BROAD OAKS
FOX HOLLIES RD
WYCHBURY
THE HAYBARN
WEBSTER WAY
4
97
3
96
2
95
1
94
14
15
16

22
14

13
8

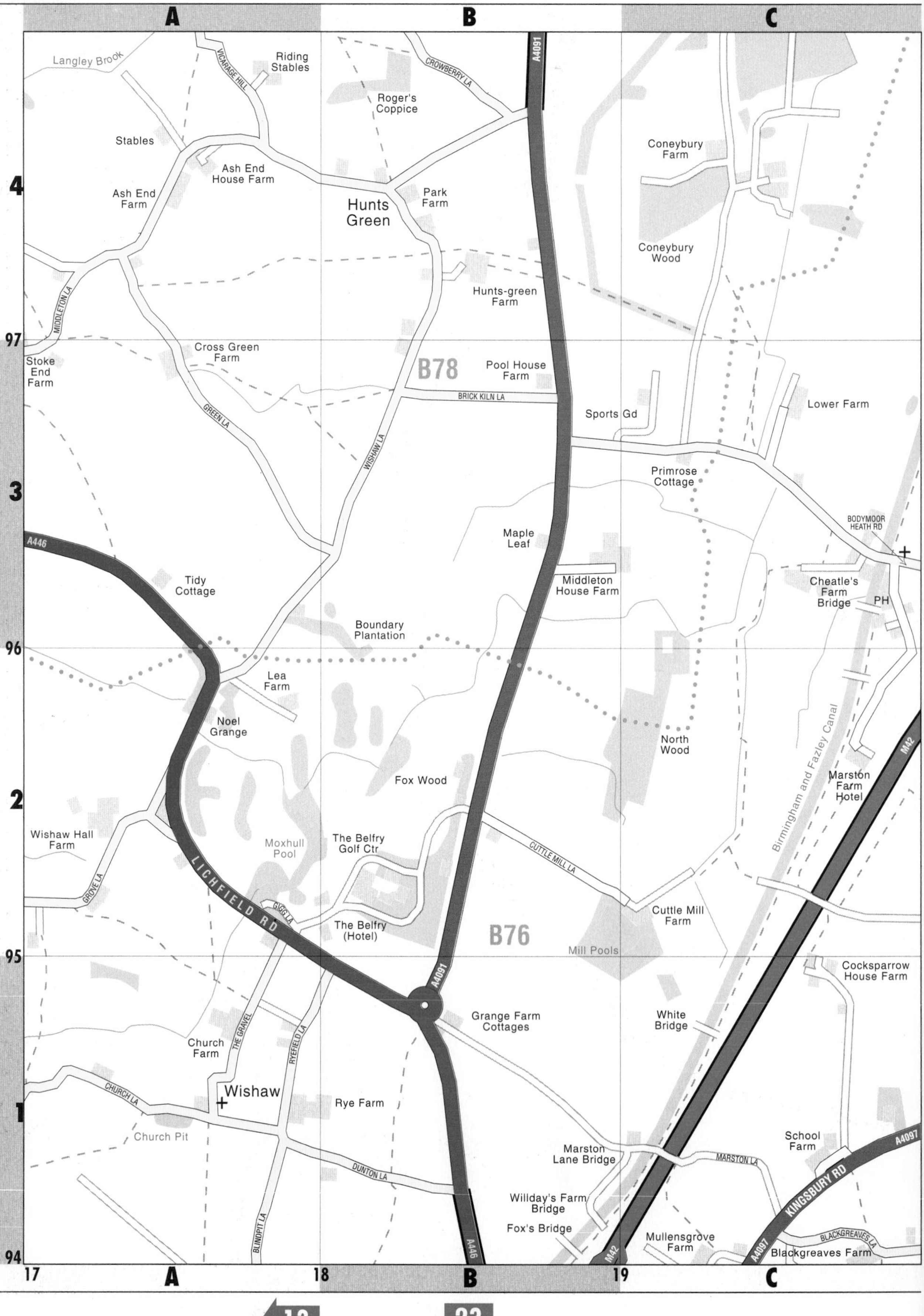
A
B
C
Langley Brook
Riding Stables
VICARAGE HILL
CROWBERRY LA
A4091
Roger's Coppice
Stables
Ash End House Farm
Ash End Farm
Hunts Green
Park Farm
Coneybury Farm
Coneybury Wood
Hunts-green Farm
MIDDLETON LA
Stoke End Farm
Cross Green Farm
B78
Pool House Farm
BRICK KILN LA
Sports Gd
Lower Farm
GREEN LA
WISHAW LA
Primrose Cottage
BODYMOOR HEATH RD
Maple Leaf
A446
Tidy Cottage
Middleton House Farm
Cheatle's Farm Bridge
PH
Boundary Plantation
Lea Farm
Noel Grange
North Wood
Birmingham and Fazley Canal
M42
Marston Farm Hotel
Fox Wood
Wishaw Hall Farm
Moxhull Pool
The Belfry Golf Ctr
CUTTLE MILL LA
GROVE LA
LICHFIELD RD
GIGG LA
The Belfry (Hotel)
Cuttle Mill Farm
B76
Mill Pools
Cocksparrow House Farm
A4091
Grange Farm Cottages
White Bridge
THE GRAVEL
RYEFIELD LA
Church Farm
Wishaw
Rye Farm
CHURCH LA
Church Pit
School Farm
A4097
Marston Lane Bridge
MARSTON LA
DUNTON LA
KINGSBURY RD
Willday's Farm Bridge
Fox's Bridge
Mullensgrove Farm
BLACKGREAVES LA
Blackgreaves Farm
BLINDPIT LA
A446
M42
4
97
3
96
2
95
1
94
17
18
19

13
23

9
16

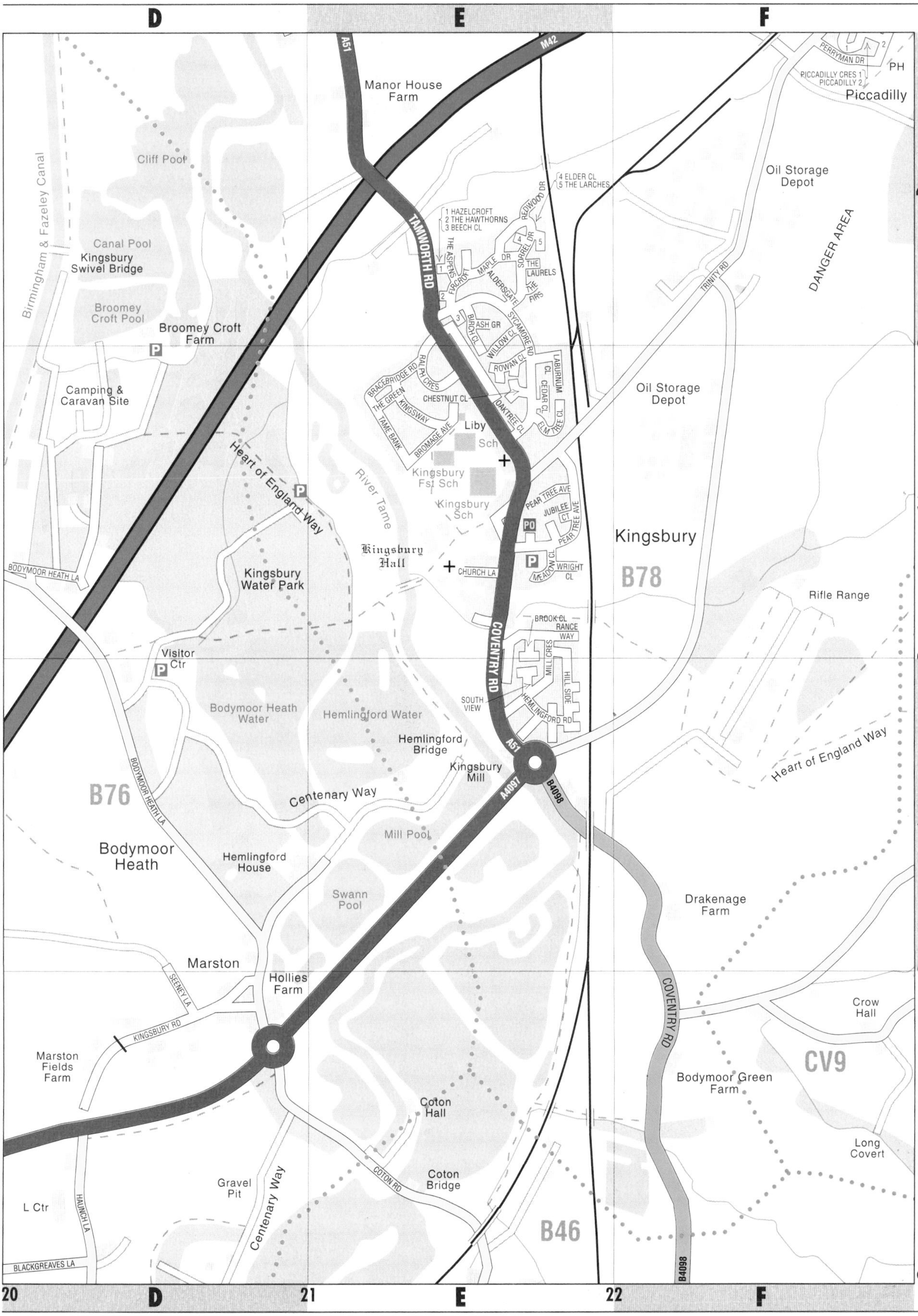
D
E
F
Manor House Farm
A51
M42
Cliff Pool
Birmingham & Fazeley Canal
Canal Pool
Kingsbury Swivel Bridge
Broomey Croft Pool
Broomey Croft Farm
Camping & Caravan Site
TAMWORTH RD
1 HAZELCROFT
2 THE HAWTHORNS
3 BEECH CL
4 ELDER CL
5 THE LARCHES
REDWOOD DR
SORREL DR
THE LAURELS
THE FIRS
THE ASPENS
FIRCROFT
MAPLE DR
ALDERSGATE
SYCAMORE RD
ASH GR
BIRCH CL
WILLOW CL
ROWAN CL
LABURNUM CL
CEDAR CL
ELM TREE CL
OAKTREE CL
CHESTNUT CL
BRACEBRIDGE RD
RALPH CRES
THE GREEN
KINGSWAY
TAME BANK
BROMAGE AVE
Liby
Sch
Kingsbury Fst Sch
Kingsbury Sch
PEAR TREE AVE
JUBILEE CT
PO
MEADOW CL
WRIGHT CL
CHURCH LA
Kingsbury Hall
River Tame
Heart of England Way
Kingsbury Water Park
BODYMOOR HEATH LA
Visitor Ctr
Bodymoor Heath Water
Hemlingford Water
Hemlingford Bridge
Kingsbury Mill
COVENTRY RD
BROOK CL
RANCE WAY
MILL CRES
HILL SIDE
SOUTH VIEW
HEMLINGFORD RD
Centenary Way
Mill Pool
Swann Pool
B76
Bodymoor Heath
Hemlingford House
Marston
Hollies Farm
SEENEY LA
KINGSBURY RD
Marston Fields Farm
A4097
B4098
Coton Hall
Coton Bridge
COTON RD
Gravel Pit
Centenary Way
L Ctr
HAUNCH LA
BLACKGREAVES LA
B46
PERRYMAN DR
PICCADILLY CRES 1
PICCADILLY 2
PH
Piccadilly
Oil Storage Depot
DANGER AREA
TRINITY RD
Oil Storage Depot
Kingsbury
B78
Rifle Range
Heart of England Way
Drakenage Farm
COVENTRY RD
Crow Hall
CV9
Bodymoor Green Farm
Long Covert
B4098
4
97
3
96
2
95
1
94
20
21
22

24
16

15
10

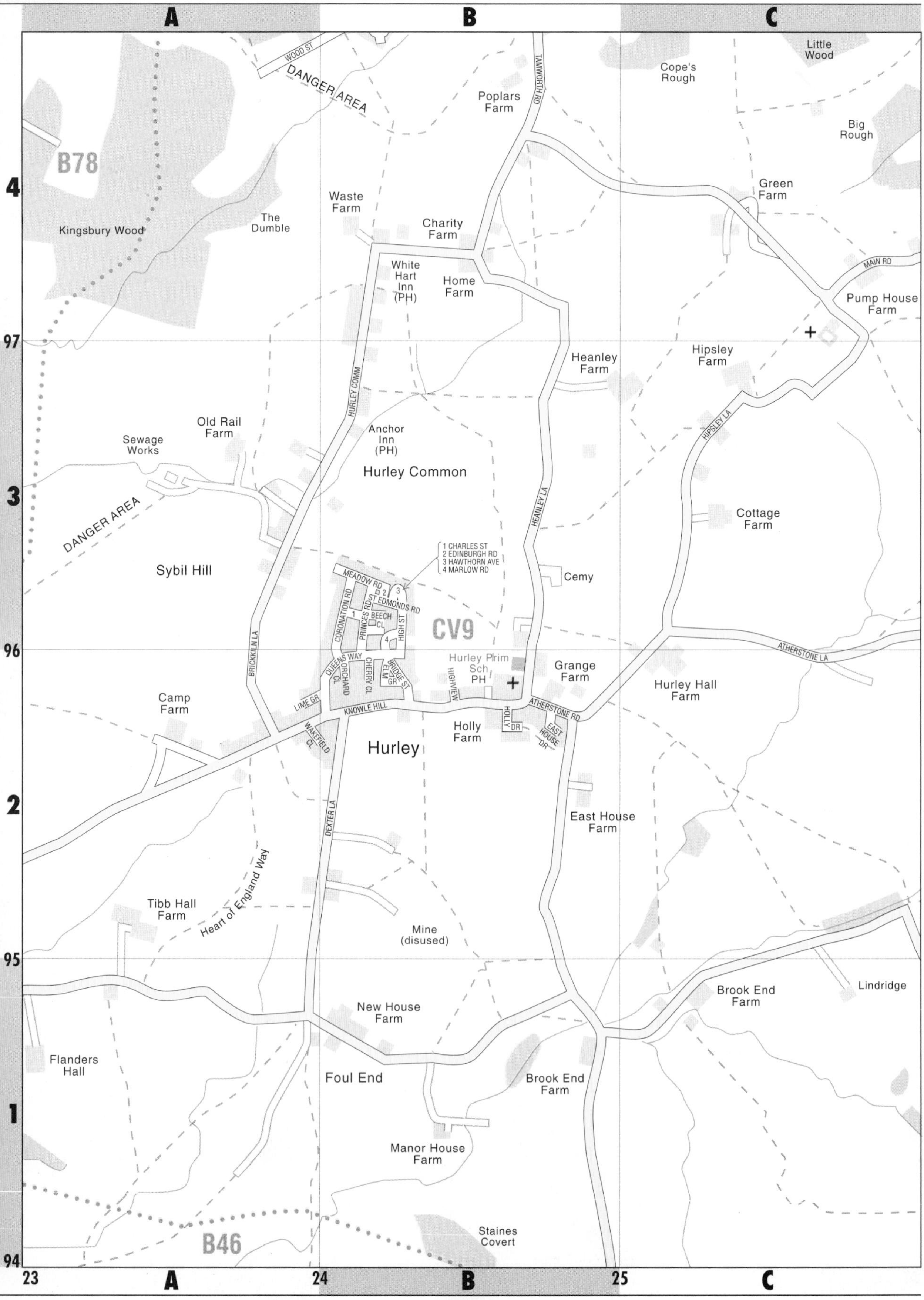
A
B
C
4
97
3
96
2
95
1
94
23
24
25
WOOD ST
DANGER AREA
TAMWORTH RD
Poplars Farm
Cope's Rough
Little Wood
Big Rough
B78
Kingsbury Wood
The Dumble
Waste Farm
Charity Farm
Green Farm
MAIN RD
Pump House Farm
White Hart Inn (PH)
Home Farm
Heanley Farm
Hipsley Farm
HURLEY COMM
Old Rail Farm
Sewage Works
Anchor Inn (PH)
Hurley Common
HIPSLEY LA
DANGER AREA
HEANLEY LA
Cottage Farm
Sybil Hill
1 CHARLES ST
2 EDINBURGH RD
3 HAWTHORN AVE
4 MARLOW RD
Cemy
MEADOW RD
ST EDMONDS RD
CORONATION RD
PRINCES RD
BEECH CL
HIGH ST
CV9
ATHERSTONE LA
BRICKKILN LA
QUEENS WAY
ORCHARD CL
CHERRY CL
ELM GR
BRIDGE ST
HIGHVIEW
Hurley Prim Sch
PH
Grange Farm
Hurley Hall Farm
Camp Farm
LIME GR
KNOWLE HILL
HOLLY DR
ATHERSTONE RD
EAST HOUSE DR
WAKEFIELD CL
Hurley
Holly Farm
East House Farm
DEXTER LA
Heart of England Way
Tibb Hall Farm
Mine (disused)
Lindridge
Brook End Farm
New House Farm
Flanders Hall
Foul End
Brook End Farm
Manor House Farm
Staines Covert
B46

15
25

11
18

D E F

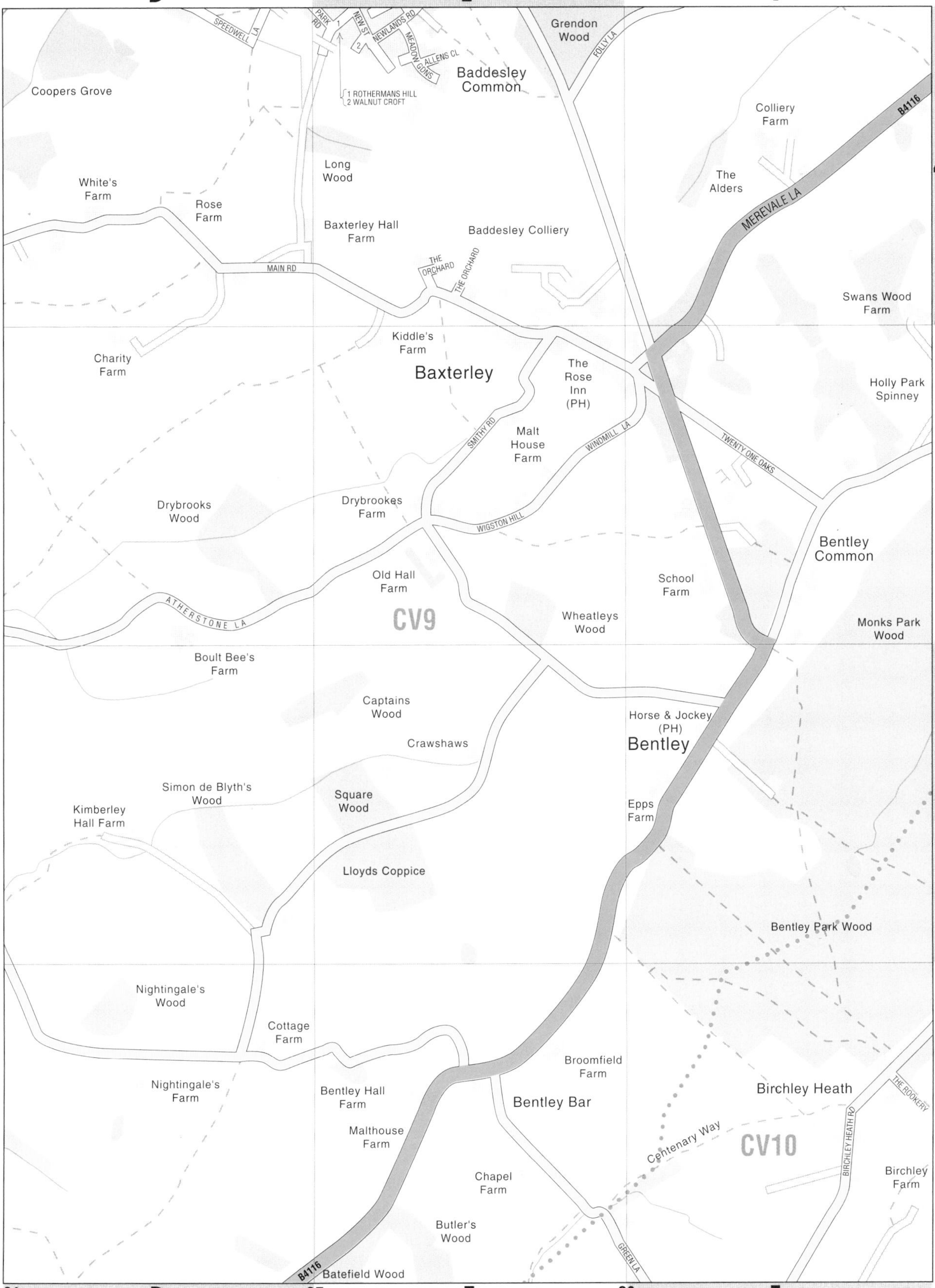
Grendon Wood
SPEEDWELL LA
PARK RD
NEW ST
NEWLANDS RD
MEADOW GDNS
ALLENS CL
FOLLY LA
Baddesley Common
1 ROTHERMANS HILL
2 WALNUT CROFT
Coopers Grove
Colliery Farm
B4116
Long Wood
White's Farm
Rose Farm
The Alders
MEREVALE LA
Baxterley Hall Farm
Baddesley Colliery
MAIN RD
THE ORCHARD
THE ORCHARD
Swans Wood Farm
Kiddle's Farm
Charity Farm
Baxterley
The Rose Inn (PH)
Holly Park Spinney
SMITHY RD
Malt House Farm
WINDMILL LA
TWENTY ONE OAKS
Drybrooks Wood
Drybrookes Farm
WIGSTON HILL
Bentley Common
Old Hall Farm
School Farm
ATHERSTONE LA
CV9
Wheatleys Wood
Monks Park Wood
Boult Bee's Farm
Captains Wood
Horse & Jockey (PH)
Bentley
Crawshaws
Simon de Blyth's Wood
Square Wood
Kimberley Hall Farm
Epps Farm
Lloyds Coppice
Bentley Park Wood
Nightingale's Wood
Cottage Farm
Broomfield Farm
Nightingale's Farm
Bentley Hall Farm
Bentley Bar
Birchley Heath
THE ROOKERY
Malthouse Farm
Centenary Way
CV10
BIRCHLEY HEATH RD
Chapel Farm
Birchley Farm
Butler's Wood
GREEN LA
B4116
Batefield Wood

4 97 3 96 2 95 1 94

26 D 27 E 28 F

26
18

17
12

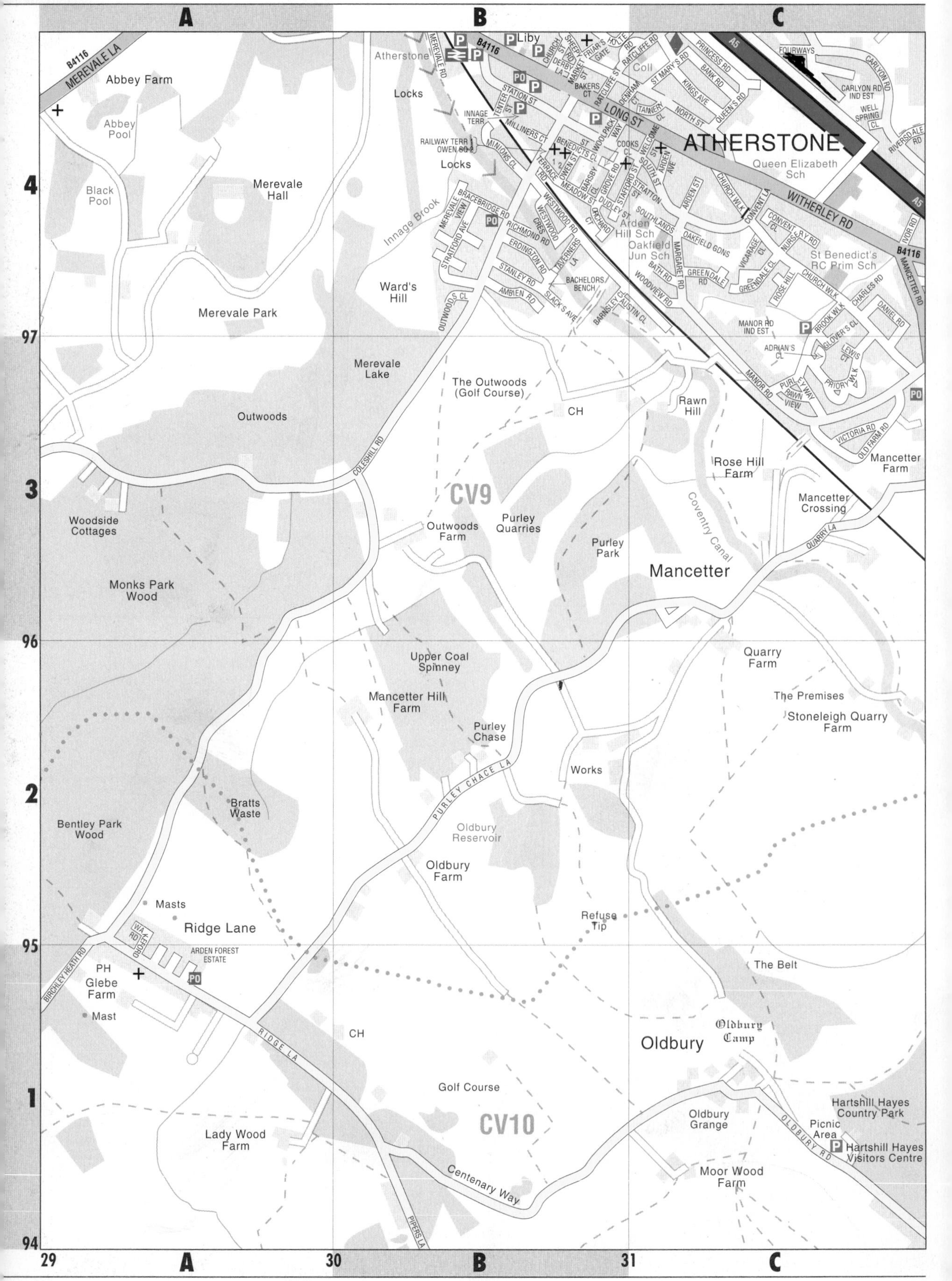
A
B
C
ATHERSTONE
Atherstone
Abbey Farm
Abbey Pool
Black Pool
Merevale Hall
Merevale Park
Locks
Ward's Hill
Merevale Lake
Outwoods
The Outwoods (Golf Course)
CH
Rawn Hill
Rose Hill Farm
Mancetter Farm
Mancetter Crossing
Woodside Cottages
CV9
Outwoods Farm
Purley Quarries
Purley Park
Coventry Canal
Mancetter
Monks Park Wood
Upper Coal Spinney
Mancetter Hill Farm
Quarry Farm
The Premises
Stoneleigh Quarry Farm
Purley Chase
Works
Bratts Waste
Bentley Park Wood
Oldbury Reservoir
Oldbury Farm
Masts
Ridge Lane
Refuse Tip
The Belt
ARDEN FOREST ESTATE
PH
Glebe Farm
Mast
CH
Oldbury
Oldbury Camp
Golf Course
CV10
Hartshill Hayes Country Park
Picnic Area
Hartshill Hayes Visitors Centre
Oldbury Grange
Lady Wood Farm
Moor Wood Farm
Centenary Way
Queen Elizabeth Sch
Arden Hill Sch
Oakfield Jun Sch
St Benedict's RC Prim Sch
MANOR RD IND EST
CARLYON RD IND EST
FOURWAYS
Coll
Liby
LONG ST
WITHERLEY RD
B4116
A5
MEREVALE LA
COLESHILL RD
PURLEY CHACE LA
RIDGE LA
OLDBURY RD
QUARRY LA
MANCETTER RD
BIRCHLEY HEATH RD
PIPERS LA
Innage Brook
4
97
3
96
2
95
1
94
29
30
31

17
27

4th R/about from M42 +/L

20

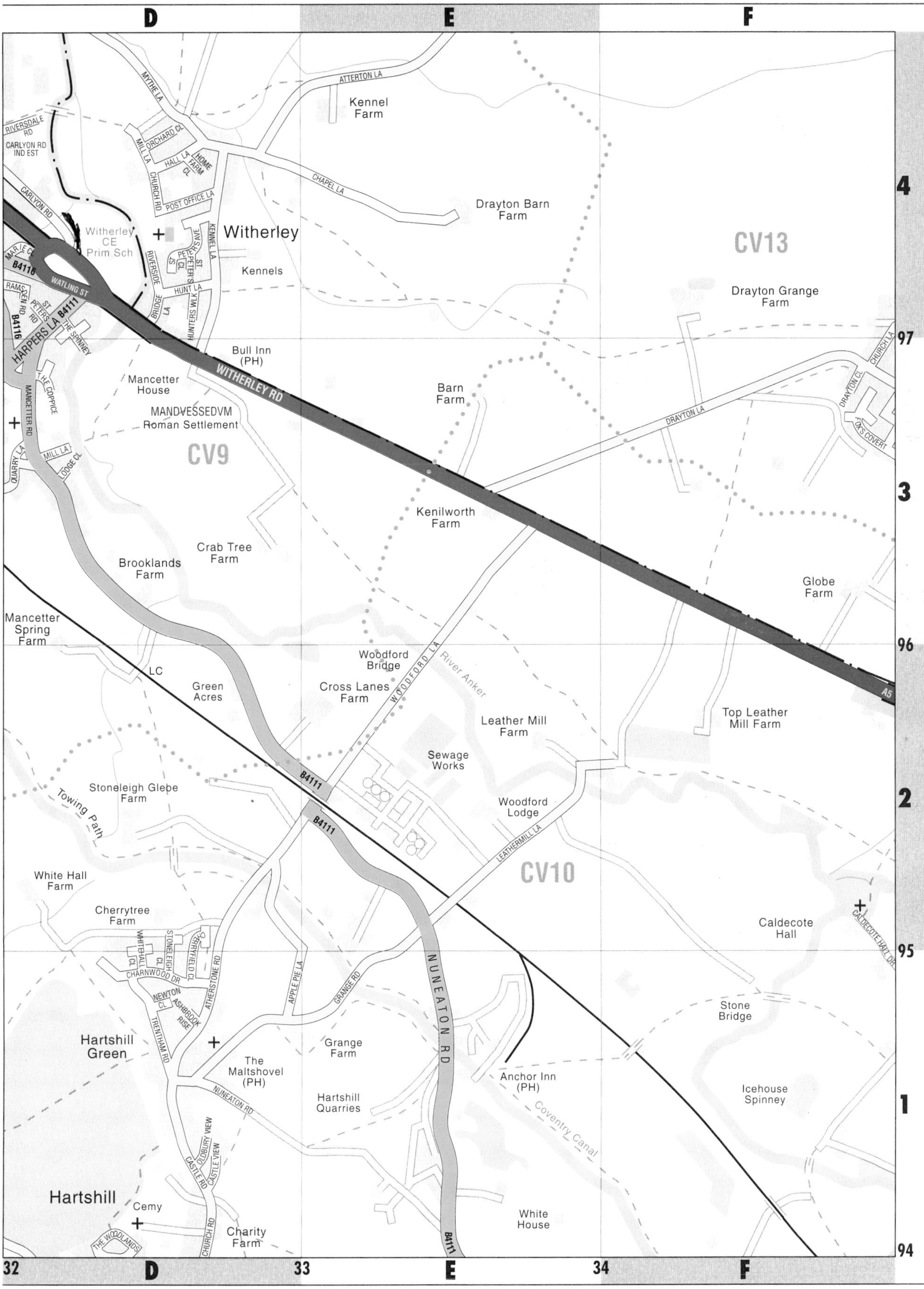
D
E
F
ATTERTON LA
Kennel Farm
MYTHE LA
RIVERSDALE RD
CARLYON RD IND EST
ORCHARD CL
MILL LA
HALL LA
HOME FARM CL
CHURCH RD
POST OFFICE LA
CHAPEL LA
Drayton Barn Farm
CARLYON RD
Witherley CE Prim Sch
Witherley
KENNEL LA
RIVERSIDE
ST PETERS CL
Kennels
HUNT LA
WATLING ST
B4116
B4111
HARPERS LA
THE SPINNEY
BRIDGE LA
HUNTERS WLK
CV13
Drayton Grange Farm
4
97
Bull Inn (PH)
WITHERLEY RD
Mancetter House
MANDVESSEDVM Roman Settlement
THE COPPICE
MANCETTER RD
Barn Farm
DRAYTON LA
CHURCH LA
DRAYTON CL
FOX'S COVERT
CV9
MILL LA
QUARRY LA
LODGE CL
3
Kenilworth Farm
Crab Tree Farm
Brooklands Farm
Globe Farm
Mancetter Spring Farm
96
LC
Woodford Bridge
River Anker
Green Acres
Cross Lanes Farm
WOODFORD LA
A5
Top Leather Mill Farm
Leather Mill Farm
Sewage Works
Stoneleigh Glebe Farm
Towing Path
B4111
2
Woodford Lodge
LEATHERMILL LA
CV10
White Hall Farm
Cherrytree Farm
Caldecote Hall
CALDECOTE HALL DR
WHITEHALL CL
STONELEIGH CL
CHERRYFIELD CL
CHARNWOOD DR
ATHERSTONE RD
APPLE PIE LA
GRANGE RD
NUNEATON RD
95
NEWTON CL
ASHBROOK RISE
TRENTHAM RD
Stone Bridge
Hartshill Green
Grange Farm
The Maltshovel (PH)
Anchor Inn (PH)
Icehouse Spinney
NUNEATON RD
Hartshill Quarries
Coventry Canal
1
OLDBURY VIEW
CASTLE VIEW
CASTLE RD
Hartshill
Cemy
Charity Farm
CHURCH RD
THE WOODLANDS
White House
B4111
94
32
D
33
E
34
F

28

20

19

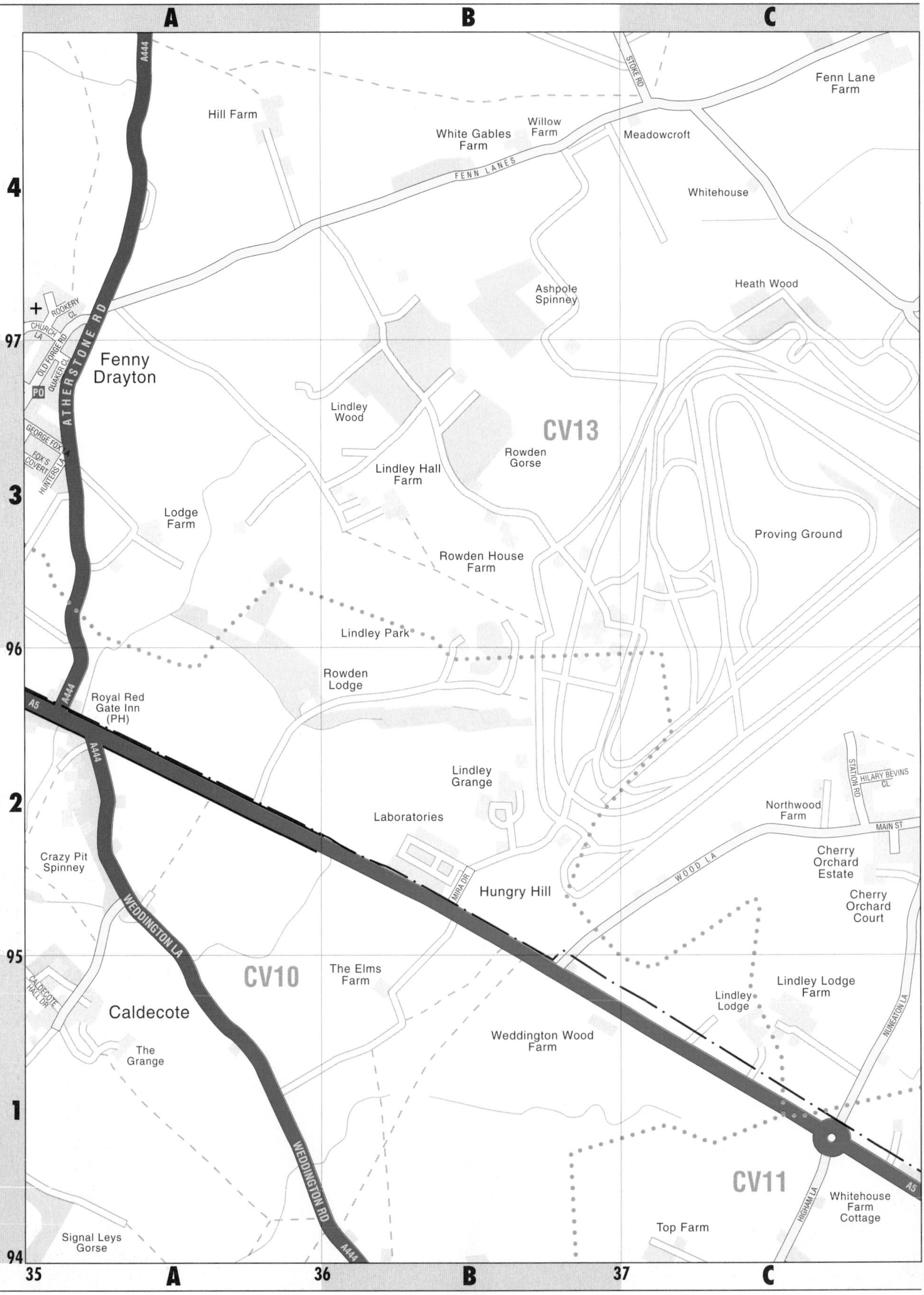
A
B
C
4
97
3
96
2
95
1
94
35
36
37
A444
ATHERSTONE RD
ROOKERY CL
CHURCH LA
OLD FORGE RD
QUAKER CL
PO
GEORGE FOX LA
FOX'S COVERT
HUNTERS LA
Fenny Drayton
Hill Farm
White Gables Farm
Willow Farm
FENN LANES
STOKE RD
Meadowcroft
Fenn Lane Farm
Whitehouse
Heath Wood
Ashpole Spinney
Lindley Wood
CV13
Rowden Gorse
Lindley Hall Farm
Lodge Farm
Proving Ground
Rowden House Farm
Lindley Park
Rowden Lodge
Royal Red Gate Inn (PH)
A5
Lindley Grange
Laboratories
STATION RD
HILARY BEVINS CL
Northwood Farm
MAIN ST
Cherry Orchard Estate
Cherry Orchard Court
WOOD LA
MIRA DR
Hungry Hill
Crazy Pit Spinney
WEDDINGTON LA
CV10
The Elms Farm
Lindley Lodge
Lindley Lodge Farm
NUNEATON LA
CALDECOTE HALL DR
Caldecote
The Grange
Weddington Wood Farm
WEDDINGTON RD
CV11
HIGHAM LA
Whitehouse Farm Cottage
Top Farm
Signal Leys Gorse

19
29

D
E
F
Grange Farm
Fox Covert Farm
FOXCOVERT LA
UPTON LA
WILLOW PARK IND EST
Crown Hill
Crown Hill Farm
Ivy House Farm
STOKE LA
THE GREEN
STAPLETON LA
Lodge Farm
CHURCH CL
HIGH ST
BLACKSMITHS YD
ANDREW CL
CHURCH WLKS
IVY CL
GREENHILL RD
ROSEWAY
SHENTON CL
WHITEMOORS RD
WHITEMOORS CL
SHERWOOD RD
GREENWOOD RD
HINCKLEY RD
St Martin's Convent
St Martin's Catholic High Sch
St Margarets CE Prim Sch
ST MARGARET RD
HALL DR
PINE CL
THORNFIELD AVE
STATION RD
PO
PH
MAIN ST
BENNET CL
ARNOLD RD
STONELY RD
TITHE CL
Brook Farm
Stoke Golding
HIGHAM LA
Higham Fields Court
Stoke Fields Farm
STOKE RD
Willow Farm
Brook House
Brook Farm
CV13
Millfield Farm
Highfield Farm
Cuckoos Nest Farm
Compass Fields Farm
Oaklands
Basin Bridge Farm
Basin Bridge
Ashby de la Zouch Canal
BASIN BRIDGE LA
Vale Farm
Wykin Fields
The Hollows
Higham on the Hill CE Prim Sch
Church Farm
Hall Farm
Spring Hill Farm
Manor Farm
PH
MAIN ST
NUNEATON LA
Higham on the Hill
Higham Hall
HINCKLEY LA
Wykin House Farm
HIGHAM LA
Wykin
Wykin Hall
Towing Path
BARR LA
LE10
A47
Grange Farm
Harper's Hill
Change Brook
Higham Grange
Higham Thorns
Higham Gorse
Hollow Farm
CV11
A5
DODWELLS RD
1 BRASCOTE RD
2 LOVETTS CL
ROSTON DR
4
97
3
96
2
95
1
94
38
39
40

13

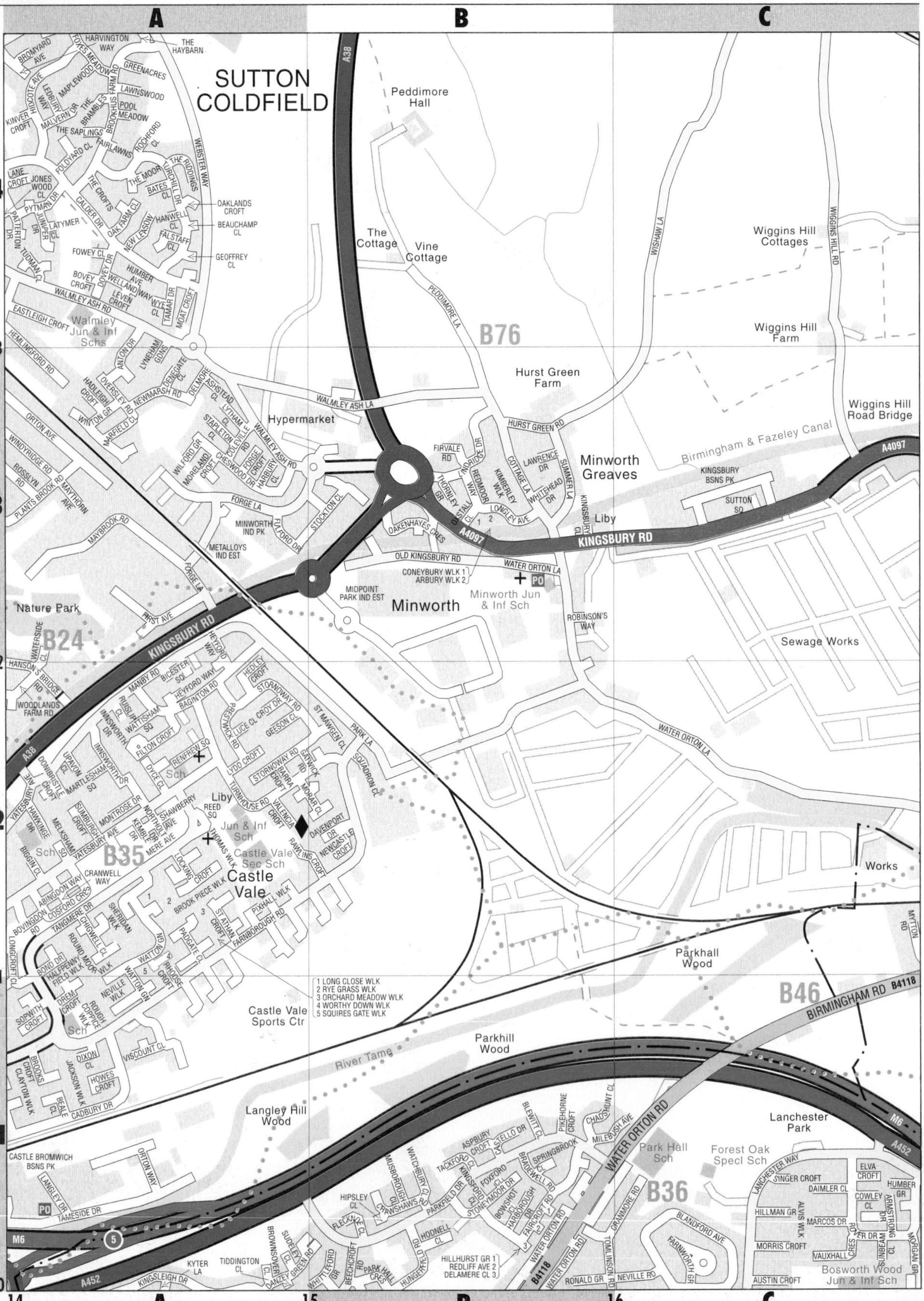

A
B
C
SUTTON COLDFIELD
Peddimore Hall
The Cottage
Vine Cottage
B76
Hurst Green Farm
Wiggins Hill Cottages
Wiggins Hill Farm
Wiggins Hill Road Bridge
Birmingham & Fazeley Canal
Minworth Greaves
KINGSBURY BSNS PK
SUTTON SQ
Liby
KINGSBURY RD
A4097
A38
Hypermarket
WALMLEY ASH LA
Walmley Jun & Inf Schs
MINWORTH IND PK
METALLOYS IND EST
MIDPOINT PARK IND EST
Minworth
Minworth Jun & Inf Sch
PO
ROBINSON'S WAY
Sewage Works
WATER ORTON LA
Nature Park
B24
Castle Vale
B35
Jun & Inf Sch
Castle Vale Sec Sch
Liby
Sch
Works
Parkhall Wood
B46
BIRMINGHAM RD
B4118
1 LONG CLOSE WLK
2 RYE GRASS WLK
3 ORCHARD MEADOW WLK
4 WORTHY DOWN WLK
5 SQUIRES GATE WLK
Castle Vale Sports Ctr
River Tame
Parkhill Wood
Langley Hill Wood
CASTLE BROMWICH BSNS PK
M6
A452
Park Hall Sch
Forest Oak Specl Sch
Lanchester Park
B36
WATER ORTON RD
HILLHURST GR 1
REDLIFF AVE 2
DELAMERE CL 3
Bosworth Wood Jun & Inf Sch
4
93
3
92
2
91
1
90
14
15
16

14
24

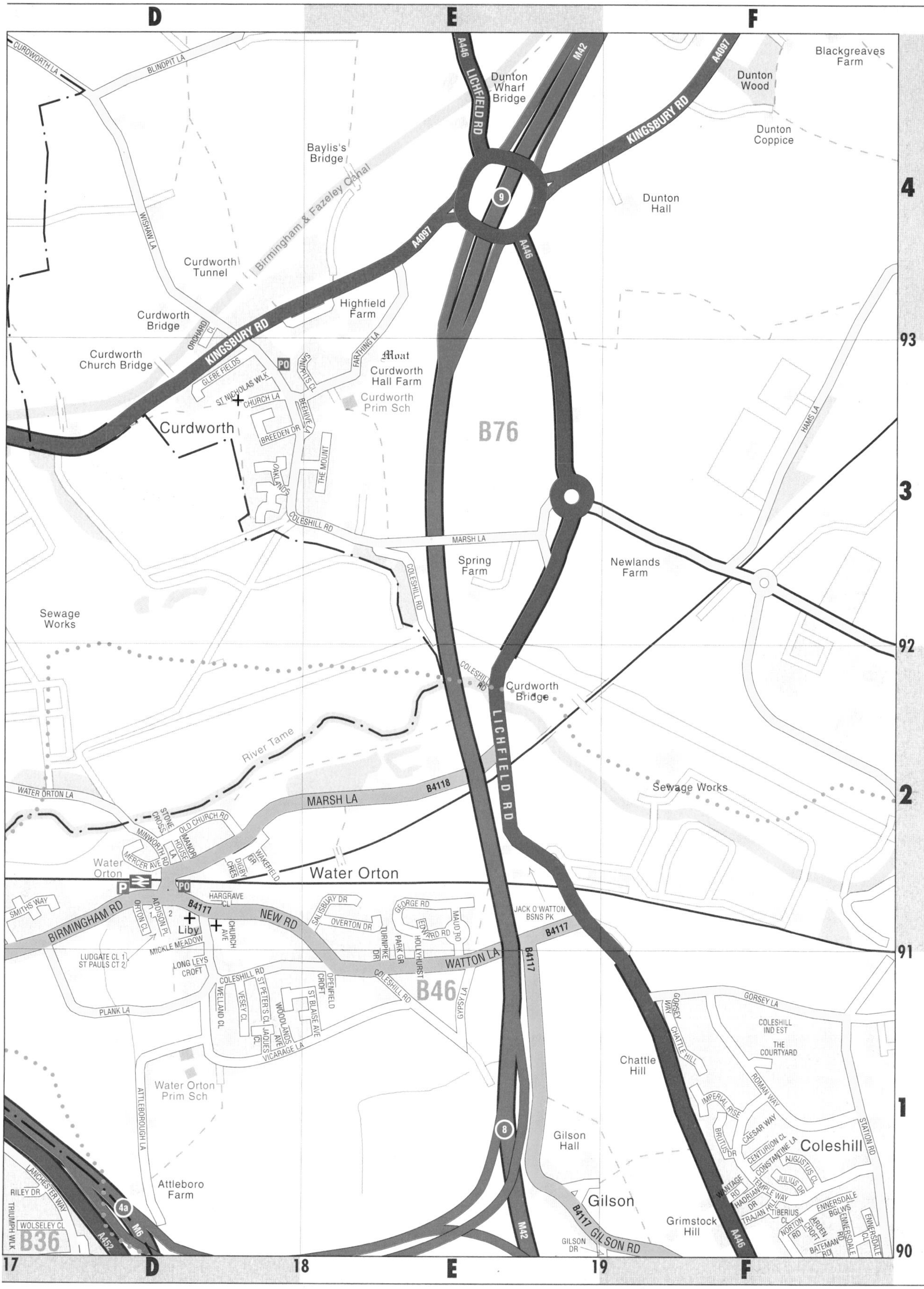
D
E
F
Blackgreaves Farm
Dunton Wood
Dunton Wharf Bridge
Dunton Coppice
Dunton Hall
Baylis's Bridge
Birmingham & Fazeley Canal
CURDWORTH LA
BLINDPIT LA
WISHAW LA
A446
LICHFIELD RD
M42
A4097
KINGSBURY RD
9
Curdworth Tunnel
Curdworth Bridge
Curdworth Church Bridge
Highfield Farm
ORCHARD CL
GLEBE FIELDS
ST NICHOLAS WLK
CHURCH LA
PO
FARTHING LA
Moat
Curdworth Hall Farm
Curdworth Prim Sch
Curdworth
BREEDEN DR
BEEHIVE LA
THE MOUNT
OAKLANDS
B76
COLESHILL RD
MARSH LA
Spring Farm
Newlands Farm
HAMS LA
Sewage Works
Curdworth Bridge
River Tame
Sewage Works
WATER ORTON LA
STONE CROSS
OLD CHURCH RD
MANOR HOUSE LA
MINWORTH RD
MERCER AVE
DIGBY GR
CRES
WAKEFIELD
B4118
Water Orton
Water Orton
P
PO
SMITHS WAY
BIRMINGHAM RD
ORTON CL
ADDISON PL
HARGRAVE CL
B4117
NEW RD
Liby
CHURCH AVE
MICKLE MEADOW
LUDGATE CL 1
ST PAULS CT 2
LONG LEYS CROFT
SALISBURY DR
OVERTON DR
GEORGE RD
EDWARD RD
MAUD RD
TURNPIKE DR
PARK GR
HOLLYHURST
WATTON LA
JACK O'WATTON BSNS PK
COLESHILL RD
OPENFIELD CROFT
B46
GYPSY LA
PLANK LA
WELLAND CL
VESEY CL
ST PETER'S CL
JAQUES CL
WOODLANDS AVE
ST BLAISE AVE
VICARAGE LA
GORSEY LA
GORSEY WAY
CHATTLE HILL
COLESHILL IND EST
THE COURTYARD
Chattle Hill
Water Orton Prim Sch
ATTLEBOROUGH LA
8
Gilson Hall
IMPERIAL RISE
ROMAN WAY
BRUTUS DR
CAESAR WAY
CENTURION CL
CONSTANTINE LA
AUGUSTUS CL
JULIUS DR
Coleshill
STATION RD
Attleboro Farm
LANCHESTER WAY
RILEY DR
4a
M6
A452
WOLSELEY CL
TRIUMPH WLK
B36
Gilson
B4117
GILSON RD
GILSON DR
Grimstock Hill
WANTAGE RD
HADRIAN DR
TEMPLE WAY
TRAJAN HILL
TIBERIUS CL
NORTON RD
ARDEN CROFT
ENNERSDALE BGLWS
ENNERSDALE RD
ENNERSDALE CL
BATEMAN RD
4
93
3
92
2
91
1
90
17
18
19

33
24

23
15

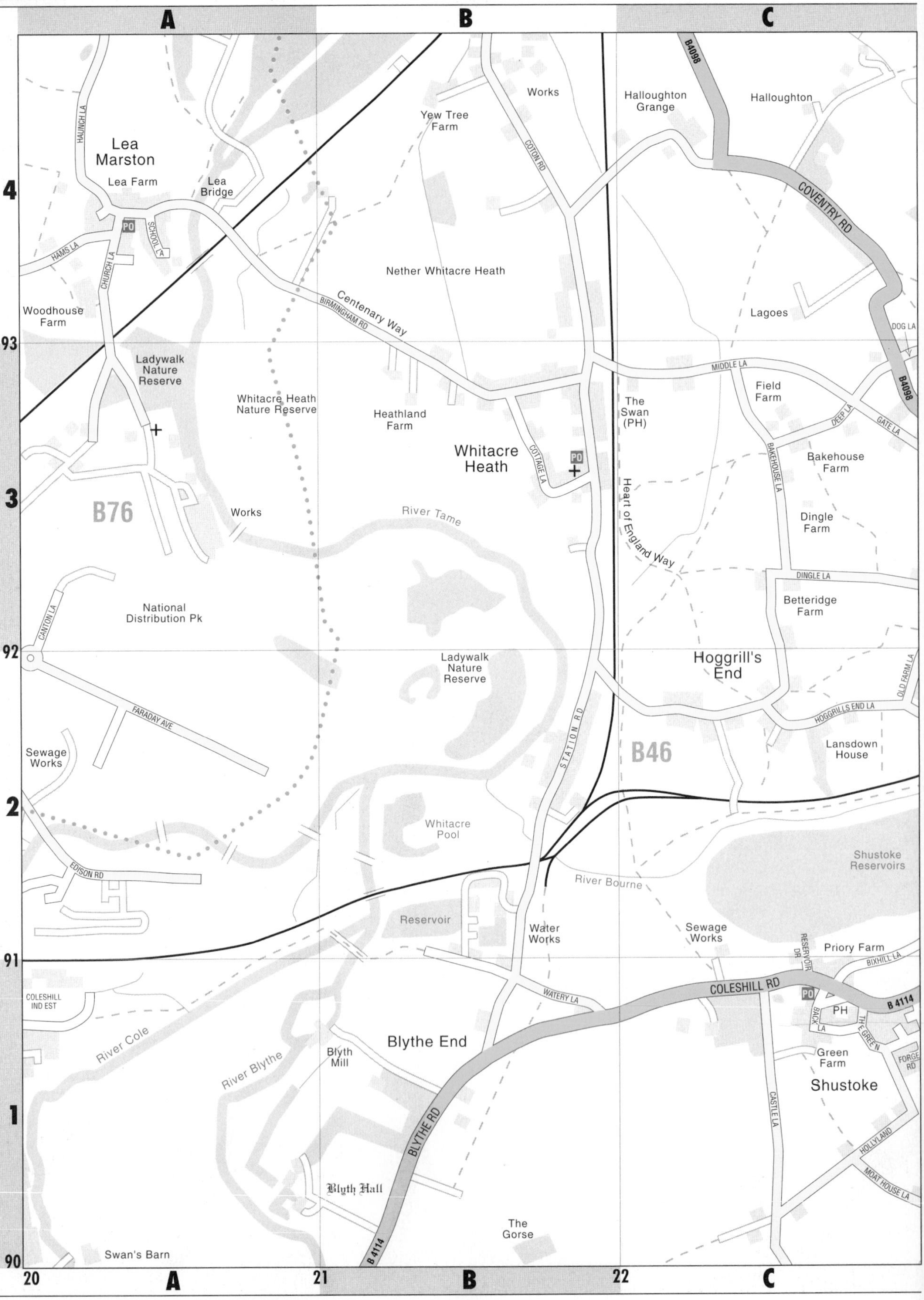
A
B
C
4
93
3
92
2
91
1
90
20
21
22
Lea Marston
Lea Farm
Lea Bridge
HAUNCH LA
HAMS LA
CHURCH LA
SCHOOL LA
PO
Woodhouse Farm
Ladywalk Nature Reserve
B76
Works
National Distribution Pk
CANTON LA
FARADAY AVE
Sewage Works
EDISON RD
COLESHILL IND EST
River Cole
River Blythe
Blyth Mill
Blythe End
Blyth Hall
Swan's Barn
B 4114
BLYTHE RD
The Gorse
Yew Tree Farm
Works
COTON RD
Nether Whitacre Heath
Centenary Way
BIRMINGHAM RD
Whitacre Heath Nature Reserve
Heathland Farm
Whitacre Heath
COTTAGE LA
River Tame
Ladywalk Nature Reserve
STATION RD
Whitacre Pool
Reservoir
Water Works
WATERY LA
River Bourne
Halloughton Grange
Halloughton
B4098
COVENTRY RD
Lagoes
DOG LA
MIDDLE LA
Field Farm
The Swan (PH)
DEEP LA
GATE LA
Bakehouse Farm
BAKEHOUSE LA
Heart of England Way
Dingle Farm
DINGLE LA
Betteridge Farm
Hoggrill's End
OLD FARM LA
HOGGRILLS END LA
B46
Lansdown House
Shustoke Reservoirs
Sewage Works
RESERVOIR DR
Priory Farm
BIXHILL LA
COLESHILL RD
B 4114
BACK LA
PH
THE GREEN
FORGE RD
Green Farm
Shustoke
CASTLE LA
HOLLYLAND
MOAT HOUSE LA

23
34

16
26

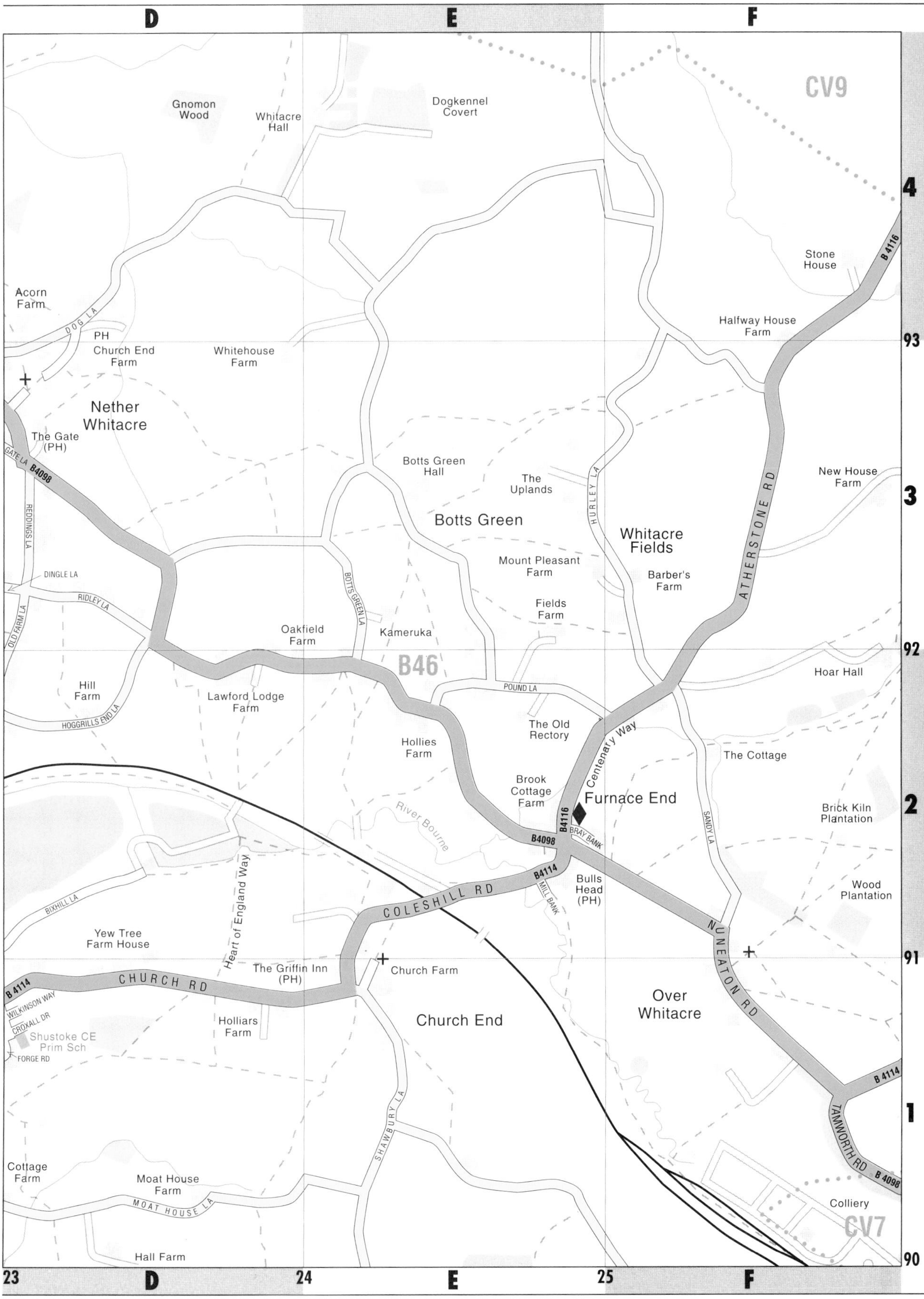
D
E
F
CV9
Gnomon Wood
Whitacre Hall
Dogkennel Covert
4
Acorn Farm
Stone House
DOG LA
PH
Church End Farm
Whitehouse Farm
Halfway House Farm
93
B4116
Nether Whitacre
The Gate (PH)
GATE LA
B4098
REDDINGS LA
Botts Green Hall
The Uplands
HURLEY LA
New House Farm
3
Botts Green
Whitacre Fields
ATHERSTONE RD
Mount Pleasant Farm
Barber's Farm
DINGLE LA
RIDLEY LA
OLD FARM LA
BOTTS GREEN LA
Fields Farm
Oakfield Farm
Kameruka
B46
92
Hill Farm
Lawford Lodge Farm
POUND LA
Hoar Hall
HOGGRILLS END LA
The Old Rectory
Centenary Way
Hollies Farm
The Cottage
Brook Cottage Farm
Furnace End
SANDY LA
Brick Kiln Plantation
2
River Bourne
B4116
BRAY BANK
B4098
B4114
MILL BANK
Bulls Head (PH)
Wood Plantation
BIXHILL LA
COLESHILL RD
Heart of England Way
NUNEATON RD
Yew Tree Farm House
The Griffin Inn (PH)
Church Farm
91
B 4114
CHURCH RD
WILKINSON WAY
CROXALL DR
Holliars Farm
Over Whitacre
Church End
Shustoke CE Prim Sch
FORGE RD
B 4114
1
SHAWBURY LA
TAMWORTH RD
B 4098
Cottage Farm
Moat House Farm
MOAT HOUSE LA
Colliery
CV7
Hall Farm
90
23
D
24
E
25
F

35
26

25
17

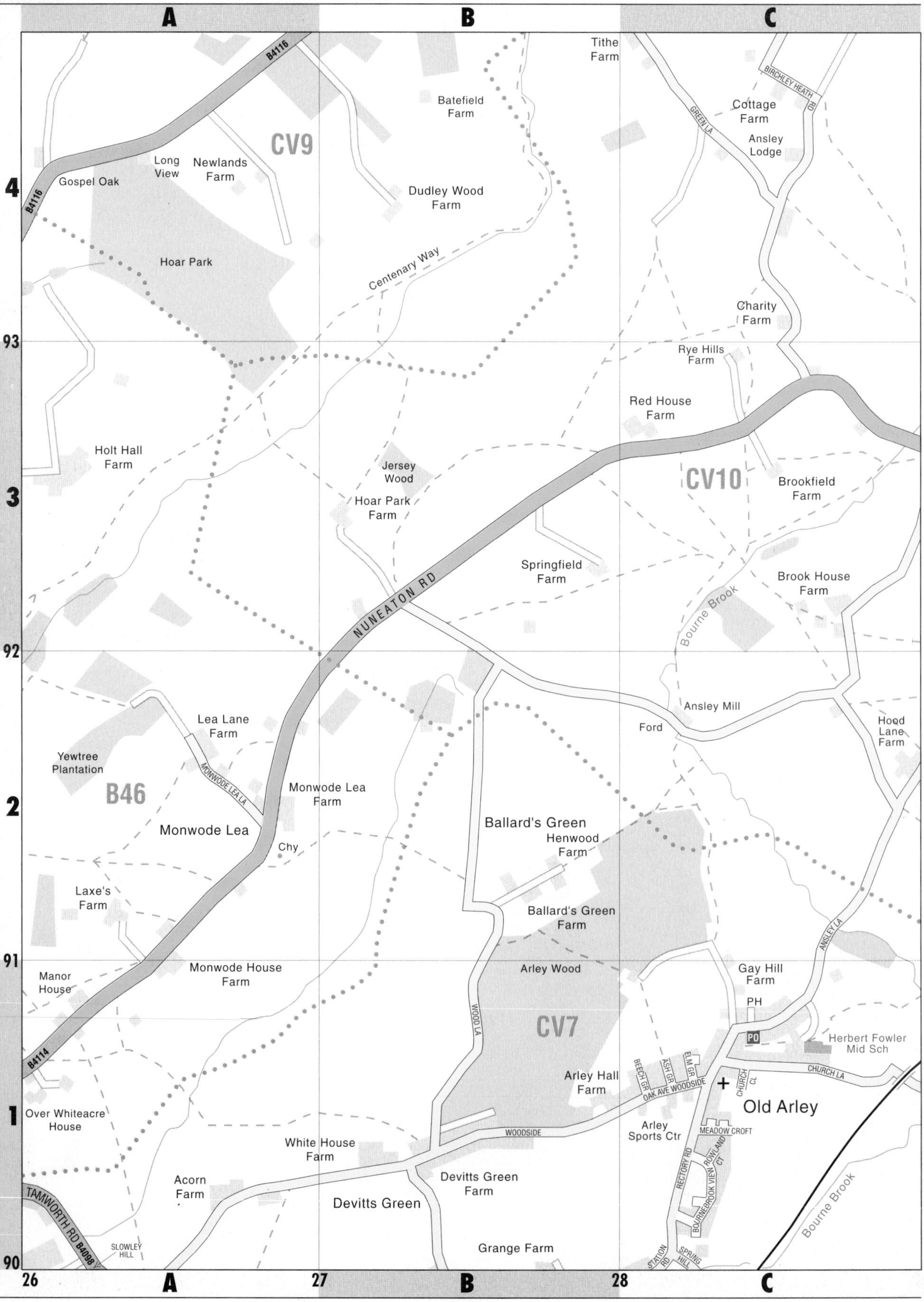
A
B
C
4
93
3
92
2
91
1
90
26
27
28
B4116
CV9
Tithe Farm
Batefield Farm
Cottage Farm
Ansley Lodge
BIRCHLEY HEATH RD
GREEN LA
Long View
Newlands Farm
Gospel Oak
Dudley Wood Farm
Hoar Park
Centenary Way
Charity Farm
Rye Hills Farm
Red House Farm
Holt Hall Farm
Jersey Wood
Hoar Park Farm
CV10
Brookfield Farm
Springfield Farm
Brook House Farm
NUNEATON RD
Bourne Brook
Ansley Mill
Ford
Hood Lane Farm
Lea Lane Farm
Yewtree Plantation
B46
MONWODE LEA LA
Monwode Lea Farm
Monwode Lea
Chy
Ballard's Green
Henwood Farm
Laxe's Farm
Ballard's Green Farm
ANSLEY LA
Manor House
Monwode House Farm
Arley Wood
Gay Hill Farm
PH
PO
Herbert Fowler Mid Sch
WOOD LA
CV7
B4114
BEECH GR
ASH GR
ELM GR
CHURCH CL
CHURCH LA
Arley Hall Farm
OAK AVE WOODSIDE
Old Arley
Over Whiteacre House
Arley Sports Ctr
MEADOW CROFT
White House Farm
WOODSIDE
ROWLAND CT
RECTORY RD
BOURNEBROOK VIEW
Devitts Green Farm
Acorn Farm
Devitts Green
TAMWORTH RD B4098
SLOWLEY HILL
Grange Farm
STATION RD
SPRING HILL
Bourne Brook

25
36

18
28

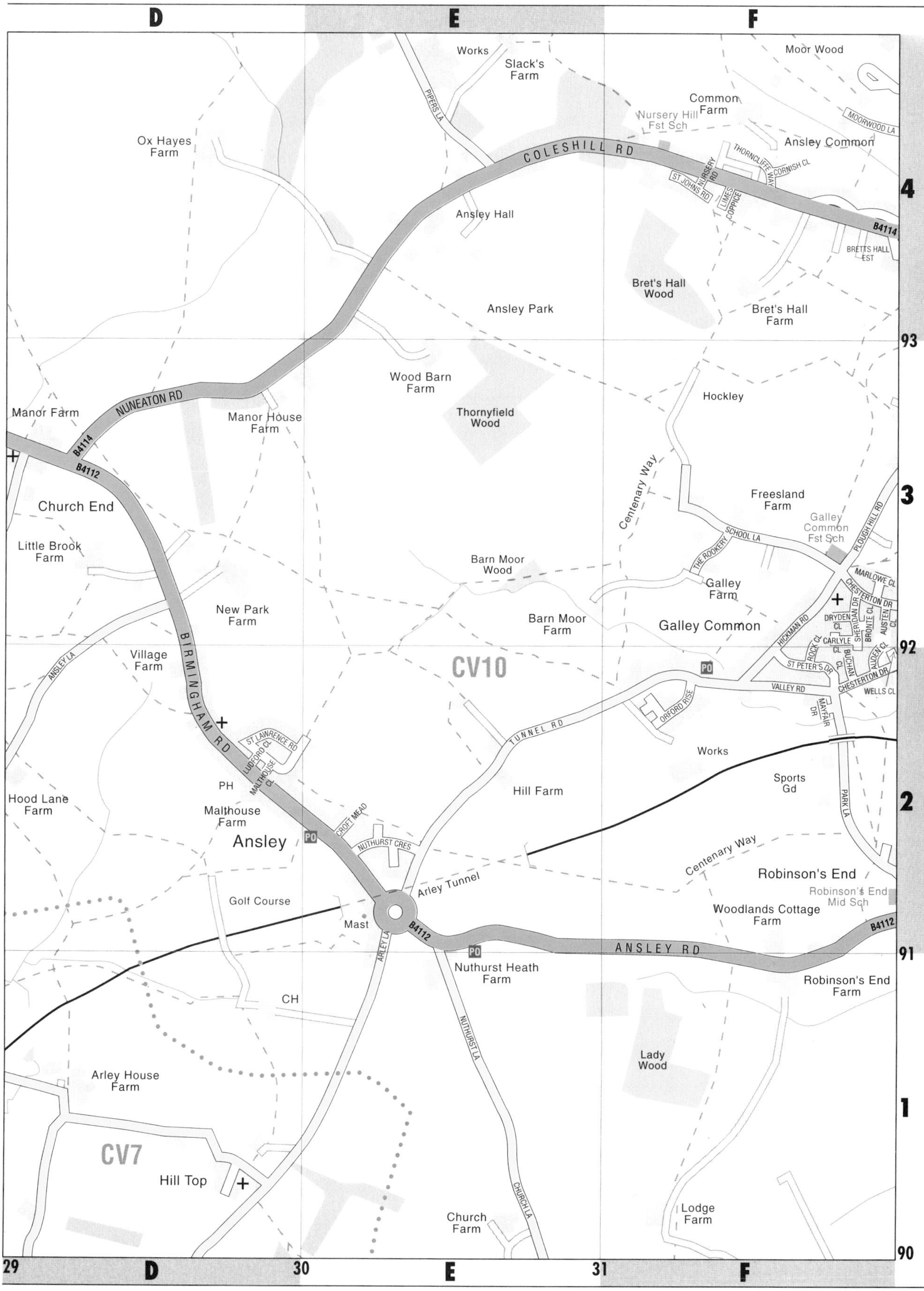
D
E
F
Works
Slack's Farm
Moor Wood
Common Farm
Nursery Hill Fst Sch
Ansley Common
MOORWOOD LA
Ox Hayes Farm
PIPERS LA
COLESHILL RD
THORNCLIFFE WAY
CORNISH CL
NURSERY RD
ST JOHNS RD
LIMES COPPICE
Ansley Hall
B4114
BRETTS HALL EST
Bret's Hall Wood
Ansley Park
Bret's Hall Farm
93
4
Wood Barn Farm
Hockley
NUNEATON RD
Manor Farm
Manor House Farm
Thornyfield Wood
B4114
B4112
Centenary Way
Church End
Freesland Farm
3
Galley Common Fst Sch
PLOUGH HILL RD
SCHOOL LA
Little Brook Farm
Barn Moor Wood
THE ROOKERY
Galley Farm
MARLOWE CL
CHESTERTON DR
New Park Farm
Barn Moor Farm
Galley Common
HICKMAN RD
DRYDEN CL
SHERIDAN DR
BRONTE CL
AUSTEN CL
CARLYLE CL
ROCK CL
BUCHAN CL
AUDEN CL
92
Village Farm
ANSLEY LA
CV10
PO
ST PETER'S DR
CHESTERTON DR
VALLEY RD
WELLS CL
BIRMINGHAM RD
ORFORD RISE
MAYFAIR DR
ST LAWRENCE RD
LUDFORD CL
MALTHOUSE CL
TUNNEL RD
Works
PH
Hill Farm
Sports Gd
Hood Lane Farm
Malthouse Farm
PARK LA
2
Ansley
PO
CROFT MEAD
NUTHURST CRES
Centenary Way
Robinson's End
Arley Tunnel
Robinson's End Mid Sch
Golf Course
Woodlands Cottage Farm
Mast
B4112
ARLEY LA
B4112
ANSLEY RD
PO
91
Nuthurst Heath Farm
Robinson's End Farm
CH
NUTHURST LA
Lady Wood
Arley House Farm
1
CV7
Hill Top
CHURCH LA
Lodge Farm
Church Farm
90
29
D
30
E
31
F

37
28

27
19

A
B
C
4
93
3
92
2
91
1
90
32
33
34
Michael Drayton Mid Sch
Hartshill Sch
Chapel End
Nathaniel Newton Fst Sch
Hartshill Quarries
Mast
Hill House
Wood Bridge
River Anker
Coventry Canal
Caldicote Hill
Mill
Judkins Quarry
OLDBURY RD
WOOD LA
THE WOODLANDS
MOORWOOD LA
HILLSIDE
SPRINGHILL
DRAYTON CL
CHURCH RD
CHURCH CL
HAYES RD
ASH DR
WOOD CRES
MOOR RD
MEADOW RD
HAWTHORN WAY
HAZEL CL
LAUREL DR
SCHOOL HILL
VICTORIA RD
ORCHARD CL
SILVERBIRCH CL
B4114
ANSLEY COMM
COLESHILL RD
WILLOW CL
ALDERS LA
BRETTS HALL EST
CHANCERY LA
SALISBURY DR
LINCOLN AVE
GRANGE CL
CAMP HILL RD
B4111
NUNEATON RD
MANCETTER RD
BERRINGTON RD
HILLSIDE DR
CLEVELEY DR
ARLON AVE
WINDMILL RD
DRAYTON WAY
CRADDOCK DR
GREEN LA
OAKROYD CRES
CAMP HILL DR
St Anne's RC Prim Sch
KAREN CL
TUTTLE HILL IND EST
TUTTLE HILL
Nuneaton Common
Plough Hill
PH
PLOUGH HILL RD
WESTMINSTER DR
BIRCHTREE RD
ORCHARD WAY
ALMOND AVE
TUDOR RD
RAMSDEN AVE
Camp Hill Cty Jun Sch
The Hollies Inf Sch
STITCHES RD
THE HEDGEROWS
B4114
Cemy
BUCKS HILL
FRESLAND RISE
HILTON AVE
FRASER CL
MERLIN AVE
TRAFFORD DR
MALLARD AVE
KINGFISHER AVE
ROWAN RD
SPRING HILL RD
LUDFORD RD
EDINBURGH RD
BEECHWOOD RD
SYCAMORE RD
CEDAR RD
LABURNUM GR
THE DINGLE
PEAR TREE AVE
CHERRY TREE AVE
CHESTNUT CRES
ASHWOOD RD
LIME GR
MOUNT PLEASANT TERR
HAWTHORNE TERR
WILLOW RD
DALE END
HAZEL RD
HILLCREST RD
GORSY WAY
QUEEN ELIZABETH RD
Camp Hill
CV11
Ind Est
POOL RD
HILARY RD
MAPLE RD
Hill Farm
Galley Common
LORRINA CL
BETTINA CL
FRENSHAM DR
GARNETTE CL
CROFT
MALLERIN
BURNABY CL
Whittleford
CV10
ACACIA RD
ADDISON CL
BROWNING CL
RUSKIN CL
BLAKE CL
CHESTERTON DR
FIELDING WAY
KEATS CL
SWINBURNE CL
SELBY WAY
WIMBOURNE CL
WALTHAM CRES
HARDY CL
CHAUCER DR
DICKENS CL
THACKERAY CL
HAMPTON AVE
SHERBOURNE AVE
BEVERLEY AVE
PORTLAND DR
KNOWLES AVE
SPINNEY LA
WHITTLEFORD RD
WOODFORD CL
HAMILTON CT
ST MICHAEL'S WAY
VALE VIEW
BLACK-A-TREE RD
TRYAN RD
VERNONS LA
BYFORD ST
BARPOOL RD
THE CIRCLE
WOOD ST
Recn Gd
OLTON PL
BEAUMONT RD
King's Wood
CHURCHDALE CL
QUARRY YD
EADIE ST
FREEMAN CL
HAUNCHWOOD RD
CULPEPPER CL
FORD ST
TOMKINSON RD
KINGSWOOD RD
BERWYN WAY
THE SPIRES
SHORT ST
HILL ST
RANDLE RD
MELDRUM RD
BEDE RD
WHITEHOUSE CRES
CROSS ST
DANIEL AVE
CHURCH RD
SOMERSET DR
MONMOUTH GDNS
HERTFORD CL
CUMBERLAND DR
WESTMORLAND AVE
NORFOLK CRES
WARWICK GDNS
HUNTINGDON WAY
RUTLAND AVE
NORTHUMBERLAND AVE
DEVON CL
DORSET CL
GRANBY RD
CLIFTON RD
NORTH ST
CLENT DR
QUANTOCK DR
PENNINE WAY
PRESCELLY CL
MENDIP DR
WENLOCK WAY
SNOWDON CL
ASHE RD
THORNTONS WAY
CROWDALE CL
BRENDON WAY
ROBINS WAY
TOWER VIEW CRES
COTSWOLD CRES
CHEVIOT CL
MALVERN AVE
WICLIF WAY
St Paul's CE Fst Sch
ST PAUL'S RD
PADDIFORD PL
Stockingford Fst & Mid Sch
WESTBURY RD
SUFFOLK CL
SUSSEX CL
SURREY CL
BERKSHIRE CL
VIRGINIA RD
MONTANA WLK
Croft Mid Sch
MARSDALE DR
HELENA CL
DENEHURST WAY
RUNNYMEDE GDNS
CROFT RD
B4102
SILVER WLK
ROBINSON PARK LA
B4112
ANSLEY RD
Stockingford
WEBB ST
PRIORY ST
GROVE PL
GROVE RD
THE POPLARS
CAMBRIDGE DR
ALBERT ST
JOHN ST
HERBERT ST
BELLE VUE
Robinson's End Mid Sch
Tower Farm
B4102
ARBURY RD
SEESWOOD CL
Alderman Smith Sch
ROSSENDALE WAY
FOREST WAY
KIELDER DR
RADNOR DR
CHARNWOOD AVE
ATHOLL CRES
B4112
HEATH END RD
LEAWARD CL
BRACKENDALE DR
LINGWOOD DR
HEATHER CL
BROOMFIELD RISE
STROMA WAY
BRODICK WAY
FAIR ISLE DR
MONTROSE DR
THE RATWOODS
KINROSS CL
SKYE CL
ASHDOWN DR
OLDANY WAY
COLLISS CRES
Heath End
Glendale Fst Sch
Heath End Farm
TENLONS RD
Centenary Way
Seeswood Pool
Coton Lawn
Coton Lawn Farm
ASTLEY LA
Sees Wood
PO
P

27
38

20
30

D E F

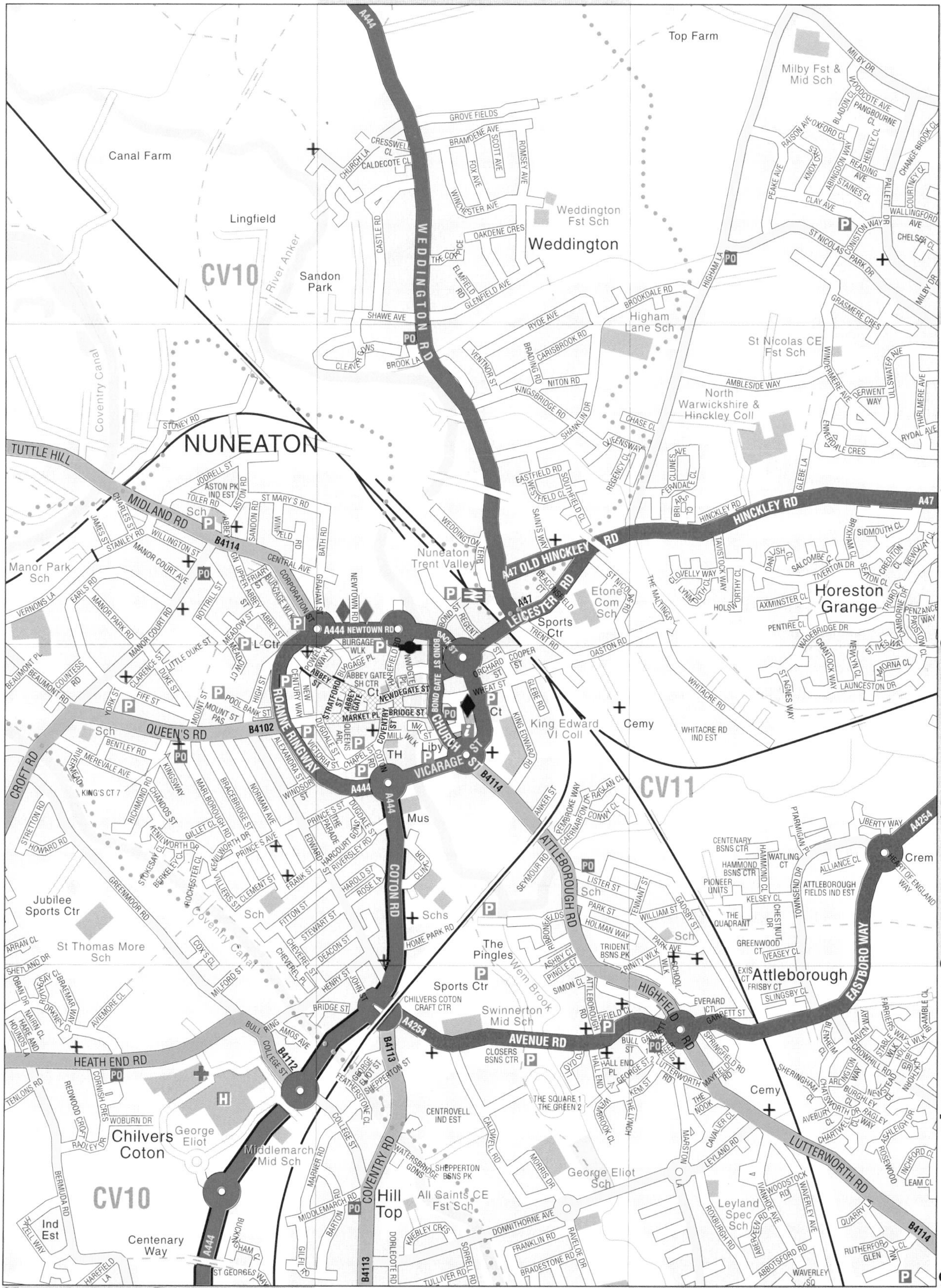

4 3 2 1
93 92 91 90
35 36 37
D E F

39
30

29
21

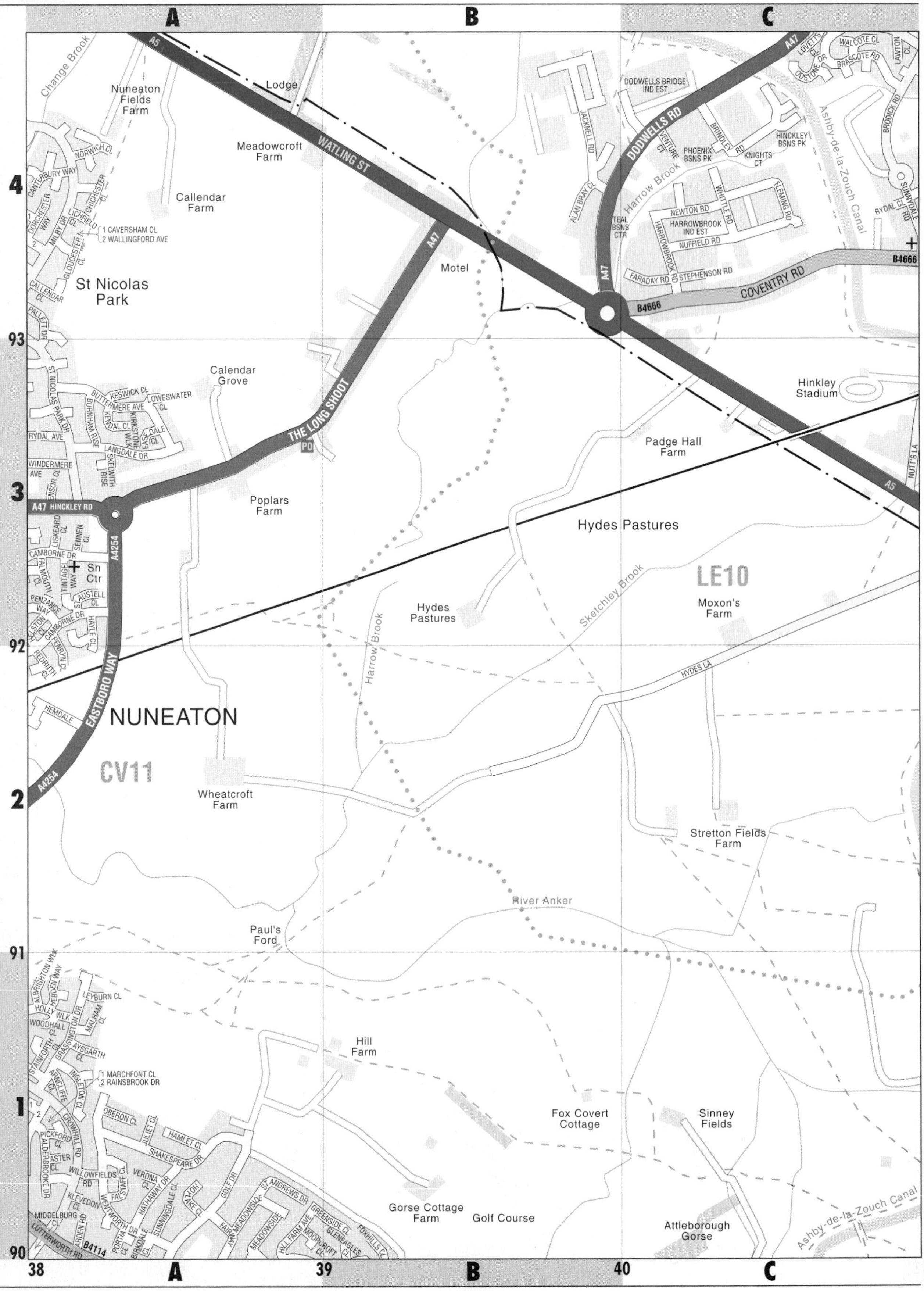
A
B
C
Change Brook
Nuneaton Fields Farm
Lodge
Meadowcroft Farm
WATLING ST
Callendar Farm
St Nicolas Park
Motel
A47
A5
DODWELLS BRIDGE IND EST
DODWELLS RD
JACKNELL RD
ALAN BRAY CL
Harrow Brook
PHOENIX BSNS PK
BRINDLEY RD
KNIGHTS CT
HINCKLEY BSNS PK
VENTURE CT
TEAL BSNS CTR
NEWTON RD
HARROWBROOK IND EST
NUFFIELD RD
WHITTLE RD
FLEMING RD
HARROWBROOK RD
FARADAY RD
STEPHENSON RD
COVENTRY RD
B4666
Ashby-de-la-Zouch Canal
LOVETTS CL
WALCOTE CL
BRASCOTE RD
LAWTON CL
ODSTONE DR
BRODICK RD
SUNNYDALE RD
RYDAL CL
NORWICH CL
CANTERBURY WAY
DORCHESTER WAY
CHICHESTER CL
LICHFIELD CL
MILBY DR
GLOUCESTER CL
1 CAVERSHAM CL
2 WALLINGFORD AVE
CALLENDAR CL
PALLETT DR
Calendar Grove
KESWICK CL
BUTTERMERE AVE
LOWESWATER CL
KENDAL CL
KIRKSTONE WLK
EASEDALE CL
BURNHAM RISE
LANGDALE DR
SKELWITH RISE
ST NICOLAS PARK DR
RYDAL AVE
WINDERMERE AVE
THE LONG SHOOT
PO
Poplars Farm
Hinkley Stadium
Padge Hall Farm
NUTT'S LA
Hydes Pastures
LE10
Sketchley Brook
Moxon's Farm
A47 HINCKLEY RD
A4254
CAMBORNE DR
LISKEARD CL
SENNEN CL
FALMOUTH CL
TINTAGEL WAY
Sh Ctr
PENZANCE WAY
ST AUSTELL CL
HELSTON CL
HAYLE CL
PENRYN CL
REDRUTH CL
Hydes Pastures
Harrow Brook
HYDES LA
EASTBORO WAY
HEMDALE
NUNEATON
CV11
Wheatcroft Farm
Stretton Fields Farm
River Anker
Paul's Ford
ALBRIGHTON WLK
HEBDEN WAY
LEYBURN CL
HOLLY WLK
WOODHALL CL
GRASSINGTON DR
MALHAM CL
AYSGARTH CL
STAINFORTH CL
ARNCLIFFE CL
INGLETON CL
1 MARCHFONT CL
2 RAINSBROOK DR
Hill Farm
CROWHILL RD
PICKFORD CL
OBERON CL
JULIET CL
HAMLET CL
SHAKESPEARE DR
ALDERBROOK DR
ASTER CL
WILLOWFIELDS RD
VERONA CL
FALSTAFF CL
HATHAWAY DR
SUNNINGDALE CL
GOLF DR
KLEVEDON CL
WENTWORTH DR
MIDDELBURG CL
ARDEN RD
PORTIA CL
BIRKDALE CL
LUTTERWORTH RD
B4114
MEADOWSIDE
ST ANDREWS DR
GREENSIDE CL
GLENEAGLES
FOXHILLS CL
HILL FARM AVE
MOORCROFT CL
Fox Covert Cottage
Sinney Fields
Gorse Cottage Farm
Golf Course
Attleborough Gorse
4
93
3
92
2
91
1
90
38
39
40

29
40

E4
1 MANSION ST
2 BRITTANIA SH CTR
3 EDWARDS CTR
4 THE HORSEFAIR

32

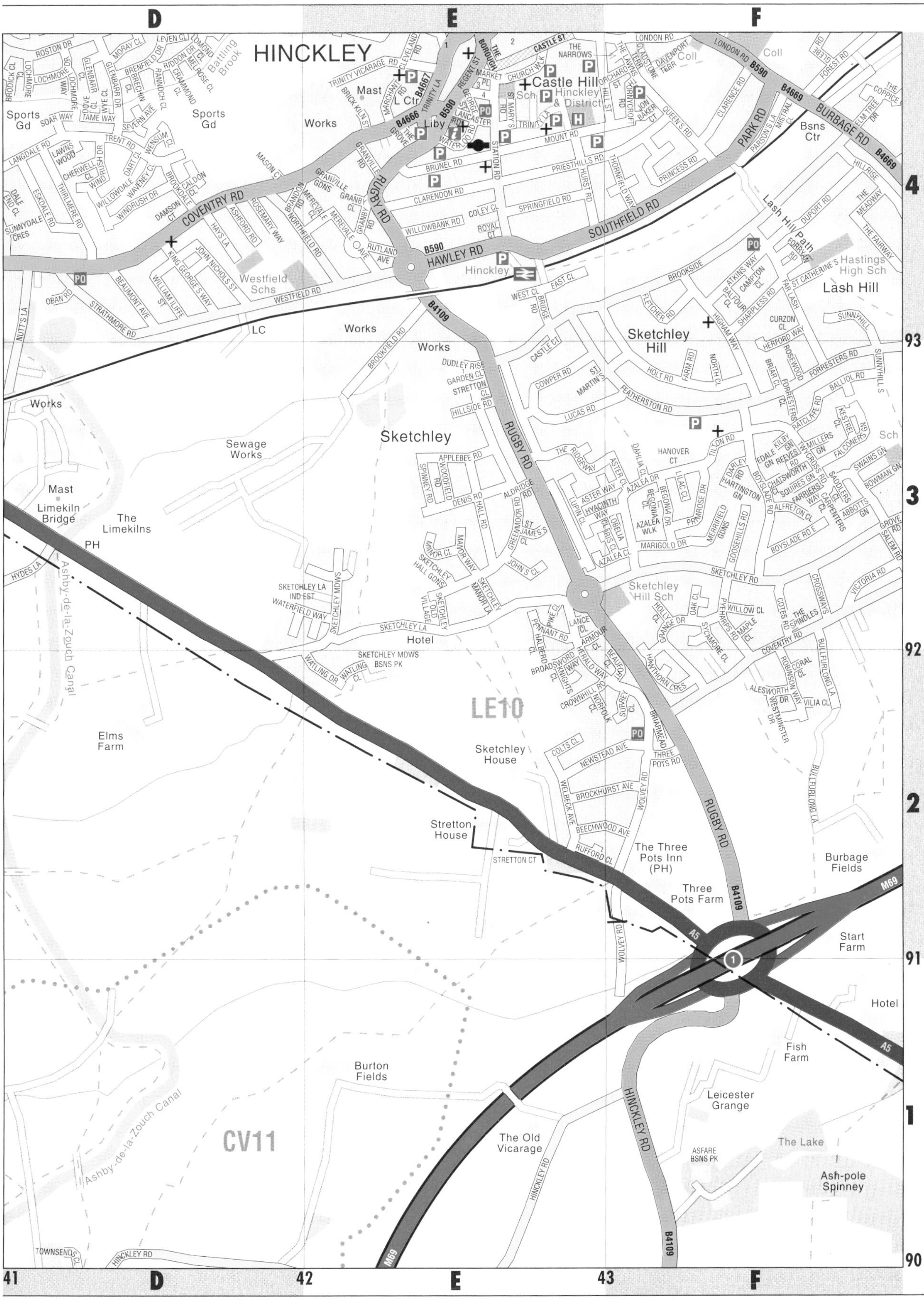

4T
32

31

A B C

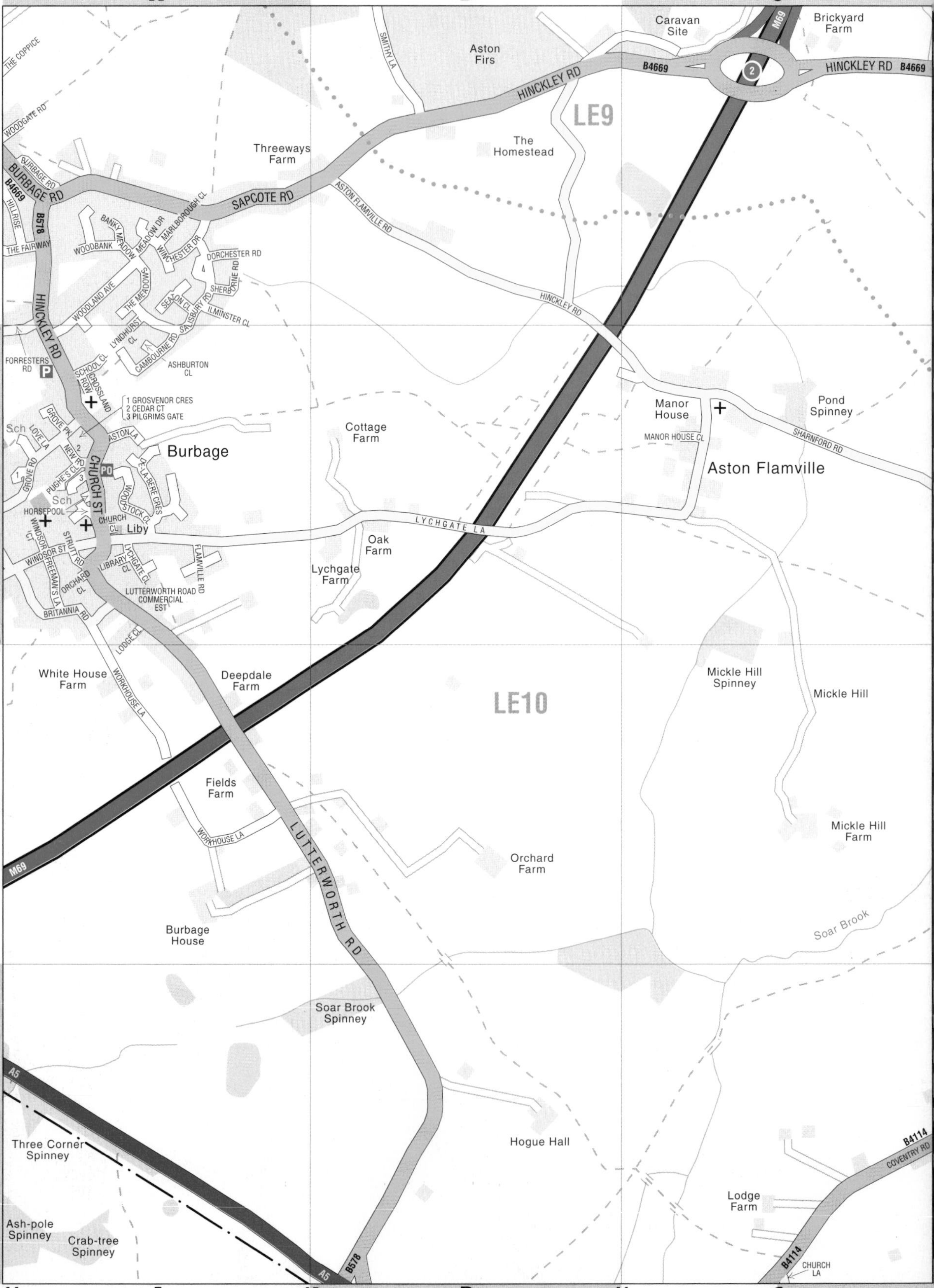

4
93
3
92
2
91
1
90
Caravan Site
Brickyard Farm
Aston Firs
SMITHY LA
HINCKLEY RD
B4669
M69
2
HINCKLEY RD B4669
LE9
THE COPPICE
WOODGATE RD
Threeways Farm
The Homestead
BURBAGE RD
B4669
BURBAGE RD
HILLRISE
B578
SAPCOTE RD
MARLBOROUGH CL
ASTON FLAMVILLE RD
THE FAIRWAY
WOODBANK
BANKY MEADOW
MEADOW DR
WINCHESTER DR
DORCHESTER RD
SHERBORNE RD
THE MEADOWS
SEATON CL
ILMINSTER CL
WOODLAND AVE
LYNDHURST CL
SALISBURY RD
CAMBOURNE RD
HINCKLEY RD
ASHBURTON CL
HINCKLEY RD
FORRESTERS RD
P
SCHOOL ROW
CROSSLAND
1 GROSVENOR CRES
2 CEDAR CT
3 PILGRIMS GATE
Manor House
Pond Spinney
Cottage Farm
MANOR HOUSE CL
SHARNFORD RD
Sch
LOVE LA
GROVE PK
ASTON LA
NEW RD
Burbage
Aston Flamville
GROVE RD
PUGHE'S CL
CHURCH ST
PO
LA BERE CRES
WOODSTOCK CL
Sch
HORSEPOOL
CHURCH CL
Liby
LYCHGATE LA
WINDSOR CT
STRUTT RD
WINDSOR ST
Oak Farm
FREEMAN'S LA
LIBRARY CL
LYCHGATE CL
FLAMVILLE RD
ORCHARD CL
Lychgate Farm
LUTTERWORTH ROAD COMMERCIAL EST
BRITANNIA RD
LODGE CL
White House Farm
WORKHOUSE LA
Deepdale Farm
LE10
Mickle Hill Spinney
Mickle Hill
Fields Farm
LUTTERWORTH RD
WORKHOUSE LA
Mickle Hill Farm
M69
Orchard Farm
Burbage House
Soar Brook
Soar Brook Spinney
A5
Three Corner Spinney
Hogue Hall
B4114
COVENTRY RD
Lodge Farm
Ash-pole Spinney
Crab-tree Spinney
B4114
B578
A5
CHURCH LA

44 A 45 B 46 C

31

42

23
34

D E F

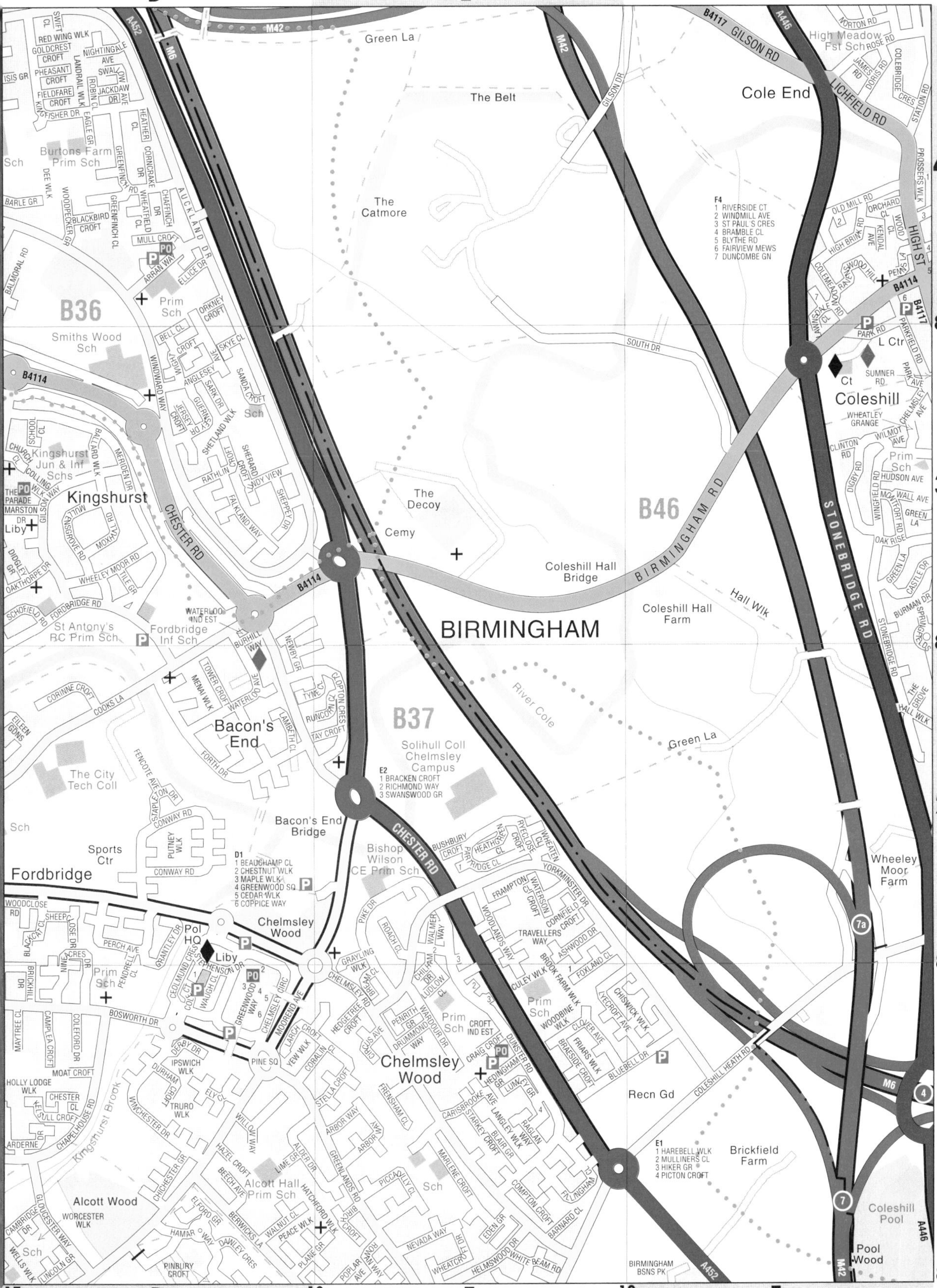

17 D 18 E 19 F

44
34

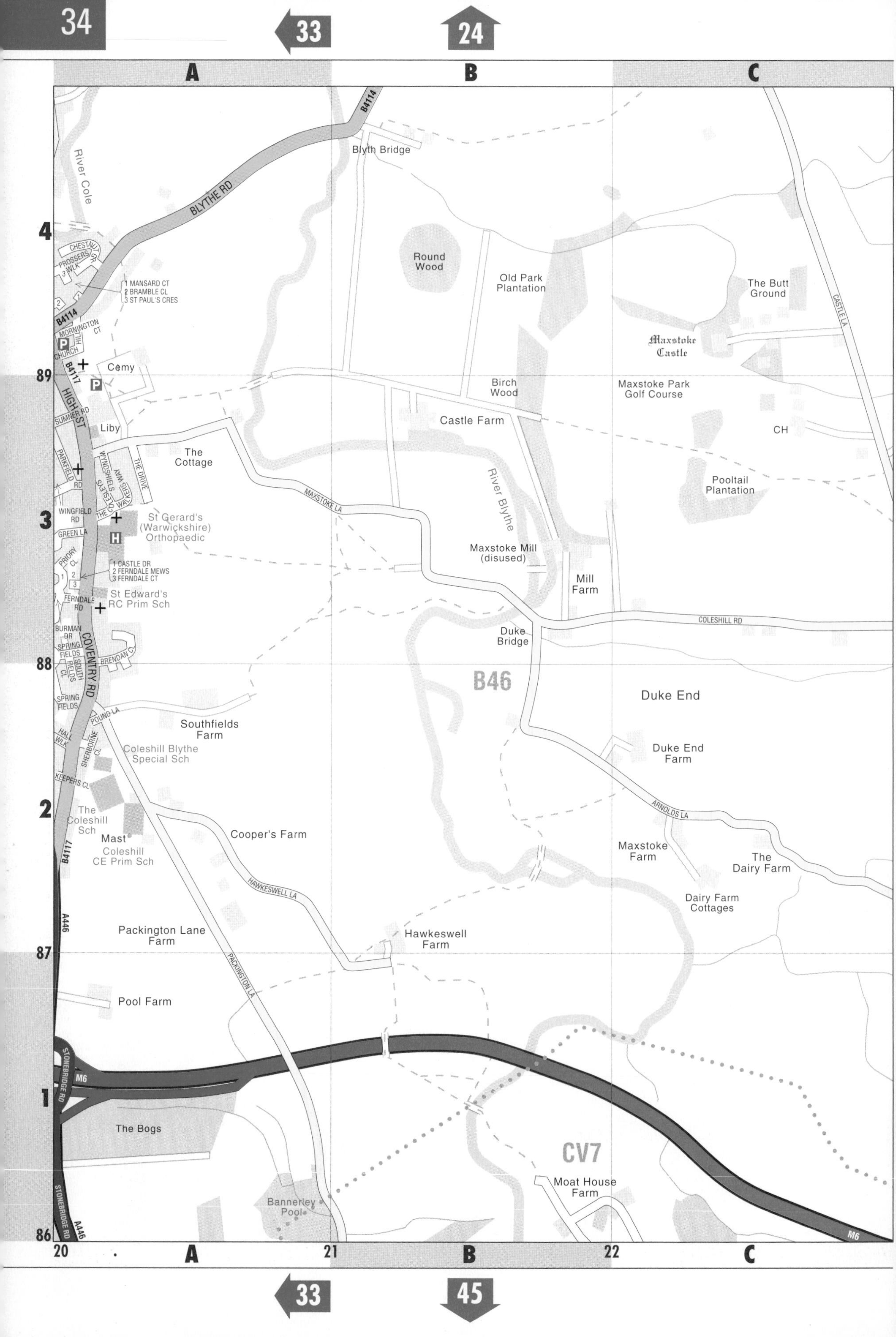
33
24
A
B
C
4
3
2
1
89
88
87
86
20
21
22
B4114
Blyth Bridge
BLYTHE RD
River Cole
CHESTNUT GR
PROSSERS WLK
1 MANSARD CT
2 BRAMBLE CL
3 ST PAUL'S CRES
B4114
MORNINGTON CT
CHURCH HILL
B4117
Cemy
HIGH ST
SUMNER RD
Liby
PARKFIELD RD
WYNDSHIELS
THE DRIVE
WALKERS WAY
THE COLESHILL
WINGFIELD RD
GREEN LA
PRIORY CL
St Gerard's (Warwickshire) Orthopaedic
1 CASTLE DR
2 FERNDALE MEWS
3 FERNDALE CT
FERNDALE RD
St Edward's RC Prim Sch
BURMAN DR
SPRING FIELDS
SOUTH FIELDS CL
BRENDAN CL
COVENTRY RD
SPRING FIELDS
POUND LA
HALL WLK
SHERBORNE CL
Coleshill Blythe Special Sch
KEEPERS CL
The Coleshill Sch
Mast
Coleshill CE Prim Sch
B4117
A446
The Cottage
Southfields Farm
Cooper's Farm
HAWKESWELL LA
Packington Lane Farm
Pool Farm
PACKINGTON LA
Hawkeswell Farm
M6
STONEBRIDGE RD
The Bogs
Bannerley Pool
STONEBRIDGE RD
A446
Round Wood
Old Park Plantation
Birch Wood
Castle Farm
MAXSTOKE LA
River Blythe
Maxstoke Mill (disused)
Mill Farm
Duke Bridge
COLESHILL RD
B46
Duke End
Duke End Farm
ARNOLDS LA
Maxstoke Farm
The Dairy Farm
Dairy Farm Cottages
CV7
Moat House Farm
M6
The Butt Ground
Maxstoke Castle
CASTLE LA
Maxstoke Park Golf Course
CH
Pooltail Plantation
33
45

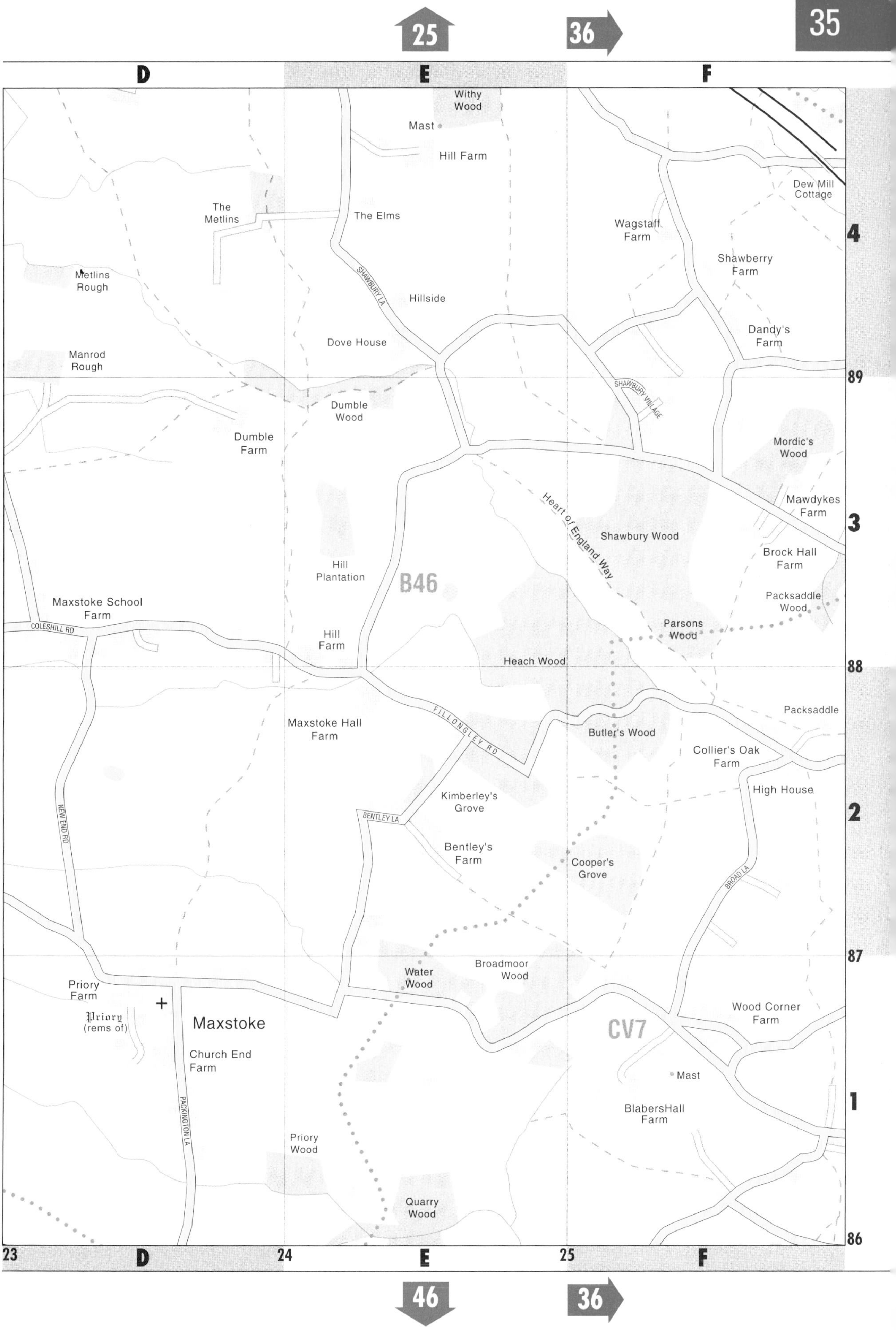
25
36
D
E
F
Withy Wood
Mast
Hill Farm
The Metlins
The Elms
Dew Mill Cottage
Wagstaff Farm
Shawberry Farm
Metlins Rough
SHAWBURY LA
Hillside
Dandy's Farm
Dove House
Manrod Rough
SHAWBURY VILLAGE
Dumble Wood
Dumble Farm
Mordic's Wood
Heart of England Way
Mawdykes Farm
Shawbury Wood
Brock Hall Farm
Hill Plantation
B46
Packsaddle Wood
Maxstoke School Farm
COLESHILL RD
Parsons Wood
Hill Farm
Heach Wood
Packsaddle
Maxstoke Hall Farm
FILLONGLEY RD
Butler's Wood
Collier's Oak Farm
High House
Kimberley's Grove
BENTLEY LA
NEW END RD
Bentley's Farm
Cooper's Grove
BROAD LA
Broadmoor Wood
Water Wood
Priory Farm
Wood Corner Farm
Priory (rems of)
Maxstoke
CV7
Church End Farm
Mast
BlabersHall Farm
PACKINGTON LA
Priory Wood
Quarry Wood
4
89
3
88
2
87
1
86
23
24
25
46
36

35
26

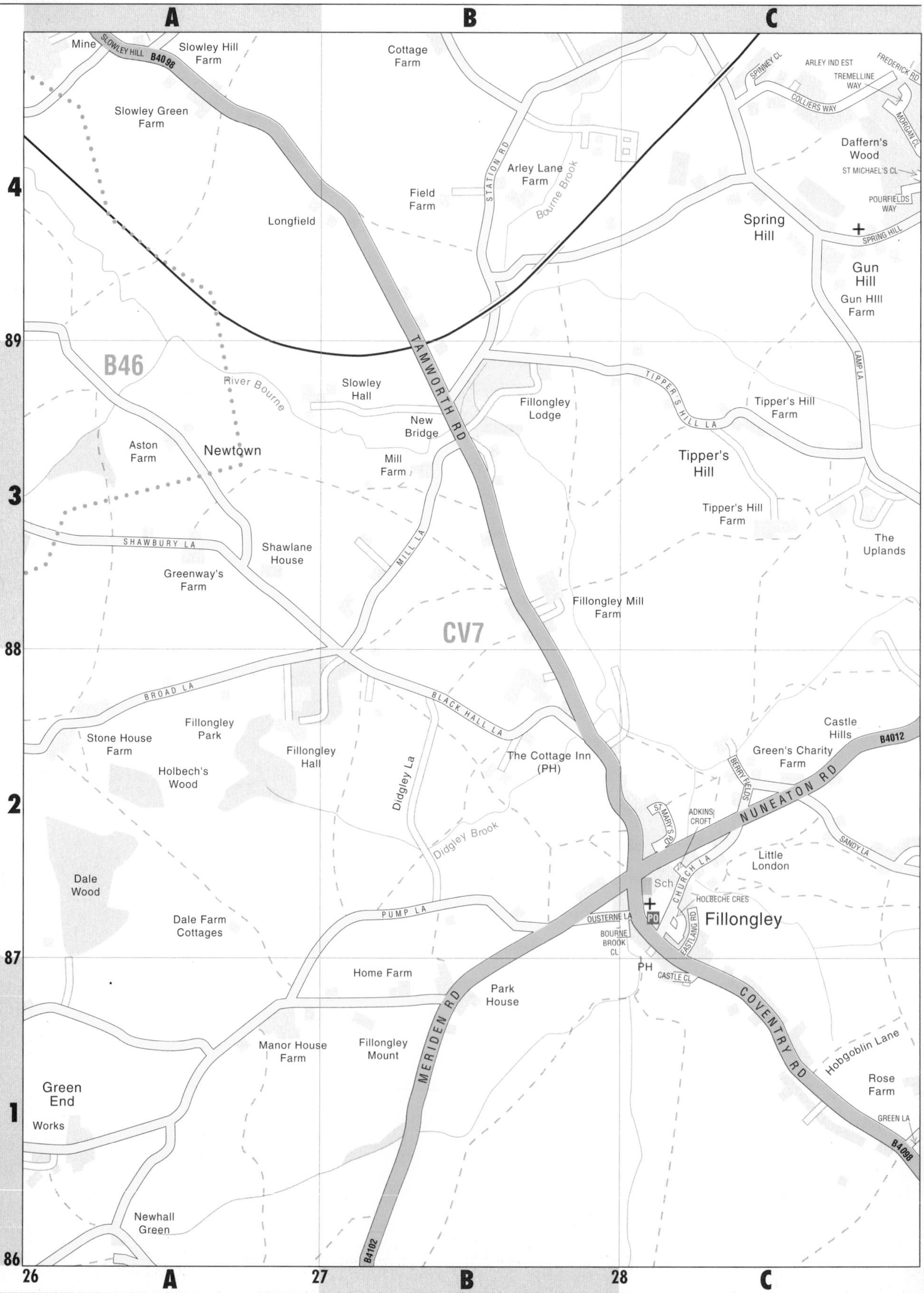
A
B
C
Mine
SLOWLEY HILL
B4098
Slowley Hill Farm
Cottage Farm
SPINNEY CL
ARLEY IND EST
FREDERICK RD
TREMELLINE WAY
COLLIERS WAY
MORGAN CL
Slowley Green Farm
Daffern's Wood
STATION RD
Arley Lane Farm
Bourne Brook
ST MICHAEL'S CL
4
Field Farm
POURFIELDS WAY
Longfield
Spring Hill
SPRING HILL
Gun Hill
Gun Hill Farm
89
TAMWORTH RD
LAMP LA
B46
River Bourne
Slowley Hall
TIPPER'S HILL LA
Fillongley Lodge
Tipper's Hill Farm
New Bridge
Aston Farm
Newtown
Mill Farm
Tipper's Hill
3
Tipper's Hill Farm
The Uplands
SHAWBURY LA
Shawlane House
MILL LA
Greenway's Farm
Fillongley Mill Farm
CV7
88
BROAD LA
BLACK HALL LA
Fillongley Park
Stone House Farm
Castle Hills
B4012
Fillongley Hall
Green's Charity Farm
Holbech's Wood
The Cottage Inn (PH)
BERRY FIELDS
Didgley La
NUNEATON RD
2
ST MARY'S RD
ADKINS CROFT
Didgley Brook
SANDY LA
Little London
CHURCH LA
Dale Wood
Sch
HOLBECHE CRES
PUMP LA
PO
Fillongley
Dale Farm Cottages
OUSTERNE LA
BOURNE BROOK CL
EASTLANG RD
87
PH
CASTLE CL
Home Farm
Park House
COVENTRY RD
MERIDEN RD
Manor House Farm
Fillongley Mount
Hobgoblin Lane
Green End
Rose Farm
1
Works
GREEN LA
B4098
Newhall Green
B4102
86
26
A
27
B
28
C

35
47

27
38

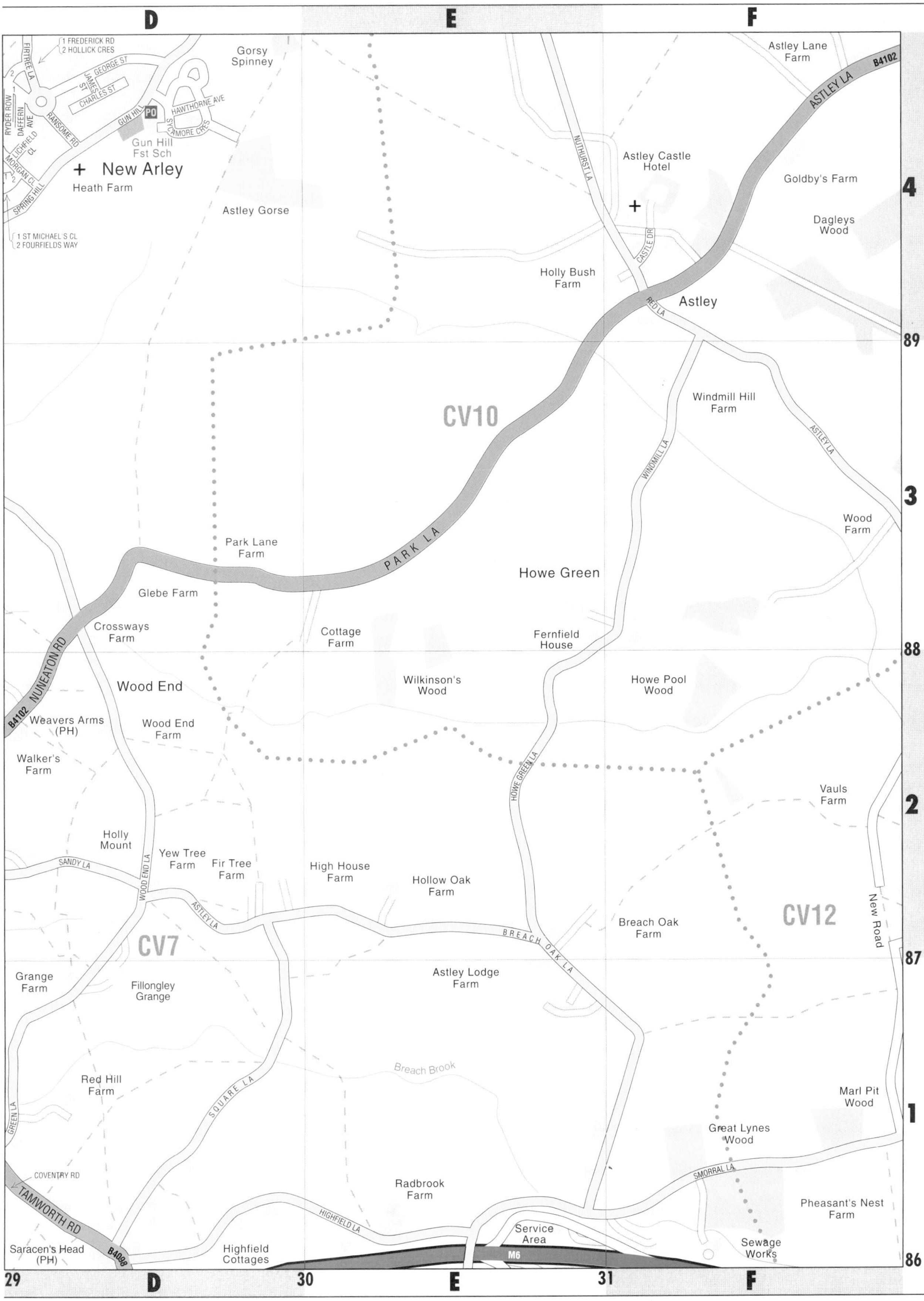
D
E
F
1 FREDERICK RD
2 HOLLICK CRES
FIRTREE LA
GEORGE ST
JAMES ST
CHARLES ST
RYDER ROW
DAFFERN AVE
RANSOME RD
LICHFIELD CL
MORGAN CL
SPRING HILL
GUN HILL
PO
HAWTHORNE AVE
SYCAMORE CRES
Gun Hill Fst Sch
New Arley
Heath Farm
1 ST MICHAEL'S CL
2 FOURFIELDS WAY
Gorsy Spinney
Astley Gorse
NUTHURST LA
Astley Castle Hotel
CASTLE DR
Holly Bush Farm
Astley
RED LA
Astley Lane Farm
B4102
ASTLEY LA
Goldby's Farm
Dagleys Wood
4
89
Windmill Hill Farm
ASTLEY LA
WINDMILL LA
CV10
PARK LA
3
Wood Farm
Park Lane Farm
Howe Green
Glebe Farm
Crossways Farm
Cottage Farm
Fernfield House
NUNEATON RD
B4102
88
Wood End
Wilkinson's Wood
Howe Pool Wood
Weavers Arms (PH)
Wood End Farm
Walker's Farm
HOWE GREEN LA
Vauls Farm
2
Holly Mount
Yew Tree Farm
Fir Tree Farm
High House Farm
Hollow Oak Farm
SANDY LA
WOOD END LA
ASTLEY LA
BREACH OAK LA
Breach Oak Farm
CV12
New Road
CV7
87
Grange Farm
Fillongley Grange
Astley Lodge Farm
Breach Brook
Red Hill Farm
SQUARE LA
Marl Pit Wood
1
GREEN LA
Great Lynes Wood
COVENTRY RD
SMORRAL LA
TAMWORTH RD
Radbrook Farm
Pheasant's Nest Farm
HIGHFIELD LA
Service Area
B4098
Saracen's Head (PH)
Highfield Cottages
M6
Sewage Works
86
29
D
30
E
31
F

48
38

37 28

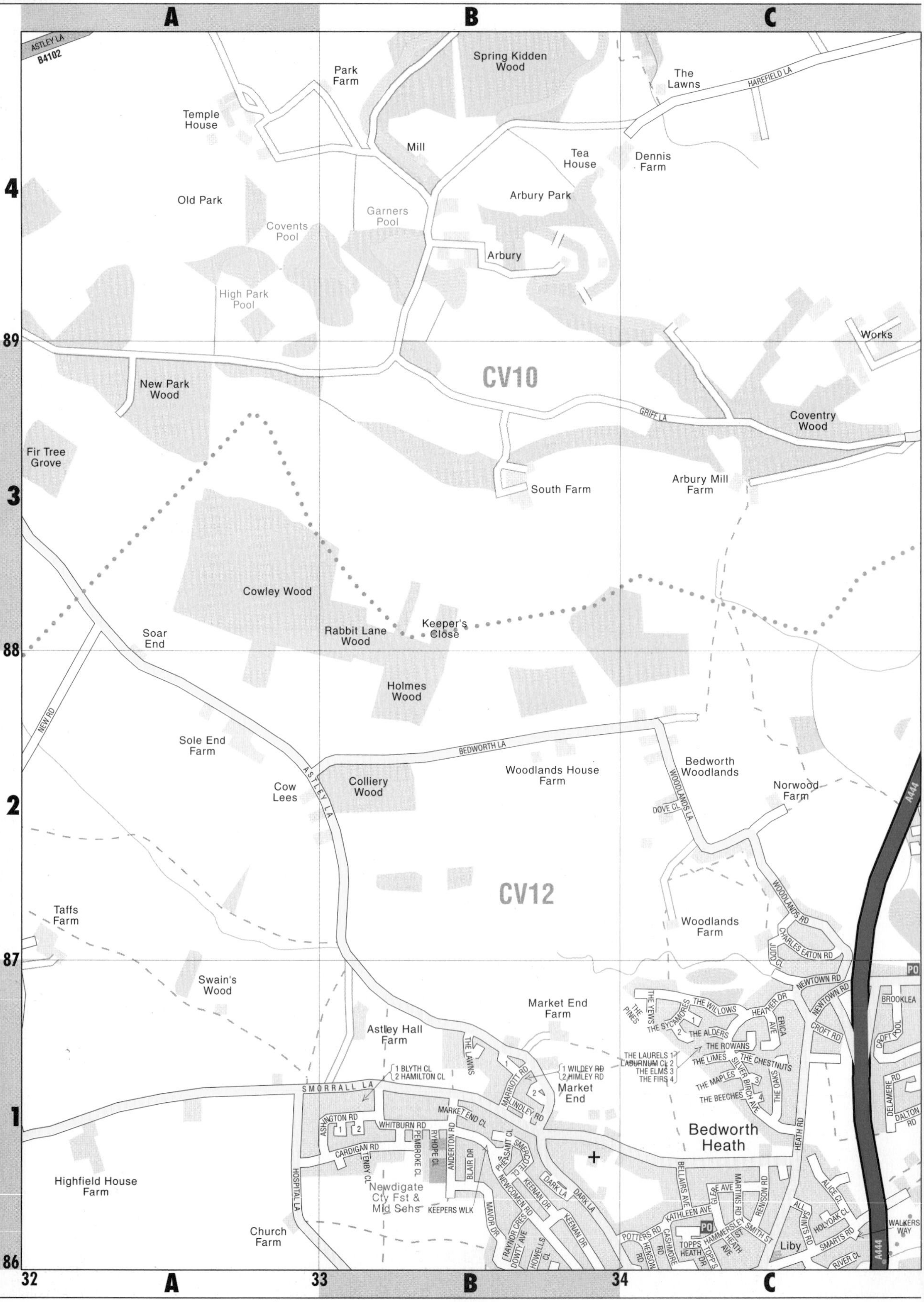
A
B
C
ASTLEY LA
B4102
Park Farm
Spring Kidden Wood
The Lawns
HAREFIELD LA
Temple House
Mill
Tea House
Dennis Farm
4
Old Park
Arbury Park
Garners Pool
Covents Pool
Arbury
High Park Pool
Works
89
CV10
New Park Wood
GRIFF LA
Coventry Wood
Fir Tree Grove
South Farm
Arbury Mill Farm
3
Cowley Wood
Rabbit Lane Wood
Keeper's Close
Soar End
88
Holmes Wood
NEW RD
Sole End Farm
BEDWORTH LA
Woodlands House Farm
Bedworth Woodlands
Cow Lees
ASTLEY LA
Colliery Wood
WOODLANDS LA
Norwood Farm
2
DOVE CL
A444
CV12
Taffs Farm
Woodlands Farm
WOODLANDS RD
CHARLES EATON RD
JUDD CL
87
Swain's Wood
Market End Farm
NEWTOWN RD
PO
BROOKLEA
THE YEWS
THE PINES
THE SYCAMORES
THE WILLOWS
HEATHER DR
ERICA AVE
THE ALDERS
THE ROWANS
CROFT RD
CROFT POOL
Astley Hall Farm
THE LAWNS
THE LAURELS 1
LABURNUM CL 2
THE ELMS 3
THE FIRS 4
THE LIMES
THE CHESTNUTS
1 BLYTH CL
2 HAMILTON CL
1 WILDEY RD
2 HIMLEY RD
Market End
THE MAPLES
SILVER BIRCH AVE
THE OAKS
THE BEECHES
DELAMERE RD
DALTON RD
SMORRALL LA
MARRIOTT RD
LINDLEY RD
1
ASHINGTON RD
WHITBURN RD
MARKET END CL
CARDIGAN RD
PEMBROKE CL
RYHOPE CL
ANDERTON RD
BLAIR DR
PHEASANT CL
SMERCOTE CL
Bedworth Heath
HEATH RD
TENBY CL
HOSPITAL LA
Highfield House Farm
Newdigate Cty Fst & Mid Schs
KEEPERS WLK
MAVOR DR
NEWCOMEN RD
KEENAN DR
DARK LA
BELLAIRS AVE
GLEBE AVE
MARTINS RD
RENISON RD
ALICE CL
ALL SAINTS RD
HOLYOAK CL
WALKERS WAY
KATHLEEN AVE
HAMMERSLEY ST
SMITH ST
Church Farm
RAYNOR CRES
DOWTY AVE
HOWELLS CL
POTTERS RD
HENSON RD
CASHMORE RD
TOPPS HEATH
TOPPS DR
HEATH AVE
Liby
SMARTS RD
RIVER CL
86
32
33
34

37 49

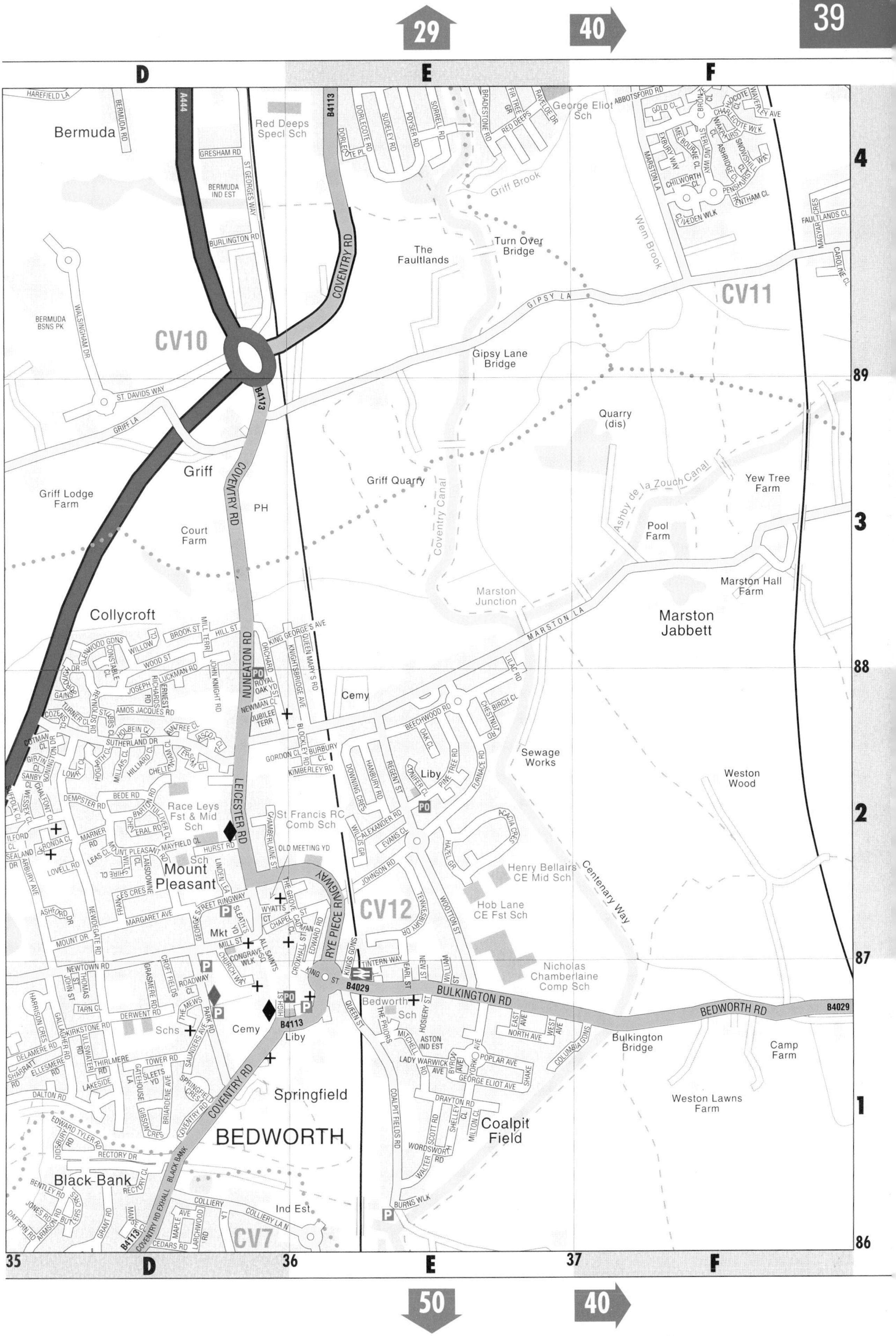

D E F

4

CV11

89

3

2

88

87

86

D E F

Bermuda

HAREFIELD LA

BERMUDA RD

A444

GRESHAM RD

ST GEORGES WAY

BERMUDA IND EST

BURLINGTON RD

COVENTRY RD

B4113

Red Deeps Specl Sch

George Eliot Sch

ABBOTSFORD RD

GOLD CL

WAVERLEY AVE

DORLECOTE RD

POYSER RD

SORRELL RD

SUDELEY RD

BRADESTONE RD

BAKER DR

FIR TREE GR

RED DEEPS

CV11

CHARLECOTE WLK

STERLING WAY

ASHRIDGE CL

PENSHAM CL

FAULTLANDS CL

CAROLINE CL

MARSTON LA

CHILWORTH

KIBWORTH CL

LIEDEN WLK

CLEEDEN WLK

KENILWAY

MAYWOOD

Griff Brook

The Faultlands

Turn Over Bridge

Wem Brook

GIPSY LA

Gipsy Lane Bridge

CV10

BERMUDA BSNS PK

WALSINGHAM DR

ST DAVIDS WAY

GRIFF LA

B4113

COVENTRY RD

Quarry (dis)

Ashby de la Zouch Canal

Yew Tree Farm

Griff

Griff Lodge Farm

PH

Court Farm

Coventry Canal

Griff Quarry

Pool Farm

Marston Hall Farm

Marston Junction

MARSTON LA

Marston Jabbett

Collycroft

NUNEATON RD

COVENTRY RD

MILL HILL

HILL ST

BROOK ST

WOOD ST

WILLOW

JOHN KNIGHT RD

ORCHARD

KING GEORGE'S AVE

QUEEN MARY'S RD

KNIGHTSBRIDGE AVE

NEWMAN CL

ROYAL OAK YD

JUBILEE TERR

PO

Cemy

BLOCKLEY RD

GORDON CL

BURBURY CL

KIMBERLEY RD

BEECHWOOD RD

OAK CL

HANBURY RD

CHESTNUT RD

BIRCH CL

PINE TREE RD

Sewage Works

Weston Wood

Race Leys Fst & Mid Sch

LEICESTER RD

St Francis RC Comb Sch

CHAMBERLAINE RD

Old Meeting Yd

Liby

PO

REGENT ST

HAZEL CL

FURNACE RD

ACACIA CL

Mount Pleasant

HURST RD

LINDEN LA

THE GROVE

WYATTS CT

CHAPEL ST

JOHNSON RD

ALEXANDER RD

EVANS CL

Henry Bellairs CE Mid Sch

Centenary Way

CV12

P

Mkt

MILL ST

CONGREVE WLK

ALL SAINTS SQ

RYE PIECE RINGWAY

KINGS GDNS

TINTERN WAY

PEARL ST

Hob Lane CE Fst Sch

WOOTTON ST

WILLIAM ST

P

NEWTOWN RD

ROADWAY

CROFT FIELDS

EDWARD ST

KING ST

B4029

BULKINGTON RD

Nicholas Chamberlaine Comp Sch

BEDWORTH RD

B4029

P

THE MEWS

PARK RD

Schs

Cemy

Liby

B4113

PO

HIGH ST

QUEEN ST

Bedworth Sch

The Priors

HOSIERY ST

MITCHELL ST

Aston Ind Est

EAST AVE

NORTH AVE

WEST AVE

COLUMBIA GDNS

Bulkington Bridge

Camp Farm

GRASMERE RD

THIRLMERE RD

TOWER RD

SAUNDERS AVE

Springfield

COVENTRY RD

LADY WARWICK AVE

BYRON AVE

POPLAR AVE

SHAKE

Weston Lawns Farm

1

BEDWORTH

COALPIT FIELDS RD

GEORGE ELIOT AVE

DRAYTON RD

SCOTT RD

SHELLEY RD

MILTON RD

Coalpit Field

Black-Bank

EDWARD TYLER RD

RECTORY DR

BLACK BANK

RECTORY RD

COLLIERY LA

Ind Est

COLLIERY LA N

CV7

WORDSWORTH RD

WALTER RD

BURNS WLK

P

B4113

COVENTRY RD BYPASS

MAPLE AVE

LARCHWOOD RD

CEDARS AVE

39 30

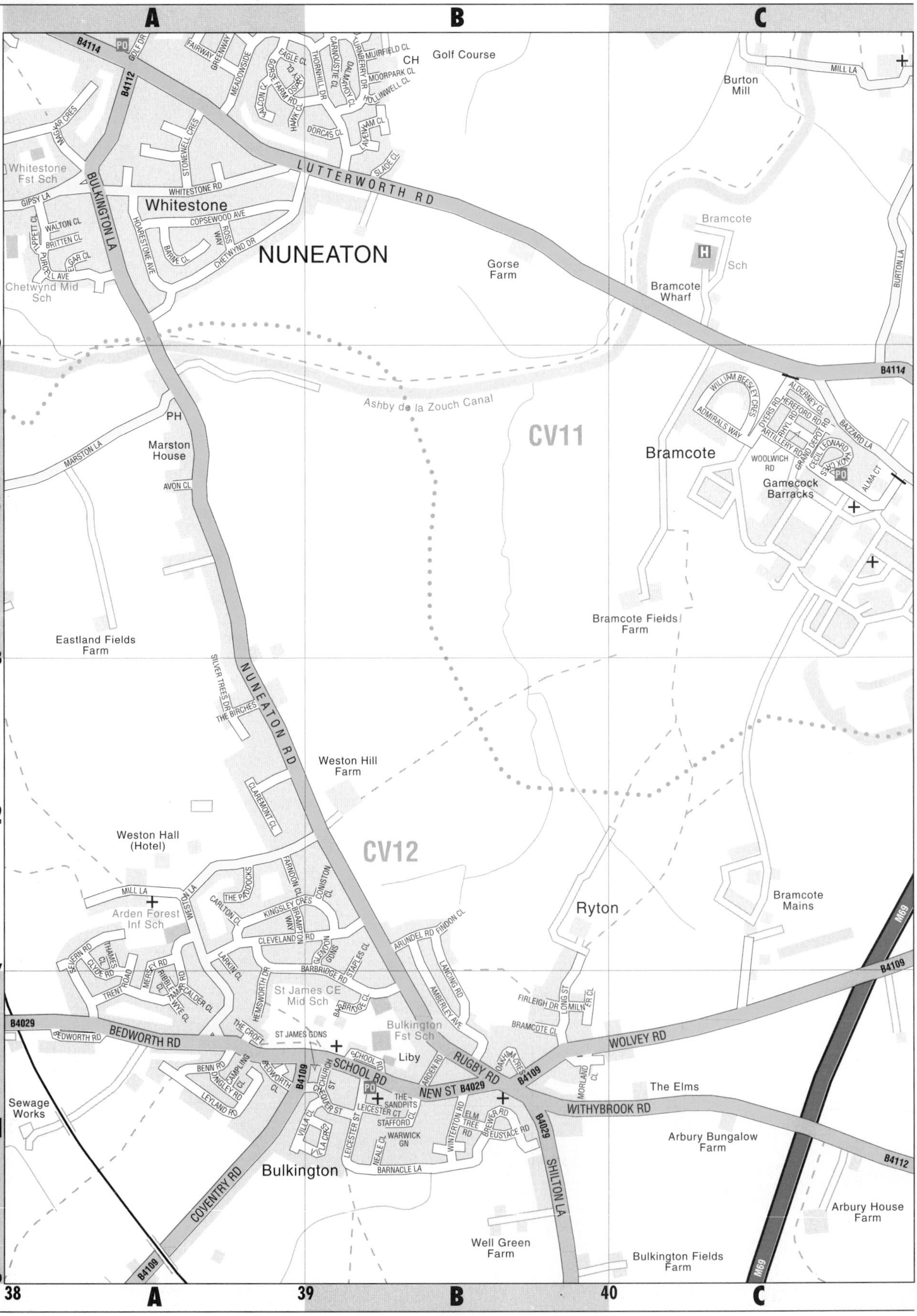
A
B
C
4
3
2
1
89
88
87
86
38
39
40
NUNEATON
Whitestone
Whitestone Fst Sch
Chetwynd Mid Sch
Golf Course
CH
LUTTERWORTH RD
BULKINGTON LA
B4114
B4112
WHITESTONE RD
GIPSY LA
COPSEWOOD AVE
HOARESTONE AVE
CHETWYND DR
STONEWELL CRES
WALTON CL
BRITTEN CL
ELGAR CL
PURCELL AVE
TIPPETT CL
FAIRWAY
GREENWAY
MEADOWSIDE
GOLF DR
EAGLE CL
GORSE FARM RD
FALCON CL
HAWK CL
THORNHILL DR
CARNOUSTIE CL
DALMAHOY CL
TURNBERRY DR
MUIRFIELD CL
MOORPARK CL
HOLLINWELL CL
DORCAS CL
SLADE CL
Burton Mill
MILL LA
BURTON LA
Bramcote
Sch
Bramcote Wharf
Gorse Farm
Ashby de la Zouch Canal
CV11
Bramcote
Gamecock Barracks
WILLIAM BEESLEY CRES
ADMIRALS WAY
ALDERNEY CL
HEREFORD RD
DYERS RD
RHYL RD
ARTILLERY RD
GRAND DEPOT RD
CECIL LEONARD
WOOLWICH RD
BAZZARD LA
ALMA CT
PH
Marston House
MARSTON LA
AVON CL
Eastland Fields Farm
Bramcote Fields Farm
NUNEATON RD
SILVER TREES DR
THE BIRCHES
Weston Hill Farm
CLAREMONT CL
Weston Hall (Hotel)
CV12
Ryton
Bramcote Mains
M69
B4109
MILL LA
Arden Forest Inf Sch
WESTON LA
THE PADDOCKS
FARNDON CL
CONISTON CL
KINGSLEY CRES
BRAMPTON WAY
CARLTON CL
CLEVELAND RD
GLENDON GDNS
BARBRIDGE RD
STAPLES CL
ARUNDEL RD
FINDON CL
LANCING RD
AMBERLEY AVE
SEVERN RD
THAMES CL
CLYDE RD
TRENT ROAD
MERSEY RD
RIBBLE CL
TAMAR RD
CALDER CL
WYE CL
LARKIN CL
HEMSWORTH DR
St James CE Mid Sch
BARBRIDGE CL
Bulkington Fst Sch
THE CROFT
ST JAMES GDNS
Liby
B4029
BEDWORTH RD
SCHOOL RD
RUGBY RD
NEW ST
FIRLEIGH DR
LONG ST
MILNER CL
BRAMCOTE CL
WOLVEY RD
MORLAND CL
The Elms
WITHYBROOK RD
Sewage Works
BENN RD
DANGLEY RD
CAMPLING CL
LEYLAND RD
CHURCH ST
LEICESTER CT
LEICESTER ST
THE SANDPITS
STAFFORD CL
WARWICK GN
NEALE CL
VILLA CL
LILAC CRES
BARNACLE LA
ARDEN RD
WINTERTON RD
ELM TREE RD
BREWER RD
EUSTACE RD
OAKHAM CRES
SHILTON LA
Arbury Bungalow Farm
Arbury House Farm
Bulkington
COVENTRY RD
Well Green Farm
Bulkington Fields Farm
PO
H

39 51

31
42

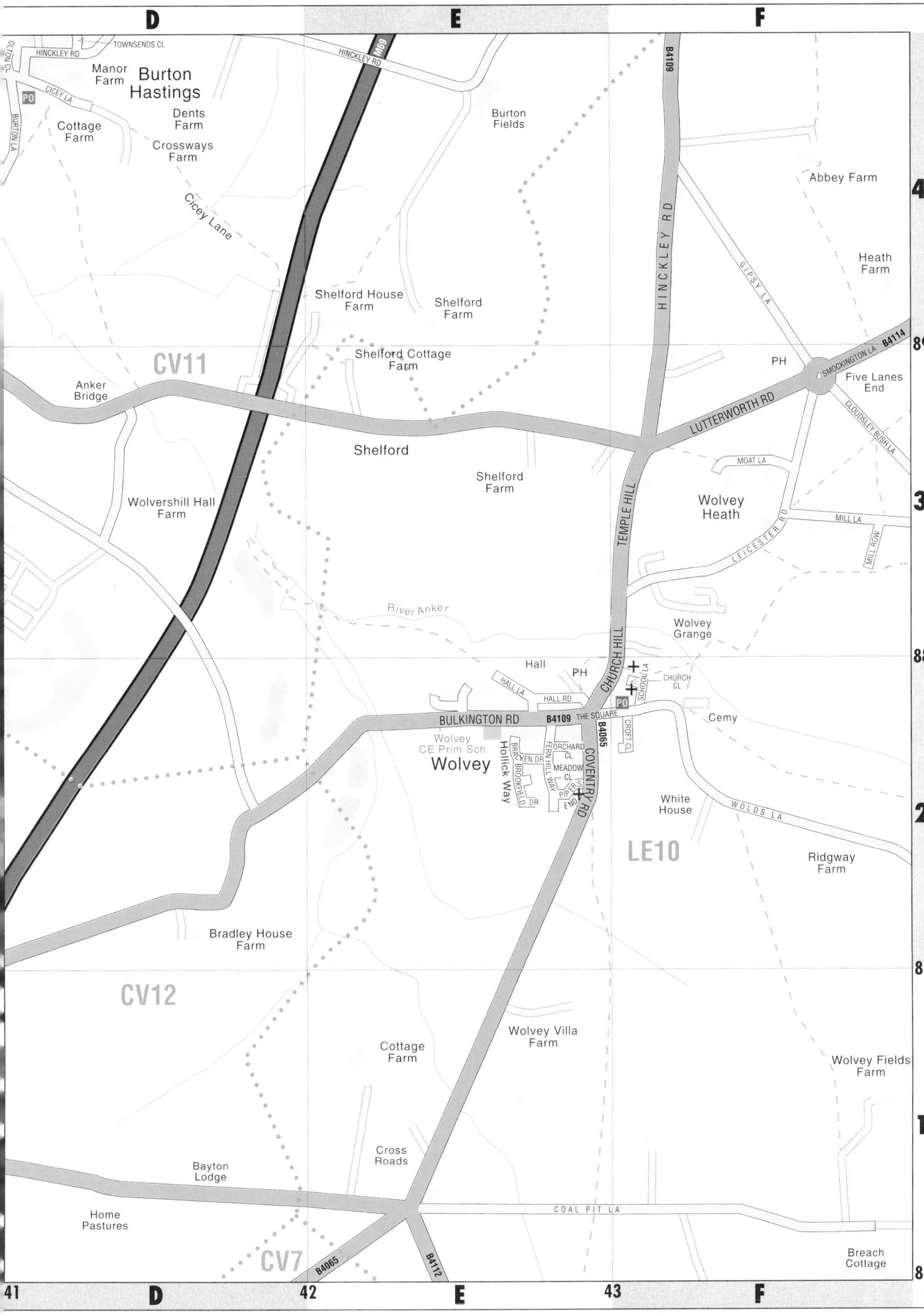
D
E
F
HINCKLEY RD
TOWNSENDS CL
OLTON CL
Manor Farm
Burton Hastings
PO
CICEY LA
BURTON LA
Cottage Farm
Dents Farm
Crossways Farm
Cicey Lane
M69
HINCKLEY RD
Burton Fields
B4109
HINCKLEY RD
Abbey Farm
4
Heath Farm
GIPSY LA
Shelford House Farm
Shelford Farm
89
Shelford Cottage Farm
CV11
PH
SMOCKINGTON LA
B4114
Five Lanes End
Anker Bridge
LUTTERWORTH RD
CLOUDSLEY BUSH LA
Shelford
MOAT LA
Shelford Farm
Wolvershill Hall Farm
TEMPLE HILL
Wolvey Heath
3
LEICESTER RD
MILL LA
MILL ROW
River Anker
Wolvey Grange
CHURCH HILL
88
Hall
PH
HALL LA
HALL RD
SCHOOL LA
CHURCH CL
PO
BULKINGTON RD
B4109
THE SQUARE
B4065
Cemy
CROFT CL
Wolvey CE Prim Sch
Wolvey
Hollick Way
BRACKEN DR
BROOKFIELD DR
ORCHARD CL
FERN HILL WAY
MEADOW CL
PIPERS END
COVENTRY RD
White House
WOLDS LA
2
LE10
Ridgway Farm
Bradley House Farm
87
CV12
Cottage Farm
Wolvey Villa Farm
Wolvey Fields Farm
1
Cross Roads
Bayton Lodge
Home Pastures
COAL PIT LA
CV7
B4065
B4112
Breach Cottage
86
41
D
42
E
43
F

52
42

41
32

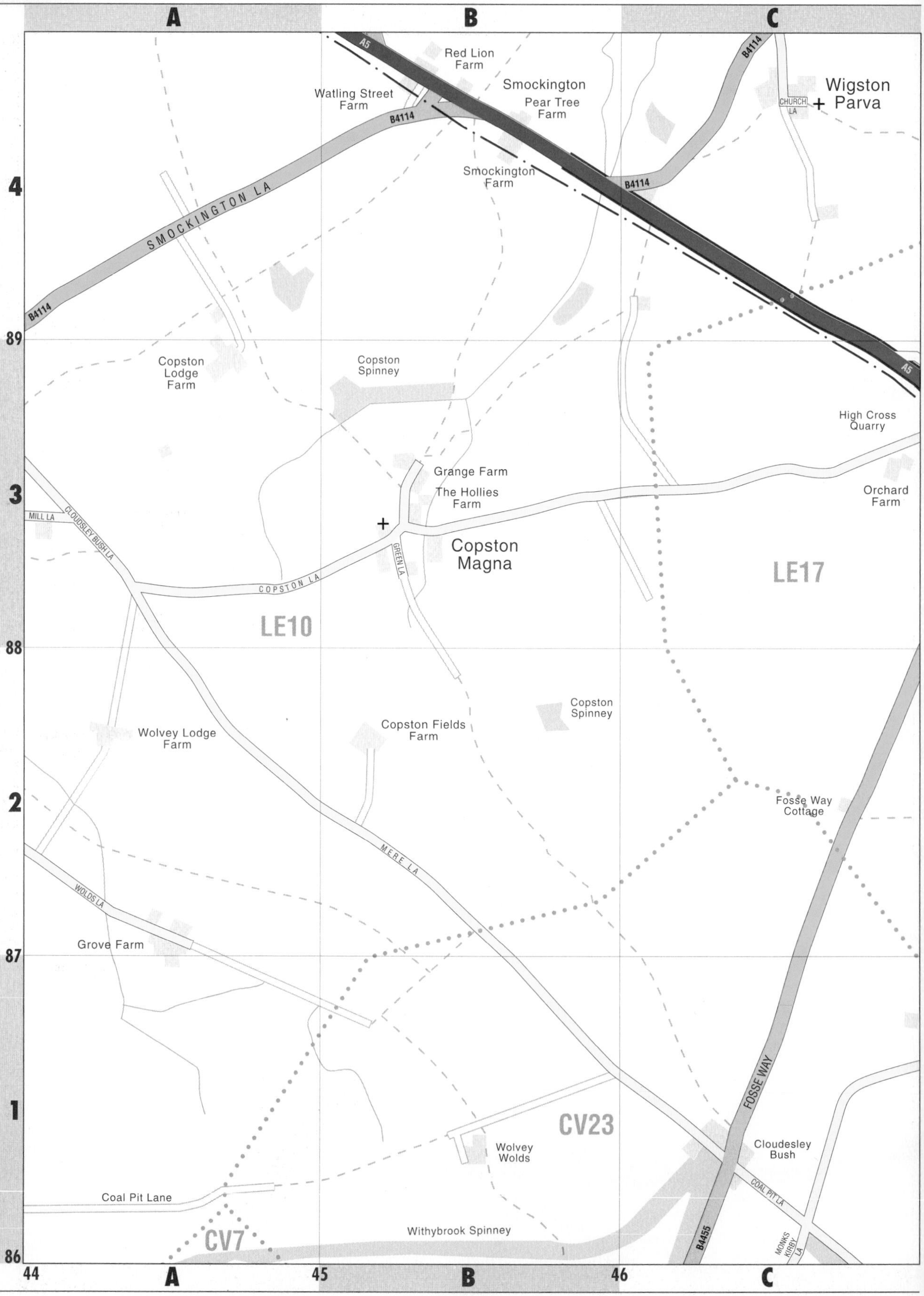
A
B
C
4
3
2
1
89
88
87
86
44
45
46
A5
B4114
Red Lion Farm
Watling Street Farm
Smockington
Pear Tree Farm
Wigston Parva
CHURCH LA
Smockington Farm
SMOCKINGTON LA
Copston Lodge Farm
Copston Spinney
High Cross Quarry
Grange Farm
The Hollies Farm
Orchard Farm
MILL LA
CLOUDSLEY BUSH LA
Copston Magna
GREEN LA
COPSTON LA
LE10
LE17
Copston Spinney
Copston Fields Farm
Wolvey Lodge Farm
Fosse Way Cottage
MERE LA
WOLDS LA
Grove Farm
FOSSE WAY
CV23
Wolvey Wolds
Cloudesley Bush
Coal Pit Lane
COAL PIT LA
Withybrook Spinney
B4455
MONKS KIRBY LA
CV7

41
53

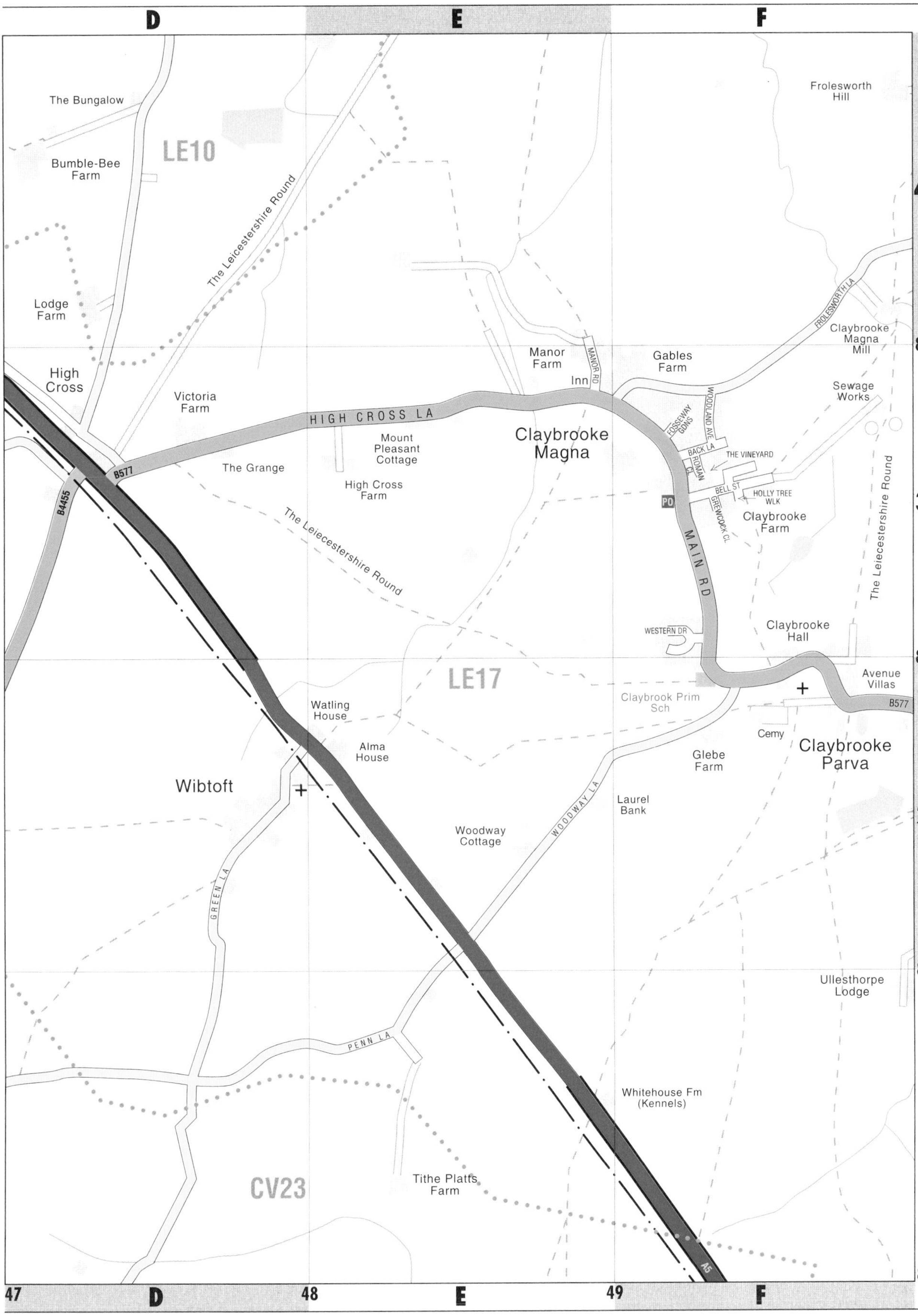

D
E
F
The Bungalow
LE10
Bumble-Bee Farm
The Leicestershire Round
Lodge Farm
High Cross
Victoria Farm
B577
B4455
HIGH CROSS LA
Mount Pleasant Cottage
The Grange
High Cross Farm
The Leicestershire Round
Manor Farm
MANOR RD
Inn
Claybrooke Magna
Gables Farm
FOSSEWAY GDNS
WOODLAND AVE
BACK LA
ROMAN CL
THE VINEYARD
BELL ST
HOLLY TREE WLK
GREWCOCK CL
PO
Claybrooke Farm
MAIN RD
Frolesworth Hill
FROLESWORTH LA
Claybrooke Magna Mill
Sewage Works
The Leicestershire Round
WESTERN DR
Claybrooke Hall
LE17
Avenue Villas
B577
Claybrook Prim Sch
Cemy
Claybrooke Parva
Glebe Farm
Watling House
Alma House
Wibtoft
Laurel Bank
WOODWAY LA
Woodway Cottage
GREEN LA
Ullesthorpe Lodge
PENN LA
Whitehouse Fm (Kennels)
CV23
Tithe Platts Farm
A5
4
89
3
88
2
87
1
86
47
48
49
D
E
F

33

A
B
C
4
85
3
84
2
83
1
82
17
18
19
Marston Green
Coleshill Heath
Sports Ctr
Heath Farm
BIRMINGHAM BSNS PK
Marston Green Jun &Inf Sch
Liby
B37
School Rough
1 ROTHERBY GR
2 WOLVERTON RD
Cemy
B46
Bickenhill Plantations
ELMDON TRAD EST
Low Brook
B40
National Exhibition Ctr
Birmingham International Airport
Birmingham International
Hotel
B26
Mast
Hotels
Depot
Hotel
COVENTRY RD
A45
The Clock Inn (PH)
Wyckhams Close
CH
Dunston Farm
B92
Caravan Park
The Jungle
Castle Hills
Grange Farm
Bickenhill
MOOREND AVE
COLESHILL RD
IVY LODGE CL
STATION RD
MALTHOUSE ROW
BICKENHILL RD
COLESHILL HEATH RD
BLACKFIRS LA
BICKENHILL PARKWAY
BICKENHILL LA
STARLEY WAY
FIRE STATION RD
CHESTER RD
A452
M42
B4438
THE CRESCENT
SOLIHULL PARKWAY
PARK SQ
NORTH AVE
NORTHWAY
PENDIGO WAY
EAST CAR PARK RD
HARBET DR
PERIMETER RD
THE UNDERPASS
EASTWAY
SOUTH WAY
SOUTH CAR PARK RD
FORUM RD
AIRPORT WAY
CATHERINE DE BARNES LA
CLOCK LA
PITT LA
CHURCH LA
ST PETERS LA
OLD STATION RD
OLD DAMSON LA
ELMDON LA
HANGER RD
COMMISSARY RD
FORWARD RD
WORKS RD
DIGBY DR
THE FORDRIFT
NEWLANDS LA
ELMDON LA
THE GREENWAY
CANTERBURY DR
SOMERTON DR
FARNDON AVE
ELMDON RD
HALL DR
LAND LA
EXHIBITION WAY
STATION WAY
MAIN AVE
NOVOTEL WAY
INTERNATIONAL DR
EUROPA WAY
RAMP RD
PARK LA
NEWINGTON RD
SYCAMORE CRES
CHELMSLEY LA
WAYSIDE
TULIP WLK
WHITE BEAM RD
BOX RD
HELMSWOOD DR
ROWAN WAY
POPLAR AVE
LEAF DR
MAPLE LA
BERWICKS LA

56

34
46

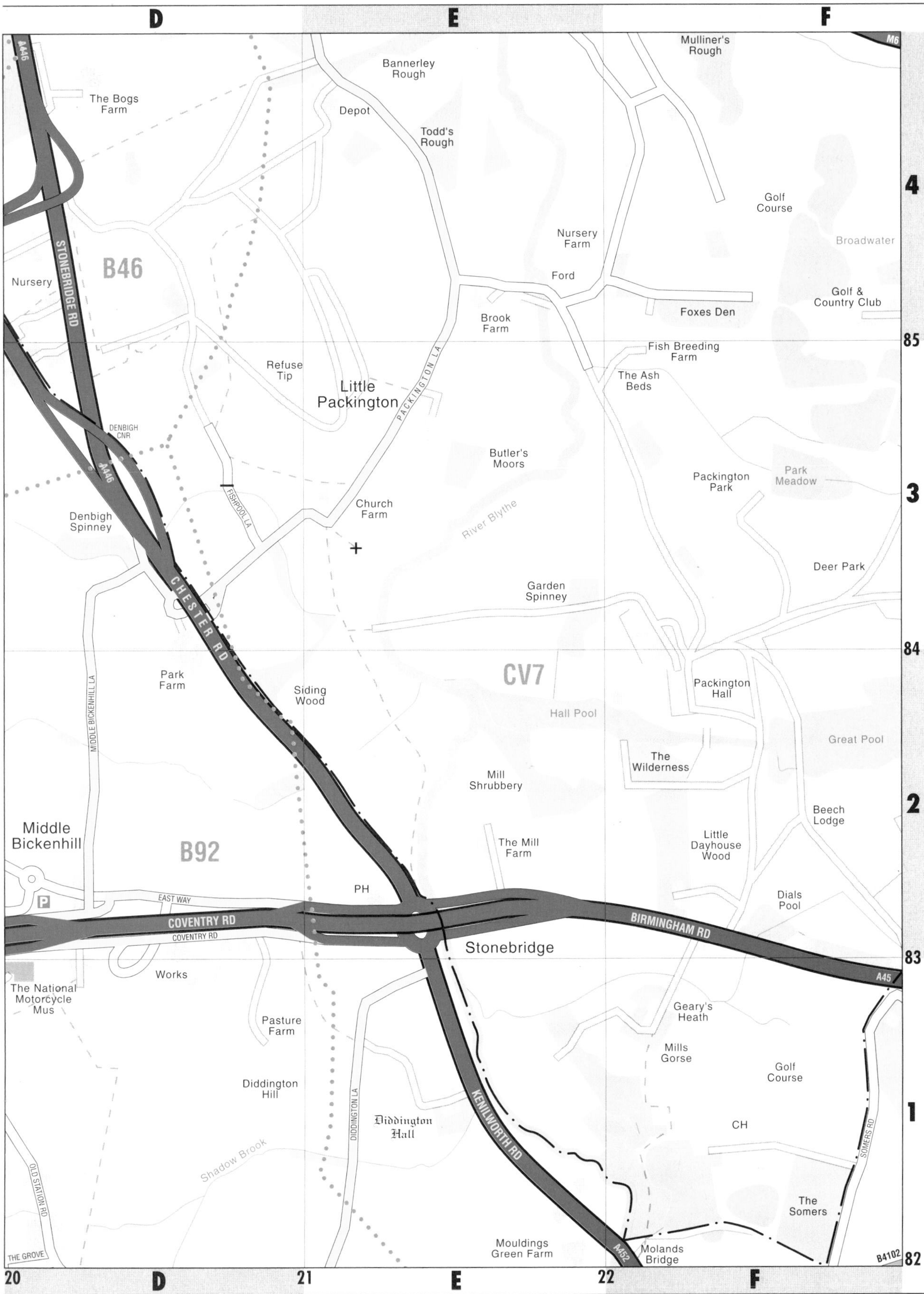
D
E
F
A446
M6
The Bogs
Farm
Bannerley
Rough
Mulliner's
Rough
Depot
Todd's
Rough
Golf
Course
Broadwater
Nursery
Farm
STONEBRIDGE RD
B46
Nursery
Ford
Golf &
Country Club
Foxes Den
Brook
Farm
Fish Breeding
Farm
The Ash
Beds
Refuse
Tip
Little
Packington
PACKINGTON LA
DENBIGH
CNR
Butler's
Moors
A446
Packington
Park
Park
Meadow
Church
Farm
FISHPOOL LA
Denbigh
Spinney
River Blythe
Deer Park
CHESTER RD
Garden
Spinney
Park
Farm
CV7
Siding
Wood
Packington
Hall
Hall Pool
MIDDLE BICKENHILL LA
Great Pool
The
Wilderness
Mill
Shrubbery
Middle
Bickenhill
B92
The Mill
Farm
Little
Dayhouse
Wood
Beech
Lodge
PH
Dials
Pool
P
EAST WAY
COVENTRY RD
COVENTRY RD
BIRMINGHAM RD
Stonebridge
A45
Works
The National
Motorcycle
Mus
Geary's
Heath
Pasture
Farm
Mills
Gorse
Golf
Course
Diddington
Hill
KENILWORTH RD
Diddington
Hall
CH
DIDDINGTON LA
SOMERS RD
Shadow Brook
OLD STATION RD
The
Somers
Mouldings
Green Farm
A452
Molands
Bridge
THE GROVE
B4102
4
85
3
84
2
83
1
82
20
21
22
D
E
F

57
46

45
35

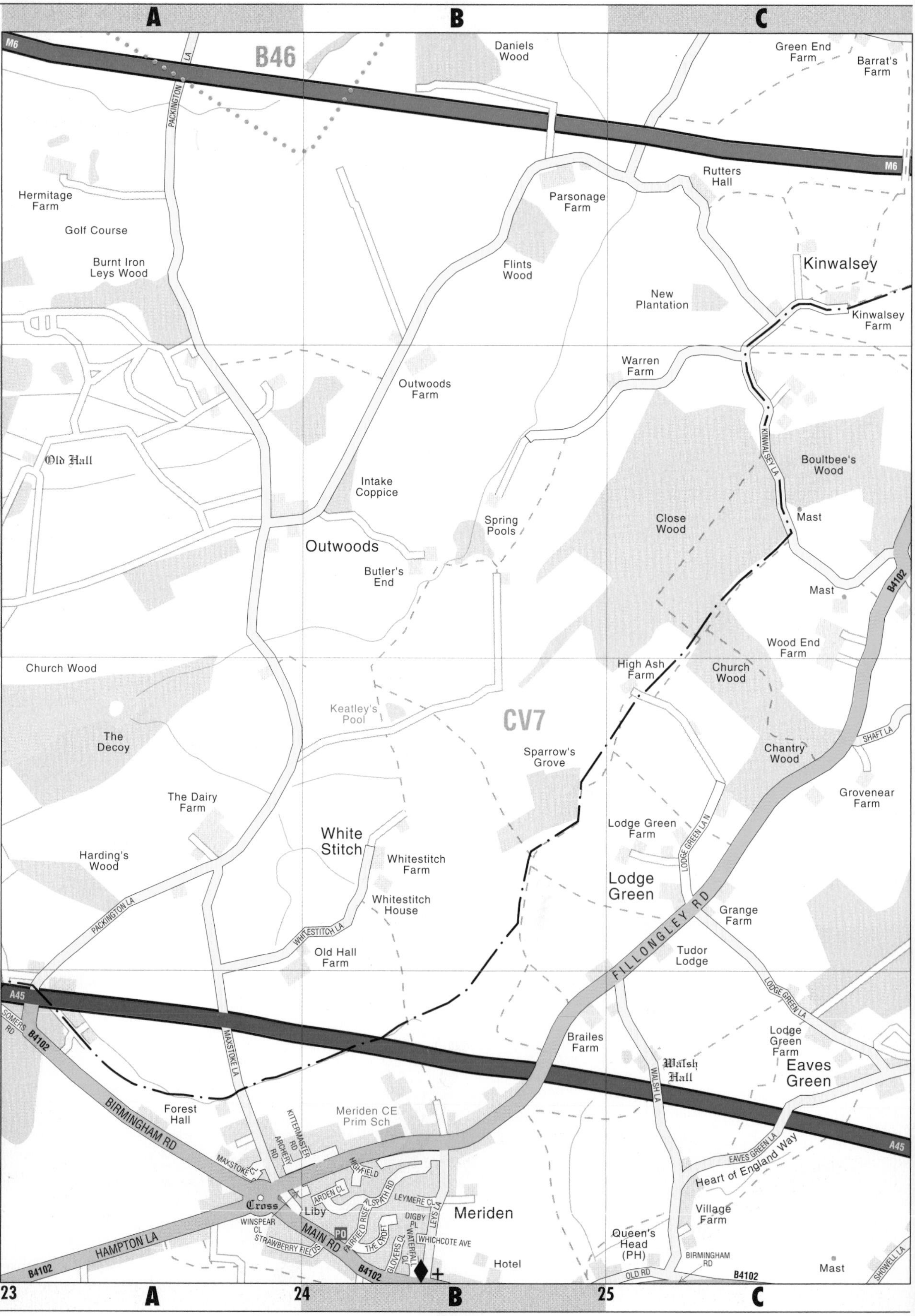
A
B
C
4
85
3
84
2
83
1
82
23
24
25
M6
B46
Daniels Wood
Green End Farm
Barrat's Farm
Rutters Hall
Parsonage Farm
Hermitage Farm
Golf Course
Burnt Iron Leys Wood
Flints Wood
Kinwalsey
New Plantation
Kinwalsey Farm
PACKINGTON LA
Warren Farm
Outwoods Farm
Old Hall
KINWALSEY LA
Boultbee's Wood
Intake Coppice
Spring Pools
Close Wood
Mast
Outwoods
Butler's End
B4102
Wood End Farm
Church Wood
High Ash Farm
Church Wood
Keatley's Pool
CV7
The Decoy
Sparrow's Grove
Chantry Wood
SHAFT LA
The Dairy Farm
Grovenear Farm
White Stitch
Whitestitch Farm
Lodge Green Farm
LODGE GREEN LA N
Harding's Wood
Lodge Green
Whitestitch House
FILLONGLEY RD
Grange Farm
WHITESTITCH LA
Old Hall Farm
Tudor Lodge
A45
LODGE GREEN LA
SOMERS RD
MAXSTOKE LA
Brailes Farm
Lodge Green Farm
Walsh Hall
Eaves Green
WALSH LA
Forest Hall
BIRMINGHAM RD
Meriden CE Prim Sch
KITTERMASTER RD
ARCHERY RD
HIGHFIELD
MAXSTOKE CL
EAVES GREEN LA
Heart of England Way
Cross
ARDEN CL
ALSPATH RD
LEYMERE CL
LEYS LA
Liby
Meriden
WINSPEAR CL
FAIRFIELD RISE
DIGBY PL
Village Farm
HAMPTON LA
STRAWBERRY FIELDS
MAIN RD
PO
THE CROFT
GLOVERS CL
WATERFALL CL
WHICHCOTE AVE
Queen's Head (PH)
BIRMINGHAM RD
Hotel
OLD RD
Mast
SHOWELL LA

45
58

36
48

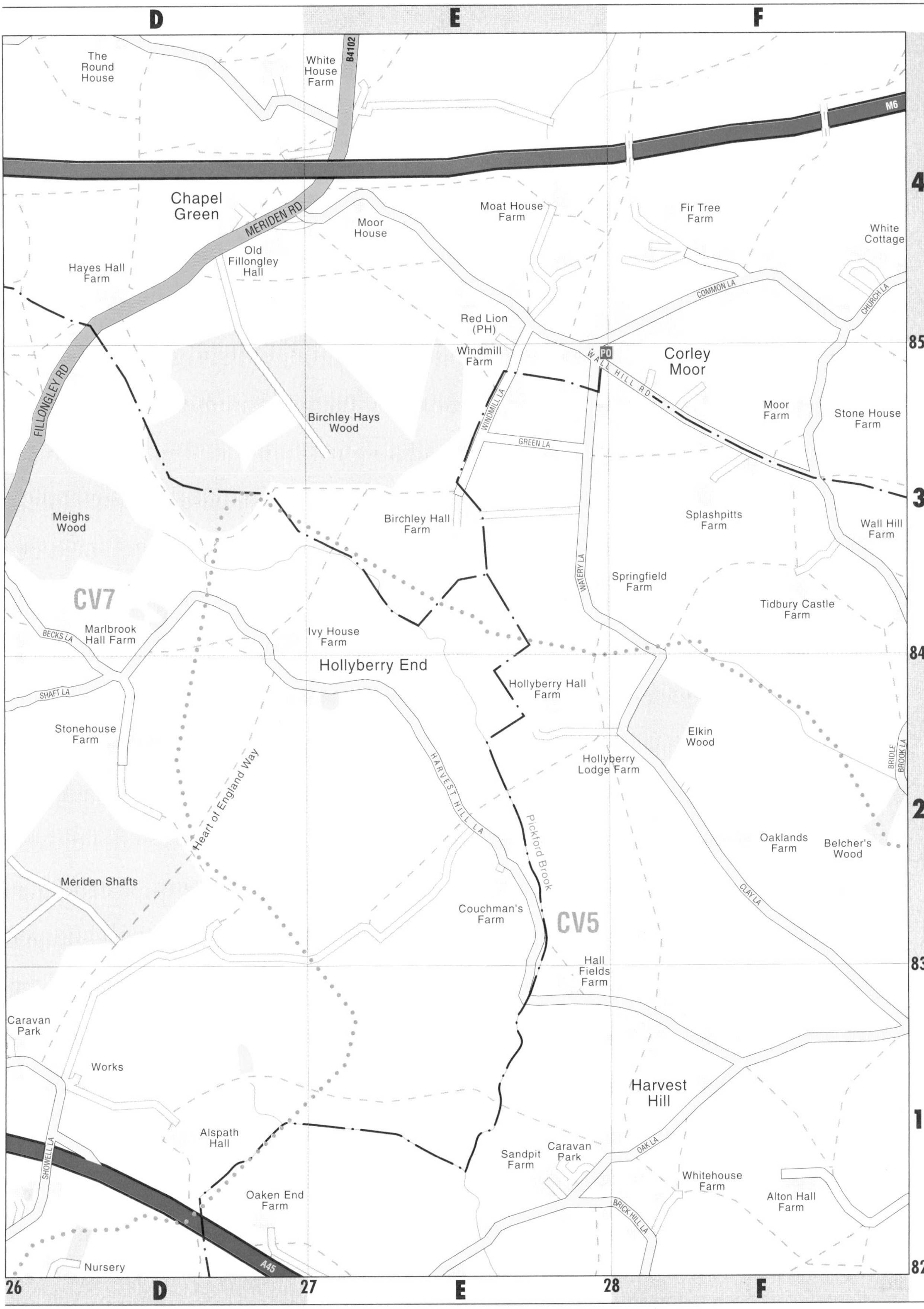
D
E
F
The Round House
White House Farm
B4102
M6
4
Chapel Green
MERIDEN RD
Moor House
Moat House Farm
Fir Tree Farm
White Cottage
Old Fillongley Hall
Hayes Hall Farm
COMMON LA
CHURCH LA
Red Lion (PH)
Windmill Farm
PO
WALL HILL RD
Corley Moor
85
FILLONGLEY RD
WINDMILL LA
Birchley Hays Wood
GREEN LA
Moor Farm
Stone House Farm
3
Meighs Wood
Birchley Hall Farm
Splashpitts Farm
Wall Hill Farm
WATERY LA
Springfield Farm
CV7
Tidbury Castle Farm
Marlbrook Hall Farm
BECKS LA
Ivy House Farm
84
Hollyberry End
SHAFT LA
Hollyberry Hall Farm
Stonehouse Farm
Elkin Wood
Hollyberry Lodge Farm
BRIDLE BROOK LA
Heart of England Way
HARVEST HILL LA
2
Pickford Brook
Oaklands Farm
Belcher's Wood
Meriden Shafts
CLAY LA
Couchman's Farm
CV5
Hall Fields Farm
83
Caravan Park
Works
Harvest Hill
1
Alspath Hall
SHOWELL LA
Sandpit Farm
Caravan Park
OAK LA
Whitehouse Farm
Alton Hall Farm
Oaken End Farm
BRICK HILL LA
A45
Nursery
82
26
D
27
E
28
F

59
48

47
37

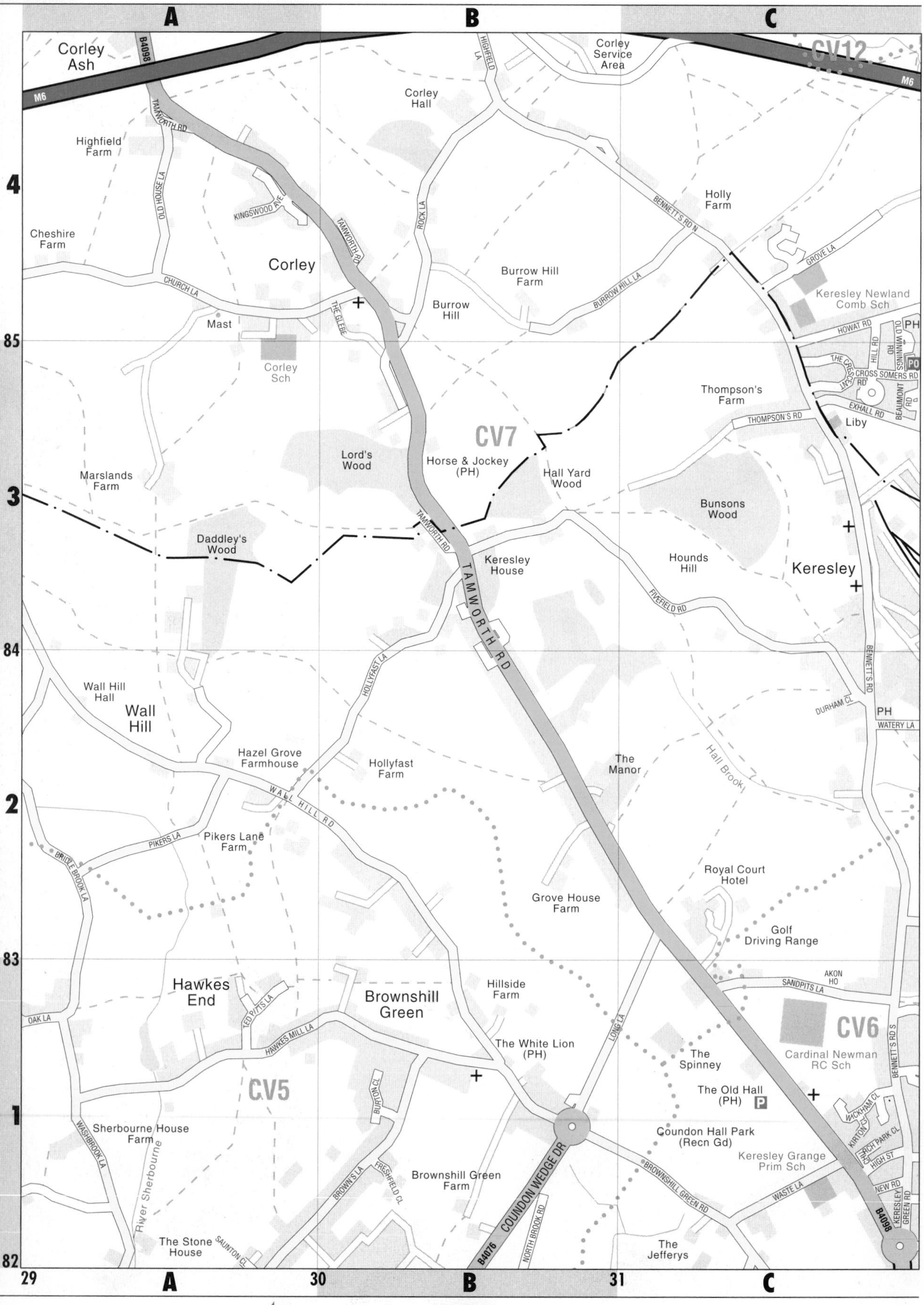
A
B
C
4
85
3
84
2
83
1
82
29
30
31
Corley Ash
Corley Service Area
CV12
M6
B4098
Corley Hall
Highfield Farm
HIGHFIELD LA
TAMWORTH RD
OLD HOUSE LA
KINGSWOOD AVE
ROCK LA
Holly Farm
BENNETT'S RD N
Cheshire Farm
Corley
Burrow Hill Farm
GROVE LA
CHURCH LA
BURROW HILL LA
Keresley Newland Comb Sch
THE GLEBE
Burrow Hill
Mast
HOWAT RD
PH
Corley Sch
THE CRESCENT
HILL RD
OLD WINNINGS RD
PO
CROSS RD
SOMERS RD
Thompson's Farm
BEAUMONT RD
EXHALL RD
THOMPSON'S RD
Liby
CV7
Lord's Wood
Horse & Jockey (PH)
Hall Yard Wood
Marslands Farm
Bunsons Wood
Daddley's Wood
Keresley House
Hounds Hill
Keresley
FIVEFIELD RD
Wall Hill Hall
HOLLYFAST LA
BENNETT'S RD
Wall Hill
DURHAM CL
PH
WATERY LA
Hazel Grove Farmhouse
Hollyfast Farm
The Manor
Hall Brook
WALL HILL RD
Pikers Lane Farm
PIKERS LA
BRIDLE BROOK LA
Royal Court Hotel
Grove House Farm
Golf Driving Range
AKON HO
SANDPITS LA
Hawkes End
Brownshill Green
Hillside Farm
CV6
OAK LA
TED PITTS LA
HAWKES MILL LA
The White Lion (PH)
LONG LA
The Spinney
Cardinal Newman RC Sch
BENNETT'S RD S
CV5
The Old Hall (PH)
P
BURTON CL
WICKHAM CL
KIRTON CL
CHURCH PARK CL
Sherbourne House Farm
WASHBROOK LA
Coundon Hall Park (Recn Gd)
Keresley Grange Prim Sch
HIGH ST
COUNDON WEDGE DR
River Sherbourne
BROWN'S LA
FRESHFIELD CL
Brownshill Green Farm
BROWNSHILL GREEN RD
WASTE LA
NEW RD
KERESLEY GREEN RD
NORTH BROOK RD
B4076
The Stone House
SAUNTON CL
The Jefferys

47
60

38
50

D E F

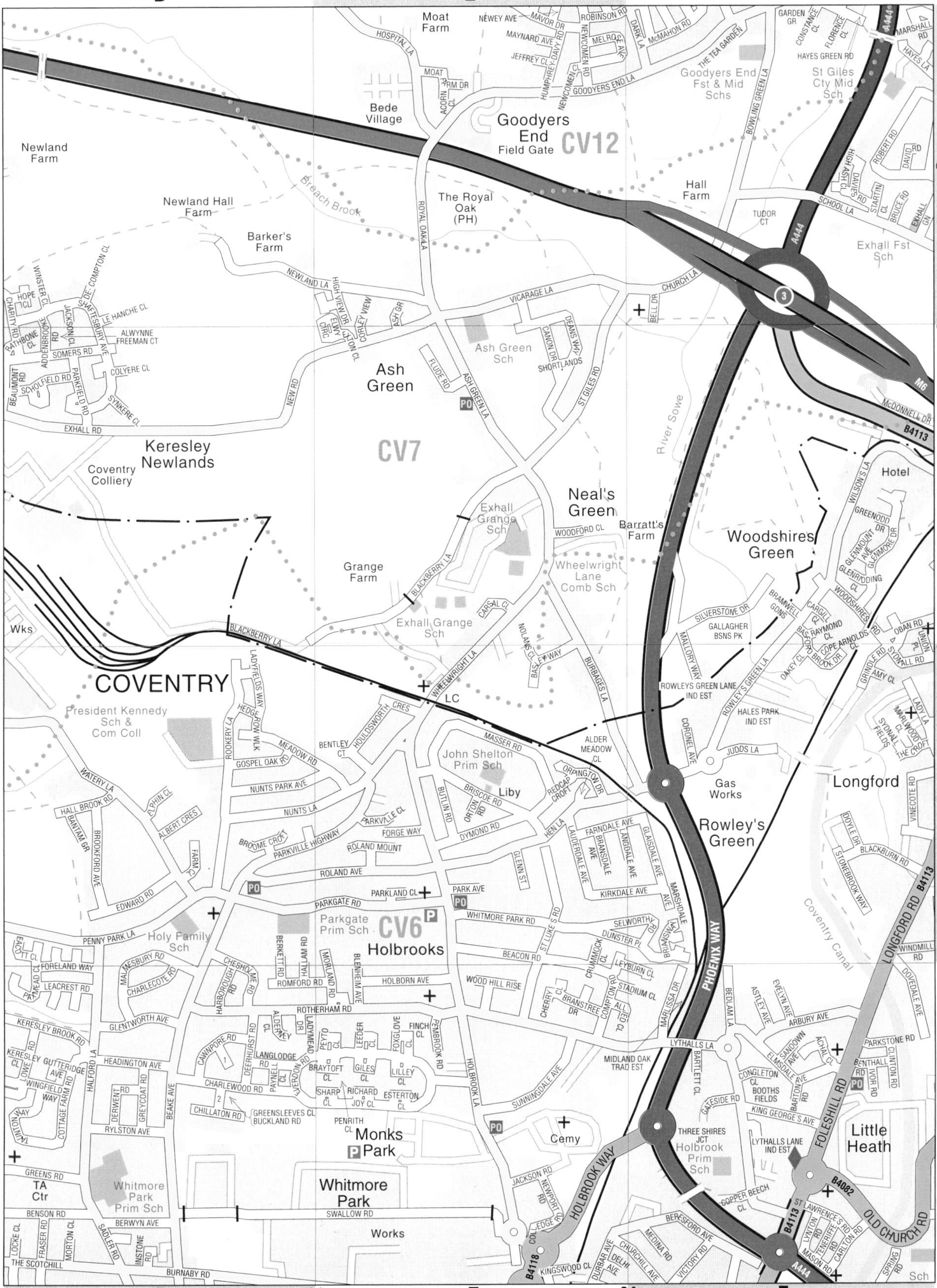

32 D 33 E 34 F

4 85 3 84 2 83 1 82

61
50

49
39

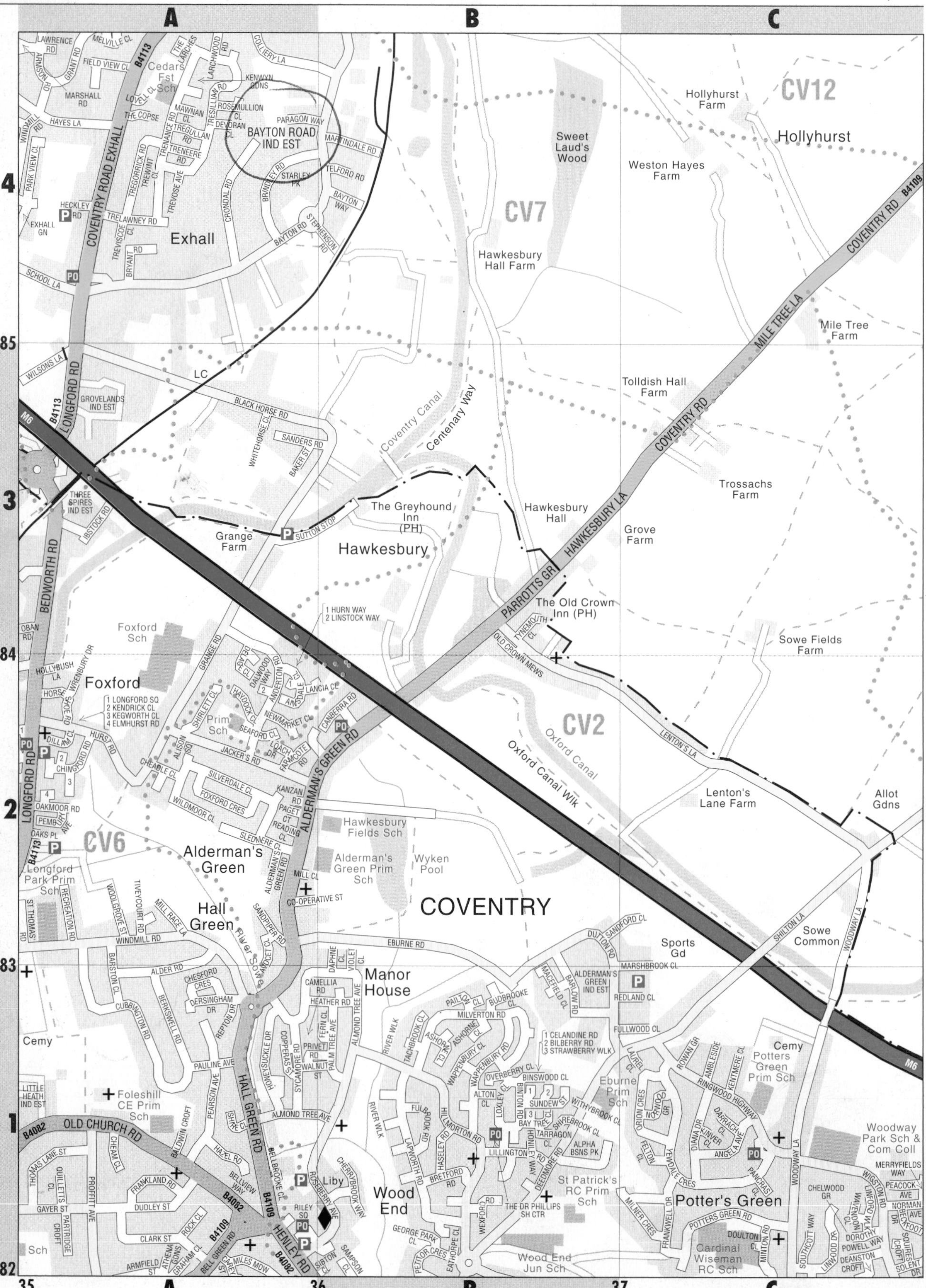
A
B
C
4
3
2
1
85
84
83
82
35
36
37
CV12
Hollyhurst Farm
Hollyhurst
Sweet Laud's Wood
Weston Hayes Farm
CV7
Hawkesbury Hall Farm
Mile Tree Farm
Tolldish Hall Farm
Trossachs Farm
Hawkesbury Hall
Grove Farm
Sowe Fields Farm
CV2
Lenton's Lane Farm
Allot Gdns
Sowe Common
Sports Gd
COVENTRY
Cedars Fst Sch
BAYTON ROAD IND EST
Exhall
GROVELANDS IND EST
THREE SPIRES IND EST
LC
Grange Farm
The Greyhound Inn (PH)
Hawkesbury
Coventry Canal
Centenary Way
The Old Crown Inn (PH)
Oxford Canal
Oxford Canal Wlk
Foxford Sch
Foxford
Prim Sch
CV6
Alderman's Green
Hall Green
River Sowe
Hawkesbury Fields Sch
Alderman's Green Prim Sch
Wyken Pool
Longford Park Prim Sch
Manor House
ALDERMAN'S GREEN IND EST
Cemy
Foleshill CE Prim Sch
Eburne Prim Sch
Potters Green Prim Sch
Woodway Park Sch & Com Coll
Liby
Wood End
St Patrick's RC Prim Sch
ALPHA BSNS PK
THE DR PHILLIPS SH CTR
Potter's Green
Cardinal Wiseman RC Sch
Wood End Jun Sch
Sch
COVENTRY ROAD EXHALL
LONGFORD RD
BEDWORTH RD
B4113
M6
COVENTRY RD
B4109
MILE TREE LA
HAWKESBURY LA
PARROTTS GR
ALDERMAN'S GREEN RD
HALL GREEN RD
HENLEY RD
OLD CHURCH RD
B4082
WOODWAY LA
SHILTON LA
LENTON'S LA
BLACK HORSE RD
SANDERS RD
SUTTON STOP
EBURNE RD
WINDMILL RD
ALMOND TREE AVE
RINGWOOD HIGHWAY
POTTERS GREEN RD
1 HURN WAY
2 LINSTOCK WAY
1 LONGFORD SQ
2 KENDRICK CL
3 KEGWORTH CL
4 ELMHURST RD
1 CELANDINE RD
2 BILBERRY RD
3 STRAWBERRY WLK

49
62

40
52

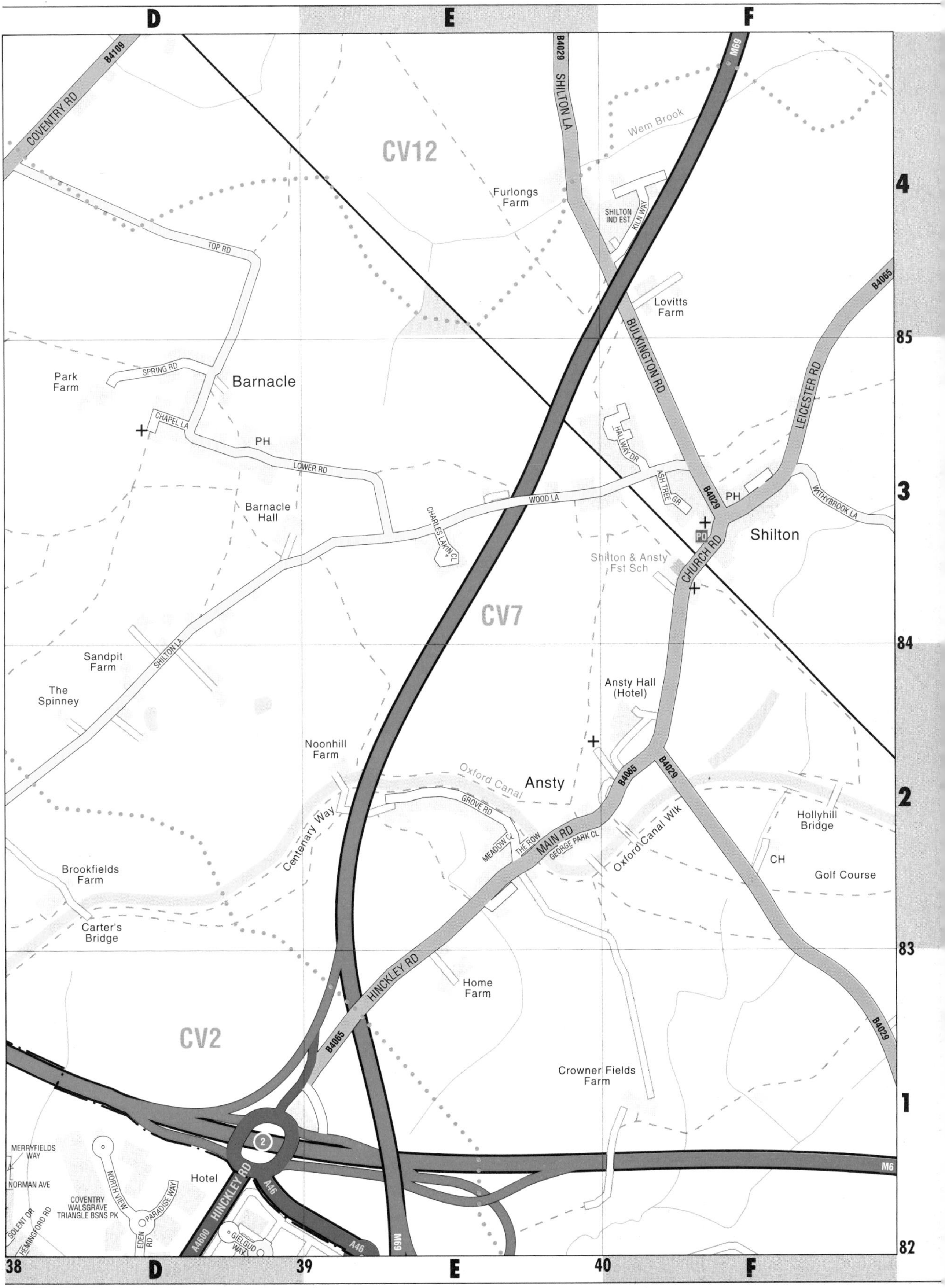
D
E
F
4
85
3
84
2
83
1
82
38
39
40
B4109
COVENTRY RD
CV12
B4029
SHILTON LA
M69
Wem Brook
Furlongs
Farm
SHILTON
IND EST
KILN WAY
TOP RD
Lovitts
Farm
BULKINGTON RD
B4065
Park
Farm
SPRING RD
Barnacle
LEICESTER RD
CHAPEL LA
PH
HALLWAY DR
LOWER RD
ASH TREE GR
B4029
PH
WITHYBROOK LA
WOOD LA
Barnacle
Hall
CHARLES LAKIN CL
PO
Shilton
CHURCH RD
Shilton & Ansty
Fst Sch
CV7
Sandpit
Farm
SHILTON LA
The
Spinney
Ansty Hall
(Hotel)
Noonhill
Farm
Oxford Canal
Ansty
B4065
B4029
Hollyhill
Bridge
Centenary Way
GROVE RD
MEADOW CL
THE ROW
MAIN RD
GEORGE PARK CL
Oxford Canal Wlk
CH
Golf Course
Brookfields
Farm
Carter's
Bridge
HINCKLEY RD
Home
Farm
B4029
CV2
B4065
Crowner Fields
Farm
2
MERRYFIELDS
WAY
NORMAN AVE
NORTH VIEW
Hotel
M6
COVENTRY
WALSGRAVE
TRIANGLE BSNS PK
PARADISE WAY
HINCKLEY RD
A46
SOLENT DR
HEMINGFORD RD
EDEN RD
A4600
GIELGUD WAY
A46
M69

63
52

51
41

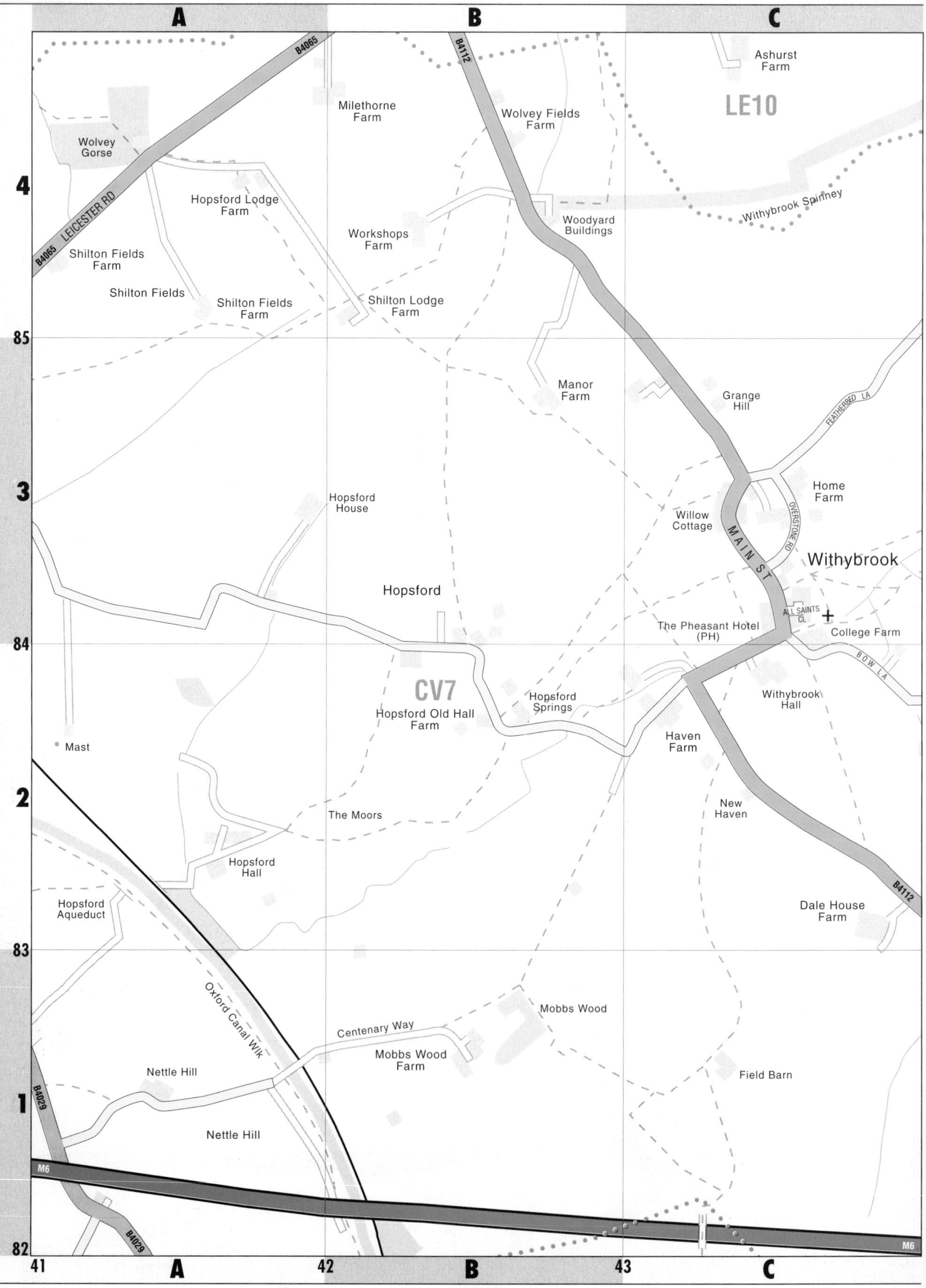
A
B
C
4
85
3
84
2
83
1
82
41
42
43
B4065
LEICESTER RD
B4112
LE10
Ashurst Farm
Milethorne Farm
Wolvey Fields Farm
Wolvey Gorse
Hopsford Lodge Farm
Workshops Farm
Woodyard Buildings
Withybrook Spinney
Shilton Fields Farm
Shilton Fields
Shilton Fields Farm
Shilton Lodge Farm
Manor Farm
Grange Hill
FEATHERBED LA
Home Farm
Hopsford House
Willow Cottage
OVERSTONE RD
MAIN ST
Withybrook
Hopsford
ALL SAINTS CL
The Pheasant Hotel (PH)
College Farm
BOW LA
CV7
Hopsford Springs
Withybrook Hall
Hopsford Old Hall Farm
Haven Farm
Mast
New Haven
The Moors
Hopsford Hall
B4112
Dale House Farm
Hopsford Aqueduct
Oxford Canal Wlk
Mobbs Wood
Centenary Way
Mobbs Wood Farm
Nettle Hill
Field Barn
B4029
Nettle Hill
M6
B4029
M6

51
64

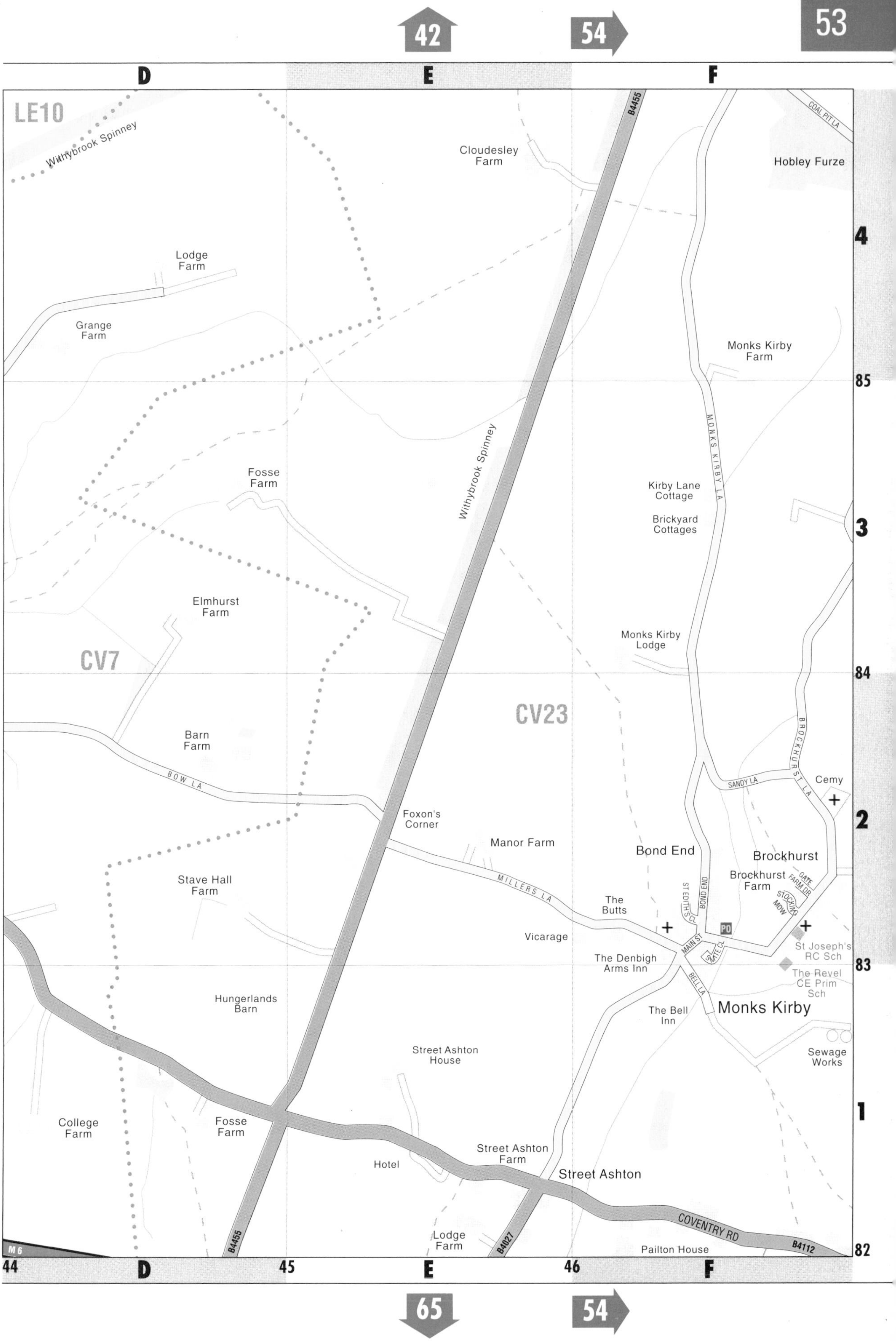
42
54
D
E
F
LE10
Withybrook Spinney
Cloudesley Farm
B4455
COAL PIT LA
Hobley Furze
4
Lodge Farm
Grange Farm
Monks Kirby Farm
85
MONKS KIRBY LA
Withybrook Spinney
Fosse Farm
Kirby Lane Cottage
Brickyard Cottages
3
Elmhurst Farm
Monks Kirby Lodge
CV7
84
CV23
BROCKHURST LA
Barn Farm
BOW LA
SANDY LA
Cemy
Foxon's Corner
2
Manor Farm
Bond End
Brockhurst
Stave Hall Farm
MILLERS LA
Brockhurst Farm
GATE FARM DR
ST EDITH'S CL
BOND END
STOCKING MDW
The Butts
PO
Vicarage
MAIN ST
GATE CL
St Joseph's RC Sch
The Denbigh Arms Inn
83
BELL LA
The Revel CE Prim Sch
Hungerlands Barn
The Bell Inn
Monks Kirby
Sewage Works
Street Ashton House
1
College Farm
Fosse Farm
Street Ashton Farm
Hotel
Street Ashton
COVENTRY RD
Lodge Farm
B4027
B4455
M6
B4112
Pailton House
82
44
45
46
D
E
F
65
54

53
43

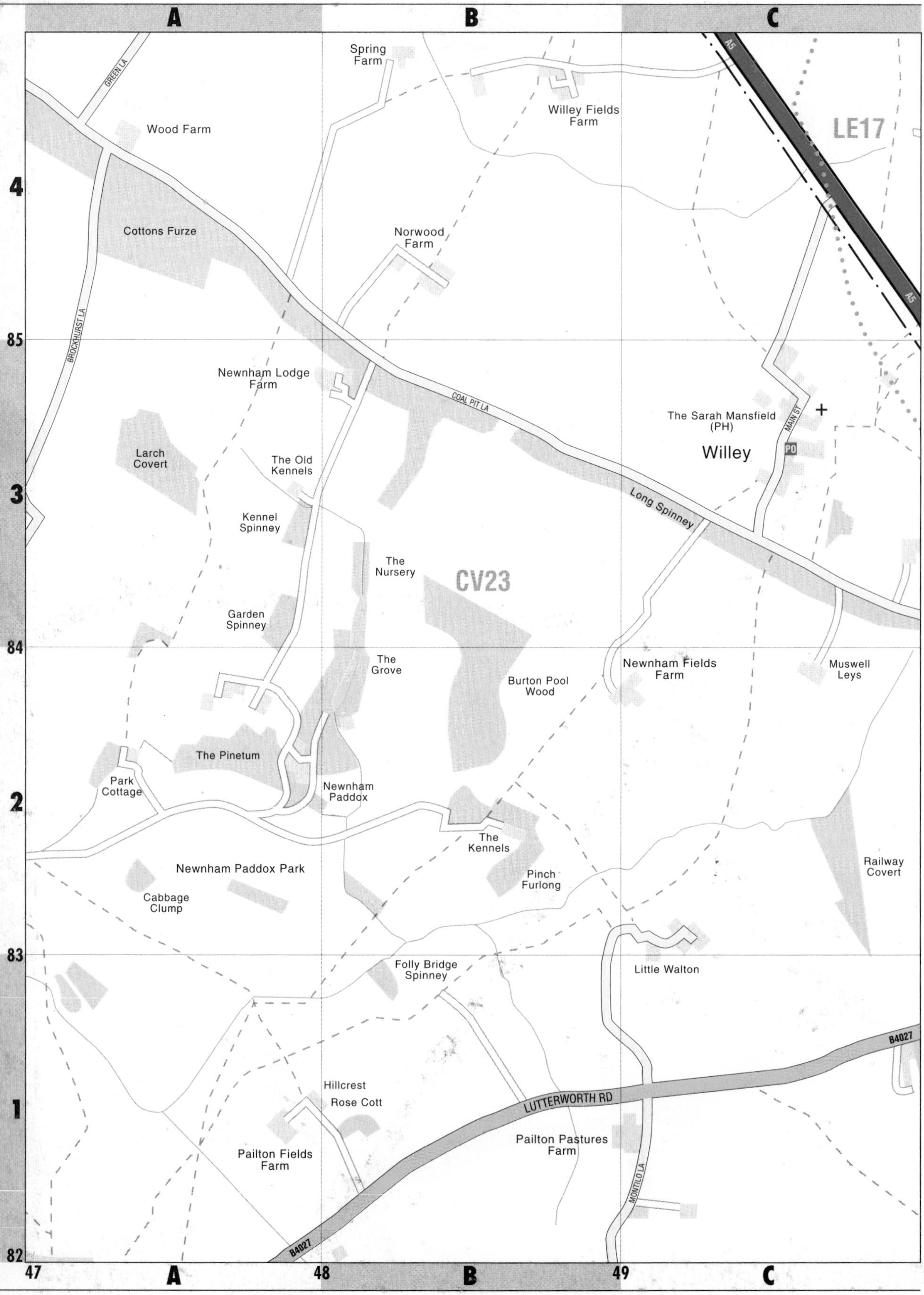
A
B
C
4
85
3
84
2
83
1
82
47
48
49
Spring Farm
Willey Fields Farm
LE17
A5
GREEN LA
Wood Farm
Cottons Furze
Norwood Farm
BROCKHURST LA
Newnham Lodge Farm
COAL PIT LA
The Sarah Mansfield (PH)
MAIN ST
PO
Willey
Larch Covert
The Old Kennels
Long Spinney
Kennel Spinney
The Nursery
CV23
Garden Spinney
The Grove
Newnham Fields Farm
Muswell Leys
Burton Pool Wood
The Pinetum
Park Cottage
Newnham Paddox
The Kennels
Railway Covert
Newnham Paddox Park
Pinch Furlong
Cabbage Clump
Folly Bridge Spinney
Little Walton
B4027
Hillcrest
Rose Cott
LUTTERWORTH RD
Pailton Fields Farm
Pailton Pastures Farm
MONTILO LA
B4027

53
66

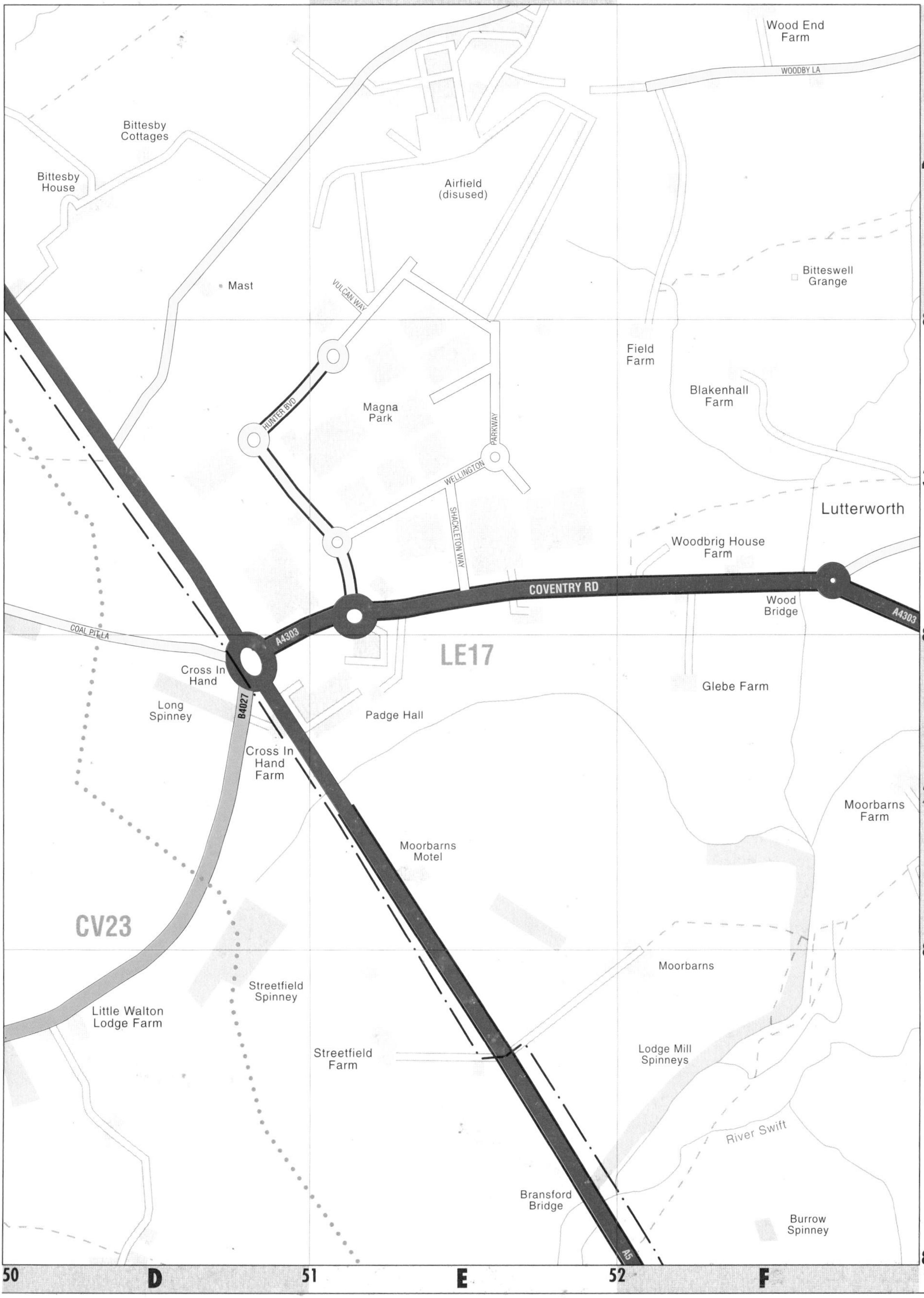
D
E
F
Wood End Farm
WOODBY LA
Bittesby Cottages
Bittesby House
Airfield (disused)
4
Bitteswell Grange
Mast
VULCAN WAY
85
Field Farm
Blakenhall Farm
Magna Park
HUNTER BVD
PARKWAY
WELLINGTON
3
Lutterworth
SHACKLETON WAY
Woodbrig House Farm
COVENTRY RD
Wood Bridge
A4303
COAL PIT LA
A4303
84
LE17
Cross In Hand
Glebe Farm
Long Spinney
B4027
Padge Hall
Cross In Hand Farm
2
Moorbarns Farm
Moorbarns Motel
CV23
83
Moorbarns
Streetfield Spinney
Little Walton Lodge Farm
Lodge Mill Spinneys
Streetfield Farm
1
River Swift
Bransford Bridge
Burrow Spinney
A5
82
50
D
51
E
52
F

67

44

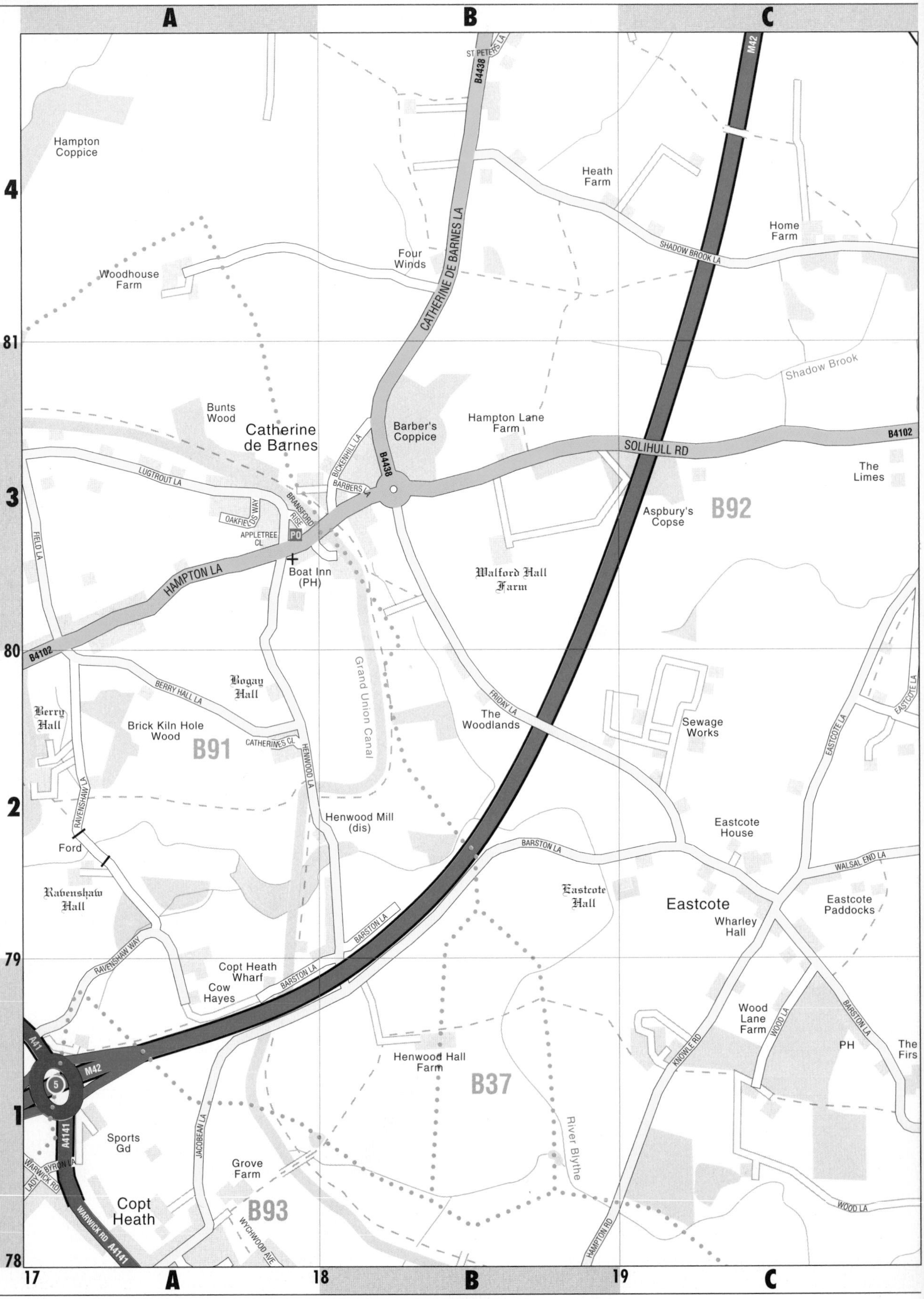
A
B
C
4
81
3
80
2
79
1
78
17
18
19
M42
B4438
ST PETERS LA
Hampton Coppice
Heath Farm
Home Farm
SHADOW BROOK LA
Four Winds
CATHERINE DE BARNES LA
Woodhouse Farm
Shadow Brook
Bunts Wood
Catherine de Barnes
Barber's Coppice
Hampton Lane Farm
SOLIHULL RD
B4102
The Limes
BICKENHILL LA
LUGTROUT LA
BARBERS LA
BRANSFORD RISE
OAKFIELDS WAY
FIELD LA
APPLETREE CL
PO
Aspbury's Copse
B92
HAMPTON LA
Boat Inn (PH)
Walford Hall Farm
Grand Union Canal
Bogay Hall
BERRY HALL LA
Berry Hall
Brick Kiln Hole Wood
B91
CATHERINES CL
HENWOOD LA
FRIDAY LA
The Woodlands
Sewage Works
EASTCOTE LA
RAVENSHAW LA
Henwood Mill (dis)
Eastcote House
Ford
BARSTON LA
WALSAL END LA
Ravenshaw Hall
Eastcote Hall
Eastcote
Eastcote Paddocks
Wharley Hall
RAVENSHAW WAY
Copt Heath Wharf
Cow Hayes
Wood Lane Farm
WOOD LA
PH
The Firs
A41
5
Henwood Hall Farm
B37
KNOWLE RD
A4141
Sports Gd
JACOBEAN LA
River Blythe
WARWICK RD
LADY BYRON LA
Grove Farm
Copt Heath
B93
WYCHWOOD AVE
HAMPTON RD

72

45
58

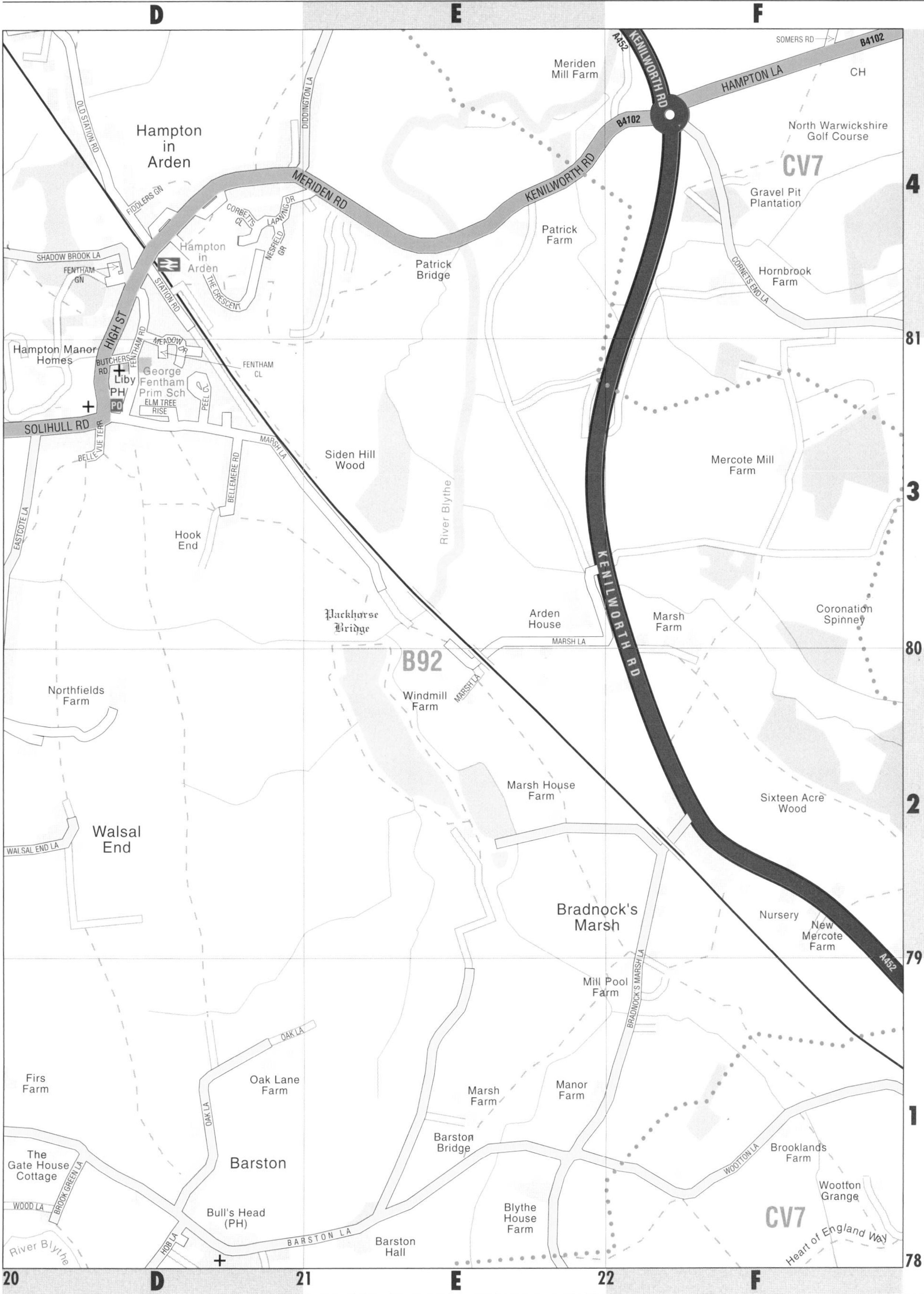
D
E
F
Hampton in Arden
Meriden Mill Farm
North Warwickshire Golf Course
CV7
Gravel Pit Plantation
Patrick Farm
Patrick Bridge
Hornbrook Farm
Hampton Manor Homes
George Fentham Prim Sch
Liby
PH
PO
Siden Hill Wood
River Blythe
Mercote Mill Farm
Hook End
Packhorse Bridge
Arden House
Marsh Farm
Coronation Spinney
B92
Northfields Farm
Windmill Farm
Marsh House Farm
Sixteen Acre Wood
Walsal End
Bradnock's Marsh
Nursery
New Mercote Farm
Mill Pool Farm
Firs Farm
Oak Lane Farm
Marsh Farm
Manor Farm
The Gate House Cottage
Barston
Barston Bridge
Brooklands Farm
Wootton Grange
Bull's Head (PH)
Blythe House Farm
Barston Hall
Heart of England Way
River Blythe
CH
SOMERS RD
B4102
HAMPTON LA
A452
KENILWORTH RD
B4102
KENILWORTH RD
MERIDEN RD
OLD STATION RD
DIDDINGTON LA
FIDDLERS GN
CORBETTS CL
LAPWING DR
NESFIELD GR
THE CRESCENT
SHADOW BROOK LA
FENTHAM GN
STATION RD
HIGH ST
FENTHAM RD
MEADOW DR
BUTCHERS RD
FENTHAM CL
ELM TREE RISE
PEEL CL
SOLIHULL RD
BELLE VUE TERR
MARSH LA
BELLEMERE RD
EASTCOTE LA
CORNETS END LA
KENILWORTH RD
MARSH LA
MARSH LA
WALSAL END LA
BRADNOCK'S MARSH LA
A452
OAK LA
OAK LA
WOOTTON LA
WOOD LA
BROOK GREEN LA
HOB LA
BARSTON LA
4
81
3
80
2
79
1
78
20
21
22

73
58

57
46

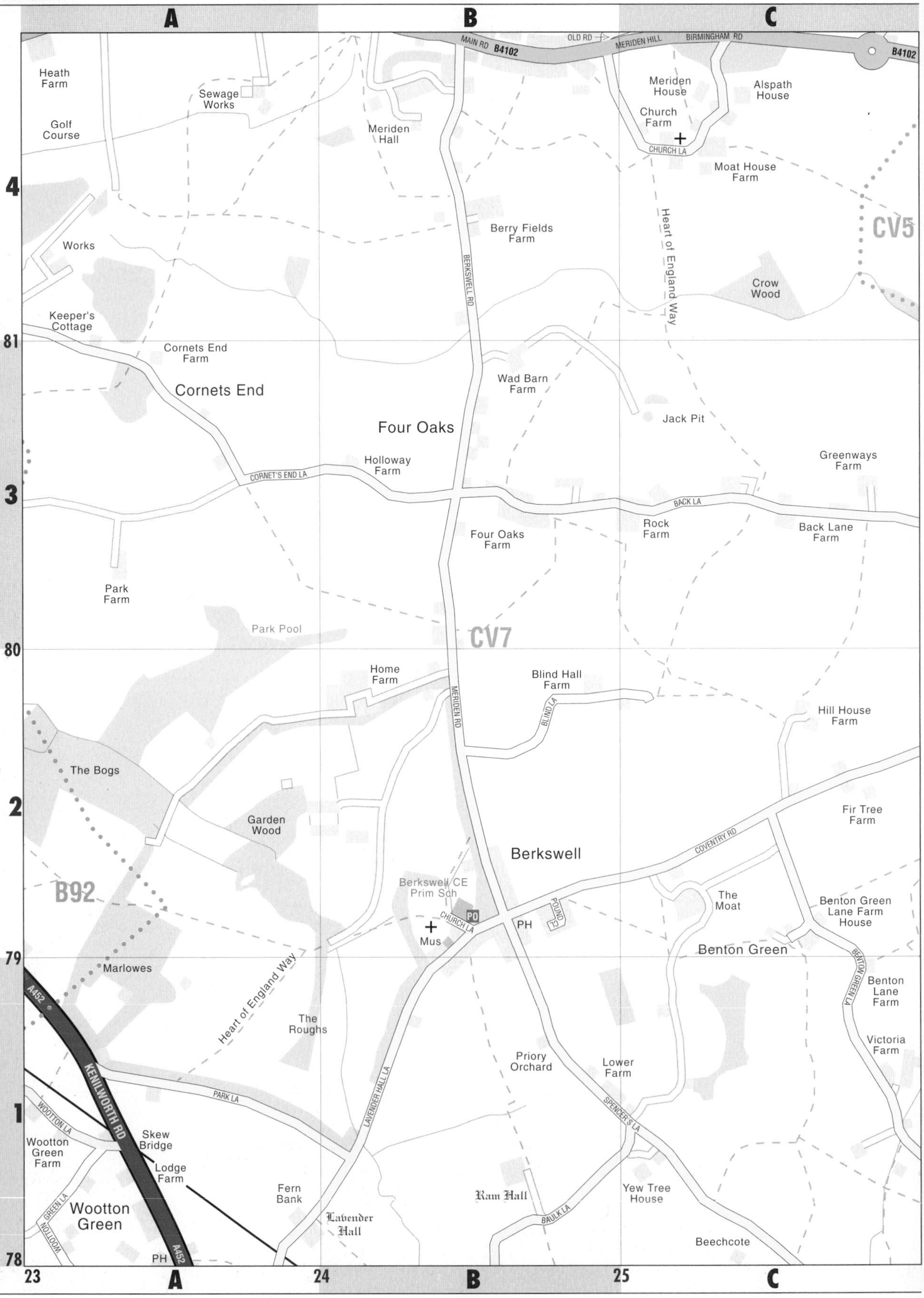
A
B
C
4
81
3
80
2
79
1
78
23
24
25
MAIN RD
B4102
OLD RD
MERIDEN HILL
BIRMINGHAM RD
B4102
Heath Farm
Sewage Works
Golf Course
Meriden Hall
Meriden House
Alspath House
Church Farm
CHURCH LA
Moat House Farm
Works
Berry Fields Farm
BERKSWELL RD
Heart of England Way
CV5
Crow Wood
Keeper's Cottage
Cornets End Farm
Cornets End
Wad Barn Farm
Four Oaks
Jack Pit
Holloway Farm
CORNET'S END LA
Greenways Farm
BACK LA
Rock Farm
Four Oaks Farm
Back Lane Farm
Park Farm
Park Pool
CV7
Home Farm
Blind Hall Farm
MERIDEN RD
BLIND LA
Hill House Farm
The Bogs
Garden Wood
Fir Tree Farm
Berkswell
COVENTRY RD
B92
Berkswell CE Prim Sch
CHURCH LA
PO
PH
POUND CL
The Moat
Benton Green Lane Farm House
Mus
Benton Green
Marlowes
BENTON GREEN LA
Benton Lane Farm
A452
Heart of England Way
The Roughs
Victoria Farm
KENILWORTH RD
Priory Orchard
Lower Farm
PARK LA
LAVENDER HALL LA
SPENCER'S LA
WOOTTON LA
Wootton Green Farm
Skew Bridge
Lodge Farm
Fern Bank
Ram Hall
Yew Tree House
WOOTTON GREEN LA
Wootton Green
Labender Hall
BAULK LA
Beechcote
PH
A452

57
74

47
60

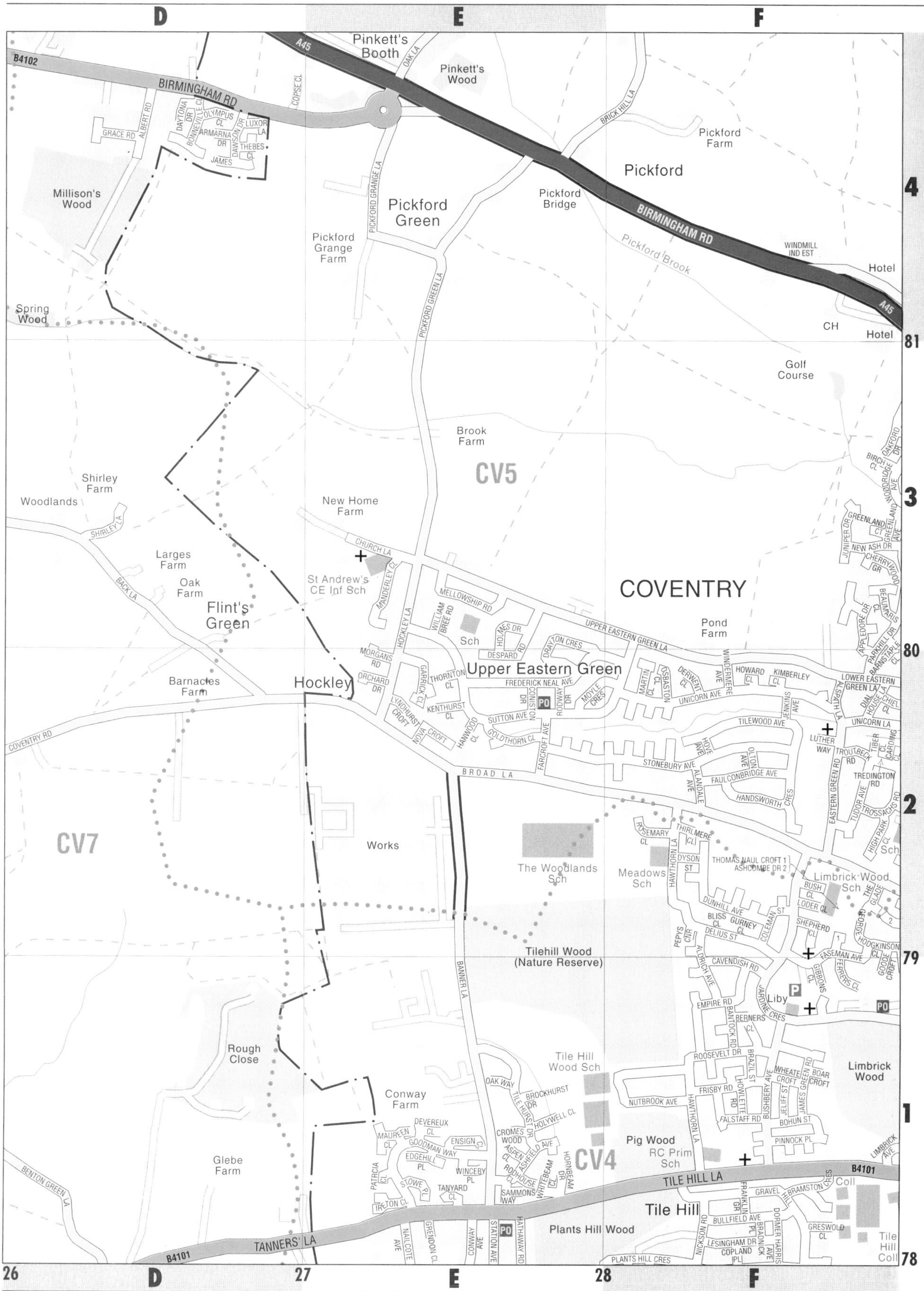
D
E
F
Pinkett's Booth
Pinkett's Wood
A45
B4102
BIRMINGHAM RD
OAK LA
COPSE CL
GRACE RD
ALBERT RD
DAYTONA DR
BONNEVILLE CL
OLYMPUS CL
ARMARNA DR
DAWSON DR
LUXOR LA
THEBES CL
JAMES
Millison's Wood
BRICK HILL LA
Pickford Farm
Pickford
Pickford Bridge
Pickford Green
PICKFORD GRANGE LA
Pickford Grange Farm
BIRMINGHAM RD
Pickford Brook
WINDMILL IND EST
Hotel
A45
CH
Hotel
Spring Wood
PICKFORD GREEN LA
Golf Course
Brook Farm
CV5
Shirley Farm
Woodlands
New Home Farm
OAKFORD DR
BIRCH CL
WOODRIDGE AVE
GREENLAND AVE
GREENLAND CT
JUNIPER DR
NEW ASH DR
CHERRYWOOD GR
SHIRLEY LA
CHURCH LA
Larges Farm
Oak Farm
BACK LA
St Andrew's CE Inf Sch
MANDERLEY CL
COVENTRY
Flint's Green
MELLOWSHIP RD
WILLIAM BREE RD
HOCKLEY LA
Sch
HOLMES DR
DESPARD RD
DRAYTON CRES
UPPER EASTERN GREEN LA
Pond Farm
APPLEDORE DR
PARKHILL DR
BEAUMARIS CL
BARNSTAPLE CL
MORGANS RD
ORCHARD DR
GARRICK CL
THORNTON CL
Upper Eastern Green
FREDERICK NEAL AVE
MARTIN CL
OSBASTON CL
DERWENT CL
WINDERMERE AVE
HOWARD CL
KIMBERLEY
LOWER EASTERN GREEN LA
Barnacles Farm
Hockley
CONISTON DR
PO
RODWAY DR
MOYLE CRES
UNICORN AVE
JENKINS AVE
ALSPATH LA
DIAL HOUSE LA
CHIEL CL
KENTHURST CL
LYNDHURST CROFT
SUTTON AVE
TILEWOOD AVE
UNICORN LA
COVENTRY RD
NOVA CROFT
HANWOOD CL
GOLDTHORN CL
FARCROFT AVE
LUTHER WAY
TIBER CL
CARDING CL
TROUTBECK RD
BROAD LA
STONEBURY AVE
HOVE AVE
OLTON AVE
FAULCONBRIDGE AVE
EASTERN GREEN RD
TREDINGTON RD
ALANDALE AVE
HANDSWORTH CRES
TUDOR AVE
TROSSACHS RD
CV7
Works
ROSEMARY CL
THIRLMERE CL
HIGH PARK CL
Sch
The Woodlands Sch
Meadows Sch
HAWTHORN LA
DYSON ST
THOMAS NAUL CROFT 1
ASHCOMBE DR 2
Limbrick Wood Sch
BUSH CL
LODER CL
THE GLADE
DUNHILL AVE
BLISS CL
GURNEY CL
COLEMAN ST
SHEPHERD CL
GEORGE
DELIUS ST
PEPYS CNR
HODGKINSON CL
Tilehill Wood (Nature Reserve)
FASEMAN AVE
GOODE CROFT
ALDRICH AVE
CAVENDISH RD
GIBBONS CL
FERRERS CL
BANNER LA
P
Liby
JARDINE CRES
PO
EMPIRE RD
BANTOCK RD
BERNERS CL
Rough Close
ROOSEVELT DR
Tile Hill Wood Sch
BRAZIL ST
BOAR CROFT
Limbrick Wood
WHEATE CROFT
JAMES GREEN RD
OAK WAY
BROCKHURST DR
TILE HURST DR
HOLYWELL CL
FRISBY RD
HOWLETTE RD
BUSHBERY AVE
JELIFF ST
Conway Farm
NUTBROOK AVE
HAWTHORN LA
FALSTAFF RD
BOHUN ST
DEVEREUX CL
MAUREEN CL
GOODMAN WAY
ENSIGN CL
CROMES WOOD
ASHFIELD AVE
Pig Wood RC Prim Sch
PINNOCK PL
LIMBRICK AVE
Glebe Farm
EDGEHILL PL
WINCEBY PL
ASPEN CL
CV4
HORNBEAM DR
B4101
BENTON GREEN LA
PATRICIA CL
STOWE PL
RODHOUSE CL
WHITEBEAM CL
TILE HILL LA
FRANKLIN GR
GRAVEL HILL
BRAMSTON CRES
Coll
TANYARD CL
SAMMONS WAY
IRETON CL
Tile Hill
NICKSON RD
BULLFIELD AVE
DORMER HARRIS AVE
GRESWOLD CL
B4101
TANNERS' LA
NAILCOTE AVE
GRENDON CL
CONWAY AVE
STATION AVE
PO
HATHAWAY RD
Plants Hill Wood
LESINGHAM DR
COPLAND PL
BRADNICK PL
Tile Hill Coll
PLANTS HILL CRES
4
81
3
80
2
79
1
78
26
D
27
E
28
F

75
60

59 48

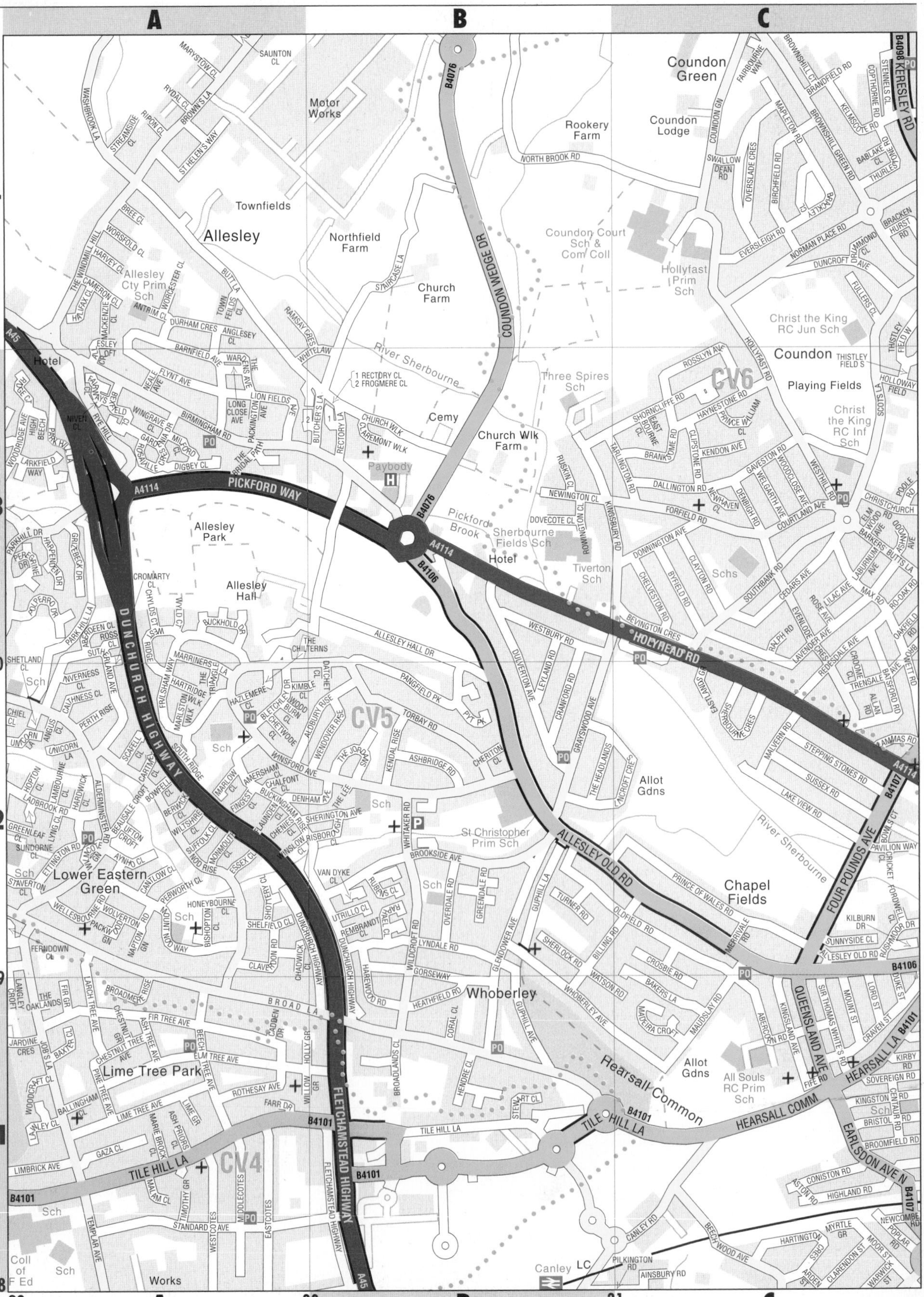
A
B
C
Coundon Green
Coundon Lodge
Rookery Farm
Motor Works
Townfields
Allesley
Northfield Farm
Allesley Cty Prim Sch
Church Farm
Coundon Court Sch & Com Coll
Hollyfast Prim Sch
Christ the King RC Jun Sch
Coundon
Playing Fields
Christ the King RC Inf Sch
Three Spires Sch
CV6
River Sherbourne
Cemy
Church Wlk Farm
Paybody
Hotel
PICKFORD WAY
A4114
B4076
B4106
COUNDON WEDGE DR
Allesley Park
Allesley Hall
Pickford Brook
Sherbourne Fields Sch
Tiverton Sch
Schs
HOLYHEAD RD
DUNCHURCH HIGHWAY
CV5
Sch
Allot Gdns
St Christopher Prim Sch
ALLESLEY OLD RD
Chapel Fields
FOUR POUNDS AVE
Lower Eastern Green
Whoberley
BROAD LA
Lime Tree Park
Hearsall Common
HEARSALL COMM
TILE HILL LA
B4101
B4107
EARLSDON AVE N
FLETCHAMSTEAD HIGHWAY
CV4
All Souls RC Prim Sch
Coll of F Ed
Works
Canley
LC
A45
KERESLEY RD
B4098
4
81
3
80
2
79
1
78
29
30
31

59 76

D2
1 BATEMAN'S ACRE S
2 CHILTERN LEYS
3 PRIORSFIELD RD N
4 PRORSFIELD RD
5 RADFORD CIRC
6 HAWKSWORTH DR
7 COLLETT WLK
8 COMPASS CT

D3
1 NETHERMILL RD
2 PAKE'S CROFT
3 HUMBERSTONE RD

49
62

D E F

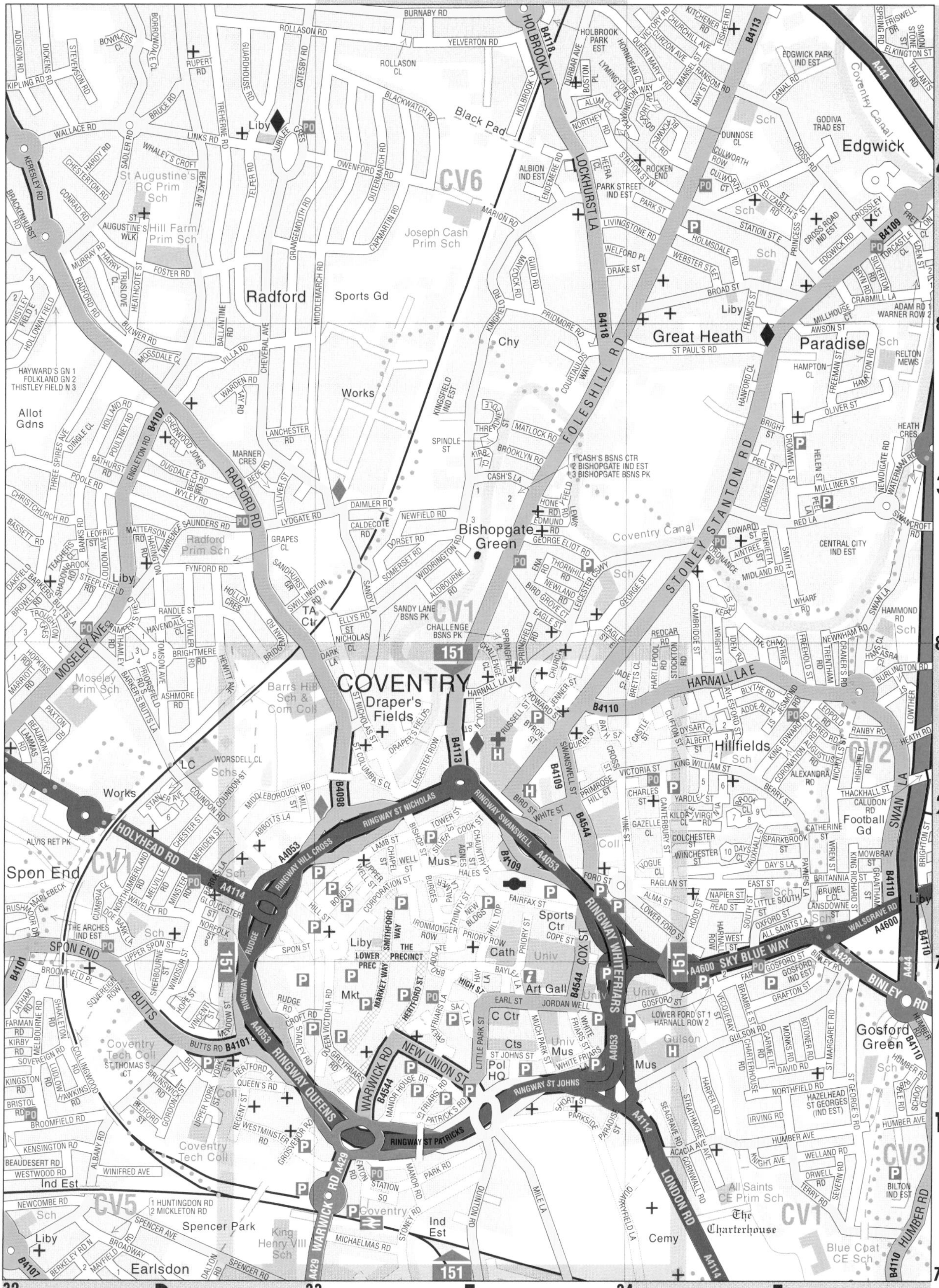

For full street detail of the highlighted area see page 151.

77
62

F2
1 CAWTHORNE CL
2 PENSILVA WAY
3 LEIGH ST
4 CLARENCE ST
5 NELSON ST
6 WATERLOO ST
7 GILBERT CL
8 VAUXHALL CL
9 VERNON CL
10 SPRING CL

61
50

A
B
C
4
3
2
1
81
80
79
78
35
36
37
Woodway Park
Henley Green
Bell Green
Deedmore Sch
Courthouse Green Prim Sch
Henley Coll
CV6
Superstore
Annie Osborn Prim Sch
Saints Peter & Paul RC Prim Sch
Frank Whittle Prim Sch
River Sowe
Clifford Bridge
Stoke Heath
Wyken Green
Lyng Hall Sch
Wyken Croft Nature Park
Stoke Heath Prim Sch
St John Fisher RC Prim Sch
Dartmouth Sch
Wyken Croft Prim Sch
Wyken
Walsgrave
Mkt
CV2
Caludon Castle (remains of)
Upper Stoke
Church End
Caludon Castle Sch
Stoke Prim Sch
Stoke Park Sch & Com Coll
Ravensdale Prim Sch
Sowe Bridge
Middle Stoke
Playing Fields
Sch
Richard Lee PrimSch
St Gregory's RC Prim Sch
Pattison Coll
Stoke Park
New Century Pk
Works
Stoke
Vicarage
Binley Bridge
Lower Stoke
Golf Course
CV3
COVENTRY
CV1
ANSTY RD
WALSGRAVE RD
BINLEY RD
HENLEY RD
BELL GREEN RD
CLIFFORD BRIDGE RD
BRANDON RD
ALLARD WAY
WOODWAY LA
SEWALL HIGHWAY
HIPSWELL HIGHWAY
A444
A4600
A428
A4082
B4082
B4109
B4110
B4027

61
78

51
64

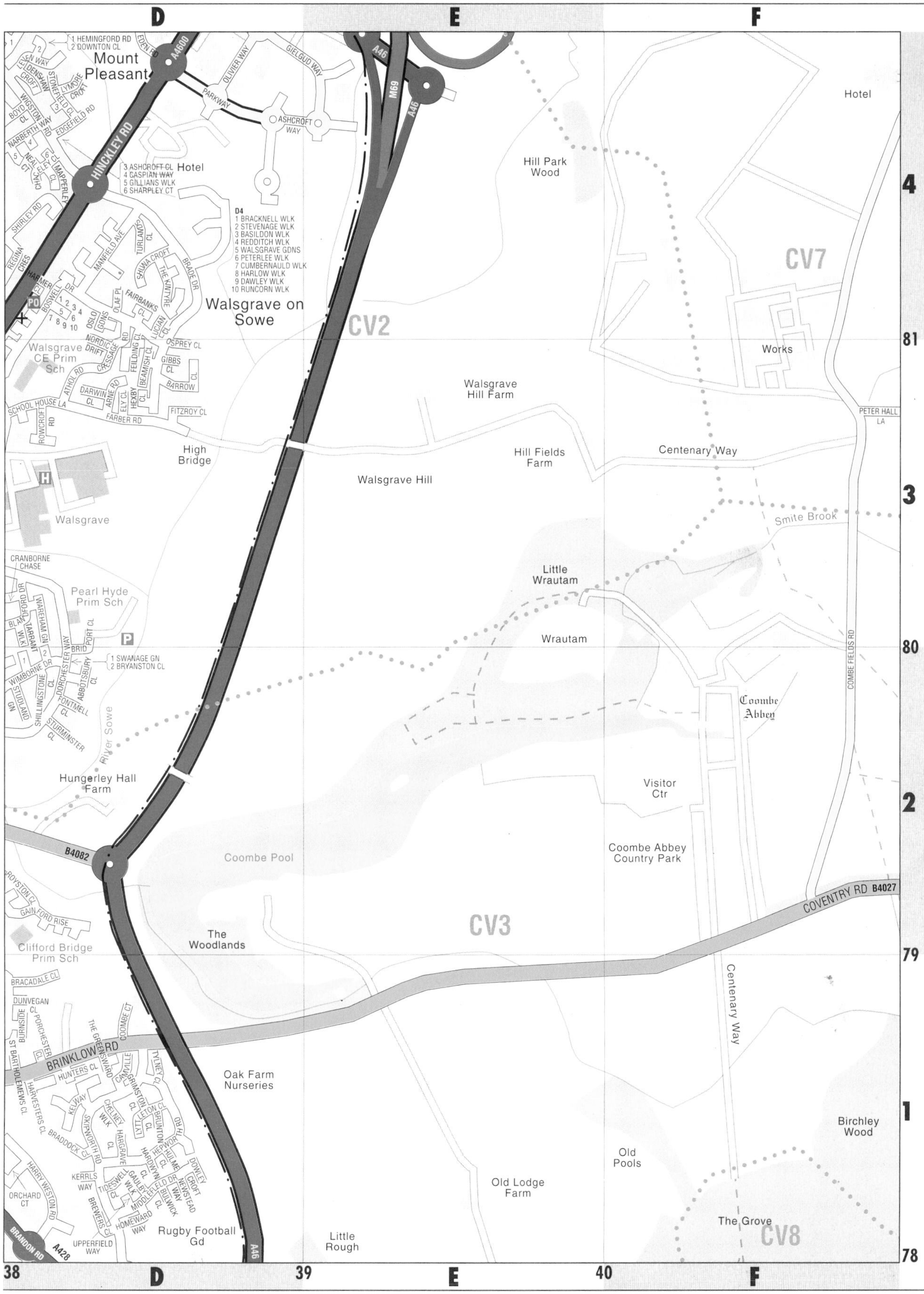
D
E
F
Mount Pleasant
1 HEMINGFORD RD
2 DOWNTON CL
A4600
HINCKLEY RD
OLIVIER WAY
GIELGUD WAY
PARKWAY
ASHCROFT WAY
A46
M69
Hotel
3 ASHCROFT CL
4 CASPIAN WAY
5 GILLIANS WLK
6 SHARPLEY CT
D4
1 BRACKNELL WLK
2 STEVENAGE WLK
3 BASILDON WLK
4 REDDITCH WLK
5 WALSGRAVE GDNS
6 PETERLEE WLK
7 CUMBERNAULD WLK
8 HARLOW WLK
9 DAWLEY WLK
10 RUNCORN WLK
Walsgrave on Sowe
CV2
Hill Park Wood
CV7
Works
Hotel
4
81
3
80
2
79
1
78
Walsgrave CE Prim Sch
SCHOOL HOUSE LA
FARBER RD
FITZROY CL
High Bridge
Walsgrave
Walsgrave Hill Farm
Walsgrave Hill
Hill Fields Farm
Centenary Way
PETER HALL LA
Smite Brook
Little Wrautam
Wrautam
COMBE FIELDS RD
Coombe Abbey
CRANBORNE CHASE
Pearl Hyde Prim Sch
1 SWANAGE GN
2 BRYANSTON CL
River Sowe
Hungerley Hall Farm
Visitor Ctr
B4082
Coombe Pool
Coombe Abbey Country Park
COVENTRY RD B4027
Clifford Bridge Prim Sch
The Woodlands
CV3
Centenary Way
BRINKLOW RD
Oak Farm Nurseries
Birchley Wood
Old Pools
Old Lodge Farm
The Grove
CV8
ORCHARD CT
Rugby Football Gd
Little Rough
BRANDON RD
A428
UPPERFIELD WAY
38
39
40

79
64

63
52

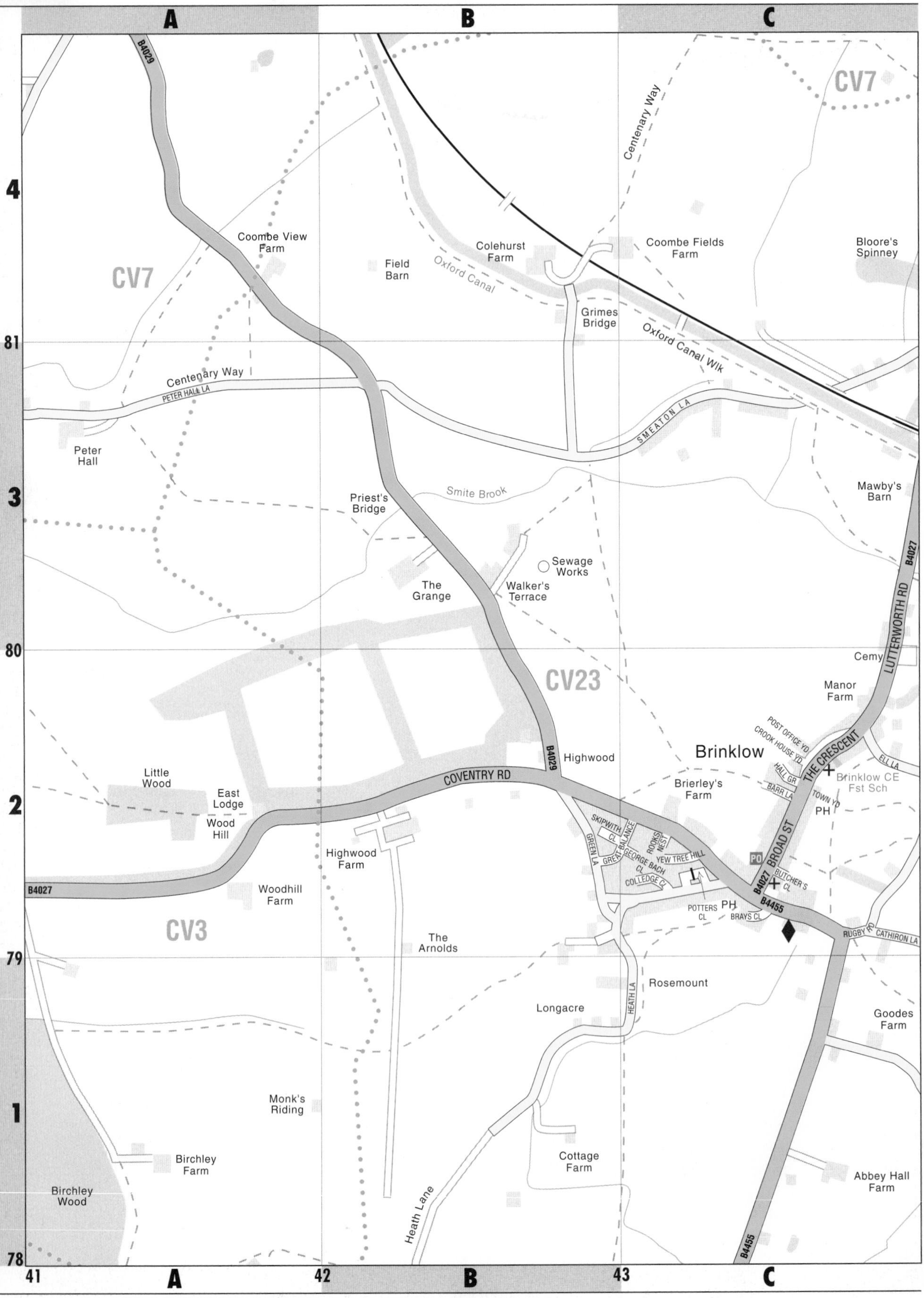
A
B
C
4
3
2
1
81
80
79
78
41
42
43
CV7
CV7
CV23
CV3
B4029
B4027
B4455
Centenary Way
Coombe View Farm
Field Barn
Colehurst Farm
Oxford Canal
Coombe Fields Farm
Bloore's Spinney
Grimes Bridge
Oxford Canal Wlk
Centenary Way
PETER HALL LA
SMEATON LA
Peter Hall
Smite Brook
Priest's Bridge
Mawby's Barn
Sewage Works
The Grange
Walker's Terrace
LUTTERWORTH RD
Cemy
Manor Farm
Highwood
Brinklow
POST OFFICE YD
CROOK HOUSE YD
THE CRESCENT
ELL LA
HALL GR
BARR LA
Brinklow CE Fst Sch
TOWN YD
PH
Little Wood
East Lodge
Wood Hill
COVENTRY RD
Brierley's Farm
SKIPWITH CL
GREAT BALANCE
ROOKS' NEST
GREEN LA
GREAT GEORGE BACH CL
YEW TREE HILL
COLLEDGE CL
BROAD ST
PO
BUTCHER'S CL
Highwood Farm
Woodhill Farm
POTTERS CL
PH
BRAYS CL
RUGBY RD
CATHIRON LA
The Arnolds
Rosemount
HEATH LA
Longacre
Goodes Farm
Monk's Riding
Birchley Farm
Cottage Farm
Abbey Hall Farm
Birchley Wood
Heath Lane

63
80

53
66

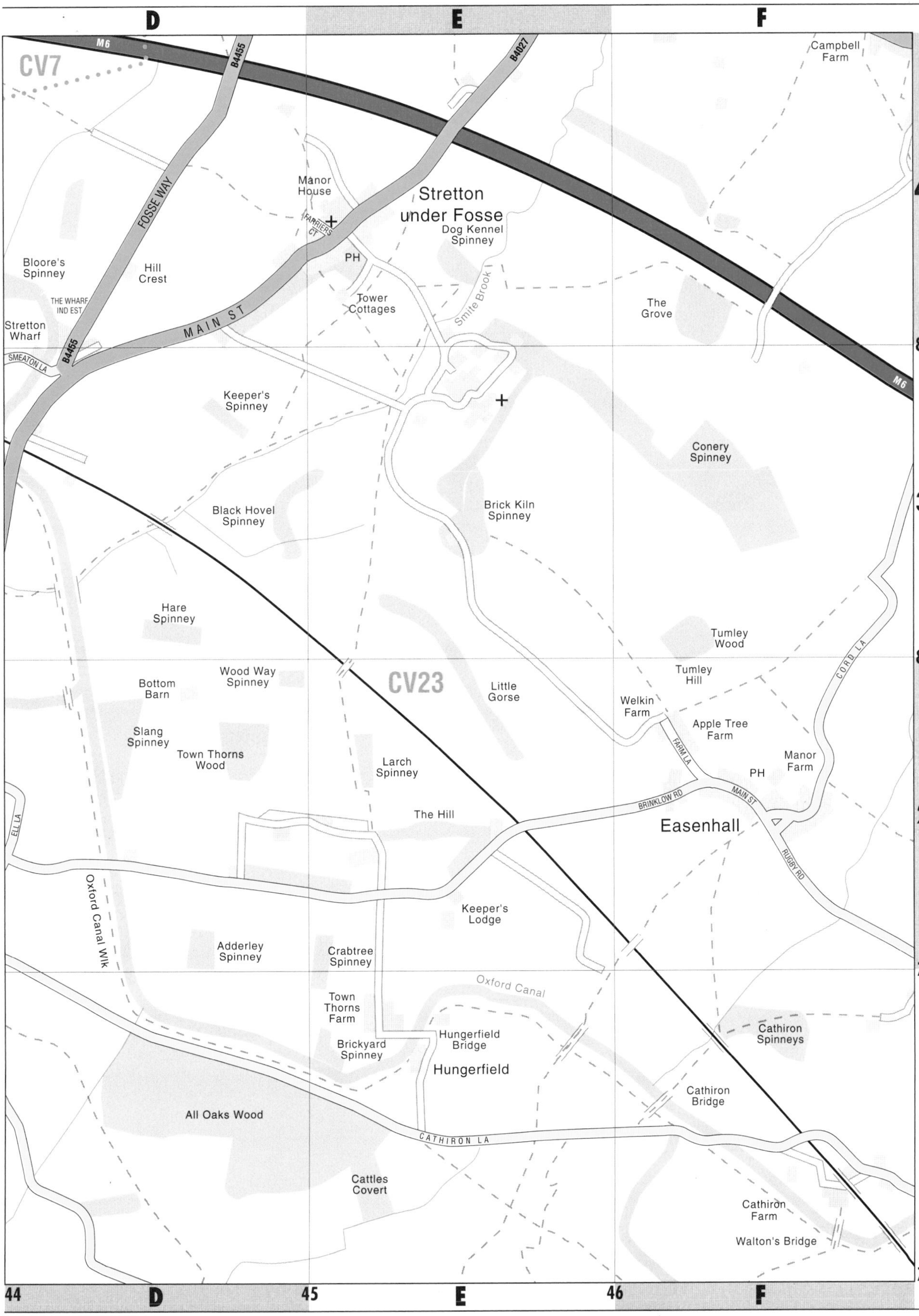
D
E
F
CV7
M6
B4455
B4027
Campbell Farm
Manor House
Stretton under Fosse
Dog Kennel Spinney
FOSSE WAY
FARRIERS CT
PH
Bloore's Spinney
Hill Crest
THE WHARF IND EST
Tower Cottages
Smite Brook
The Grove
Stretton Wharf
MAIN ST
SMEATON LA
Keeper's Spinney
Conery Spinney
Black Hovel Spinney
Brick Kiln Spinney
Hare Spinney
Tumley Wood
Tumley Hill
CV23
Wood Way Spinney
Bottom Barn
Little Gorse
Welkin Farm
Apple Tree Farm
CORD LA
Slang Spinney
Town Thorns Wood
FARM LA
Larch Spinney
Manor Farm
PH
MAIN ST
BRINKLOW RD
The Hill
Easenhall
ELL LA
RUGBY RD
Oxford Canal Wlk
Keeper's Lodge
Adderley Spinney
Crabtree Spinney
Oxford Canal
Town Thorns Farm
Brickyard Spinney
Hungerfield Bridge
Hungerfield
Cathiron Spinneys
Cathiron Bridge
All Oaks Wood
CATHIRON LA
Cattles Covert
Cathiron Farm
Walton's Bridge
4
81
3
80
2
79
1
78
44
45
46
D
E
F

81
66

65
54

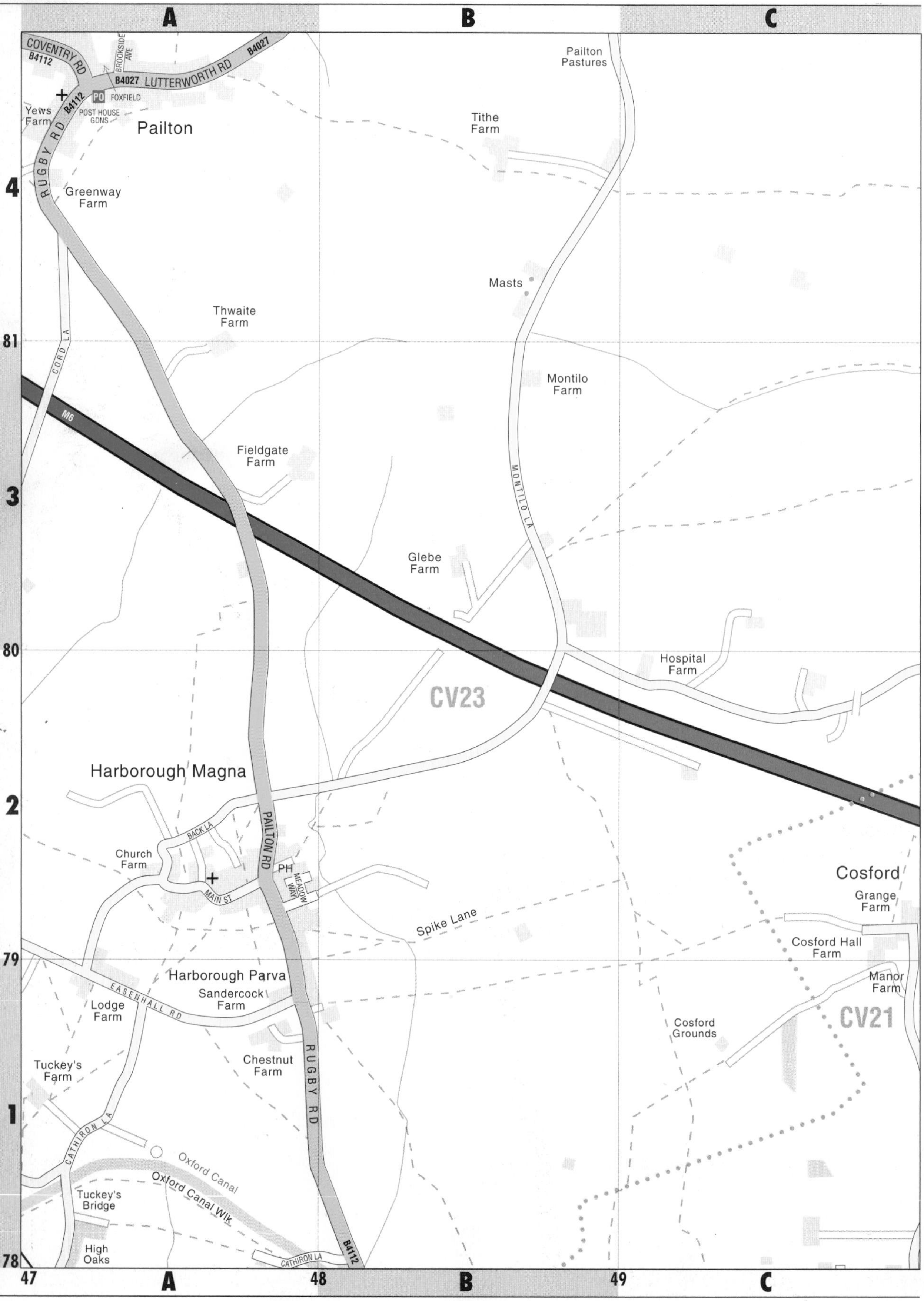
A
B
C
COVENTRY RD
B4112
BROOKSIDE AVE
B4027
LUTTERWORTH RD
B4027
PO
FOXFIELD
POST HOUSE GDNS
Yews Farm
Pailton
RUGBY RD
Greenway Farm
Pailton Pastures
Tithe Farm
Masts
Thwaite Farm
CORD LA
M6
Montilo Farm
Fieldgate Farm
MONTILO LA
Glebe Farm
Hospital Farm
CV23
Harborough Magna
BACK LA
PAILTON RD
Church Farm
PH
MEADOW WAY
MAIN ST
Spike Lane
Cosford
Grange Farm
Cosford Hall Farm
Manor Farm
Harborough Parva
Sandercock Farm
EASENHALL RD
Lodge Farm
CV21
Cosford Grounds
Chestnut Farm
Tuckey's Farm
RUGBY RD
CATHIRON LA
Oxford Canal
Oxford Canal Wlk
Tuckey's Bridge
High Oaks
CATHIRON LA
B4112
4
81
3
80
2
79
1
78
47
48
49

65
82

55
68
83
68

D E F

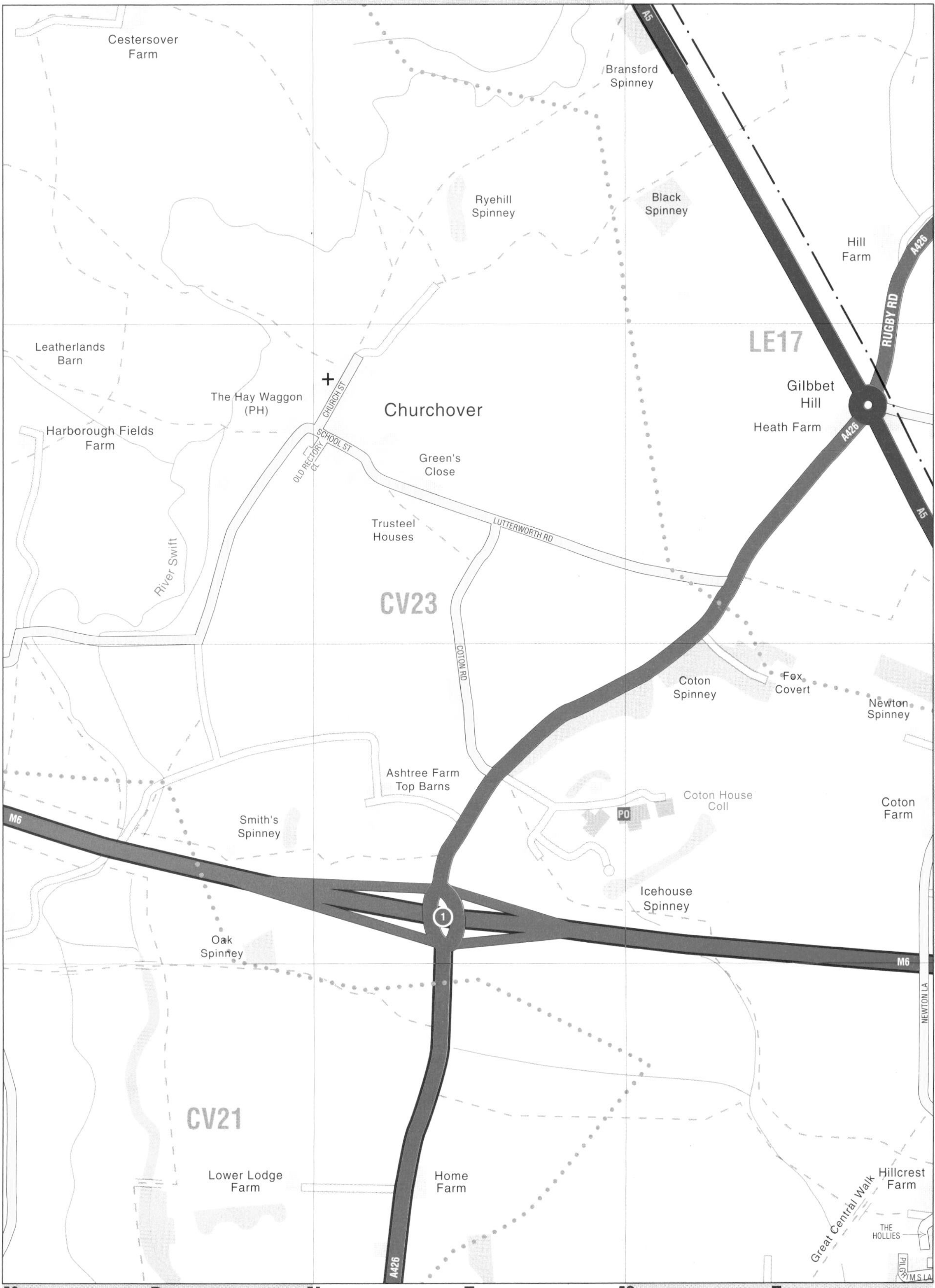
Cestersover Farm
Bransford Spinney
A5
Ryehill Spinney
Black Spinney
Hill Farm
A426
RUGBY RD
Leatherlands Barn
LE17
Gilbbet Hill
Heath Farm
The Hay Waggon (PH)
CHURCH ST
Churchover
Harborough Fields Farm
SCHOOL ST
OLD RECTORY CL
Green's Close
Trusteel Houses
LUTTERWORTH RD
River Swift
CV23
COTON RD
Coton Spinney
Fox Covert
Newton Spinney
Ashtree Farm Top Barns
Coton House Coll
PO
Coton Farm
M6
Smith's Spinney
Icehouse Spinney
1
Oak Spinney
NEWTON LA
CV21
Lower Lodge Farm
Home Farm
Hillcrest Farm
Great Central Walk
THE HOLLIES
PILGRIMS LA

4
81
3
80
2
79
1
78

50 D 51 E 52 F

67

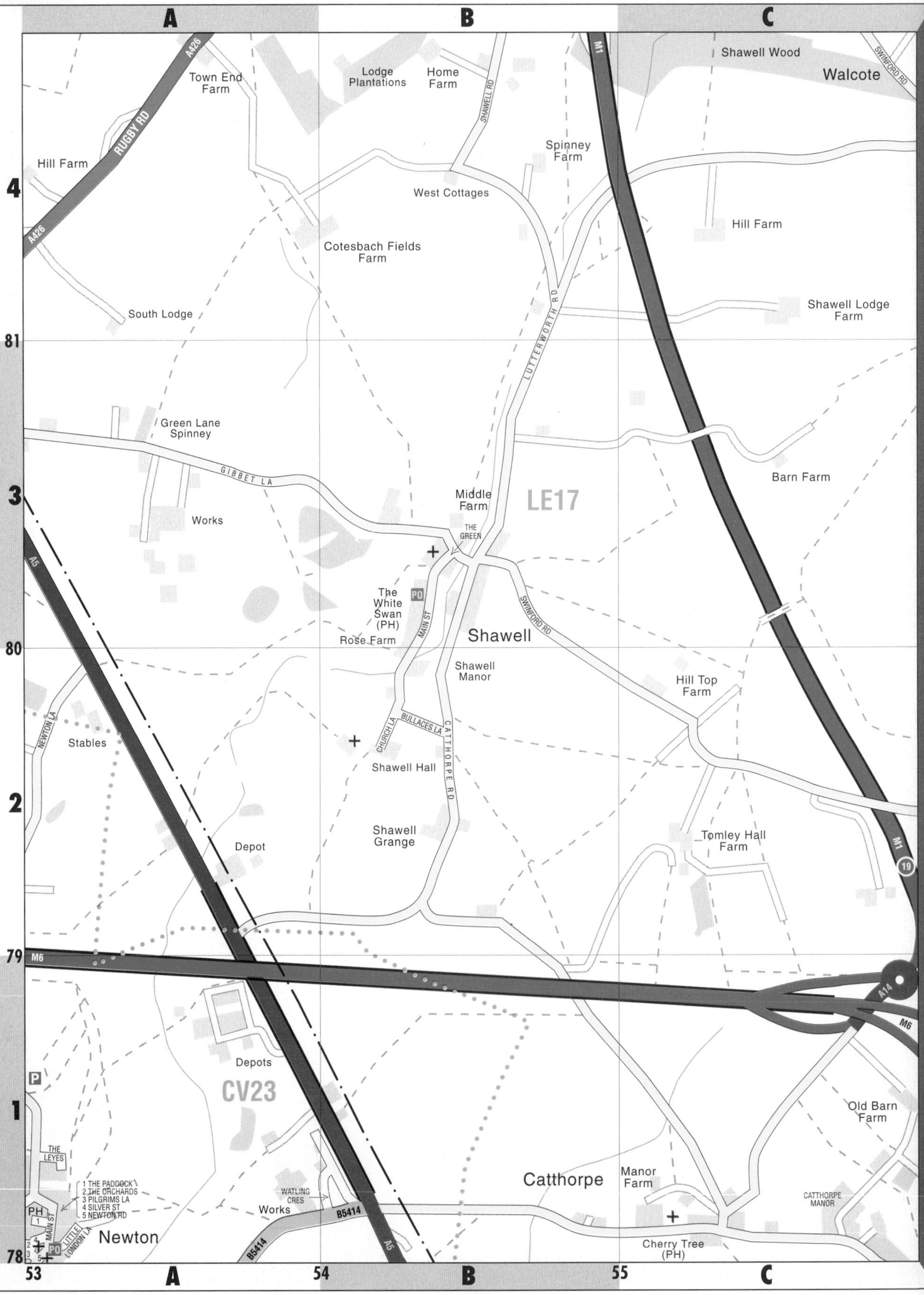
A
B
C
4
81
3
80
2
79
1
78
53
54
55
Shawell Wood
Walcote
SWINFORD RD
Town End Farm
Lodge Plantations
Home Farm
SHAWELL RD
M1
A426
RUGBY RD
Hill Farm
Spinney Farm
West Cottages
Hill Farm
Cotesbach Fields Farm
LUTTERWORTH RD
South Lodge
Shawell Lodge Farm
Green Lane Spinney
Barn Farm
GIBBET LA
Middle Farm
LE17
Works
THE GREEN
A5
The White Swan (PH)
PO
MAIN ST
SWINFORD RD
Rose Farm
Shawell
Shawell Manor
Hill Top Farm
NEWTON LA
Stables
BULLACES LA
CHURCH LA
CATTHORPE RD
Shawell Hall
Shawell Grange
Tomley Hall Farm
Depot
19
M6
A14
Depots
P
CV23
Old Barn Farm
THE LEYES
1 THE PADDOCK
2 THE ORCHARDS
3 PILGRIMS LA
4 SILVER ST
5 NEWTON RD
WATLING CRES
Catthorpe
Manor Farm
CATTHORPE MANOR
PH
Works
B5414
LITTLE LONDON LA
Newton
Cherry Tree (PH)

67
84

70

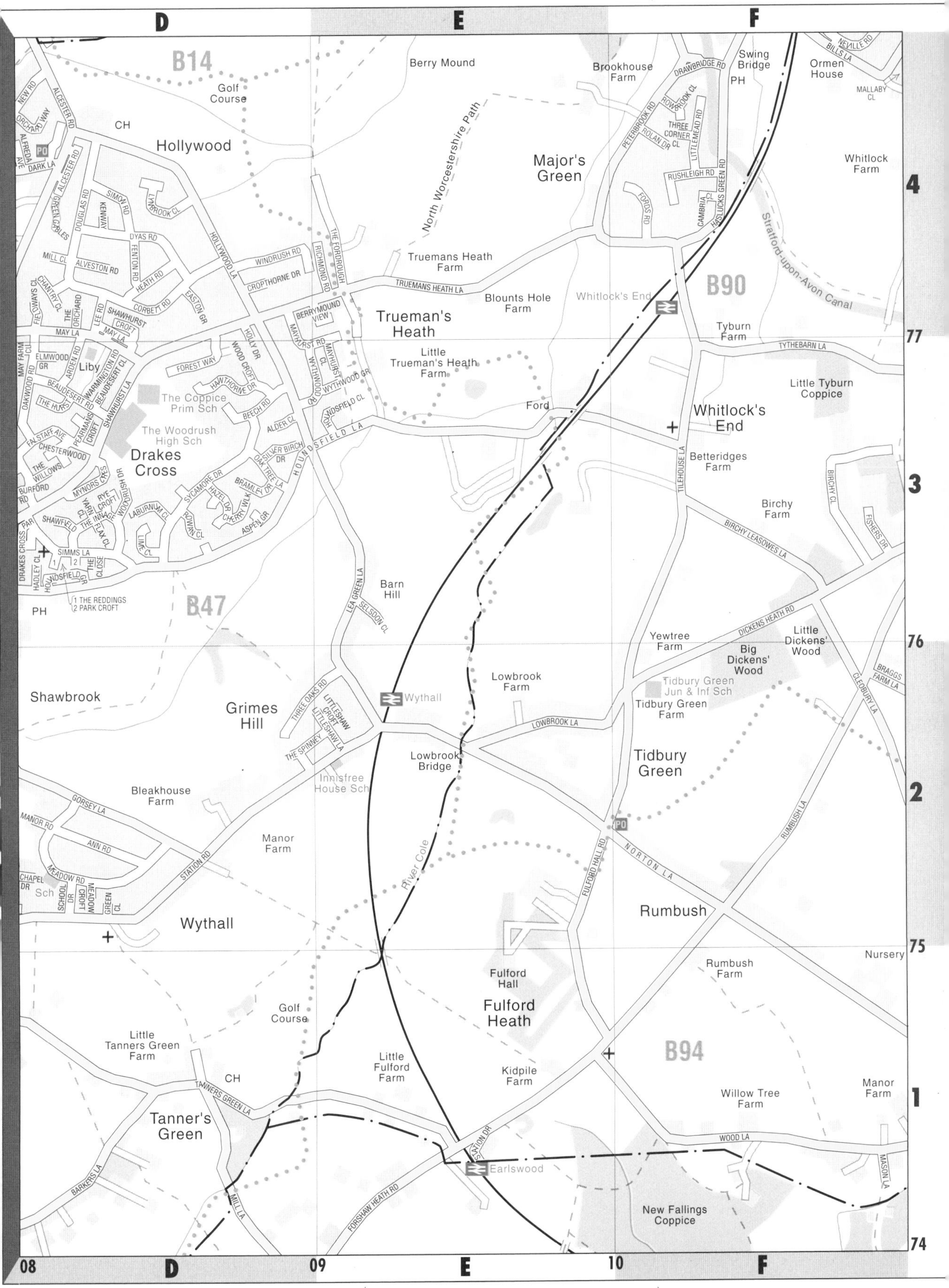

D
E
F
B14
Golf Course
Berry Mound
Brookhouse Farm
Swing Bridge
PH
Ormen House
Whitlock Farm
Mallaby Cl
Bills La
Neville Rd
Drawbridge Rd
Rowbrook Cl
Peterbrook Rd
Three Corner Cl
Rolan Dr
Littlemead Rd
Rushleigh Rd
Hasluck's Green Rd
Cambria Cl
Fords Rd
Major's Green
Hollywood
CH
PO
New Rd
Alcester Rd
Orchard Way
Alfreda Ave
Dark La
Green Gables
Douglas Rd
Simon Rd
Kenway
Lynbrook Cl
Dyas Rd
Fenton Rd
Mill Cl
Alveston Rd
Heath Rd
Chantry Cl
Fieldways Cl
The Orchard
Lee Rd
Corbett Rd
Shawhurst Croft
Easton Gr
May La
May Farm Cl
Elmwood Gr
Arden Rd
Liby
Oakwood Rd
Beaudesert Rd
Warmington Rd
Beaudesert Cl
Shawhurst La
The Hurst
Pearmans Croft
Falstaff Ave
Chesterwood
The Willows
Burford Rd
Mynors Cres
Pye Croft
Yarn Cl
The Inhedge
Flax Cl
Woodrush Dr
Shawfield
Simms La
The Close
Drakes Cross Par
Hadley Cl
Houndsfield Gr
1 The Reddings
2 Park Croft
The Coppice Prim Sch
The Woodrush High Sch
Drakes Cross
Hollywood La
Windrush Rd
Cropthorne Dr
Richmond Rd
The Fordrough
Berrymound View
Forest Way
Wood Croft
Holly Dr
Hawthorne Dr
Beech Rd
Alder Cl
Silver Birch Dr
Oak Tree La
Bramley Dr
Sycamore Dr
Hazel Dr
Cherry Wlk
Rowan Cl
Laburnum Cl
Lime Cl
Aspen Gr
Mayhurst Rd
Mayhurst Cl
Wythwood Rd
Wythwood Gr
Houndsfield Cl
Houndsfield La
Truemans Heath Farm
Truemans Heath La
Trueman's Heath
North Worcestershire Path
Blounts Hole Farm
Little Trueman's Heath Farm
Ford
Whitlock's End
B90
Stratford-upon-Avon Canal
Tyburn Farm
Tythebarn La
Little Tyburn Coppice
Whitlock's End
Betteridges Farm
Tilehouse La
Birchy Cl
Birchy Farm
Fishers Dr
Birchy Leasowes La
Barn Hill
Lea Green La
Selsdon Cl
B47
PH
Dickens Heath Rd
Yewtree Farm
Big Dickens' Wood
Little Dickens' Wood
Braggs Farm La
Cleobury La
Tidbury Green Jun & Inf Sch
Tidbury Green Farm
Lowbrook Farm
Lowbrook La
Shawbrook
Grimes Hill
Three Oaks Rd
Littleshaw Croft
Littleshaw La
The Spinney
Wythall
Lowbrook Bridge
Tidbury Green
Innisfree House Sch
Bleakhouse Farm
Gorsey La
Manor Rd
Ann Rd
Manor Farm
Station Rd
PO
Norton La
Rumbush La
Fulford Hall Rd
River Cole
Chapel Dr
Sch
Meadow Rd
School Dr
Meadow Croft
Green Cl
Wythall
Rumbush
Nursery
Rumbush Farm
Fulford Hall
Fulford Heath
Golf Course
Little Tanners Green Farm
Little Fulford Farm
Kidpile Farm
B94
Manor Farm
CH
Tanners Green La
Tanner's Green
Willow Tree Farm
Wood La
Station Dr
Earlswood
Barkers La
Mill La
Forshaw Heath Rd
New Fallings Coppice
Mason La
4
77
3
76
2
75
1
74
08
09
10

86

70

69

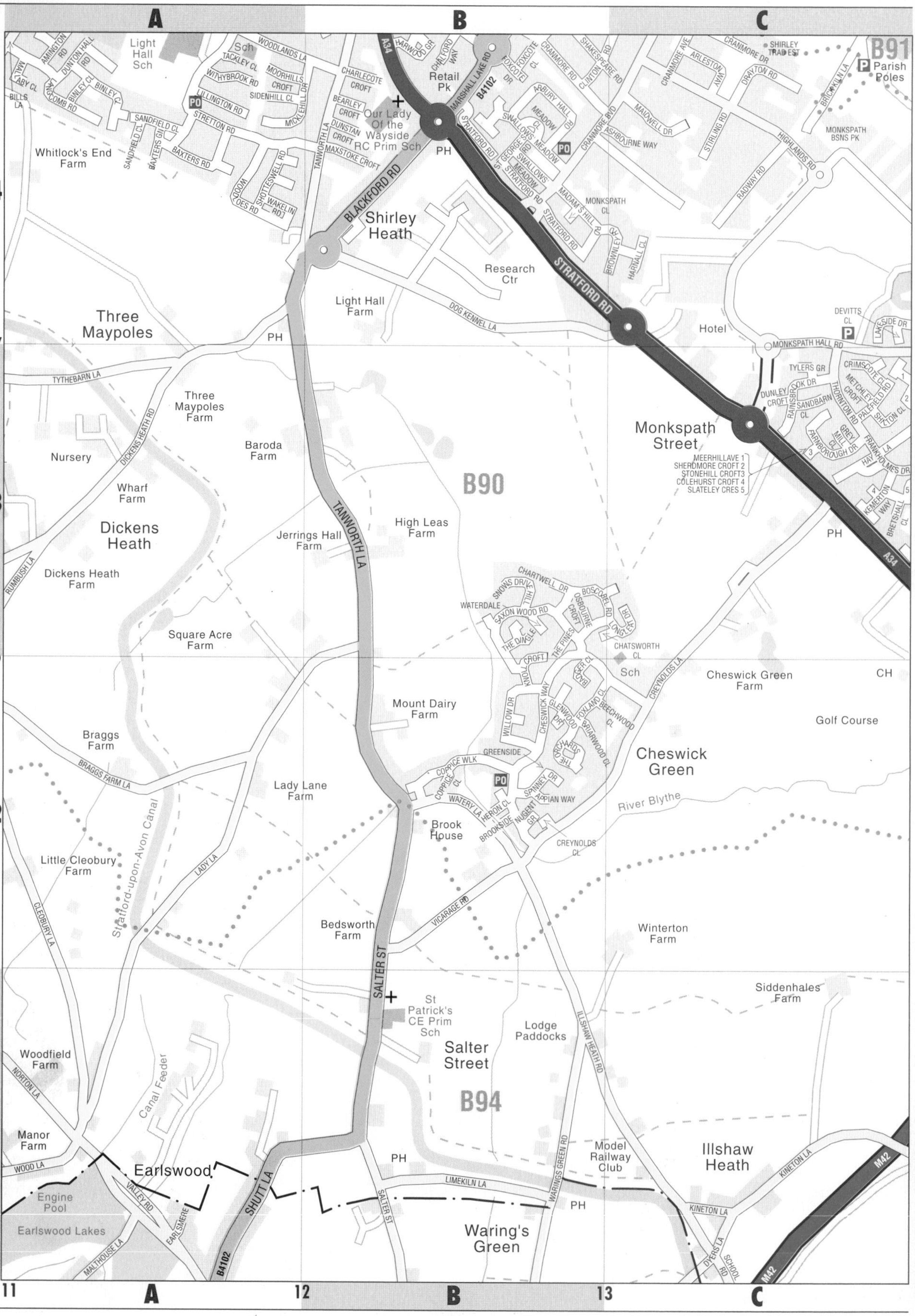
A
B
C
B91
B90
B94
Light Hall Sch
Sch
Retail Pk
Our Lady Of the Wayside RC Prim Sch
PH
Parish Poles
SHIRLEY TRAD EST
MONKSPATH BSNS PK
Whitlock's End Farm
Shirley Heath
Research Ctr
Light Hall Farm
Three Maypoles
Hotel
DEVITTS CL
Three Maypoles Farm
Baroda Farm
Nursery
Wharf Farm
Monkspath Street
MEERHILLAVE 1
SHERDMORE CROFT 2
STONEHILL CROFT 3
COLEHURST CROFT 4
SLATELEY CRES 5
Dickens Heath
High Leas Farm
Jerrings Hall Farm
Dickens Heath Farm
Square Acre Farm
CHATSWORTH CL
Sch
Cheswick Green Farm
CH
Mount Dairy Farm
Golf Course
Braggs Farm
Cheswick Green
Lady Lane Farm
River Blythe
Brook House
Little Cleobury Farm
Stratford-upon-Avon Canal
Bedsworth Farm
Winterton Farm
St Patrick's CE Prim Sch
Siddenhales Farm
Lodge Paddocks
Salter Street
Woodfield Farm
Canal Feeder
Manor Farm
Earlswood
Model Railway Club
Illshaw Heath
Engine Pool
Earlswood Lakes
Waring's Green
A34
B4102
M42
STRATFORD RD
BLACKFORD RD
TANWORTH LA
SALTER ST
SHUTT LA
DOG KENNEL LA
TYTHEBARN LA
DICKENS HEATH RD
RUMBUSH LA
BRAGGS FARM LA
LADY LA
CLEOBURY LA
NORTON LA
WOOD LA
VALLEY RD
MALTHOUSE LA
EARLSMERE
LIMEKILN LA
WARINGS GREEN RD
ILLSHAW HEATH RD
KINETON LA
DYERS LA
SCHOOL RD
VICARAGE RD
CREYNOLDS LA
CREYNOLDS CL
MONKSPATH HALL RD
HIGHLANDS RD
CRANMORE BLVD
CRANMORE AVE
CRANMORE DR
DRAYTON RD
STIRLING RD
RADWAY RD
BRICKILN LA
WOODLANDS LA
MOORHILLS CROFT
MICKLEHILL DR
CHARLECOTE CROFT
BEARLEY CROFT
DUNSTAN CROFT
MAXSTOKE CROFT
STRETTON RD
BAXTERS RD
SANDFIELD CL
LILLINGTON RD
WITHYBROOK RD
TACKLEY CL
SIDENHILL CL
SHOTTESWELL RD
WAKELIN RD
MARSHALL LAKE RD
FOXCOTE DR
ASBURY HALL
SWALLOWS MEADOW
MADAM'S HILL RD
MONKSPATH CL
BROWNLEY RD
HARVALL CL
ASHBOURNE WAY
MAIDWELL DR
CLINTON RD
SHAKESPEARE RD
ARLESTON WAY
TYLERS GR
DUNLEY CROFT
RAINSBROOK DR
SANDBARN CL
THORNTON RD
METCHLEY CROFT
PALEFIELD RD
SHELTON CL
GREY MILL CL
FARNBOROUGH DR
FRANKHOLMES DR
HAY LA
KEMERTON WAY
BRETSHALL CL
LAKESIDE DR
CHARTWELL DR
SNOWS DR
WATERDALE
SAXON WOOD RD
OSBOURNE CROFT
BOSCOBEL RD
LONGLEAT DR
THE DINGLE
THE PINES
KNOLL CROFT
CHESWICK WAY
WILLOW DR
GLENWOOD DR
FOXLAND CL
BEECHWOOD CL
BRIARWOOD CL
THE ORCHARDS
GREENSIDE
COPPICE WLK
COPPICE CL
WATERY LA
HERON CL
SPINNEY DR
APPIAN WAY
BROOKSIDE
NUGENT GR
11
12
13
74
75
76
77
1
2
3
4

69
87

D3
1 HIMBLETON CROFT
2 SLIMBRIDGE CL
3 HIGHDOWN CRES
4 OLDBERROW CL
5 BELLINGTON CROFT
6 WESTGROVE AVE
7 BARHAM CL
8 ELKINGTON CROFT
9 APPLEBY GR
10 TIMBERLAKE CL

D4
1 CHADBURY CROFT
2 LITTLEWOOD CL
3 HILLFIELD MEWS
4 MAYTHORN GR
5 GREYHURST CROFT
6 HUNNINGHAM GR
7 CRYERSOAK CL
8 BAYWELL CL
9 KITEBROOK CL
10 LAKESIDE DR

E4
1 CHIPSTONE CL
2 GLENFIELD CL
3 CHERRYWOOD CRES
4 LIBBARDS GATE
5 MERRINGTON CL
6 LITTLETON CROFT
7 THORNGROVE AVE

72

D E F

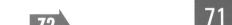

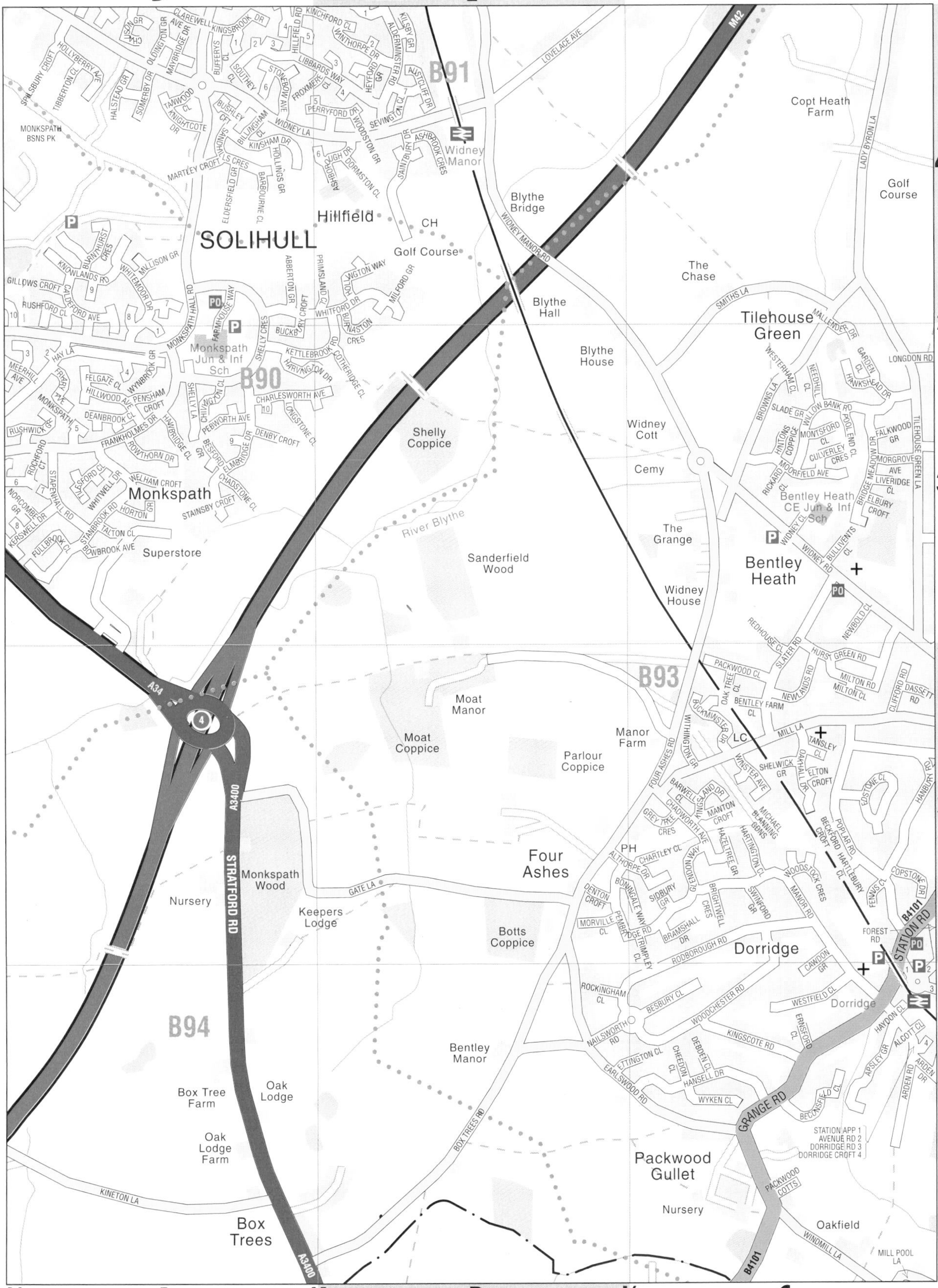

88

72

71 56

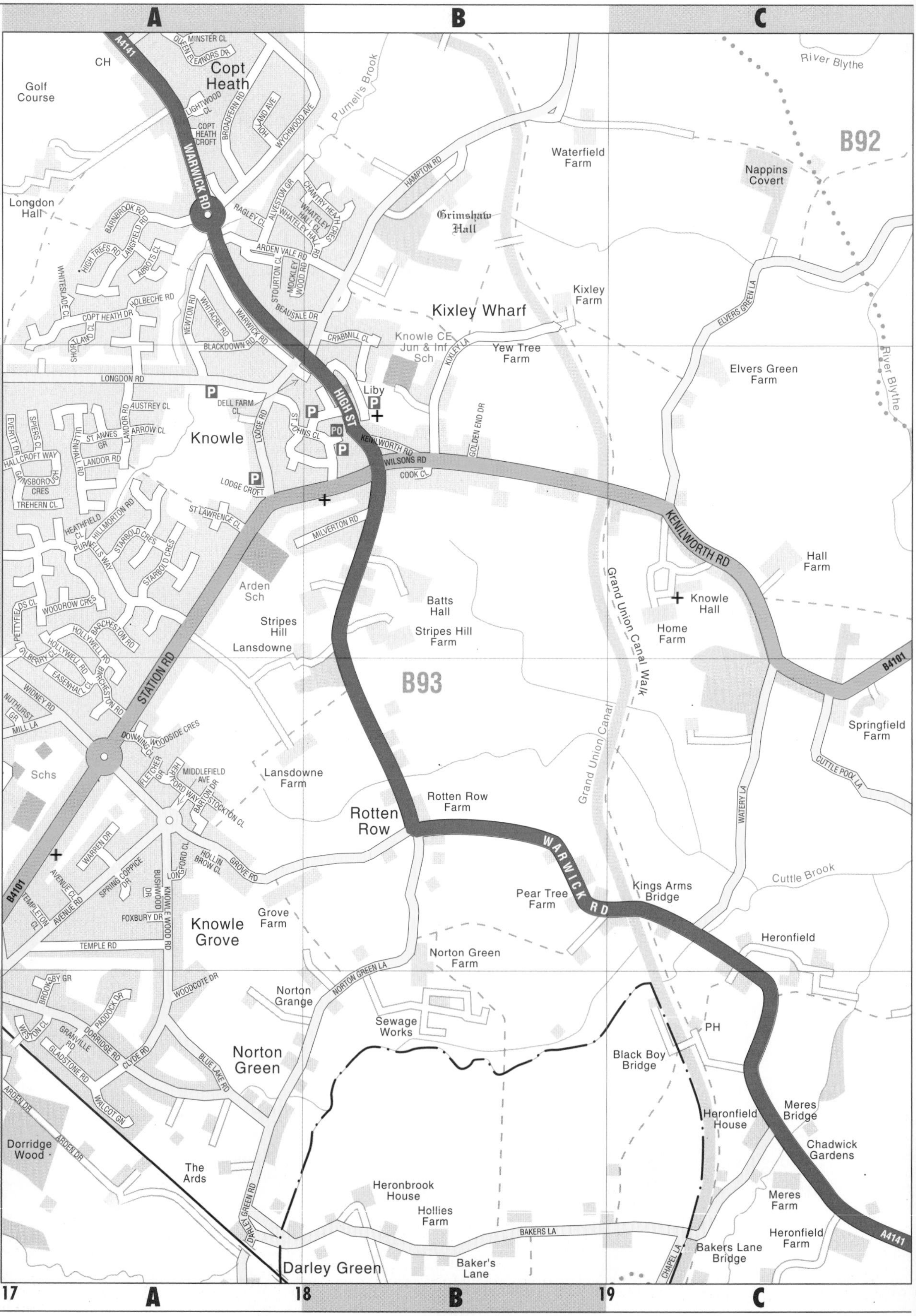
A
B
C
4
77
3
76
2
75
1
74
17
18
19
CH
Golf Course
Copt Heath
A4141
MINSTER CL
QUEEN ELEANORS DR
LIGHTWOOD CL
COPT HEATH CROFT
BROADFERN RD
HOLLAND AVE
WYCHWOOD AVE
WARWICK RD
Purnell's Brook
HAMPTON RD
River Blythe
B92
Waterfield Farm
Nappins Covert
Longdon Hall
BARNBROOK RD
LANGFIELD RD
RAGLEY CL
ALVESTON GR
CHANTRY HEATH CRES
WHATELEY HALL CL
WHATELEY HALL RD
Grimshaw Hall
HIGH TREES RD
ABBOTS CL
ARDEN VALE RD
WHITESLADE CL
HOLBECHE RD
NEWTON RD
WHITACRE RD
STOURTON CL
MOCKLEY WOOD RD
BEAUSALE DR
Kixley Wharf
Kixley Farm
ELVERS GREEN LA
COPT HEATH DR
SHORTLAND CL
BLACKDOWN RD
CRABMILL CL
Knowle CE Jun & Inf Sch
KIXLEY LA
Yew Tree Farm
Elvers Green Farm
LONGDON RD
P
DELL FARM CL
HIGH ST
Liby
AUSTREY CL
LODGE RD
ST JOHNS CL
PO
GOLDEN END DR
EVERITT DR
SPIERS CL
ULLENHALL RD
ST ANNES GR
ARROW CL
LANDOR RD
Knowle
KENILWORTH RD
HALLCROFT WAY
GAINSBOROUGH CRES
WILSONS RD
COOK CL
LODGE CROFT
TREHERN CL
HILLMORTON RD
ST LAWRENCE CL
HEATHFIELD CL
PURNELLS WAY
STARBOLD CRES
MILVERTON RD
Grand Union Canal Walk
Hall Farm
Arden Sch
Knowle Hall
PETTYFIELDS CL
WOODROW CRES
Batts Hall
Stripes Hill
Stripes Hill Farm
Home Farm
HOLLYWELL RD
BARCHESTON RD
Lansdowne
GYLBERRY CL
EASENHALL CL
B93
B4101
WIDNEY RD
STATION RD
NUTHURST GR
MILL LA
WOODSIDE CRES
DOWNING CL
Springfield Farm
Schs
FLETCHER GR
MIDDLEFIELD AVE
HEPFORD WAY
BARTON DR
STOCKTON CL
Lansdowne Farm
Grand Union Canal
CUTTLE POOL LA
Rotten Row Farm
Rotten Row
WATERY LA
WARREN DR
HOLLIN BROW CL
GROVE RD
WARWICK RD
SPRING COPPICE DR
LONGFORD CL
BUSHWOOD DR
KNOWLE WOOD RD
Cuttle Brook
AVENUE CL
AVENUE RD
TEMPLETON CL
FOXBURY DR
Kings Arms Bridge
Pear Tree Farm
Knowle Grove
Grove Farm
TEMPLE RD
Norton Green Farm
Heronfield
BROOKSBY GR
WOODCOTE DR
NORTON GREEN LA
Norton Grange
PADDOCK DR
Sewage Works
PH
WESTON CL
GRANVILLE RD
DORRIDGE RD
CLYDE RD
Norton Green
GLADSTONE RD
BLUE LAKE RD
Black Boy Bridge
ARDEN DR
WALCOT GN
Heronfield House
Meres Bridge
Dorridge Wood
Chadwick Gardens
The Ards
Heronbrook House
Hollies Farm
Meres Farm
DARLEY GREEN RD
BAKERS LA
Heronfield Farm
CHAPEL LA
Bakers Lane Bridge
Darley Green
Baker's Lane

71 89

57
74

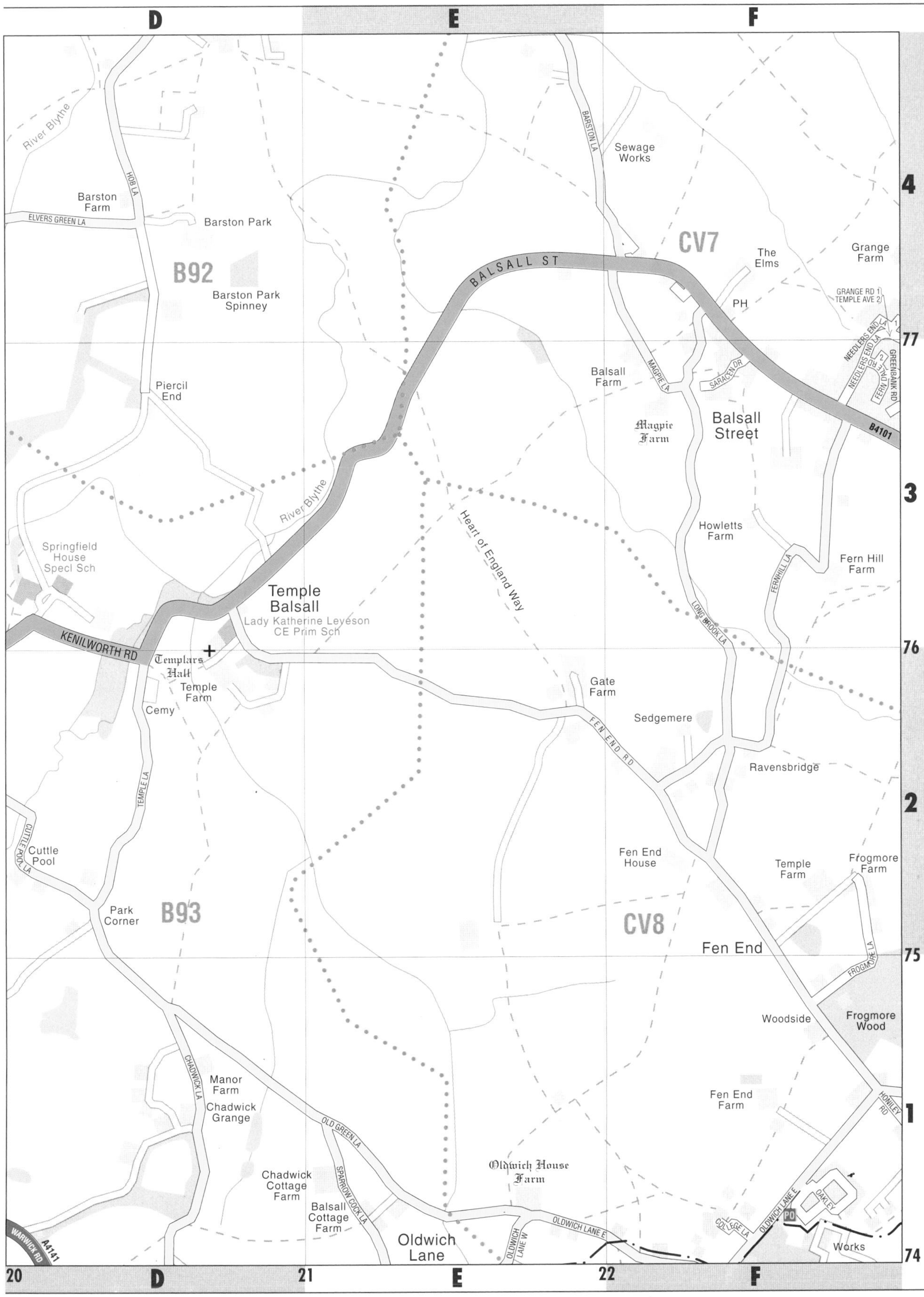
D
E
F
4
3
2
1
77
76
75
74
20
21
22
River Blythe
Barston Farm
ELVERS GREEN LA
HOB LA
Barston Park
B92
Barston Park Spinney
Piercil End
BARSTON LA
Sewage Works
CV7
The Elms
Grange Farm
GRANGE RD 1
TEMPLE AVE 2
BALSALL ST
PH
NEEDLERS END LA
GREENBANK RD
FERN HILL
Balsall Farm
MAGPIE LA
SARACEN DR
Magpie Farm
Balsall Street
B4101
Springfield House Specl Sch
River Blythe
Heart of England Way
Howletts Farm
Fern Hill Farm
FERNHILL LA
LONG BROOK LA
Temple Balsall
Lady Katherine Leveson CE Prim Sch
KENILWORTH RD
Templars Hall
Temple Farm
Cemy
Gate Farm
Sedgemere
FEN END RD
Ravensbridge
TEMPLE LA
CUTTLE POOL LA
Cuttle Pool
Fen End House
Temple Farm
Frogmore Farm
Park Corner
B93
CV8
Fen End
FROGMORE LA
Woodside
Frogmore Wood
CHADWICK LA
Manor Farm
Chadwick Grange
Fen End Farm
HONILEY RD
OLD GREEN LA
Oldwich House Farm
Chadwick Cottage Farm
SPARROW COCK LA
Balsall Cottage Farm
OLDWICH LANE E
OLDWICH LANE W
COLLEGE LA
OLDWICH LANE E
PO
OAKLEY
Oldwich Lane
Works
WARWICK RD
A4141

90
74

73
58

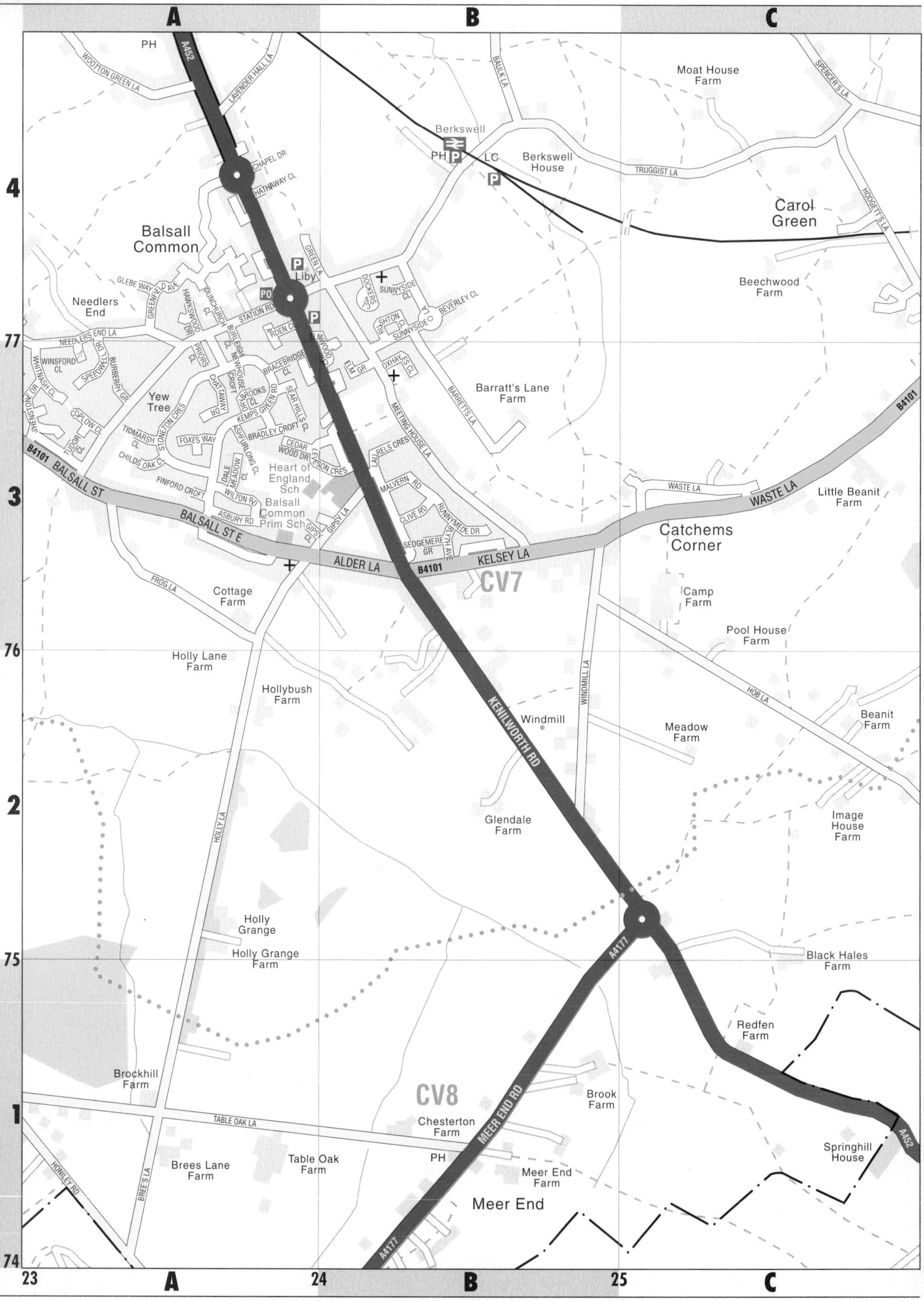
A
B
C
4
77
3
76
2
75
1
74
23
24
25
PH
WOOTTON GREEN LA
LAVENDER HALL LA
A452
BAULK LA
Moat House
Farm
SPENCER'S LA
Berkswell
PH
LC
Berkswell
House
TRUGGIST LA
CHAPEL DR
HATHAWAY CL
Carol
Green
HODGETTS LA
Balsall
Common
GREEN LA
Liby
PO
GLEBE WAY
GREENFIELD AVE
HAWKSWOOD DR
DUNCHURCH CL
STATION RD
DOCKERS CL
SUNNYSIDE CL
BEVERLEY CL
SUNNYSIDE LA
Beechwood
Farm
Needlers
End
NEEDLERS END LA
WINSFORD CL
SPEEDWELL DR
BURBERRY GR
WHITNASH CL
PRIORS CL
BURLEIGH CL
NEWHOUSE CROFT
BRACEBRIDGE CL
ELM GR
OXHAYES CL
BARRETTS LA
Barratt's Lane
Farm
Yew
Tree
CHATAWAY DR
BROOKS CL
KEMPS GREEN RD
SEAR HILLS CL
MEETING HOUSE LA
COPLOW CL
TUDOR CL
TIDMARSH CL
STONETON CRES
FOXES WAY
BRADLEY CROFT
ASHFURLONG CL
CEDAR WOOD DR
LEVESON CRES
LAURELS CRES
CHILDS OAK CL
B4101
BALSALL ST
FINFORD CROFT
DALE MEADOW CL
Heart of
England
Sch
WILTON RD
Balsall
Common
Prim Sch
ASBURY RD
GIPSY LA
GIPSY CL
MALVERN RD
CLIVE RD
RUNNYMEDE DR
BLYTH AVE
SEDGEMERE GR
BALSALL ST E
ALDER LA
KELSEY LA
WASTE LA
Little Beanit
Farm
Catchems
Corner
CV7
FROG LA
Cottage
Farm
Camp
Farm
Pool House
Farm
Holly Lane
Farm
Hollybush
Farm
KENILWORTH RD
Windmill
WINDMILL LA
HOB LA
Meadow
Farm
Beanit
Farm
Glendale
Farm
Image
House
Farm
HOLLY LA
Holly
Grange
Holly Grange
Farm
A4177
Black Hales
Farm
Redfen
Farm
Brockhill
Farm
CV8
MEER END RD
Brook
Farm
TABLE OAK LA
Chesterton
Farm
HONILEY RD
BREE'S LA
Brees Lane
Farm
Table Oak
Farm
PH
Meer End
Farm
Springhill
House
Meer End

73
91

59
76

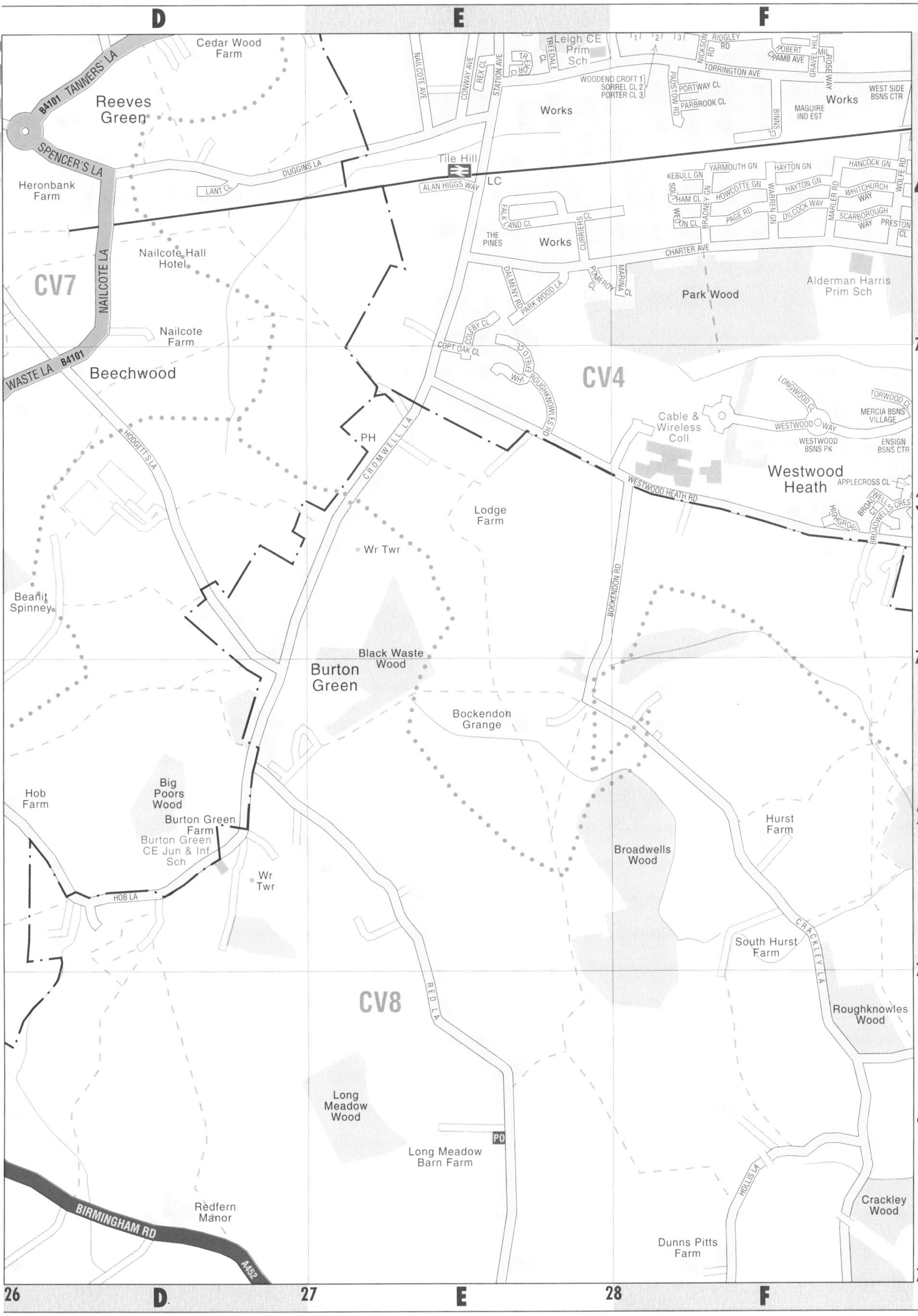
D
E
F
Cedar Wood Farm
TANNERS' LA
B4101
Reeves Green
SPENCER'S LA
Heronbank Farm
Nailcote Hall Hotel
CV7
NAILCOTE LA
Nailcote Farm
WASTE LA
Beechwood
HODGETT'S LA
Beanit Spinney
Hob Farm
Big Poors Wood
Burton Green Farm
Burton Green CE Jun & Inf Sch
HOB LA
Wr Twr
BIRMINGHAM RD
A452
Redfern Manor
DUGGINS LA
LANT CL
NAILCOTE AVE
CONWAY AVE
REX CL
STATION AVE
Leigh CE Prim Sch
TREEDALE CL
Works
WOODEND CROFT 1
SORREL CL 2
PORTER CL 3
PADSTOW RD
PORTWAY CL
PARBROOK CL
NICKSON RD
RIDGLEY RD
TORRINGTON AVE
ROBERT CRAMB AVE
GRAVEL HILL
MILROSE WAY
WEST SIDE BSNS CTR
MAGUIRE IND EST
BINNS CL
Tile Hill
ALAN HIGGS WAY
LC
KEBULL GN
YARMOUTH GN
HAYTON GN
HANCOCK GN
WOLFE RD
HOWCOTTE GN
WARREN GN
MARLER RD
WHITCHURCH WAY
DILCOCK WAY
SCARBOROUGH WAY
PRESTON CL
PAGE RD
BRADNEY GN
FALKLAND CL
THE PINES
CURRIERS CL
CHARTER AVE
DALMENY RD
PARK WOOD LA
POMEROY CL
MARINA CL
Park Wood
Alderman Harris Prim Sch
COLEBY CL
COPT OAK CL
ROUGHKNOWLES RD
CV4
Cable & Wireless Coll
LONGWOOD CL
TORWOOD CL
MERCIA BSNS VILLAGE
WESTWOOD WAY
WESTWOOD BSNS PK
ENSIGN BSNS CTR
Westwood Heath
APPLECROSS CL
WESTWOOD HEATH RD
BROADWELLS CRES
HIGHGROVE
PH
CROMWELL LA
Lodge Farm
Wr Twr
BOCKENDON RD
Black Waste Wood
Burton Green
Bockendon Grange
Broadwells Wood
Hurst Farm
South Hurst Farm
CRACKLEY LA
Roughknowles Wood
CV8
RED LA
Long Meadow Wood
PO
Long Meadow Barn Farm
HOLLIS LA
Crackley Wood
Dunns Pitts Farm
4
77
3
76
2
75
1
74
26
27
28

92
76

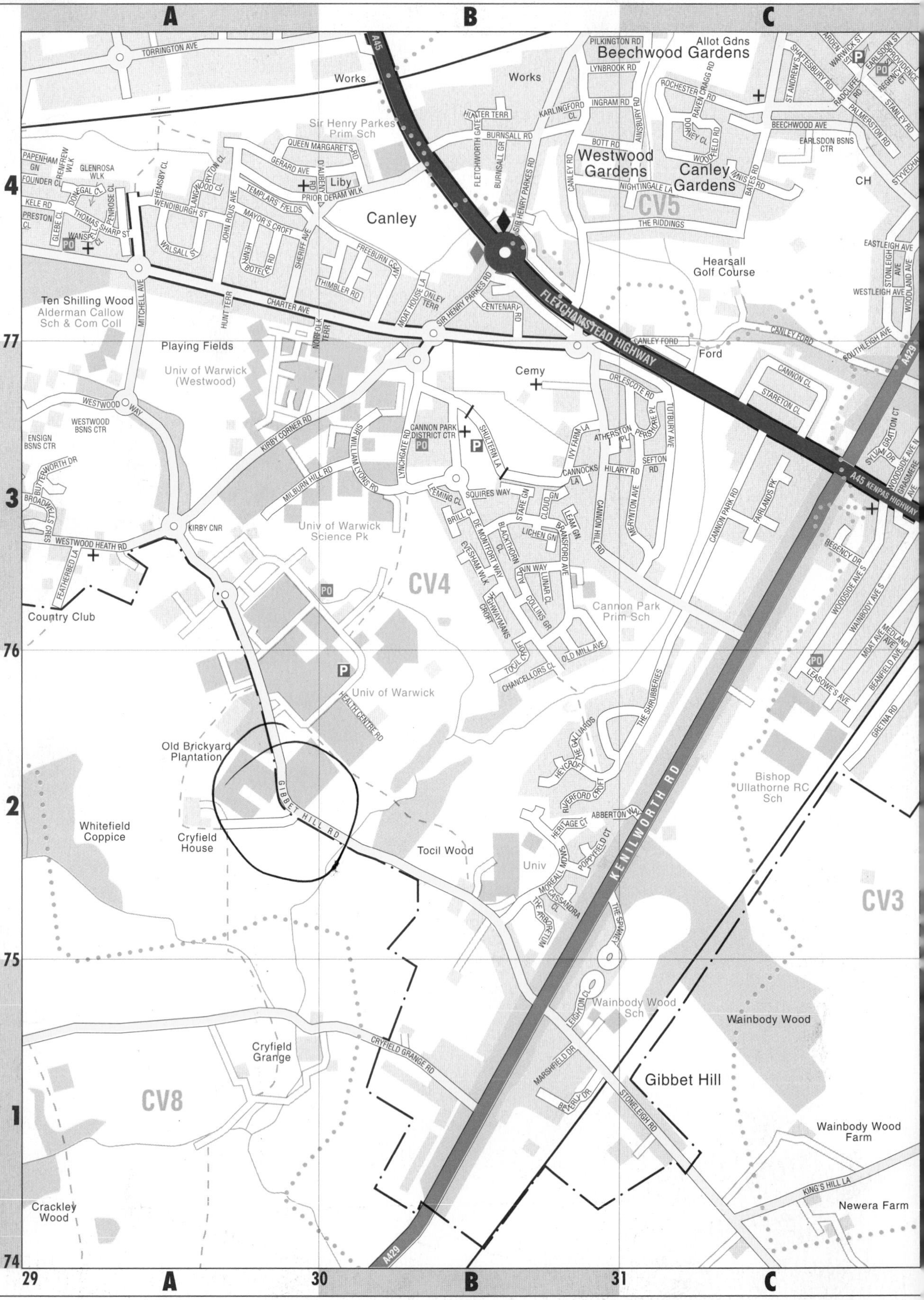
A
B
C
4
3
2
1
77
76
75
74
29
30
31
Torrington Ave
Works
Sir Henry Parkes Prim Sch
Queen Margaret's Rd
Gerard Ave
Liby
Canley
Templars' Fields
Mayor's Croft
Prior Deram Wlk
Pilkington Rd
Allot Gdns
Beechwood Gardens
Lynbrook Rd
Ingram Rd
Karlingford Cl
Hunter Terr
Burnsall Rd
Bott Rd
Westwood Gardens
Canley Gardens
CV5
Nightingale La
The Riddings
Rochester Rd
Beechwood Ave
Earlsdon Bsns Ctr
CH
Hearsall Golf Course
Eastleigh Ave
Westleigh Ave
Canley Ford
Ford
Southleigh Ave
Papenham Gn
Founder Cl
Kele Rd
Preston Cl
Glenrosa Wlk
Thomas Sharp St
Penrose Cl
Hemsby Cl
Wendiburgh St
Walsall St
John Rous Ave
Henry Boteler Rd
Sheriff Ave
Thimbler Rd
Freeburn Cswy
Moat House La
Onley Terr
Sir Henry Parkes Rd
Centenary Rd
Fletchamstead Highway
A45
A429
Ten Shilling Wood
Alderman Callow Sch & Com Coll
Mitchell Ave
Hunt Terr
Charter Ave
Norfolk Terr
Playing Fields
Univ of Warwick (Westwood)
Westwood Way
Westwood Bsns Ctr
Ensign Bsns Ctr
Butterworth Dr
Broadwells Cres
Kirby Corner Rd
Kirby Cnr
Westwood Heath Rd
Featherbed La
Country Club
Milburn Hill Rd
Sir William Lyons Rd
Lynchgate Rd
Cannon Park District Ctr
PO
P
Shultern La
Cemy
Orlescote Rd
Ivy Farm La
Atherston Pl
Pershore Pl
Tutbury Ave
Cannocks La
Hilary Rd
Sefton Rd
Squires Way
Leeming Cl
Brill Cl
De Montfort Way
Stare Gn
Cloud Gn
Lichen Gn
Leam Gn
Blackthorn Cl
Bransford Ave
Evesham Wlk
Alvin Way
Lunar Cl
Collins Gr
Hathaways Croft
Tocil Croft
Chancellors Cl
Old Mill Ave
Cannon Hill Rd
Merynton Ave
Cannon Park Rd
Fairlands Pk
Cannon Cl
Stareton Cl
Cannon Park Prim Sch
CV4
Univ of Warwick Science Pk
Univ of Warwick
Health Centre Rd
Old Brickyard Plantation
Gibbet Hill Rd
Whitefield Coppice
Cryfield House
Tocil Wood
The Shrubberies
The Galliards
Heycroft
Riverford Croft
Abberton Way
Heritage Ct
Poppyfield Ct
Univ
Moreall Mdws
Cassandra Cl
The Arboretum
Kenilworth Rd
The Spinney
A45 Kenpas Highway
Regency Dr
Woodside Ave S
Wainbody Ave S
Moat Ave
Medland Ave
Beanfield Ave
Leasowes Ave
Gretna Rd
Bishop Ullathorne RC Sch
CV3
Wainbody Wood Sch
Leighton Cl
Wainbody Wood
Cryfield Grange
Cryfield Grange Rd
Marshfield Dr
Beverly Dr
Stoneleigh Rd
Gibbet Hill
CV8
Wainbody Wood Farm
King's Hill La
Newera Farm
Crackley Wood

61
78

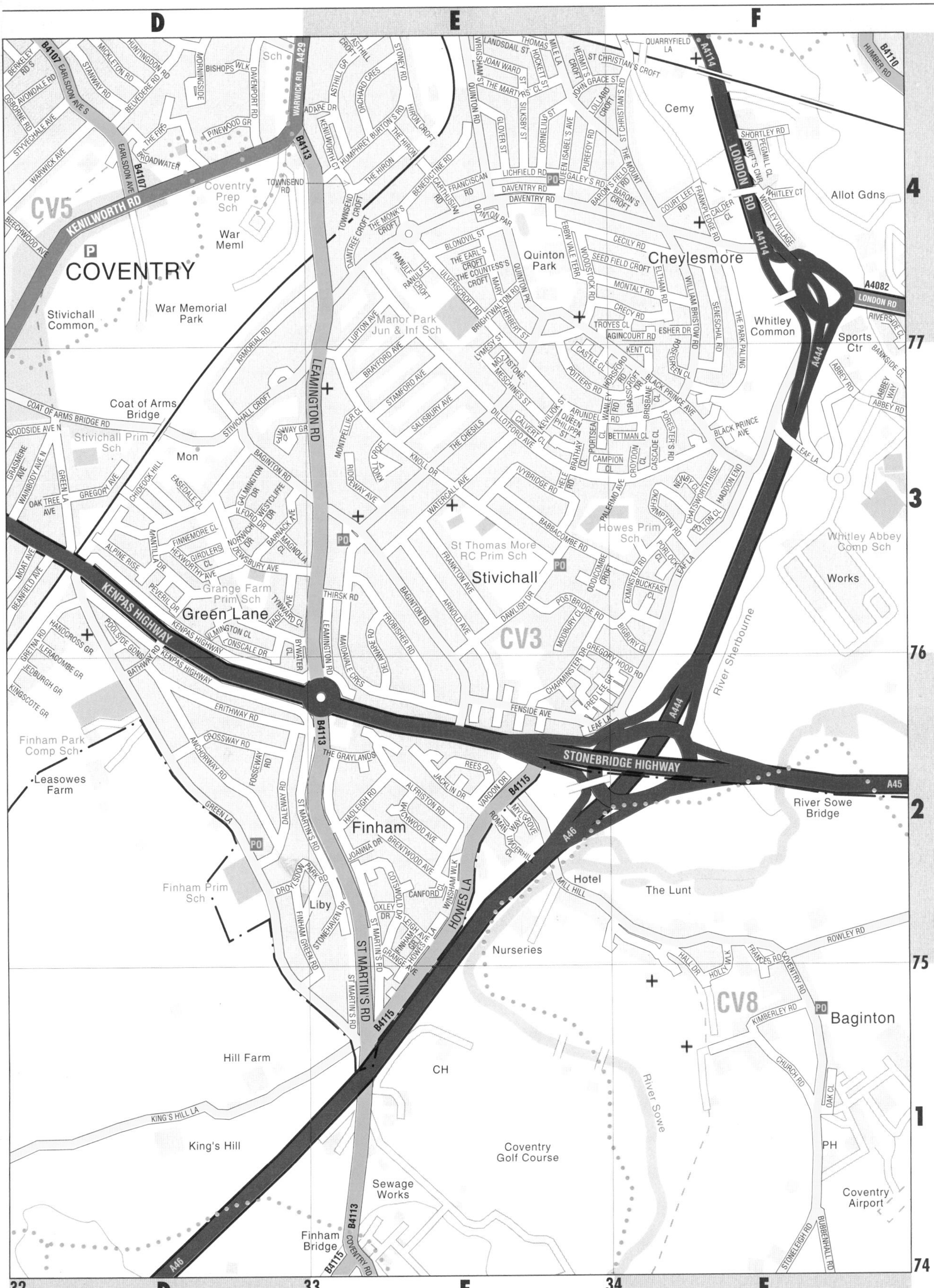
D
E
F
COVENTRY
CV5
KENILWORTH RD
Coventry Prep Sch
War Meml
War Memorial Park
Stivichall Common
Coat of Arms Bridge
Stivichall Prim Sch
Mon
Green Lane
Grange Farm Prim Sch
KENPAS HIGHWAY
LEAMINGTON RD
WARWICK RD
Manor Park Jun & Inf Sch
Quinton Park
Cheylesmore
LONDON RD
Cemy
Allot Gdns
Whitley Common
Sports Ctr
Whitley Abbey Comp Sch
Works
Howes Prim Sch
St Thomas More RC Prim Sch
Stivichall
CV3
River Sherbourne
STONEBRIDGE HIGHWAY
A45
River Sowe Bridge
Finham Park Comp Sch
Leasowes Farm
Finham
Finham Prim Sch
Liby
Hotel
The Lunt
Nurseries
CV8
Baginton
Hill Farm
CH
King's Hill
Coventry Golf Course
River Sowe
PH
Coventry Airport
Sewage Works
Finham Bridge
ST MARTIN'S RD
HOWES LA
A46
A444
A4114
A4082
B4113
B4115
B4107
B4110
A429
4
77
3
76
2
75
1
74
32
33
34

94
78

77
62

C4
1 CARDALE CROFT
2 KESTREL CROFT
3 RUTLAND CROFT
4 JIM FORREST CL
5 WILLOWHERB CL
6 WASPERTON CL
7 JOE WILLIAMS CL

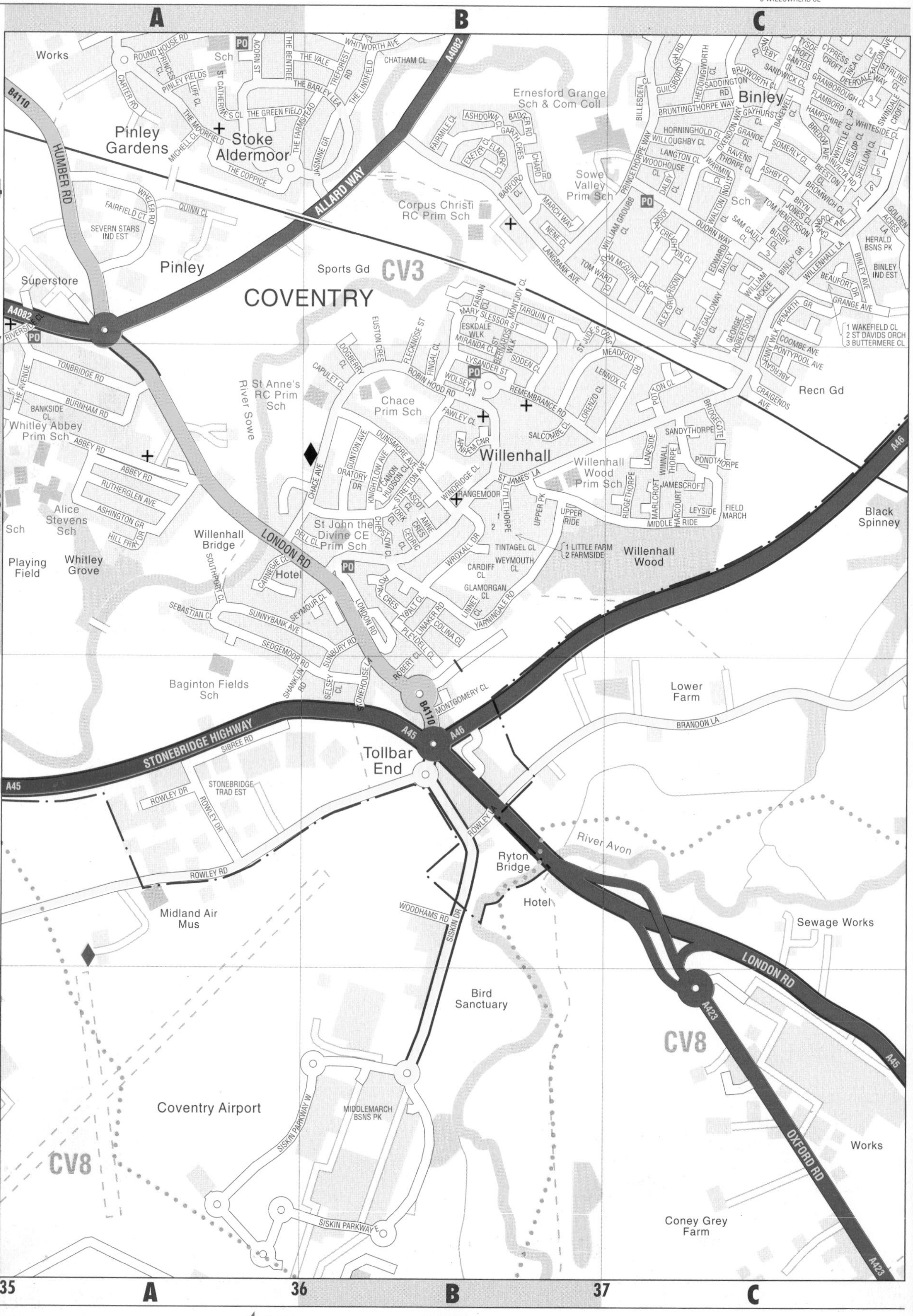

77
95

63
80

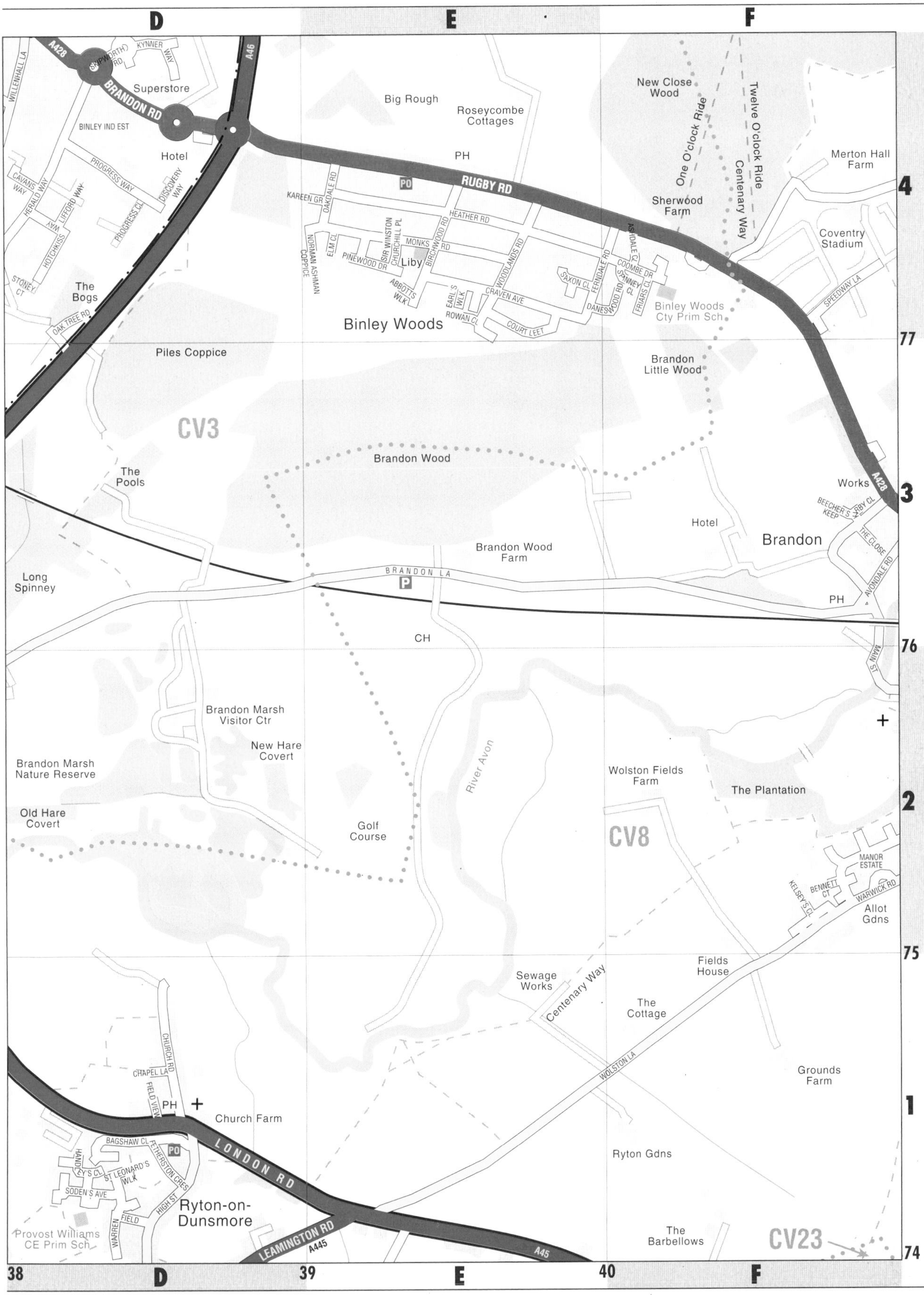
D
E
F
A428
A46
BRANDON RD
SKIPWORTH RD
KYNNER WAY
WILLENHALL LA
Superstore
BINLEY IND EST
Hotel
PROGRESS WAY
PROGRESS CL
DISCOVERY WAY
CAVANS WAY
HERALD WAY
LIFFORD WAY
HOTCHKISS WAY
STONEY CT
The Bogs
OAK TREE RD
Big Rough
Roseycombe Cottages
PH
PO
RUGBY RD
KAREEN GR
OAKDALE RD
HEATHER RD
NORMAN ASHMAN COPPICE
ELM CL
SIR WINSTON CHURCHILL PL
MONKS RD
PINEWOOD DR
Liby
BIRCHWOOD RD
ABBOTTS WLK
EARLS WLK
ROWAN CL
CRAVEN AVE
WOODLANDS RD
COURT LEET
SAXON CL
FERNDALE RD
DANES
WOOD RD
ASHDALE CL
COOMBE DR
SPINNEY CL
FRIARS CL
Binley Woods
Binley Woods Cty Prim Sch
New Close Wood
One O'clock Ride
Twelve O'clock Ride
Centenary Way
Sherwood Farm
Merton Hall Farm
Coventry Stadium
SPEEDWAY LA
4
77
Piles Coppice
Brandon Little Wood
CV3
Brandon Wood
The Pools
Works
BEECHER'S KEEP
ARBY CL
THE CLOSE
AVONDALE RD
3
Hotel
Brandon
Brandon Wood Farm
BRANDON LA
P
PH
Long Spinney
CH
76
MAIN ST
Brandon Marsh Visitor Ctr
New Hare Covert
Brandon Marsh Nature Reserve
River Avon
Wolston Fields Farm
The Plantation
Old Hare Covert
2
Golf Course
CV8
MANOR ESTATE
BENNETT CT
KELSEY'S CL
WARWICK RD
Allot Gdns
75
Fields House
Sewage Works
Centenary Way
The Cottage
CHURCH RD
CHAPEL LA
FIELD VIEW
PH
Church Farm
WOLSTON LA
Grounds Farm
1
BAGSHAW CL
FETHERSTON CRES
PO
LONDON RD
HANDLEY'S CL
ST LEONARD'S WLK
SODEN'S AVE
HIGH ST
Ryton Gdns
Ryton-on-Dunsmore
WARREN FIELD
Provost Williams CE Prim Sch
LEAMINGTON RD
A445
A45
The Barbellows
CV23
74
38
D
39
E
40
F

96
80

79
64

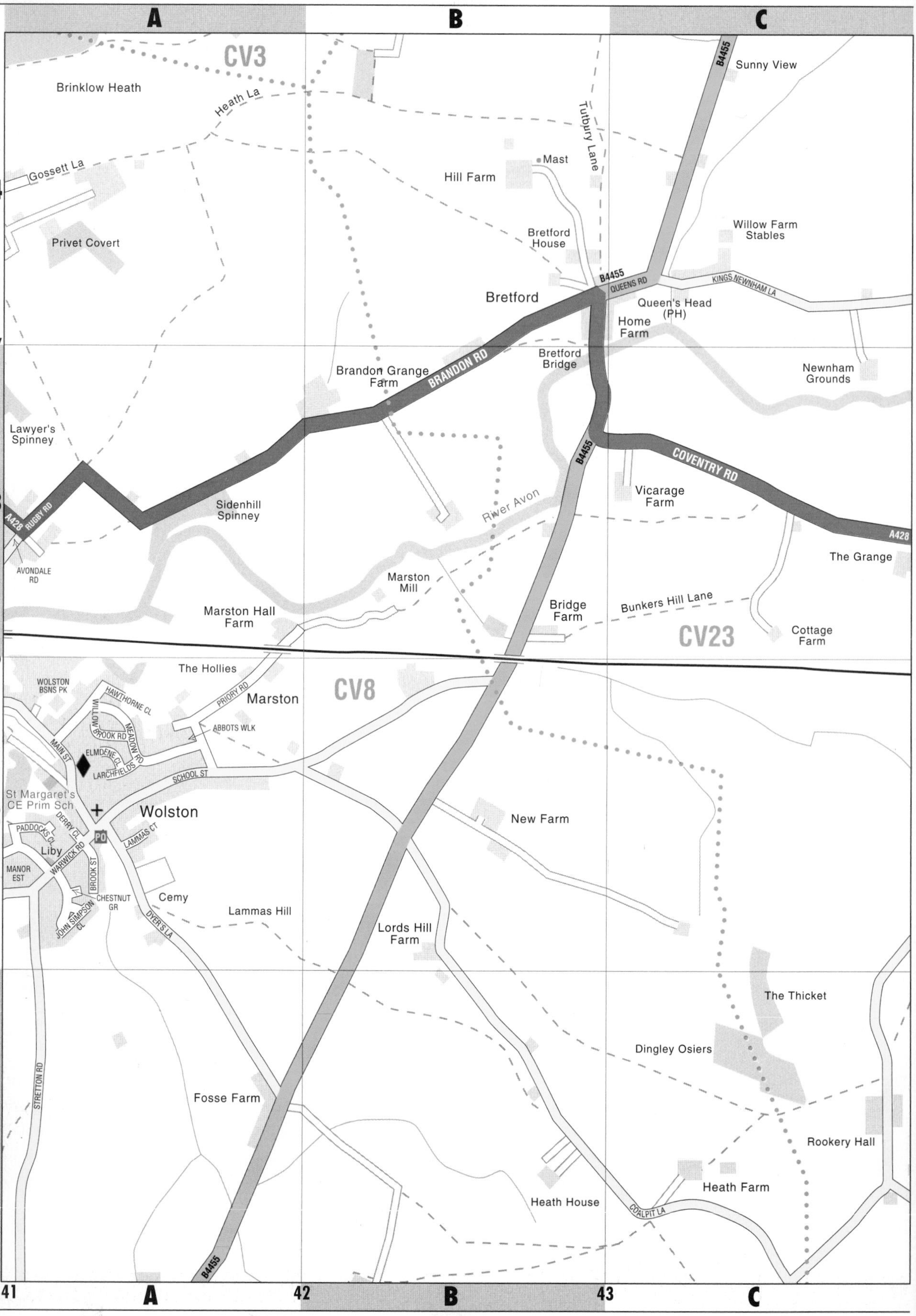
A
B
C
CV3
Brinklow Heath
Heath La
Gossett La
Privet Covert
Tutbury Lane
Mast
Hill Farm
Sunny View
B4455
Willow Farm Stables
Bretford House
B4455
QUEENS RD
KINGS NEWNHAM LA
Bretford
Queen's Head (PH)
Home Farm
Bretford Bridge
Newnham Grounds
Brandon Grange Farm
BRANDON RD
Lawyer's Spinney
B4455
COVENTRY RD
Vicarage Farm
Sidenhill Spinney
River Avon
A428
RUGBY RD
A428
The Grange
AVONDALE RD
Marston Mill
Marston Hall Farm
Bridge Farm
Bunkers Hill Lane
CV23
Cottage Farm
The Hollies
WOLSTON BSNS PK
HAWTHORNE CL
PRIORY RD
Marston
CV8
WILLOW BROOK RD
MEADOW RD
ABBOTS WLK
MAIN ST
ELMDENE CL
LARCHFIELDS
SCHOOL ST
St Margaret's CE Prim Sch
Wolston
DERRY CL
PADDOCKS CL
LAMMAS CT
PO
Liby
WARWICK RD
MANOR EST
BROOK ST
New Farm
CHESTNUT GR
JOHN SIMPSON CL
Cemy
DYER'S LA
Lammas Hill
Lords Hill Farm
The Thicket
Dingley Osiers
STRETTON RD
Fosse Farm
Rookery Hall
Heath Farm
Heath House
COALPIT LA
B4455
4
77
3
76
2
75
1
74
41
42
43

79
97

65
82

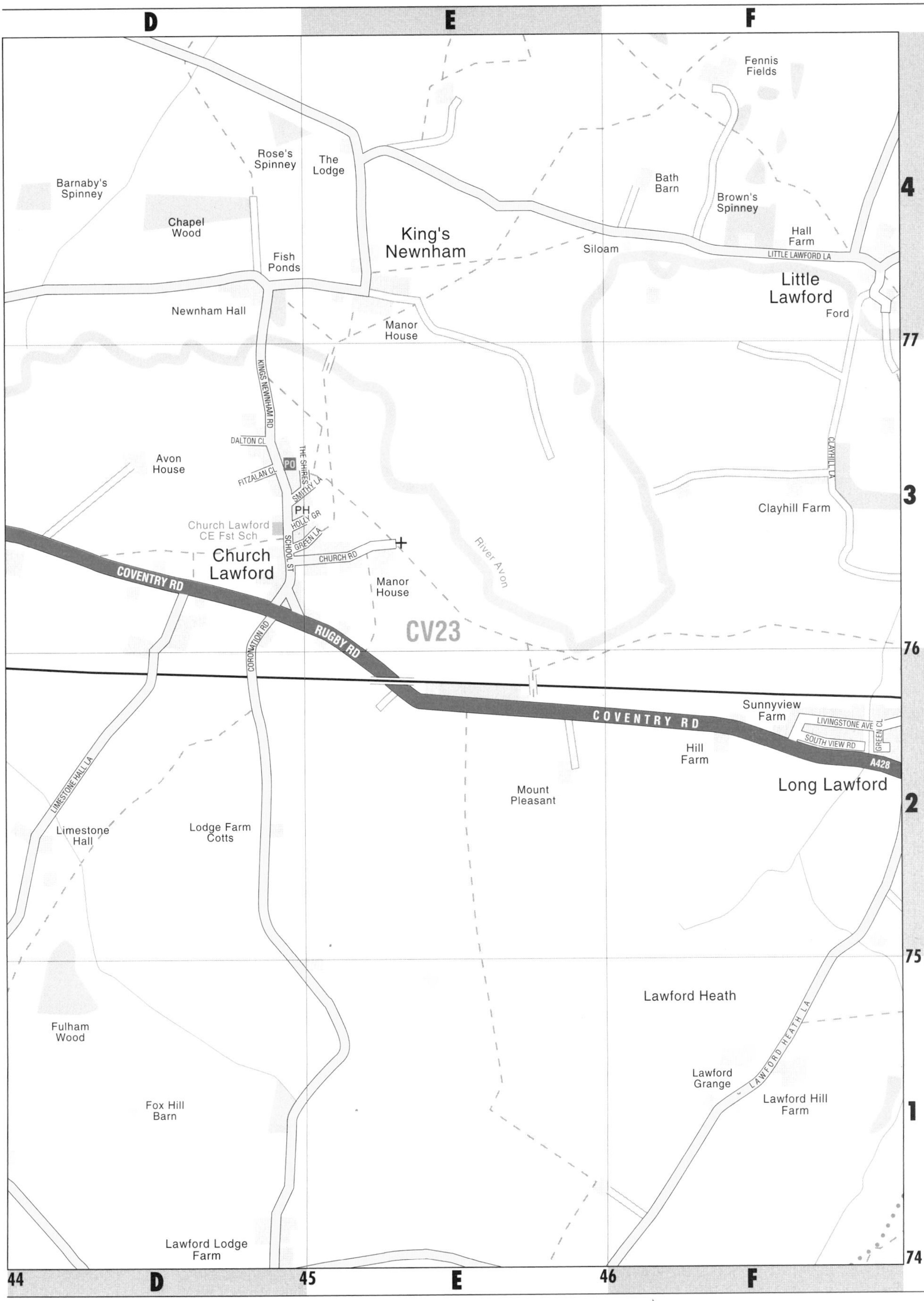
D
E
F
Fennis
Fields
Rose's
Spinney
The
Lodge
Barnaby's
Spinney
Bath
Barn
Brown's
Spinney
4
Chapel
Wood
King's
Newnham
Hall
Farm
Siloam
LITTLE LAWFORD LA
Fish
Ponds
Little
Lawford
Newnham Hall
Ford
Manor
House
77
KINGS NEWNHAM RD
DALTON CL
Avon
House
PO
THE SHIRES
FITZALAN CL
SMITHY LA
CLAYHILL LA
3
PH
HOLLY GR
Clayhill Farm
Church Lawford
CE Fst Sch
GREEN LA
River Avon
Church
Lawford
CHURCH RD
SCHOOL ST
COVENTRY RD
Manor
House
CORONATION RD
RUGBY RD
CV23
76
Sunnyview
Farm
COVENTRY RD
LIVINGSTONE AVE
SOUTH VIEW RD
GREEN CL
Hill
Farm
A428
Mount
Pleasant
Long Lawford
LIMESTONE HALL LA
2
Limestone
Hall
Lodge Farm
Cotts
75
Lawford Heath
LAWFORD HEATH LA
Fulham
Wood
Lawford
Grange
Lawford Hill
Farm
Fox Hill
Barn
1
Lawford Lodge
Farm
74
44
D
45
E
46
F

98
82

81
66

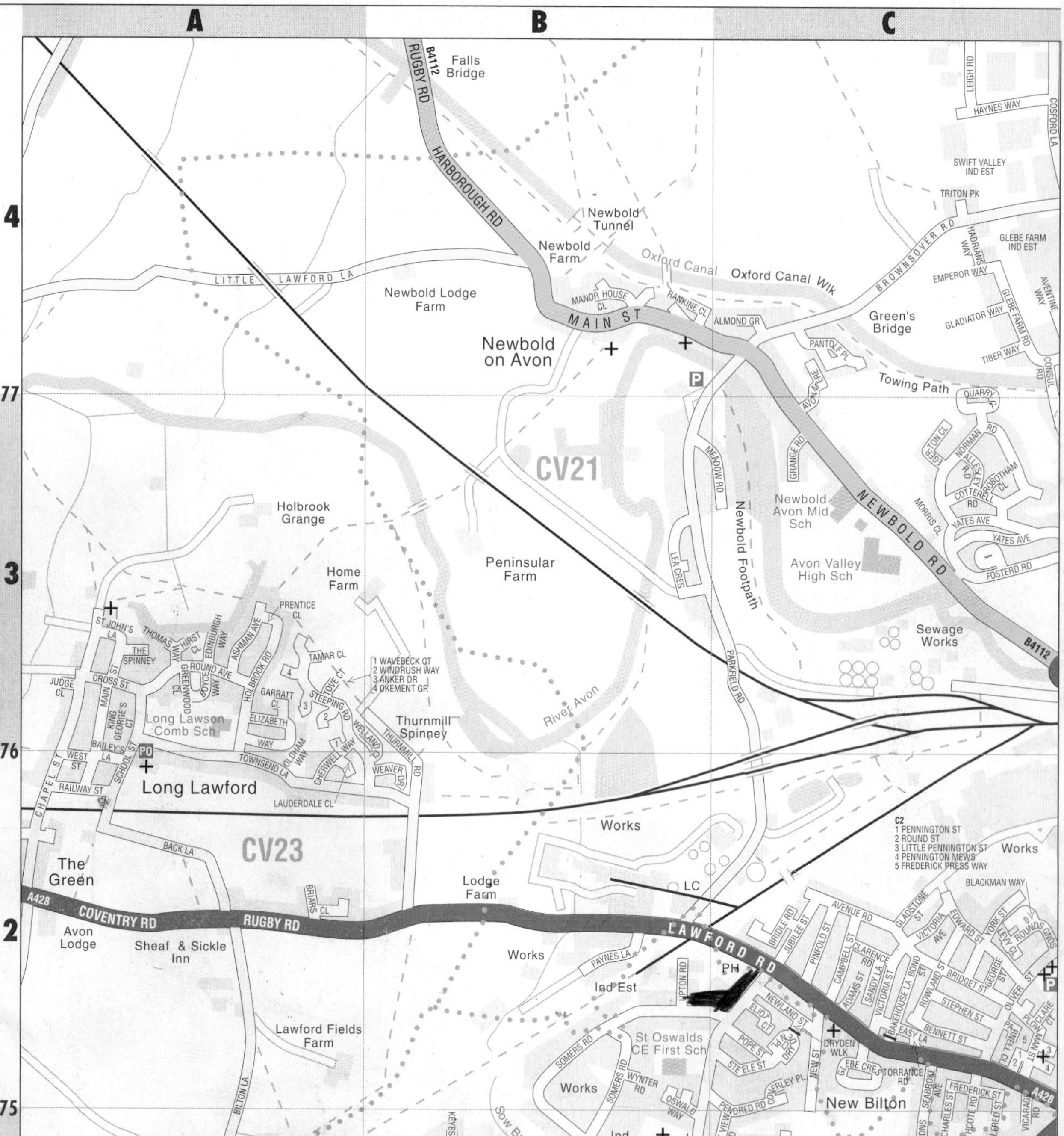
A
B
C
4
3
2
1
77
76
75
74
47
48
49
B4112
RUGBY RD
HARBOROUGH RD
Falls Bridge
Newbold Tunnel
Newbold Farm
Oxford Canal
Oxford Canal Wlk
LITTLE LAWFORD LA
Newbold Lodge Farm
MANOR HOUSE CL
MAIN ST
RANKINE CL
ALMOND GR
Newbold on Avon
Green's Bridge
PANTOLF PL
Towing Path
BROWNSOVER RD
LEIGH RD
HAYNES WAY
COSFORD LA
SWIFT VALLEY IND EST
TRITON PK
GLEBE FARM IND EST
EMPEROR WAY
GLADIATOR WAY
TIBER WAY
AVENTINE WAY
QUARRY
NORMAN RD
YATES AVE
FOSTERD RD
MORRIS CL
CV21
MEADOW RD
GRANGE RD
Newbold Avon Mid Sch
NEWBOLD RD
Holbrook Grange
Peninsular Farm
Newbold Footpath
LEA CRES
Avon Valley High Sch
Home Farm
Sewage Works
PRENTICE CL
TAMAR CL
1 WAVEBECK CT
2 WINDRUSH WAY
3 ANKER DR
4 OKEMENT GR
River Avon
Thurnmill Spinney
THURNMILL RD
PARKFIELD RD
ST JOHN'S LA
THE SPINNEY
THOMAS WAY
HIRST CL
EDINBURGH WAY
ASHMAN AVE
HOLBROOK RD
ROUND AVE
GREENWOOD CL
JUDGE CL
CROSS ST
MAIN ST
KING GEORGE'S CT
Long Lawson Comb Sch
GARRATT CL
ELIZABETH WAY
OLDHAM WAY
BAILEY'S LA
WEST ST
SCHOOL ST
PO
TOWNSEND LA
CHERWELL WAY
WELLAND RD
WEAVER DR
RAILWAY ST
Long Lawford
CHAPEL ST
LAUDERDALE CL
Works
CV23
BACK LA
The Green
LC
Lodge Farm
A428
COVENTRY RD
RUGBY RD
BRIARS CL
LAWFORD RD
Avon Lodge
Sheaf & Sickle Inn
Works
PAYNES LA
PH
Ind Est
C2
1 PENNINGTON ST
2 ROUND ST
3 LITTLE PENNINGTON ST
4 PENNINGTON MEWS
5 FREDERICK PRESS WAY
Works
BLACKMAN WAY
BRIDLE RD
JUBILEE ST
AVENUE RD
PINFOLD ST
GLADSTONE ST
VICTORIA AVE
EDWARD ST
YORK ST
CAMPBELL ST
CLARENCE RD
ADAMS ST
SANDY LA
VICTORIA ST
BAKEHOUSE LA
BOND ST
ROWLAND ST
BRIDGET ST
GEORGE ST
OLIVER ST
STEPHEN ST
BENNETT ST
EASY LA
NEWLAND ST
ELIOT CT
POPE ST
DRYDEN WLK
Lawford Fields Farm
SOMERS RD
St Oswalds CE First Sch
WYNTER RD
STEELE ST
COVERLEY PL
NEW ST
EBE CRES
TORRANCE RD
SEABROOKE AVE
FREDERICK ST
CHARLES ST
NORTHCOTE RD
ALFRED ST
VICARAGE RD
A428
Works
OSWALD WAY
PENDRED RD
New Bilton
Sow Brook
Ind Est
Cemy
WEST VIEW RD
JOHNSON AVE
Bloxam Mid Sch
BLOXAM GDNS
A4071
KEYES DR
WILSON CL
Allot Gdns
ADDISON RD
BILTON LA
BIRCH DR 1
ROWAN DR 2
HAWTHORN WAY 3
ELDER CL 4
LAUREL DR 5
Henry Hinde Mid Sch
KENNEDY DR
MADDEN PL
DREYER CL
CORNWALLIS RD
ANSON CL
FREEMANTLE RD
CV22
GILBERT AVE
1 BRACKEN CL
2 FERNDOWN CT
3 ARMSTRONG CL
4 FERNDOWN TERR
5 MELVILLE CL
6 NARES CL
7 HAWKINS CL
8 BAFFIN CL
9 BATHURST CL
WEBB ELLIS RD
Westfield Cty Fst Sch
WESTFIELD RD
OAKFIELD RD
MERTTENS DR
FIRS DR
APPLE GR
LARCH CL
MULBERRY RD
EVANS RD
FROBISHER RD
TROUBRIDGE WLK
BLAKE CL
HARDY CL
BEATTY DR
HOOD'S WAY
BLACKWOOD AVE
COLLINGWOOD AVE
BILTON RD
BURNSIDE
Mid Sch
Sow Brook (North)
Brooke Specl Sch
ACORN DR
LILAC DR
WALNUT WAY
WYCH-ELM CL
LESTOCK CL
CUNNINGHAM WAY N
BARRINGTON RD
KEPPEL CL
COWAN CL
CUNNINGHAM WAY S
GRENVILLE CL
MAY LA
PO
GREENHILL RD
WESTBOURNE GR
WENTWORTH RD
PEAR TREE WAY
LAWFORD LA
WHEATFIELD RD
ST ANNE'S RD
MELLISH CT
FERNDOWN RD
SAUNTON RD
Henry Hinde Fst Sch
RODNEY CL
DITTON CL
NELSON WAY
HILLFIELD RD
PLEXFIELD RD
SPICER PL
HUDSON RD
BROOM CL
PEAT CL
BRACKEN DR
BUCHANAN RD
MELLISH RD
ELMORE RD
Harris CE High Sch
Cawston Old Farm
Bilton High Sch
MONTGOMERY DR
PIPEWELL CL
BEECH DR
CARLTON RD
EPSOM RD
LYTHAM RD
DEEPMORE RD
MOSS CL
HEATHER CL
GORSE CL
HARRIS DR
A426

81
99

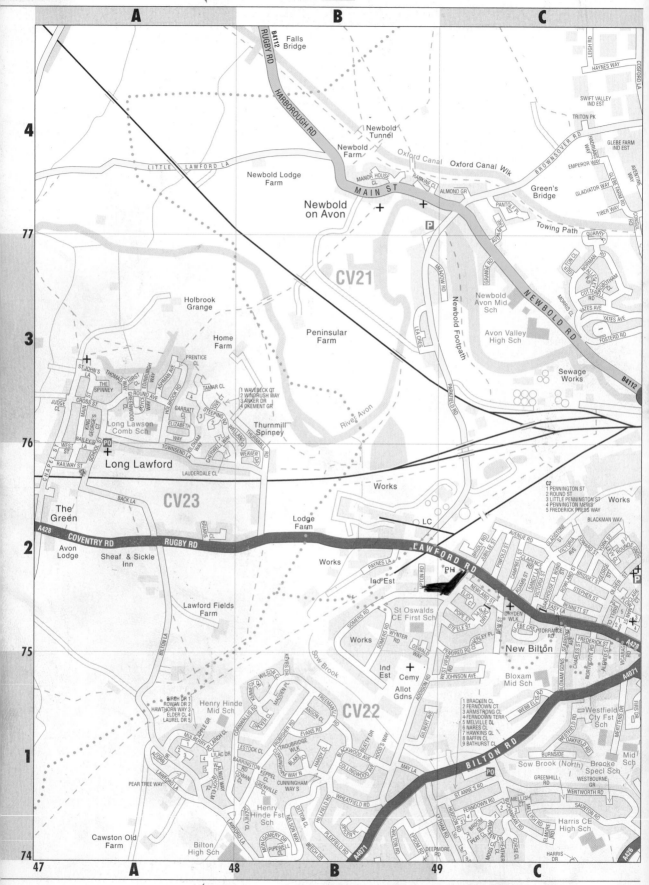

67
84

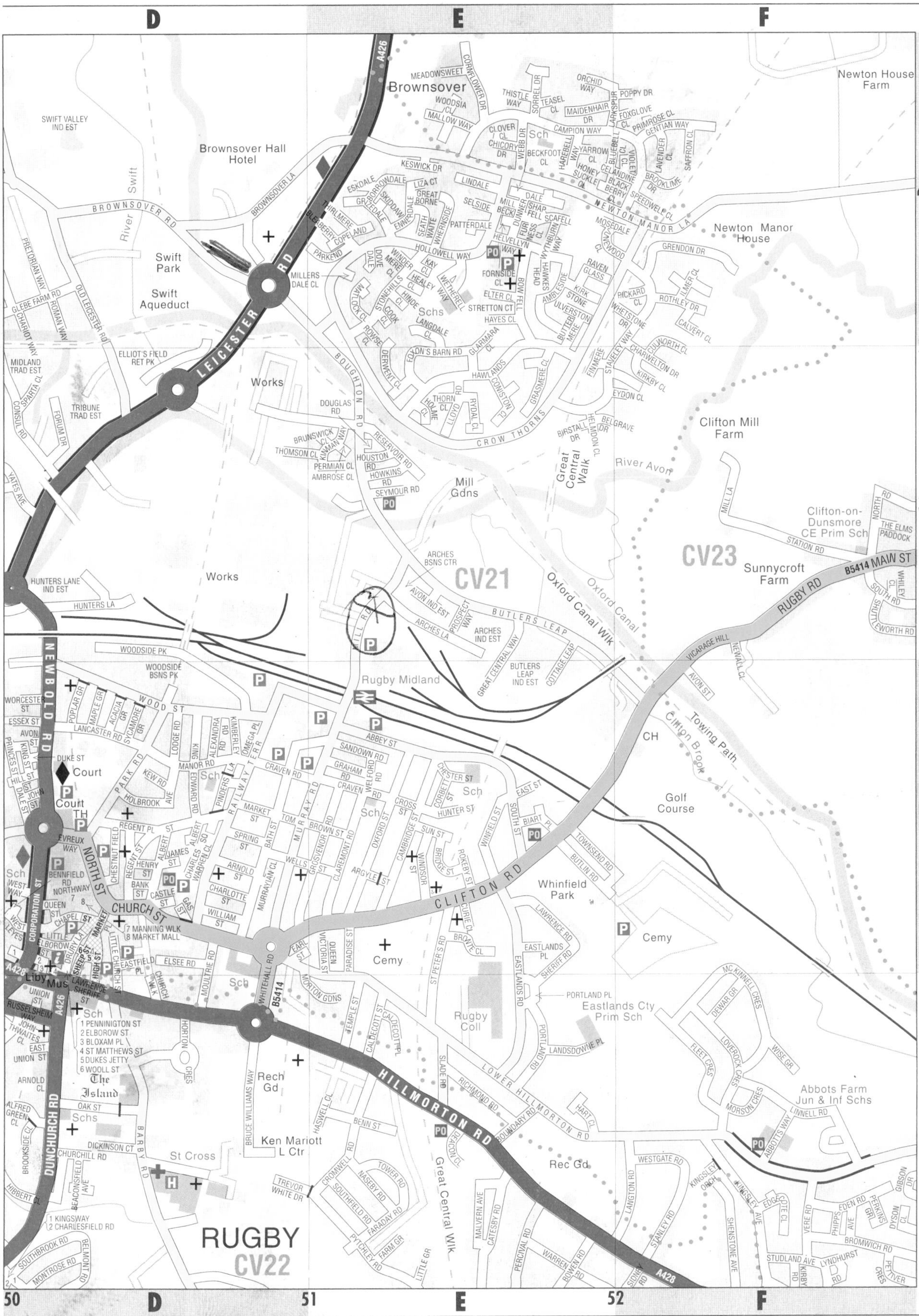
D
E
F
Brownsover
Brownsover Hall Hotel
SWIFT VALLEY IND EST
River Swift
Swift Park
Swift Aqueduct
BROWNSOVER RD
BROWNSOVER LA
LEICESTER RD
A426
MEADOWSWEET
CORNFLOWER DR
WOODSIA CL
MALLOW WAY
THISTLE WAY
SORREL DR
TEASEL CL
ORCHID WAY
POPPY DR
MAIDENHAIR DR
LARKSPUR
FOXGLOVE CL
PRIMROSE CL
GENTIAN WAY
CAMPION WAY
CLOVER CL
CHICORY DR
WEBB DR
BECKFOOT CL
HAREBELL WAY
YARROW CL
BLUEBELL CL
VIOLET CL
LAVENDER CL
SAFFRON CL
HONEYSUCKLE CL
CELANDINE
BLACKBERRY LA
BROOKLIME DR
SPEEDWELL CL
KESWICK DR
ESKDALE
BORROWDALE
LIZA CT
GREAT BORNE
LINDALE
SELSIDE
DALE
SHAP FELL
SCAFELL
NEWTON MANOR LA
MOSEDALE
NEWDOOD
THIRLMERE
BLEABERRY
COPELAND
PARKEND
SKIDDAW
ENNERDALE
SEATHWAITE
WHERNSIDE
PATTERDALE
MILL BECK
DUNNERHEAD
FURNESS CL
HELVELLYN WAY
HOLLOWELL WAY
WINDERMERE CL
KAY CL
HEALEY WAY
WETHERELL WAY
FORNSIDE CL
ELTER CL
BOWFELL
HAWKESHEAD
AMBLESIDE
KIRKSTONE
ULVERSTON
BUTTERMERE
RAVENGLASS
RICKARD CL
ROTHLEY DR
GRENDON DR
FILMER CL
CALVERT CL
WHETSTONE DR
STANLEY WAY
NORTH CL
CHARWELTON DR
KIRKBY CL
EYDON CL
FINMERE
MILLERS DALE CL
DOVE DALE
STONEHILLS
HINDE CL
COOK CL
MATLOCK CL
ROWSE CL
DERWENT CL
LANGDALE CL
STRETTON CT
HAYES CL
FOLLON'S BARN RD
GLARMARA CL
HAWLANDS
CONISTON CL
GRASMERE CL
THORN
HOLME
LLOYD
RYDAL CL
CROW THORNS
BIRSTALL DR
HELMDON CL
BELGRAVE DR
Newton House Farm
Newton Manor House
Clifton Mill Farm
River Avon
Great Central Walk
Mill Gdns
PRETORIAN WAY
GLEBE FARM RD
CHARIOT WAY
ROMAN WAY
OLD LEICESTER RD
MIDLAND TRAD EST
SPARTA CL
CONSUL RD
ELLIOT'S FIELD RET PK
TRIBUNE TRAD EST
FORUM DR
Works
BOUGHTON RD
DOUGLAS RD
BRUNSWICK CL
KINMAN WAY
THOMSON CL
PERMIAN CL
AMBROSE CL
RESERVOIR RD
HOUSTON RD
HOWKINS RD
SEYMOUR RD
YATES AVE
MILL LA
NORTH RD
Clifton-on-Dunsmore CE Prim Sch
THE ELMS PADDOCK
STATION RD
CV23
Sunnycroft Farm
B5414 MAIN ST
RUGBY RD
WHITLEY CL
SOUTH RD
SHUTTLEWORTH RD
ARCHES BSNS CTR
CV21
HUNTERS LANE IND EST
HUNTERS LA
AVON IND EST
PROSPECT WAY
ARCHES LA
ARCHES IND EST
MILL RD
BUTLERS LEAP
Oxford Canal Wlk
Oxford Canal
BUTLERS LEAP IND EST
GREAT CENTRAL WAY
COTTAGE LEAP
VICARAGE HILL
NEWALL CL
AVON ST
Towing Path
Clifton Brook
CH
Golf Course
Rugby Midland
WOODSIDE PK
WOODSIDE BSNS PK
NEWBOLD RD
WORCESTER ST
ESSEX ST
AVON ST
KING ST
PRINCES ST
HILL ST
DALE ST
JOHN ST
DUKE ST
Court
TH
POPLAR GR
MAPLE GR
ACACIA GR
SYCAMORE GR
WOOD ST
LANCASTER RD
LODGE RD
ALEXANDRA RD
KIMBERLEY RD
OMEGA PL
KING EDWARD RD
MANOR RD
KEW RD
PARK RD
HOLBROOK AVE
PINDERS LA
RAILWAY TERR
ABBEY ST
SANDOWN RD
GRAHAM RD
CRAVEN RD
WELFORD RD
CHESTER ST
CORBETT ST
MURRAY RD
TOM BROWN ST
MARKET ST
SPRING ST
BATH ST
OXFORD ST
CROSS ST
CAMBRIDGE ST
HUNTER ST
SUN ST
WINFIELD ST
SOUTH ST
EAST ST
BIART PL
TOWNSEND RD
BUTLIN RD
REGENT PL
REGENT ST
ALBERT ST
JAMES ST
HENRY ST
BANK ST
CASTLE ST
GAS ST
CHARLES WARREN CL
ARNOLD ST
CHARLOTTE ST
WILLIAM ST
MURRAYIAN CL
WELLS ST
GROSVENOR RD
CLAREMONT RD
ARGYLE ST
WINDSOR ST
BRIDGE ST
ROKEBY ST
CLIFTON RD
Whinfield Park
Cemy
EVREUX WAY
NORTH ST
CHESTNUT FIELD
BENNFIELD RD
NORTHWAY
WEST WAY
CORPORATION ST
QUEEN ST
CHAPEL ST
MARKET PL
CHURCH ST
7 MANNING WLK
8 MARKET MALL
WEST LEYES
ELBOROW ST
DRURY LA
SHEEP ST
HIGH ST
LITTLE CHURCH ST
EASTFIELD PL
ELSEE RD
MOULTRIE RD
WHITEHALL RD
EARL ST
VICTORIA ST
QUEEN ST
PARADISE ST
ST PETER'S RD
CURIE CL
BRONTE CL
LAWRENCE RD
EASTLANDS PL
SHERIFF RD
EASTLANDS RD
PORTLAND PL
PORTLAND RD
Eastlands Cty Prim Sch
LANDSDOWNE PL
MC KINNELL CRES
DEWAR GR
LOVEROCK CRES
FLEET CRES
WISE GR
MORSON CRES
Abbots Farm Jun & Inf Schs
LINNELL RD
ABBOTTS WAY
Liby
Mus
LAWRENCE SHERIFF ST
UNION ST
RUSSELSHEIM WAY
JOHN THWAITES CL
EAST UNION ST
B5414
MORTON GDNS
TEMPLE ST
CALDECOTT ST
CALDECOTT PL
Rugby Coll
1 PENNINGTON ST
2 ELBOROW ST
3 BLOXAM PL
4 ST MATTHEWS ST
5 DUKES JETTY
6 WOOLL ST
HORTON CRES
Rech Gd
BRUCE WILLIAMS WAY
HILLMORTON RD
LOWER HILLMORTON RD
RICHMOND RD
BOUNDARY RD
HART CL
SLADE RD
ARNOLD CL
The Island
ALFRED GREEN CL
OAK ST
Schs
DUNCHURCH RD
DICKINSON CT
CHURCHILL RD
BARBY RD
BROOKSIDE CL
HASWELL CL
BENN ST
Ken Mariott L Ctr
DEACON CL
St Cross
H
WESTGATE RD
KINGSLEY ORCH
KINGSLEY AVE
LANGTON RD
Rec Gd
GIBSON CL
BEACONSFIELD AVE
HIBBERT CL
TREVOR WHITE DR
CROMWELL RD
TOWER RD
NASEBY RD
SOUTHFIELD RD
FARADAY RD
Great Central Wlk
MALVERN AVE
CATESBY RD
STANLEY RD
EDGECOTE CL
VERE RD
PHIPPS AVE
EDEN RD
PERKINS GR
DOSAD CL
1 KINGSWAY
2 CHARLESFIELD RD
RUGBY
CV22
SOUTHBROOK RD
MONTROSE RD
BELMONT RD
PYTCHLEY RD
FARM GR
LITTLE GR
PERCIVAL RD
WARREN RD
BOWEN RD
SIDNEY RD
A428
SHENSTONE AVE
STUDLAND AVE
LYNDHURST RD
BROMWICH RD
PETIVER CRES
KIRBY RD
4
77
3
76
2
75
1
74
50
51
52

100
84

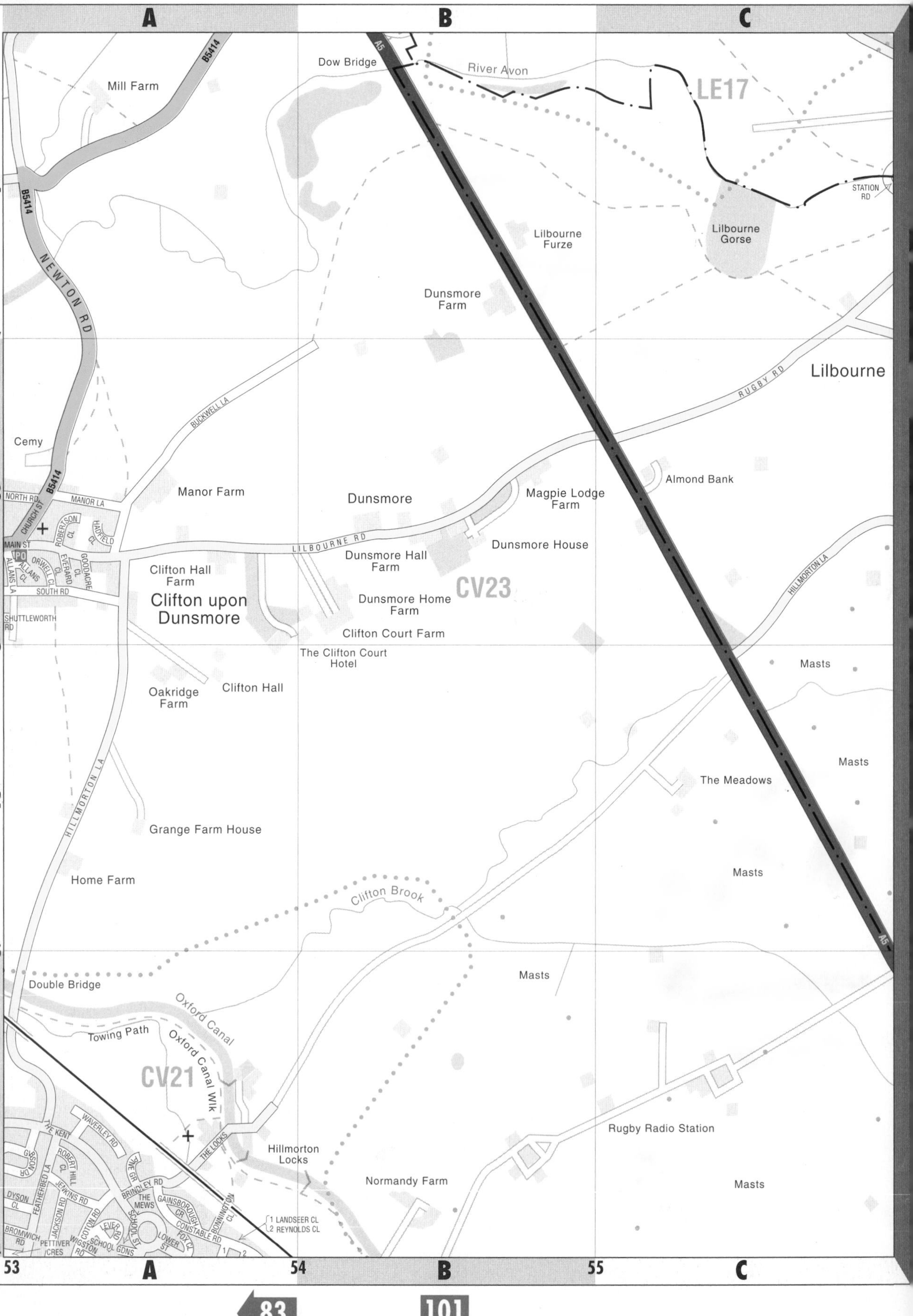
A
B
C
4
77
3
76
2
75
1
74
53
54
55
Dow Bridge
A5
River Avon
LE17
Mill Farm
B5414
STATION RD
Lilbourne Gorse
Lilbourne Furze
NEWTON RD
Dunsmore Farm
Lilbourne
RUGBY RD
BUCKWELL LA
Cemy
Manor Farm
Dunsmore
Magpie Lodge Farm
Almond Bank
NORTH RD
CHURCH ST
MANOR LA
ROBERTSON CL
HADFIELD CL
MAIN ST
PO
ORWELL CL
EVERARD CL
GOODACRE CL
ALLANS CL
ALLANS LA
SOUTH RD
SHUTTLEWORTH RD
LILBOURNE RD
Dunsmore House
Dunsmore Hall Farm
Clifton Hall Farm
Clifton upon Dunsmore
Dunsmore Home Farm
CV23
HILLMORTON LA
Clifton Court Farm
The Clifton Court Hotel
Clifton Hall
Oakridge Farm
Masts
The Meadows
Grange Farm House
Home Farm
Clifton Brook
Double Bridge
Oxford Canal
Towing Path
Oxford Canal Wlk
CV21
THE LOCKS
Hillmorton Locks
Rugby Radio Station
Normandy Farm
THE KENT
WAVERLEY RD
ROBERT HILL CL
FEATHERBED LA
JENKINS RD
DYSON CL
JACKSON RD
COTON RD
BROMWICH RD
PETTIVER CRES
WIGSTON RD
LEVER RD
SCHOOL GDNS
SCHOOL ST
THE MEWS
BRINDLEY RD
GAINSBOROUGH CR
CONSTABLE RD
FOX CL
LOWER ST
BONNINGTON CL
1 LANDSEER CL
2 REYNOLDS CL

86

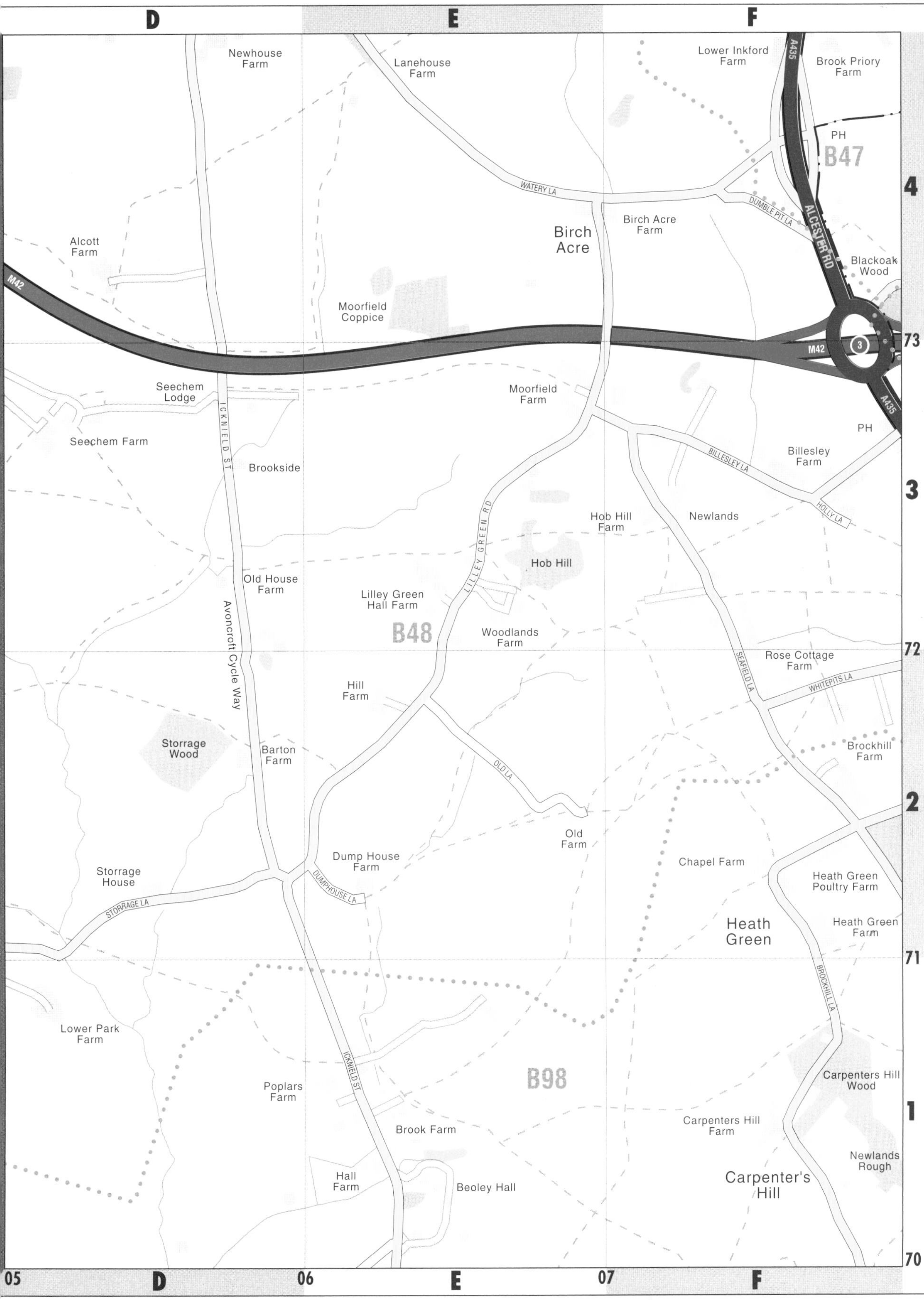
D
E
F
Newhouse Farm
Lanehouse Farm
Lower Inkford Farm
Brook Priory Farm
A435
PH
B47
4
WATERY LA
DUMBLE PIT LA
ALCESTER RD
Birch Acre
Birch Acre Farm
Alcott Farm
Blackoak Wood
M42
Moorfield Coppice
73
3
Seechem Lodge
Moorfield Farm
Seechem Farm
ICKNIELD ST
Brookside
BILLESLEY LA
Billesley Farm
Hob Hill Farm
Newlands
HOLLY LA
3
LILLEY GREEN RD
Hob Hill
Old House Farm
Lilley Green Hall Farm
Avoncroft Cycle Way
B48
Woodlands Farm
72
SEAFIELD LA
Rose Cottage Farm
WHITEPITS LA
Hill Farm
Storrage Wood
Barton Farm
OLD LA
Brockhill Farm
2
Old Farm
Dump House Farm
Chapel Farm
Storrage House
DUMPHOUSE LA
Heath Green Poultry Farm
STORRAGE LA
Heath Green
Heath Green Farm
71
BROCKHILL LA
Lower Park Farm
ICKNIELD ST
B98
Carpenters Hill Wood
Poplars Farm
Carpenters Hill Farm
1
Brook Farm
Newlands Rough
Hall Farm
Beoley Hall
Carpenter's Hill
70
05
06
07

86

85
69

A
B
C
4
73
3
72
2
71
1
70
08
09
10
River Cole
Mill La
Forshaw Heath Rd
The Poplars
Clowes Wood
Terry's Pool
B47
Pound Close Farm
Cloweswood La
The Lakes
Terry's Green
Forshaw Heath
Graves Coppice
Poolhead La
Malthouse La
Springbrook La
White House Farm
Forshaw Heath La
Juggins La
Oaktree Farm Mobile Homes Pk
Yew Tree Farm
Forshaw Park Farm
Springbrook Farm
Glebe Farm
Checkley's Coppice
M42
The Plantation
The Lyndons
Small Lane Farm
Small La
Earlswood Trad Est
Biddles Hill
Sewage Works
Spring Brook
Rugby Football Ground
A435
Tyler's Grove
Windmill Naps
B48
Portway
Ladbrookpark Coppice
B94
Poolhead Farm
Wood End La
Pool House Farm
Holly Farm
Whitepits La
Alcester Rd
Golf Course
Cottage Farm
Little Ladbrooke Farm
Ladbrooke Hall
Ladbrooke Hall Farm
Wood End
PH
B4101
Lion Wood
Penn La
CH
Brockhill La
Alcester Rd
Brockhill Wood
Rushbrook La
Woodcock Cl
Wood End
Hill Barn
High Park Farm
Rushbrook Farm
Rushbrook
Broad La
Gilbert's Green
Vicarage Hill
Spring Brook
Highpark Wood
B98
Seafield La
Arden Leys
Aspley Heath La
Park Farm
Branson's Cross
Aspley Heath
River Alne
PH
Baylis Green
Cherry Pit La
Beoley La
Broad La
Blind La
Branson's Cross Farm
Pinkfield Wood
Aspley Farm
Bates La
Alderhanger Wood

85
112

70
88

D
E
F
Waring's Green
Warren Farm
Windmill Pool
VALLEY RD
PH
SHUTT LA
B4102
PO
P
MALTHOUSE LA
Earlswood Court
Waring's Green Farm
WARINGS GREEN RD
SALTER ST
DYERS LA
M42
SCHOOL RD
TINKERS LA
Stratford-upon-Avon Canal
Rotheram's Oak Farm
High Chimneys Farm
The Old Moathouse
Flower Knott Cottage
Terry's Green
Clay Bank Farm
CUT THROAT LA
SCHOOL RD
Acorn Coppice
Woodlands Farm
Cottage Farm
UMBERSLADE RD
Mast
ROTHERHAMS OAK LA
SPRINGBROOK LA
EARLSWOOD COMM
Old Grove Wood
Heathfield Farm
Wychpitts Farm
73
Arnold's Wood
Old Grove
The Beeches
TITHE BARN LA
3a
Three Gables Wood Farm
Abbey Farm
The Priory
Chamber's Coppice
Chalcot Wood
3
Jonathan's Farm
Wood's Coppice
Bissell's Coppice
M42
M40
Clarksland Coppice
B94
Birchy Cross
72
B4102
M40
Beaumont Hill Farm
BROAD LA
Birchy Cross Farm
Brown's Green
POUND HOUSE LA
B4101
Works
Brown's Green
Tom Hill
2
Brook House Farm
Brown's Green Wood
Umberslade Hall
TOM HILL
UMBERSLADE RD
71
South Lodge
Knowlebury Cross
VICARAGE HILL
BELLFIELD
BUTTS LA
The Vicarage
Tanworth-in-Arden
Tanworth-in-Arden CE Sch
The Leasowes Children's Farm
Dairy House Farm
PO
BATES LA
WELL LA
1
Oxstalls Farm House
KEMPS GREEN RD
Cank Farm
Sewage Works
DANZEY GREEN LA
Robin Hood Farm
70
11
D
12
E
13
F

112
88

87
71

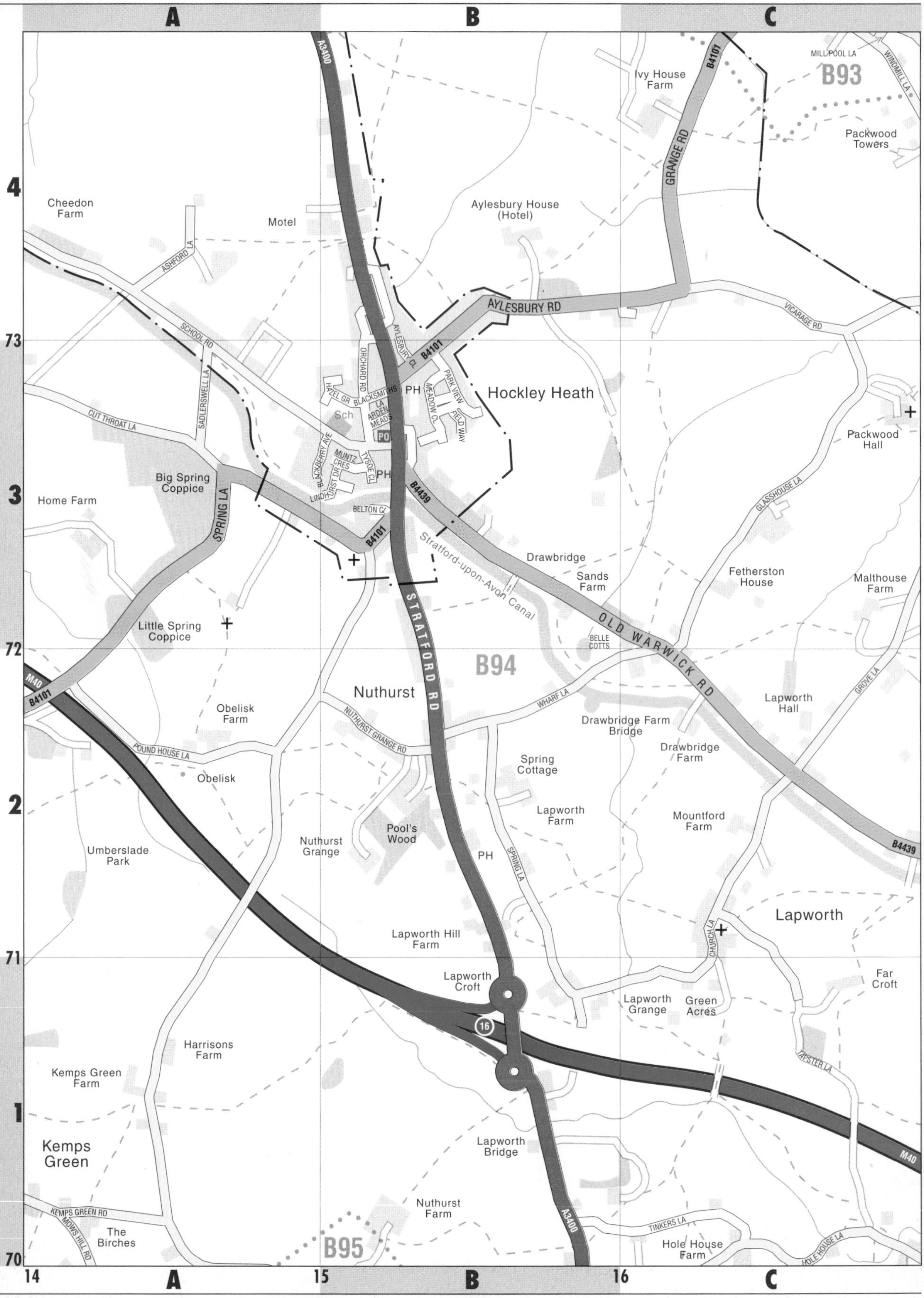
A
B
C
4
73
3
72
2
71
1
70
14
15
16
A
B
C
A3400
B4101
MILL POOL LA
WINDMILL LA
B93
Ivy House Farm
Packwood Towers
GRANGE RD
Cheedon Farm
Motel
Aylesbury House (Hotel)
ASHFORD LA
AYLESBURY RD
VICARAGE RD
SCHOOL RD
AYLESBURY CL
ORCHARD RD
SADLERSWELL LA
HAZEL GR
BLACKSMITHS LA
ARDEN MEADS
PH
MEADOW CL
PARK VIEW
FIELD WAY
Hockley Heath
CUT THROAT LA
Sch
PO
Packwood Hall
BLACKBERRY AVE
MUNTZ CRES
TYSOE CL
LYNDHURST DR
PH
Big Spring Coppice
Home Farm
SPRING LA
B4439
GLASSHOUSE LA
BELTON CL
B4101
Stratford-upon-Avon Canal
Drawbridge
Sands Farm
Fetherston House
Malthouse Farm
STRATFORD RD
OLD WARWICK RD
Little Spring Coppice
BELLE COTTS
B94
72
M40
B4101
Nuthurst
Lapworth Hall
GROVE LA
Obelisk Farm
NUTHURST GRANGE RD
WHARF LA
Drawbridge Farm Bridge
POUND HOUSE LA
Obelisk
Spring Cottage
Drawbridge Farm
Lapworth Farm
Mountford Farm
Pool's Wood
Umberslade Park
Nuthurst Grange
PH
SPRING LA
B4439
Lapworth
CHURCH LA
Lapworth Hill Farm
Lapworth Croft
Far Croft
Lapworth Grange
Green Acres
16
Harrisons Farm
TAPSTER LA
Kemps Green Farm
Lapworth Bridge
M40
Kemps Green
Nuthurst Farm
KEMPS GREEN RD
MOWS HILL RD
The Birches
A3400
TINKERS LA
B95
Hole House Farm
HOLE HOUSE LA

87
113

72
90

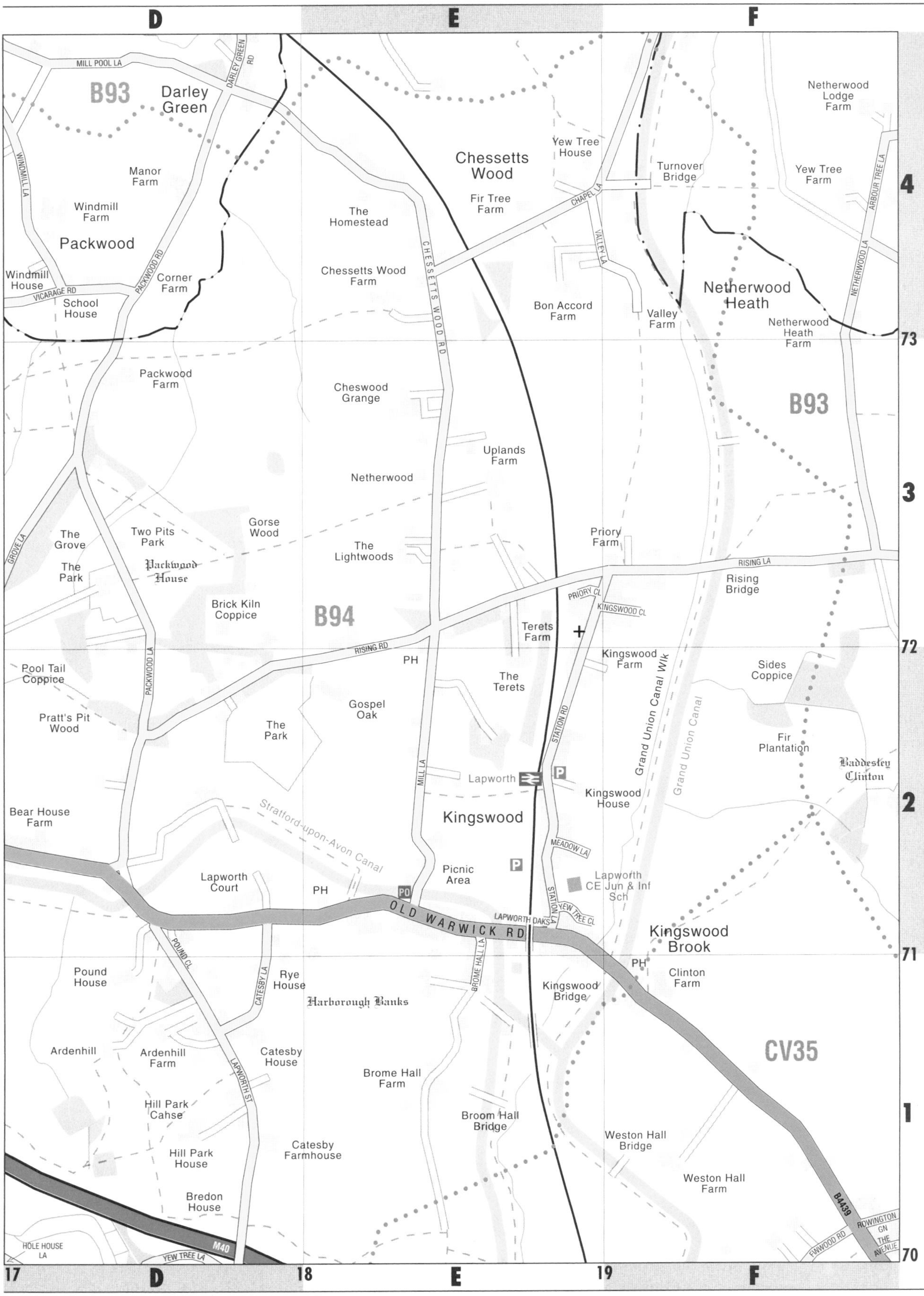
D
E
F
MILL POOL LA
B93
Darley Green
DARLEY GREEN RD
WINDMILL LA
Manor Farm
Windmill Farm
Packwood
PACKWOOD RD
Windmill House
VICARAGE RD
Corner Farm
School House
The Homestead
Chessetts Wood Farm
CHESSETTS WOOD RD
Chessetts Wood
Fir Tree Farm
Yew Tree House
CHAPEL LA
VALLEY LA
Bon Accord Farm
Turnover Bridge
Valley Farm
Netherwood Lodge Farm
Yew Tree Farm
ARBOUR TREE LA
NETHERWOOD LA
Netherwood Heath
Netherwood Heath Farm
4
73
Packwood Farm
Cheswood Grange
Uplands Farm
B93
Netherwood
3
The Grove
GROVE LA
Two Pits Park
Gorse Wood
The Lightwoods
Priory Farm
The Park
Packwood House
RISING LA
Rising Bridge
Brick Kiln Coppice
B94
PRIORY CL
KINGSWOOD CL
Terets Farm
72
Pool Tail Coppice
RISING RD
PH
Kingswood Farm
Sides Coppice
PACKWOOD LA
The Terets
Grand Union Canal Wlk
Pratt's Pit Wood
Gospel Oak
The Park
STATION RD
Grand Union Canal
Fir Plantation
Baddesley Clinton
MILL LA
Lapworth
Kingswood House
Bear House Farm
Stratford-upon-Avon Canal
Kingswood
2
MEADOW LA
Lapworth Court
PH
Picnic Area
Lapworth CE Jun & Inf Sch
PO
OLD WARWICK RD
LAPWORTH OAKS
STATION LA
YEW TREE CL
Kingswood Brook
71
POUND CL
PH
Pound House
Rye House
BROME HALL LA
Kingswood Bridge
Clinton Farm
CATESBY LA
Harborough Banks
Ardenhill
Ardenhill Farm
Catesby House
CV35
LAPWORTH ST
Brome Hall Farm
Hill Park Cahse
Broom Hall Bridge
1
Weston Hall Bridge
Hill Park House
Catesby Farmhouse
Weston Hall Farm
Bredon House
B4439
ROWINGTON GN
FIRWOOD RD
THE AVENUE
HOLE HOUSE LA
M40
YEW TREE LA
70
17
D
18
E
19
F

113
90

89
73

A
B
C
4
3
2
1
73
72
71
70
20
21
22
A4141
WARWICK RD
ARBOUR TREE LA
Arbour Tree Farm
CHADWICK LA
Chadwick End Farm
OLDWICH LA W
Rosemary Farm
SPARROW COCK LA
Brookside Grange
Dadkin Farm
Sewage Works
OLDWICH LA E
HILLTOP CL
CV8
Hill Farm
Chadwick End
NETHERWOOD LA
PO
WHEELER CL
BAKEHOUSE LA
PH
Priests Park Wood
Heart of England Way
Nunley Farm
Proving Ground
Works
Bedlam's End
B93
THISTLEWOOD GR
CHADWICK MEWS
Priests Park Farm
Baddesley Clinton
Convent
RISWG LA
Warren Farm
Nunley Pit
Breach Wood
Manor Park Farm
Haywood Farm
Nunnery Coppice
Manor Wood
Brome's Park
SCHOOL LA
Cemy
Glendale
Abbey Farm
CV35
MANOR LA
BIRMINGHAM RD
Wroxall
Old Keeper's Lodge
HAY WOOD LA
Hay Wood
Wroxall CE Jun & Inf Sch
Heart of England Way
Wood Corner Farm
P
Picnic Area
Wroxall Abbey (Sch)
Rowington Coppice
The Park
Gilbert's Coppice
Rowington Green
Lyons Farm
QUARRY LA
A4141
A4177
FIVE WAYS
Shrewley Lodge Farm
ROWINGTON GN
Rowington Mill
Quarry Farm
QUEEN'S DR
THE AVENUE
BEECH CL
CASE LA
PH
FIVE WAYS RD
A4177

89
114

74
92

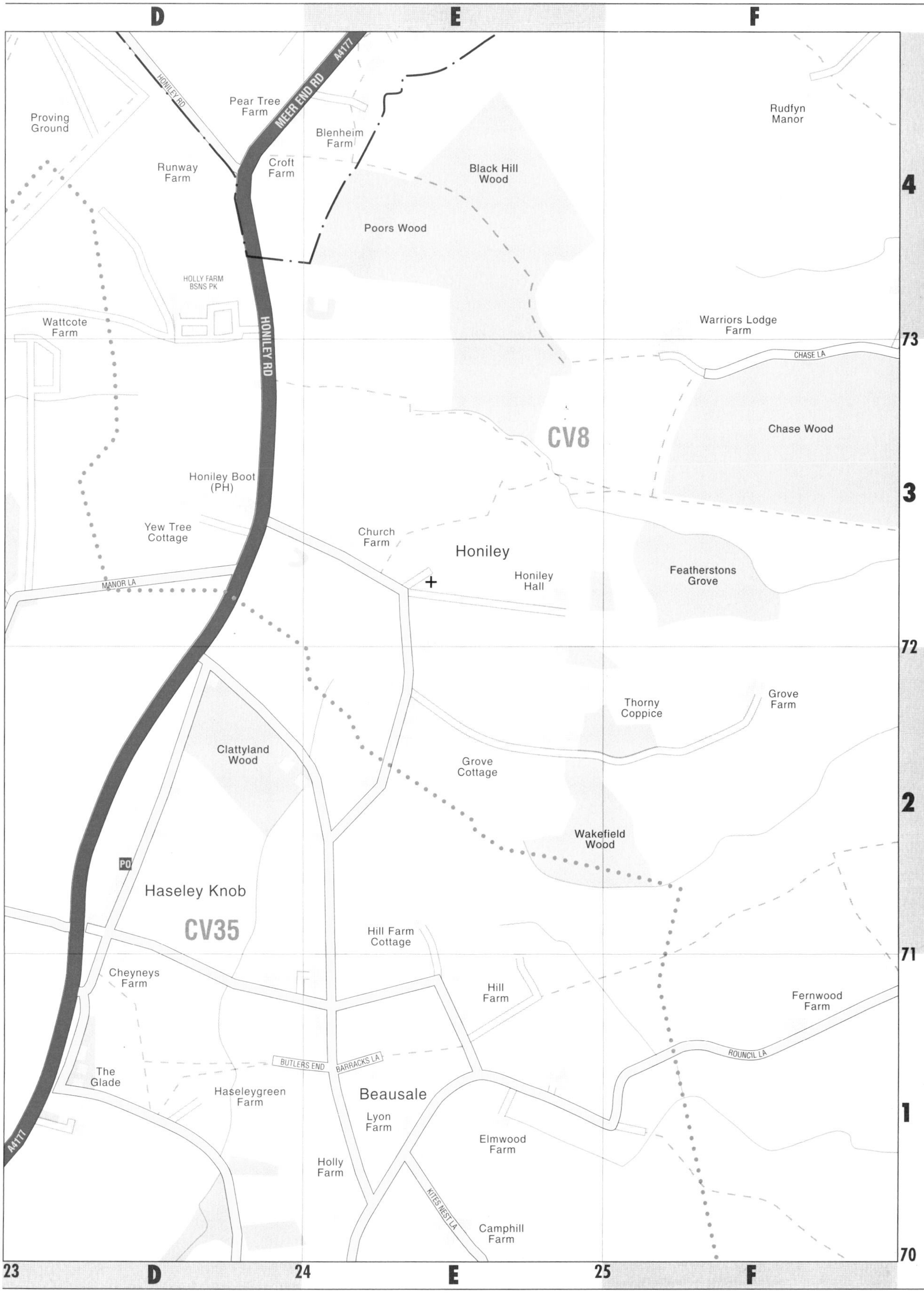
D
E
F
HONILEY RD
MEER END RD
A4177
Pear Tree Farm
Proving Ground
Blenheim Farm
Rudfyn Manor
Runway Farm
Croft Farm
Black Hill Wood
4
Poors Wood
HOLLY FARM BSNS PK
Wattcote Farm
Warriors Lodge Farm
73
CHASE LA
Chase Wood
CV8
Honiley Boot (PH)
3
Yew Tree Cottage
Church Farm
Honiley
Honiley Hall
Featherstons Grove
MANOR LA
72
Thorny Coppice
Grove Farm
Clattyland Wood
Grove Cottage
2
Wakefield Wood
PO
Haseley Knob
CV35
Hill Farm Cottage
71
Cheyneys Farm
Hill Farm
Fernwood Farm
ROUNCIL LA
BUTLERS END
BARRACKS LA
The Glade
Haseleygreen Farm
Beausale
1
Lyon Farm
Elmwood Farm
A4177
Holly Farm
KITES NEST LA
Camphill Farm
70
23
24
25

114
92

91
75

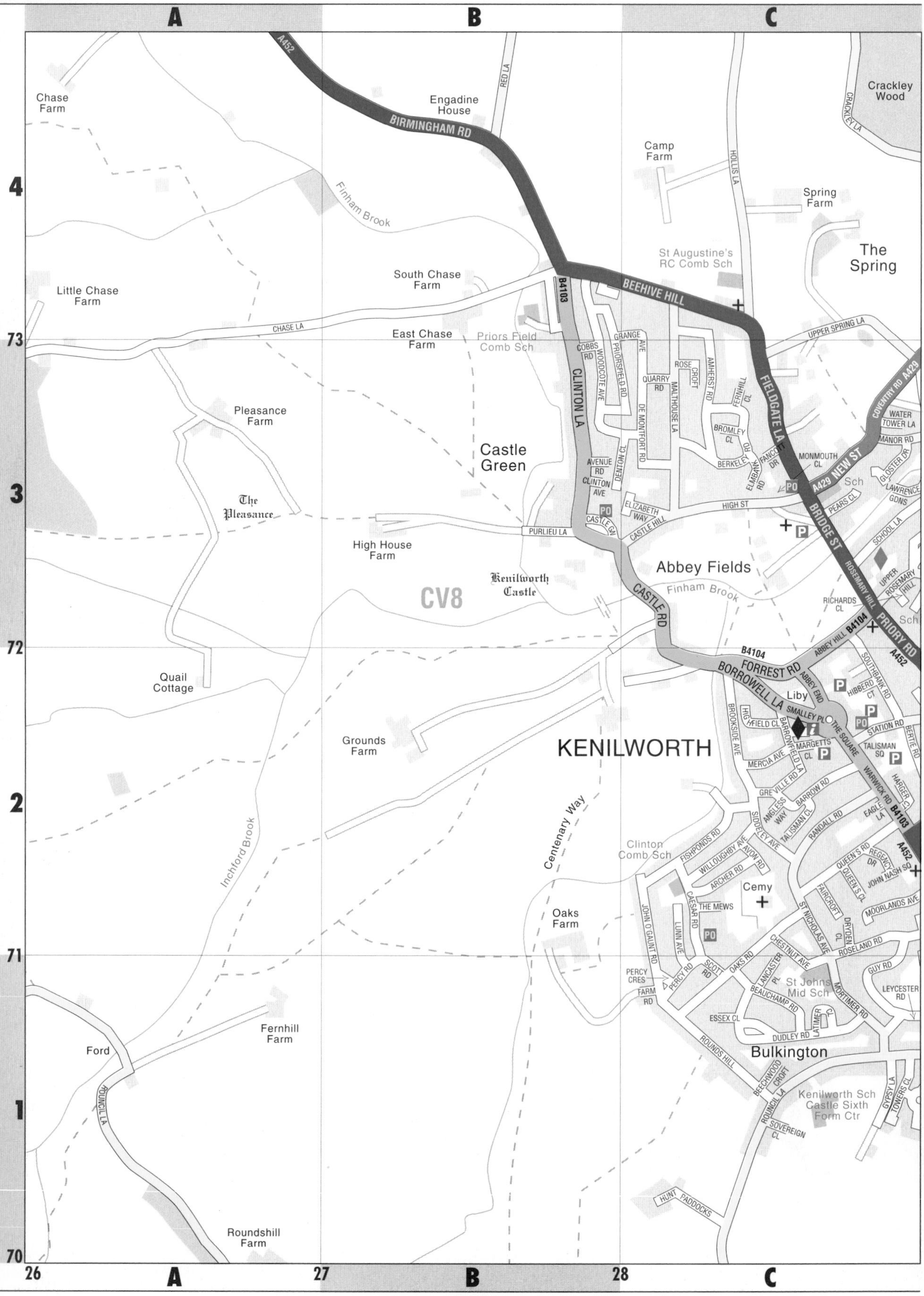
A
B
C
4
3
2
1
73
72
71
70
26
27
28
A452
BIRMINGHAM RD
RED LA
Engadine House
Chase Farm
Finham Brook
Camp Farm
HOLLIS LA
Crackley Wood
CRACKLEY LA
Spring Farm
The Spring
St Augustine's RC Comb Sch
South Chase Farm
Little Chase Farm
B4103
BEEHIVE HILL
CHASE LA
East Chase Farm
Priors Field Comb Sch
UPPER SPRING LA
COBBS RD
GRANGE AVE
WOODCOTE AVE
PRIORSFIELD RD
QUARRY RD
ROSE CROFT
AMHERST RD
FERNHILL CL
CLINTON LA
DE MONTFORT RD
MALTHOUSE LA
FIELDGATE LA
COVENTRY RD A429
WATER TOWER LA
MANOR RD
Pleasance Farm
BROMLEY CL
BERKELEY RD
FANCOTT DR
MONMOUTH CL
Castle Green
AVENUE RD
DENTON CL
ELMBANK RD
A429 NEW ST
GLOSTER DR
CLINTON AVE
PO
Sch
LAWRENCE GDNS
The Pleasance
ELIZABETH WAY
HIGH ST
PEARS CL
CASTLE GN
CASTLE HILL
BRIDGE ST
SCHOOL LA
PURLIEU LA
High House Farm
Abbey Fields
Kenilworth Castle
UPPER ROSEMARY HILL
CV8
CASTLE RD
Finham Brook
ROSEMARY HILL
RICHARDS CL
PRIORY RD
ABBEY HILL B4104
72
B4104
FORREST RD
A452
Quail Cottage
BORROWELL LA
ABBEY END
SOUTHBANK RD
HIBBERD CT
Liby
SMALLEY PL
BROOKSIDE AVE
HIGHFIELD CL
THE SQUARE
STATION RD
BERTIE RD
Grounds Farm
KENILWORTH
BARROWFIELD LA
MARGETTS CL
TALISMAN SQ
MERCIA AVE
GREVILLE RD
BARROW RD
HARGER CT
ANGLESEY WAY
TALISMAN CL
RANDALL RD
EAGLE LA
WARWICK RD
B4103
Centenary Way
SIDDELEY AVE
Clinton Comb Sch
FISHPONDS RD
WILLOUGHBY AVE
AVON RD
QUEEN'S RD
REGENCY DR
JOHN NASH SQ
Inchford Brook
ARCHER RD
Cemy
CAESAR RD
THE MEWS
QUEEN'S CL
FAIRCROFT
MOORLANDS AVE
Oaks Farm
LUNN AVE
JOHN O GAUNT RD
ST NICHOLAS AVE
DRYDEN CL
ROSELAND RD
CHESTNUT AVE
GUY RD
PERCY CRES
PERCY RD
SCOTT RD
OAKS RD
LANCASTER PL
St Johns Mid Sch
LEYCESTER RD
FARM RD
BEAUCHAMP RD
MORTIMER RD
ESSEX CL
LATIMER CL
Fernhill Farm
DUDLEY RD
Ford
ROUNDS HILL
Bulkington
BEECHWOOD CROFT
ROUNCIL LA
GYPSY LA
TOWERS CL
Kenilworth Sch Castle Sixth Form Ctr
SOVEREIGN CL
HUNT PADDOCKS
Roundshill Farm

91
104

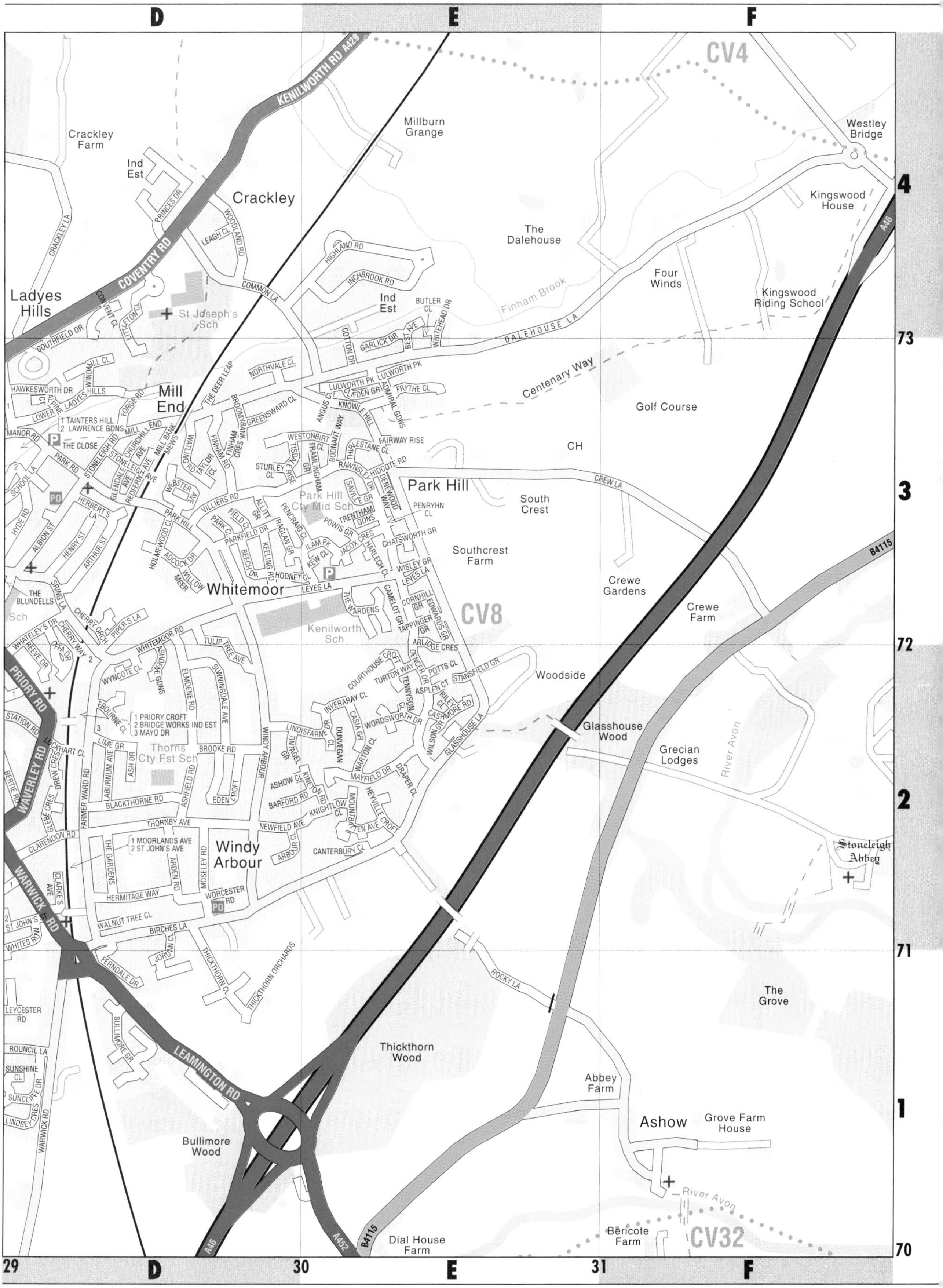
D
E
F
CV4
Millburn Grange
Westley Bridge
Crackley Farm
Ind Est
Crackley
Kingswood House
The Dalehouse
Ladyes Hills
St Joseph's Sch
Ind Est
Four Winds
Kingswood Riding School
Finham Brook
Centenary Way
Golf Course
Mill End
CH
Park Hill
South Crest
Park Hill Cty Mid Sch
Southcrest Farm
Crewe Gardens
Whitemoor
Crewe Farm
Kenilworth Sch
CV8
Woodside
Glasshouse Wood
Grecian Lodges
River Avon
Thorns Cty Fst Sch
Windy Arbour
Stoneleigh Abbey
The Grove
Thickthorn Wood
Abbey Farm
Ashow
Grove Farm House
Bullimore Wood
River Avon
Bericote Farm
CV32
Dial House Farm
KENILWORTH RD A429
COVENTRY RD
LEAMINGTON RD
WARWICK RD
PRIORY RD
WAVERLEY RD
A46
A452
B4115
DALEHOUSE LA
CREW LA
ROCKY LA
COMMON LA
1 TAINTERS HILL
2 LAWRENCE GDNS
1 PRIORY CROFT
2 BRIDGE WORKS IND EST
3 MAYO DR
1 MOORLANDS AVE
2 ST JOHN'S AVE
4
73
3
72
2
71
1
70
29
30
31

93
77

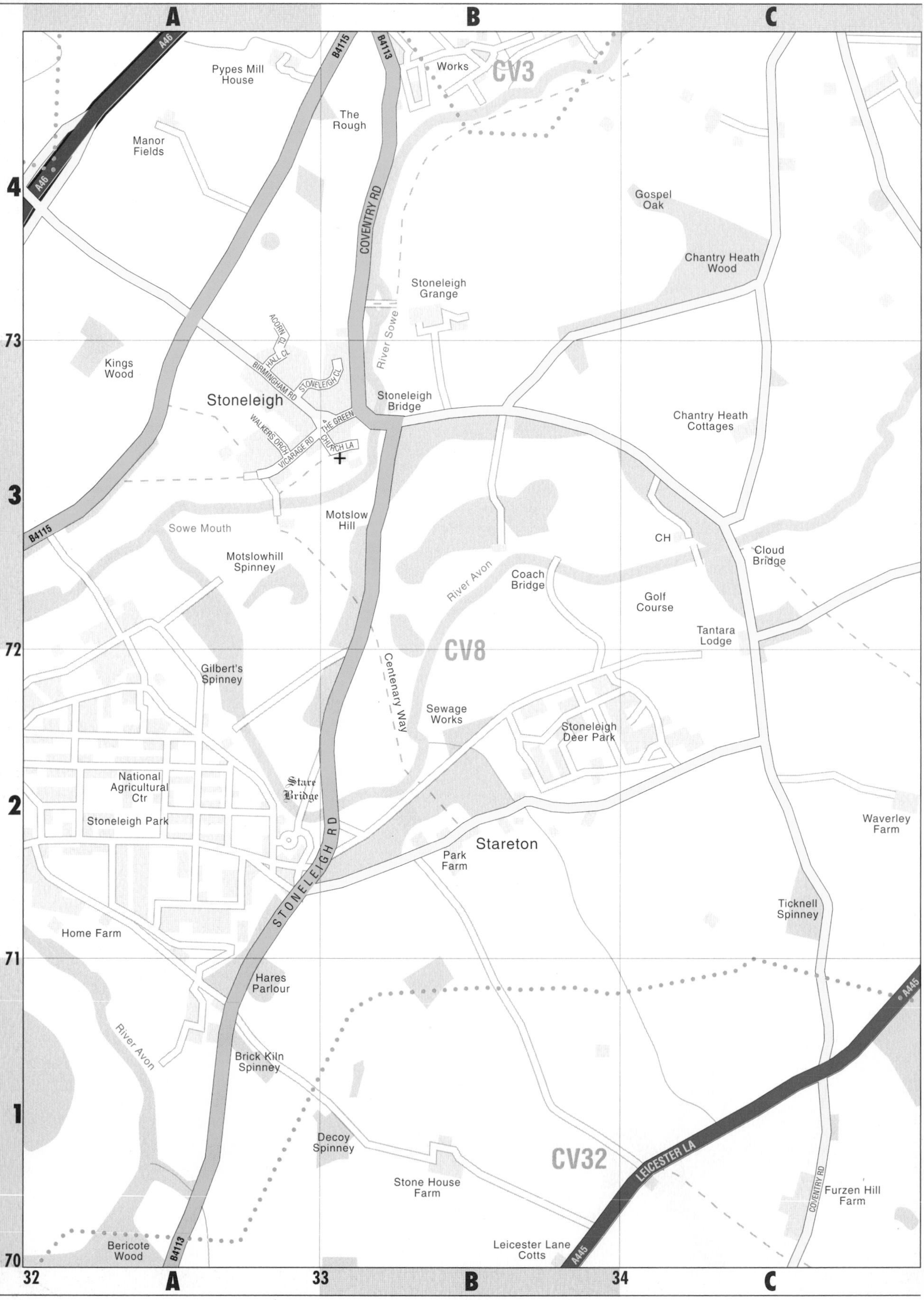
A
B
C
4
73
3
72
2
71
1
70
32
33
34
A46
B4115
B4113
Pypes Mill House
Works
CV3
The Rough
Manor Fields
COVENTRY RD
Gospel Oak
Chantry Heath Wood
Stoneleigh Grange
River Sowe
ACORN CL
HALL CL
BIRMINGHAM RD
STONELEIGH CL
Kings Wood
Stoneleigh
Stoneleigh Bridge
Chantry Heath Cottages
THE GREEN
WALKERS ORCH
VICARAGE RD
CHURCH LA
Motslow Hill
Sowe Mouth
CH
Cloud Bridge
Motslowhill Spinney
Coach Bridge
River Avon
Golf Course
Tantara Lodge
CV8
Gilbert's Spinney
Centenary Way
Sewage Works
Stoneleigh Deer Park
National Agricultural Ctr
Stare Bridge
Stoneleigh Park
STONELEIGH RD
Stareton
Park Farm
Waverley Farm
Ticknell Spinney
Home Farm
Hares Parlour
A445
River Avon
Brick Kiln Spinney
Decoy Spinney
CV32
LEICESTER LA
Stone House Farm
COVENTRY RD
Furzen Hill Farm
Bericote Wood
Leicester Lane Cotts

93
106

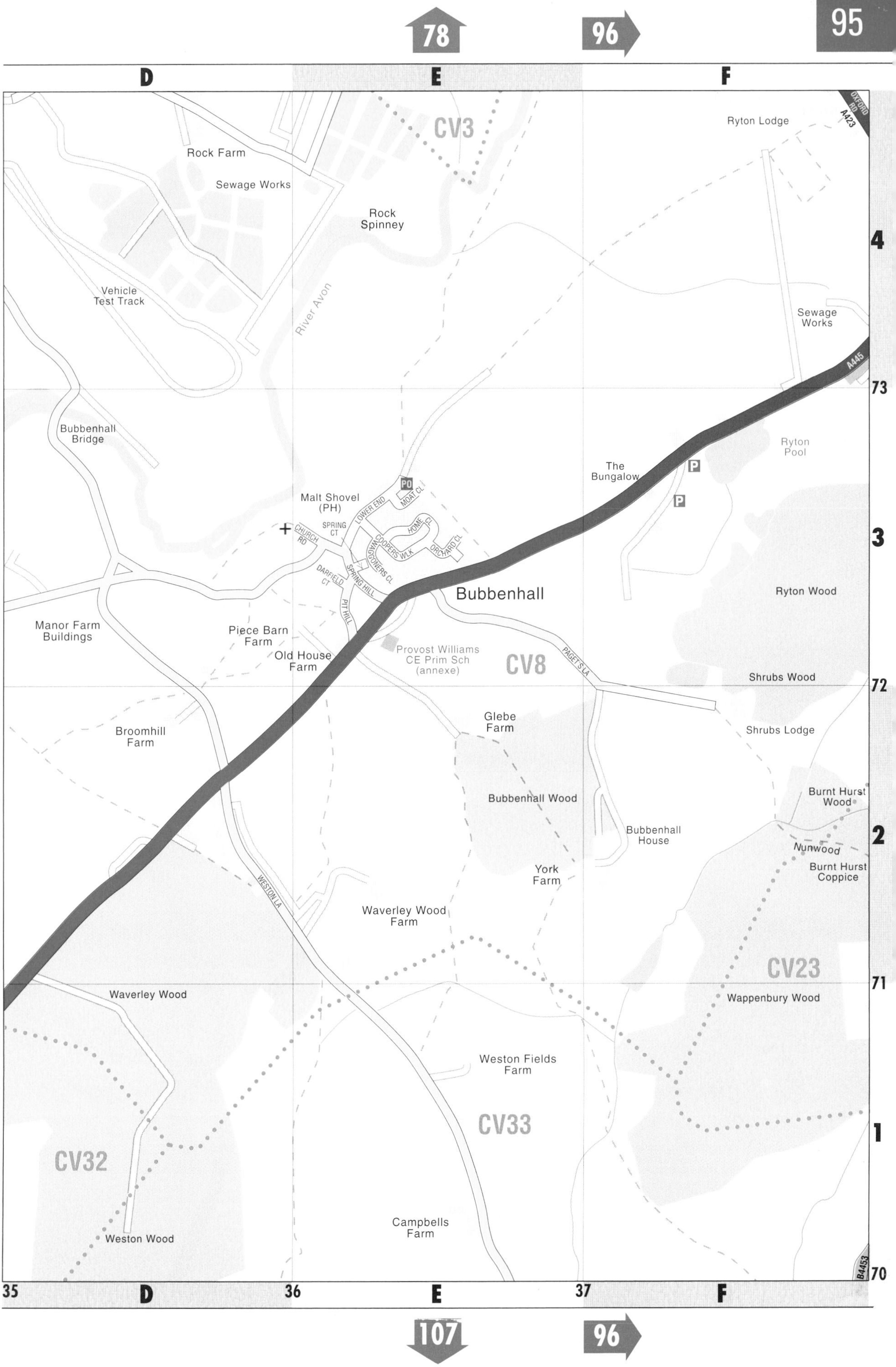
78
96
D
E
F
CV3
Ryton Lodge
OXFORD RD
A423
Rock Farm
Sewage Works
Rock Spinney
Vehicle Test Track
River Avon
Sewage Works
A445
Bubbenhall Bridge
Ryton Pool
The Bungalow
P
PO
MOAT CL
LOWER END
Malt Shovel (PH)
SPRING CT
CHURCH RD
HOME CL
COOPERS WLK
WAGGONERS CL
ORCHARD CL
DARFIELD CT
SPRING HILL
PIT HILL
Bubbenhall
Ryton Wood
Manor Farm Buildings
Piece Barn Farm
Old House Farm
Provost Williams CE Prim Sch (annexe)
CV8
PAGET'S LA
Shrubs Wood
Glebe Farm
Broomhill Farm
Shrubs Lodge
Burnt Hurst Wood
Bubbenhall Wood
Bubbenhall House
Nunwood
Burnt Hurst Coppice
York Farm
WESTON LA
Waverley Wood Farm
CV23
Waverley Wood
Wappenbury Wood
Weston Fields Farm
CV33
CV32
Weston Wood
Campbells Farm
B4453
4
73
3
72
2
71
1
70
35
36
37
107
96

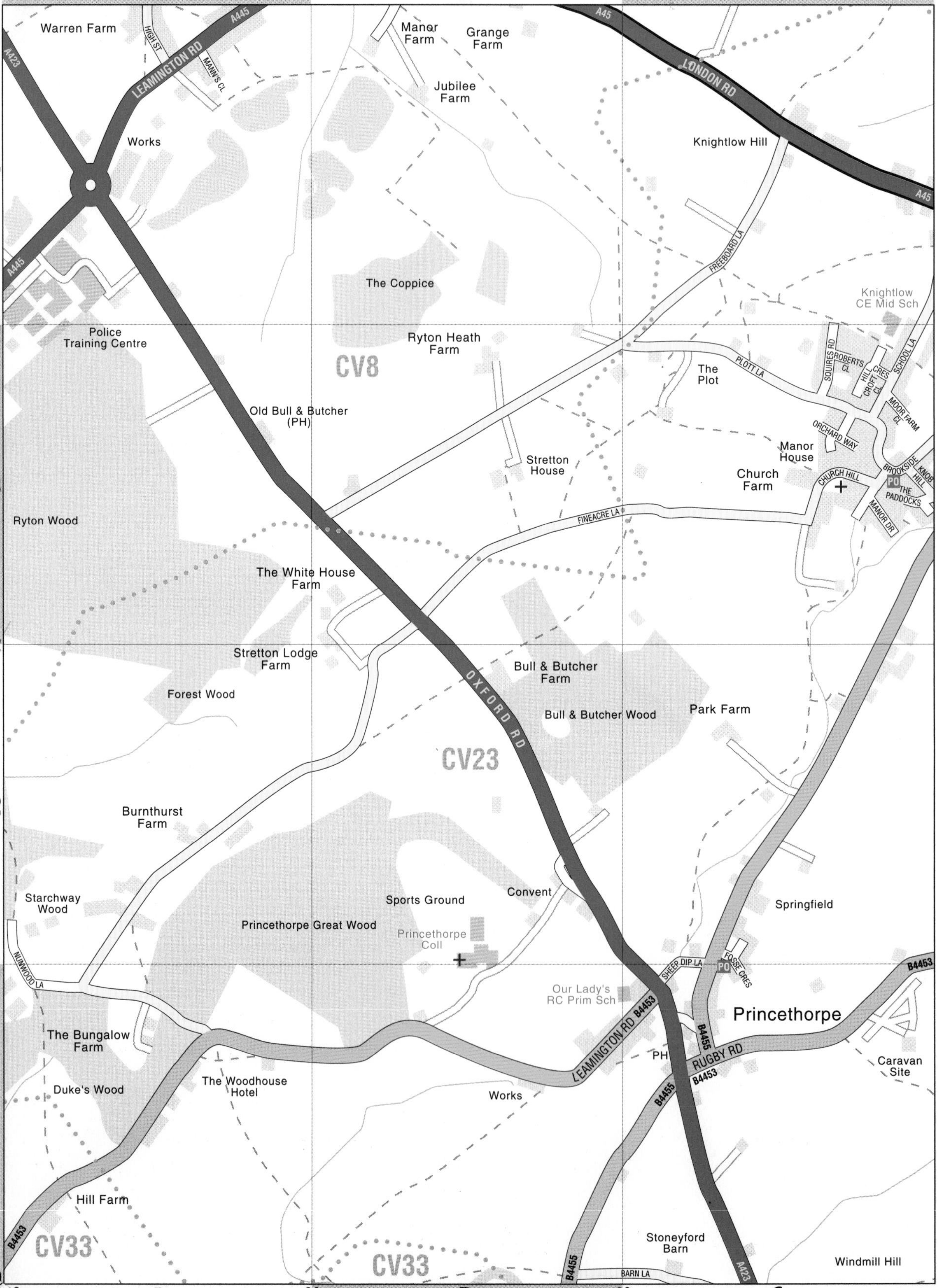
A
B
C
Warren Farm
HIGH ST
A445
LEAMINGTON RD
MANN'S CL
A423
Manor Farm
Grange Farm
Jubilee Farm
A45
LONDON RD
Works
Knightlow Hill
4
A445
FREEBOARD LA
The Coppice
Knightlow CE Mid Sch
73
Police Training Centre
Ryton Heath Farm
CV8
SQUIRES RD
ROBERTS CL
HILL CRES
CROFT CL
SCHOOL LA
The Plot
PLOTT LA
MOOR FARM CL
Old Bull & Butcher (PH)
ORCHARD WAY
Manor House
Stretton House
BROOKSIDE
KNOB HILL
3
Church Farm
CHURCH HILL
PO
THE PADDOCKS
MANOR DR
Ryton Wood
FINEACRE LA
The White House Farm
72
Stretton Lodge Farm
OXFORD RD
Bull & Butcher Farm
Forest Wood
Bull & Butcher Wood
Park Farm
CV23
2
Burnthurst Farm
Starchway Wood
Sports Ground
Convent
Springfield
Princethorpe Great Wood
Princethorpe Coll
71
NUNWOOD LA
SHEEP DIP LA
PO
FOSSE CRES
B4453
Our Lady's RC Prim Sch
LEAMINGTON RD B4453
Princethorpe
The Bungalow Farm
B4455
PH
RUGBY RD
B4453
Caravan Site
The Woodhouse Hotel
B4455
Duke's Wood
Works
1
Hill Farm
B4453
CV33
CV33
Stoneyford Barn
Windmill Hill
B4455
BARN LA
A423
70
38
A
39
B
40
C

80
98

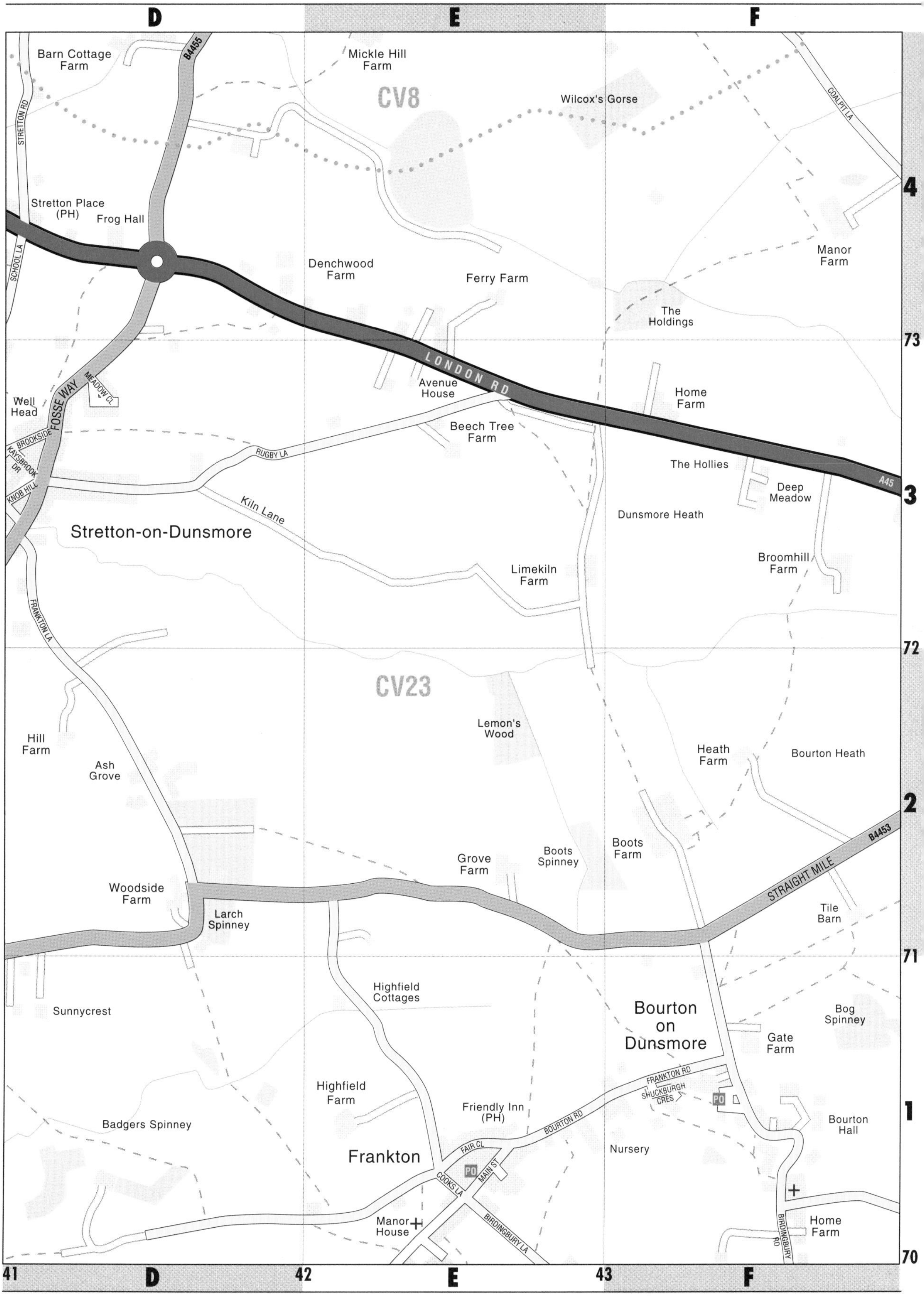
D
E
F
Barn Cottage Farm
Mickle Hill Farm
CV8
Wilcox's Gorse
B4455
STRETTON RD
COALPIT LA
Stretton Place (PH)
Frog Hall
SCHOOL LA
Denchwood Farm
Ferry Farm
Manor Farm
The Holdings
LONDON RD
Avenue House
Home Farm
MEADOW CL
Well Head
FOSSE WAY
BROOKSIDE
KAYSBROOK DR
KNOB HILL
Beech Tree Farm
RUGBY LA
The Hollies
Deep Meadow
A45
Kiln Lane
Dunsmore Heath
Stretton-on-Dunsmore
Limekiln Farm
Broomhill Farm
FRANKTON LA
CV23
Lemon's Wood
Hill Farm
Ash Grove
Heath Farm
Bourton Heath
B4453
STRAIGHT MILE
Woodside Farm
Grove Farm
Boots Spinney
Boots Farm
Larch Spinney
Tile Barn
Sunnycrest
Highfield Cottages
Bourton on Dunsmore
Bog Spinney
Gate Farm
FRANKTON RD
SHUCKBURGH CRES
PO
Highfield Farm
Friendly Inn (PH)
BOURTON RD
Bourton Hall
Badgers Spinney
FAIR CL
Frankton
Nursery
MAIN ST
COOKS LA
Manor House
BIRDINGBURY LA
BIRDINGBURY RD
Home Farm
4
73
3
72
2
71
1
70
41
42
43

115
98

97
81

A
B
C
4
73
3
72
2
71
1
45
46
Lawford Heath
Lawford Heath Farm
Rose Grove Farm
LAWFORD HEATH IND EST
Works
North Lodge Farm
Nursery
COALPIT LA
LAWFORD HEATH LA
THE RYELANDS
Reservoir
CV22
A4071
Wolston Grange
THE CRESCENT
Potford's Dam Farm
Cawston Farm
Cawston Spinney
A45
Park Farm
South Lodge Farm
Blue Boar Farm
Nursery
LONDON RD
DUNCHURCH TRAD EST
Station Farm
B4453
Motel
STRAIGHT MILE
CV23
The Mill House
Northampton Lane
Hotel
CH
COVENTRY RD
B4429
M45
Barnwells Barn Farm
Far Popehill Spinney
Golf Course
Thurlaston
STOCKS LA
THE GARDENS
BEECH DR
MAIN ST
CHURCH WLK
Poultry Farm
BIGGIN HALL LA
Popehill Spinneys
Biggin Hall
PUDDING BAG LA
MOAT CL
Little Mead
Grange Farm
Biggin House
GRAYS ORCHARD
Hill Farm
Thurlaston Grange
Draycote Fields Farm
Draycote Water (Reservoir)
Chapel Farm

97
116

82
100

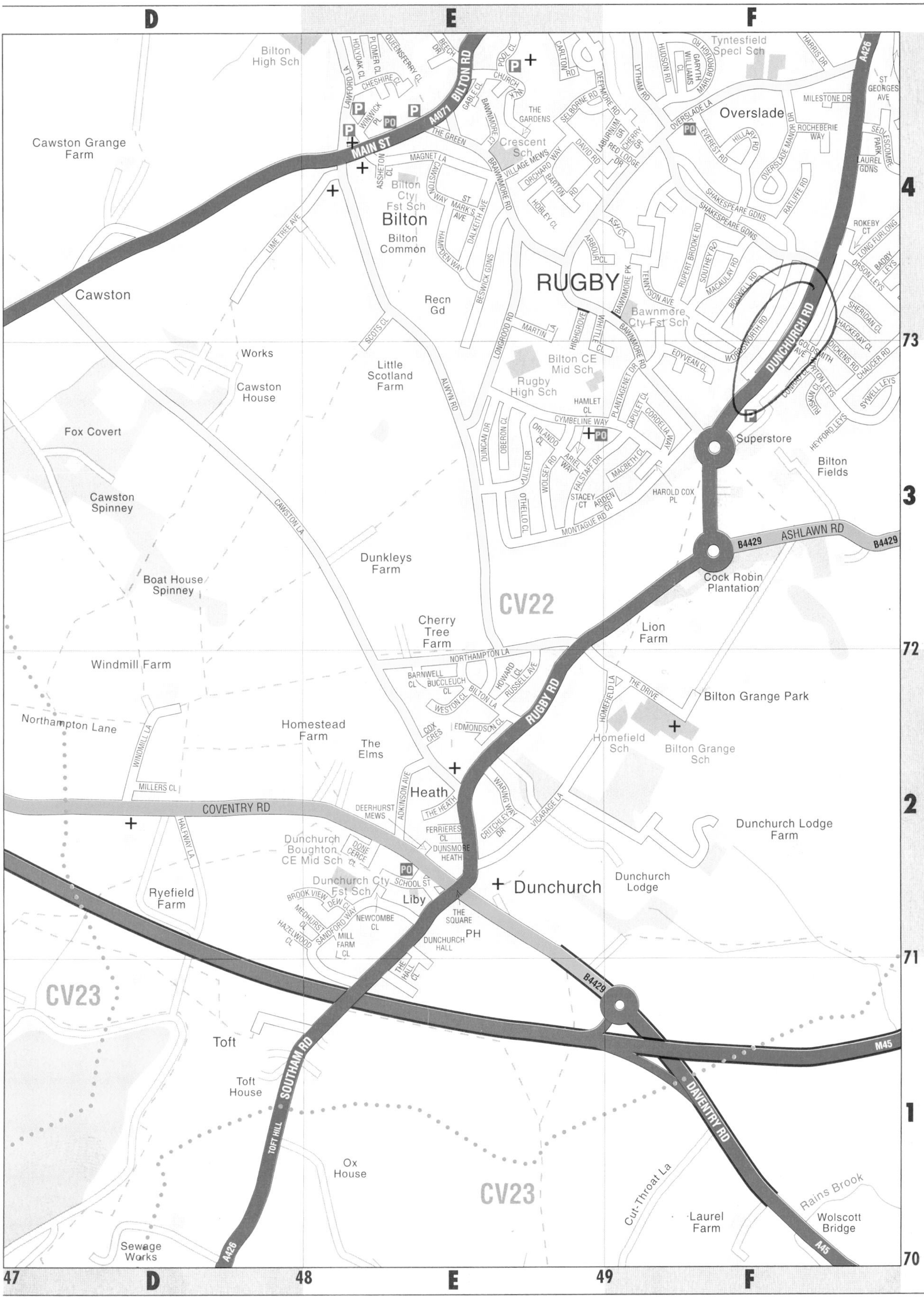

116
100

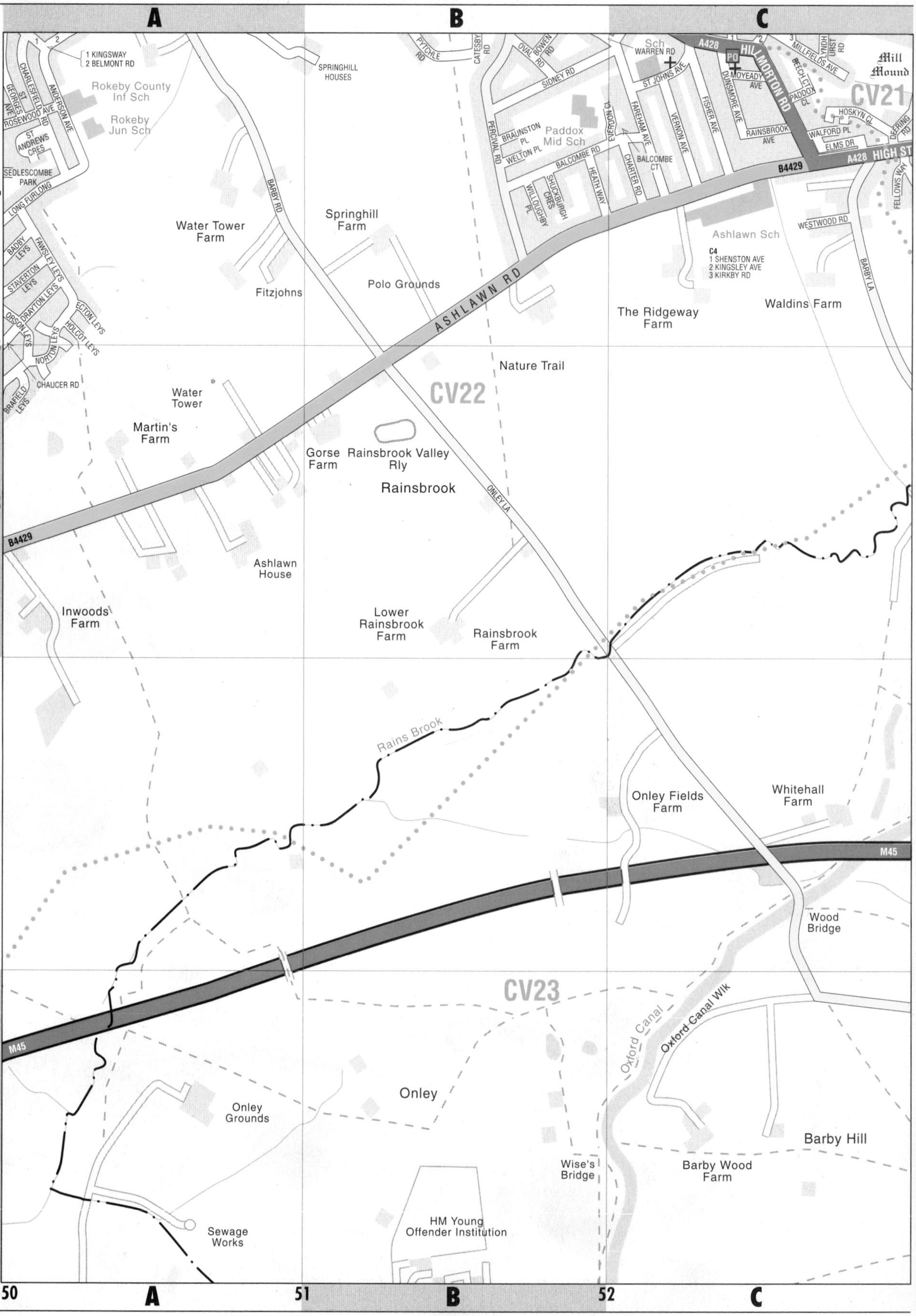
A
B
C
1 KINGSWAY
2 BELMONT RD
SPRINGHILL HOUSES
Rokeby County Inf Sch
Rokeby Jun Sch
ANDERSON AVE
CHARLESFIELD RD
ST GEORGES AVE
ROSEWOOD AVE
ST ANDREWS CRES
SEDLESCOMBE PARK
LONG FURLONG
BADBY LEYS
FAWSLEY LEYS
STAVERTON LEYS
DRAYTON LEYS
ORSON LEYS
ECTON LEYS
HOLCOT LEYS
NORTON LEYS
CHAUCER RD
BRAFIELD LEYS
PYTCHLEY RD
CATESBY RD
OVAL RD
BOWEN RD
SIDNEY RD
Sch
WARREN RD
A428
HILLMORTON RD
PO
ST JOHNS AVE
MOYEADY AVE
DUNSMORE AVE
FISHER AVE
VERNON AVE
FAREHAM AVE
EVERTON CL
Paddox Mid Sch
PERCIVAL RD
BRAUNSTON PL
WELTON PL
BALCOMBE RD
BALCOMBE CT
CHARTER RD
HEATH WAY
SHUCKBURGH CRES
WILLOUGHBY PL
RAINSBROOK AVE
MILLFIELDS AVE
BEECH CT
PADDOX CL
HOSKYN CL
WALFORD PL
ELMS DR
DEERING RD
HIGH ST
Mill Mound
CV21
B4429
FELLOWS WAY
WESTWOOD RD
Ashlawn Sch
C4
1 SHENSTON AVE
2 KINGSLEY AVE
3 KIRKBY RD
BARBY LA
Waldins Farm
The Ridgeway Farm
4
BARBY RD
Water Tower Farm
Springhill Farm
Fitzjohns
Polo Grounds
ASHLAWN RD
73
Nature Trail
CV22
Water Tower
Martin's Farm
Gorse Farm
Rainsbrook Valley Rly
Rainsbrook
ONLEY LA
3
B4429
Ashlawn House
Inwoods Farm
Lower Rainsbrook Farm
Rainsbrook Farm
72
Rains Brook
2
Onley Fields Farm
Whitehall Farm
M45
Wood Bridge
71
CV23
Oxford Canal
Oxford Canal Wlk
M45
Onley
Onley Grounds
1
Barby Hill
Wise's Bridge
Barby Wood Farm
HM Young Offender Institution
Sewage Works
70
50
A
51
B
52
C

84

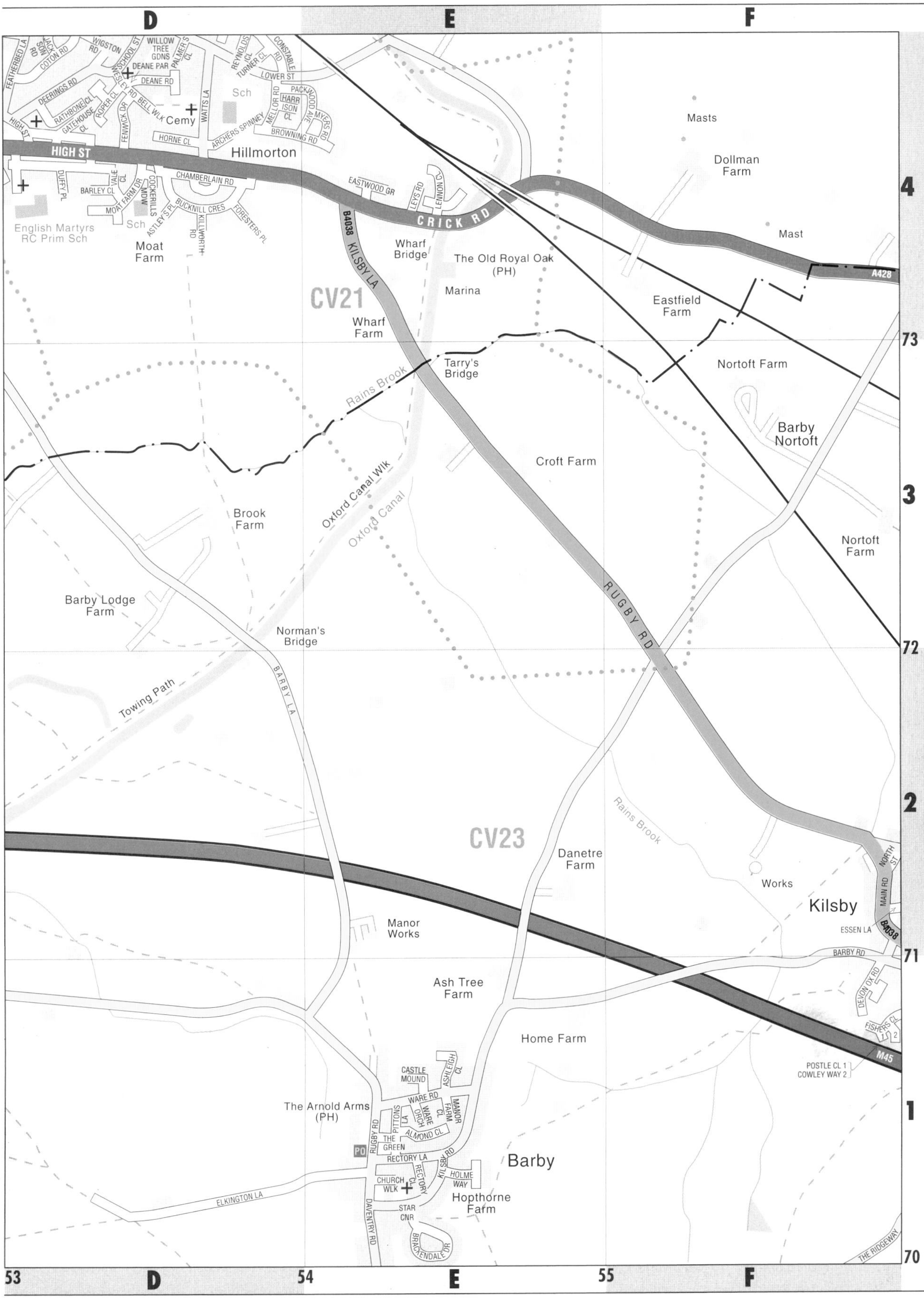
D
E
F
FEATHERBED LA
JACKSON RD
COTON RD
WIGSTON RD
SCHOOL ST
WILLOW TREE GDNS
PALMER'S CL
REYNOLDS CL
TURNER CL
CONSTABLE RD
LOWER ST
DEANE PAR
DEANE RD
DEERINGS RD
RATHBONE CL
GATEHOUSE CL
ROPER CL
WESLEY RD
BELL WLK
FENWICK DR
Cemy
WATTS LA
Sch
ARCHERS SPINNEY
MELLOR RD
HARRISON CL
PACKWOOD AVE
MYERS RD
BROWNING RD
HIGH ST
HORNE CL
Hillmorton
HIGH ST
DUFFY PL
BARLEY CL
VALE CL
MOAT FARM DR
COCKERILLS MDW
CHAMBERLAIN RD
BUCKNILL CRES
ASTLEY'S PL
KILLWORTH RD
FORESTERS PL
EASTWOOD GR
LEYS RD
LENNON CL
English Martyrs RC Prim Sch
Sch
Moat Farm
B4038
KILSBY LA
CRICK RD
Wharf Bridge
The Old Royal Oak (PH)
Marina
CV21
Wharf Farm
Masts
Dollman Farm
Mast
A428
Eastfield Farm
Nortoft Farm
Tarry's Bridge
Rains Brook
Barby Nortoft
Croft Farm
Oxford Canal Wlk
Oxford Canal
Brook Farm
Nortoft Farm
Barby Lodge Farm
Norman's Bridge
RUGBY RD
BARBY LA
Towing Path
Rains Brook
CV23
Danetre Farm
Works
NORTH ST
MAIN RD
Kilsby
ESSEN LA
B4038
Manor Works
BARBY RD
Ash Tree Farm
DEVON OX RD
FISHERS CL
M45
Home Farm
POSTLE CL 1
COWLEY WAY 2
CASTLE MOUND
ASHLEIGH CL
WARE RD
MANOR FARM CL
The Arnold Arms (PH)
PITTONS LA
WARE ORCH
ALMOND CL
RUGBY RD
THE GREEN
PO
RECTORY LA
KILSBY RD
Barby
HOLME WAY
CHURCH WLK
RECTORY CL
Hopthorne Farm
ELKINGTON LA
STAR CNR
DAVENTRY RD
BRACKENDALE DR
THE RIDGEWAY
4
73
3
72
2
71
1
70
53
54
55

117

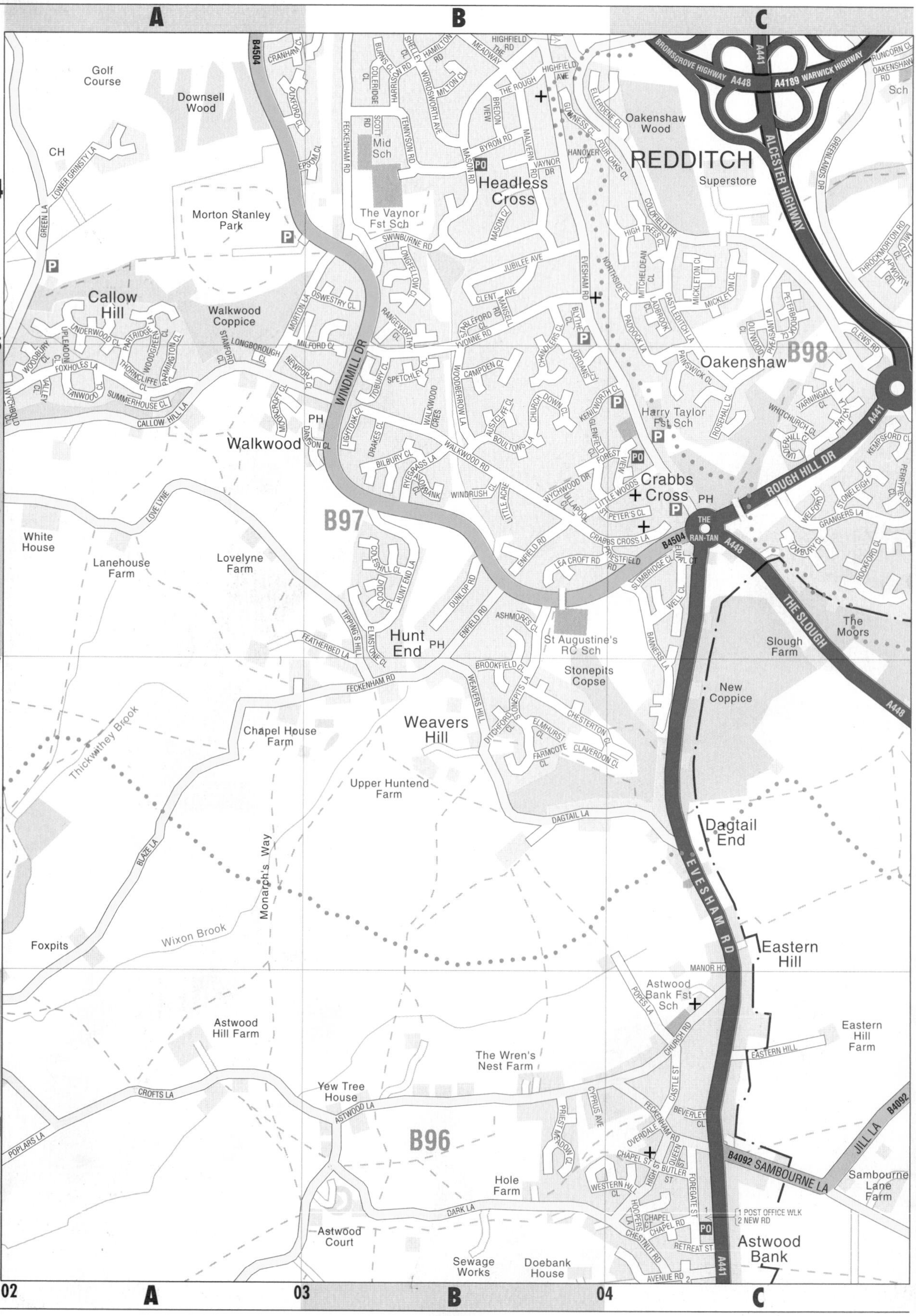
A
B
C
4
65
3
64
2
63
1
62
02
03
04
Golf Course
Downsell Wood
CH
Morton Stanley Park
Callow Hill
Walkwood Coppice
Walkwood
PH
White House
Lanehouse Farm
Lovelyne Farm
B97
Hunt End
Weavers Hill
Chapel House Farm
Upper Huntend Farm
Thickwithey Brook
Monarch's Way
Wixon Brook
Foxpits
Astwood Hill Farm
Yew Tree House
B96
Hole Farm
Astwood Court
Sewage Works
Doebank House
The Wren's Nest Farm
Mid Sch
The Vaynor Fst Sch
Headless Cross
REDDITCH
Superstore
Oakenshaw Wood
Oakenshaw
B98
Harry Taylor Fst Sch
Crabbs Cross
THE RAN-TAN
St Augustine's RC Sch
Stonepits Copse
Slough Farm
The Moors
New Coppice
Dagtail End
Eastern Hill
Astwood Bank Fst Sch
Eastern Hill Farm
Sambourne Lane Farm
Astwood Bank
B4504
A441
A448
A4189
B4092
WINDMILL DR
ALCESTER HIGHWAY
BROMSGROVE HIGHWAY
WARWICK HIGHWAY
ROUGH HILL DR
THE SLOUGH
EVESHAM RD
B4092 SAMBOURNE LA
JILL LA
FECKENHAM RD
CALLOW HILL LA
LOVE LYNE
FEATHERBED LA
BLAZE LA
DAGTAIL LA
CROFTS LA
POPLARS LA
ASTWOOD LA
DARK LA
CYPRUS AVE
CHURCH RD
CASTLE ST
EASTERN HILL
MANOR HO
1 POST OFFICE WLK
2 NEW RD

118

112

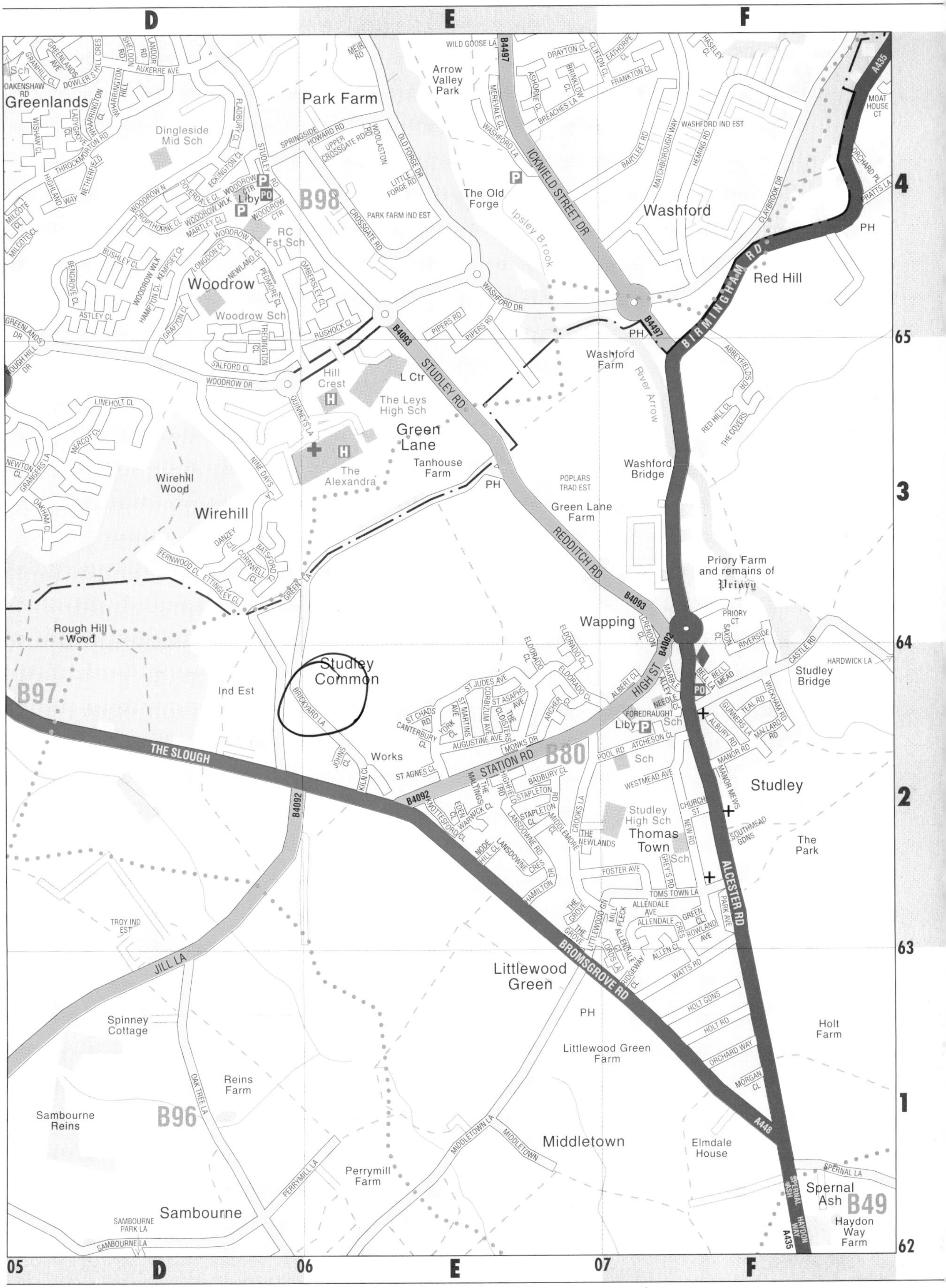
D
E
F
4
65
3
64
2
63
1
62
05
06
07
Greenlands
Park Farm
Arrow Valley Park
Dingleside Mid Sch
Liby
RC Fst Sch
Woodrow
Woodrow Sch
B98
The Old Forge
Ipsley Brook
Washford
Red Hill
PH
MOAT HOUSE CT
WASHFORD IND EST
PARK FARM IND EST
ICKNIELD STREET DR
BIRMINGHAM RD
B4497
A435
B4093
STUDLEY RD
Hill Crest
L Ctr
The Leys High Sch
Green Lane
Tanhouse Farm
The Alexandra
Washford Farm
River Arrow
Washford Bridge
POPLARS TRAD EST
Green Lane Farm
REDDITCH RD
Wirehill Wood
Wirehill
Rough Hill Wood
Priory Farm and remains of Priory
Wapping
B4092
HIGH ST
Studley Common
Ind Est
B97
THE SLOUGH
Works
STATION RD
B80
Sch
Studley Bridge
Studley
Studley High Sch
Thomas Town
The Park
ALCESTER RD
TROY IND EST
JILL LA
BROMSGROVE RD
Littlewood Green
Littlewood Green Farm
Spinney Cottage
Holt Farm
Reins Farm
Sambourne Reins
B96
Middletown
Elmdale House
Perrymill Farm
Sambourne
Spernal Ash
B49
Haydon Way Farm
A448
SPERNAL LA

118
112

114
92

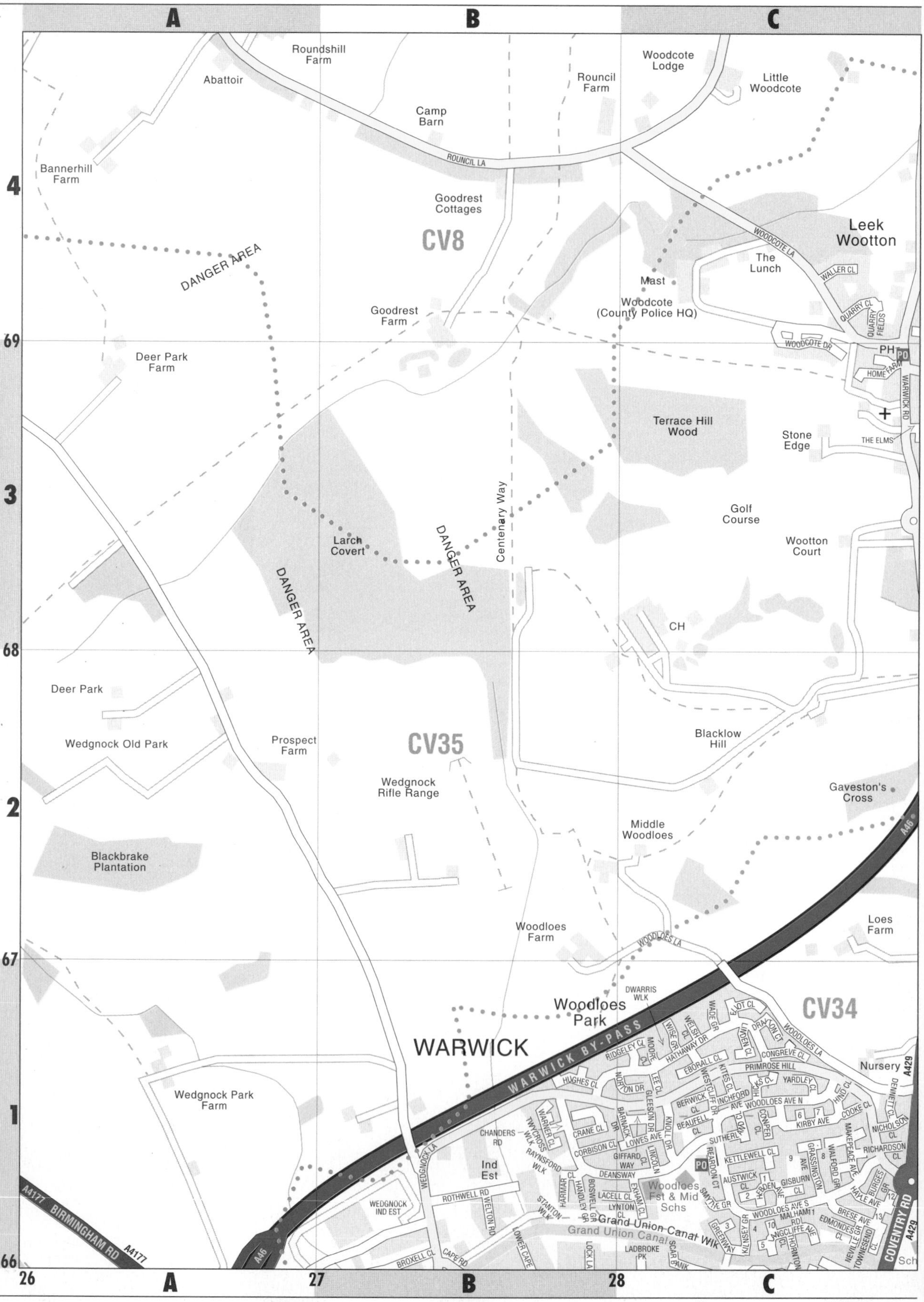

114
108

C1
1 NEWSHOLME CL
2 ADDINGHAM CL
3 WATSON CL
4 RYLSTONE WAY
5 KILDWICK WAY
6 SHELDON GR
7 WEALE GR
8 HETTON CL
9 BUCKDEN CL
10 LEYBURN CL
11 ARNCLIFFE WAY
12 HUDDISDON CL
13 PHILLIPPES RD

93
106

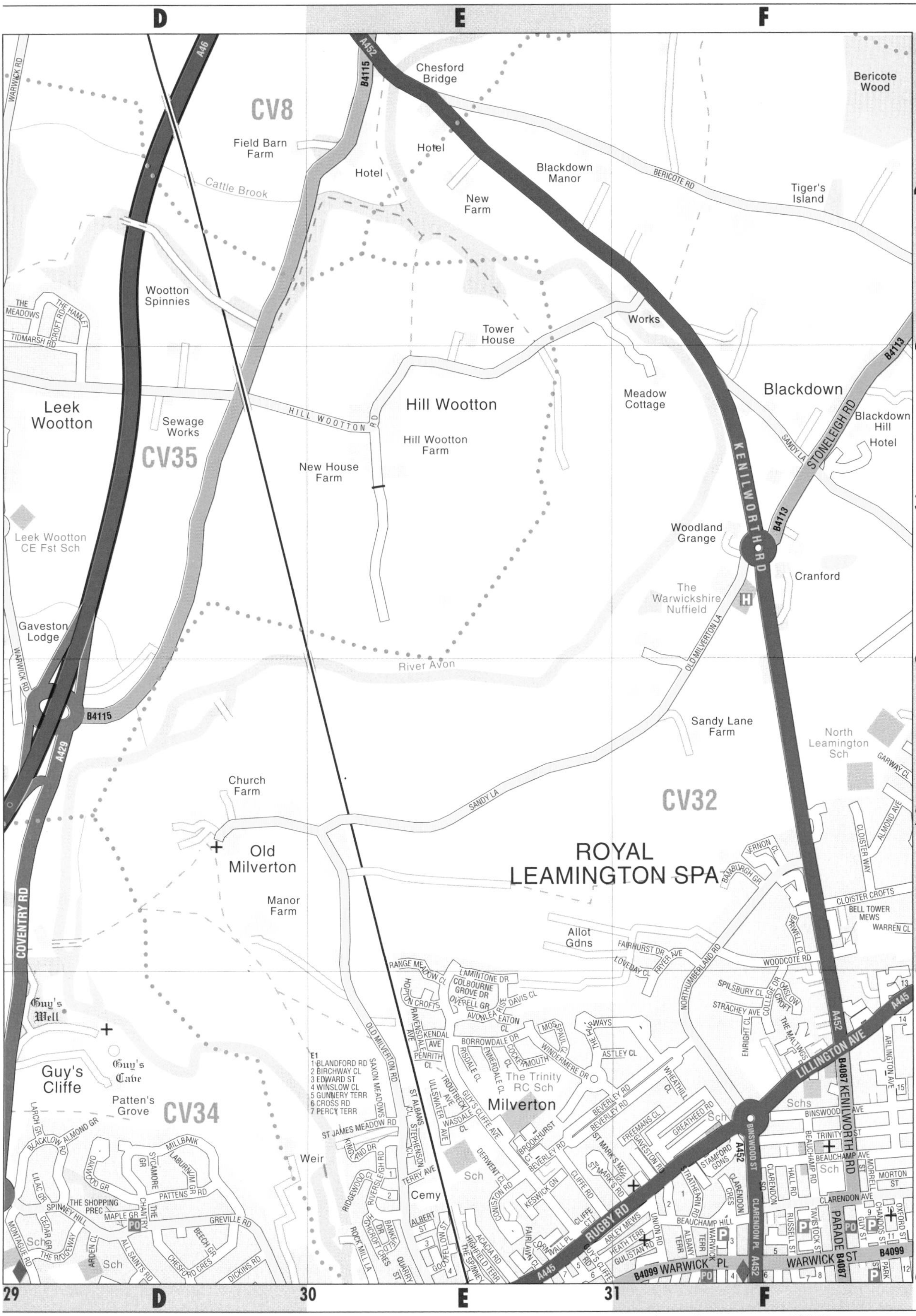
D
E
F
4
69
3
68
2
67
1
66
29
30
31
CV8
CV35
CV32
CV34
A46
A452
B4115
B4113
A429
A445
B4087
B4099
Chesford Bridge
Field Barn Farm
Hotel
Hotel
Cattle Brook
Blackdown Manor
BERICOTE RD
Bericote Wood
Tiger's Island
New Farm
Wootton Spinnies
THE MEADOWS
THE HAMLET
CROFT RD
TIDMARSH RD
Tower House
Works
Leek Wootton
Sewage Works
HILL WOOTTON RD
Hill Wootton
Hill Wootton Farm
New House Farm
Meadow Cottage
Blackdown
Blackdown Hill Hotel
SANDY LA
STONELEIGH RD
KENILWORTH RD
Woodland Grange
Cranford
The Warwickshire Nuffield
Leek Wootton CE Fst Sch
Gaveston Lodge
WARWICK RD
River Avon
OLD MILVERTON LA
Sandy Lane Farm
North Leamington Sch
GARWAY CL
Church Farm
SANDY LA
Old Milverton
ROYAL LEAMINGTON SPA
Manor Farm
COVENTRY RD
CLOISTER WAY
ALMOND AVE
VERNON CL
BAMBURGH GR
CLOISTER CROFTS
BELL TOWER MEWS
WARREN CL
BARWELL CL
Allot Gdns
FAIRHURST DR
FRYER AVE
LOVEDAY CL
NORTHUMBERLAND RD
WOODCOTE RD
RANGE MEADOW CL
LAMINTONE DR
COLBOURNE GROVE DR
OVERELL GR
DAVIS CL
HOPTON CROFTS
RAVENSDALE AVE
AVONLEA RISE
EATON CL
KENDAL AVE
PENRITH CL
BORROWDALE DR
MOSSPAUL CL
WINDERMERE DR
THE FAIRWAYS
ASTLEY CL
SPILSBURY CL
COLLEGE DR
ONSLOW CROFT
STRACHEY AVE
ENRIGHT CL
THE MALTINGS
LILLINGTON AVE
KENILWORTH RD
ARLINGTON AVE
Guy's Well
Guy's Cave
Guy's Cliffe
Patten's Grove
E1
1 BLANDFORD RD
2 BIRCHWAY CL
3 EDWARD ST
4 WINSLOW CL
5 GUNNERY TERR
6 CROSS RD
7 PERCY TERR
OLD MILVERTON RD
SAXON MEADOWS
ST ALBANS CL
STEPHENSON CL
TROUTBECK AVE
ULLSWATER AVE
RYSDALE CL
ENNERDALE CL
COCKERMOUTH CL
The Trinity RC Sch
Milverton
WHEATHILL CL
BEVERLEY RD
GREATHEED RD
Sch
Schs
BINSWOOD AVE
TRINITY ST
BEAUCHAMP AVE
BEAUCHAMP RD
MORRELL ST
MORTON ST
LARCH GR
ALMOND GR
BLACKLOW RD
MILLBANK
LABURNUM GR
SYCAMORE GR
OAKWOOD GR
LILAC GR
THE SHOPPING PREC
SPINNEY HILL
MAPLE GR
CHANTRY
PATTENS RD
ST JAMES MEADOW RD
KING AND DR
GUY'S CLIFFE AVE
DERWENT CL
BROOKHURST CT
BEVERLEY RD
ST MARK'S MEWS
FREEMANS CL
GAVESTON RD
STAMFORD GDNS
A452
BINSWOOD ST
CLARENDON SQ
CLARENDON CRES
HALL RD
CLARENDON AVE
Weir
RIDGEWOOD CL
RIVERSLEIGH RD
TERRY AVE
Cemy
Sch
CONISTON RD
KESWICK GN
CLIFFE RD
ST MARK'S RD
RUGBY RD
STRATHEARN RD
BEAUCHAMP HILL
CLARENDON PL
RUSSELL ST
TAVISTOCK ST
PARADE
GUY ST
CHANDOS ST
OXFORD ST
CEDAR GR
GREVILLE RD
BEECH GR
MONTAGUE RD
THE RIDGEWAY
ARDEN CL
ALL SAINTS RD
CHESFORD CRES
DICKINS RD
ROCK MILL LA
BANKCROFT CRES
ASHCROFT DR
QUARRY ST
ALBERT ST
GOODFELLOW ST
THE SPINNEY
HIGHFIELD TERR
ACACIA RD
FAIRLAWN CL
CROMWELL PL
GUY'S CLIFFE RD
ARLEY MEWS
HEATH TERR
GULISTAN RD
UNION RD
ALBANY TERR
WARWICK TERR
B4099 WARWICK PL
WARWICK ST
PARK ST
PO
P
H
Sch

109
106

F1
1 MILVERTON CRES
2 MILVERTON CRES W
3 UPPER GROVE ST
4 GROVE ST
5 WATERLOO PL
6 CLARENCE TERR
7 WINDSOR PL
8 BEDFORD ST
9 GUY PL W
10 GUY PL E
11 OXFORD ROW
12 KENILWORTH ST
13 RIPLINGHAM
14 ARLINGTON MEWS
15 BINSWOOD MANS

105
94

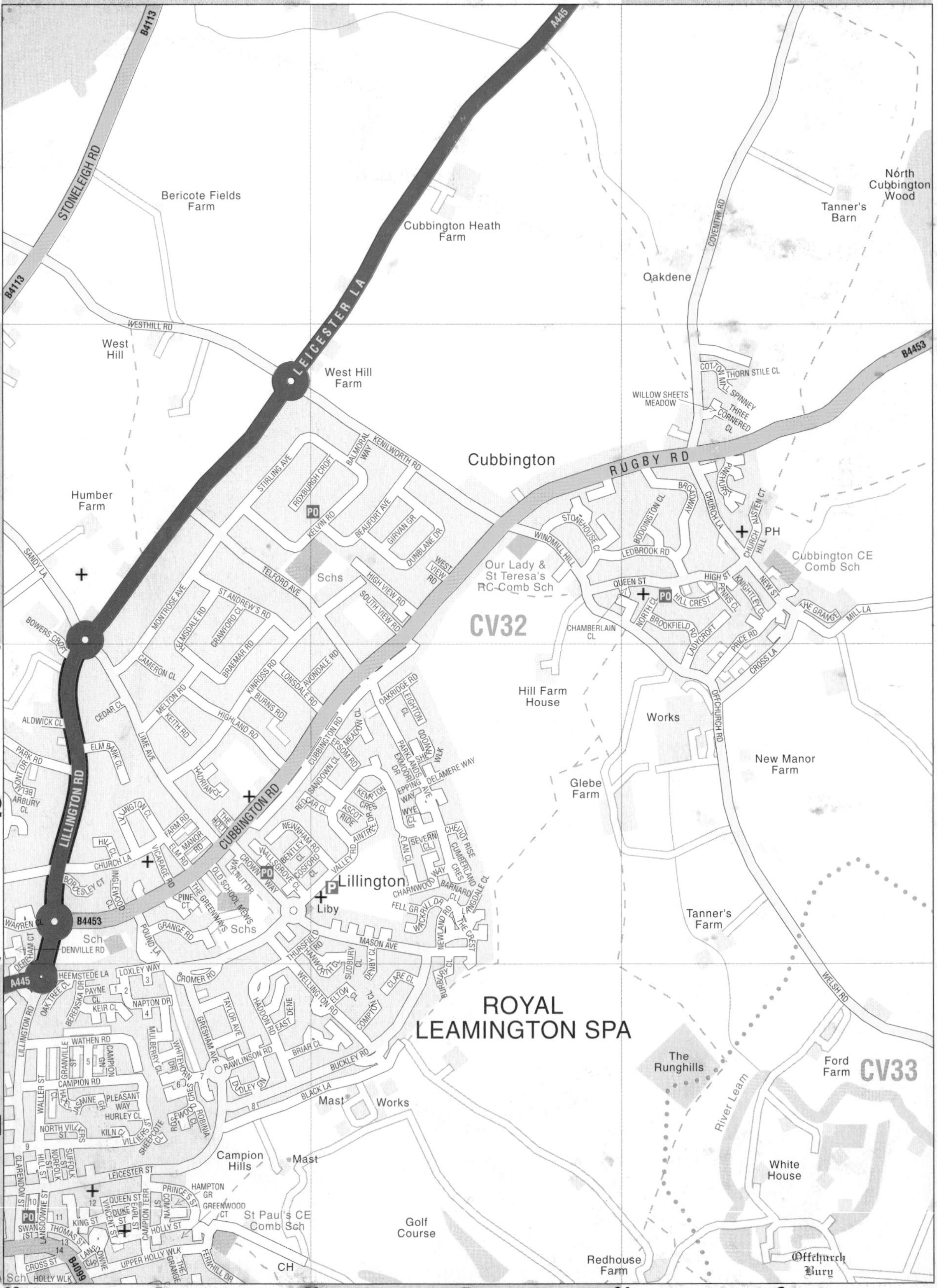
A
B
C
4
3
2
1
69
68
67
66
32
33
34
Bericote Fields Farm
Cubbington Heath Farm
North Cubbington Wood
Tanner's Barn
Oakdene
West Hill
West Hill Farm
Humber Farm
Cubbington
Our Lady & St Teresa's RC Comb Sch
Cubbington CE Comb Sch
CV32
Schs
Hill Farm House
Works
New Manor Farm
Glebe Farm
Lillington
Liby
Tanner's Farm
ROYAL LEAMINGTON SPA
The Runghills
Ford Farm
CV33
River Leam
White House
Mast
Works
Campion Hills
Golf Course
St Paul's CE Comb Sch
Redhouse Farm
Offchurch Bury
CH
PH
PO
STONELEIGH RD
B4113
A445
LEICESTER LA
WESTHILL RD
RUGBY RD
B4453
COVENTRY RD
OFFCHURCH RD
WELSH RD
CUBBINGTON RD
LILLINGTON RD
KENILWORTH RD
TELFORD AVE
HIGHLAND RD
BUCKLEY RD
BLACK LA
LEICESTER ST
MILL LA
THORN STILE CL
WILLOW SHEETS MEADOW
THREE CORNERED CL
QUEEN ST
HIGH ST
CHURCH LA
WINDMILL HILL
CHAMBERLAIN CL
CROSS LA
PRICE RD
MASON AVE
CHURCH LA
UPPER HOLLY WLK
HOLLY WLK
CROSS ST
B4099

A
B
C

105
110

A1
1 STOCKTON GR
2 WHITACRE RD
3 SHUCKBURGH GR
4 HELLIDON CL
5 BROWNLOW ST
6 CHESTNUT SQ
7 GRESHAM PL
8 MARSTON CL
9 LOWER VILLIERS ST
10 LANSDOWNE RD
11 KENNEDY SQ
12 ST PAUL'S SQ
13 LANSDOWNE CRES
14 WILLES RD

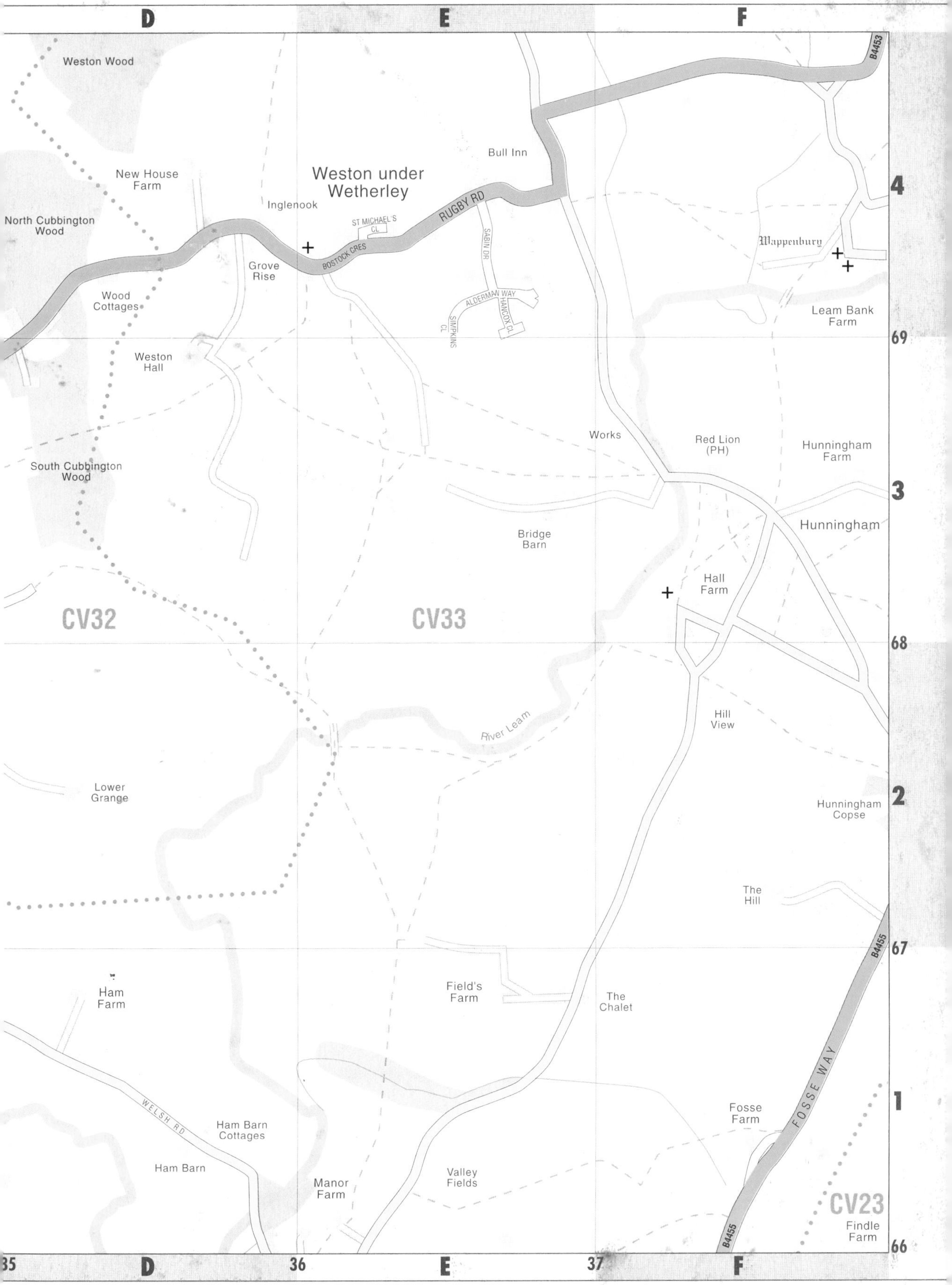
D
E
F
Weston Wood
New House Farm
North Cubbington Wood
Weston under Wetherley
Bull Inn
Inglenook
ST MICHAEL'S CL
RUGBY RD
BOSTOCK CRES
SABIN DR
ALDERMAN WAY
HANCOX CL
SIMPKINS CL
Grove Rise
Wood Cottages
Weston Hall
Wappenbury
Leam Bank Farm
B4453
Works
Red Lion (PH)
Hunningham Farm
Hunningham
South Cubbington Wood
Bridge Barn
Hall Farm
CV32
CV33
River Leam
Hill View
Lower Grange
Hunningham Copse
The Hill
B4455
Ham Farm
Field's Farm
The Chalet
FOSSE WAY
Fosse Farm
WELSH RD
Ham Barn Cottages
Ham Barn
Manor Farm
Valley Fields
CV23
Findle Farm
4
69
3
68
2
67
1
66
35
36
37

114
104

C3
1 OLD SQ
2 MARKET PL
3 PUCKERING'S LA
4 GERRARD ST

C4
1 PEMBROKE CL
2 ARUNDEL CL
3 CORNWALL CL
4 CROSS FIELDS RD
5 MULBERRY DR
6 ROWAN DR
7 GAVESTON CL
8 BARTLETT CL
9 ST JOHN'S CT
10 YEOMANRY CL
11 GARDEN CT
12 CROSS ST
13 THE KNIBBS SH CTR
14 CHAPEL ROW
15 JOYCE POOL

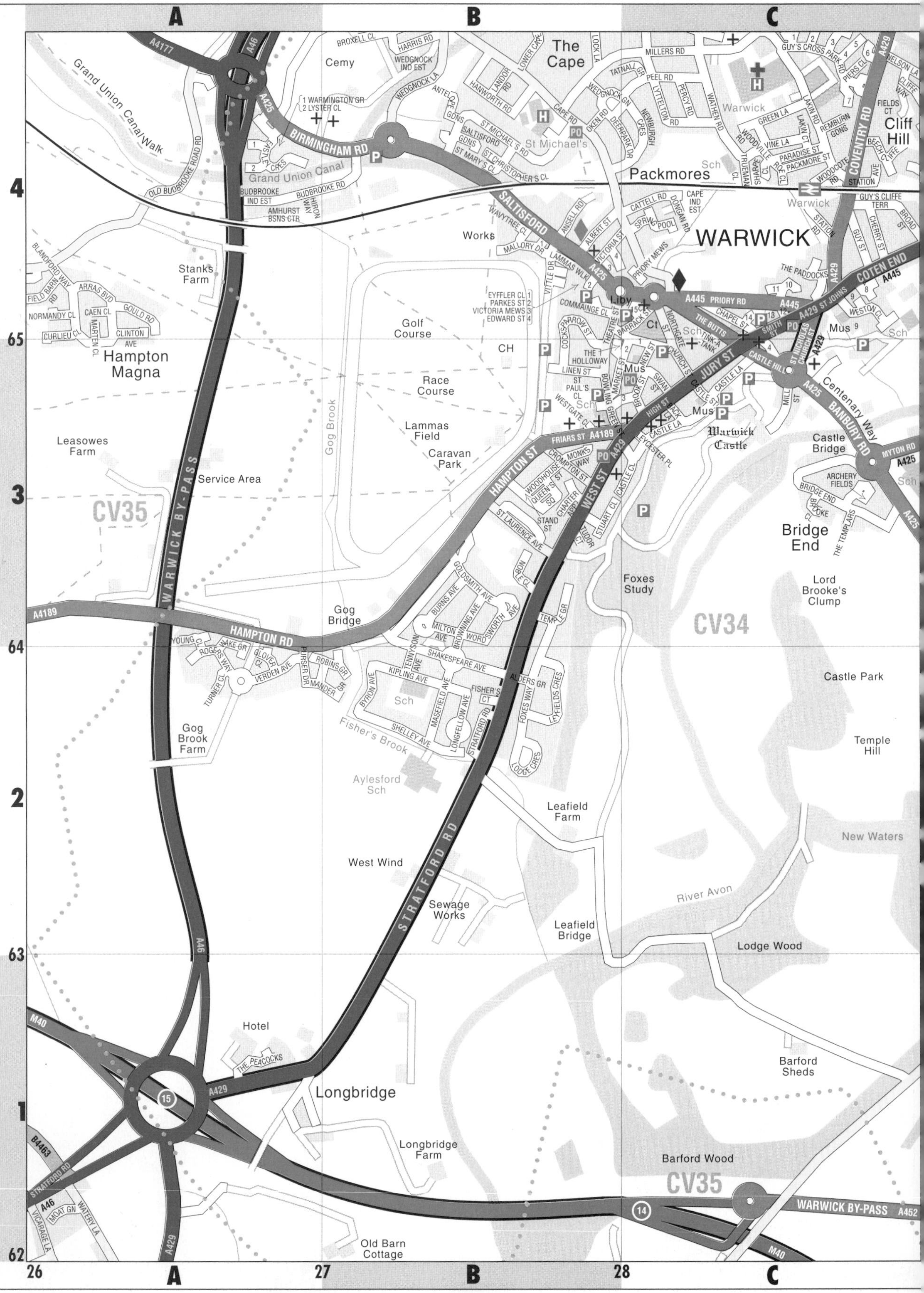

114
122

D4
1 ST EDITH'S GN
2 AUSTIN EDWARDS DR

F4
1 WOODBINE ST
2 NEW BROOK ST
3 SOMERS PL
4 PORTLAND PLACE W
5 POTLAND PLACE E
6 PORTLAND PL
7 ST PETER'S RD
8 SATCHWELL WLK
9 ROSEFIELD WLK
10 ROSEFIELD PL
11 VICTORIA TERR
12 CHURCH WLK
13 SMITH ST
14 BATH PL
15 ABBOTTS ST

105
110

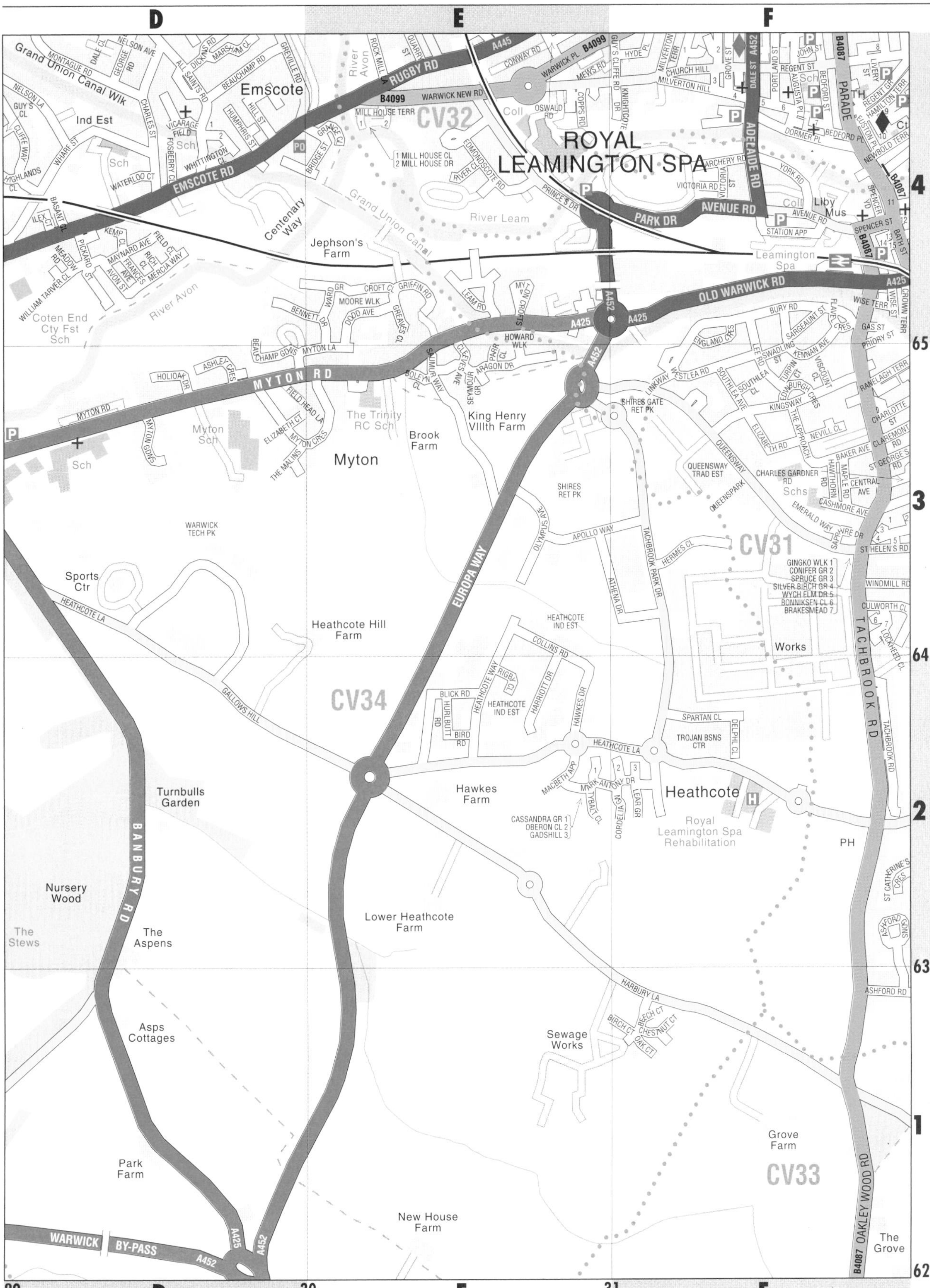

A3
1 GROVE PL
2 PRINCE REGENT CT
3 CHRISTINE LEDGER SQ

A4
1 GLOUCESTER ST
2 REGENT PL
3 CHAPEL ST
4 PACKINGTON PL
5 TOWER ST
6 CUMMING ST

109

A4
7 ALTHORPE IND EST
8 MOSS ST
9 BAXTER CT
10 VICTORIA BSNS CTR

106

A4
11 SOUTHLANDS
12 NORTHCOTE ST
13 RUSHMORE TERR

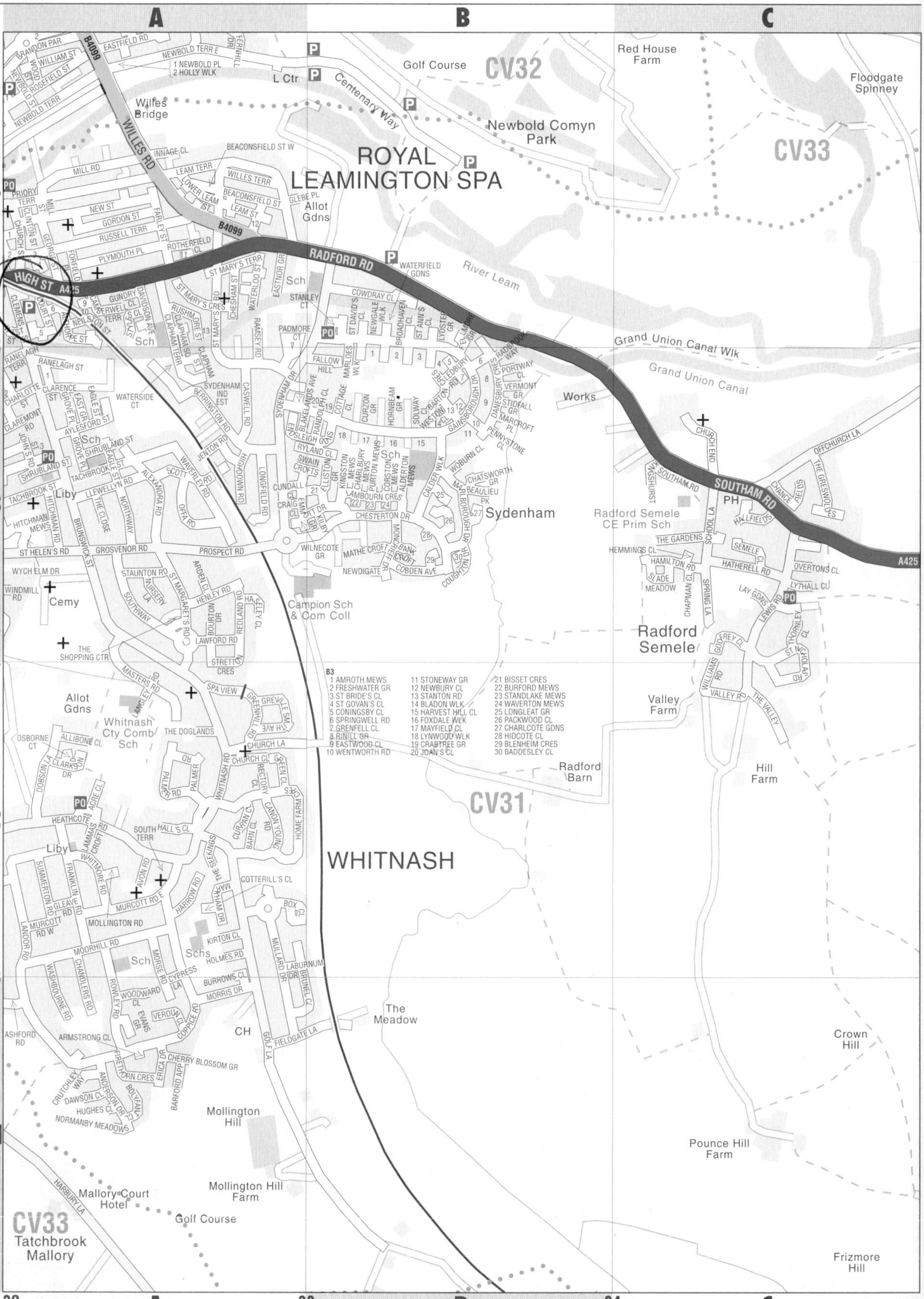

107
115

D E F

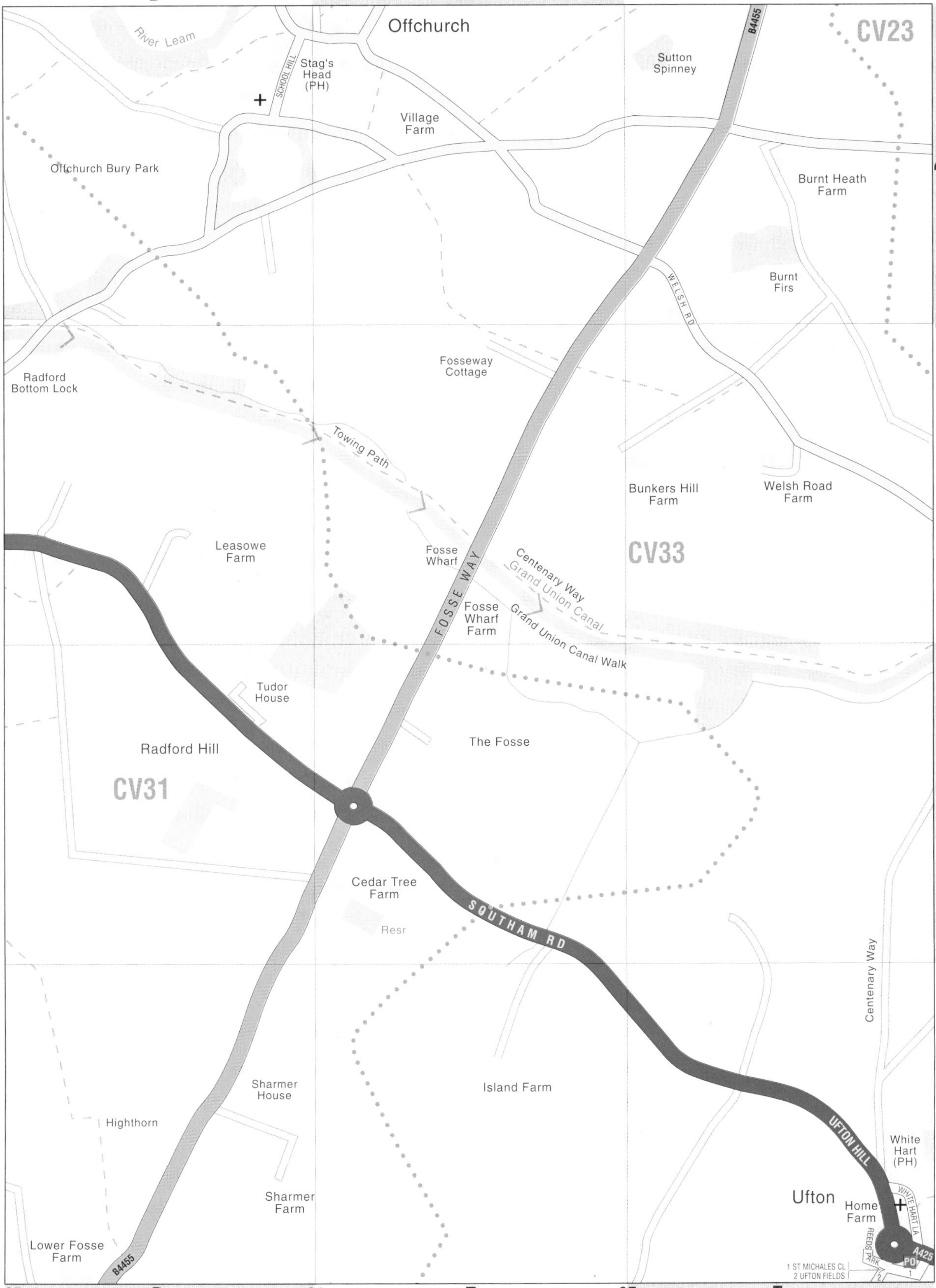

4 65 3 64 2 63 1 62

35 D 36 E 37 F

123
115

86

87

Scale: 1¾ inches to 1 mile
0 ¼ ½ mile
0 250m 500m 750m 1km

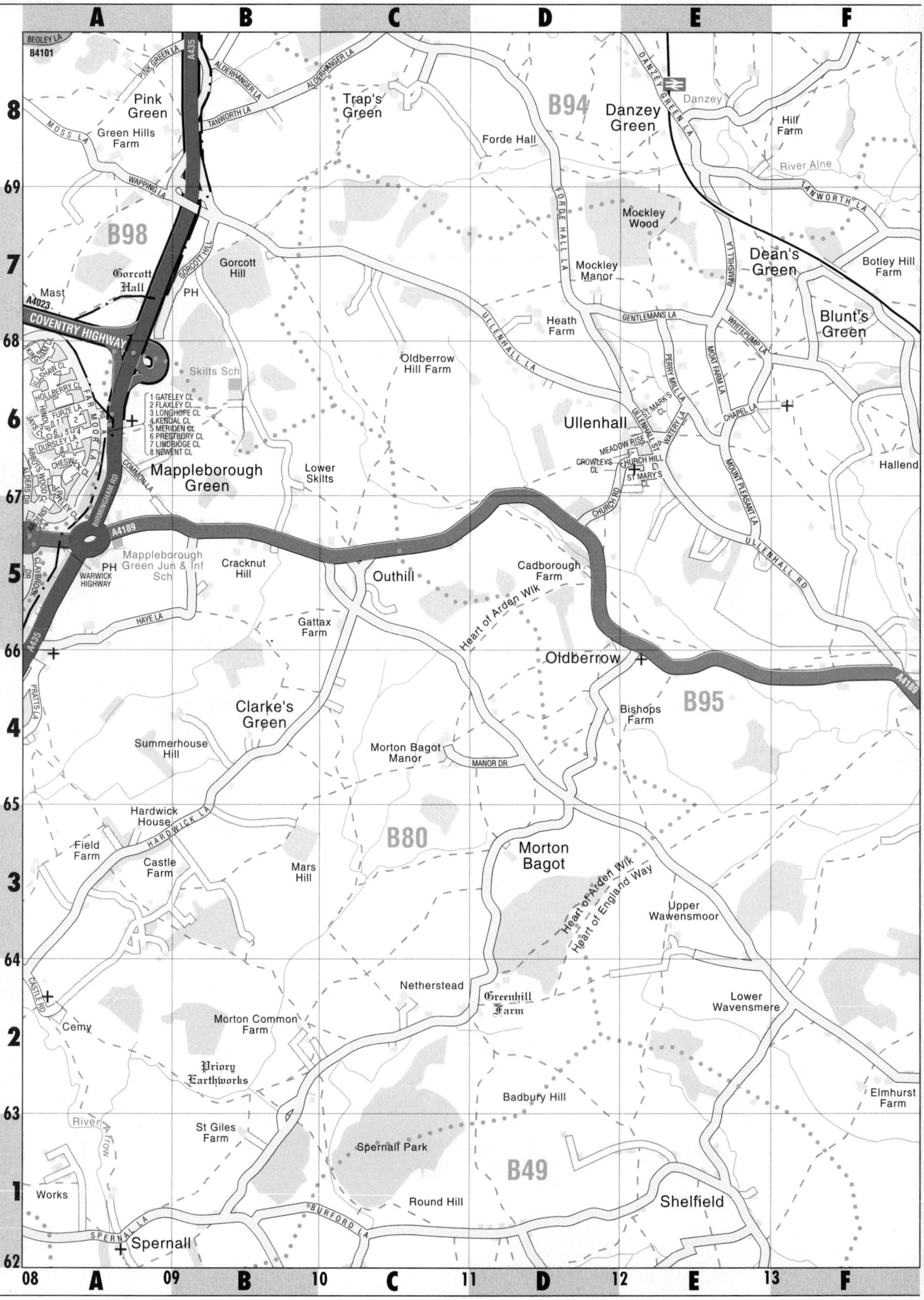
A
B
C
D
E
F
8
69
7
68
6
67
5
66
4
65
3
64
2
63
1
62
08
09
10
11
12
13
BEOLEY LA
B4101
PINK GREEN LA
A435
ALDERHANGER LA
TANWORTH LA
Pink Green
MOSS LA
Green Hills Farm
WAPPING LA
B98
Trap's Green
B94
Danzey Green
Danzey
DANZEY GREEN LA
Hill Farm
River Alne
TANWORTH LA
Forde Hall
FORDE HALL LA
Mockley Wood
Dean's Green
RAMSHILL LA
Botley Hill Farm
Gorcott Hall
GORCOTT HILL
Gorcott Hill
PH
Mast
A4023
COVENTRY HIGHWAY
Mockley Manor
GENTLEMANS LA
Heath Farm
WHITEPUMP LA
Blunt's Green
ULLENHALL LA
Oldberrow Hill Farm
Skilts Sch
PERRY MILL LA
MOAT FARM LA
ST MARK'S CL
CHAPEL LA
HOLLBERRY CL
FURZE LA
FAR MOOR LA
1 GATELEY CL
2 FLAXLEY CL
3 LONGHOPE CL
4 KENDAL CL
5 MERIDEN CL
6 PRESTBURY CL
7 LINDRIDGE CL
8 NEWENT CL
Ullenhall
ULLENHALL ST
WATERY LA
MEADOW RISE
CROWLEYS CL
CHURCH HILL
ST MARY'S CL
MOUNT PLEASANT LA
Hallend
COMMON LA
Mappleborough Green
Lower Skilts
BIRMINGHAM RD
CHURCH RD
A4189
ULLENHALL RD
PH
Mappleborough Green Jun & Inf Sch
Cracknut Hill
Outhill
Cadborough Farm
CLAYBROOK DR
WARWICK HIGHWAY
HAYE LA
Gattax Farm
Heart of Arden Wlk
A435
Oldberrow
PRATTS LA
B95
A4189
Bishops Farm
Clarke's Green
Summerhouse Hill
Morton Bagot Manor
MANOR DR
Hardwick House
HARDWICK LA
Field Farm
Castle Farm
B80
Mars Hill
Morton Bagot
Heart of Arden Wlk
Heart of England Way
Upper Wawensmoor
Netherstead
Greenhill Farm
Lower Wavensmere
CASTLE RD
Cemy
Morton Common Farm
Priory Earthworks
Badbury Hill
Elmhurst Farm
River Arrow
St Giles Farm
Spernall Park
B49
Works
Round Hill
Shelfield
BURFORD LA
SPERNALL LA
Spernall

103

119

Scale: 1¾ inches to 1 mile
0 ¼ ½ mile
0 250m 500m 750m 1km

88 89 114

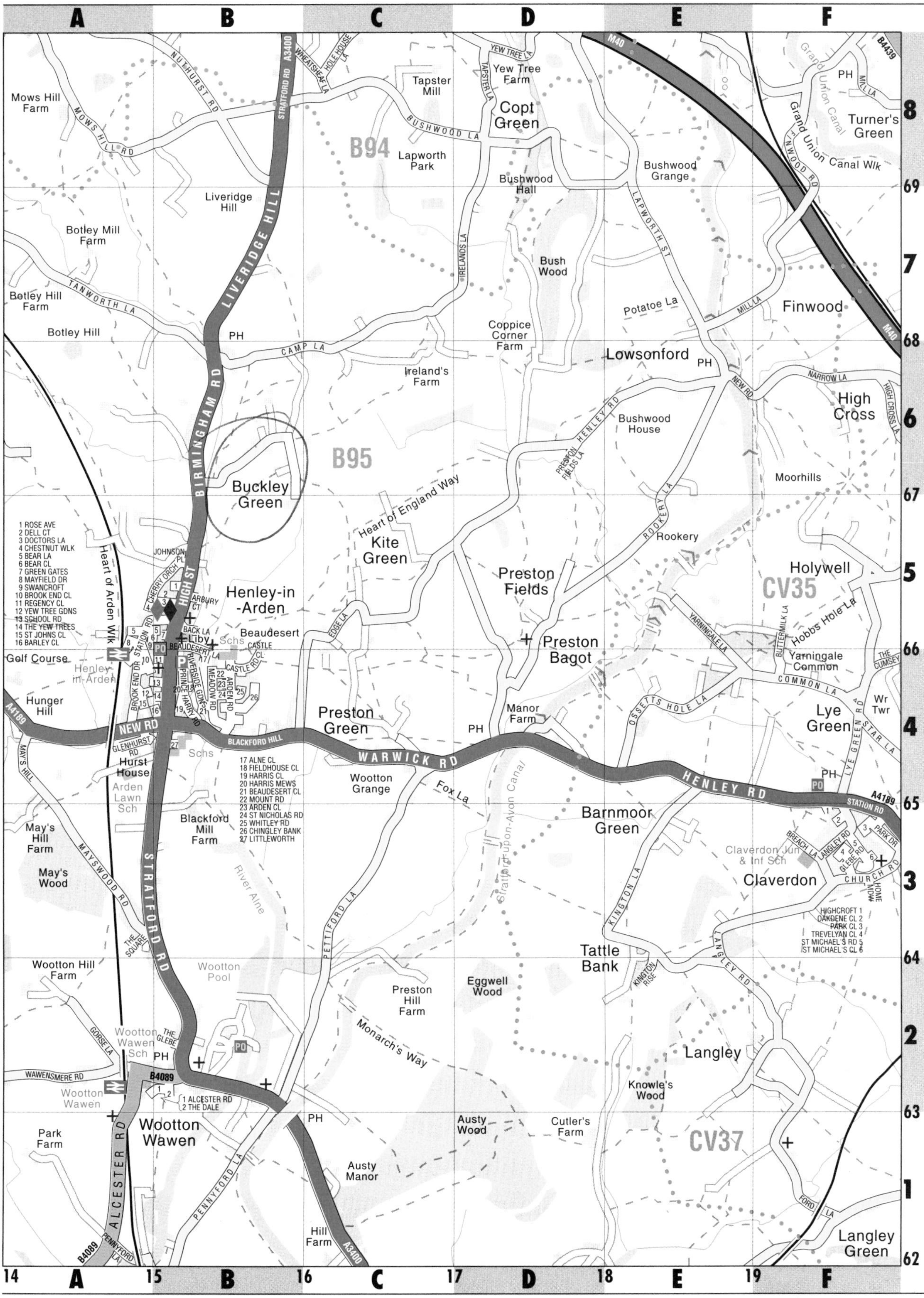

120 114

Scale: 1¾ inches to 1 mile

0 ¼ ½ mile

0 250m 500m 750m 1km

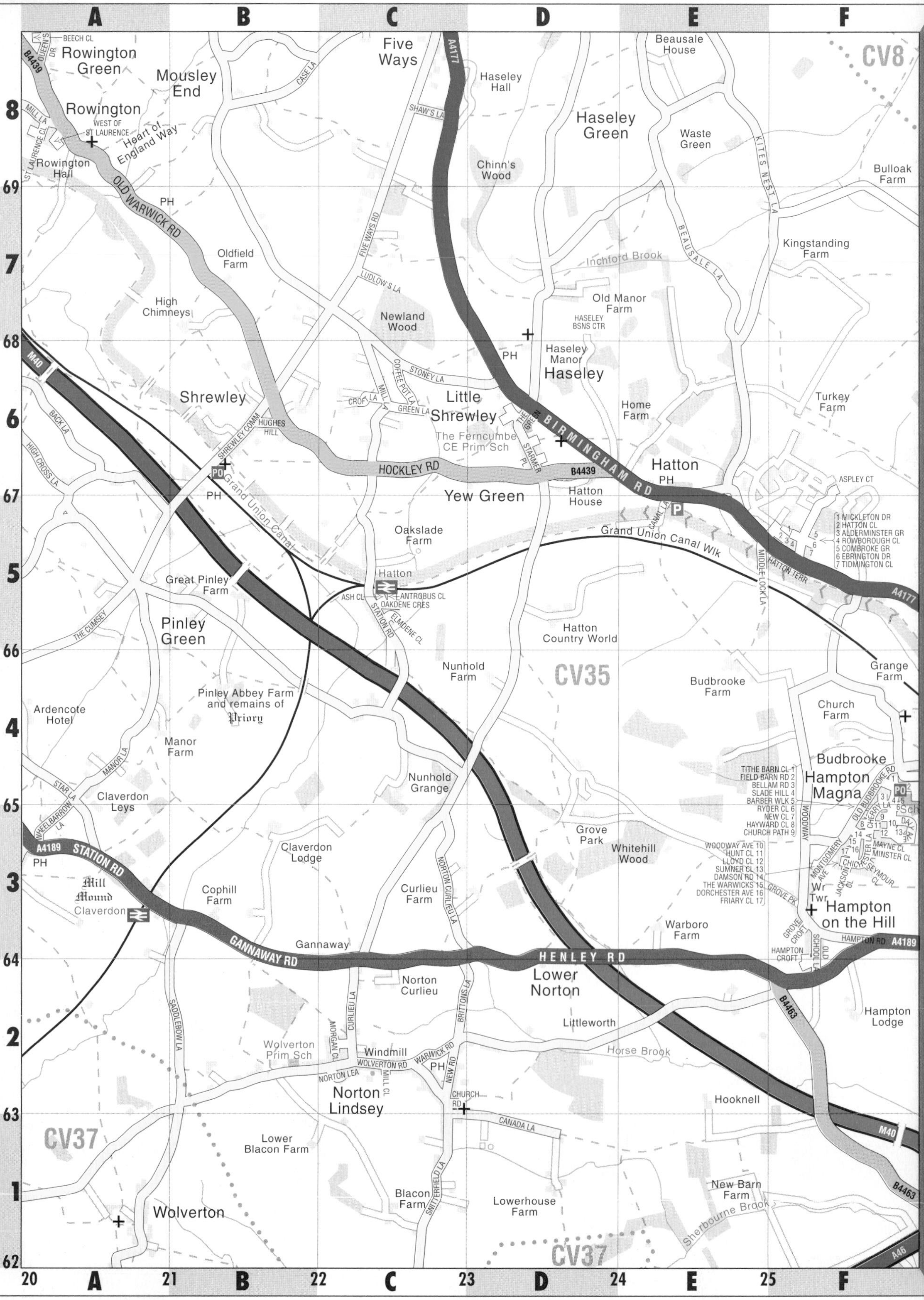
A
B
C
D
E
F
Rowington Green
Mousley End
Rowington
Five Ways
Haseley Hall
Beausale House
CV8
Haseley Green
Waste Green
Rowington Hall
Heart of England Way
OLD WARWICK RD
Chinn's Wood
Bulloak Farm
PH
Oldfield Farm
Kingstanding Farm
Inchford Brook
BEAUSALE LA
KITES NEST LA
High Chimneys
Newland Wood
Old Manor Farm
HASELEY BSNS CTR
Haseley Manor
Haseley
Shrewley
Little Shrewley
Home Farm
Turkey Farm
The Ferncumbe CE Prim Sch
HOCKLEY RD
B4439
BIRMINGHAM RD
Hatton
Yew Green
Hatton House
ASPLEY CT
Grand Union Canal
Grand Union Canal Wlk
Oakslade Farm
1 MICKLETON DR
2 HATTON CL
3 ALDERMINSTER GR
4 ROWBOROUGH CL
5 COMBROKE GR
6 EBRINGTON DR
7 TIDMINGTON CL
Great Pinley Farm
Pinley Green
Hatton Country World
CV35
THE CUMSEY
STATION RD
Nunhold Farm
Budbrooke Farm
Grange Farm
Ardencote Hotel
Pinley Abbey Farm and remains of Priory
Church Farm
Manor Farm
Budbrooke
Hampton Magna
Nunhold Grange
Claverdon Leys
TITHE BARN CL 1
FIELD BARN RD 2
BELLAM RD 3
SLADE HILL 4
BARBER WLK 5
RYDER CL 6
NEW CL 7
HAYWARD CL 8
CHURCH PATH 9
Grove Park
Whitehill Wood
WOODWAY AVE 10
HUNT CL 11
LLOYD CL 12
SUMNER CL 13
DAMSON RD 14
THE WARWICKS 15
DORCHESTER AVE 16
FRIARY CL 17
A4189
STATION RD
Claverdon Lodge
Mill Mound
Claverdon
Cophill Farm
Curlieu Farm
NORTON CURLIEU LA
Warboro Farm
Hampton on the Hill
Gannaway
GANNAWAY RD
HENLEY RD
Lower Norton
Norton Curlieu
Hampton Lodge
Littleworth
Wolverton Prim Sch
Windmill
Horse Brook
Norton Lindsey
Hooknell
CV37
Lower Blacon Farm
CANADA LA
New Barn Farm
Blacon Farm
Lowerhouse Farm
Wolverton
Sherbourne Brook
M40
B4463
A46
A4177
20
21
22
23
24
25
62
63
64
65
66
67
68
69

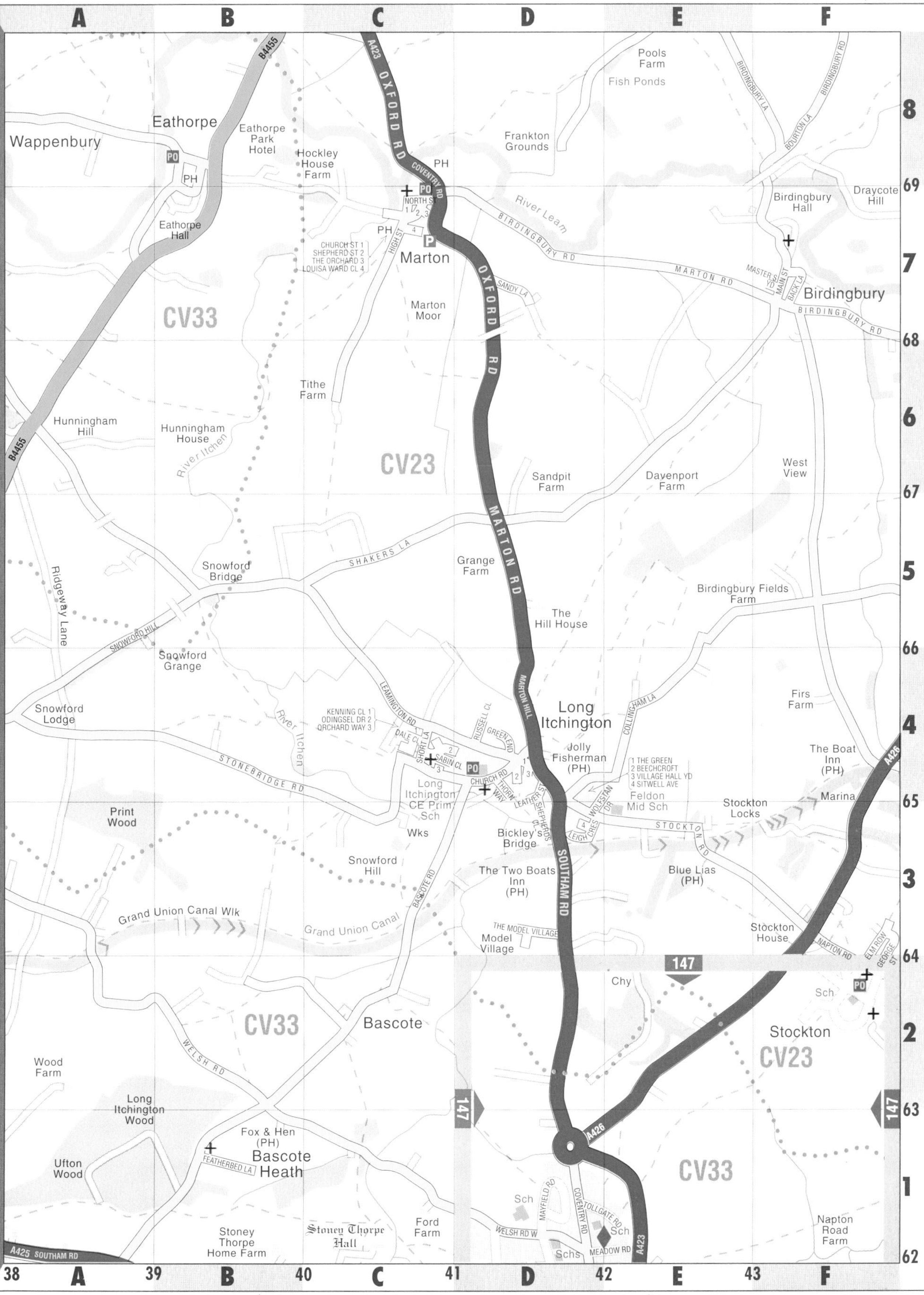
A
B
C
D
E
F
Wappenbury
Eathorpe
PO
PH
Eathorpe Hall
Eathorpe Park Hotel
Hockley House Farm
B4455
A423
OXFORD RD
COVENTRY RD
PH
PO
NORTH ST
PH
HIGH ST
P
Marton
CHURCH ST 1
SHEPHERD ST 2
THE ORCHARD 3
LOUISA WARD CL 4
Pools Farm
Fish Ponds
Frankton Grounds
River Leam
BIRDINGBURY RD
SANDY LA
Marton Moor
BIRDINGBURY LA
BIRDINGBURY RD
BOURTON LA
Draycote Hill
Birdingbury Hall
MARTON RD
MASTERS YD
MAIN ST
BACK LA
Birdingbury
BIRDINGBURY RD
CV33
Tithe Farm
Hunningham Hill
Hunningham House
River Itchen
CV23
Sandpit Farm
Davenport Farm
West View
MARTON RD
SHAKERS LA
Grange Farm
Snowford Bridge
Ridgeway Lane
Birdingbury Fields Farm
The Hill House
SNOWFORD HILL
Snowford Grange
Snowford Lodge
LEAMINGTON RD
KENNING CL 1
ODINGSEL DR 2
ORCHARD WAY 3
RUSSELL CL
GREEN END
MARTON HILL
Long Itchington
COLLINGHAM LA
Firs Farm
River Itchen
STONEBRIDGE RD
DALE CL
SHORT LA
SABIN CL
PO
CHURCH RD
THORN WAY
Jolly Fisherman (PH)
1 THE GREEN
2 BEECHCROFT
3 VILLAGE HALL YD
4 SITWELL AVE
The Boat Inn (PH)
A426
Long Itchington CE Prim Sch
LEATHER ST
SHEPHERDS CL
WOLESTAN DR
Feldon Mid Sch
Stockton Locks
Marina
Print Wood
Wks
Bickley's Bridge
LEIGH CRES
STOCKTON RD
Snowford Hill
BASCOTE RD
The Two Boats Inn (PH)
SOUTHAM RD
Blue Lias (PH)
Grand Union Canal Wlk
Grand Union Canal
THE MODEL VILLAGE
Model Village
Stockton House
NAPTON RD
ELM ROW
GEORGE ST
147
Chy
Sch
PO
CV33
Bascote
Stockton
CV23
WELSH RD
Wood Farm
Long Itchington Wood
147
147
A426
Fox & Hen (PH)
Bascote Heath
FEATHERBED LA
Ufton Wood
CV33
Sch
MAYFIELD RD
COVENTRY RD
TOLLGATE RD
Sch
Stoney Thorpe Home Farm
Stoney Thorpe Hall
Ford Farm
WELSH RD W
Schs
MEADOW RD
A423
Napton Road Farm
A425 SOUTHAM RD
8
69
7
68
6
67
5
66
4
65
3
64
2
63
1
62
38
39
40
41
42
43

For full street detail of the highlighted area see page 147

115
98
99

Scale: 1¾ inches to 1 mile
0 ¼ ½ mile
0 250m 500m 750m 1km

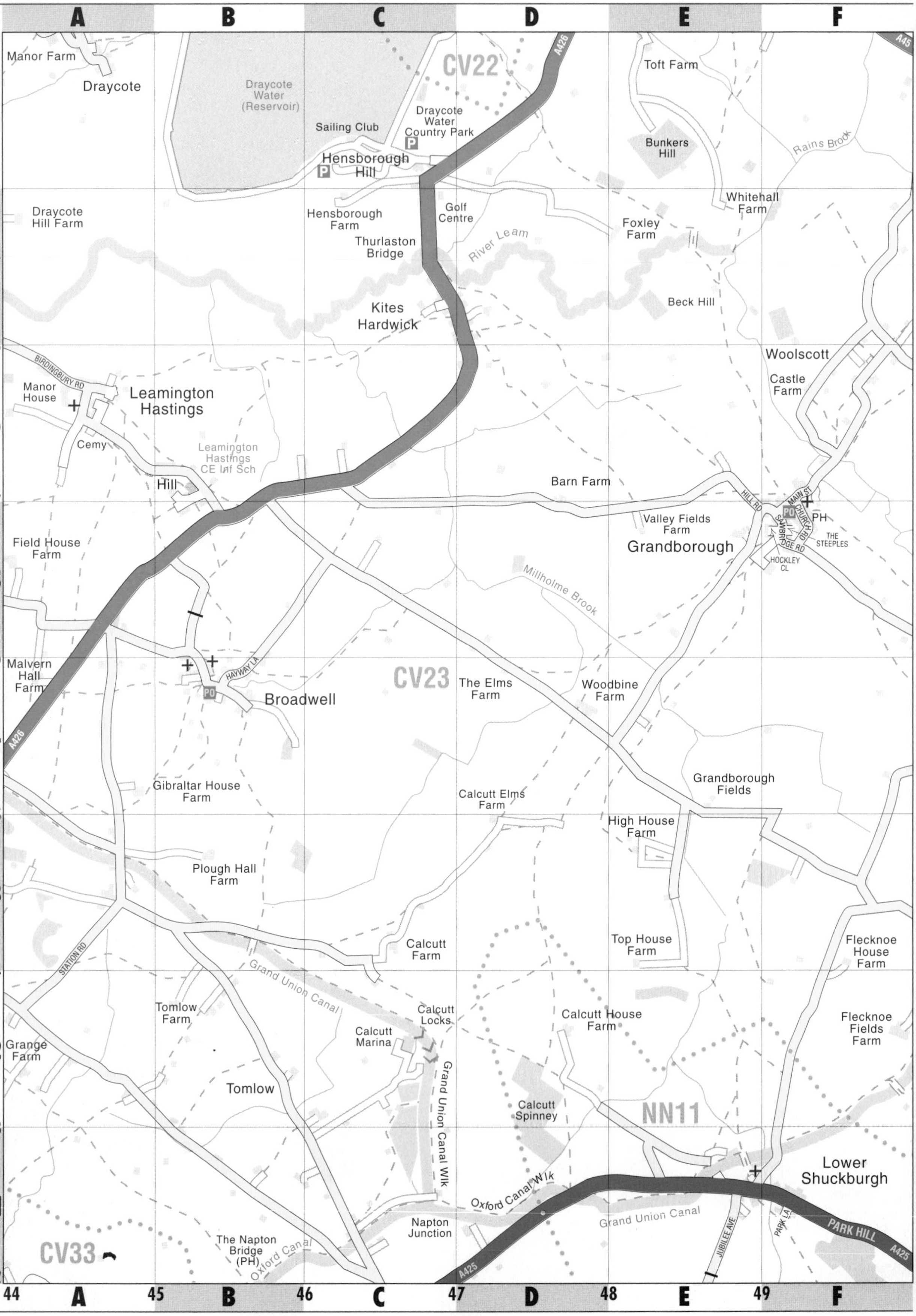

115
125

Scale: 1¾ inches to 1 mile

100
101

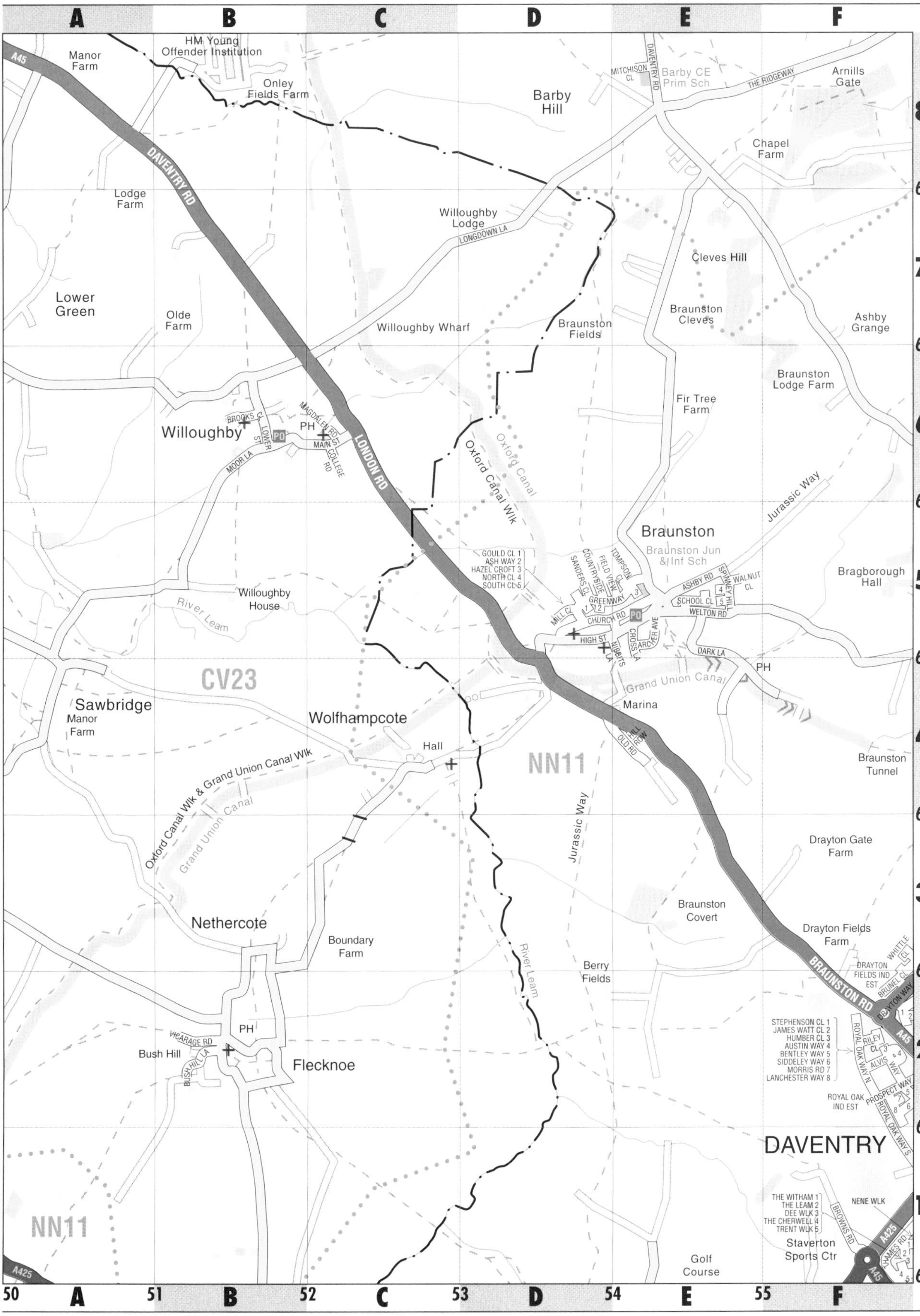
Manor Farm
HM Young Offender Institution
Onley Fields Farm
Barby Hill
Barby CE Prim Sch
MITCHISON CL
DAVENTRY RD
THE RIDGEWAY
Arnills Gate
Chapel Farm
Lodge Farm
DAVENTRY RD
Willoughby Lodge
LONGDOWN LA
Cleves Hill
Lower Green
Olde Farm
Willoughby Wharf
Braunston Fields
Braunston Cleves
Ashby Grange
Braunston Lodge Farm
Fir Tree Farm
Willoughby
BROOKS CL
LOWER ST
MAGDALEN RD
MAIN
COLLEGE RD
MOOR LA
LONDON RD
Oxford Canal Wlk
Oxford Canal
Jurassic Way
Braunston
Braunston Jun &Inf Sch
Bragborough Hall
GOULD CL 1
ASH WAY 2
HAZEL CROFT 3
NORTH CL 4
SOUTH CL 5
Willoughby House
River Leam
MILL CL
HIGH ST
CHURCH RD
GREENWAY
ASHBY RD
SCHOOL CL
WELTON RD
WALNUT CL
DARK LA
PH
CV23
Grand Union Canal
Marina
Sawbridge Manor Farm
Wolfhampcote
Hall
NN11
HILL ROW
OLD RD
Braunston Tunnel
Oxford Canal Wlk & Grand Union Canal Wlk
Grand Union Canal
Jurassic Way
Drayton Gate Farm
Nethercote
Boundary Farm
Braunston Covert
River Leam
Drayton Fields Farm
BRAUNSTON RD
DRAYTON FIELDS IND EST
Berry Fields
PH
VICARAGE RD
Bush Hill
BUSH HILL LA
Flecknoe
STEPHENSON CL 1
JAMES WATT CL 2
HUMBER CL 3
AUSTIN WAY 4
BENTLEY WAY 5
SIDDELEY WAY 6
MORRIS RD 7
LANCHESTER WAY 8
ROYAL OAK IND EST
ROYAL OAK WAY N
ROYAL OAK WAY S
PROSPECT WAY
DAVENTRY
NN11
THE WITHAM 1
THE LEAM 2
DEE WLK 3
THE CHERWELL 4
TRENT WLK 5
BROWNS RD
NENE WLK
Staverton Sports Ctr
Golf Course
A45
A425

102
103

Scale: 1¾ inches to 1 mile
0 ¼ ½ mile
0 250m 500m 750m 1km

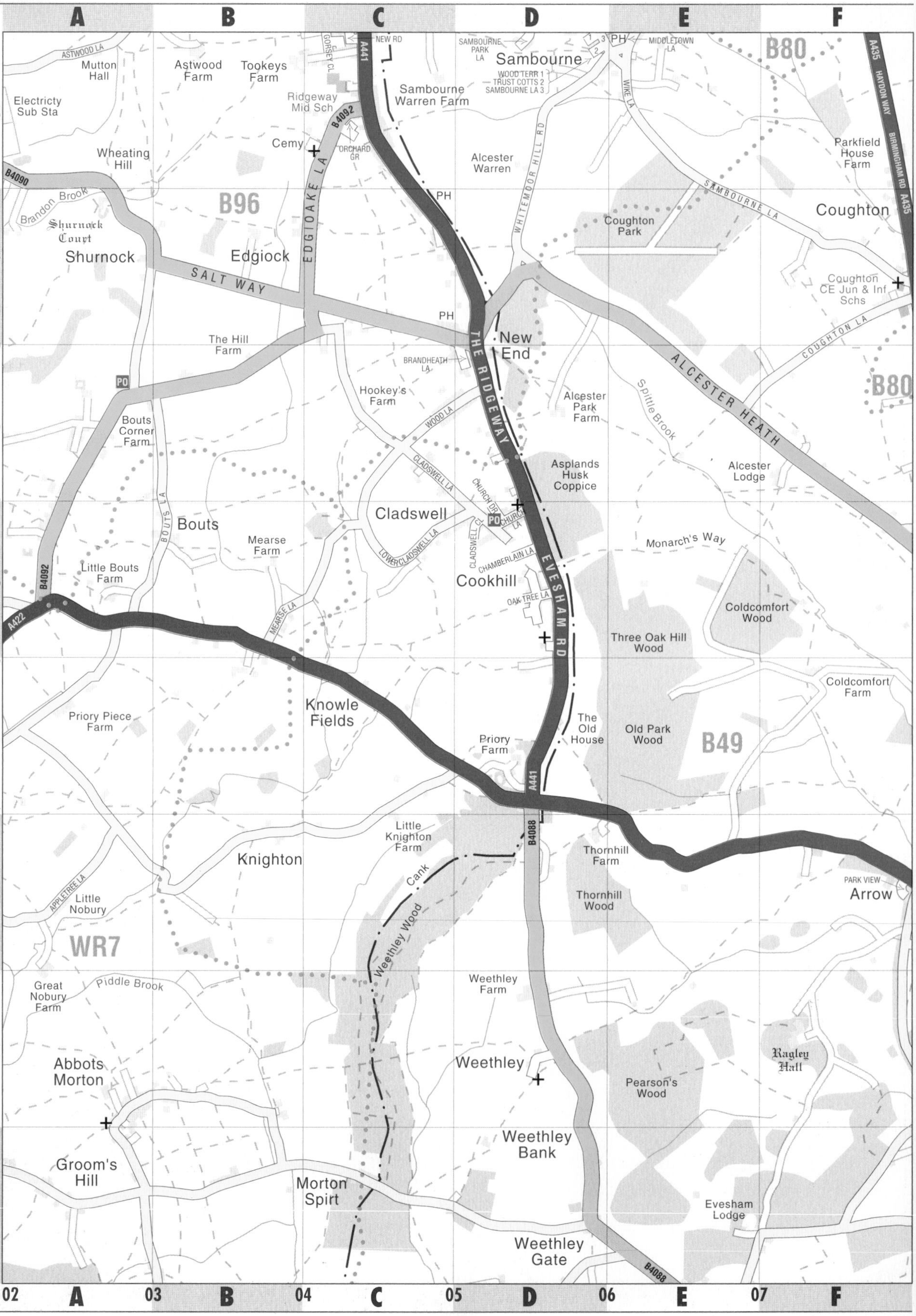

127

Scale: 1¾ inches to 1 mile
0 ¼ ½ mile
0 250m 500m 750m 1km

112
120

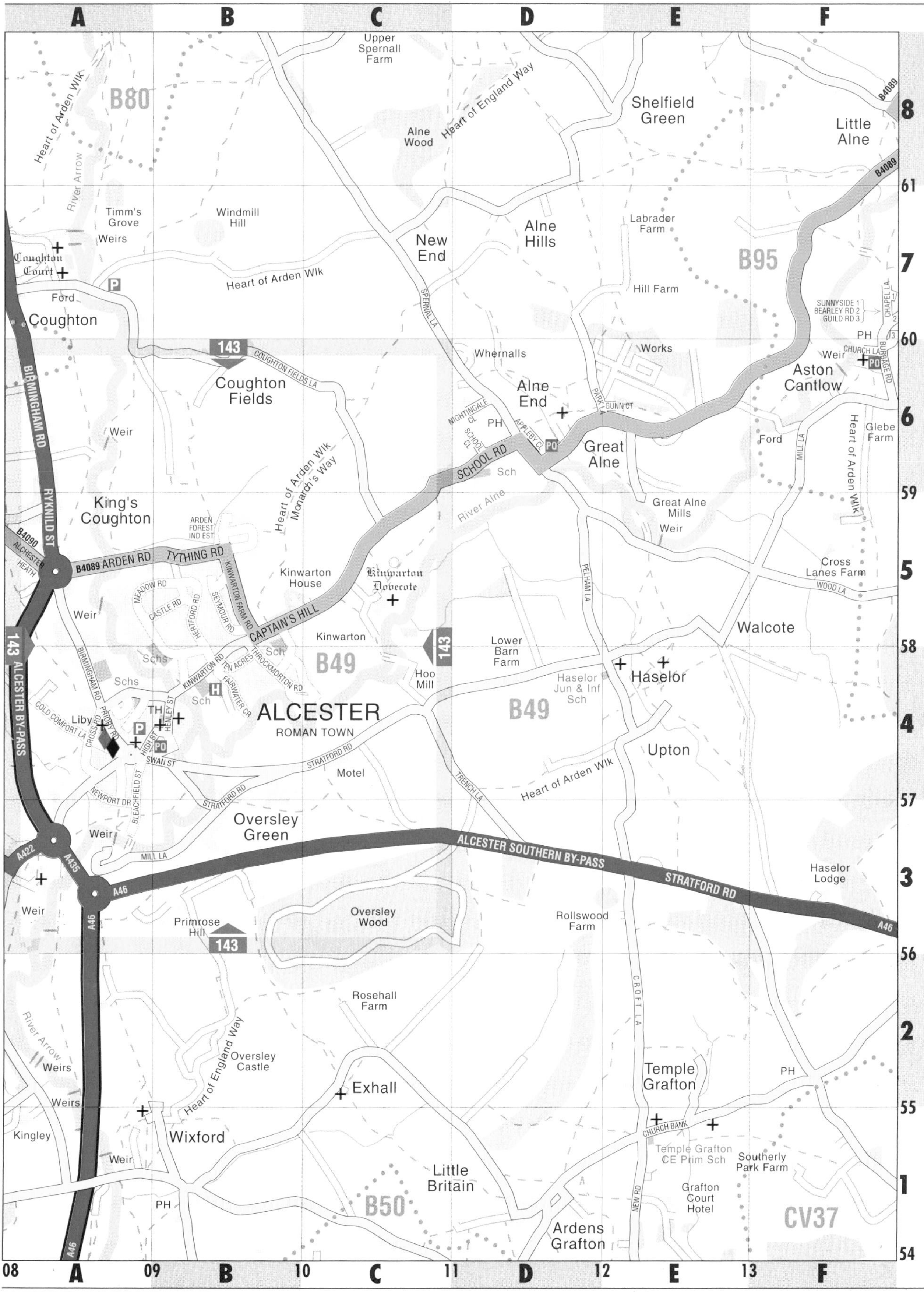

For full street detail of the highlighted area see page 143

128
120

Scale: 1¾ inches to 1 mile
0 ¼ ½ mile
0 250m 500m 750m 1km

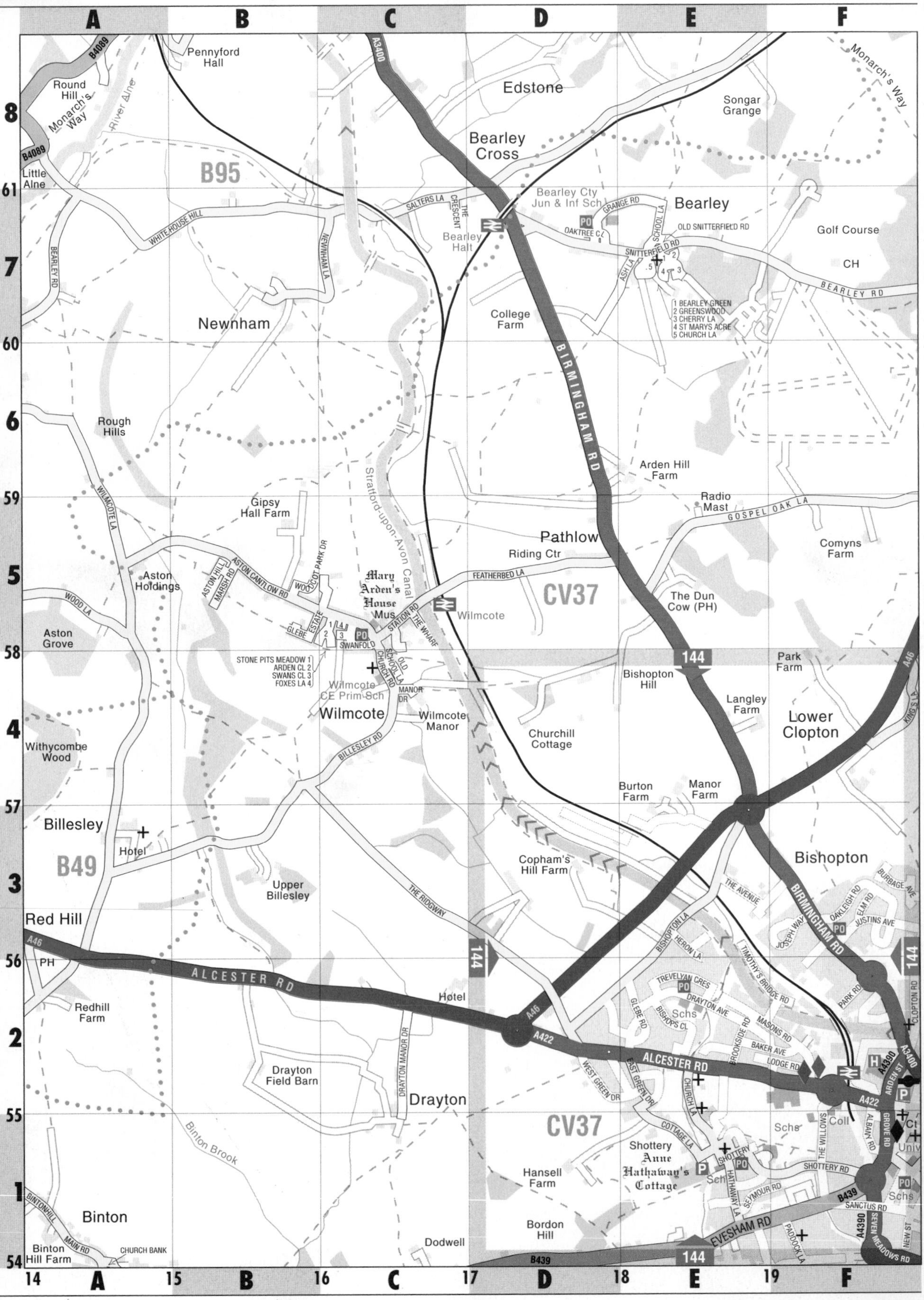
A
B
C
D
E
F
8
61
7
60
6
59
5
58
4
57
3
56
2
55
1
54
14
15
16
17
18
19
A3400
B4089
Pennyford Hall
Round Hill
Monarch's Way
River Alne
Little Alne
B95
Edstone
Bearley Cross
Songar Grange
SALTERS LA
THE CRESCENT
Bearley Halt
Bearley Cty Jun & Inf Sch
GRANGE RD
OAKTREE CL
PO
SCHOOL LA
Bearley
OLD SNITTERFIELD RD
SNITTERFIELD RD
ASH LA
Golf Course
CH
BEARLEY RD
1 BEARLEY GREEN
2 GREENSWOOD
3 CHERRY LA
4 ST MARYS ACRE
5 CHURCH LA
WHITE HOUSE HILL
NEWNHAM LA
Newnham
College Farm
BIRMINGHAM RD
Rough Hills
WILMCOTE LA
Stratford-upon-Avon Canal
Arden Hill Farm
Radio Mast
GOSPEL OAK LA
Gipsy Hall Farm
Pathlow
Riding Ctr
Comyns Farm
Aston Holdings
ASTON HILL
MARSH RD
ASTON CANTLOW RD
WOODCOT PARK DR
Mary Arden's House Mus
FEATHERBED LA
CV37
The Dun Cow (PH)
WOOD LA
Aston Grove
GLEBE
ESTATE
SWANFOLD
STATION RD
THE WHARF
Wilmcote
STONE PITS MEADOW 1
ARDEN CL 2
SWANS CL 3
FOXES LA 4
CHURCH RD
SCHOOL LA
OLD
MANOR DR
144
Park Farm
Bishopton Hill
A46
KINGS LA
Wilmcote CE Prim Sch
Wilmcote
Wilmcote Manor
Langley Farm
Lower Clopton
Withycombe Wood
BILLESLEY RD
Churchill Cottage
Burton Farm
Manor Farm
Billesley
Hotel
B49
Copham's Hill Farm
Bishopton
Upper Billesley
THE RIDGWAY
THE AVENUE
BIRMINGHAM RD
BURBAGE AVE
OAKLEIGH RD
ELM RD
JUSTINS AVE
JOSEPH WAY
Red Hill
BISHOPTON LA
HERON LA
TIMOTHY'S BRIDGE RD
PH
ALCESTER RD
TREVELYAN CRES
DRAYTON AVE
PARK RD
CLOPTON RD
Redhill Farm
Hotel
GLEBE RD
Schs
BISHOPS CL
BROOKSIDE RD
MASONS RD
A422
BAKER AVE
LODGE RD
ALCESTER RD
WEST GREEN DR
EAST GREEN DR
CHURCH LA
H
A4390
ARDEN ST
A3400
Drayton Field Barn
DRAYTON MANOR DR
Drayton
Coll
ALBANY RD
GROVE RD
Ct
Univ
Binton Brook
CV37
COTTAGE LA
THE WILLOWS
Schs
Shottery
Anne Hathaway's Cottage
SHOTTERY
P
Hansell Farm
Sch
HATHAWAY LA
SEYMOUR RD
SHOTTERY RD
B439
SANCTUS RD
BINTON HILL
Binton
EVESHAM RD
Bordon Hill
PADDOCK LA
SEVEN MEADOWS RD
NEW ST
MAIN RD
Binton Hill Farm
CHURCH BANK
Dodwell
B439

For full street detail of the highlighted area see page 144

114
122

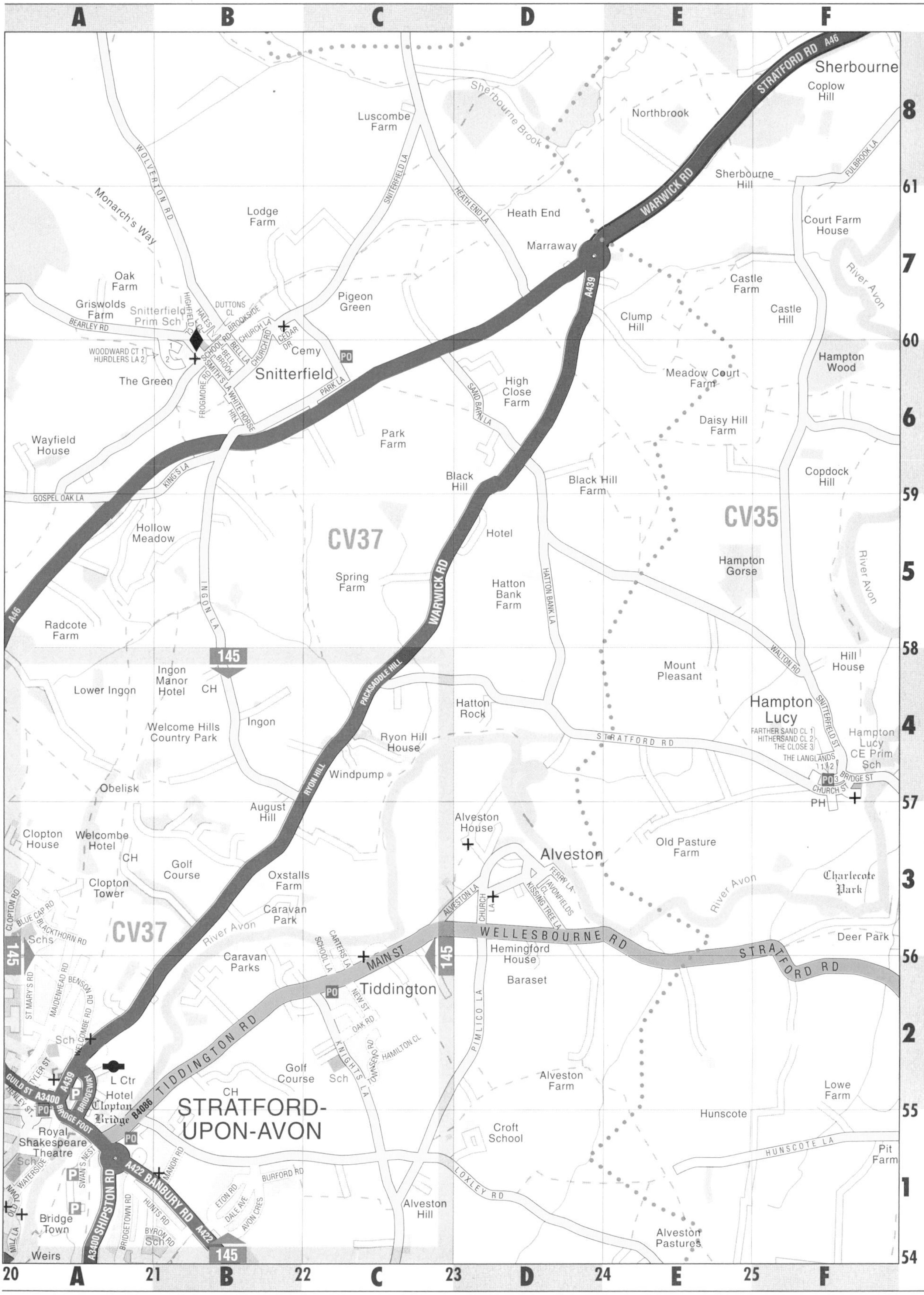

130
122

For full street detail of the highlighted area see page 145

Scale: 1¾ inches to 1 mile
0 ¼ ½ mile
0 250m 500m 750m 1km

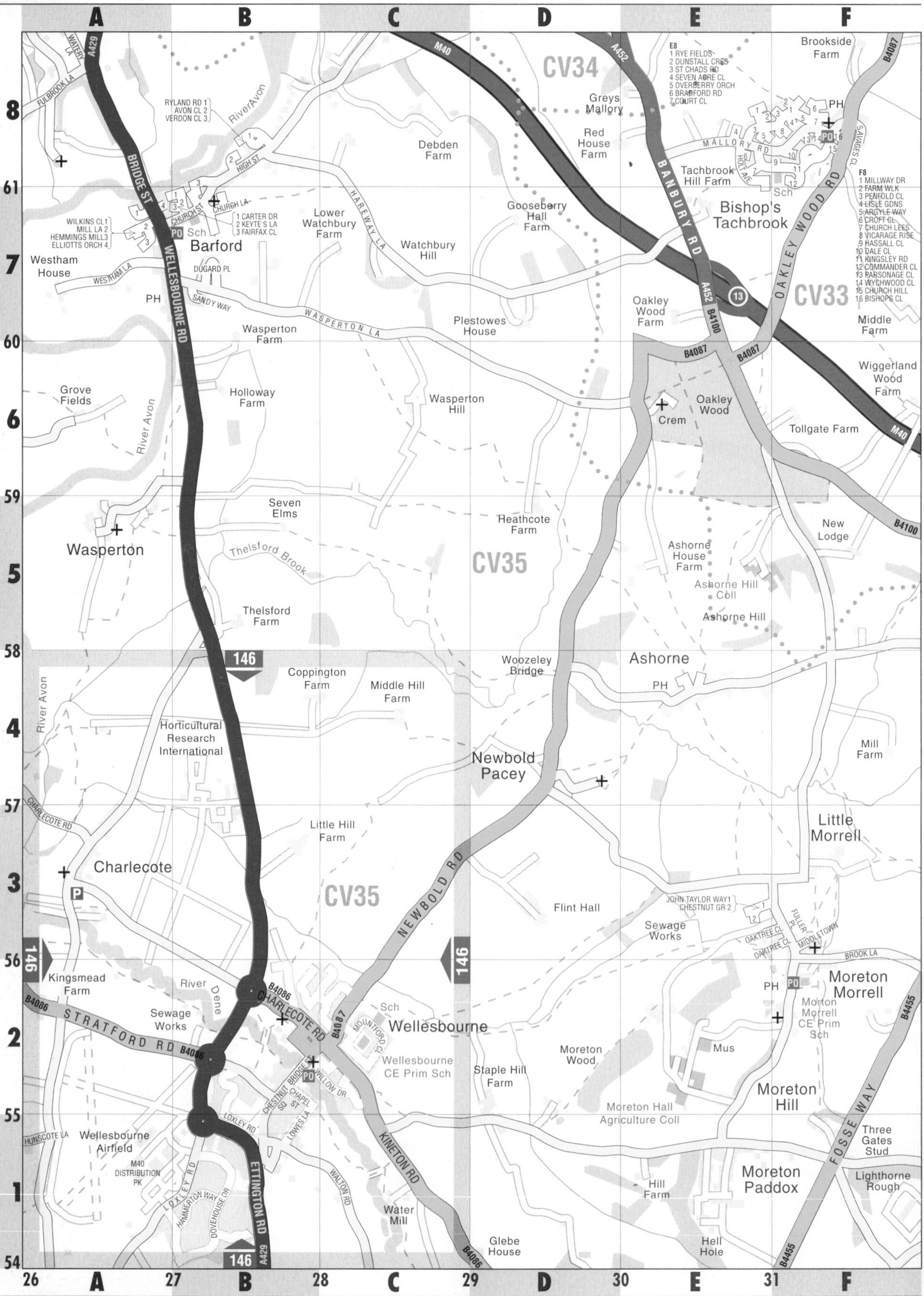

Scale: 1¾ inches to 1 mile
0 ¼ ½ mile
0 250m 500m 750m 1km

110 111 124

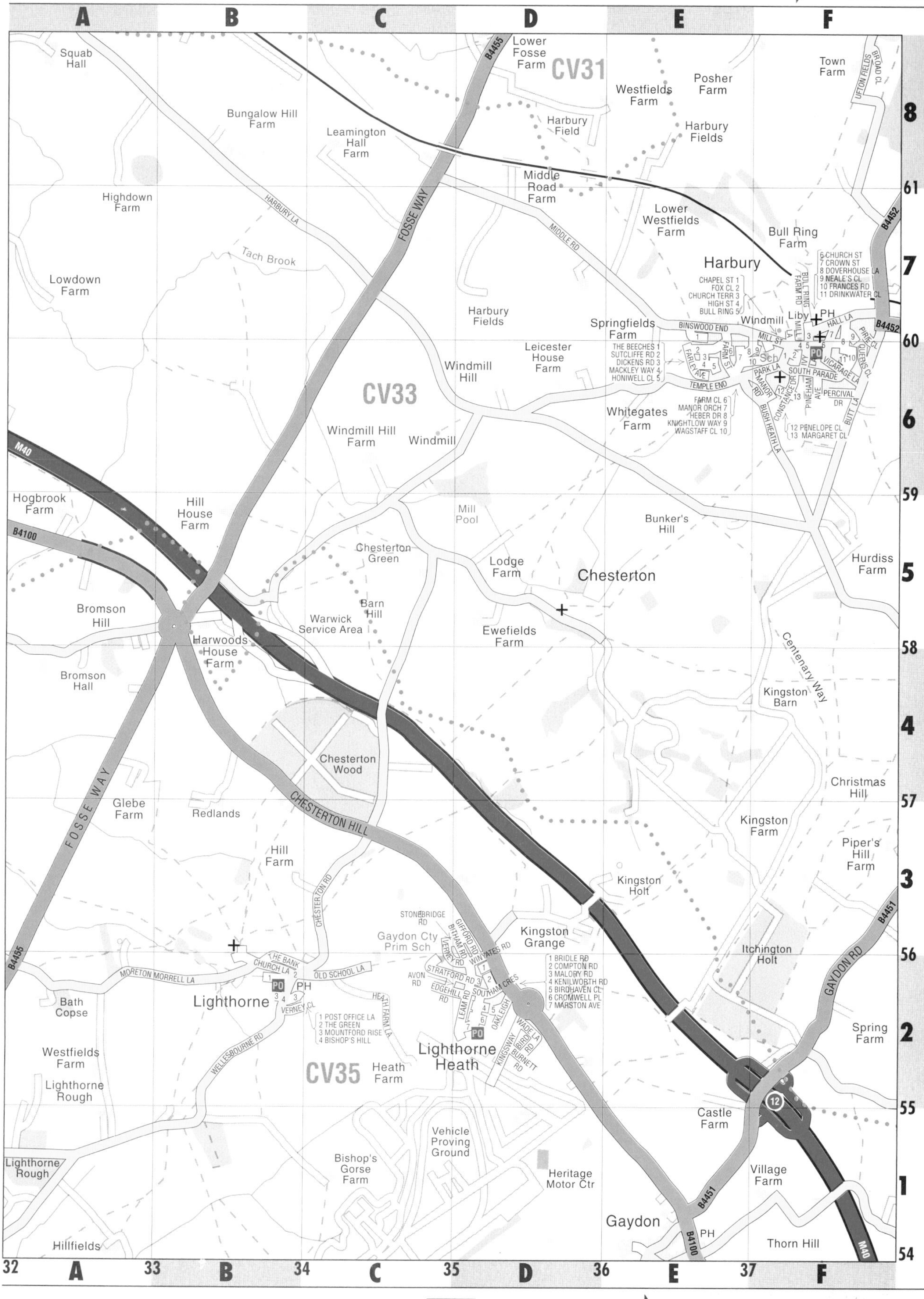

132 124

123
115
For full street detail of the highlighted area see page 147

Scale: 1¾ inches to 1 mile
0 ¼ ½ mile
0 250m 500m 750m 1km

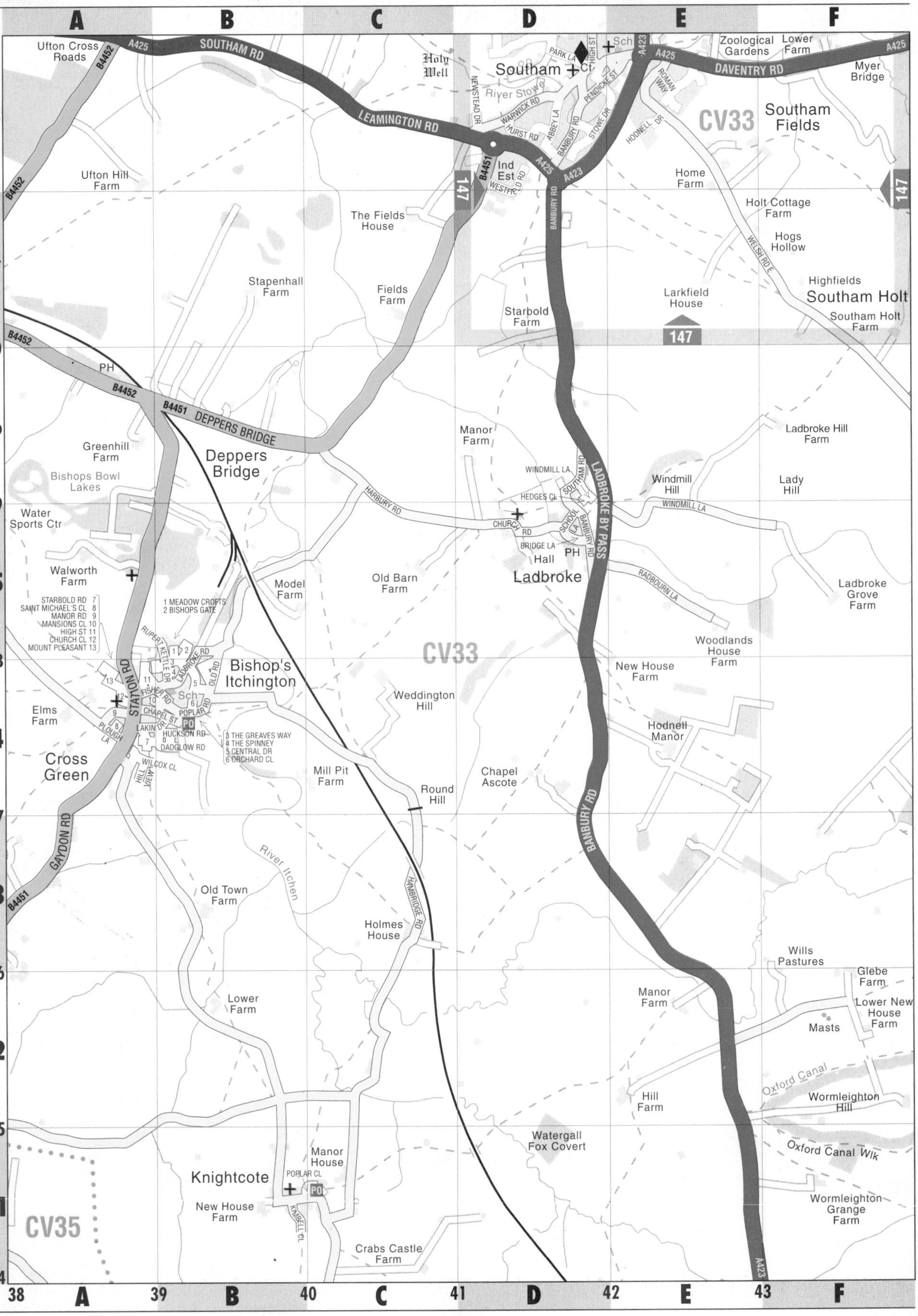
A
B
C
D
E
F
Ufton Cross Roads
B4452
A425
SOUTHAM RD
Holy Well
Southam
PARK LA
HIGH ST
Ct
Sch
Zoological Gardens
Lower Farm
A423
A425
DAVENTRY RD
Myer Bridge
NEWSTEAD DR
River Stowe
WARWICK RD
PENDICKE ST
ROMAN WAY
LEAMINGTON RD
HURST RD
ABBEY LA
BANBURY RD
STOWE DR
HODNELL DR
CV33
Southam Fields
Ufton Hill Farm
B4451
Ind Est
WESTFIELD RD
A425
A423
147
Home Farm
Holt Cottage Farm
Hogs Hollow
The Fields House
BANBURY RD
WELSH RD E
Stapenhall Farm
Fields Farm
Highfields
Larkfield House
Southam Holt
Starbold Farm
Southam Holt Farm
147
B4452
PH
B4452
B4451
DEPPERS BRIDGE
Manor Farm
Ladbroke Hill Farm
Greenhill Farm
Deppers Bridge
WINDMILL LA
SOUTHAM RD
LADBROKE BY PASS
Windmill Hill
Lady Hill
Bishops Bowl Lakes
HARBURY RD
HEDGES CL
WINDMILL LA
Water Sports Ctr
CHURCH RD
SCHOOL LA
BANBURY RD
BRIDGE LA
PH
Hall
Walworth Farm
Model Farm
Old Barn Farm
Ladbroke
RADBOURN LA
Ladbroke Grove Farm
STARBOLD RD 7
SAINT MICHAEL'S CL 8
MANOR RD 9
MANSIONS CL 10
HIGH ST 11
CHURCH CL 12
MOUNT PLEASANT 13
1 MEADOW CROFTS
2 BISHOPS GATE
RUPERT KETTLE DR
LADBROKE RD
OLD RD
Woodlands House Farm
CV33
Bishop's Itchington
New House Farm
STATION RD
FISHER RD
Sch
POPLAR RD
Weddington Hill
Elms Farm
CHAPEL ST
LAKIN DR
PO
HUCKSON RD
DADGLOW RD
3 THE GREAVES WAY
4 THE SPINNEY
5 CENTRAL DR
6 ORCHARD CL
Hodnell Manor
PLOUGH LA
Cross Green
WILCOX CL
HILL VIEW
Mill Pit Farm
Chapel Ascote
Round Hill
GAYDON RD
BANBURY RD
B4451
River Itchen
Old Town Farm
HAMBRIDGE RD
Holmes House
Wills Pastures
Glebe Farm
Lower Farm
Manor Farm
Lower New House Farm
Masts
Oxford Canal
Hill Farm
Wormleighton Hill
Watergall Fox Covert
Oxford Canal Wlk
Manor House
Knightcote
POPLAR CL
PO
New House Farm
KNIGHTCOTE CL
Wormleighton Grange Farm
CV35
Crabs Castle Farm
A423
8
61
7
60
6
59
5
58
4
57
3
56
2
55
1
54
38
39
40
41
42
43

123
133

Scale: 1¾ inches to 1 mile
0 ¼ ½ mile
0 250m 500m 750m 1km

116
126

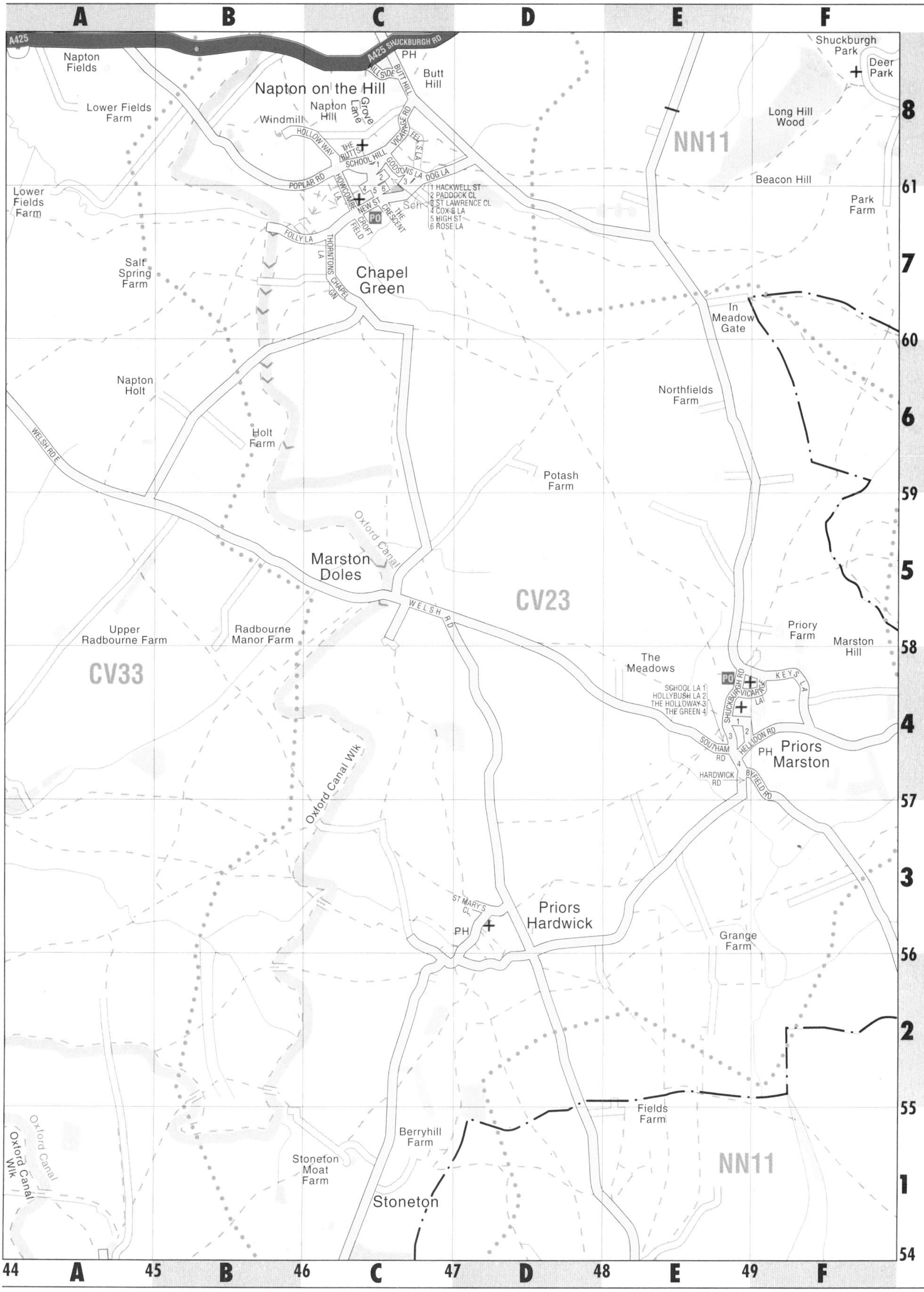

134
126

125
117

Scale: 1¾ inches to 1 mile
0 ¼ ½ mile
0 250m 500m 750m 1km

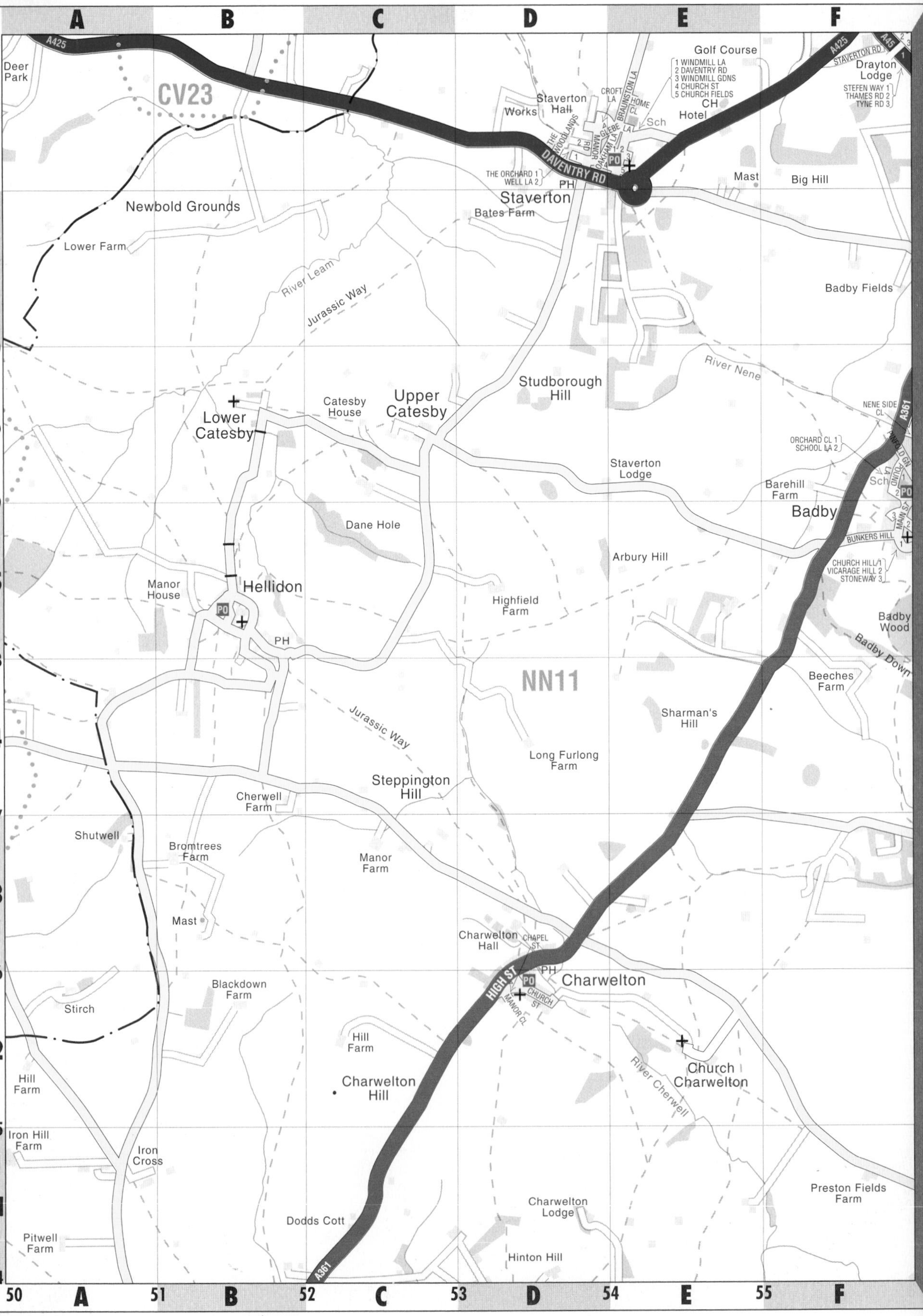

125

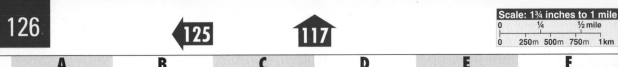

Scale: 1¾ inches to 1 mile
0 ¼ ½ mile
0 250m 500m 750m 1 km

118
128

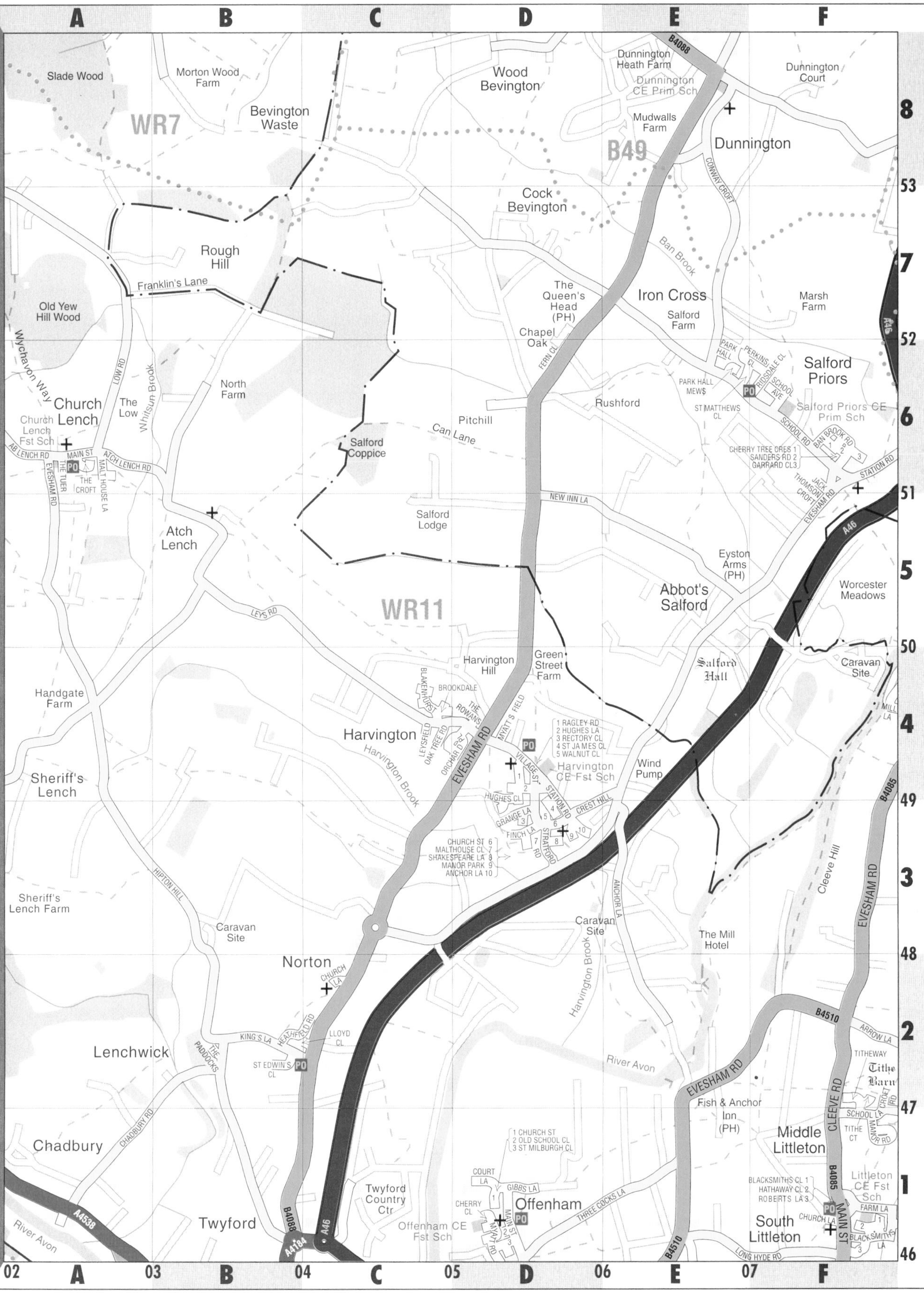

128

For full street detail of the highlighted area see page 148.

127

119

Scale: 1¾ inches to 1 mile
0 ¼ ½ mile
0 250m 500m 750m 1km

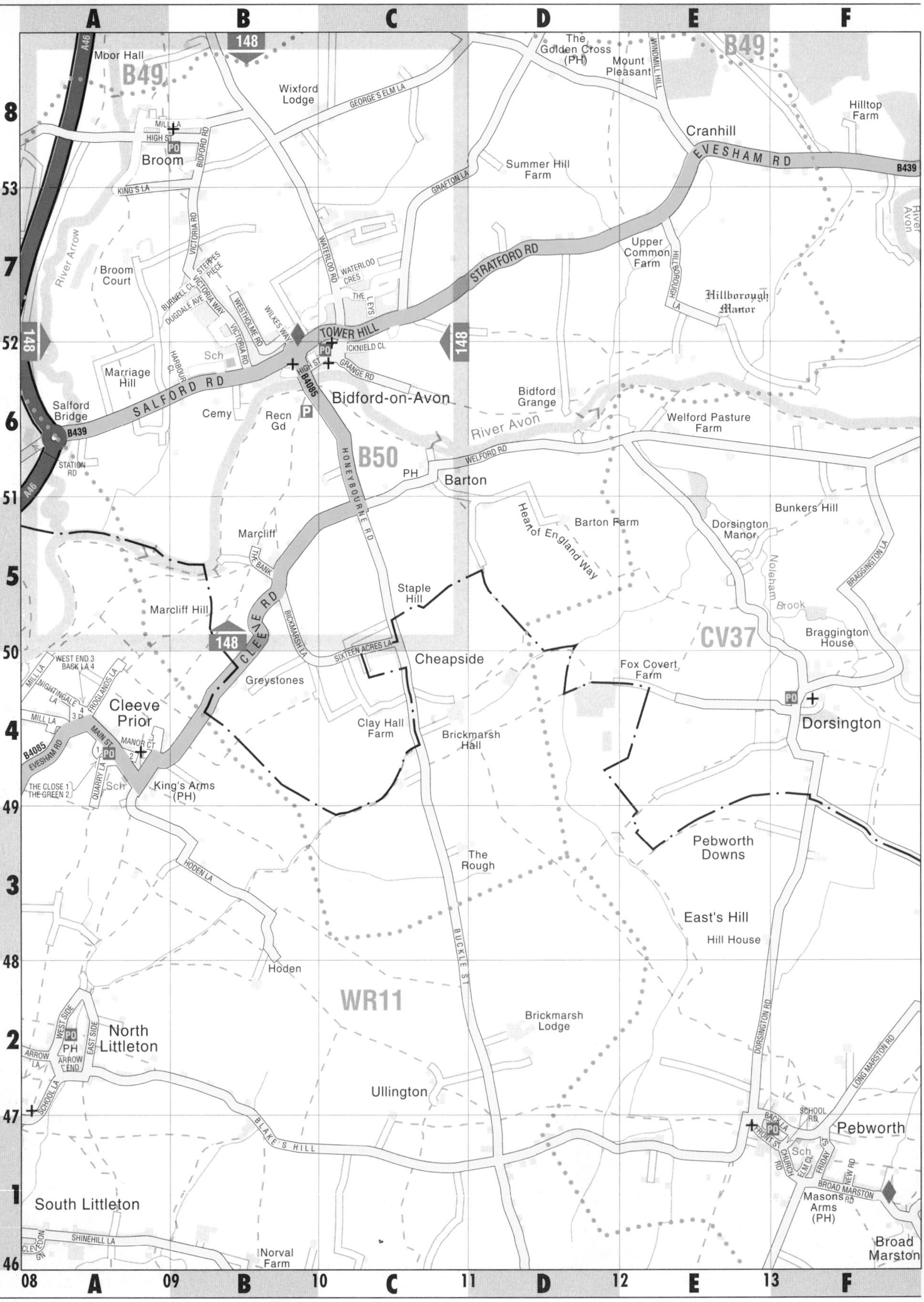

Scale: 1¾ inches to 1 mile
0 ¼ ½ mile
0 250m 500m 750m 1km

120
130

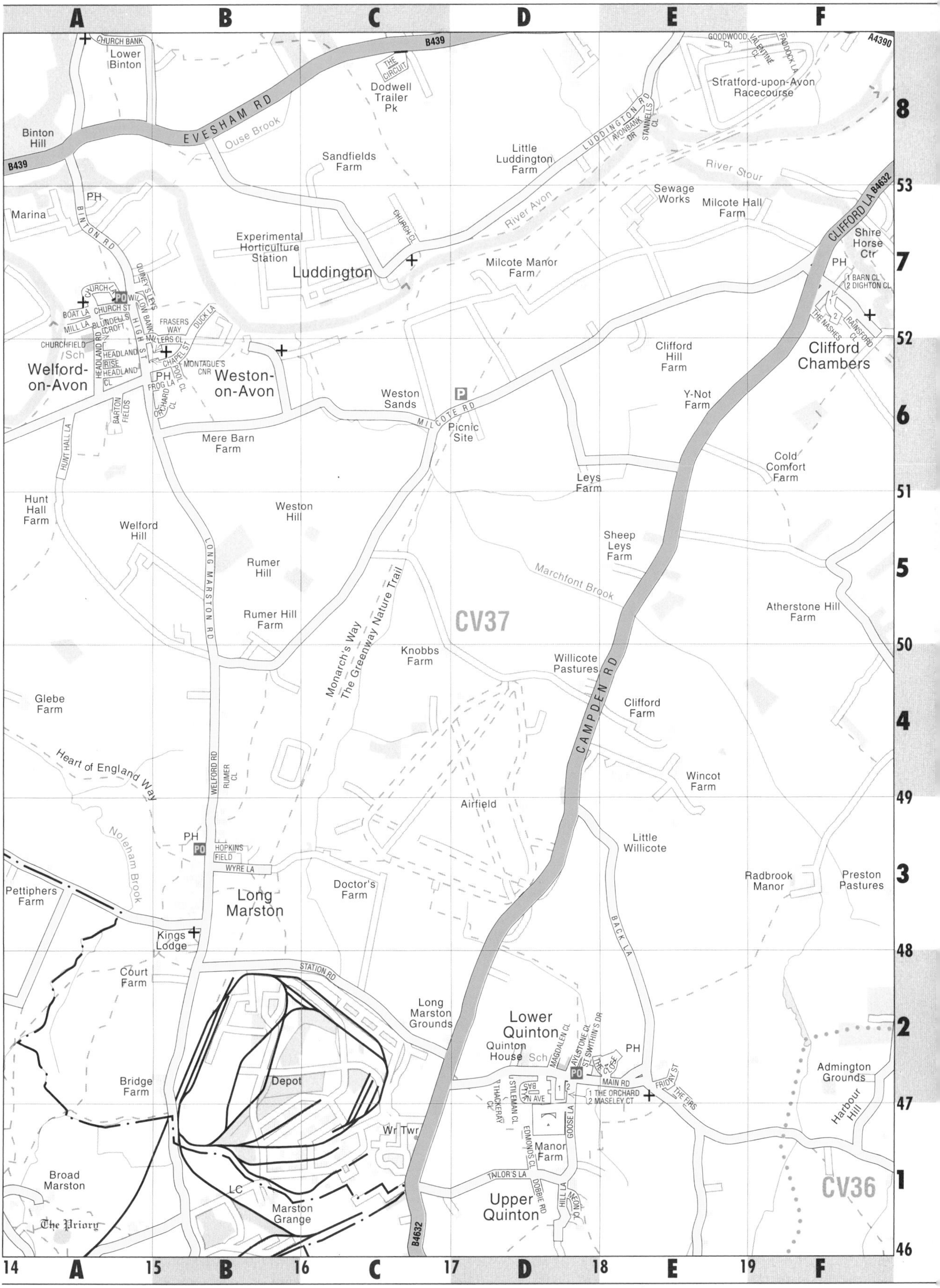

135
130

129
121

Scale: 1¾ inches to 1 mile
0 ¼ ½ mile
0 250m 500m 750m 1km

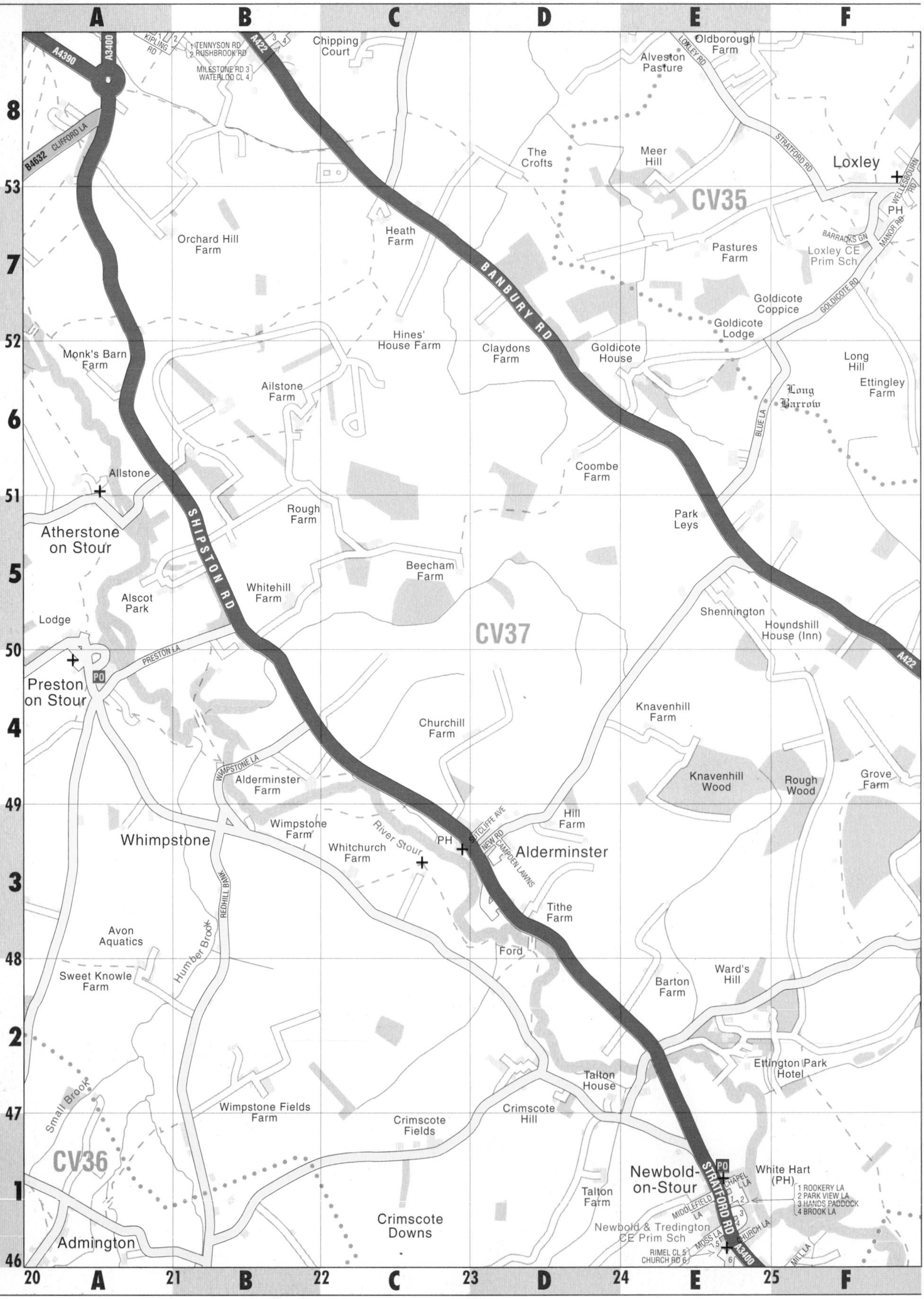

129
136

Scale: 1¾ inches to 1 mile
0 ¼ ½ mile
0 250m 500m 750m 1km

122
132

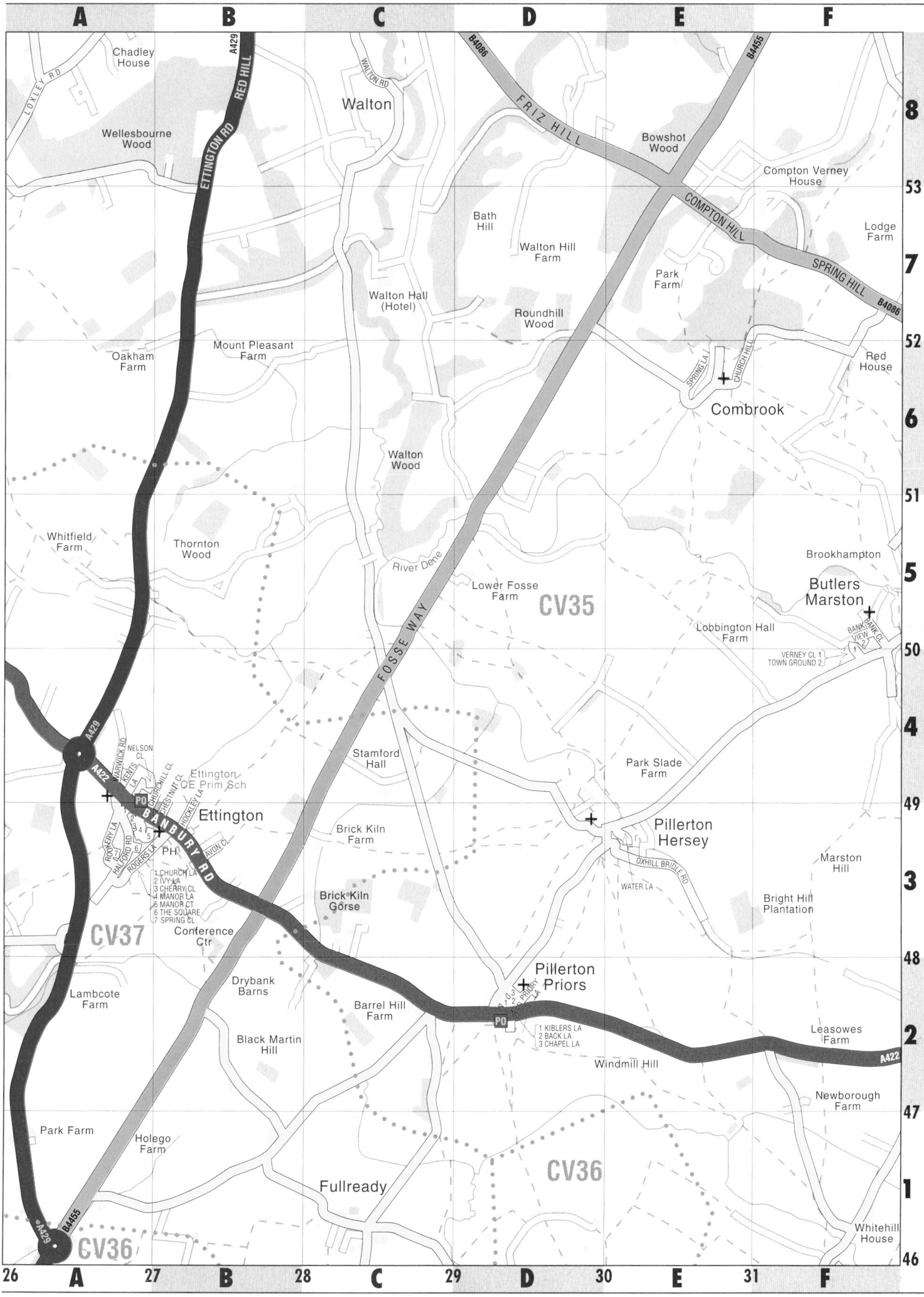

137
132

131
123

Scale: 1¾ inches to 1 mile
0 ¼ ½ mile
0 250m 500m 750m 1km

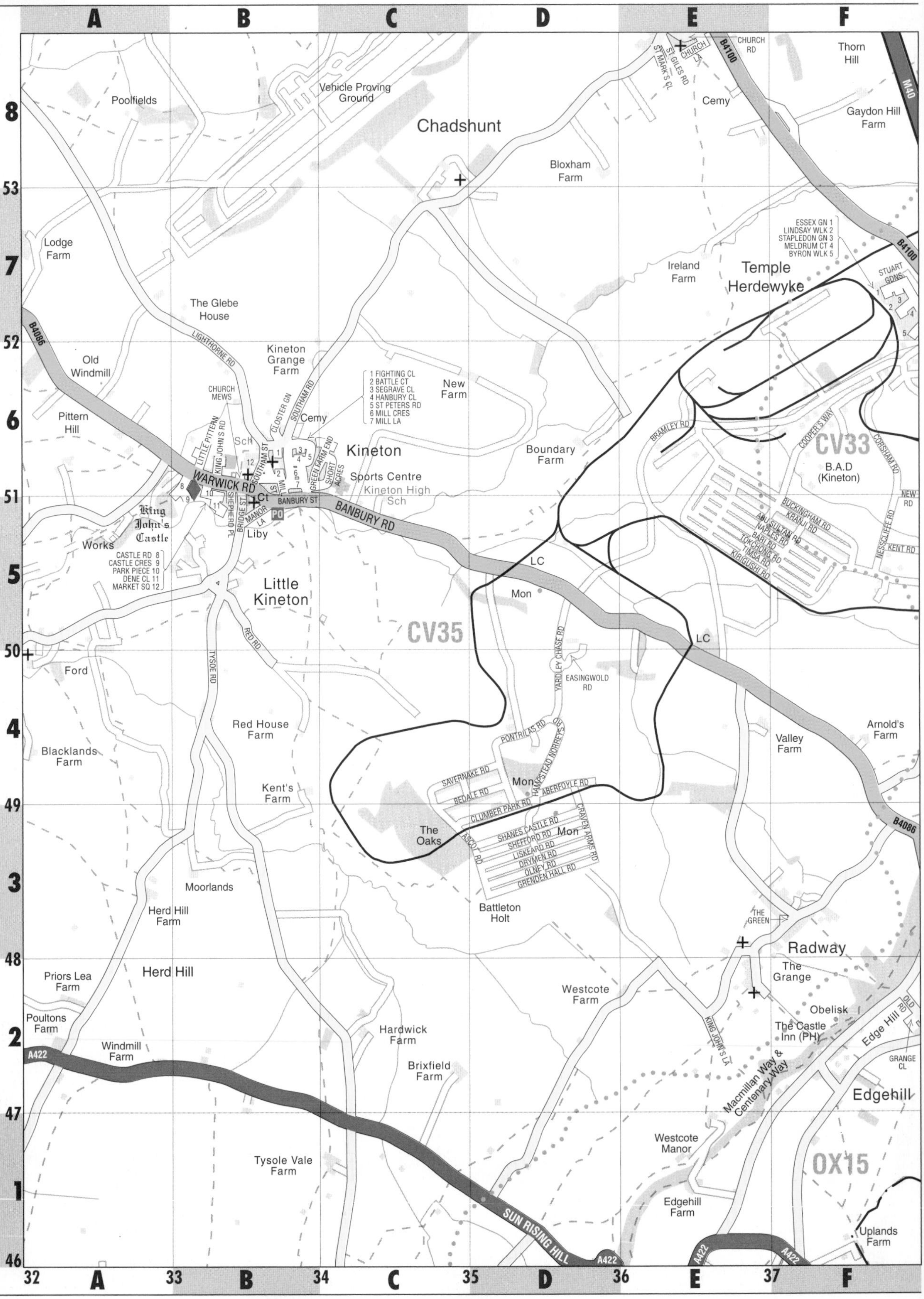

131
138

124
134

Scale: 1¾ inches to 1 mile
0 ¼ ½ mile
0 250m 500m 750m 1km

139
134

133

125

Scale: 1¾ inches to 1 mile

0 ¼ ½ mile

0 250m 500m 750m 1km

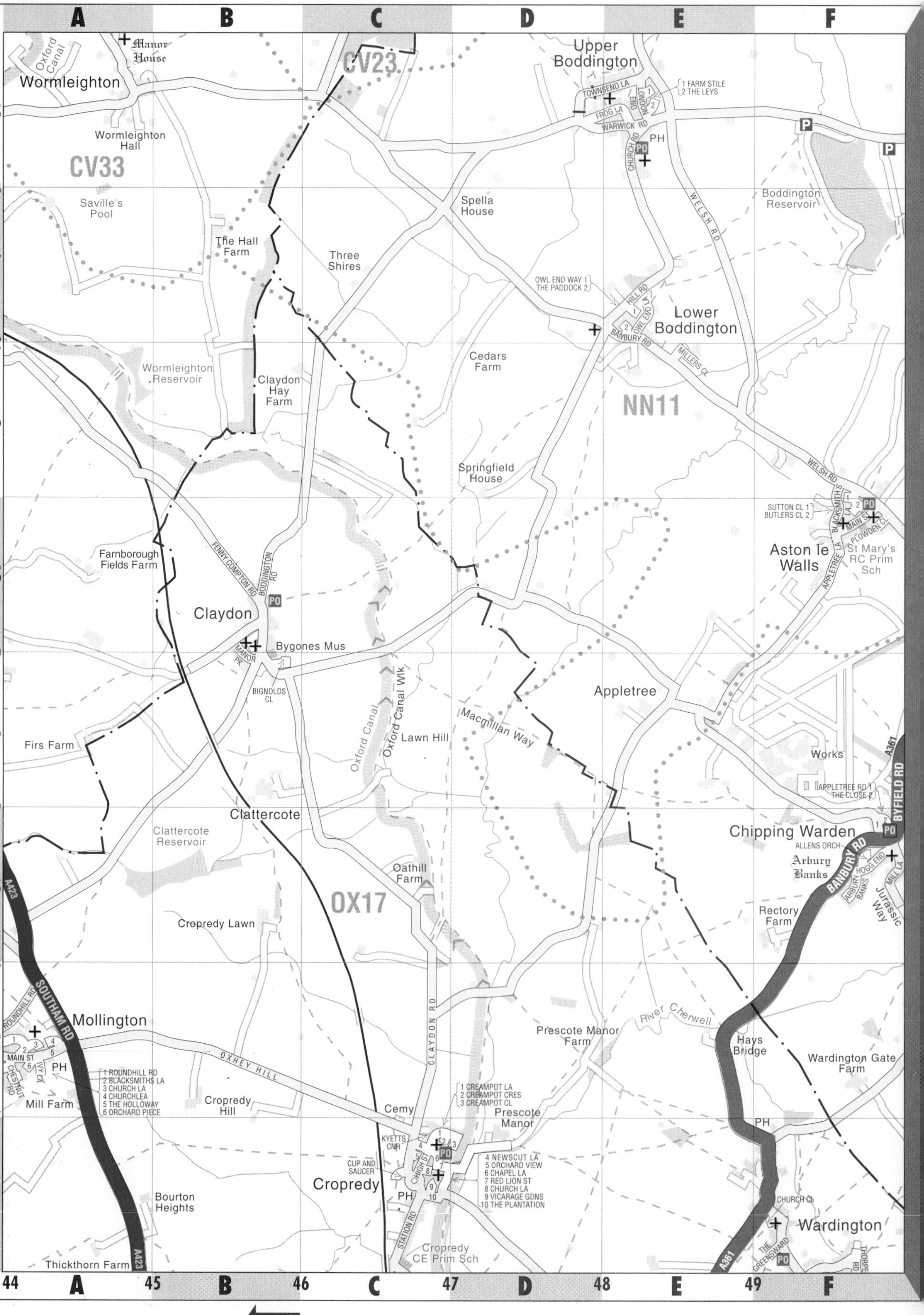
A
B
C
D
E
F
Manor House
Oxford Canal
Wormleighton
CV23
Upper Boddington
TOWNSEND LA
FROG LA
WARWICK RD
OWL END
LONDON
1 FARM STILE
2 THE LEYS
PH
CHURCH RD
Wormleighton Hall
CV33
Saville's Pool
Spella House
WELSH RD
Boddington Reservoir
The Hall Farm
Three Shires
OWL END WAY 1
THE PADDOCK 2
HILL RD
OWL END LA
Lower Boddington
BANBURY RD
MILLERS CL
Cedars Farm
Wormleighton Reservoir
Claydon Hay Farm
NN11
Springfield House
SUTTON CL 1
BUTLERS CL 2
BLACKSMITH'S LA
MAIN ST
PLOWDEN CL
Farnborough Fields Farm
FENNY COMPTON RD
BODDINGTON RD
Aston le Walls
St Mary's RC Prim Sch
APPLETREE LA
Claydon
Bygones Mus
MANOR PK
BIGNOLDS CL
Appletree
Macmillan Way
Oxford Canal
Oxford Canal Wlk
Lawn Hill
Firs Farm
Works
A361
BYFIELD RD
APPLETREE RD 1
THE CLOSE 2
Clattercote
Clattercote Reservoir
Chipping Warden
ALLENS ORCH
BANBURY RD
HOGGS END
MILL LA
Arbury Banks
Oathill Farm
OX17
Jurassic Way
Rectory Farm
Cropredy Lawn
A423
SOUTHAM RD
ROUNDHILL RD
Mollington
River Cherwell
Prescote Manor Farm
Hays Bridge
Wardington Gate Farm
CLAYDON RD
OXHEY HILL
MAIN ST
CHESTNUT RD
IVY LA
1 ROUNDHILL RD
2 BLACKSMITHS LA
3 CHURCH LA
4 CHURCHLEA
5 THE HOLLOWAY
6 ORCHARD PIECE
Mill Farm
Cropredy Hill
1 CREAMPOT LA
2 CREAMPOT CRES
3 CREAMPOT CL
Cemy
Prescote Manor
KYETTS CNR
CUP AND SAUCER
HIGH ST
4 NEWSCUT LA
5 ORCHARD VIEW
6 CHAPEL LA
7 RED LION ST
8 CHURCH LA
9 VICARAGE GDNS
10 THE PLANTATION
Cropredy
Bourton Heights
STATION RD
Cropredy CE Prim Sch
CHURCH CL
Wardington
THE GREENSWARD
THORPE RD
Thickthorn Farm
8
53
7
52
6
51
5
50
4
49
3
48
2
47
1
46
44
45
46
47
48
49

133

Scale: 1¾ inches to 1 mile
0 ¼ ½ mile
0 250m 500m 750m 1km

129
136

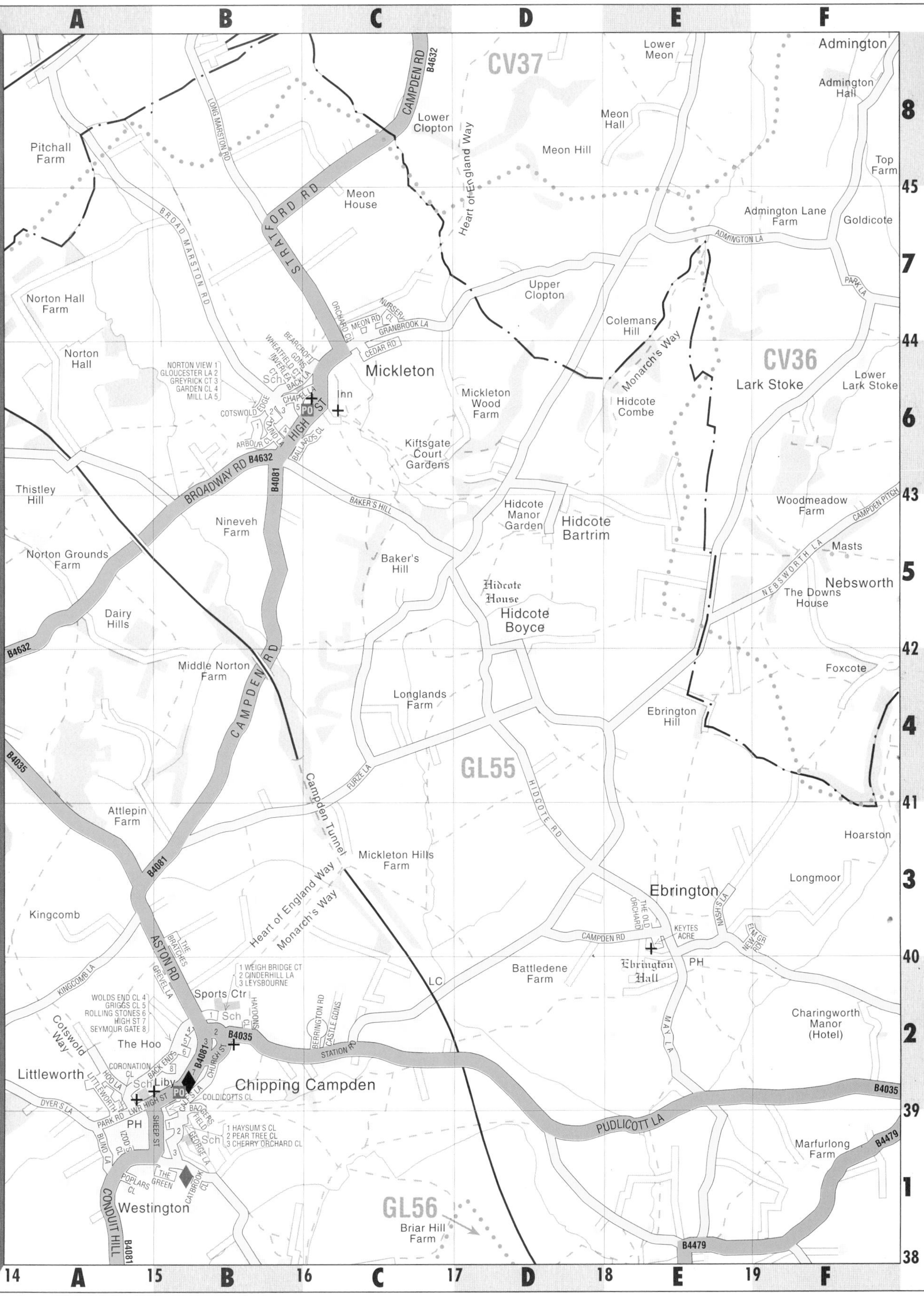

136

135
130

Scale: 1¾ inches to 1 mile
0 ¼ ½ mile
0 250m 500m 750m 1km

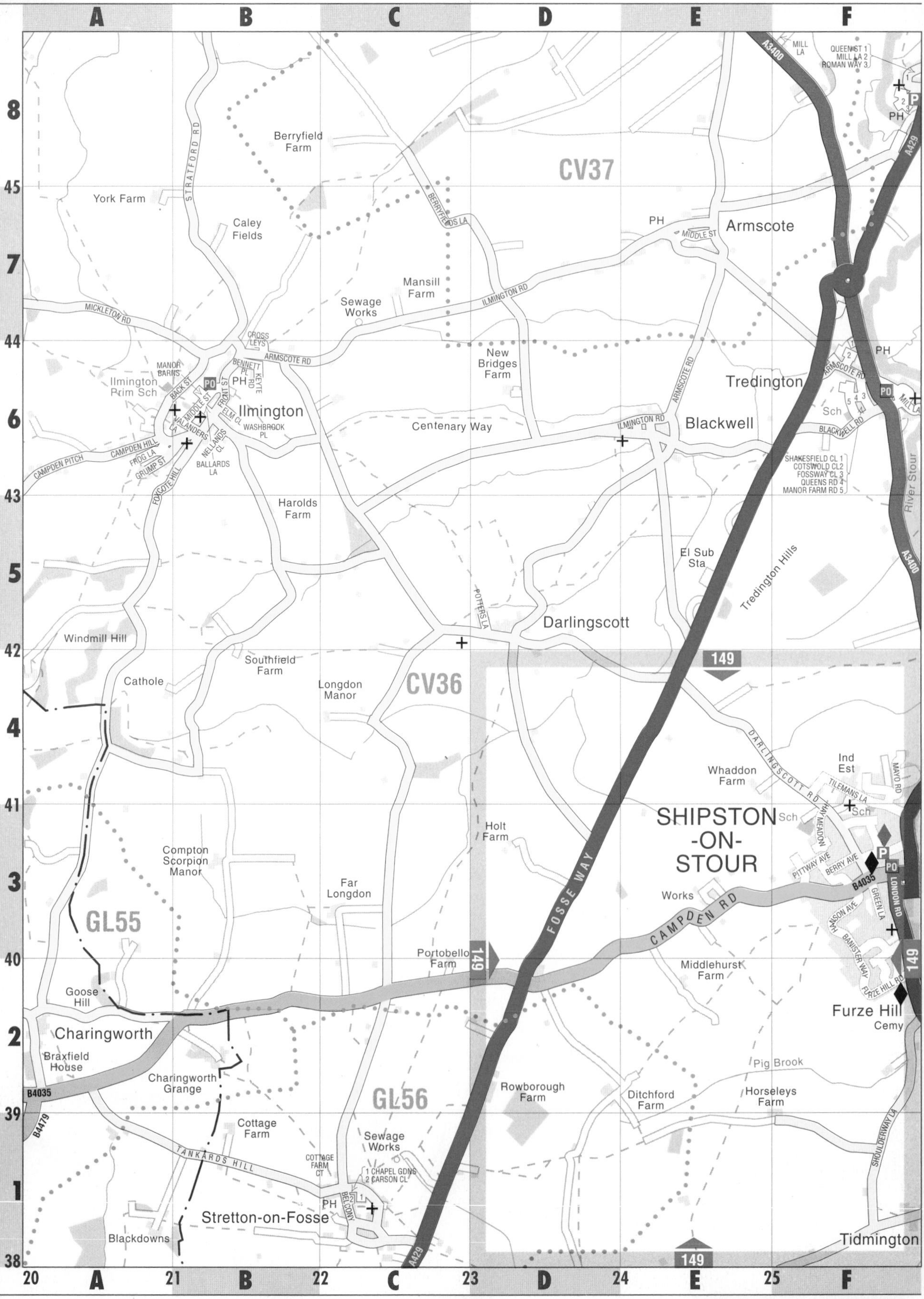

135
140

For full street detail of the highlighted area see page 149 .

Scale: 1¾ inches to 1 mile
0 ¼ ½ mile
0 250m 500m 750m 1km

131
138

141
138

137
132

Scale: 1¾ inches to 1 mile
0 ¼ ½ mile
0 250m 500m 750m 1km

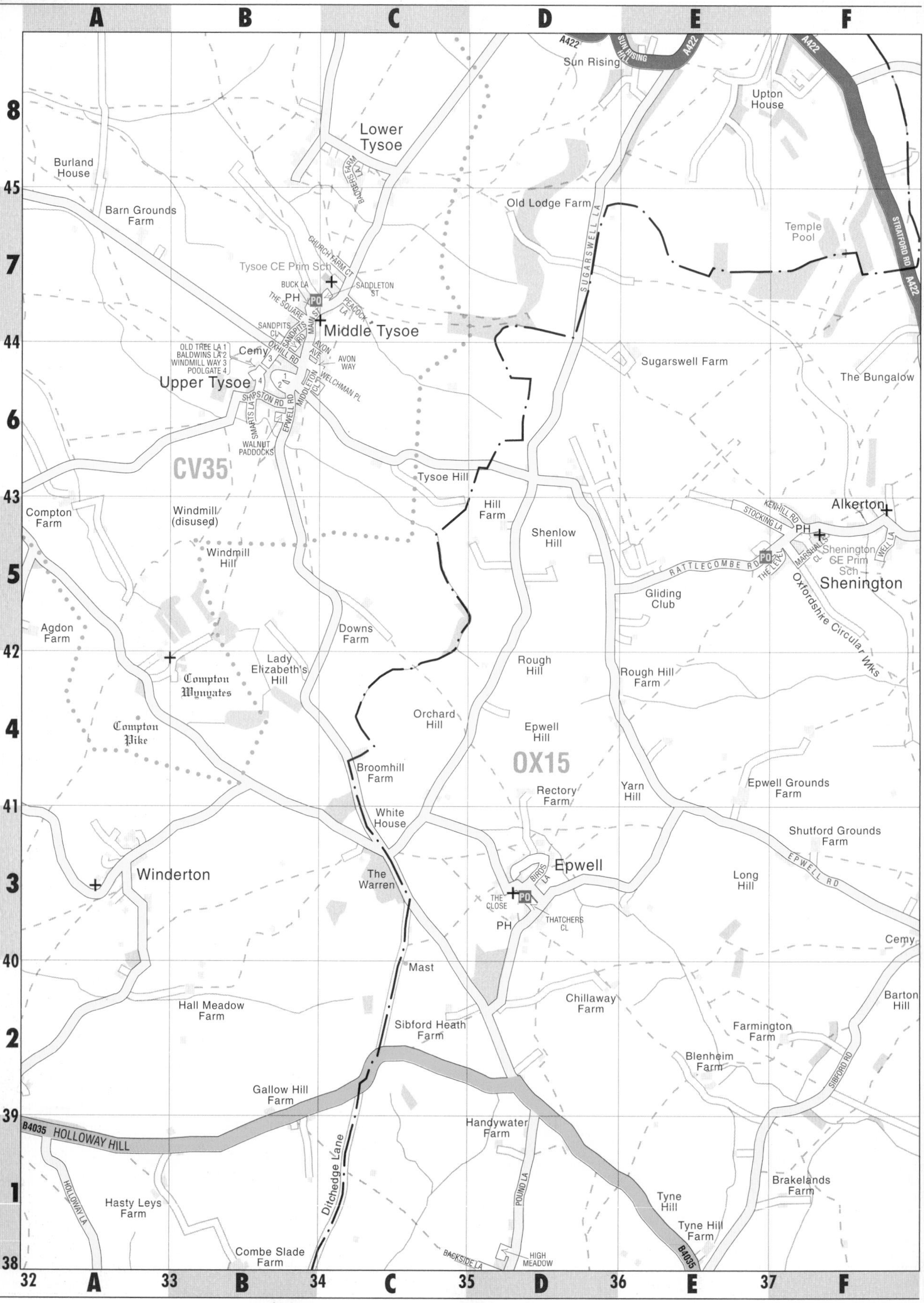

137
142

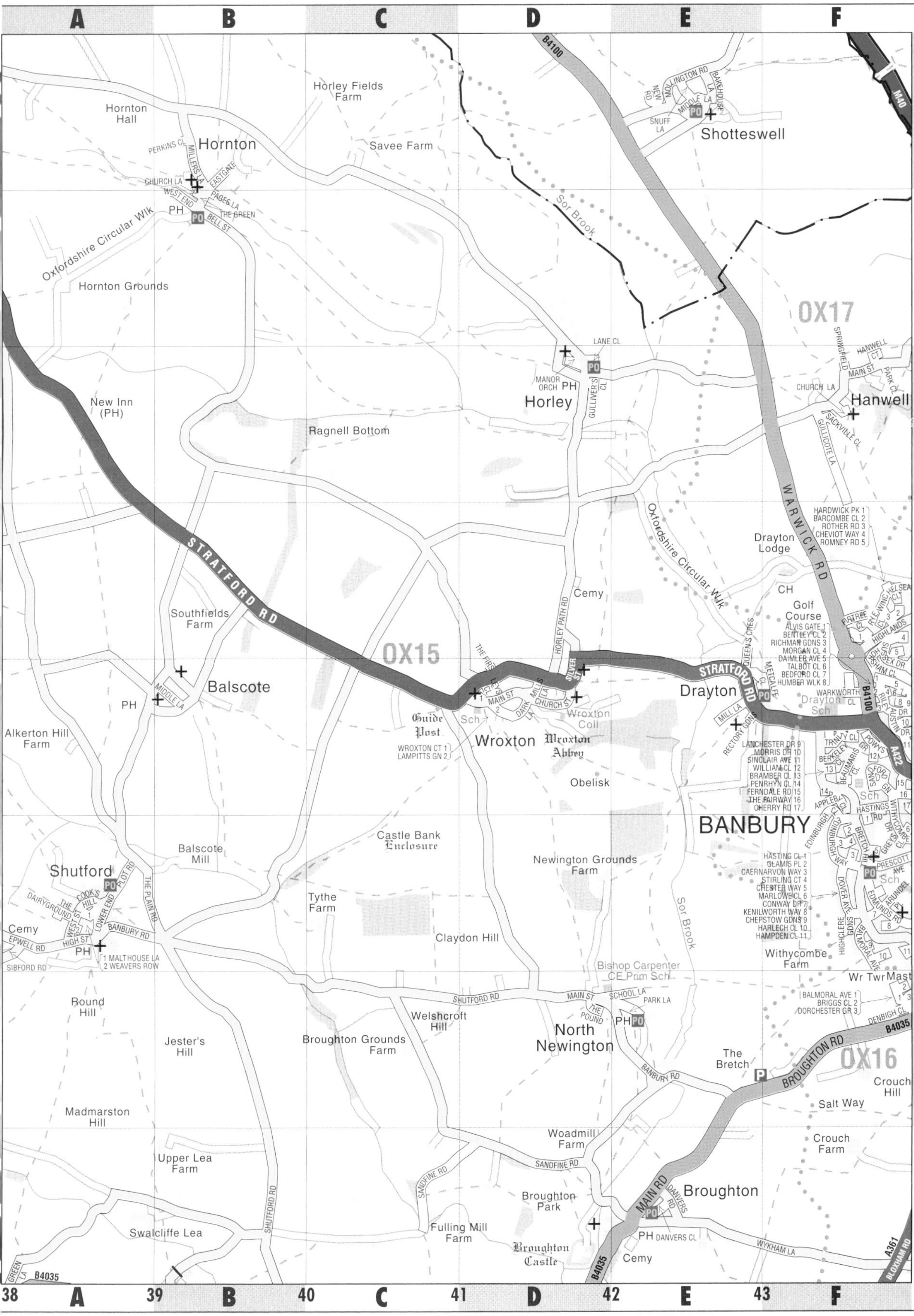
A
B
C
D
E
F
Horley Fields Farm
Hornton Hall
Hornton
Savee Farm
Shotteswell
MOLLINGTON RD
BAKEHOUSE LA
MIDDLE LA
NEW RD
SNUFF LA
B4100
M40
PERKINS CL
MILLERS LA
CHURCH LA
EASTGATE
WEST END
PAGES LA
THE GREEN
BELL ST
PH
PO
Sor Brook
Oxfordshire Circular Wlk
Hornton Grounds
OX17
LANE CL
MANOR ORCH
GULLIVER'S CL
Horley
SPRINGFIELD
HANWELL CT
MAIN ST
PARK CL
CHURCH LA
Hanwell
SACKVILLE CL
GULLICOTE LA
New Inn (PH)
Ragnell Bottom
WARWICK RD
HARDWICK PK 1
BARCOMBE CL 2
ROTHER RD 3
CHEVIOT WAY 4
ROMNEY RD 5
Drayton Lodge
STRATFORD RD
Southfields Farm
Cemy
CH
Golf Course
HORLEY PATH RD
ALVIS GATE 1
BENTLEY CL 2
RICHMAN GDNS 3
MORGAN CL 4
DAIMLER AVE 5
TALBOT CL 6
BEDFORD CL 7
HUMBER WLK 8
OX15
THE FIRS
SILVER ST
QUEEN'S CRES
METCALFE CL
Balscote
MIDDLE LA
MAIN ST
DARK LA
MILLS LA
CHURCH ST
Drayton
Drayton Sch
Alkerton Hill Farm
Guide Post
Sch
Wroxton
Wroxton Coll
Wroxton Abbey
WROXTON CT 1
LAMPITTS GN 2
MILL LA
RECTORY GDNS
LANCHESTER DR 9
MORRIS DR 10
SINCLAIR AVE 11
WILLIAM CL 12
BRAMBER CL 13
PENRHYN CL 14
FERNDALE RD 15
THE FAIRWAY 16
CHERRY RD 17
Obelisk
A422
Castle Bank Enclosure
BANBURY
Balscote Mill
Newington Grounds Farm
Shutford
HASTING CL 1
GLAMIS PL 2
CAERNARVON WAY 3
STIRLING CT 4
CHESTER WAY 5
MARLOWE CL 6
CONWAY DR 7
KENILWORTH WAY 8
CHEPSTOW GDNS 9
HARLECH CL 10
HAMPDEN CL 11
DAIRYGROUND
COOK'S HILL
PLOT RD
LOWER END
THE PLAIN RD
WEST ST
HIGH ST
BANBURY RD
Tythe Farm
Cemy
EPWELL RD
SIBFORD RD
1 MALTHOUSE LA
2 WEAVERS ROW
Claydon Hill
Sor Brook
Withycombe Farm
Bishop Carpenter CE Prim Sch
Wr Twr Mast
SHUTFORD RD
MAIN ST
SCHOOL LA
PARK LA
THE POUND
BALMORAL AVE 1
BRIGGS CL 2
DORCHESTER GR 3
Round Hill
Welshcroft Hill
North Newington
DENBIGH CL
B4035
Jester's Hill
Broughton Grounds Farm
The Bretch
BROUGHTON RD
OX16
BANBURY RD
Crouch Hill
Salt Way
Madmarston Hill
Woadmill Farm
Crouch Farm
Upper Lea Farm
SANDFINE RD
Broughton Park
Broughton
MAIN RD
DANVERS RD
SHUTFORD RD
Swalcliffe Lea
Fulling Mill Farm
DANVERS CL
WYKHAM LA
A361
BLOXHAM RD
Broughton Castle
Cemy
GREEN LA
B4035
B4035
8
45
7
44
6
43
5
42
4
41
3
40
2
39
1
38
38
39
40
41
42
43

136

Scale: 1¾ inches to 1 mile

0 ¼ ½ mile

0 250m 500m 750m 1km

Paddle Brook

High Furze

Middle
Ditchford

Ditchford
Frary

Neighbrook

Ditchford
Hill

Lower
Farm

Knee Brook

River Stour

BECKET
CL

Farriers Arms
(PH)

STONE BRIDGE

CHURCH
VIEW

Aston Magna

CHURCH FARM
LA

Aston Hale

Oldborough
Farm

Todenham

WOLFORD RD

CV36

Nethercote Brook

Dorn

Lower
Lemington

Manor
Farm

GL56

Woodhills
Farm

Mount
Sorrell

Great
Wolford

CARTERS
LEGGE
PH

PO

THE GREEN

Nethercote

Lemington
Grange

Lemington
Manor

NORTH CIRCULAR
RD

5TH AVE

Rectory
Farm

Stanford Brook

6TH AVE

1ST AVE

Wolford Wood

Old
Covert

Moreton-
in-Marsh
District

Moreton-
in-Marsh

NURSERY RD

2ND AVE

3RD AVE

4TH AVE

ULVERTON PL

STATION
RD

DAVIES
RD

MOSSDALE

Fire Service
Tech Coll

CLARKE
AVE

MASSEY
SEAN
AVE
KERR WAY

6TH AVE

FIRTH AVE

Barton-
on-the-Heath

PO

CAMDEN
...

H

PO

BOWLING
GREEN CT

P

OXFORD
ST

A44

STOW RD

LONDON RD

Gravels
Coppice

HOSP

HIGH ST

SWAN CL

A44 BOURTON RD

EAST ST

PRIN...

STOCKWELLS

Cemy

Schl

CH ST

The Four Shires Stone

Mus

PARKERS

Liby

CH ST

KEBLE RD

GREAT ...

COLDSIDE RD

EVENLODE RD

COTSWOLD
BSNS VILLAGE

WELLINGTON RD

Bedesdale ...

FOSSEWAY ...

FOSSEWAY R...

EVENLODE
GDNS

1 GRAY'S LA
2 WARNEFORD PL
3 ST GEORGE'S CL

Moreton-in-Marsh

Fosseway
Farm

1 ST JAMES CT
2 BOWES LYON CL
3 FOSSEWAY CL
4 SANKEY GR

Kitebrook

Salter's Well
Farm

Wells Folly

Coldicote
Farm

Brookend
House

Pool Close Cotts 1
Deerhurst Cl 2
Brewery Row 3

Frogmore Farm

Middle Brookend
Farm

Grove Farm

PAUL'S ...
COL CL
...
CL

River Evenlode

Chastleton
Glebe

Little Compton

Inn

A44

A29

River Stour

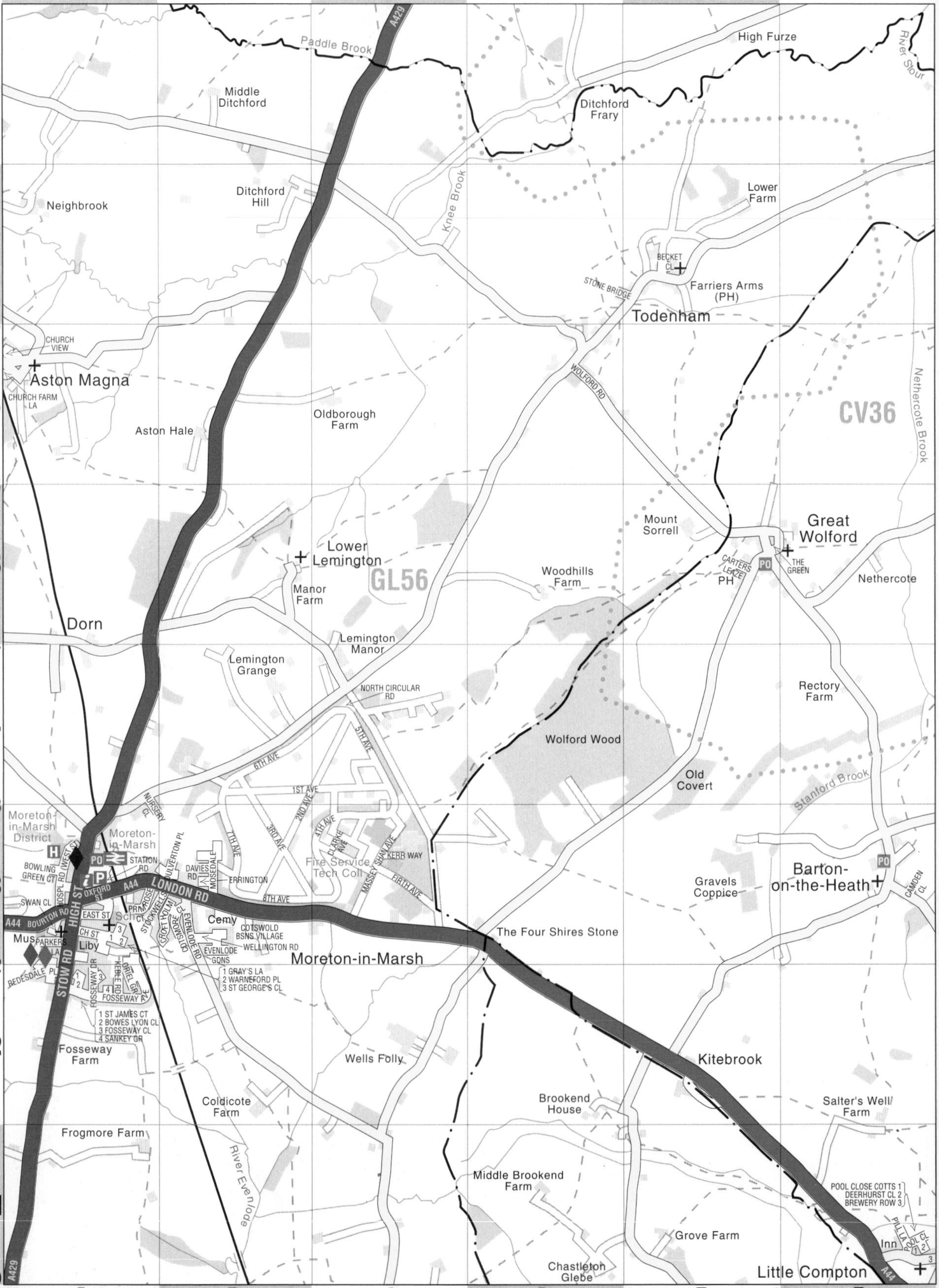

Scale: 1¾ inches to 1 mile
0 ¼ ½ mile
0 250m 500m 750m 1km

137
142

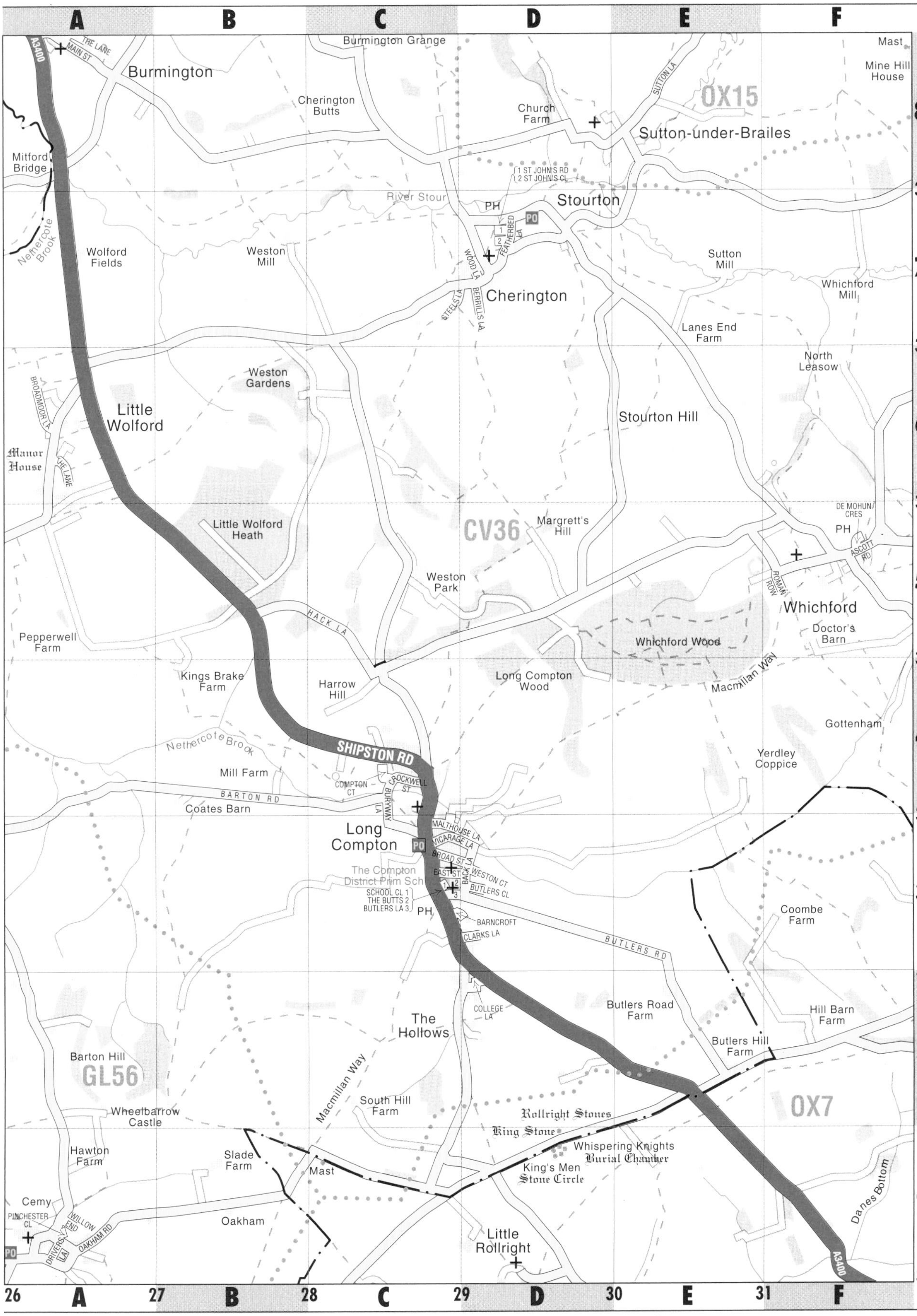

150
142

141
138

Scale: 1¾ inches to 1 mile
0 ¼ ½ mile
0 250m 500m 750m 1km

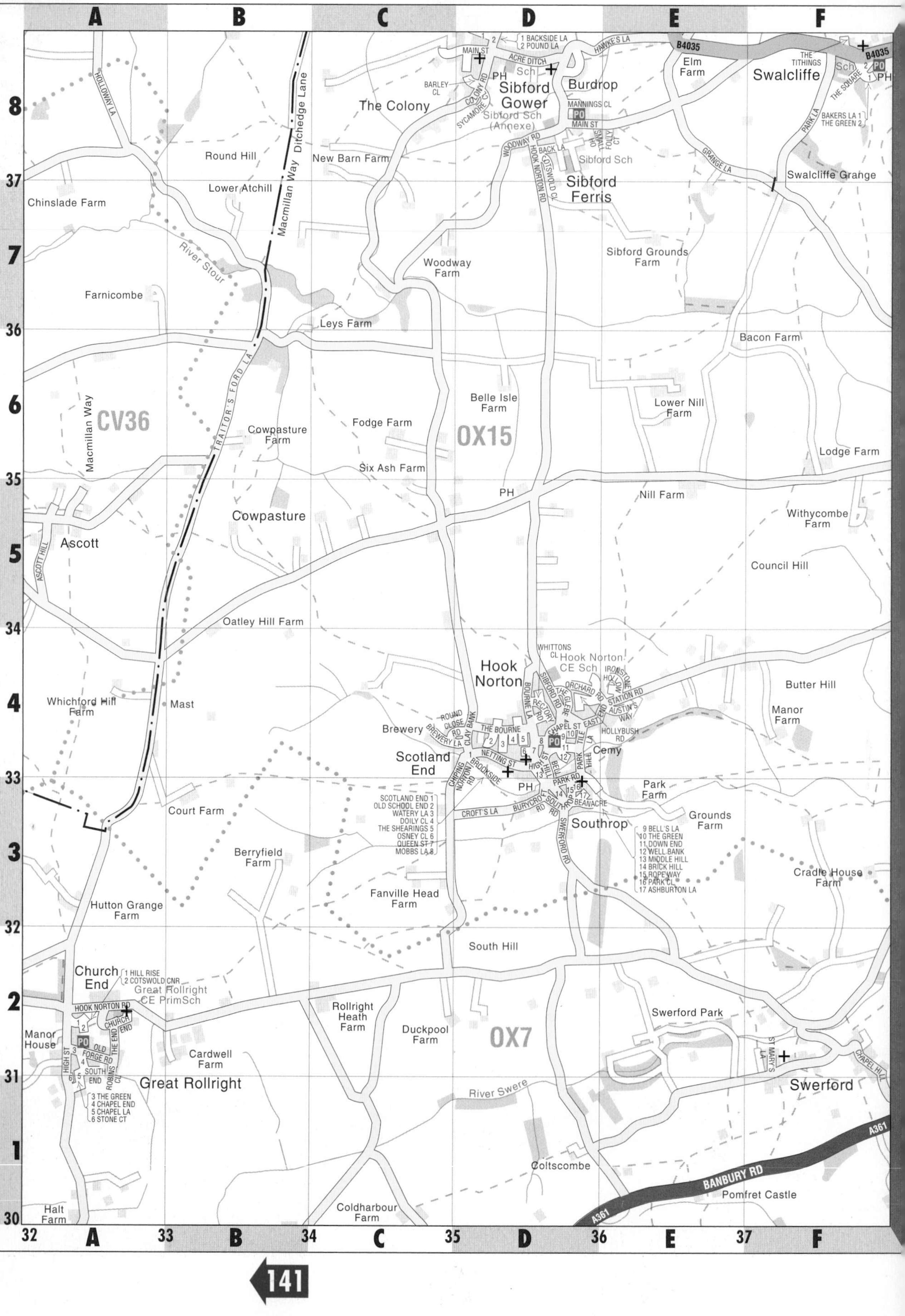

141

118 119 119

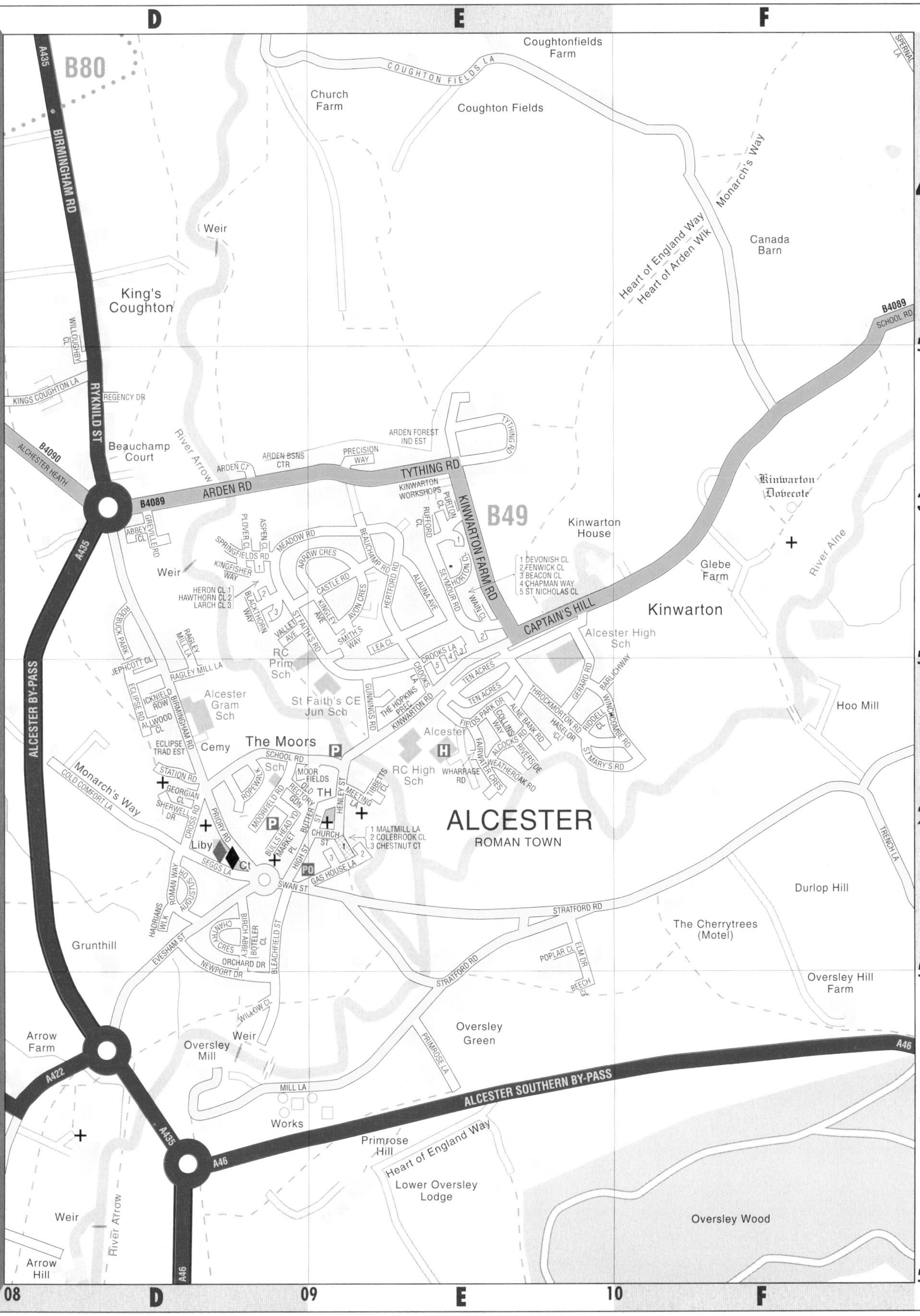

118 119 119

120
120

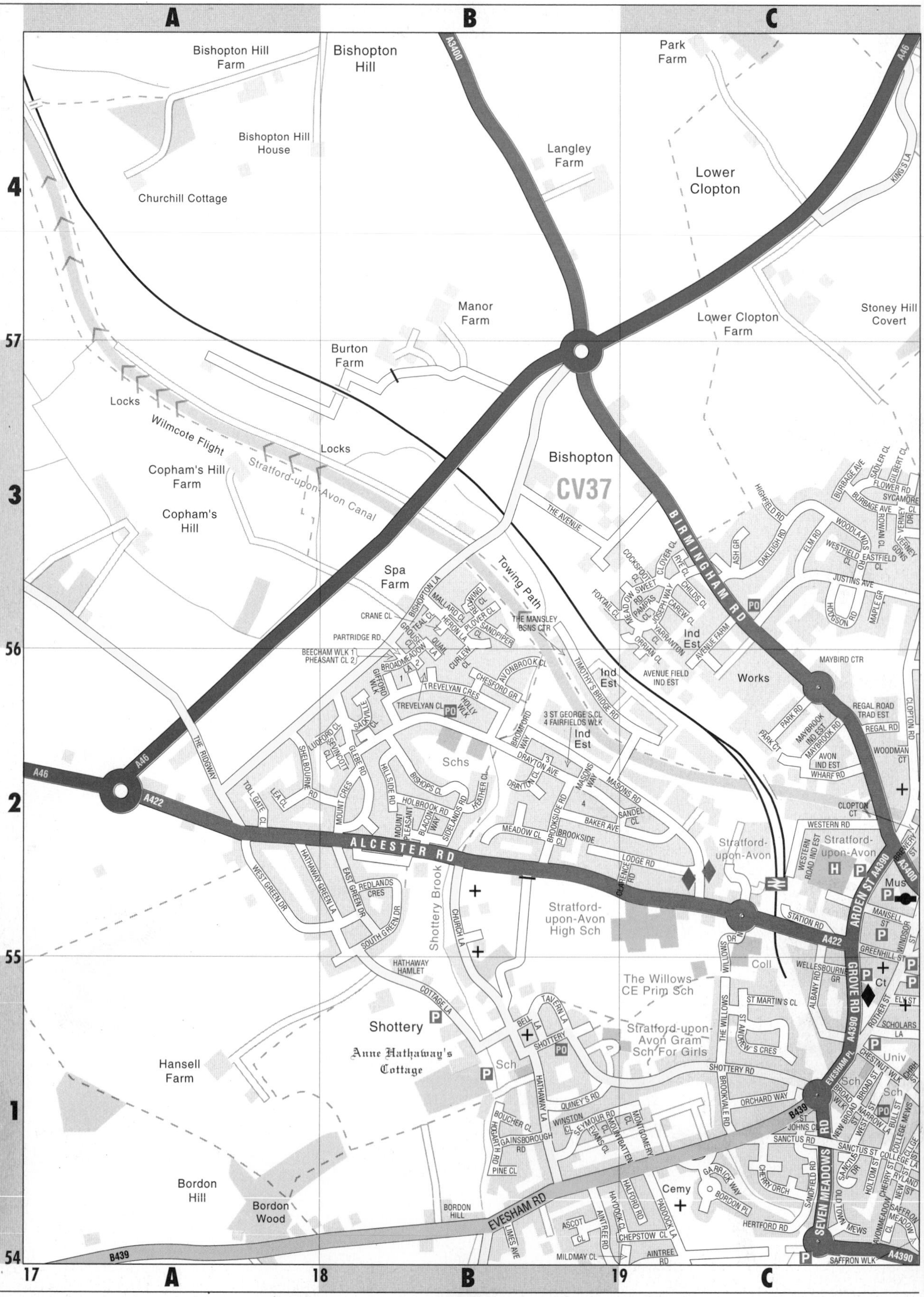

120
129

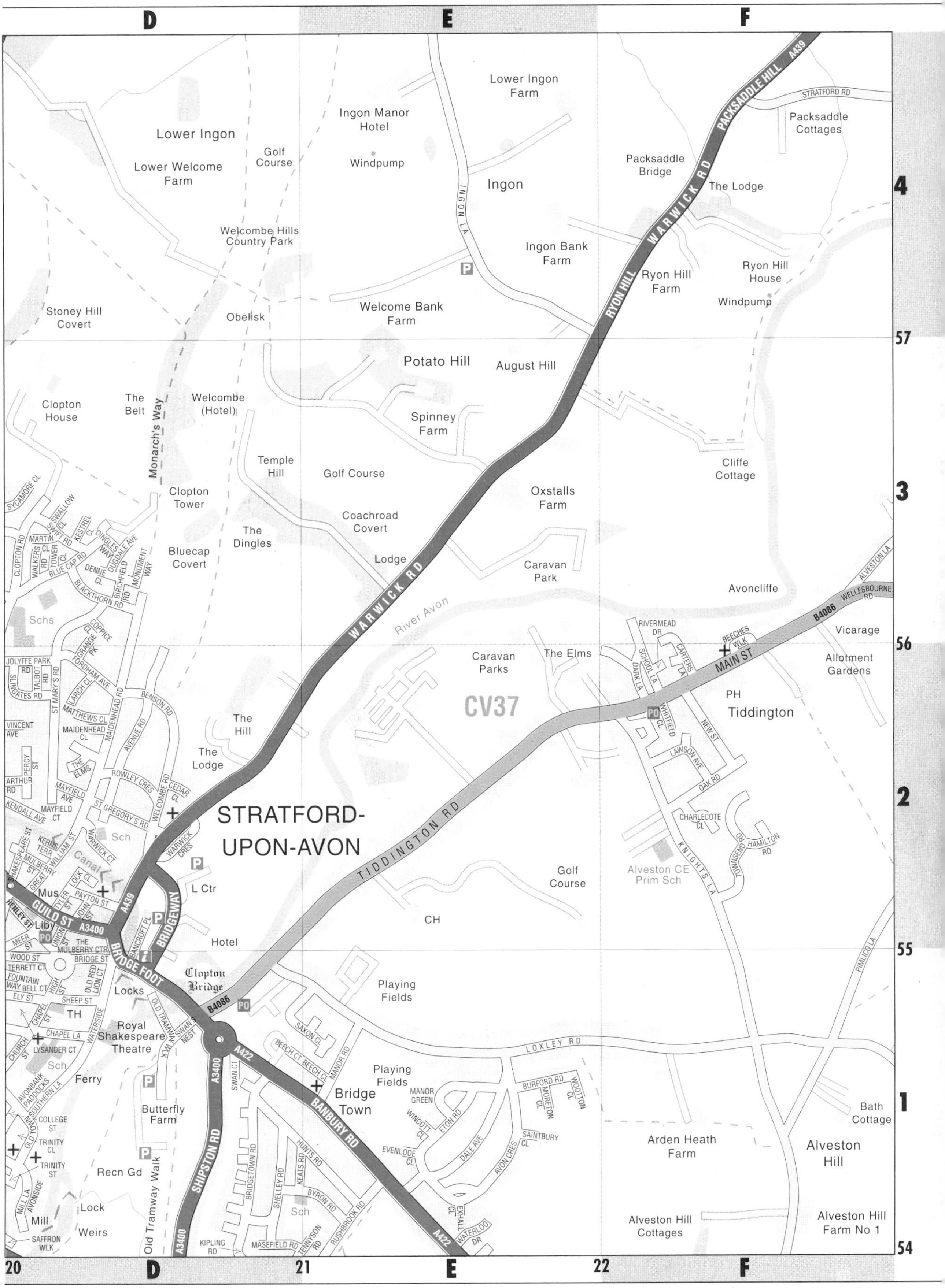
D
E
F
4
57
3
56
2
55
1
54
20
D
21
E
22
F
Lower Ingon Farm
Ingon Manor Hotel
Lower Ingon
Golf Course
Lower Welcome Farm
Windpump
Ingon
INGON LA
Packsaddle Bridge
PACKSADDLE HILL
A439
STRATFORD RD
Packsaddle Cottages
The Lodge
WARWICK RD
Welcombe Hills Country Park
Ingon Bank Farm
Ryon Hill Farm
RYON HILL
Ryon Hill House
Windpump
Welcome Bank Farm
Stoney Hill Covert
Obelisk
Potato Hill
August Hill
Clopton House
The Belt
Welcombe (Hotel)
Monarch's Way
Spinney Farm
Temple Hill
Golf Course
Cliffe Cottage
Clopton Tower
Oxstalls Farm
Coachroad Covert
The Dingles
Bluecap Covert
Lodge
Caravan Park
Avoncliffe
ALVESTON LA
WELLESBOURNE RD
B4086
River Avon
Schs
Vicarage
RIVERMEAD DR
Caravan Parks
The Elms
BEECHES WLK
Allotment Gardens
SCHOOL LA
CARTERS LA
DARK LA
MAIN ST
PH
CV37
WHITFIELD CL
Tiddington
NEW ST
The Hill
LAWSON AVE
The Lodge
OAK RD
STRATFORD-UPON-AVON
TIDDINGTON RD
CHARLECOTE CL
HAMILTON RD
TOWNSEND RD
KNIGHTS LA
Golf Course
Alveston CE Prim Sch
L Ctr
CH
Hotel
Clopton Bridge
Playing Fields
PO
B4086
LOXLEY RD
Playing Fields
SAXON CL
BEECH CT
BEECH CL
MANOR RD
Bridge Town
MANOR GREEN
WINCOTT CL
ETON RD
BURFORD RD
MORETON CL
WOOTTON CL
SAINTBURY CL
Bath Cottage
PIMLICO LA
Arden Heath Farm
Alveston Hill
EVENLODE CL
DALE AVE
AVON CRES
BANBURY RD
A422
Alveston Hill Cottages
Alveston Hill Farm No 1
EXHALL CL
WATERLOO DR
SYCAMORE CL
SWALLOW CL
SWIFT RD
KESTREL CL
MARTIN CL
CLOPTON RD
WALKERS RD
TOWER CL
BLUE CAP RD
DINGLES WAY
DUGDALE AVE
DENNE CL
BIRCHFIELD RD
MONUMENT WAY
BLACKTHORN RD
COPPICE CL
GRANGE PK
JOLYFFE PARK RD
TALBOT RD
SLINGATES RD
ST MARY'S RD
FORDHAM AVE
LARCH CL
MAIDENHEAD RD
BENSON RD
MATTHEWS CL
MAIDENHEAD CL
VINCENT AVE
AVENUE RD
PERCY ST
THE ELMS
ARTHUR RD
ROWLEY CRES
CEDAR CL
MAYFIELD AVE
WELCOMBE RD
KENDALL AVE
MAYFIELD CT
ST GREGORY'S RD
Sch
WARWICK CRES
SHAKESPEARE ST
KERNS TERR
WILLIAM ST
WARWICK CT
MULBERRY ST
GREAT WILLIAM ST
Canal
LOCK CL
BRIDGEWAY
Mus
TYLER ST
PAYTON ST
JOHN ST
A439
GUILD ST
A3400
HENLEY ST
Liby
UNION ST
BANCROFT PL
MEER ST
THE MULBERRY CTR
BRIDGE FOOT
WOOD ST
BRIDGE ST
TERRETT CT
FOUNTAIN WAY
BELL CT
HIGH ST
OLD RED LION CT
ELY ST
Locks
SHEEP ST
CHAPEL ST
TH
WATERSIDE
OLD TRAMWAY WLK
SWANS NEST
Royal Shakespeare Theatre
CHAPEL LA
CHURCH ST
LYSANDER CT
A422
A3400
Sch
SWAN CT
AVONBANK PADDOCKS
SOUTHERN LA
Ferry
COLLEGE ST
OLD TOWN
Butterfly Farm
TRINITY CL
TRINITY ST
SHIPSTON RD
BRIDGETOWN RD
HUNTS RD
Recn Gd
SHELLEY RD
KEATS RD
BYRON RD
MILL LA
AVONSIDE
Lock
Old Tramway Walk
Mill
Sch
RUSHBROOK RD
Weirs
SAFFRON WLK
A3400
KIPLING RD
MASEFIELD RD
TENNYSON RD

121 122 122

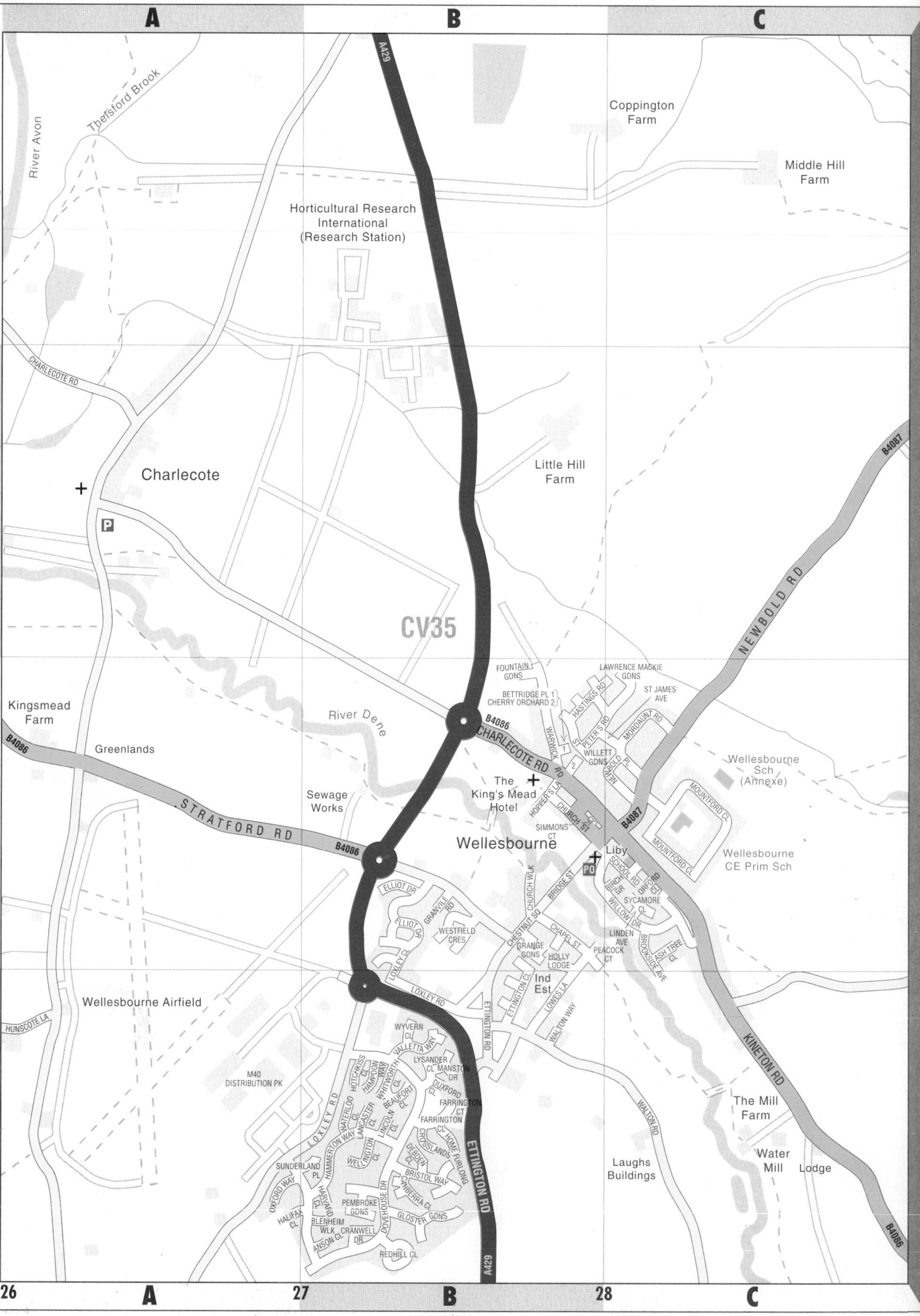

121 131 122

115 115 116

D E F

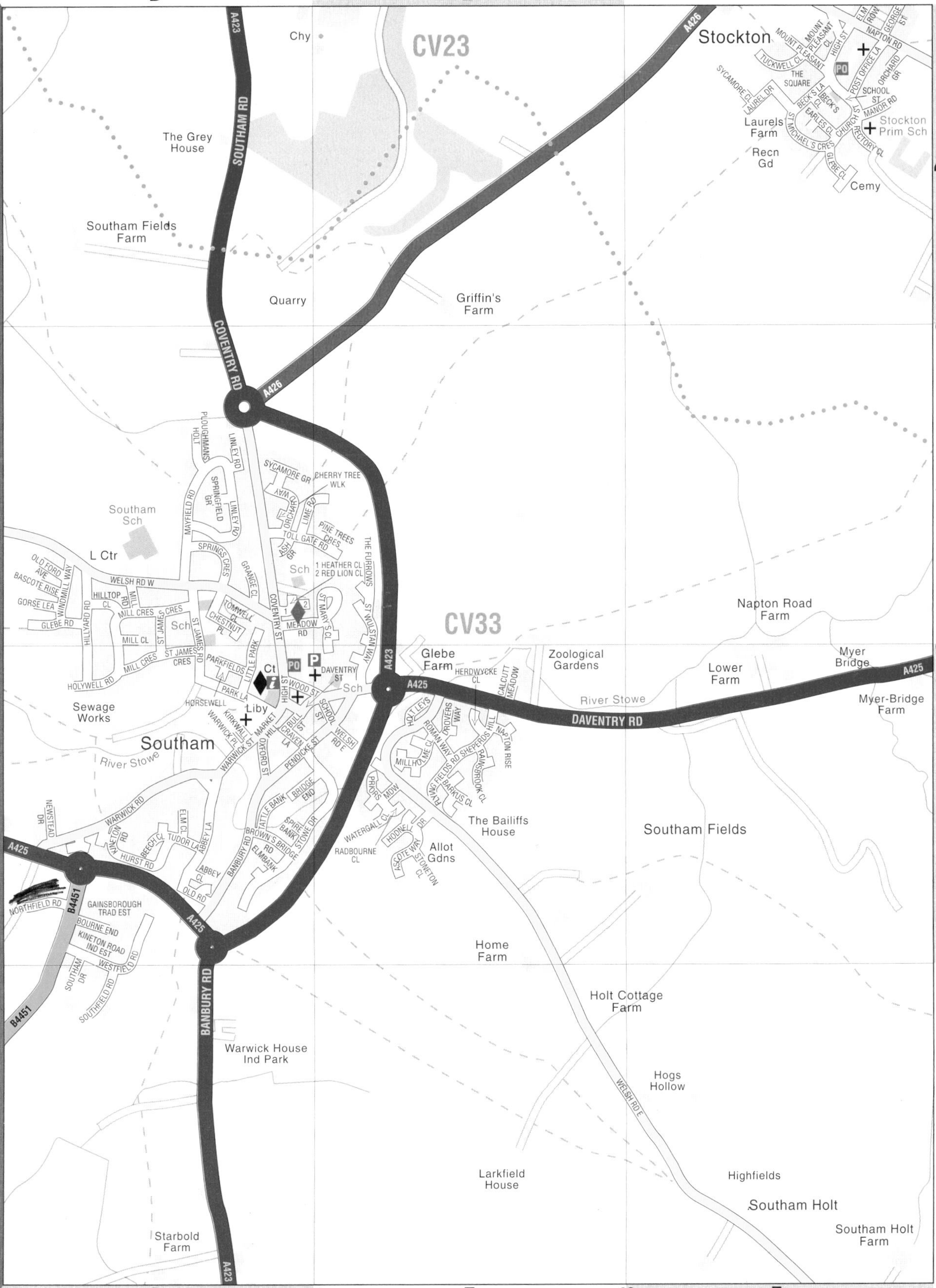

CV23
CV33
Chy
Stockton
The Grey House
Southam Fields Farm
Quarry
Griffin's Farm
SOUTHAM RD
COVENTRY RD
A423
A426
A425
B4451
MOUNT PLEASANT
MOUNT PLEASANT CL
TUCKWELL CL
THE SQUARE
SYCAMORE CL
LAUREL DR
BECK'S LA
BECK'S CL
EARLES CL
ST MICHAEL'S CRES
GLEBE CL
CHURCH ST
POST OFFICE LA
HIGH ST
ELM ROW
GEORGE ST
NAPTON RD
ORCHARD GR
SCHOOL ST
MANOR RD
RECTORY CL
Laurels Farm
Recn Gd
Stockton Prim Sch
Cemy
PO
PLOUGHMANS HOLT
LINLEY RD
SYCAMORE GR
CHERRY TREE WLK
SPRINGFIELD GR
ORCHARD WAY
LIME RD
PINE TREES CRES
TOLL GATE RD
ASH GR
THE FURROWS
Southam Sch
L Ctr
MAYFIELD RD
SPRINGS CRES
GRANGE CL
1 HEATHER CL
2 RED LION CL
Sch
OLD FORD AVE
BASCOTE RISE
WINDMILL WAY
WELSH RD W
HILLTOP
GORSE LEA
GLEBE RD
HILLYARD RD
MILL RD
MILL CRES
ST JAMES CRES
MILL CL
ST JAMES RD
TOMWELL CL
CHESTNUT PL
COVENTRY ST
MEADOW RD
ST MARY'S CL
ST WULSTAN WAY
PARKFIELDS
LITTLE PARK
PARK LA
HOLYWELL RD
Ct
PO
P
DAVENTRY ST
WOOD ST
HIGH ST
SCHOOL ST
Sewage Works
HORSEWELL
Liby
KIRKWALL
WARWICK PL
WARWICK ST
MARKET HILL
OXFORD ST
BULL ST
CRAVEN LA
PENDICKE ST
WELSH RD E
Southam
River Stowe
Glebe Farm
HERDWYCKE CL
CALCUTT MEADOW
Zoological Gardens
River Stowe
DAVENTRY RD
Napton Road Farm
Lower Farm
Myer Bridge
Myer-Bridge Farm
HOLT LEYS
DROVERS WAY
ROMAN WAY
MILLHOLME CL
FLYING FIELDS RD
SHEPERDS HILL
NAPTON RISE
RAINSBROOK CL
BARKUS CL
PRIORS MDW
WATERGALL CL
HODNELL DR
ASCOTE WAY
STONETON CL
RADBOURNE CL
Allot Gdns
The Bailiffs House
Southam Fields
NEWSTEAD DR
WARWICK RD
KINETON RD
BEECH CL
ELM CL
TUDOR LA
ABBEY LA
HURST RD
TATTLE BANK
BRIDGE END
SPIRE BANK
STOWE DR
BROWN'S BRIDGE RD
BANBURY RD
ELMBANK
ABBEY CL
OLD RD
NORTHFIELD RD
GAINSBOROUGH TRAD EST
BOURNE END
KINETON ROAD IND EST
WESTFIELD RD
SOUTHAM DR
SOUTHFIELD RD
Home Farm
Holt Cottage Farm
Warwick House Ind Park
Hogs Hollow
WELSH RD E
Larkfield House
Highfields
Southam Holt
Southam Holt Farm
Starbold Farm
4
63
3
62
2
61
1
60

41 D 42 E 43 F

124 124 125

127
119
128

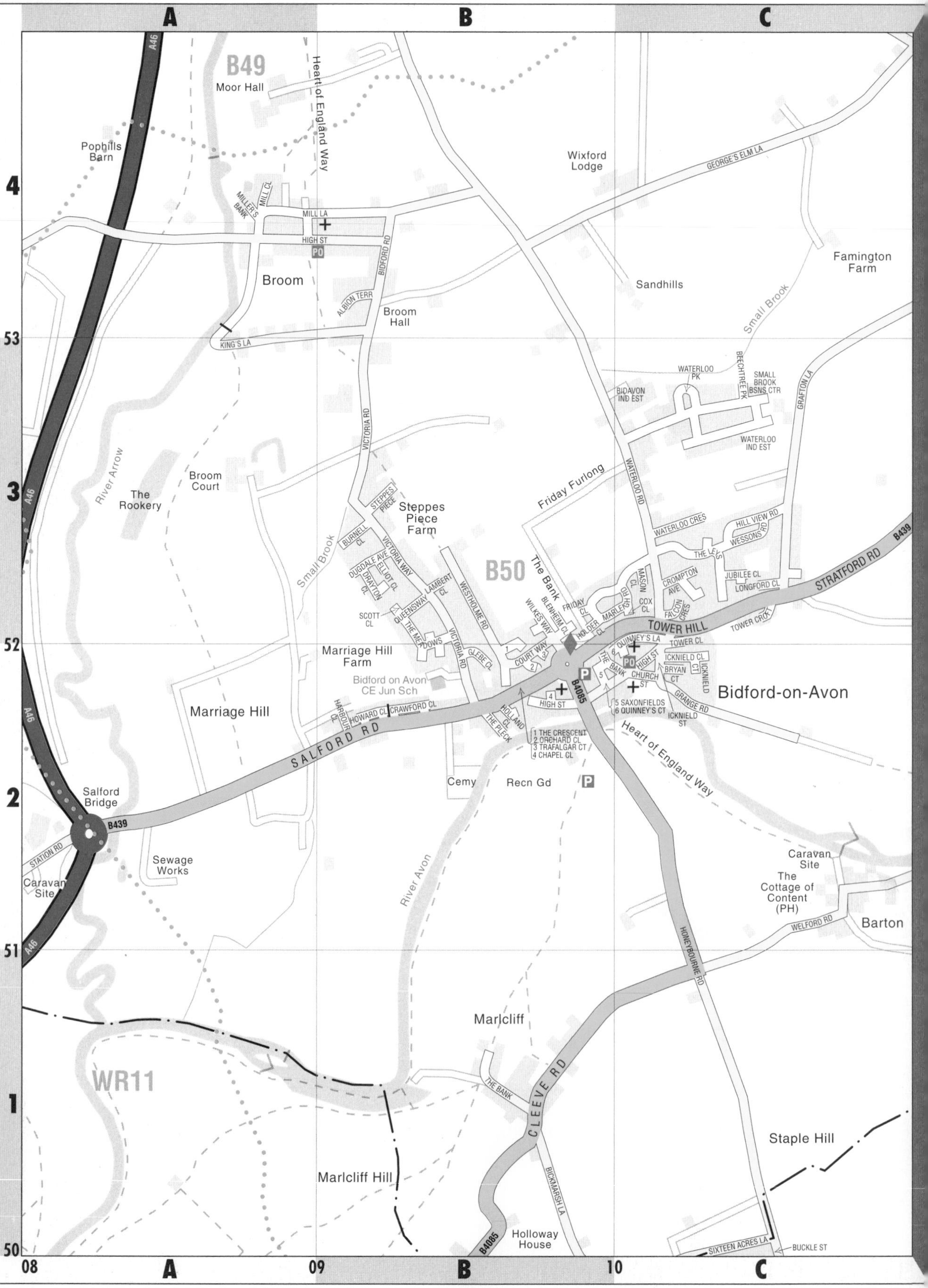

127
128
128

136 136 137

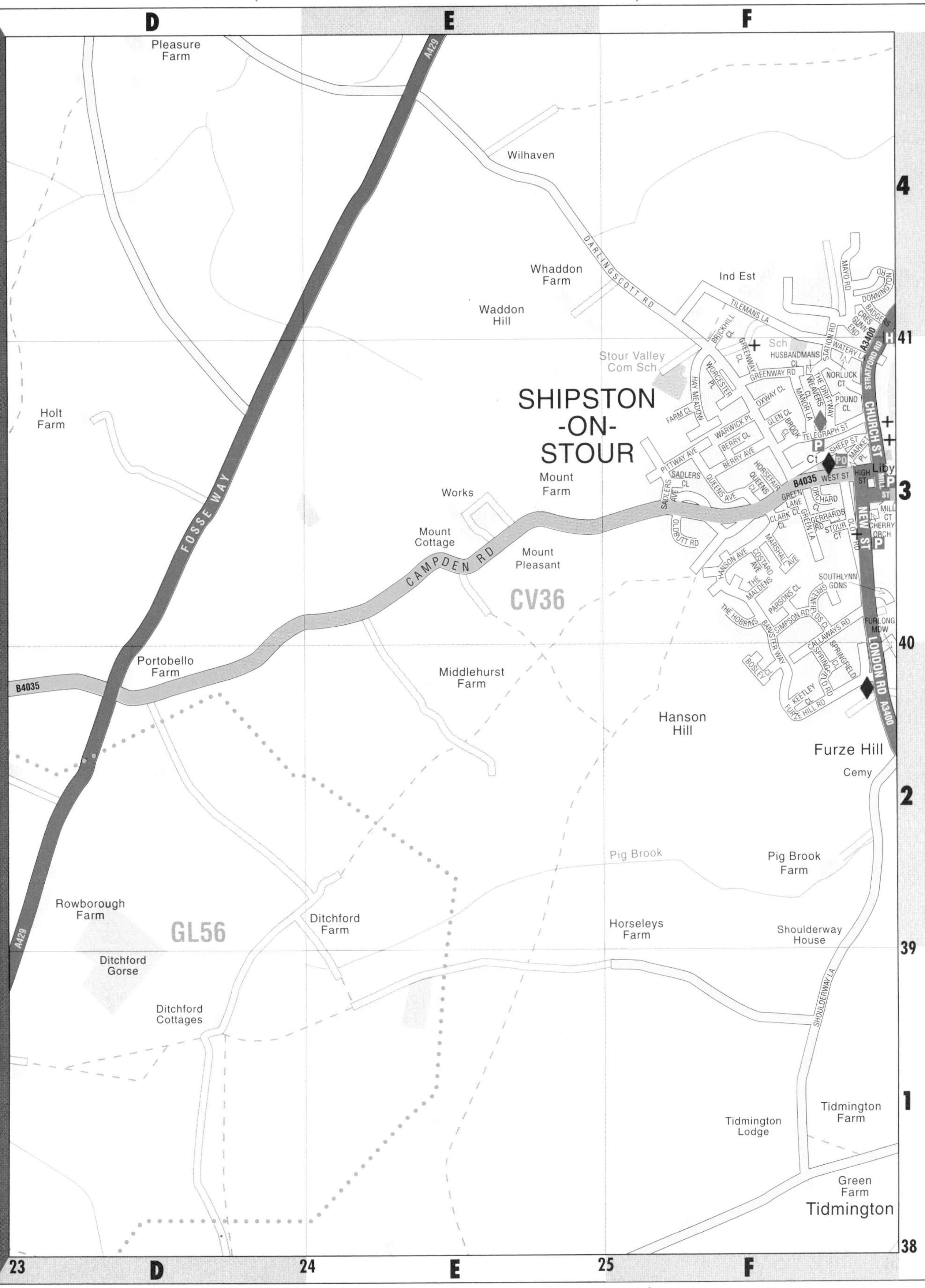

136 140 137

141

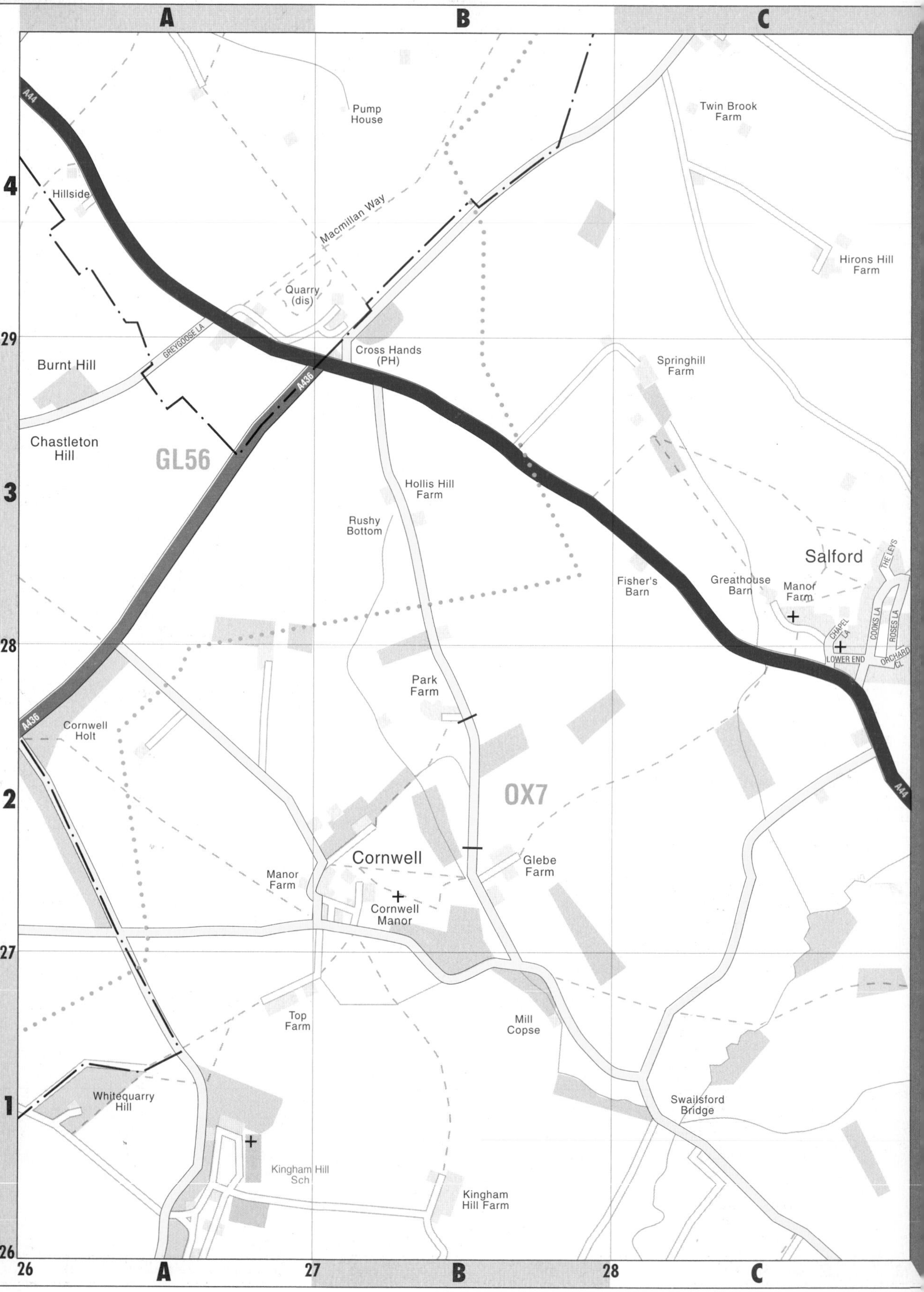
A
B
C
4
29
3
28
2
27
1
26
26
27
28
A44
A436
Pump House
Twin Brook Farm
Hillside
Macmillan Way
Hirons Hill Farm
Quarry (dis)
GREYGOOSE LA
Cross Hands (PH)
Springhill Farm
Burnt Hill
Chastleton Hill
GL56
Hollis Hill Farm
Rushy Bottom
Salford
THE LEYS
Fisher's Barn
Greathouse Barn
Manor Farm
CHAPEL LA
COOKS LA
ROSES LA
LOWER END
ORCHARD CL
Park Farm
Cornwell Holt
OX7
Cornwell
Glebe Farm
Manor Farm
Cornwell Manor
Top Farm
Mill Copse
Whitequarry Hill
Swailsford Bridge
Kingham Hill Sch
Kingham Hill Farm

61
61

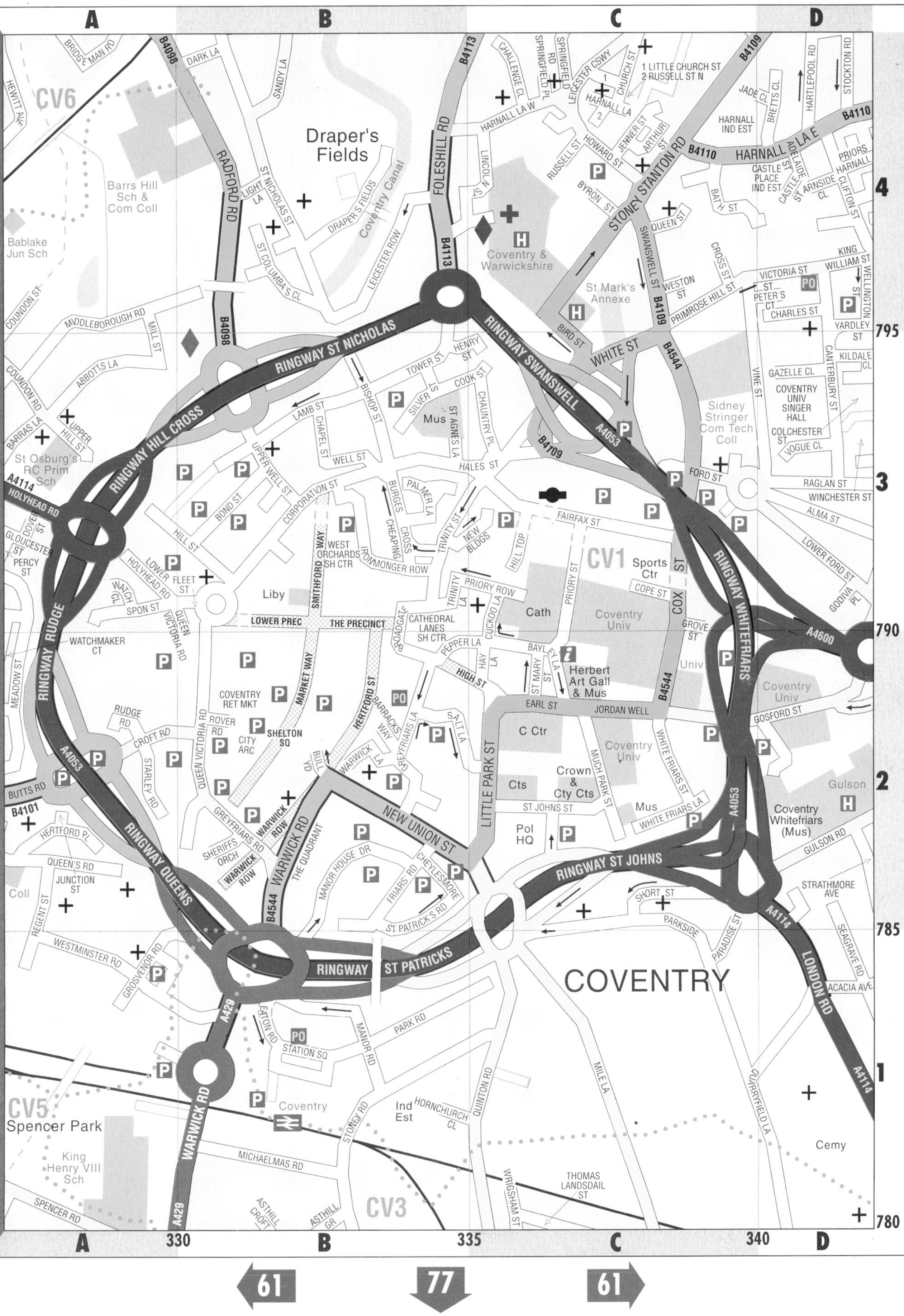
A
B
C
D
4
795
3
790
2
785
1
780
330
335
340
CV6
CV1
CV5
CV3
COVENTRY
Draper's Fields
Barrs Hill Sch & Com Coll
Bablake Jun Sch
St Osburg's RC Prim Sch
Coventry & Warwickshire
St Mark's Annexe
Sidney Stringer Com Tech Coll
COVENTRY UNIV SINGER HALL
HARNALL IND EST
CASTLE PLACE IND EST
Sports Ctr
Cath
Coventry Univ
Herbert Art Gall & Mus
Mus
Liby
C Ctr
Crown & Cty Cts
Cts
Pol HQ
COVENTRY RET MKT
CITY ARC
SHELTON SQ
WEST ORCHARDS SH CTR
CATHEDRAL LANES SH CTR
Coventry Whitefriars (Mus)
Gulson
Coll
Coventry
Spencer Park
King Henry VIII Sch
Ind Est
Cemy
Coventry Canal
RINGWAY ST NICHOLAS
RINGWAY SWANSWELL
RINGWAY HILL CROSS
RINGWAY RUDGE
RINGWAY QUEENS
RINGWAY ST PATRICKS
RINGWAY ST JOHNS
RINGWAY WHITEFRIARS
A4053
A4114
A4600
A429
B4098
B4113
B4109
B4110
B4544
B4709
B4101
FOLESHILL RD
RADFORD RD
STONEY STANTON RD
HARNALL LA E
HARNALL LA W
LONDON RD
WARWICK RD
LITTLE PARK ST
NEW UNION ST
SWANSWELL ST
WHITE ST
BIRD ST
COX ST
GOSFORD ST
JORDAN WELL
EARL ST
HIGH ST
LOWER PREC
THE PRECINCT
SMITHFORD WAY
MARKET WAY
HERTFORD ST
CORPORATION ST
UPPER WELL ST
BISHOP ST
HALES ST
FAIRFAX ST
PRIORY ST
PRIORY ROW
TRINITY ST
BURGES
CHEAPING
IRONMONGER ROW
HOLYHEAD RD
SPON ST
QUEEN VICTORIA RD
GREYFRIARS RD
GREYFRIARS LA
WARWICK ROW
MANOR HOUSE DR
FRIARS RD
CHEYLESMORE
ST PATRICK'S RD
STATION SQ
MANOR RD
PARK RD
QUINTON RD
MILE LA
QUARRYFIELD LA
PARKSIDE
PARADISE ST
MICHAELMAS RD
SPENCER RD
COUNDON RD
MIDDLEBOROUGH RD
ABBOTTS LA
BUTTS RD
HERTFORD PL
QUEEN'S RD
WESTMINSTER RD
GROSVENOR RD
REGENT ST
WHITE FRIARS ST
WHITE FRIARS LA
MUCH PARK ST
ST JOHNS ST
GULSON RD
STRATHMORE AVE
SEAGRAVE RD
ACACIA AVE
VICTORIA ST
KING WILLIAM ST
PRIMROSE HILL ST
RAGLAN ST
WINCHESTER ST
ALMA ST
LOWER FORD ST
FORD ST
1 LITTLE CHURCH ST
2 RUSSELL ST N
COVENTRY

61
77
61

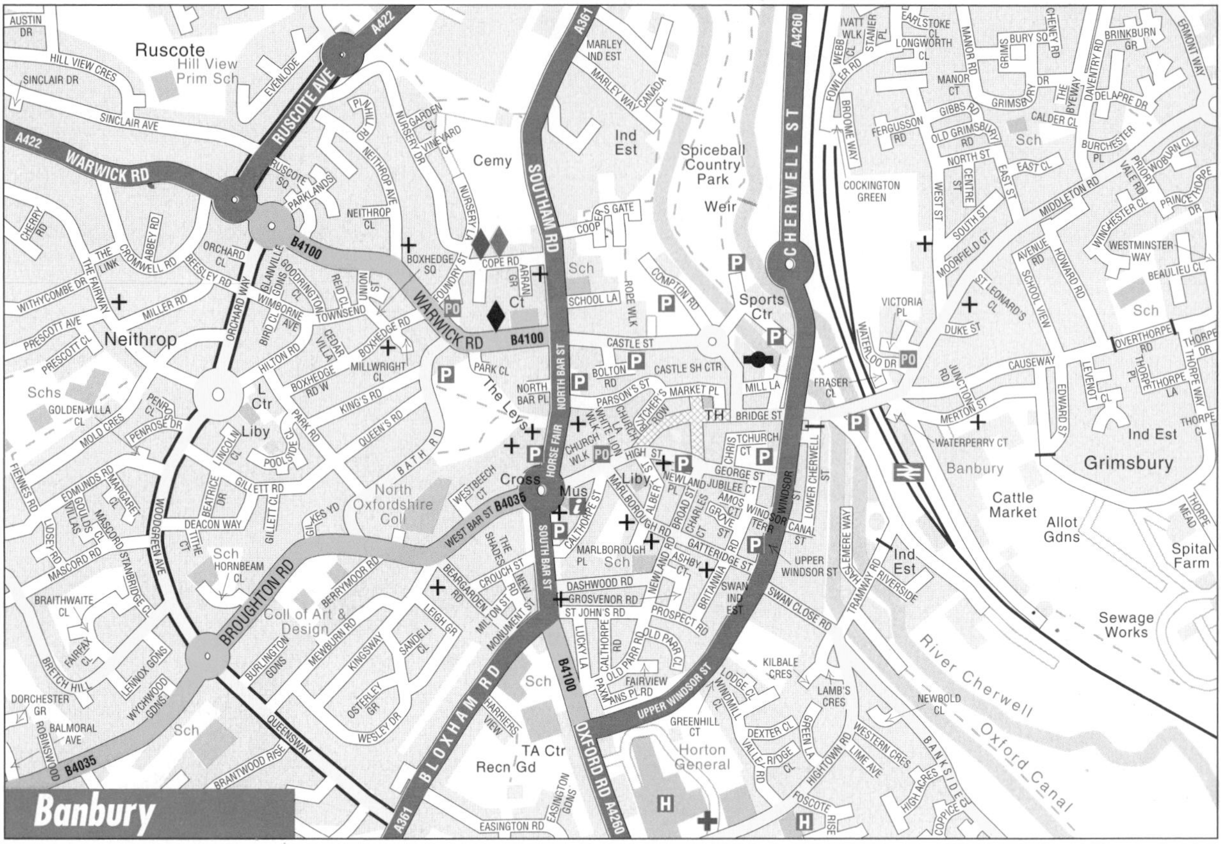
Banbury
Ruscote
Hill View Prim Sch
Neithrop
Cemy
Ind Est
Spiceball Country Park
Weir
Sports Ctr
North Oxfordshire Coll
Coll of Art & Design
Banbury
Cattle Market
Grimsbury
Ind Est
Allot Gdns
Spital Farm
Sewage Works
River Cherwell
Oxford Canal
Horton General
TA Ctr
Recn Gd
Cross
Mus
Liby
WARWICK RD
SOUTHAM RD
CHERWELL ST
BROUGHTON RD
BLOXHAM RD
OXFORD RD
UPPER WINDSOR ST
WEST BAR ST
SOUTH BAR ST
NORTH BAR ST
HORSE FAIR
RUSCOTE AVE
WOODGREEN AVE
MIDDLETON RD
CASTLE ST

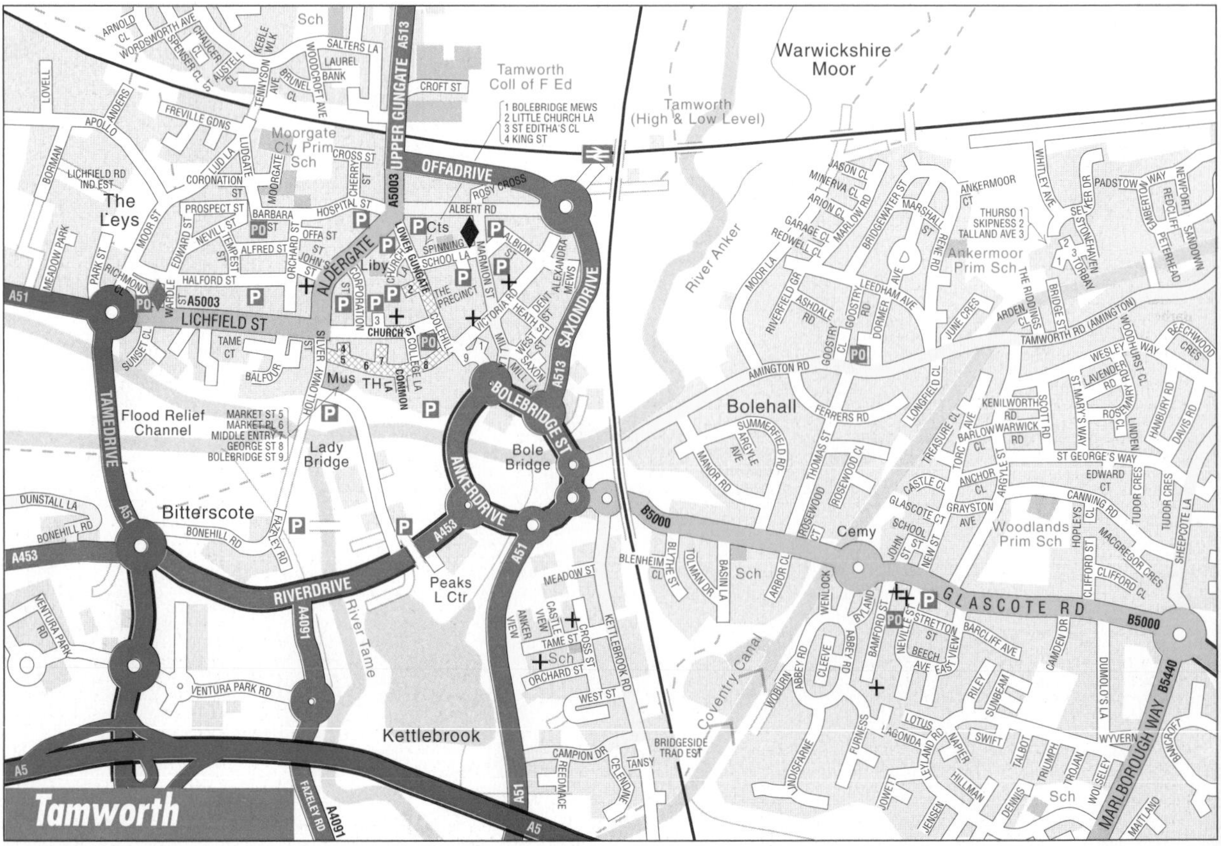
Tamworth
Warwickshire Moor
Tamworth Coll of F Ed
Tamworth (High & Low Level)
Moorgate Cty Prim Sch
The Leys
Flood Relief Channel
Lady Bridge
Bole Bridge
Bitterscote
Peaks L Ctr
River Tame
River Anker
Kettlebrook
Bolehall
Ankermoor Prim Sch
Woodlands Prim Sch
Cemy
Coventry Canal
1 BOLEBRIDGE MEWS
2 LITTLE CHURCH LA
3 ST EDITHA'S CL
4 KING ST
MARKET ST 5
MARKET PL 6
MIDDLE ENTRY 7
GEORGE ST 8
BOLEBRIDGE ST 9
OFFADRIVE
SAXONDRIVE
TAMEDRIVE
RIVERDRIVE
ANKERDRIVE
LICHFIELD ST
UPPER GUNGATE
ALDERGATE
BOLEBRIDGE ST
GLASCOTE RD
AMINGTON RD
MARLBOROUGH WAY

Street names are listed alphabetically and show the locality, the Postcode District, the page number and a reference to the square in which the name falls on the map page

Vernon Cl 9 Coventry CV1 .... **61** F2

Full street name
This may have been abbreviated on the map

Location Number
If present, this indicates the street's position on a congested area of the map instead of the name

Town, village or locality in which the street falls.

Postcode District for the street name

Page number of the map on which the street name appears

Grid square in which the centre of the street falls

Schools, hospitals, sports centres, railway stations, shopping centres, industrial estates, public amenities and other places of interest are also listed. These are highlighted in magenta

Abbreviations used in the index

App	**Approach**	Comm	**Common**	Est	**Estate**	N	**North**	Sq	**Square**
Arc	**Arcade**	Cnr	**Corner**	Gdns	**Gardens**	Orch	**Orchard**	Strs	**Stairs**
Ave	**Avenue**	Cotts	**Cottages**	Gn	**Green**	Par	**Parade**	Stps	**Steps**
Bvd	**Boulevard**	Ct	**Court**	Gr	**Grove**	Pk	**Park**	St	**Street, Saint**
Bldgs	**Buildings**	Ctyd	**Courtyard**	Hts	**Heights**	Pas	**Passage**	Terr	**Terrace**
Bsns Pk	**Business Park**	Cres	**Crescent**	Ho	**House**	Pl	**Place**	Trad Est	**Trading Estate**
Bsns Ctr	**Business Centre**	Dr	**Drive**	Ind Est	**Industrial Estate**	Prec	**Precinct**	Wlk	**Walk**
Bglws	**Bungalows**	Dro	**Drove**	Intc	**Interchange**	Prom	**Promenade**	W	**West**
Cswy	**Causeway**	E	**East**	Junc	**Junction**	Ret Pk	**Retail Park**	Yd	**Yard**
Ctr	**Centre**	Emb	**Embankment**	La	**Lane**	Rd	**Road**		
Cir	**Circus**	Ent	**Enterprise**	Mans	**Mansions**	Rdbt	**Roundabout**		
Cl	**Close**	Espl	**Esplanade**	Mdw	**Meadows**	S	**South**		

Town and village index

Alcester 143 E2
Alderminster 130 D3
Allesley 60 A4
Alvecote 4 B3
Alveston 121 D3
Ansley 27 D2
Ansty 51 E2
Appleby Magna 3 F4
Arley 26 C1
Ash Green 49 E3
Astley 37 F4
Aston Cantlow 119 F6
Aston Flamville 32 C3
Aston le Walls 134 F5
Aston Magna 140 A6
Astwood Bank 102 C1
Atherstone 18 C4
Austrey 3 D1
Avon Dassett 133 C5
Badby 126 F5
Baddesley Ensor 11 E1
Baginton 77 F2
Balsall Common 74 A4
Banbury 139 F3
Barby 101 E1
Barford 122 B7
Barnacle 51 D3
Barston 57 D1
Barton-on-the-Heath ... 140 F1
Bascote 115 C2
Baxterley 17 E3
Bearley 120 E7
Beausale 91 E1
Bedworth 39 D1
Bentley Heath 71 F3
Berkswell 58 B2
Bickenhill 44 B1
Bidford-on-Avon 148 C2
Binley Woods 79 E4
Binton 120 A1
Birchmoor 10 B4
Birdingbury 115 F7
Birmingham 33 E3
Bishops Itchington 124 B4
Bishops Tachbrook 122 E7
Blackdown 105 F3
Bourton on Dunsmore 97 F1
Bradnock's Marsh 57 E2
Bramcote 40 C3
Brandon 79 F3
Braunston 117 E5
Bretford 80 B4
Brinklow 64 C2
Broadwell 116 B4
Broom 148 A4
Broughton 139 E1
Bubbenhall 95 E3
Bulkington 40 A1
Burmington 141 A8
Burton Green 75 E2
Burton Hastings 41 D4
Butlers Marston 131 F5
Catherine de Barnes 56 A3
Catthorpe 68 B1
Chadwick End 90 A4
Charwelton 126 D2
Cherington 141 D7
Chesterton 123 D5
Cheswick Green 70 C2
Chipping Campden 135 B2
Chipping Warden 134 F3
Church Lawford 81 D3
Church Lench 127 A6
Churchover 67 E3
Claverdon 113 F3
Claybrooke Magna 43 E3
Claybrooke Parva 43 F2
Claydon 134 B5
Cleeve Prior 128 A4
Cliff 9 D1
Clifford Chambers 129 F6
Clifton upon Dunsmore ... 84 A3
Coleshill 33 F3
Combrook 131 E6
Cookhill 118 D5
Corley 48 A4
Coughton 118 F7
Coventry 61 D2
Coventry 151 C1
Cropredy 134 C1
Cubbington 106 B3
Curdworth 23 D3
Darlingscott 136 D5
Daventry 117 F1
Dordon 10 C3
Dorridge 71 F2
Drayton 139 E4
Drayton Bassett 8 B3
Dunchurch 99 E2
Dunnington 127 E8
Earlswood 70 A1
Easenhall 65 F2
Ebrington 135 E3
Epwell 138 D3
Ettington 131 B3
Farnborough 133 E4
Fazeley 8 C4
Fenny Compton 133 D7
Fenny Drayton 20 A3
Fillongley 36 C2
Flecknoe 117 B2
Frankton 97 E1
Furnace End 25 F2
G Wolford 140 F5
Gaydon 123 E1
Grandborough 116 E5
Great Alne 119 D6
Great Rollright 142 B1
Grendon 11 E2
Halford 137 A8
Hampton in Arden 57 D4
Hampton Lucy 121 F4
Hampton Magna 114 F4
Hanwell 139 F6
Harborough Magna 66 A2
Harbury 123 E7
Hartshill 19 D1
Harvington 127 C4
Hatton 114 E6
Henley-in-Arden 113 B5
Higham-on-the-Hill 21 D2
Hinckley 31 E4
Hockley Heath 88 B3
Hollywood 69 D4
Honiley 91 E3
Honington 137 A5
Hook Norton 142 D4
Horley 139 D6
Hornton 139 B8
Hurley 16 B2
Ilmington 136 B6
Kenilworth 92 C2
Keresley 48 C3
Kilsby 101 F2
Kineton 132 C6
Kingsbury 15 F3
Knightcote 124 B1
Knowle 72 A3
Ladbroke 124 D5
Lapworth 88 C2
Lawford Heath 98 B4
Lea Marston 24 A4
Leamington Hastings 116 A6
Leek Wootton 104 C4
Lighthorne 123 B2
Lighthorne Heath 123 D2
Lilbourne 84 C3
Little Compton 140 F1
Little Packington 45 E3
Littleton 127 F1
Long Compton 141 C3
Long Itchington 115 D4
Long Lawford 82 A2
Long Marston 129 B3
Lower Boddington 134 E7
Lower Brailes 137 F2
Lower Quinton 129 D2
Lower Shuckburgh 116 F1
Lowsonford 113 E6
Loxley 130 F8
Luddington 129 C7
Lutterworth 55 F3
Mappleborough Green .. 112 B6
Marton 115 C7
Maxstoke 35 D1
Meriden 46 B1
Mickleton 135 C6
Middleton 8 A1
Mile Oak 8 A4
Minworth 22 B3
Mollington 134 A2
Monks Kirby 53 F1
Moreton Morrell 122 F2
Moreton-in-Marsh 140 C3
Napton 125 C8
Nether Whitacre 25 D3
Newbold on Stour 130 E1
Newton 68 A1
Newton Regis 2 B2
North Newington 139 D2
Northend 133 B7
Norton 127 C2
Norton Lindsey 114 C2
Nuneaton 29 D3
Offchurch 111 E4
Offenham 127 D1
Orton-on-the-Hill 6 C2
Oxhill 137 F8
Pailton 66 A4
Pebworth 128 F1
Piccadilly 9 F1
Pillerton Hersey 131 E3
Pillerton Priors 131 D2
Polesworth 5 D1
Portway 86 A3
Preston Bagot 113 D5
Princethorpe 96 C1
Priors Hardwick 125 D3
Priors Marston 125 F4
Radford Semele 110 C3
Ratley 133 A2
Redditch 102 C4
Rowington 114 A8
Rowington Green 90 A1
Royal Leamington Spa ... 109 F4
Rugby 83 D1
Ryton-on-Dunsmore 79 D1
Salford 150 C3
Salford Priors 127 F6
Sambourne 118 D8
Shawell 68 B3
Sheepy Magna 12 C4
Shenington 138 F5
Sherbourne 121 F8
Shilton 51 F3
Shipston-on-Stour 149 E3
Shotteswell 139 E8
Shrewley 114 B6
Shustoke 24 C1
Shutford 139 A3
Shuttington 4 C4
Sibford Ferris 142 D7
Sibford Gower 142 D8
Snitterfield 121 B6
Southam 147 D2
Staverton 126 D7
Stockton 147 F4
Stoke Golding 21 E3
Stoneleigh 94 A3
Stratford-upon-Avon 145 D2
Stretton on Dunsmore 97 D3
Stretton on Fosse 136 B1
Stretton under Fosse 65 E4
Studley 103 F2
Sutton Coldfield 13 D2
Swalcliffe 142 F8
Swerford 142 F1
Tamworth 9 E3
Tanworth-in-Arden 87 D1
Temple Grafton 119 E2
Temple Herdewyke 132 C6
Thorpe Constantine 1 C3
Thurlaston 98 C2
Tidbury Green 69 F2
Tiddington 145 F2
Todenham 140 E7
Tredington 136 F6
Twycross 6 C4
Tysoe 138 B6
Ufton 111 F1
Ullenhall 112 D6
Upper Boddington 134 D8
Upper Brailes 137 E2
Upper Quinton 129 D1
Wardington 134 F1
Warmington 133 D2
Warton 5 F2
Warwick 108 C4
Water Orton 23 E2
Welford on Avon 129 A6
Wellesbourne 146 B2
Weston under Wetherley 107 E4
Whatcote 137 D7
Whateley 9 F2
Whichford 141 F5
White Stitch 46 B2
Whitnash 110 B2
Wibtoft 43 D2
Wigston Parva 42 C4
Willey 54 C3
Willoughby 117 B6
Wilmcote 120 C4
Wishaw 14 A1
Witherley 19 D4
Withybrook 52 C3
Wolston 80 A2
Wolvey 41 E2
Wood End 10 B1
Wootton Wawen 113 B1
Wroxall 90 C2
Wroxton 139 D4
Wythall 69 D2

1st Ave GL56 140 B4
2nd Ave GL56 140 B4
3rd Ave GL56 140 B3
4th Ave GL56 140 C3
5th Ave GL56 140 C4
6th Ave GL56 140 B4
7th Ave GL56 140 B3
8th Ave GL56 140 B3
Ab Lench Rd WR11 127 A6
Abberley B77 4 B1
Abberton Gr B90 71 D4
Abberton Way CV4 76 C2
Abbey CE Fst Sch CV11 29 D3
Abbey Cl Alcester B49 143 D3
Southam CV33 147 D2
Abbey Croft B78 5 D1
Abbey End CV8 92 C2
Abbey Est CV2 62 C3
Abbey Gate CV11 29 E2
Abbey Gate Sh Ctr CV11 29 E2
Abbey Gn CV11 29 D3
Abbey Hill CV8 92 C3
Abbey La CV33 147 D2
Abbey Rd CV3 78 A3
Abbey St Nuneaton CV11 29 D3
Rugby CV21 83 E2
Abbey View B78 11 D4
Abbey Way CV3 77 F3
Abbeydale Cl CV3 62 C1
Abbeyfields Dr B80 103 F3
Abbots Cl B93 72 A4
Abbots Farm Jun & Inf Schs CV21 83 F1
Abbots Wlk CV8 80 A2
Abbots Wood Cl B98 112 A6
Abbotsbury Cl CV2 63 D2
Abbotsford Rd CV11 29 F1
Abbotsford Sch CV8 92 C3
Abbotts Gn LE10 31 F3
Abbotts La CV1 151 A3
Abbotts St 15 CV31 109 F4
Abbotts Way CV21 83 F1
Abbotts Wlk CV3 79 E4
Abeles Way CV9 12 B1
Abelia B77 4 A2
Abercorn Rd CV5 60 C1
Aberdeen Cl CV5 60 A3
Aberdeen Rd CV11 29 F1
Aberfoyle Rd CV35 132 D4
Abergavenny Wlk CV3 78 C3
Abingdon Way
Birmingham B35 22 A2
Nuneaton CV11 29 F4
Abu Sultan Rd CV35 132 F5
Acacia Ave CV1 61 F1
Acacia Gr CV21 83 D2
Acacia Rd Nuneaton CV10 28 C3
Royal Leamington Spa CV32 105 E1
Achal Cl CV6 49 F1
Achilles Rd CV6 62 A4
Acorn Cl Bedworth CV12 49 E4
Stoneleigh CV8 94 A4
Acorn Dr CV22 82 A1
Acorn St CV3 78 A4
Acre Cl CV31 110 A2
Acre Ditch OX15 142 D8
Adam Rd CV6 61 F4
Adams St CV21 82 C2
Adare Dr CV3 77 E4
Adcock Dr CV8 93 D3
Addenbrooke Rd CV7 49 D3
Adderley St CV1 61 F2
Addingham Cl 2 CV34 104 C1
Addison Cl CV10 28 A3
Addison Pl B46 23 D2
Addison Rd Coventry CV6 61 D4
Rugby CV22 82 B1
Adelaide Rd CV31 109 F4
Adelaide St CV1 151 D4
Adkins Croft CV7 36 C2
Adkinson Ave CV22 99 E2
Admington La CV36 135 E7
Admiral Gdns CV8 93 E3
Admirals Way CV11 40 C3
Agincourt Rd CV3 77 F4
Ainsbury Rd CV5 76 C4
Ainsdale Cl CV6 50 A2
Aintree Cl Bedworth CV12 39 D2
Coventry CV6 61 F3
Aintree Dr CV32 106 B2
Aintree Rd CV37 144 B1
Airport Way B26 44 B2
Akon Ho CV6 48 C1
Alan Bray Cl LE10 30 B4
Alan Higgs Way CV4 75 E4
Alandale Ave CV5 59 F2
Alauna Ave B49 143 E3
Albany Rd Coventry CV5 61 D1
Stratford-u-A CV37 144 C1
Albany Terr CV32 105 F1
Albert Cl B80 103 F2
Albert Cres CV6 49 D2
Albert Rd Allesley CV5 59 D4
Fazeley B78 9 D4
Albert Sq CV21 83 D2
Albert St Coventry CV1 61 F2
Nuneaton CV10 28 C1
Royal Leamington Spa CV32 105 E1
Rugby CV21 83 D2
Warwick CV34 108 B4
Albion Ind Est CV6 61 E4
Albion St CV8 93 D3
Albion Terr B50 148 B4
Albrighton Wlk CV11 30 A1
Albury Rd B80 103 F2
Alcester By-Pass B49 143 D2
Alcester Gram Sch B49 143 D2
Alcester Heath B49 118 E6
Alcester High Sch B49 143 E3
Alcester Highway B98 102 C4
Alcester Hospl B49 143 E2
Alcester Inf Sch B49 143 D2
Alcester Rd Hollywood B47 69 D4
Portway B48 85 F4
Stratford-u-A CV37 144 B2
Studley B80 103 F2
Wootton Wawen B95 113 A1
Wootton Wawen B95 113 B2
Alcester Southern By-Pass B49 143 E1
Alcocks Rd B49 143 E2
Alcott Cl B93 71 F1
Alcott Hall Prim Sch B37 33 D1
Aldbourne Rd CV1 61 E3
Aldbury Rise CV5 60 B2
Alder Cl B47 69 D3
Alder Dr B37 33 D1
Alder La CV7 74 B3
Alder Meadow Cl CV6 49 E2
Alder Rd CV6 50 A1
Alderbrooke Dr CV11 30 A1
Alderhanger La B98 112 B8
Alderman Callow Sch & Com Coll CV4 76 A3
Alderman Harris Prim Sch CV4 75 F4
Alderman Smith Sch CV10 28 B1
Alderman Way CV33 107 E4
Alderman's Green Ind Est CV2 50 B1
Alderman's Green Prim Sch CV2 50 B2
Alderman's Green Rd CV2 50 A2
Alderminster Gr CV35 114 F5
Alderminster Rd
Coventry CV5 60 A2
Solihull B90 71 E4
Aldermoor Farm Prim Sch CV3 78 A4
Aldermoor La CV3 62 A1
Alderney Cl Bramcote CV11 40 C3
Coventry CV6 49 D1
Alders Dr B98 112 A6
Alders Gr CV34 108 B2
Alders La CV10 28 A4
Alders The CV12 38 C1
Aldersgate B78 15 E4
Alderton Mews CV31 110 B3
Aldrich Ave CV4 59 F1
Aldridge Cl B78 10 C4
Aldridge Rd LE10 31 E3
Aldrin Way CV4 76 B3
Aldwick Cl CV32 106 A2
Alesworth Dr LE10 31 F2
Alex Grierson Cl CV3 78 C4
Alexander Rd CV12 39 E2
Alexandra Ct CV9 18 C4
Alexandra Hospl The B98 103 E3
Alexandra Rd Coventry CV1 61 F2
Royal Leamington Spa CV31 110 A3
Rugby CV21 83 D2
Alexandra St CV11 29 D2
Alfall Rd CV2 62 A3
Alfred Green Cl CV22 83 D1
Alfred Rd CV1 61 F2
Alfred St CV21 82 C1
Alfreda Ave B47 69 D4
Alfreton Cl LE10 31 F3
Alfriston Rd CV3 77 E2
Alice Cl CV12 38 C1
Alice Stevens Sch CV3 78 A3
Alison Sq CV6 50 A2
All Saints CE Fst Sch
Bedworth CV12 39 E1
Nuneaton CV10 29 E1
All Saints CE Mid Sch CV34 105 D1
All Saints CE Prim Sch CV1 61 F1
All Saints Cl CV7 52 C3
All Saints La CV1 61 F2
All Saints Rd Bedworth CV12 38 C1
Warwick CV34 109 D4
All Saints Sq CV12 39 D2
All Souls RC Prim Sch CV5 60 B1
Allan Rd CV6 60 C2
Allans Cl CV23 84 A3
Allans La CV23 84 A3
Allard Way CV3 78 B4
Allen Cl B80 103 F2
Allendale Ave B80 103 F2
Allendale Cres B80 103 F2
Allendale Ct B80 103 F2
Allens Cl CV9 17 E4
Allens Orch OX17 134 F3
Allerton Cl CV2 62 C1
Allesley Croft CV5 60 A4
Allesley Cty Prim Sch CV5 60 A4
Allesley Hall Dr CV5 60 B3
Allesley Hall Prim Sch CV5 60 A2
Allesley Old Rd CV5 60 B2
Allesley Rd CV21 82 C3
Alliance Cl CV11 29 F2
Alliance Way CV2 62 A3
Allibone Cl CV31 110 A2
Allied Cl CV6 49 E1
Allitt Gr CV8 93 D3
Allwood Cl B49 143 D2
Alma Ct CV11 40 C3
Alma St CV1 151 D3
Almond Ave Nuneaton CV10 28 B3
Royal Leamington Spa CV32 105 F2
Almond Cl CV23 101 E1
Almond Gr Rugby CV21 82 C4
Warwick CV34 105 D1
Almond Tree Ave CV2 50 B1
Almshouses B78 8 A1
Alne Bank Rd B49 143 E2
Alne Cl B95 113 B4
Alpha Bsns Pk CV2 50 B1
Alpine Ct CV8 93 D3
Alpine Rise CV3 77 D3
Alspath La CV5 59 F2
Alspath Rd CV7 46 B1
Althorpe Dr B93 71 F2
Althorpe Ind Est 7 CV31 110 A4
Althorpe St CV31 110 A4
Alton Cl CV2 50 B1
Alum Cl CV6 61 E4
Alvecote Pools Nature Reserve B79 4 B4
Alverstone Rd CV2 62 A2
Alveston CE Prim Sch CV37 145 F2
Alveston Gr B93 72 A4
Alveston La CV37 121 D3
Alveston Rd B47 69 D4
Alvin Cl CV3 62 C1
Alvis Gate OX16 139 F4
Alvis Ret Pk CV5 61 D2
Alvis Way NN11 117 F2
Alvis Wlk B36 22 C1
Alwyn B77 9 F4
Alwyn Rd CV22 99 E3
Alwynne Freeman Ct CV7 49 D3
Amber Bsns Village B77 4 A2
Amber Cl B77 4 A2
Amberley Ave CV12 40 B1
Ambien Rd CV9 18 B4
Ambler Gr CV2 62 B2
Ambleside Coventry CV2 50 C1
Rugby CV21 83 E4
Ambleside Way CV11 29 F3
Ambrose Cl CV21 83 E3
Amersham Cl CV5 60 A2
Amherst Rd CV8 92 C3
Amhurst Bsns Ctr CV34 108 A4
Amicombe B77 4 B1
Amington Heath Prim Sch B77 4 A2
Amington Ind Est B77 4 A1
Amington Rd B90 70 A4
Amos Ave CV10 29 D1
Amos Jacques Rd CV12 39 D2
Amroth Mews 1 CV31 110 B3
Amy Cl CV6 49 F2
Anchor La WR11 127 E3
Anchorway Rd CV3 77 D2
Anderson Ave CV22 100 A4
Anderson Dr CV31 110 A1
Anderton Rd Bedworth CV12 38 B1
Coventry CV6 50 A2
Andrew Cl CV13 21 E4
Angela Ave CV2 50 C1
Anglesey Ave B36 33 D3
Anglesey Cl CV5 60 A4
Angless Way CV8 92 C2
Angus Cl Coventry CV5 60 A2
Kenilworth CV8 93 E3
Anker Dr CV23 82 A3
Anker St CV11 29 E2
Anker View B78 11 D4
Ankerside B78 5 D2
Ann Rd B47 69 D2
Anne Cres CV3 78 B3
Annie Osborn Prim Sch CV2 62 B4
Ansell Rd CV34 108 B4
Ansley Comm CV10 28 A4
Ansley La CV7 26 C2
Ansley Rd CV10 27 F2
Anson Cl Rugby CV22 82 B1
Wellesbourne CV35 146 B1
Anson Way CV2 62 C4
Ansty Rd CV2 62 C3
Antelope Gdns CV34 108 B4
Anthony Way CV2 62 B1
Anton Dr B76 22 A3
Antrim Cl CV5 60 A4
Antrobus Cl CV35 114 C5
Apollo Way CV34 109 E3
Appian Cl B77 9 E4
Appian Way B90 70 B2
Apple Gr CV22 82 A1
Apple Pie La CV10 19 D1
Applebee Rd LE10 31 E3
Appleby Cl Banbury OX16 139 F4
Great Alne B49 119 D6
Appleby Gr 9 B90 71 D3
Appleby Hill CV9 3 D2
Applecross Cl CV4 75 F3
Appledore Dr CV5 59 F3
Appletree Cl B91 56 A3
Appletree La Cookhill WR7 118 A3
Cropredy NN11 134 F5
Appletree Rd OX17 134 F3
Approach The CV31 109 F3
Apsley Gr B93 71 F1
Aragon Dr CV34 109 E3
Arbor Way B37 33 E1
Arboretum The CV4 76 B2
Arbour Cl Kenilworth CV8 93 D2
Mickleton GL55 135 B6
Rugby CV22 99 E4
Arbour Tree La B93 89 F4
Arbury Ave Bedworth CV12 39 D2
Coventry CV6 49 F1
Arbury Banks OX17 134 F3
Arbury Cl CV32 106 A2
Arbury Ct B95 113 B5
Arbury Hall Rd B90 70 B4
Arbury Rd CV10 28 B1
Arbury Wlk B76 22 B3
Arch Rd CV2 62 C3
Archer Ave NN11 117 E5
Archer Cl B80 103 E2
Archer Rd CV8 92 C2
Archers Spinney CV21 101 D4
Archery Fields CV34 108 C3
Archery Rd Meriden CV7 46 A1
Royal Leamington Spa CV31 109 F4
Arches Bsns Ctr CV21 83 E3
Arches Ind Est CV21 83 E3
Arches Ind Est The CV5 61 D2
Arches La CV21 83 E3
Arden Ave CV9 18 C4
Arden Bsns Ctr B49 143 D3
Arden Cl Balsall Common CV7 74 A4
Henley-in-A B95 113 B4
Meriden CV7 46 B1
Royal Leamington Spa CV31 110 A3
Rugby CV22 99 E3
Warwick CV34 105 D1
Wilmcote CV37 120 C5
Arden Croft B46 23 F1
Arden Ct B49 143 D3
Arden Dr Dorridge B93 72 A1
Sutton Coldfield, Falcon Lodge B75 13 D3
Arden Forest Est CV10 18 A1
Arden Forest Ind Est B49 143 E3
Arden Forest Inf Sch CV12 40 A2
Arden Hill Inf Sch CV9 18 C4
Arden Lawn Sch B95 113 A4
Arden Leys B94 86 B1
Arden Meads B94 88 B3
Arden Rd Alcester B49 143 D3
Bulkington CV12 40 B1
Dorridge B93 71 F1
Henley-in-A B95 113 B4
Hollywood B47 69 D3
Kenilworth CV8 93 D2
Nuneaton CV11 30 A1
Tamworth B77 9 F3
Arden Sch B93 72 A3
Arden St Atherstone CV9 18 C4
Coventry CV5 76 C4
Stratford-u-A CV37 144 C2
Arden Vale Rd B93 72 A4
Ardens Cl B98 112 A5
Arderne Dr B37 33 D1
Argyle St CV21 83 E2
Argyle Way 5 CV33 122 F8
Argyll St CV2 62 A2
Ariel Way CV22 99 E3
Arkle B77 9 E2
Arkle Dr CV2 62 C4
Arleston Way B90 70 C4
Arley Ind Est CV7 36 C4
Arley La CV10 27 E2
Arley Mews CV32 105 F1
Arlidge Cres CV8 93 E3
Arlington Ave CV32 105 F1
Arlington Mews 14 CV32 105 F1
Arlington Way CV11 29 F1
Arlon Ave CV10 28 B4
Armarna Dr CV5 59 D4
Armfield St CV6 62 A4
Armorial Rd CV3 77 D4
Armour Cl LE10 31 E3
Armscote Rd
Ilmington CV36 136 B6
Tredington CV36 136 E6
Armscott Rd CV2 62 B3
Armson Rd CV7 39 D1
Armstrong Ave CV3 62 A1
Armstrong Cl Rugby CV22 82 C1
Whitnash CV31 110 A1
Armstrong Dr B36 22 C1
Arncliffe Cl CV11 30 A1
Arncliffe Way 11 CV34 104 C1
Arne Rd CV2 63 D3
Arnhem Cnr CV3 78 B3
Arnold Ave CV3 77 E3
Arnold Cl CV22 83 D1
Arnold Lodge Prep Sch CV32 105 F1
Arnold Rd CV13 21 E3
Arnold St CV21 83 D2
Arnolds La B46 34 C2
Arnside Cl CV1 151 D4
Arran Cl CV10 29 D2
Arran Way B36 33 D4
Arras Bvd CV35 108 A4
Arrow Cl B93 72 A3
Arrow Cres B49 143 E3
Arrow End WR11 128 A2
Arrow La WR11 127 F2
Arthingworth Cl CV3 62 C1
Arthur Rd CV37 145 D2
Arthur St Coventry CV1 151 C4
Kenilworth CV8 93 D3
Artillery Rd CV11 40 C3
Arun Way B76 13 D1
Arundel B77 9 E4
Arundel Cl 2 CV34 108 C4
Arundel Pl OX16 139 F3
Arundel Rd Bulkington CV12 40 B2
Coventry CV3 77 E3
Asbury Rd CV7 74 A3
Ascot Cl Bedworth CV12 39 D2
Coventry CV3 78 B3
Stratford-u-A CV37 144 B1
Ascot Rd CV35 132 D3
Ascot Ride CV32 106 B2
Ascote Way CV33 147 E2
Ascott Hill CV36 142 A5
Ascott Rd CV36 141 F5
Asfare Bsns Pk LE10 31 F1
Ash Cl CV35 114 C5
Ash Ct CV22 99 F4
Ash Dr Hartshill CV10 28 A4
Kenilworth CV8 93 D2
Ash Gr Arley CV7 26 C1
Ash Green CV7 49 E4
Kingsbury B78 15 E4
Southam CV33 147 D3
Stratford-u-A CV37 144 C3
Tamworth B77 9 F3
Ash Green La CV7 49 E3
Ash Green Sch CV7 49 E3
Ash La CV37 120 E7
Ash Priors Cl CV4 60 A1
Ash Tree Ave CV4 60 A1
Ash Tree Cl CV35 146 C2
Ash Tree Gr CV7 51 F3
Ash Way NN11 117 D5
Ashborough Dr B91 71 E4
Ashbourne Way B90 70 C4
Ashbridge Rd CV5 60 B2
Ashbrook Cres B91 71 E4
Ashbrook Rise CV10 19 D1
Ashburton Cl LE10 32 A3
Ashburton La OX15 142 D3
Ashburton Rd CV2 62 C4
Ashby Cl CV3 78 C4
Ashby Ct CV11 29 E2
Ashby Rd NN11 117 E5
Ashcombe Dr CV4 59 F2
Ashcroft Cl CV2 63 D4
Ashcroft Way CV2 63 D4
Ashdale Cl CV3 79 F4
Ashdene Gdns CV8 93 D2
Ashdown Cl CV3 78 B4
Ashdown Dr CV10 28 C1
Ashe Rd CV10 28 A2
Ashfield Ave CV4 59 E1
Ashfield Rd CV8 93 D2
Ashford Dr CV12 39 D2
Ashford Gdns CV31 109 F2
Ashford La B94 88 A4
Ashford Rd Hinckley LE10 31 D4
Whitnash CV31 109 F1
Ashfurlong Cl CV7 74 A3
Ashington Gr CV3 78 A3
Ashington Rd CV12 38 B1
Ashlawn Rd CV22 100 B4
Ashlawn Sch CV22 100 C4
Ashlea B78 10 C3
Ashleigh Cl CV23 101 E1
Ashleigh Dr Nuneaton CV11 29 F1
Tamworth B77 9 F4
Ashley Cres CV34 109 D3
Ashman Ave CV23 82 A3
Ashmore Rd CV6 61 D2
Ashmores Cl B97 102 B3
Ashorne Cl Coventry CV2 50 B1
Redditch B98 103 E4
Ashorne Hill Coll CV33 122 E5
Ashow Cl CV8 93 D2
Ashridge Cl CV11 39 F4
Ashstead Cl B76 22 A3
Ashwood Ave CV6 60 C3
Ashwood Dr B37 33 E2
Ashwood Rd CV10 28 C3
Aspbury Croft B36 22 B1
Aspen Cl Alcester B49 143 D3
Coventry CV4 59 E1
Aspen Dr B37 44 B4
Aspen Gr B47 69 D3
Aspens The B78 15 E4
Asplen Ct CV8 93 E2
Aspley Ct CV35 114 F6
Aspley Heath B94 86 B1
Aspley Heath La B94 86 B1
Asra Cl CV2 61 F2
Assheton Cl CV22 99 E4
Aster Cl Hinckley LE10 31 F3
Nuneaton CV11 30 A1
Aster Way LE10 31 E3
Asthill Croft CV3 77 E4
Asthill Gr CV3 77 E4
Astley Ave CV6 49 F1
Astley Cl Redditch B98 103 D4
Royal Leamington Spa CV32 105 E1
Astley La Bedworth CV12 38 B2
Fillongley CV7 37 D2
Nuneaton CV10 28 A1
Astley Wlk CV33 133 A7
Astley's Pl CV21 101 D4
Aston Cantlow Rd CV37 120 B5
Aston Flamville Rd LE10 32 B4
Aston Hill CV37 120 B5
Aston Ind Est CV12 39 E1
Aston La LE10 32 A3
Aston Pk Ind Est CV11 29 D3
Aston Rd
Chipping Campden GL55 135 B3
Coventry CV5 60 C1
Nuneaton CV11 29 D3
Astwood Bank Fst Sch B96 102 C1
Astwood La B96 102 B1
Atch Lench Rd WR11 127 A6
Atcheson Cl B80 103 F2
Athena Dr CV34 109 F3
Athena Gdns CV6 50 A1
Atherston Pl CV4 76 B3
Atherstone Coll CV9 18 C4
Atherstone La CV9 16 C3
Atherstone Rd
Appleby Magna DE12 3 F3
Fenny Drayton CV13 20 A3
Furnace End B46 25 F3
Hartshill CV10 19 D1
Hurley CV9 16 B2
Sheepy Magna CV9 12 B2
Twycross DE12 3 F3

Atherstone St B78 9 D4
Atherstone Sta CV9 18 B4
Athol Rd CV2 63 D3
Atholl Cres CV10 28 C1
Atkins Way LE10 31 F4
Atterton La CV9 19 E4
Attleborough Fields Ind Est CV11 29 F2
Attleborough Fst Sch CV11 29 F2
Attleborough La B46 23 D1
Attleborough Rd CV11 29 E2
Attoxhall Rd CV2 62 C2
Attwood Cres CV2 62 B4
Auckland Dr B36 33 D4
Auden Cl CV10 27 F2
Augusta Pl CV32 109 F4
Augustine Ave B80 103 E2
Augustus Cl B46 23 F1
Augustus Dr B49 143 D2
Augustus Rd CV1 61 F2
Austcliff Cl B97 102 B3
Austcliff Dr B91 71 E4
Austen Cl CV10 27 F3
Austen Ct CV32 106 C3
Austin Cl CV9 18 B4
Austin Croft B36 22 C1
Austin Dr Banbury OX16 139 F4
Coventry CV6 62 A4
Austin Edwards Dr 2 CV34 109 D4
Austin Way NN11 117 F2
Austin's Way OX15 142 E4
Austrey CE Prim Sch CV9 3 D1
Austrey Cl B93 72 A3
Austrey La Austrey B79 3 D3
Newton Regis B79 2 C2
Austrey Rd Appleby Magna CV9 3 E3
Warton B79 5 F3
Austwick Cl CV34 104 C1
Auxerre Ave B98 103 D4
Avebury Cl CV11 29 F1
Aventine Way CV21 82 C4
Avenue Cl B93 72 A2
Avenue Farm CV37 144 C3
Avenue Field Ind Est CV37 144 C2
Avenue Rd
Astwood Bank B96 102 C1
Dorridge B93 72 A2
Kenilworth CV8 92 B3
Nuneaton CV11 29 E1
Royal Leamington Spa CV31 109 F4
Rugby CV21 82 C2
Stratford-u-A CV37 145 D2
Avenue The Coventry CV3 78 A3
Rowington Green CV35 90 A1
Stratford-u-A CV37 144 B3
Aviemore Cl CV10 29 D1
Avill B77 10 A3
Avocet Cl CV2 50 A2
Avon B77 10 A3
Avon Aquatics CV37 130 A3
Avon Ave CV35 138 B6
Avon Carrow CV33 133 D4
Avon Cl Barford CV35 122 B8
Bulkington CV12 40 A3
Ettington CV37 131 B3
Avon Cres Alcester B49 143 E3
Stratford-u-A CV37 145 E1
Avon Ct CV8 92 C3
Avon Dassett Rd CV33 133 D6
Avon Ind Est Rugby CV21 83 E3
Stratford-u-A CV37 144 C2
Avon Rd Kenilworth CV8 92 C2
Lighthorne Heath CV35 123 D2
Whitnash CV31 110 A2
Avon St Clifton u D CV21 83 F2
Coventry CV2 62 A3
Rugby CV21 83 D2
Warwick CV34 109 D4
Avon Valley High Sch CV21 82 C3
Avon Way CV35 138 B6
Avonbank Cl B97 102 B3
Avonbank Dr CV37 129 E8
Avonbank Paddocks CV37 145 D1
Avonbrook Cl CV37 144 B2
Avondale Rd Brandon CV8 79 F3
Coventry CV5 77 D4
Royal Leamington Spa CV32 106 B2
Avonfields Cl CV37 121 D3
Avonlea Rise CV32 105 E1
Avonmeadow Cl CV37 144 C1
Avonmere CV21 82 C4
Avonside CV37 145 D1
Awson St CV6 61 F3
Axholme Rd CV2 62 C2
Axminster Cl CV11 29 F3
Aylesbury Cl B94 88 B3
Aylesbury Rd B94 88 B4
Aylesford Dr B37 44 A4
Aylesford Sch CV34 108 B2
Aylesford St Coventry CV1 61 F2
Royal Leamington Spa CV31 110 A3
Aylstone Cl CV37 129 D2
Aynho Cl CV5 60 A2
Aysgarth Cl CV11 30 A1
Azalea Cl LE10 31 F3
Azalea Dr LE10 31 F3
Azalea Wlk LE10 31 F3

Babbacombe Rd CV3 77 E3
Bablake Cl CV6 60 C4
Bablake Jun Sch CV1 151 A4
Bablake Sch CV1 61 D2
Bachelors Bench CV9 18 B4
Back Ends GL55 135 B2
Back La Birdingbury CV23 115 F7
Claverdon CV35 114 A6
Claybrooke Magna LE17 43 F3
Back La continued
Cleeve Prior WR11 128 A4
Harborough Magna CV23 66 A2
Henley-in-A B95 113 B5
Long Compton CV36 141 D3
Long Lawford CV23 82 A2
Lower Quinton CV37 129 E3
Meriden CV7 58 C3
Mickleton GL55 135 B6
Pebworth CV37 128 E1
Pillerton Priors CV35 131 D2
Shustoke B46 24 C1
Sibford Ferris OX15 142 D8
Warwick CV34 108 C3
Back St Ilmington CV36 136 B6
Nuneaton CV11 29 E3
Backside La OX15 142 D8
Badbury Cl B80 103 E2
Badby Cty Prim Sch NN11 126 F6
Badby Leys CV22 100 A4
Baddesley Cl 30 CV31 110 B3
Baddesley Clinton B93 89 F2
Baddesley Ensor CE Inf Sch CV9 11 E1
Baddesley Ensor Jun Sch CV9 11 E1
Badger Cl B90 70 B2
Badger Rd CV3 78 B4
Badgers Cres CV36 149 F4
Badgers Farm La CV35 138 C8
Badgers Field GL55 135 B2
Baffin Cl CV22 82 C1
Baginton Fields Sch CV3 78 A2
Baginton Rd Birmingham B35 22 A2
Coventry CV3 77 E3
Bagshaw Cl CV8 79 D1
Bailey Ave B77 9 F3
Bailey's La CV23 82 A2
Bakehouse La
Chadwick End B93 90 A3
Nether Whitacre B46 24 C3
Rugby CV21 82 C2
Shotteswell OX17 139 E8
Baker Ave
Royal Leamington Spa CV31 109 F3
Stratford-u-A CV37 144 B2
Baker St CV6 50 A3
Baker's Hill GL55 135 C5
Bakers Croft CV9 11 E1
Bakers Ct CV9 18 B4
Bakers La Coventry CV5 60 C1
Knowle B93 72 B1
Swalcliffe OX15 142 F8
Bakers Wlk B77 9 F3
Bakewell Cl CV3 78 C4
Balcombe Ct CV22 100 C4
Balcombe Rd CV22 100 B4
Baldwin Croft CV6 50 A1
Baldwins La CV35 138 B6
Balfour Cl LE10 31 F4
Ballantine Rd CV6 61 D3
Ballard Wlk B37 33 D3
Ballards Cl GL55 135 B6
Ballards La CV36 136 B6
Ballingham Cl CV4 60 A1
Balliol Rd Coventry CV2 62 B2
Hinckley LE10 31 F3
Balmoral Ave Banbury OX16 139 F3
Banbury, Crouch Hill OX16 139 F2
Balmoral Cl CV2 62 C3
Balmoral Rd B36 33 D4
Balmoral Way CV32 106 B3
Balsall Common Prim Sch CV7 74 A3
Balsall St B93, CV7 73 E4
Balsall St E CV7 74 A3
Bamburgh B77 9 E4
Bamburgh Gr CV32 105 F2
Ban Brook Rd WR11 127 F6
Banbury Rd
Bishops Tachbrook CV33 122 E7
Chipping Warden OX17 134 F3
Ettington CV37 131 B3
Kineton CV35 132 C5
Ladbroke CV33 124 D4
Lower Boddington NN11 134 E7
North Newington OX15 139 E2
Shutford OX15 139 A3
Southam CV33 147 D1
Southam CV33 147 D2
Stratford-u-A CV37 130 D7
Swerford OX7 142 E1
Warmington OX17 133 D1
Warwick CV34 109 D2
Banbury St CV35 132 B5
Bancroft Pl CV37 145 D2
Bangley La Drayton Bassett B78 7 F3
Mile Oak B78 8 A4
Banister Way CV36 149 F3
Bank Cl CV35 131 F5
Bank Croft CV31 110 B3
Bank Rd CV9 18 C4
Bank St CV21 83 D2
Bank The Bidford-on-A B50 148 B2
Bidford-on-A, Marlcliff B50 148 B1
Lighthorne CV35 123 B2
Bank View CV35 131 F5
Bankfield Dr CV32 105 E1
Banks Rd CV6 61 D3
Bankside Cl CV3 78 A3
Banky Mdw LE10 32 A4
Banner La CV4 59 E1
Banners La B97 102 C3
Bantam Gr CV6 49 D2
Bantock Rd CV4 59 F1
Barber Wlk CV35 114 F4
Barbers La B91 56 B3
Barbican Rise CV2 62 C1
Barbourne Cl B91 71 D4
Barbridge Cl CV12 40 B1
Barbridge Rd CV12 40 B2
Barby CE Prim Sch CV23 117 E8
Barby La CV22 101 D2
Barby Rd Kilsby CV23 101 F2
Rugby CV22 100 A4
Barcheston Rd B93 72 A2
Barcombe Cl OX16 139 F5
Bardon View Rd B78 11 D4
Barford App CV31 110 A1
Barford Cl CV3 78 B4
Barford Rd CV8 93 D2
Barham Cl 7 B90 71 D3
Bari Rd CV35 132 E5
Barker's Butts La CV6 61 D2
Barkers' Butts La CV1 61 D3
Barkers La B47 69 D1
Barkus Cl CV33 147 E2
Barle Gr B36 33 D4
Barley Cl Henley-In-A B95 113 B4
Rugby CV21 101 D4
Sibford Gower OX15 142 D8
Barley Lea The CV3 78 B4
Barlichway B49 143 E2
Barlow Rd CV2 50 B1
Barn Cl
Clifford Chambers CV37 129 F7
Dordon B78 10 C3
Whitnash CV31 110 A2
Barn End Rd B79 5 F2
Barn La CV23 96 B1
Barnack Ave CV3 77 D3
Barnack Dr CV34 104 C1
Barnacle La CV12 40 B1
Barnard Cl Birmingham B37 33 E1
Royal Leamington Spa CV32 106 B2
Barnbrook Rd B93 72 A4
Barncroft CV36 141 C3
Barne Cl CV11 40 A4
Barnfield Ave CV5 60 A3
Barnsley Cl CV9 18 B4
Barnstaple Cl CV5 59 F3
Barnwell Cl CV22 99 E2
Baron's Croft CV3 77 F4
Baron's Field Rd CV3 77 F4
Barons Croft CV10 28 B2
Barpool Rd CV10 28 C2
Barr La Brinklow CV23 64 C2
Higham-on-t-H CV13 21 D2
Barra Croft B35 22 A2
Barrack St CV34 108 C4
Barracks Gn CV35 130 F7
Barracks La CV35 91 E1
Barracks Way CV1 151 B2
Barras Gn CV2 62 A2
Barras La CV1 61 D2
Barretts La CV7 74 B3
Barrington Rd CV22 82 B1
Barrow Cl CV2 63 D3
Barrow Rd CV8 92 C2
Barrowfield La CV8 92 C2
Barrs Hill Sch & Com Coll CV1 151 A4
Barsby Cl CV9 18 B4
Barston Cl CV6 50 A1
Barston La
Balsall Common CV7 73 E4
Barston B92 57 E1
Catherine de B B91 56 A1
Hampton in A B92 56 B2
Bartleet Rd B98 103 F4
Bartlett Cl Coventry CV6 49 F1
8 Warwick CV34 108 C4
Barton Cres CV31 110 B3
Barton Dr B93 72 A2
Barton Fields CV37 129 A6
Barton Rd Bedworth CV12 39 D2
Coventry CV6 49 F1
Long Compton CV36 141 B4
Nuneaton CV10 29 E1
Rugby CV22 99 E4
Barton's Mdw CV2 62 A3
Barwell Cl Dorridge B93 71 F2
Royal Leamington Spa CV32 105 F2
Basant Cl CV34 109 D4
Bascote Rd CV33 115 C3
Bascote Rise CV33 147 D3
Basford Brook Dr CV6 49 F2
Basildon Wlk 3 CV2 63 D4
Basin Bridge La CV13 21 E2
Basley Way CV6 49 E2
Bassett Rd CV6 61 D3
Bastyan Ave CV37 129 D2
Bateman Rd B46 23 F1
Bateman's Acre S 1 CV6 61 D2
Bates Cl B76 22 A4
Bates La B94 86 C1
Bates Rd CV5 76 C4
Bath Pl 14 CV31 109 F4
Bath Rd Atherstone CV9 18 C4
Nuneaton CV11 29 E3
Bath St Coventry CV1 151 C4
Royal Leamington Spa CV31 109 F4
Rugby CV21 83 D2
Bathurst Rd CV6 61 D3
Bathway Rd CV3 77 D2
Batsford Cl B98 103 D3
Batsford Rd CV6 60 C2
Battle Ct CV35 132 B6
Baulk La CV7 58 B1
Bawnmore Ct CV22 99 E4
Bawnmore Cty Fst Sch CV22 99 F4
Bawnmore Pk CV22 99 F4
Bawnmore Rd CV22 99 E4
Baxter Cl CV4 60 A1
Baxter Ct 9 CV31 110 A4
Baxters Gn B90 70 A4
Baxters Rd B90 70 A4
Bay Tree Cl CV2 50 B1
Bayley La CV1 151 C2
Bayton Rd CV7 50 A4
Bayton Road Ind Est CV7 50 A4
Bayton Way CV7 50 B4
Baywell Cl 8 B90 71 D4
Bazzard La CV11 40 C3
Beacon Cl B49 143 E3
Beacon Rd CV6 49 E2
Beaconsfield Ave CV22 83 D1
Beaconsfield Ct CV11 29 E3
Beaconsfield Rd CV2 62 A1
Beaconsfield St CV31 110 A4
Beaconsfield St W CV31 110 A4
Beake Ave CV6 61 D4
Beale Cl B35 22 A1
Beamish Cl CV2 63 D3
Beanacre Rd OX15 142 D3
Beanfield Ave CV3 76 C2
Bear Cl B95 113 B5
Bear La B95 113 A5
Bear La Cl B78 5 D1
Bearcroft Gdns GL55 135 C6
Bearley Croft B90 70 B4
Bearley Cty Jun & Inf Sch CV37 120 D7
Bearley Gn CV37 120 E7
Bearley Halt B95 120 D7
Bearley Rd
Aston Cantlow B95 120 A7
Snitterfield CV37 121 A7
Beatty Dr CV22 82 B1
Beauchamp Ave CV32 105 F1
Beauchamp Cl
1 Birmingham B37 33 D1
Sutton Coldfield B76 22 A4
Beauchamp Gdns CV34 109 D3
Beauchamp Hill CV32 105 F1
Beauchamp Ind Pk B77 9 E4
Beauchamp Rd
Alcester B49 143 E3
Kenilworth CV8 92 C1
Royal Leamington Spa CV32 105 F1
Tamworth B77 9 F3
Warwick CV34 109 D4
Beaudesert Cl
Henley-in-A B95 113 B4
Hollywood B47 69 D3
Beaudesert La B95 113 B5
Beaudesert Rd Coventry CV5 61 D1
Hollywood B47 69 D3
Beaudesert St Mary's RC Prim Sch B95 113 B4
Beaufell Cl CV34 104 C1
Beaufort Ave CV32 106 B3
Beaufort Cl Hinckley LE10 31 F2
Wellesbourne CV35 146 B1
Beaufort Dr CV3 78 C4
Beaulieu Pk CV31 110 B3
Beaumaris Cl Banbury OX16 139 F4
Coventry CV5 59 F3
Beaumont Ave LE10 31 D4
Beaumont Cl CV33 133 A7
Beaumont Cres CV6 61 D2
Beaumont Pl CV11 29 D2
Beaumont Rd Keresley CV7 49 D3
Nuneaton CV11 29 D2
Beausale Croft CV5 60 A2
Beausale Dr B93 72 B4
Beausale La CV35 114 E7
Beck's Cl CV23 147 F4
Beck's La CV23 147 F4
Beckbury Rd CV2 62 C3
Becket Cl GL56 140 E7
Beckfoot Cl CV21 83 E4
Beckfoot Dr CV2 50 C1
Beckford Croft B93 71 F2
Becks La CV7 47 D3
Beconsfield Cl B93 71 F1
Bedale Rd CV35 132 D4
Bede Rd Bedworth CV12 39 D2
Coventry CV6 61 D3
Nuneaton CV10 28 B2
Bedford Cl OX16 139 F4
Bedford Pl CV32 109 F4
Bedford St Coventry CV1 61 D1
Royal Leamington Spa CV32 109 F4
Bedlam La CV6 49 F1
Bedworth Cl CV12 40 A1
Bedworth La CV12 38 B2
Bedworth Rd Bedworth CV12 39 F1
Bulkington CV12 40 A1
Coventry CV6 50 A3
Bedworth Sta CV12 39 E1
Beech Ave B37 33 D1
Beech Cl Alcester B49 143 E1
Hartshill CV10 28 A4
Hurley CV9 16 B3
Kingsbury B78 15 E4
Rowington CV35 114 A8
Southam CV33 147 D2
Stratford-u-A CV37 145 E1
Beech Cliffe CV34 108 C4
Beech Ct
Royal Leamington Spa CV34 109 F1
Rugby CV22 100 C4
Stratford-u-A CV37 145 D1
Beech Dr Kenilworth CV8 93 D3
Rugby CV22 99 E4
Thurlaston CV23 98 C2
Beech Gr Arley CV7 26 C1
Warwick CV34 105 D1
Beech Rd Coventry CV6 61 D3
Hollywood B47 69 D3
Oxhill CV35 137 F8
Beech Tree Ave CV4 60 A1
Beecham Wlk CV37 144 B2
Beechcroft Birmingham B36 22 B1
Long Itchington CV23 115 D4
Beecher's Keep CV8 79 F3
Beeches The Bedworth CV12 38 C1
Harbury CV33 123 E7
Polesworth B78 11 D4
Beeches Wlk CV37 145 F2
Beechtree Pk B50 148 C3
Beechwood Ave
Coventry CV5 76 C4
Hinckley LE10 31 E2
Beechwood Cl B90 70 B2
Beechwood Croft CV8 92 C1
Beechwood Rd
Bedworth CV12 39 E2
Nuneaton CV10 28 B3
Beehive Hill CV8 92 C4
Beehive La B76 23 E3
Beeston Cl CV3 78 C4
Begonia Cl LE10 31 F3
Begonia Dr LE10 31 F3
Belcony GL56 136 C1
Belgrave Dr CV21 83 E3
Belgrave Rd Coventry CV2 62 C2
Tamworth B77 9 F4
Belgrave Sq CV2 62 C2
Bell Brook CV37 121 B6
Bell Cl B36 33 D3
Bell Ct CV37 145 D1
Bell Dr CV7 49 F4
Bell Green Rd CV6 62 A4
Bell Hill OX15 142 D4
Bell La Monks Kirby CV23 53 F1
Snitterfield CV37 121 B6
Stratford-u-A CV37 144 B1
Studley B80 103 F2
Bell Mead B80 103 F2
Bell St Claybrooke Magna LE17 43 F3
Hornton OX15 139 B7
Bell Tower Mews CV32 105 F2
Bell Wlk CV21 101 D4
Bell's La OX15 142 D4
Bellairs Ave CV12 38 C1
Bellam Rd CV35 114 F4
Bellbrooke Cl CV6 50 A1
Belle Cotts B94 88 C3
Belle Vue CV10 28 C2
Belle Vue Terr B92 57 D3
Bellemere Rd B92 57 D3
Bellfield B94 87 D1
Bellingham B77 4 B1
Bellington Croft 5 B90 71 D3
Bells La OX15 137 E3
Bellview Way CV6 50 A1
Belmont Dr CV32 106 A2
Belmont Rd Coventry CV6 62 A4
Rugby CV22 83 D1
Tamworth B77 9 F4
Belton Cl B94 88 B3
Belvedere Rd CV5 77 D4
Belvoir B77 9 E4
Benedictine Rd CV3 77 E4
Bengrove Cl B98 103 D4
Benn Rd CV12 40 A1
Benn St CV22 83 E1
Bennet Cl CV13 21 E4
Bennett Ct CV8 79 F2
Bennett Dr CV34 109 E4
Bennett Pl CV36 136 B6
Bennett St CV21 82 C2
Bennett's Rd CV7 48 C2
Bennett's Rd N CV7 48 C4
Bennett's Rd S CV6 48 C1
Bennfield Rd CV21 83 D2
Benson Rd Coventry CV6 49 D1
Stratford-u-A CV37 145 D2
Benthall Rd CV6 49 F1
Bentley Cl Banbury OX16 139 F4
Royal Leamington Spa CV32 106 A2
Bentley Ct CV6 49 E2
Bentley Farm Cl B93 71 F2
Bentley Heath CE Jun & Inf Sch B93 71 F3
Bentley La B46 35 E2
Bentley Rd Bedworth CV7 39 D1
Nuneaton CV11 29 D2
Bentley Way NN11 117 F2
Benton Green La CV7 58 C1
Bentree The CV3 78 A4
Beoley La B98 86 A1
Berenska Dr CV32 106 A1
Beresford Ave CV6 49 F1
Bericote Rd CV32 105 F4
Berkeley Cl Banbury OX16 139 F4
Nuneaton CV11 29 D2
Redditch B98 112 A6
Berkeley Rd CV8 92 C3
Berkeley Rd N CV5 61 D1
Berkeley Rd S CV5 77 D4
Berkett Rd CV6 49 D1
Berkshire Cl CV10 28 C2
Berkswell CE Prim Sch CV7 58 B2
Berkswell Rd Coventry CV6 50 A1
Meriden CV7 58 B4
Berkswell Sta CV7 74 B4
Bermuda Bsns Pk CV10 39 D4
Bermuda Ind Est CV10 39 D4
Bermuda Rd CV10 29 D1
Berners Cl CV4 59 F1
Berrills La CV36 141 D7
Berrington Rd
Chipping Campden GL55 135 C2
Nuneaton CV10 28 B4
Royal Leamington Spa CV31 110 A3
Berry Ave CV36 149 F3

Berry Cl CV36 149 F3
Berry Hall La B91 56 A2
Berry Mdw CV33 133 E7
Berry St CV1 61 F2
Berryfields CV7 36 C2
Berryfields La CV37 136 C7
Berrymound View B47 69 E4
Bertie Rd CV8 93 D2
Berwick Cl Coventry CV5 60 A2
Warwick CV34 104 C1
Berwicks La B37 33 D1
Berwyn Ave CV6 49 D1
Berwyn Way CV10 28 B2
Besbury Cl B93 71 F1
Besford Gr B90 71 D3
Best Ave CV8 93 E4
Beswick Gdns CV22 99 E4
Bettina Cl CV10 28 A3
Bettman Cl CV3 77 F3
Bettridge Pl CV35 146 B2
Beverley Ave CV10 28 A2
Beverley Cl
Astwood Bank B96 102 C1
Balsall Common CV7 74 B4
Beverley Rd CV32 105 E1
Beverly Dr CV4 76 B1
Bevington Cres CV6 60 C3
Bexfield Cl CV5 60 A3
Beyer Cl B77 4 A1
Biart Pl CV21 83 E2
Bicester Sq B35 22 A2
Bickenhill La Birmingham B40 44 B2
Catherine de B B91 56 B3
Bickenhill Parkway B37 44 B3
Bickenhill Rd B37 44 A4
Bickmarsh La B50 148 B1
Bidavon Ind Est B50 148 C3
Biddles Hill B94 86 B3
Bideford Rd CV2 62 B4
Bidford on Avon CE Jun Sch B50 148 B2
Bidford Rd B50 148 B4
Bigbury Cl CV3 77 F3
Biggin Cl B35 22 A2
Biggin Hall Cres CV3 62 A1
Biggin Hall La CV23 98 C1
Bignolds Cl OX17 134 B4
Bigwood Dr B75 13 D3
Bilberry Rd CV2 50 B1
Bilbury Cl B97 102 B3
Billesden Cl CV3 78 C4
Billesley La B48 85 F3
Billesley Rd CV37 120 C4
Billing Rd CV5 60 B2
Billingham Cl B91 71 D4
Billinton Cl CV2 62 C1
Bills La B90 69 F4
Bilton CE Mid Sch CV22 99 E3
Bilton Cty Fst Sch CV22 99 E4
Bilton Grange Sch CV22 99 F2
Bilton High Sch CV22 82 A1
Bilton Ind Est CV3 61 F1
Bilton La Dunchurch CV22 99 E2
Long Lawford CV23 82 A2
Bilton Rd CV22 82 C1
Binley Ave CV3 78 C4
Binley Cl B90 70 A4
Binley Gr CV3 78 C4
Binley Ind Est CV3 79 D4
Binley Rd CV2, CV3 62 B1
Binley Woods Cty Prim Sch CV3 79 F4
Binns Cl CV4 75 F4
Binswood Ave CV32 105 F1
Binswood Cl CV2 50 B1
Binswood End CV33 123 E7
Binswood Mans 15 CV32 105 F1
Binswood St CV32 105 F1
Binton Rd Coventry CV2 50 B1
Welford on A CV37 129 A7
Bintonhill CV37 120 A1
Birch Abbey B49 143 D2
Birch Cl Bedworth CV12 39 E2
Coventry CV5 59 F3
Kingsbury B78 15 E4
Birch Croft B37 33 E1
Birch Ct CV34 109 F1
Birch Dr CV22 82 A1
Birch Gr Birchmoor B78 10 B4
Wellesbourne CV35 146 C2
Birches La CV8 93 D2
Birches The CV12 40 A2
Birchfield Cl CV9 10 B1
Birchfield Rd Coventry CV6 60 C4
Stratford-u-A CV37 145 D3
Birchgrave Cl CV6 62 A4
Birchley Heath Rd CV10 17 F1
Birchmoor Rd B78 10 C4
Birchtree Rd CV10 28 B3
Birchway Cl 2 CV32 105 E1
Birchwood Ave B78 10 C4
Birchwood Prim Sch B78 10 C4
Birchwood Rd CV3 79 E4
Birchy Cl B90 69 F3
Birchy Leasowes La B90 69 F3
Bird Grove Ct CV1 61 E3
Bird Rd
Lighthorne Heath CV35 123 D2
Royal Leamington Spa CV34 109 E2
Bird St CV1 151 C3
Birdhaven Cl CV35 123 D2
Birdhope B77 4 B1
Birdingbury La CV23 115 E8
Birdingbury Rd
Birdingbury CV23 115 F8
Marton CV23 115 D7
Birds Bush Cty Prim Sch B77 9 F4
Birds Bush Rd B77 9 F4
Birds La OX15 138 D3
Birkdale Cl CV11 30 A1
Birmingham Bsns Pk B37 44 C4
Birmingham Int Airport B40 44 A2
Birmingham Int Sta B40 44 B2
Birmingham Rd
Alcester B49 143 D2
Allesley CV5 59 F4
Ansley CV10 27 D2
Burton Green CV8 75 D1
Coleshill B46 33 F3
Henley-In-A B95 113 B6
Kenilworth CV8 92 B4
Little Packington CV7 45 F2
Nether Whitacre B46 24 B4
Shrewley CV35 114 D6
Stoneleigh CV8 94 A3
Stratford-u-A CV37 144 C3
Studley B80 103 F4
Warwick CV34 108 B4
Water Orton B46 23 D2
Wilmcote CV37 120 D6
Wroxall B93, CV35 90 B2
Birstall Dr CV21 83 E3
Bishop Carpenter CE Prim Sch Ox15 139 D2
Bishop St CV1 151 B3
Bishop Ullathorne RC Sch CV3 76 C2
Bishop Wilson CE Prim Sch B37 33 E2
Bishop Wulstan RC High Sch CV22 83 D1
Bishop's Hill CV35 123 B2
Bishop's Itchington Sch CV33 124 B4
Bishop's Tachbrook CE Prim Sch CV35 122 F8
Bishopgate Bsns Pk CV1 61 E3
Bishopgate Ind Est CV1 61 E3
Bishops Bowl Lakes Water Sports Ctr CV33 124 A5
Bishops Cl
16 Bishops Tachbrook CV33 122 F8
Stratford-u-A CV37 144 B2
Bishops Cleeve CV9 3 D1
Bishops Gate CV33 124 B5
Bishops Wlk CV5 77 D4
Bishopton Cl CV5 60 A2
Bishopton La CV37 144 B3
Bishopton Prim Sch CV37 144 B2
Bisset Cres 21 CV31 110 B3
Bitham Rd CV35 123 D3
Bixhill La B46 25 D2
Black Bank CV7 39 D1
Black Hall La CV7 36 B2
Black Horse Hill DE12 3 F4
Black Horse Rd CV6 50 A3
Black La CV32 106 B1
Black Prince Ave CV3 77 F3
Black-A-Tree Rd CV10 28 C2
Blackberry Ave B94 88 B3
Blackberry Cl CV23 83 E4
Blackberry La Ash Green CV7 49 E3
Coventry CV2 62 B3
Blackbird Croft B36 33 D4
Blackburn Rd CV6 49 F2
Blackcat Cl B37 33 D2
Blackdown B77 4 B1
Blackdown Rd B93 72 A3
Blackfirs La B37, B46 44 B4
Blackford Hill B95 113 B4
Blackford Rd B90 70 B4
Blackford Way CV35 137 F8
Blackgreaves La B76 14 C1
Blacklow Rd CV34 105 D1
Blackman Way CV21 82 C2
Blackshaw Dr CV2 62 C3
Blacksmith's La NN11 134 F5
Blacksmiths Cl WR11 127 F1
Blacksmiths La
Hockley Heath B94 88 B3
Littleton WR11 127 F1
Mollington OX17 134 A2
Blacksmiths Yd CV13 21 E4
Blackthorn Cl CV4 76 B3
Blackthorn Gr CV11 29 F1
Blackthorn Rd CV37 145 D3
Blackthorn Way B49 143 D3
Blackthorne Rd CV8 93 D2
Blackwatch Rd CV6 61 E4
Blackwell Rd Coventry CV6 61 F4
Tredington CV36 136 F6
Blackwood Ave CV22 82 B1
Blackwood Rd B77 9 E4
Blacon Way CV37 144 B2
Bladon Cl CV11 29 F4
Bladon Wlk 14 CV31 110 B3
Blair Dr CV12 38 B1
Blair Gr B37 33 E1
Blake Cl Nuneaton CV10 28 A3
Rugby CV22 82 B1
Blake's Hill WR11, CV37 128 B1
Blakelands Ave CV31 110 A3
Blakenhurst WR11 127 C4
Blandford Ave B36 22 C1
Blandford Dr CV2 62 C3
Blandford Rd 1 CV32 105 E1
Blandford Way CV35 108 A4
Blaze La B96, B97 102 A2
Bleaberry CV21 83 E4
Bleachfield St B49 143 D2
Blenheim Ave CV6 49 E1
Blenheim Cl
Bidford-on-A B50 148 B3
Nuneaton CV11 29 F1
Blenheim Cres 29 CV31 110 B3
Blenheim Wlk CV35 146 B1
Bletchley Dr CV5 60 A2
Blewgates OX15 137 F2
Blewitt Cl B36 22 B1
Blick Rd CV34 109 E2
Blind La Berkswell CV7 58 B2
Chipping Campden GL55 135 A1
Tanworth-In-A B94 86 B1
Blindpit La B76 23 D4
Bliss Cl CV4 59 F2
Blockley Rd CV12 39 E2
Blondvil St CV3 77 E4
Bloxam Gdns CV22 82 C1
Bloxam Mid Sch CV22 82 C1
Bloxam Pl CV21 83 D2
Bloxham Rd OX16 139 F1
Blue Cap Rd CV37 145 D3
Blue Coat CE Sch CV1 61 F1
Blue La CV35 130 E6
Blue Lake Rd B93 72 A1
Bluebell Cl CV23 83 E4
Bluebell Dr B37 33 F1
Bluebellwood Cl B76 13 D2
Blundells Croft CV37 129 A7
Blundells The CV8 93 D3
Blyth Ave CV7 74 B3
Blyth Cl CV12 38 B1
Blythe Cl B97 102 B4
Blythe Rd Coleshill B46 34 A4
Coventry CV1 61 F2
Boar Croft CV4 59 F1
Boat La CV37 129 A7
Bockendon Rd CV4 75 F3
Boddington Cl CV32 106 C3
Boddington Rd OX17 134 B5
Bodmin Rd CV2 62 C3
Bodnant Way CV8 93 E3
Bodymoor Heath La B76 15 D2
Bohun St CV4 59 F1
Boleyn Cl CV34 109 E3
Bolingbroke Rd CV3 62 A1
Bolton Cl CV3 77 F3
Bolyfant Cl CV31 110 A1
Bond Dr B35 22 A2
Bond End CV23 53 F2
Bond Gate CV11 29 E2
Bond St Coventry CV1 151 B3
Nuneaton CV11 29 E3
Rugby CV21 82 C2
Boningale Way B93 71 F2
Bonington Dr CV12 39 D2
Bonneville Cl CV5 59 D4
Bonniksen Cl CV31 109 F3
Bonnington Cl CV21 84 A1
Boot Hill CV9 11 E1
Booths Fields CV6 49 F1
Bordesley Ct CV32 106 A2
Bordon Hill CV37 144 B1
Bordon Pl CV37 144 C1
Borough The LE10 31 E4
Borrowdale CV21 83 E4
Borrowdale Cl CV6 61 D4
Borrowdale Dr CV32 105 E1
Borrowell La CV8 92 C2
Boscobel Rd B90 70 B3
Bosley Cl CV36 149 F2
Bostock Cres CV33 107 E4
Boston Pl CV6 61 E4
Boswell Dr CV2 63 D4
Boswell Gr CV34 104 B1
Boswell Rd CV22 99 F4
Bosworth Dr B37 33 D1
Bosworth Wood Jun & Inf Sch B36 22 C1
Boteler Cl B49 143 D2
Botoner Rd CV1 61 F1
Bott Rd CV5 76 B4
Bott's La DE12 3 F4
Bottrill St CV11 29 D3
Botts Green La B46 25 E3
Boucher Cl CV37 144 B1
Boughton Leigh Cty Inf Sch CV21 83 E4
Boughton Leigh Jun Sch CV21 83 E4
Boughton Rd CV21 83 E3
Boulters La CV9 10 B1
Boultons La B97 102 B3
Boundary Rd CV21 83 E1
Bourne Brook Cl CV7 36 C2
Bourne Cl CV9 12 C1
Bourne End CV33 147 D2
Bourne La OX15 142 D4
Bourne Rd CV3 62 B1
Bourne The OX15 142 D4
Bournebrook View CV7 26 C1
Bourton Dr CV31 110 A3
Bourton La CV23 115 F8
Bourton Rd Frankton CV23 97 E1
Moreton-in-M GL56 140 A3
Bouts La WR7 118 B5
Bovey Croft B76 22 A4
Bovingdon Rd B35 22 A2
Bow Fell CV21 83 E4
Bow La CV7 53 D2
Bowbrook Ave B90 71 D3
Bowden Way CV3 62 C1
Bowen Rd CV22 83 E1
Bowers Croft CV32 106 A3
Bowes Lyon Cl GL56 140 A2
Bowfell Cl CV5 60 A2
Bowley's La DE12 3 F4
Bowling Green Ave B77 9 F4
Bowling Green Ct GL56 140 A3
Bowling Green La CV7, CV12 49 F4
Bowling Green St CV34 108 B3
Bowls Ct CV5 60 C2
Bowman Gn LE10 31 F3
Bowness Cl CV6 61 D4
Bowshot Cl B36 22 B1
Box Cl CV31 110 A2
Box Rd B37 44 B4
Box Trees Rd B93 71 E1
Boxhill The CV3 62 A1
Boyce Way CV23 82 A3
Boyd Cl CV2 63 D4
Boyslade Rd LE10 31 F3
Boyslade Rd E LE10 31 F3
Bracadale Cl CV3 63 D1
Bracebridge Cl CV7 74 A3
Bracebridge Rd
Atherstone CV9 18 B4
Kingsbury B78 15 E3
Bracebridge St CV11 29 D2
Bracken Cl CV22 82 C1
Bracken Croft 1 B37 33 E2
Bracken Dr Rugby CV22 82 C1
Sutton Coldfield B75 13 D3
Wolvey LE10 41 E2
Brackendale Dr Barby CV23 101 E1
Nuneaton CV10 28 C2
Brackenhurst Rd CV6 61 D4
Bracklesham Way B77 4 A3
Brackley Cl CV6 60 C4
Bracknell Wlk 1 CV2 63 D4
Braddock Cl CV3 63 D1
Brade Dr CV2 63 D4
Bradestone Rd CV11 29 E1
Bradewell Rd B36 22 B1
Bradford Rd 6 CV33 122 E8
Brading Rd CV10 29 E3
Bradley Croft CV7 74 A3
Bradney Gn CV4 75 F4
Bradnick Pl CV4 59 F1
Bradnock's Marsh La B92 57 F1
Braemar Cl CV2 62 C3
Braemar Rd CV32 106 A2
Braemar Way CV10 29 D1
Braeside Croft B37 33 E1
Brafield Leys CV22 100 A3
Braggington La CV37 128 F5
Braggs Farm La B90 70 A2
Brailes CE Prim Sch OX15 137 E2
Brain St B77 4 A1
Brakesmead CV31 109 F3
Bramber Cl OX16 139 F4
Bramble Cl 4 Coleshill B46 33 F4
Nuneaton CV11 29 F1
Bramble St CV1 61 F1
Brambles The B76 22 A4
Brambling B77 10 A4
Bramcote Cl CV12 40 B1
Bramcote Hospl CV11 40 C4
Bramdene Ave CV10 29 E4
Bramley Dr B47 69 D3
Bramley Rd CV35 132 E6
Brampton Way CV12 40 A2
Bramshall Dr B93 71 F2
Bramston Cres CV4 59 F1
Bramwell Gdns CV6 49 F3
Brancaster Cl B77 4 A3
Brandfield Rd CV6 60 C4
Brandon La CV3, CV8 79 E3
Brandon Marsh Nature Reserve CV8 79 D2
Brandon Marsh Visitor Ctr CV8 79 D2
Brandon Par CV32 110 A4
Brandon Rd Bretford CV23 80 B3
Coventry CV3 79 D4
Hinckley LE10 31 D4
Branksome Rd CV6 60 C3
Bransdale Ave CV6 49 E2
Bransford Ave CV4 76 B3
Bransford Rise B91 56 A3
Branstree Dr CV6 49 E1
Brascote Rd LE10 30 C4
Bratches The GL55 135 B3
Brathay Cl CV3 77 E3
Braunston Cl B76 13 D1
Braunston Jun & Inf Sch NN11 117 E5
Braunston La NN11 126 E8
Braunston Pl CV22 100 B4
Braunston Rd NN11 117 F2
Bray Bank B46 25 E2
Bray's La CV2 62 A2
Brayford Ave CV3 77 E3
Brays Cl CV23 64 C2
Braytoft Cl CV6 49 E1
Brazil St CV4 59 F1
Breach La CV35 113 F3
Breach Oak La CV7 37 E2
Breaches La B98 103 E4
Bream B77 9 E4
Bream Cl B37 33 E1
Brechin Cl LE10 31 D4
Bredon Ave CV3 78 C4
Bredon View B97 102 B4
Bree Cl CV5 60 A4
Bree's La CV8 74 A1
Breeden Dr B76 23 D3
Brendan Cl B46 34 A3
Brendon B77 4 A1
Brendon Way CV10 28 A2
Brenfield Dr LE10 31 D4
Brent B77 9 F4
Brentwood Ave CV3 77 E2
Brese Ave CV34 104 C1
Bretch Hill OX16 139 F3
Bretford Rd CV2 50 B1
Bretshall Cl B90 70 C3
Bretts Cl CV1 151 D4
Brewer Rd CV12 40 B1
Brewers Cl CV3 63 D1
Brewery La OX15 142 C4
Brewery Row GL56 140 F1
Brewery St CV37 144 C2
Brewster Cl CV2 62 C1
Briansway CV6 49 F2
Briar B77 4 A2
Briar Cl Hinckley LE10 31 F3
Royal Leamington Spa CV32 106 A1
Briar Hill Cty Fst Sch CV31 110 A2
Briardene Ave CV12 39 D1
Briarmead LE10 31 F2
Briars Cl Coventry CV2 62 B1
Long Lawford CV23 82 A2
Nuneaton CV11 29 F3
Briarwood Cl B90 70 B2
Brick Hill OX15 142 D3
Brick Hill La CV5 59 F4
Brick Kiln La Middleton B78 14 B3
Solihull B90 70 C4
Brick Kiln St LE10 31 E4
Brickhill Cl CV36 149 F3
Brickhill Dr B37 33 D1
Brickkiln La CV9 16 A2
Brickyard La B80 103 E2
Bridal Path The CV5 60 A3
Bridge End Southam CV33 147 D2
Warwick CV34 108 C3
Bridge Foot CV37 145 D1
Bridge La Ladbroke CV33 124 D5
Witherley CV9 19 D4
Bridge Meadow Dr B93 71 F3
Bridge Rd LE10 31 E4
Bridge St Barford CV35 122 A7
Coventry CV6 62 A4
Fenny Compton CV33 133 D7
Hampton Lucy CV35 121 F4
Hurley CV9 16 B2
Kenilworth CV8 92 C3
Kineton CV35 132 B5
Nuneaton CV11 29 E2
Nuneaton, Chilvers Coton CV11 29 E1
Polesworth B78 5 D1
Rugby CV21 83 E2
Stratford-u-A CV37 145 D1
Warwick CV34 109 E4
Wellesbourne CV35 146 B2
Bridge Town Prim Sch CV37 145 D1
Bridgeacre Gdns CV3 62 C1
Bridgecote CV3 78 C3
Bridgeman Rd CV6 61 D2
Bridget St CV22 82 C2
Bridgetown Rd CV37 145 D1
Bridgeway CV37 145 D2
Bridle Brook La CV5, CV7 48 A2
Bridle Rd
Lighthorne Heath CV35 123 D2
Rugby CV21 82 C2
Bridport Cl CV2 63 D2
Brierley Rd CV2 62 B4
Briggs Cl OX16 139 F2
Bright St CV6 61 F3
Brightmere Rd CV6 61 D2
Brighton St CV2 61 F2
Brightwalton Rd CV3 77 E4
Brightwell Cres B93 71 F2
Brill Cl CV4 76 B3
Brindle Ave CV3 62 B1
Brindley Rd Bedworth CV7 50 A4
Hinckley LE10 30 C4
Rugby CV21 84 A1
Brinklow CE Fst Sch CV23 64 C2
Brinklow Cl B98 103 E4
Brinklow Rd Coventry CV3 63 D1
Easenhall CV23 65 F2
Brisbane Cl CV3 77 F3
Briscoe Rd CV6 49 E2
Bristol Rd CV5 60 C1
Bristol Way CV35 146 B1
Britannia Rd LE10 32 A3
Britannia St CV2 61 F2
Briton Rd CV2 62 A2
Brittania Sh Ctr 2 LE10 31 E4
Britten Cl CV11 40 A4
Brittons La CV35 114 C2
Brixham Cl CV11 29 F3
Brixham Dr CV2 62 B4
Brixworth Cl CV3 78 C4
Broad Cl CV33 123 F8
Broad Heath Com Prim Sch CV6 61 F4
Broad La Coventry CV5 59 E2
Fillongley CV7 35 F2
Tanworth-in-A B98 86 C2
Broad Marston Rd
Mickleton CV37,GL55 135 B7
Pebworth CV37 128 F1
Broad Oaks B76 13 D1
Broad Park Rd CV2 62 B4
Broad St Brinklow CV23 64 C2
Coventry CV6 61 F4
Long Compton CV36 141 C3
Stratford-u-A CV37 144 C1
Warwick CV34 108 C4
Broad Wlk CV37 144 C1
Broadfern Rd B93 72 A4
Broadgate CV1 151 B3
Broadhaven Cl CV31 110 B4
Broadlands Cl CV5 60 B1
Broadlee B77 4 B1
Broadmeadow La CV37 144 C3
Broadmere Rise CV5 60 A1

Broadmoor La CV36 141 A6
Broadsword Way LE10 31 E2
Broadwater CV5 77 D4
Broadway Coventry CV5 61 D1
Cubbington CV32 106 C3
Broadway Rd GL55 135 B6
Broadwell Ct CV4 75 F3
Broadwells Cres CV4 76 A3
Brockhill La B98 85 F1
Brockhurst Ave LE10 31 E2
Brockhurst Dr CV4 59 E1
Brockhurst La
Monks Kirby CV23 53 F2
Sutton Coldfield B75 7 D4
Brodick Cl LE10 31 D4
Brodick Rd LE10 30 C4
Brodick Way CV10 28 C2
Bromage Ave B78 15 E3
Brome Hall La B94 89 E1
Bromford Way CV37 144 B2
Bromleigh Dr CV2 62 B1
Bromley Cl CV8 92 C3
Bromsgrove Highway B98 102 C4
Bromsgrove Rd B80 103 E1
Bromwich Cl CV3 78 C4
Bromwich Rd CV21 83 F1
Bromyard Ave B76 22 A4
Bronte Cl Nuneaton CV10 27 F3
Rugby CV21 83 E2
Bronze Cl CV11 39 F4
Brook Ave B77 10 A4
Brook Cl Coventry CV1 61 F2
Kingsbury B78 15 E3
Shipston-on-S CV36 149 F3
Brook Croft B37 44 A4
Brook End B78 9 D4
Brook End Cl B95 113 A4
Brook End Dr B95 113 A4
Brook Farm Wlk B37 33 E1
Brook Green La B92 57 D1
Brook La
Moreton Morrell CV35 122 F3
Newbold-on-S CV37 130 E1
Nuneaton CV10 29 E3
Brook Piece Wlk B35 22 A2
Brook St Bedworth CV12 39 D3
Fenny Compton CV33 133 D7
Warwick CV34 108 C3
Wolston CV8 80 A2
Brook View CV22 99 E2
Brook Wlk CV9 18 C4
Brookdale Harvington WR11 127 C4
Hinckley LE10 31 D4
Brookdale Rd CV10 29 F4
Brooke Cl CV34 108 C3
Brooke Rd CV8 93 D2
Brooke Specl Sch CV22 82 C1
Brookfield Cl B97 102 B2
Brookfield Dr LE10 41 E2
Brookfield Rd
Cubbington CV32 106 C3
Hinckley LE10 31 E3
Brookford Ave CV6 49 D2
Brookhurst Ct CV32 105 E1
Brookhurst Cty Comb Sch
CV32 105 E1
Brookhus Farm Rd B76 22 A4
Brooklea CV12 38 C1
Brooklime Dr CV23 83 F4
Brooklyn Rd CV1 61 E3
Brooks Cl CV23 117 B6
Brooks Croft B35 22 A1
Brooksby Gr B93 72 A1
Brookshaw Way CV2 62 C4
Brookside
Cheswick Green B90 70 B2
Hinckley LE10 31 F4
Hook Norton OX15 142 D4
Snitterfield CV37 121 B7
Stretton on D CV23 96 C3
Brookside Ave Coventry CV5 60 B2
Kenilworth CV8 92 C2
Pailton CV23 66 A4
Wellesbourne CV35 146 C2
Brookside Cl Rugby CV22 83 D1
Stratford-u-A CV37 144 B2
Brookside Rd CV37 144 B2
Brookside Way B77 10 A3
Brookvale Ave CV3 62 C1
Brookvale Rd CV37 144 C1
Brookweed B77 4 A2
Broom Cl CV22 82 C1
Broome Croft CV6 49 D2
Broomey Croft Farm B76 15 D4
Broomfield Ave B78 9 D4
Broomfield Pl CV5 61 D1
Broomfield Rd CV5 61 D1
Broomfield Rise CV10 28 C1
Broomybank CV8 93 D3
Broughton Rd OX16 139 F2
Brownett Rd CV6 61 D3
Brown's Bridge Rd CV33 147 D2
Brown's La Allesley CV5 48 B1
Dordon B78 11 D3
Browning Ave CV34 108 B3
Browning Cl CV10 28 A3
Browning Rd Coventry CV2 62 B2
Rugby CV21 101 D4
Brownley Rd B90 70 C4
Brownlow St 5 CV32 106 A1
Browns La B93 71 F3
Browns Rd NN11 117 F1
Brownshill Ct CV6 60 C4
Brownshill Green Rd CV6 48 C1
Brownsover Cl B36 22 A1
Brownsover Com Inf Sch
CV23 83 E4
Brownsover La CV21 83 D4
Brownsover Rd CV21 82 C4
Broxell Cl CV34 104 B1
Bruce Rd Bedworth CV7 49 F4
Coventry CV6 61 D4
Bruce Williams Way CV22 83 D1
Brunel Cl Coventry CV2 61 F2
Daventry NN11 117 F2
Whitnash CV31 110 A1
Brunel Rd LE10 31 E4
Brunel Wlk B78 5 D2
Brunswick Cl CV21 83 E3
Brunswick Rd CV1 61 D1
Brunswick St CV31 110 A3
Bruntingthorpe Way CV3 78 C4
Brunton Cl CV3 63 D1
Brutus Dr B46 23 F1
Bryan Ct B50 148 C2
Bryanston Cl CV2 63 D2
Bryant Rd CV7 50 A4
Brympton Rd CV3 62 B1
Bryn Jones Cl CV3 78 C4
Bryn Rd CV6 61 F4
Buccleuch Cl CV22 99 E2
Buchan Cl CV10 27 F2
Buchannan Rd CV22 82 C1
Buck La CV35 138 B7
Buckbury Croft B90 71 D3
Buckden B77 4 B1
Buckden Cl 9 CV34 104 C1
Buckfast Cl CV3 77 F3
Buckhold Dr CV5 60 A3
Buckingham Cl CV10 29 D1
Buckingham Rd CV33 132 F5
Buckingham Rise CV5 60 A2
Buckland Rd CV6 49 D1
Buckle St WR11,B50 128 C3
Buckley Rd CV32 106 B1
Buckminster Dr B93 71 F2
Bucks Hill CV10 28 B3
Buckwell La CV23 84 A3
Budbrooke Cl CV2 50 B1
Budbrooke Ind Est CV34 108 A4
Budbrooke Prim Sch CV35 114 F4
Budbrooke Rd CV34 108 A4
Bufferys Cl B91 71 D4
Bulkington Fst Sch CV12 40 B1
Bulkington La CV11 40 A4
Bulkington Rd
Bedworth CV12 39 E1
Shilton CV7 51 F3
Wolvey LE10 41 E2
Bull Ring Harbury CV33 123 F6
Nuneaton CV10 29 D1
Bull Ring Farm Rd CV33 123 F7
Bull St Nuneaton CV11 29 E1
Southam CV33 147 D2
Stratford-u-A CV37 144 C1
Bull Yd CV1 151 B2
Bull's Head La CV3 62 A1
Bull's La B76 13 F1
Bullaces La LE17 68 B2
Bullfield Ave CV4 59 F1
Bullfurlong La LE10 31 F2
Bullimore Gr CV8 93 D1
Bullivents Cl B93 71 F3
Bulls Head Yd B49 143 D2
Bulwer Rd CV6 61 D3
Bulwick Cl CV3 63 D1
Bunkers Hill NN11 126 F5
Burbage Ave CV37 144 C3
Burbage Cty Jun Sch LE10 31 F3
Burbage Rd
Aston Cantlow B95 119 F6
Hinckley LE10 32 A4
Burbages La CV6 49 E2
Burberry Gr CV7 74 A3
Burbury Cl Bedworth CV12 39 E2
Royal Leamington Spa CV32 106 B1
Burford La B49 112 C1
Burford Mews 22 CV31 110 B3
Burford Rd Hollywood B47 69 D3
Stratford-u-A CV37 145 E1
Burgage Pl CV11 29 E2
Burgage Wlk CV11 29 D3
Burges CV1 151 B3
Burges Gr CV34 104 C1
Burghley Cl CV11 29 F1
Burhill Way B37 33 D3
Burleigh Cl CV7 74 A4
Burlington Rd Coventry CV2 61 F2
Nuneaton CV10 39 D4
Burman Dr B46 34 A3
Burnaby Cl CV10 28 A3
Burnaby Rd CV6 49 D1
Burnaston Cres B90 71 E3
Burnell Cl B50 148 B3
Burnett Rd CV35 123 D2
Burnham Rd CV3 78 A3
Burnham Rise CV11 30 A3
Burns Ave CV34 108 B3
Burns Cl B97 102 B4
Burns Rd Coventry CV2 62 A2
Royal Leamington Spa CV32 106 A2
Burns Wlk CV12 39 E1
Burnsall Gr CV5 76 B4
Burnsall Rd CV5 76 B4
Burnside Coventry CV3 63 D1
Rugby CV22 82 C1
Burnthurst Cres B90 71 D4
Burrow Hill La CV7 48 B4
Burrows Cl CV31 110 A1
Burton Cl CV5 48 B1
Burton Dassett Hills
Ctry Pk CV33 133 B7
Burton Green CE
Jun & Inf Sch CV8 75 D2
Burton La CV11 40 C4
Burton Rd CV9 3 F1
Burtons Farm Prim Sch
B36 33 D4
Bury Rd CV31 109 F4
Burycroft Rd OX15 142 D3
Buryway La CV36 141 C4
Busby Cl CV3 78 C4
Bush Cl CV4 59 F2
Bush Heath La CV33 123 F6
Bush Hill La CV23 117 B2
Bush La B77 9 E2
Bushbery Ave CV4 59 F1
Bushbury Croft B37 33 E2
Bushley Cl B98 103 D4
Bushley Croft B91 71 D4
Bushwood Dr B93 72 A2
Bushwood La B94 113 C8
Butcher's Cl CV23 64 C2
Butcher's La CV5 60 B3
Butchers La OX15 137 F2
Butchers Rd B92 57 D3
Butler Cl CV8 93 E4
Butler St B96 102 C1
Butlers Cl Aston le W NN11 134 F5
Long Compton CV36 141 D3
Butlers Cres CV7 39 D1
Butlers End CV35 91 E1
Butlers La Grendon CV9 11 E1
Long Compton CV36 141 C3
Butlers Leap CV21 83 E3
Butlers Leap Ind Est CV21 83 E2
Butlers Rd CV36 141 E3
Butlin Rd Coventry CV6 49 E2
Rugby CV21 83 E2
Butt Hill CV23 125 C8
Butt La Allesley CV5 60 A4
Harbury CV33 123 F6
Butter St B49 143 E2
Buttermere Rugby CV21 83 E4
Tamworth B77 10 A4
Buttermere Ave CV11 30 A3
Buttermere Cl CV3 78 C4
Buttermilk La CV35 113 F5
Butterworth Dr CV4 76 A3
Butts CV1 61 D1
Butts Cl CV9 3 D1
Butts La B94 87 D1
Butts Rd CV1 61 D1
Butts The
Long Compton CV36 141 C3
Napton CV23 125 C8
Warwick CV34 108 C4
Buxton Ave B78 9 D4
By Pass Rd B77 4 A3
Byfield Rd
Chipping Warden OX17 134 F4
Coventry CV6 60 C3
Priors Marston CV23 125 F4
Byford St CV10 28 C2
Bygones Mus OX17 134 B4
Byron Ave Bedworth CV12 39 E1
Warwick CV34 108 B2
Byron Rd Redditch B97 102 B4
Stratford-u-A CV37 145 E1
Byron St CV1 151 C4
Byron Wlk CV33 132 F7
Bywater Cl CV3 77 D3

Cable & Wireless Coll CV4 75 F3
Cadbury Dr B35 22 A1
Cadden Dr CV4 60 A1
Cadman Cl CV12 39 E2
Cadogan Rd B77 9 E3
Caen Cl CV35 108 A4
Caernarfon Dr CV11 29 E2
Caernarvon Way OX16 139 F3
Caesar Rd CV8 92 C2
Caesar Way B46 23 F1
Caister B77 4 A3
Caistor Cl B78 8 A4
Caithness Cl CV5 60 A2
Calcutt Mdw CV33 147 E2
Caldecote Cl CV10 29 E4
Caldecote Hall Dr CV10 19 F2
Caldecote Rd CV6 61 E3
Caldecott Pl CV21 83 E1
Caldecott St CV21 83 E1
Caldeford Ave B90 71 D4
Calder B77 4 A1
Calder Cl Bulkington CV12 40 A1
Coventry CV3 77 F4
Calder Dr B76 22 A4
Calder Wlk CV31 110 B3
Caldon Cl LE10 31 D4
Caldwell Rd CV11 29 E1
Calf's La GL55 135 B2
Callaways Rd CV36 149 F2
Callendar Cl CV11 30 A4
Callow Hill La B97 102 A3
Calmere Cl CV2 62 C4
Caludon Castle Sch CV2 62 C2
Caludon Park Ave CV2 62 C3
Caludon Rd CV2 62 A2
Calvert Cl Coventry CV3 77 E3
Rugby CV21 83 F4
Camberwell Terr CV31 110 A4
Camborne Dr CV11 29 F3
Cambourne Rd LE10 32 A3
Cambria Cl B90 69 F4
Cambrian B77 4 A1
Cambridge Dr
Birmingham B37 33 D1
Nuneaton CV10 28 C2
Cambridge St Coventry CV1 61 F3
Rugby CV21 83 E2
Camden Cl GL56 140 F3
Camden St CV2 62 A2
Camellia Rd CV2 50 A1
Camelot Gr CV8 93 E3
Cameron Cl Allesley CV5 60 A4
Royal Leamington Spa CV32 106 A2
Camhouses B77 4 A1
Camp Hill Cty Jun Sch CV10 28 C3
Camp Hill Dr CV10 28 B4
Camp Hill Rd CV10 28 B4
Camp La Henley-in-A B95 113 B6
Warmington OX17 133 B2
Campbell St CV21 82 C2
Campden Cl B97 102 B3
Campden Lawns CV37 130 D3
Campden Pitch CV36 136 A6
Campden Rd
Ebrington GL55 135 D3
Lower Quinton CV37 129 D4
Mickleton GL55 135 B4
Shipston-on-S CV36 149 E3
Campden St CV36 136 A6
Campion Cl CV3 77 E3
Campion Gn CV32 106 A1
Campion Rd CV32 106 A1
Campion Sch & Com Coll
CV31 110 B3
Campion Terr CV32 106 A1
Campion Way CV23 83 E4
Camplea Croft B37 33 D1
Campling Cl CV12 40 A1
Campton Cl LE10 31 F4
Camville CV3 63 D1
Canada La CV35 114 D1
Canal La CV35 114 E5
Canal Rd CV6 61 F4
Canberra Cl CV35 146 B1
Canberra Rd CV2 50 B2
Canford Cl CV3 77 E2
Canley Ford CV5 76 C4
Canley Rd CV5 76 B4
Canley Sta CV5 60 B1
Cannocks La CV5 76 B3
Cannon Cl CV4 76 C3
Cannon Hill Rd CV4 76 B3
Cannon Park District Ctr
CV4 76 B3
Cannon Park Prim Sch CV4 76 B3
Cannon Park Rd CV4 76 C3
Canon Dr CV7 49 E3
Canon Evans CE Fst Sch
CV12 39 D1
Canon Hudson Cl CV3 78 B3
Canon Maggs CE Mid Sch
CV12 39 D1
Canon Young Rd CV31 110 A2
Canterbury Cl Kenilworth CV8 93 E2
Studley B80 103 E2
Canterbury Dr B37 44 A4
Canterbury St CV1 151 D3
Canterbury Way CV11 30 A4
Cantlow Cl CV5 60 A2
Canton La B76 24 A3
Canwell Dr B75 7 D3
Cape Ind Est CV34 108 C4
Cape Rd CV34 108 B4
Capmartin Rd CV6 61 F4
Captain's Hill B49 143 E3
Capulet Cl Coventry CV3 78 B3
Rugby CV22 99 F3
Caradoc B77 4 A1
Caradoc Cl CV2 62 B4
Cardale Croft 1 CV3 78 C4
Cardiff Cl CV3 78 B3
Cardigan Rd CV12 38 B1
Cardinal Newman RC Sch
CV6 48 C1
Cardinal Wiseman RC Sch
CV2 50 C1
Carding Cl CV5 59 F2
Carew Cl CV37 144 C3
Carey B77 10 A3
Carey St CV6 62 A4
Cargill Cl CV6 49 F3
Carhampton Rd B75 13 D3
Carisbroke B77 4 A1
Carisbrook Rd CV10 29 E3
Carisbrooke Ave B37 33 E1
Carlcroft B77 4 A1
Carlton Cl CV12 40 A2
Carlton Rd Coventry CV6 49 F1
Rugby CV22 82 B1
Carlyle Cl CV10 27 F3
Carlyon Rd CV9 18 C4
Carlyon Road Ind Est CV9 12 C1
Carmelite Rd CV1 61 F1
Carnbroe Ave CV3 78 C4
Carnegie Cl CV3 78 A3
Carnoustie B77 4 B3
Carnoustie Cl CV11 40 B4
Caroline Cl CV11 39 F4
Carpenters Cl LE10 31 F3
Carroway Head Hill B78 7 E2
Carsal Cl CV7 49 E3
Carson Cl GL56 136 C1
Cart's La CV9 11 E1
Carter Dr CV35 122 A7
Carter Rd CV3 78 A4
Carters La CV37 145 F2
Carters Leaze CV36 140 E5
Carthusian Rd CV3 77 E4
Cartmel Cl CV5 60 A2
Carver Cl CV2 62 C1
Cascade Cl CV3 77 F3
Case La CV35 114 B8
Cash's Bsns Ctr CV1 61 E3
Cash's La CV1 61 E3
Cashmore Ave CV31 109 F3
Cashmore Mid Sch CV31 109 F3
Cashmore Rd Bedworth CV12 38 C1
Kenilworth CV8 93 E2
Casia Gr CV8 93 E2
Caspian Way CV2 63 D4
Cassandra Cl CV4 76 B2
Cassandra Gr CV34 109 E2
Castello Dr B36 22 B1
Castle Bromwich Bsns Pk
B35 22 A1
Castle Cl Coventry CV3 77 E3
Fillongley CV7 36 C1
Henley-in-A B95 113 B4
Warwick CV34 108 C3
Castle Cres CV35 132 B5
Castle Ct LE10 31 E3
Castle Dr Astley CV10 37 F4
Coleshill B46 33 F3
Castle Gdns GL55 135 C2
Castle Gn CV8 92 B3
Castle Hill Kenilworth CV8 92 C3
Upper Brailes OX15 137 E3
Warwick CV34 108 C3
Castle Hill La OX15 137 E2
Castle La Maxstoke B46 34 C4
Warwick CV34 108 C3
Castle Mound CV23 101 E1
Castle Place Ind Est CV1 151 D4
Castle Rd Alcester B49 143 E3
Henley-in-A B95 113 B4
Kenilworth CV8 92 C3
Kineton CV35 132 B6
Nuneaton CV10 29 E4
Studley B80 103 F2
Tamworth B77 9 F3
Castle St Astwood Bank B96 102 C1
Coventry CV1 151 D4
Hinckley LE10 31 E4
Rugby CV21 83 D2
Warwick CV34 108 C3
Castle Vale Sec Sch B35 22 A2
Castle Vale Sports Ctr B35 22 A1
Castle View CV10 19 D1
Castleditch La B98 102 C4
Castlehall B77 4 A1
Caswell Rd CV31 110 A3
Catbrook Cl GL55 135 B1
Catesby La B94 89 D1
Catesby Rd Coventry CV6 61 D4
Rugby CV22 83 E1
Cathedral Lanes Sh Ctr
CV1 151 B3
Catherine de Barnes La
Bickenhill B92 44 B1
Catherine de B B92 56 B4
Catherine St CV2 61 F2
Catherines Cl B91 56 A2
Cathiron La CV23 65 E1
Cattell Dr B75 13 D3
Cattell Rd CV34 108 C4
Catthorpe Manor LE17 68 C1
Catthorpe Rd LE17 68 B2
Cavalier Cl CV11 29 F1
Cavans Way CV3 79 D4
Cavendish Rd CV4 59 F1
Caversham Cl CV11 30 A4
Cawdon Gr B93 71 F2
Cawnpore Rd CV6 49 D1
Cawston La CV22 99 D3
Cawston Way CV22 99 E4
Cawthorne Cl 1 CV1 61 F2
Cecil Leonard Knox Cres
CV11 40 C3
Cecily Rd CV3 77 F4
Cedar Cl Kingsbury B78 15 E3
Royal Leamington Spa CV32 106 A2
Stratford-u-A CV37 145 D2
Cedar Ct LE10 32 A3
Cedar Dr CV37 121 B7
Cedar Gr CV34 105 D1
Cedar Rd Mickleton GL55 135 C6
Nuneaton CV10 28 B3
Cedar Wlk 5 B37 33 D1
Cedar Wood Dr CV7 74 A3
Cedars Ave CV6 60 C3
Cedars Fst Sch CV7 50 A4
Cedars Rd CV7 39 D1
Cedric Cl CV3 78 B3
Celandine CV23 83 E4
Celandine Rd CV2 50 B1
Centaur Rd CV5 60 C1
Centenary Bsns Ctr CV11 29 F2
Centenary Rd CV4 76 B4
Central Ave Coventry CV2 62 A1
Nuneaton CV11 29 D3
Royal Leamington Spa CV31 109 F3
Central City Ind Est CV6 61 F3
Central Dr CV33 124 B4
Centrovell Ind Est CV11 29 E1
Centurion Cl B46 23 F1
Centurion Pk B77 10 A3
Centurion Way B77 10 A3
Ceolmund Cres B37 33 D1
Chace Ave CV3 78 B3
Chace Prim Sch CV3 78 B3
Chaceley Cl CV2 63 D4
Chadbury Croft 1 B91 71 D4
Chadbury Rd WR11 127 A1
Chadshunt Cl B36 22 B1
Chadstone Cl B90 71 D3
Chadwick Cl CV5 60 A2
Chadwick La
Chadwick End B93 90 A4
Knowle B93 73 D1
Chadwick Mews B93 90 A3
Chadworth Ave B93 71 F2
Chaffinch Dr B36 33 D4
Chalfont Cl Bedworth CV12 39 D2
Coventry CV5 60 A2

Challenge Bsns Pk CV1 61 E3
Challenge Cl CV1 151 C4
Chamberlain Cl CV32 106 C3
Chamberlain La B49 118 D5
Chamberlain Rd CV21 101 D4
Chamberlaine St CV12 39 D2
Chance Fields CV31 110 C3
Chancellors Cl CV4 76 B2
Chancery La CV10 28 A4
Chanders Rd CV34 104 B1
Chandlers Cl B97 102 B4
Chandlers Dr B77 4 A3
Chandlers Rd CV31 110 A1
Chandos St Coventry CV2 62 A2
Nuneaton CV11 29 D2
Royal Leamington Spa CV32 105 F1
Change Brook Cl CV11 29 F4
Chantries The CV1 61 F3
Chantry Cl B47 69 D4
Chantry Cres B49 143 D2
Chantry Heath Cres B93 72 B4
Chantry The CV34 105 D1
Chapel Cl B50 148 B2
Chapel Ct B96 102 C1
Chapel Dr
Balsall Common CV7 74 A4
Wythall B47 69 D2
Chapel End OX7 142 A2
Chapel Gdns GL56 136 C1
Chapel Gn CV23 125 C7
Chapel Hill OX7 142 F2
Chapel La Aston Cantlow B95 119 F7
Barnacle CV7 51 D3
Cropredy OX17 134 C1
Great Rollright OX7 142 A2
Lapworth B94 89 E4
Mickleton GL55 135 B6
Newbold-on-S CV37 130 E1
Pillerton Priors CV35 131 D2
Ratley OX15 133 A2
Ryton-on-D CV8 79 D1
Salford OX7 150 C3
Stratford-u-A CV37 145 D1
Ullenhall B95 112 E6
Witherley CV9 19 E4
Chapel Rd B96 102 C1
Chapel Row 14 CV34 108 C4
Chapel St
Astwood Bank B96 102 C1
Bedworth CV12 39 E2
Bishops Itchington CV33 124 A4
Charwelton NN11 126 D2
Coventry CV1 151 B3
Harbury CV33 123 F6
Hook Norton OX15 142 D4
Long Lawford CV23 82 A2
Nuneaton CV11 29 E2
3 Royal Leamington Spa CV31 110 A4
Rugby CV21 83 D2
Stratford-u-A CV37 145 D1
Warmington OX17 133 D2
Warwick CV34 108 C4
Welford on A CV37 129 B6
Wellesbourne CV35 146 B2
Chapelhouse Rd B37 33 D1
Chapelon B77 4 A1
Chapman Cl CV31 110 C3
Chapman Way B49 143 E3
Chard Rd CV3 78 B4
Chariot Way CV21 83 D4
Charity Rd CV7 49 D4
Charlbury Mews CV31 110 B3
Charlecote Cl CV37 145 F2
Charlecote Croft B90 70 B4
Charlecote Gdns 27 CV31 110 B3
Charlecote Park CV35 121 F3
Charlecote Rd Coventry CV6 49 D1
Wellesbourne CV35 146 B2
Wellesbourne, Charlcote CV35 146 A3
Charlecote Wlk CV11 39 F4
Charles Eaton Rd CV12 38 C2
Charles Gardner Rd CV31 109 F3
Charles Lakin Cl CV7 51 E3
Charles Rd CV9 18 C4
Charles St Arley CV7 37 D4
Coventry CV1 151 D4
Hurley CV9 16 B3
Nuneaton CV11 29 D3
Rugby CV21 82 C2
Warwick CV34 109 D4
Charles Warren Cl CV21 83 D2
Charlesfield Rd CV22 100 A4
Charlesworth Ave B90 71 D3
Charlewood Rd CV6 49 D1
Charlotte St
Royal Leamington Spa CV31 109 F3
Rugby CV21 83 D2
Charminster Dr CV3 77 E2
Charnwood Ave CV10 28 C1
Charnwood Dr CV10 19 D1
Charnwood Way CV32 106 B2
Charter App CV34 108 B3
Charter Ave CV4 76 A4
Charter Rd CV22 100 C4
Charterhouse Rd CV1 61 F1
Chartley Cl B93 71 F2
Chartwell Cl CV11 29 F1
Chartwell Dr B90 70 B3
Charwelton Dr CV21 83 F3
Chase Cl CV11 29 F3
Chase La CV8 92 A4
Chater Dr B76 13 D1
Chatham Cl CV3 78 B4
Chatsworth Cl
Cheswick Green B90 70 C3
Hinckley LE10 31 F3
Chatsworth Dr CV11 29 F1
Chatsworth Gr
Kenilworth CV8 93 E3
Royal Leamington Spa CV31 110 B3
Chatsworth Rise CV3 77 F3
Chattaway Dr CV7 74 A3
Chattle Hill B46 23 F1
Chaucer Dr CV10 28 A2
Chaucer Rd CV22 99 F3
Chauntry Pl CV1 151 C3
Chauson Gr B91 71 D4
Chaytor Rd B78 11 D4
Cheadle Cl CV2 50 A2
Cheam Cl CV6 50 A1
Cheedon Cl B93 71 F1
Chelmsley Ave B46 33 F3
Chelmsley Circ B37 33 D2
Chelmsley La B37 44 A4
Chelmsley Rd B37 33 E1
Chelney Wlk CV3 63 D1
Chelsea Cl CV11 29 F4
Chelsey Rd CV2 62 C4
Cheltenham Cl CV12 39 D2
Cheltenham Croft CV2 62 C4
Chelveston Rd CV6 60 C3
Chelwood Gr CV2 50 C1
Chenies Cl CV5 60 A2
Chepstow Cl Coventry CV3 78 B3
Stratford-u-A CV37 144 C1
Chepstow Gdns OX16 139 F3
Chequer St CV12 40 B1
Cheriton Cl CV5 60 B2
Cherry Blossom Gr CV31 110 A1
Cherry Cl Coventry CV6 49 E1
Ettington CV37 131 A3
Hurley CV9 16 B2
Offenham WR11 127 D1
Cherry Gr CV22 99 F4
Cherry La Bearley CV37 120 E7
Hampton Magna CV35 114 F4
Cherry Orch
Henley-in-A B95 113 B5
Kenilworth CV8 93 D3
Shipston-on-S CV36 149 F3
Stratford-u-A CV37 144 C1
Wellesbourne CV35 146 B2
Cherry Orchard Cl GL55 135 B1
Cherry Pit La B98 86 A1
Cherry Rd OX16 139 F4
Cherry St
Stratford-u-A CV37 144 C1
Warwick CV34 108 C4
Cherry Tree Ave CV10 28 C3
Cherry Tree Cres WR11 127 F6
Cherry Tree Wlk CV33 147 D3
Cherry Way CV8 93 D3
Cherry Wlk B47 69 D3
Cherrybrook Way CV2 50 B1
Cherryfield Cl CV10 19 D1
Cherrywood Cres 3 B91 71 E4
Cherrywood Gr CV5 59 F3
Cherwell Cl LE10 31 D4
Cherwell The NN11 117 F1
Cherwell Way CV23 82 A2
Chesford Cres Coventry CV6 50 A1
Warwick CV34 105 D1
Chesford Gr CV37 144 B2
Chesham St CV31 110 A4
Cheshire Cl CV22 99 E4
Chesholme Rd CV6 49 D1
Chesils The CV3 77 E3
Chessetts Wood Rd B94 89 E4
Chester Cl B37 33 D1
Chester Rd Birmingham B36 33 D3
Birmingham, Chelmsley Wood B37 44 C4
Hampton in A B46, B92, CV7 45 D3
Chester St Coventry CV1 61 D2
Rugby CV21 83 E2
Chester Way OX16 139 F3
Chesterton Cl B97 102 B2
Chesterton Dr
Nuneaton CV10 28 A3
Royal Leamington Spa CV31 110 B3
Chesterton Hill CV35 123 C3
Chesterton Rd Coventry CV6 61 D4
Lighthorne CV35 123 B2
Chesterwood B47 69 D3
Chestnut Ave CV8 92 C2
Chestnut Cl Ettington CV37 131 B3
Kingsbury B78 15 E3
Chestnut Cres CV10 28 C3
Chestnut Ct Alcester B49 143 E2
Royal Leamington Spa CV34 109 F1
Chestnut Dr CV11 29 F2
Chestnut Field CV21 83 D2
Chestnut Gr Coleshill B46 34 A4
Coventry CV4 60 A1
Moreton Morrell CV35 122 E3
Wolston CV8 80 A2
Chestnut Pl CV33 147 D3
Chestnut Rd
Astwood Bank B96 102 C1
Bedworth CV12 39 E2
Mollington OX17 134 A2
Chestnut Sq
6 Royal Leamington Spa CV32 106 A1
Wellesbourne CV35 146 B2
Chestnut Tree Ave CV4 60 A1
Chestnut Wlk
2 Birmingham B37 33 D1
Henley-in-A B95 113 A5
Stratford-u-A CV37 144 C1
Chestnuts The CV12 38 C1
Cheswick Cl Coventry CV6 62 A4
Redditch B98 112 A6
Cheswick Green Jun & Inf Sch B94 70 C2
Cheswick Way B90 70 B2
Cheswood Dr B76 22 A3
Chetwode Cl CV5 60 A2
Chetwynd Dr CV11 40 A4
Chetwynd Mid Sch CV11 40 A4
Chetwynd Rd B78 11 D4
Cheveral Ave CV6 61 D3
Cheveral Rd CV12 39 D2
Cheverel Pl CV11 29 D1
Cheverel St CV11 29 D2
Cheviot B77 4 B1
Cheviot Cl CV10 28 A2
Cheviot Rise CV32 106 B2
Cheviot Way OX16 139 F5
Cheylesmore CV1 151 B2
Chichester Cl CV11 30 A4
Chichester Gr B37 33 D1
Chichester La CV35 114 F3
Chicory Dr CV23 83 E4
Chideock Hill CV3 77 D3
Chiel Cl CV5 59 F2
Chigwell Cl B35 22 A2
Childs Cl CV37 144 C3
Childs Oak Cl CV7 74 A3
Chilham Dr B37 33 E1
Chillaton Rd CV6 49 D1
Chillingham B77 9 E4
Chiltern Leys 2 CV6 61 D2
Chiltern Rd B77 4 B1
Chilterns The CV5 60 A2
Chilvers Coton Craft Ctr CV11 29 E1
Chilvers Coton Fst Sch CV11 29 D2
Chilworth Cl CV11 39 F4
Chingford Rd CV6 50 A2
Chingley Bank B95 113 B4
Chipping Campden Sch GL55 135 B2
Chipping Norton Rd OX15 142 D4
Chipstone Cl 1 B91 71 E4
Chiswick Wlk B37 33 F1
Chivenor Prim Sch B35 22 A1
Chivington Cl B90 71 D3
Choyce Cl CV9 12 B1
Christ the King RC Inf Sch CV6 60 C3
Christ the King RC Jun Sch CV6 60 C4
Christchurch Rd CV6 61 D3
Christine Ledger Sq 3 CV31 110 A3
Chub B77 9 E4
Chudleigh Rd CV2 62 C4
Church Ave B46 23 D2
Church Bank Binton CV37 129 A8
Temple Grafton B49 119 E1
Church Cl Arley CV10 26 C1
Birmingham B37 33 D3
Bishops Itchington CV33 124 A4
Drayton Bassett B78 8 C3
Hartshill CV10 28 A4
Hinckley LE10 32 A3
Luddington CV37 129 C7
Stoke Golding CV13 21 E4
Wardington OX17 134 F1
Whitnash CV31 110 A2
Wolvey LE10 41 F2
Wood End CV9 10 B1
Church Down Cl B97 102 B3
Church Dr B49 118 D5
Church End
Great Rollright OX7 142 A2
Radford Semele CV31 110 C3
Church Farm Ct CV35 138 C7
Church Farm La GL56 140 A6
Church Fields NN11 126 E8
Church Hill Badby NN11 126 F5
15 Bishops Tachbrook CV33 122 F8
Coleshill B46 34 A4
Combrook CV35 131 E6
Cubbington CV32 106 C3
Royal Leamington Spa CV32 109 F4
Stretton on D CV23 96 C3
Ullenhall B95 112 E6
Warmington OX17 133 D2
Wolvey LE10 41 F2
Church La Alveston CV37 121 D3
Ansley CV10 27 E1
Arley CV7 26 C1
Ash Green CV7 49 F4
Aston Cantlow B95 119 F6
Austrey CV9 3 D1
Austrey, No Man's Heath CV9 3 D3
Barford CV35 122 B7
Bearley CV37 120 E7
Berkswell CV7 58 B2
Bickenhill B92 44 C1
Cookhill B49 118 D5
Corley CV7 48 A4
Coventry, Middle Stoke CV2 62 A2
Coventry, Upper Eastern Green CV5 59 E3
Cropredy OX17 134 C1
Cubbington CV32 106 C3
Curdworth B76 23 D3
Ettington CV37 131 A3
Fenny Drayton CV13 19 F3
Fillongley CV7 36 C2
Gaydon CV35 132 E8
Hanwell OX17 139 F6
Hornton OX15 139 B7
Kingsbury B78 15 E3
Lapworth B94 88 C2
Church La continued
Lea Marston B76 24 A4
Lighthorne CV35 123 B2
Littleton WR11 127 F1
Meriden CV7 58 C4
Middleton B78 8 B1
Mollington OX17 134 A2
Newbold-on-S CV37 130 E1
Norton WR11 127 C2
Nuneaton CV10 29 E4
Oxhill CV35 137 F8
Royal Leamington Spa CV32 106 A2
Shawell LE17 68 B3
Shuttington B79 4 C4
Snitterfield CV37 121 B7
Stoneleigh CV8 94 B3
Stratford-u-A CV37 144 B2
Thurlaston CV23 98 C1
Welford on A CV37 129 A7
Whatcote CV36 137 D7
Whitnash CV31 110 A2
Wigston Parva LE10 42 C4
Wishaw B76 14 A1
Church Lees 7 CV33 122 F8
Church Lench Fst Sch WR11 127 A6
Church Mews CV35 132 B6
Church Park Cl CV6 48 C1
Church Path CV35 114 F3
Church Rd
Astwood Bank B96 102 C1
Baginton CV8 77 F1
Braunston NN11 117 D5
Bubbenhall CV8 95 E3
Church Lawford CV23 81 E3
Claverdon CV35 113 F3
Dordon B78 11 D3
Gaydon CV35 132 E8
Grandborough CV23 116 F5
Hartshill CV10 28 A4
Ladbroke CV33 124 D5
Long Itchington CV23 115 D4
Newbold-on-S CV37 130 E1
Norton Lindsey CV35 114 C2
Nuneaton CV10 28 B2
Pebworth CV37 128 F1
Ryton-on-D CV8 79 D1
Shilton CV7 51 F3
Shustoke B46 25 D1
Snitterfield CV37 121 B6
Tamworth B77 9 E2
Ullenhall B95 112 D5
Upper Boddington NN11 134 E8
Warton B79 5 E2
Wilmcote CV37 120 C4
Witherley CV9 19 D4
Church St Alcester B49 143 E2
Appleby Magna DE12 3 F4
Atherstone CV9 18 B4
Barford CV35 122 B7
Bidford-on-A B50 148 C2
Bulkington CV12 40 B1
Charwelton NN11 126 D2
Chipping Campden GL55 135 B2
Churchover CV23 67 E3
Clifton u D CV23 84 A3
Coventry CV1 151 C4
Fenny Compton CV33 133 D7
Hampton Lucy CV35 121 F4
Harbury CV33 123 F6
Harvington WR11 127 D3
Hinckley LE10 32 A3
Marton CV23 115 C7
Moreton-in-M GL56 140 A3
Nuneaton CV11 29 E2
Offenham WR11 127 D1
Royal Leamington Spa CV31 110 A4
Rugby CV21 83 D2
Shipston-on-S CV36 149 F3
Staverton NN11 126 D8
Stockton CV23 147 F4
Stratford-u-A CV37 144 C1
Studley B80 103 F2
Warwick CV34 108 C3
Welford on A CV37 129 A7
Wellesbourne CV35 146 B2
Wroxton OX15 139 D4
Church Terr Harbury CV33 123 F7
Royal Leamington Spa CV31 110 A4
Church View
Aston Magna GL56 140 A6
Tamworth B77 9 F4
Warton B79 5 F2
Church Way CV12 39 D1
Church Wlk Allesley CV5 60 B3
Atherstone CV9 18 C4
Barby CV23 101 E1
Hinckley LE10 31 E4
12 Royal Leamington Spa CV31 109 F4
Rugby CV22 83 D1
Rugby, Bilton CV22 99 E4
Thurlaston CV23 98 C2
Wellesbourne CV35 146 B2
Church Wlks CV13 21 E4
Churchdale Cl CV10 28 B2
Churchfield CV37 129 A7
Churchill Ave Coventry CV6 61 F4
Kenilworth CV8 93 D3
Churchill Cl CV37 131 A4
Churchill Rd Rugby CV22 83 D1
Sutton Coldfield B75 13 D3
Churchlea OX17 134 A2
Chylds Ct CV5 60 A3
Cicey La CV11 41 D4
Cinder La CV9 6 A4
Cinderhill La GL55 135 B2
Circle The CV10 28 C2
Circuit The CV37 129 C8
Circus Ave B37 33 E1
City Arc CV1 151 B2
City Tech Coll The B37 33 D2
Cladswell Cl B49 118 D5
Cladswell La B49 118 C6
Clapham Sq CV31 110 A4
Clapham St CV31 110 A3
Clapham Terr CV31 110 A4
Clapham Terrace Com Prim Sch CV31 110 A4
Clara St CV2 62 A1
Clare Cl CV32 106 B1
Clare Ct CV21 82 C2
Claremont Cl CV12 40 A2
Claremont Rd
Royal Leamington Spa CV31 109 F3
Rugby CV21 83 E2
Claremont Wlk CV5 60 B3
Clarence Rd Hinckley LE10 31 F4
Rugby CV21 82 C2
Stratford-u-A CV37 144 B2
Clarence St 4 Coventry CV1 61 F2
Nuneaton CV11 29 D2
Royal Leamington Spa CV31 110 A3
Clarence Terr 6 CV32 105 F1
Clarendon Ave CV32 105 F1
Clarendon Cres CV32 105 F1
Clarendon Pl CV32 105 F1
Clarendon Rd Hinckley LE10 31 E4
Kenilworth CV8 93 D2
Clarendon Sq CV32 105 F1
Clarendon St Coventry CV5 60 C1
Royal Leamington Spa CV32 106 A1
Clarewell Ave B91 71 D4
Clark Cl CV36 149 F3
Clark St CV6 50 A1
Clarke Ave GL56 140 C3
Clarke's Ave CV8 93 D2
Clarks La CV36 141 D3
Clarkson Dr CV31 110 A2
Claverdon Cl B97 102 B2
Claverdon Jun & Inf Sch CV35 113 F3
Claverdon Rd CV5 60 A2
Claverdon Sta CV35 114 A3
Clay Ave CV11 29 F4
Clay Bank OX15 142 D4
Clay La Allesley CV5 47 F2
Coventry CV2 62 A2
Claybrook Dr B98 103 F4
Claybrook Prim Sch LE17 43 F2
Claydon Rd OX17 134 C2
Claymore B77 9 E4
Clayton Rd CV6 60 C3
Clayton Wlk B35 22 A1
Cleasby B77 4 B1
Cleaver Gdns CV10 29 E3
Cleeve Prior CE Fst Sch WR11 128 A4
Cleeve Rd Bidford-on-A B50 148 B1
Littleton WR11 127 F2
Cleeves Ave CV34 109 E3
Clemens St CV31 110 A4
Clement St CV11 29 D2
Clements St CV2 62 A2
Clennon Rise CV2 62 B4
Clent Ave B97 102 B4
Clent Dr CV10 28 A2
Cleobury La B94 70 A2
Clevedon Gn WR11 128 A1
Cleveland Rd
Bulkington CV12 40 A2
Coventry CV2 62 A2
Hinckley LE10 31 E4
Cleveley Dr CV10 28 B4
Clews Rd B98 102 C4
Clifden Gr CV8 93 E3
Cliff Hall La B78 9 E1
Cliffe Ct CV32 105 E1
Cliffe Rd CV32 105 E1
Cliffe Way CV34 109 D4
Clifford Bridge Prim Sch CV3 63 D2
Clifford Bridge Rd CV3 62 C2
Clifford La CV37 130 A8
Clifford Rd B93 71 F2
Clifton Cl B98 103 F4
Clifton La B79 1 A2
Clifton Rd Nuneaton CV10 28 C2
Rugby CV21 83 E2
Clifton St CV1 151 D4
Clifton-on-Dunsmore CE Prim Sch CV23 83 F3
Clinic Dr CV11 29 E2
Clinton Ave Kenilworth CV8 92 B3
Warwick CV35 108 A4
Clinton Comb Sch CV8 92 C2
Clinton La CV8 92 B3
Clinton Rd Coleshill B46 33 F3
Coventry CV6 49 F1
Solihull B90 70 B4
Clinton St CV31 110 A4
Clipstone Rd CV6 60 C3
Clive Rd CV7 74 B3
Cliveden Wlk CV11 39 F4
Clock La B92 44 B1
Cloister Croft CV2 62 C3
Cloister Crofts CV32 105 F2
Cloister Way CV32 105 F2
Cloisters The Atherstone CV9 18 C4
Studley B80 103 E2
Clopton Cres B37 33 E2
Clopton Ct CV37 144 C2
Clopton Rd CV37 144 C2
Close The Brandon CV8 79 F3
Chipping Warden OX17 134 F3
Cleeve Prior WR11 128 A4

Close The continued
Epwell OX15 138 D3
Halford CV36 137 A8
Hampton Lucy CV35 121 F4
Hollywood B47 69 D3
Kenilworth CV8 93 D3
Lower Quinton CV37 129 E2
Royal Leamington Spa CV31 110 A3
Closers Bsns Ctr CV11 29 E1
Closter Gn CV35 132 B6
Cloud Gn CV4 76 B3
Cloudsley Bush La LE10 42 A3
Clovelly Gdns CV2 62 B3
Clovelly Rd CV2 62 A3
Clovelly Way CV11 29 F3
Clover Ave B37 33 E1
Clover Cl Rugby CV23 83 E4
Stratford-u-A CV37 144 C3
Cloweswood La B94 86 C4
Clumber Park Rd CV35 132 D3
Clunes Ave CV11 29 F3
Clyde Rd Bulkington CV12 40 A1
Dorridge B93 72 A1
Co-operative St CV2 50 A2
Coach House Rise B77 9 F4
Coal Pit La Willey CV23 54 B3
Wolvey LE10 41 E1
Coalpit Fields Rd CV12 39 E1
Coalpit La CV8 80 C1
Coat Of Arms Bridge Rd CV3 77 D3
Cobbs Rd CV8 92 B3
Cobden Ave CV31 110 B3
Cobden St CV6 61 F3
Cobia B77 9 E4
Cockerills Mdw CV21 101 D4
Cockermouth Cl CV32 105 E1
Cocksfoot Cl CV37 144 C3
Cocksparrow St CV34 108 B4
Cockspur St B78 10 C4
Coffee Pot La CV35 114 C6
Colbourne Grove Dr CV32 105 E1
Cold Comfort La B49 143 D2
Coldfield Dr B98 102 C4
Coldicotts Cl GL55 135 B2
Cole Ct B37 33 D1
Colebridge Cres B46 33 F4
Colebrook Cl Alcester B49 143 E2
Coventry CV3 62 C1
Coleby Cl CV4 75 E4
Coleford Dr B37 33 D1
Colehurst Croft B90 70 C3
Coleman St CV4 59 F2
Colemeadow Rd B46 33 F4
Coleridge Cl B97 102 B4
Coleridge Rd CV2 62 B2
Coleshill Blythe Specl Sch B46 34 A2
Coleshill CE Prim Sch
Coleshill B46 33 F3
Coleshill B46 34 A2
Coleshill Cl B97 102 B3
Coleshill Heath Rd
Birmingham B37 44 B4
Coleshill B37, B46 33 F1
Coleshill Heath Sch B37 33 E1
Coleshill Ind Est B46 23 F1
Coleshill Rd Ansley CV10 27 E4
Atherstone CV9 18 B3
Birmingham, Marston Green B37 44 A4
Curdworth B76 23 E3
Fazeley B78 9 D4
Furnace End B46 25 E2
Maxstoke B46 34 C3
Shustoke B46 24 C1
Water Orton B46 23 D1
Coleshill Sch The B46 34 A2
Coleshill St B78 9 D4
Colesleys The B46 34 A3
Coleville Rd B76 22 A3
Coley Cl LE10 31 E4
Colina Cl CV3 78 B3
Colledge Cl CV23 64 C2
Colledge Rd CV6 49 E1
College Dr CV32 105 F1
College La
Balsall Common CV8 73 F1
Long Compton CV36 141 D2
Stratford-u-A CV37 144 C1
College Mews CV37 144 C1
College Rd CV23 117 C6
College St Nuneaton CV10 29 E1
Stratford-u-A CV37 144 C1
Collets Brook B75 7 D1
Collett B77 4 A1
Collett Wlk 7 CV1 61 D2
Colliers Way CV7 36 C4
Colliery La CV7 39 D1
Colliery La N CV7 39 D1
Colling Wlk B37 33 D3
Collingham La CV23 115 E4
Collingwood Ave CV22 82 B1
Collingwood Rd CV5 61 D1
Collins Gr CV4 76 B3
Collins Rd CV34 109 E3
Collins Way B49 143 E2
Colmore Dr B75 13 D3
Colony Rd OX15 142 D8
Colts Cl LE10 31 E2
Columbia Gdns CV12 39 F1
Colyere Cl CV7 49 D3
Combe Fields Rd CV3 63 F2
Combroke Gr CV35 114 F5
Commainge Cl CV34 108 B4
Commander Cl 11 CV33 122 F8
Commissary Rd B26 44 A2
Common La Claverdon CV35 113 F4
Corley CV7 47 F4
Kenilworth CV8 93 D4
Mappleborough Green B80 112 A6
Polesworth B78 11 D4
Common The CV9 11 E1
Common Way CV2 62 A3
Compass Ct 8 CV1 61 D2
Compton Cl CV32 106 B1
Compton Croft B37 33 E1
Compton Ct CV36 141 C4
Compton District Prim Sch The CV36 141 C3
Compton Hill CV35 131 E7
Compton Rd Coventry CV6 49 E1
Lighthorne Heath CV35 123 D2
Compton Verney House CV35 131 F7
Comrie Cl CV2 62 C3
Comyn St CV32 106 A1
Conduit Hill GL55 135 A1
Coneybury Wlk B76 22 B3
Congleton Cl CV6 49 F1
Congrave Wlk CV12 39 D1
Congreve Cl CV34 104 C1
Conifer Cl CV12 39 E2
Conifer Gr CV31 109 F3
Conifer Paddock CV3 62 C1
Coningsby Cl 5 CV31 110 B3
Coniston B77 10 A4
Coniston Cl Bulkington CV12 40 B2
Rugby CV21 83 E3
Coniston Dr CV5 59 E2
Coniston Rd Coventry CV5 60 C1
Royal Leamington Spa CV32 105 E1
Coniston Way CV11 29 F4
Conrad Cl CV22 99 F3
Conrad Rd CV6 61 D4
Constable Cl CV12 39 D3
Constable Rd CV21 84 A1
Constance Cl CV12 49 F4
Constance Dr CV33 123 F6
Constantine La B46 23 F1
Consul Rd CV21 83 D3
Convent Cl Atherstone CV9 18 C4
Kenilworth CV8 93 D4
Convent La CV9 18 C4
Conway Ave CV4 75 E4
Conway Croft B49 127 E8
Conway Dr OX16 139 F3
Conway Rd
Birmingham, Fordbridge B37 33 D2
Royal Leamington Spa CV32 109 E4
Conwy Cl CV11 29 E2
Cook Cl Knowle B93 72 B3
Rugby CV21 83 E4
Cook St CV1 151 C3
Cook's Hill OX15 139 A3
Cooke Cl CV34 104 C1
Cooks Cl CV9 18 B4
Cooks La Birmingham B37 33 D2
Frankton CV23 97 E1
Salford OX7 150 C3
Coombe Abbey Ctry Pk CV3 63 F2
Coombe Ave CV3 78 C4
Coombe Ct CV3 63 D1
Coombe Dr CV3 79 F4
Coombe Park Rd CV3 62 C1
Coombe St CV3 62 A1
Cooper St CV11 29 E2
Cooper's Way CV33 132 F6
Coopers Wlk CV8 95 E3
Cope Arnolds Cl CV6 49 F2
Cope St CV1 151 C3
Copeland CV21 83 E4
Copeland Cl B79 5 F2
Copland Pl CV4 59 F1
Coplow Cl CV7 74 A3
Copper Beech Cl CV6 49 F1
Copperas St CV2 50 A1
Copperfield Rd CV2 62 A2
Coppice Cl
Cheswick Green B90 70 B2
Stratford-u-A CV37 145 D3
Coppice Dr B78 11 D3
Coppice La Middleton B78 7 E1
Thorpe Constantine B79 1 C4
Coppice Prim Sch The B47 69 D3
Coppice Rd CV31 110 A1
Coppice The Atherstone CV9 19 D3
Coventry CV3 78 A4
Hinckley LE10 31 F4
Nuneaton CV10 29 E4
Coppice Way 6 B37 33 D1
Coppice Wlk B90 70 B2
Copps Rd CV32 109 E4
Copse Cl CV5 59 D4
Copse The CV7 50 A4
Copsewood Ave CV11 40 A4
Copsewood Terr CV3 62 B1
Copston La LE10 42 A3
Copstone Dr B93 71 F2
Copt Heath Croft B93 72 A4
Copt Heath Dr B93 72 A4
Copt Oak Cl CV4 75 E3
Copthorne Rd CV6 60 C4
Coral Cl Coventry CV5 60 B1
Hinckley LE10 31 F2
Coralin Cl B37 33 E1
Corbett Rd B47 69 D4
Corbett St CV21 83 E2
Corbetts Cl B92 57 D4
Corbin Rd B78 11 D3
Corbison Cl CV34 104 B1
Corbizum Ave B80 103 E2
Cord La CV23 65 F2
Cordelia Gn CV34 109 F2
Cordelia Way CV22 99 F3
Corfe Cl CV2 62 C3
Corinne Croft B37 33 D2
Corley Sch CV7 48 A3
Corley View CV7 49 E3
Corncrake Dr B36 33 D4
Cornel Cl B37 44 B4
Cornelius St CV3 77 E4
Cornet's End La CV7 58 A3
Cornets End La CV7 57 F4
Cornfield Croft B37 33 E2
Cornfield The CV3 62 B1
Cornflower Dr CV23 83 E4
Cornhill Gr CV8 93 E3
Cornish Cl CV10 27 F4
Cornish Cres CV10 29 D1
Cornwall Cl 3 CV34 108 C4
Cornwall Pl CV32 105 E1
Cornwall Rd CV1 61 F1
Cornwallis Rd CV22 82 B1
Cornwell Cl B98 103 D3
Coronation Ave B78 5 D1
Coronation Cl GL55 135 A2
Coronation Cres B79 4 C4
Coronation Rd
Church Lawford CV23 81 D3
Coventry CV1 61 F2
Hurley CV9 16 B3
Coronel Ave CV6 49 F2
Corporation St
Coventry CV1 151 B3
Nuneaton CV11 29 D3
Rugby CV21 83 D2
Corpus Christi RC Prim Sch CV3 78 B4
Correen B77 4 B1
Corsham Rd CV33 132 F6
Corston Mews CV31 110 B3
Cosford Cl CV32 106 A2
Cosford Cres B35 22 A2
Cosford La CV21 82 C4
Costard Ave CV36 149 F3
Coten End CV34 108 C4
Coten End Cty Fst Sch CV34 109 D4
Coten End Prim Sch CV34 108 C4
Cotes Rd LE10 31 F3
Cotheridge Cl B90 71 E3
Cotman Cl CV12 39 D2
Coton House Coll CV23 67 F2
Coton Rd Churchover CV23 67 E2
Nether Whitacre B46 15 E1
Nuneaton CV11 29 E2
Rugby CV21 84 A1
Cotsmore Cl GL56 140 B3
Cotswold Bsns Village GL56 140 B3
Cotswold Cl
Sibford Ferris OX15 142 D8
Tredington CV36 136 F6
Cotswold Cnr OX7 142 A2
Cotswold Cres CV10 28 A2
Cotswold Dr CV3 77 E2
Cotswold Edge GL55 135 B6
Cottage Cl CV31 110 B3
Cottage Farm Ct GL56 136 C1
Cottage Farm Rd
Coventry CV6 49 D1
Tamworth B77 9 E4
Cottage La Minworth B76 22 B3
Nether Whitacre B46 24 B3
Stratford-u-A CV37 144 B1
Cottage Leap CV21 83 E3
Cottage Wlk B77 9 F3
Cotterell Rd CV21 82 C3
Cotterill's Cl CV31 110 A2
Cotters Croft CV33 133 D7
Cottesbrook Cl CV3 62 C1
Cotton Dr CV8 93 E3
Cotton Mill Spinney CV32 106 C3
Coughton CE Jun & Inf Schs B49 118 F7
Coughton Court B49 119 A7
Coughton Dr CV31 110 B3
Coughton Fields La B49 143 E4
Coughton La B49 118 F7
Coundon Court Sch & Com Coll CV6 60 C4
Coundon Gn CV6 60 C4
Coundon Prim Sch CV6 60 C3
Coundon Rd CV1 61 D2
Coundon St CV1 151 A4
Coundon Wedge Dr CV5 60 B4
Countess Rd CV11 29 D3
Countess's Croft The CV3 77 E4
Countryside NN11 117 D5
Court Cl
7 Bishops Tachbrook CV33 122 E8
Warmington OX17 133 D2
Court La WR11 127 D1
Court Leet CV3 79 E4
Court Leet Rd CV3 77 F4
Court St CV31 110 A4
Court Way B50 148 B2
Courtaulds Way CV6 61 E3
Courthouse Croft CV8 93 E2
Courthouse Green Prim Sch CV6 62 A4
Courtland Ave CV6 60 C3
Courtney Cl CV11 29 F4
Courtyard The B46 23 F1
Cove Pl CV2 62 B4
Coventry Airport CV8 78 A1
Coventry Cath Church of St Michael CV1 151 C3
Coventry City FC CV1 61 F2
Coventry Golf Course CV8 77 E1
Coventry Highway B98 112 A7
Coventry Prep Sch CV3 77 D4
Coventry Rd Baginton CV8 77 F1
Barnacle CV12 51 D4
Bedworth, Hawkesbury CV2, CV7 50 C3
Bedworth, Springfield CV12 39 D1
Berkswell CV7 58 C2
Brinklow CV23 64 B2
Bulkington CV12 40 A1
Church Lawford CV23 80 C3
Coleshill B46 34 A3
Cubbington CV32 106 C4
Dunchurch CV23 99 D2
Hampton in A B92 45 D2
Hinckley LE10 31 D4
Hinckley, Sketchley LE10 31 F3
Kenilworth CV8 93 D4
Kingsbury B78 15 F2
Long Lawford CV23 81 D3
Lutterworth LE17 55 E3
Marton CV23 115 C8
Nuneaton CV10 39 E4
Pailton CV23 66 A4
Solihull B26, B92 44 B1
Southam CV33 147 D3
Stoneleigh CV8 94 B4
Warwick CV34 108 C4
Wigston Parva LE10 32 C1
Coventry Ret Mkt CV1 151 B2
Coventry Road Exhall CV7 50 A4
Coventry St Coventry CV2 62 A2
Nuneaton CV11 29 E2
Southam CV33 147 D3
Coventry Sta CV1 151 B1
Coventry Tech Coll CV1 61 D1
Coventry Univ CV1 151 C3
Coventry Univ Singer Hall CV1 151 D3
Coventry Walsgrave Triangle Bsns Pk CV2 51 D1
Coventry & Warwickshire Hospl CV1 151 C4
Coventry Whitefriars (Mus) CV1 151 D2
Coverley Pl CV22 82 C2
Covers The B80 103 F3
Cow La Lower Brailes OX15 137 F2
Whateley B78 9 F2
Cowan Cl CV22 82 B1
Cowdray Cl CV31 110 B4
Cowley Cl B36 22 C1
Cowley Rd CV2 62 B2
Cowley Way CV23 101 F1
Cowper Cl CV34 104 C1
Cowper Rd LE10 31 E3
Cox Cl B50 148 C3
Cox Cres CV22 99 E2
Cox St CV1 151 C3
Cox's Cl CV10 29 D2
Cox's La CV23 125 C7
Cozens Cl CV12 39 D2
Crabbs Cross La B97 102 C3
Crabmill Cl B93 72 B4
Crabmill La CV6 61 F4
Crabtree Gr 10 CV31 110 B3
Crackley La Coventry CV4 75 F2
Kenilworth CV8 93 D4
Craddock Dr CV10 28 B4
Craig Cl CV31 110 A3
Craig Croft B37 33 E1
Craigends Ave CV3 78 C3
Crakston Cl CV2 62 C1
Crammond Cl LE10 31 D4
Cramper's Field CV6 61 D3
Cranborne Chase CV2 63 D3
Crane Cl Stratford-u-A CV37 144 B3
Warwick CV34 104 B1
Cranebrook Hill B78 7 F3
Craner's Rd CV1 61 F2
Cranford Rd CV5 60 B2
Cranham Cl B97 102 A4
Cranmore Ave B90 70 C4
Cranmore Bvd B90 70 B4
Cranmore Rd
Birmingham B36 22 C1
Solihull B90 70 B4
Crantock Way CV11 29 F2
Cranwell Dr CV35 146 B1
Cranwell Rise B78 8 A4
Cranwell Way B35 22 A2
Crathie Cl CV2 62 C3
Craven B77 4 A1
Craven Arms Rd CV35 132 D3
Craven Ave CV3 79 E4
Craven La CV33 147 D2
Craven Rd CV21 83 E2
Craven St CV5 60 C1
Crawford Cl
Bidford-on-A B50 148 B2
Royal Leamington Spa CV32 106 A3
Crawshaws Rd B36 22 B1
Creampot Cl OX17 134 C1
Creampot Cres OX17 134 C1
Creampot La OX17 134 C1
Crecy Rd CV3 77 F4
Crediton Cl CV11 29 F3
Crendon Cl B80 103 F3
Crescent Ave CV3 62 B1
Crescent Sch CV22 99 E4
Crescent The
Baddesley Ensor CV9 11 E2
Bidford-on-A B50 148 B2
Birmingham, Coleshill Heath B37 44 C4
Brinklow CV23 64 C2
Hampton in A B92 57 D4
Keresley CV7 48 C3
Lawford Heath CV23 98 B3
Crescent The continued
Napton CV23 125 C7
Wootton Wawen B95 120 C7
Cressage Rd CV2 63 D3
Cresswell Cl CV10 29 E4
Crest Hill WR11 127 D3
Crest The CV32 106 B2
Crestwood B77 4 A3
Crew La CV8 93 F3
Creynolds Cl B90 70 B2
Creynolds La B90 70 C2
Crick Rd CV21 101 E4
Cricket Cl CV5 60 C2
Crigdon B77 4 B1
Crimscote Cl B90 70 C3
Cringlebrook B77 9 E4
Critchley Dr CV22 99 E2
Crockwell St CV36 141 C4
Croft Cl
6 Bishops Tachbrook CV33 122 F8
Stretton on D CV23 96 C3
Warwick CV34 109 E4
Wolvey LE10 41 F2
Croft Field CV23 125 C7
Croft Fields CV12 39 D1
Croft Holm GL56 140 B3
Croft Ind Est B37 33 E1
Croft La Shrewley CV35 114 C6
Staverton NN11 126 D8
Temple Grafton B49 119 E2
Croft Mead CV10 27 E2
Croft Mid Sch CV10 28 C2
Croft Pool CV12 38 C1
Croft Rd Atherstone CV9 12 B1
Bedworth CV12 38 C1
Coventry CV1 151 A2
Leek Wootton CV35 105 D4
Littleton WR11 127 F2
Nuneaton CV10 28 C2
Croft Sch The CV37 144 C1
Croft The Bulkington CV12 40 A1
Church Lench WR11 127 A6
Coventry CV6 49 F2
Meriden CV7 46 B1
Warton B79 5 F2
Croft's La OX15 142 D3
Crofts La B96 102 A1
Crofts The B76 22 A4
Cromarty Cl CV5 60 A3
Cromdale B77 4 B1
Cromdale Cl CV10 28 A2
Cromer Rd CV32 106 A1
Cromes Wood CV4 59 E1
Crompton Ave B50 148 C3
Crompton St CV34 108 B3
Cromwell La CV4 75 E3
Cromwell Pl CV35 123 D2
Cromwell Rd CV22 83 E1
Cromwell St CV6 61 F3
Crondal Rd CV7 50 A4
Crook House Yd CV23 64 C2
Crooks La Alcester B49 143 E3
Studley B80 103 E2
Croome Cl CV6 60 C2
Cropredy CE Prim Sch OX17 134 C1
Cropthorne Cl B98 103 D4
Cropthorne Dr B47 69 D4
Crosbie Rd CV5 60 C2
Cross Cheaping CV1 151 B3
Cross Fields Rd 4 CV34 108 C4
Cross La Braunston NN11 117 E5
Cubbington CV32 106 C2
Cross Leys CV36 136 B6
Cross Rd Alcester B49 143 D2
Coventry CV6 61 F4
Keresley CV7 48 C3
6 Royal Leamington Spa CV32 105 E1
Cross Road Ind Est CV6 61 F4
Cross St Coventry CV1 151 C4
Long Lawford CV23 82 A3
Nuneaton CV10 28 B2
Royal Leamington Spa CV32 106 A1
Rugby CV21 83 E2
12 Warwick CV34 108 C4
Cross Wlk B78 11 D3
Crossfell B77 4 A1
Crossgate Rd B98 103 E4
Crossland Row LE10 32 A3
Crosslands CV35 146 B1
Crossley Ct CV6 61 F4
Crossway Rd CV3 77 D2
Crossways LE10 31 F3
Crow Hill CV9 11 E1
Crow Thorns CV21 83 E3
Crowberry La B78 14 B4
Crowden Rd B77 4 A1
Crowhill Rd CV11 30 A1
Crowleys Cl B95 112 E6
Crowmere Rd CV2 62 C4
Crown St CV33 123 F7
Crown Terr CV32 109 F4
Crown Way CV32 106 A2
Crownhill Rd LE10 31 E2
Croxall Dr B46 25 D1
Croxhall St CV12 39 E2
Croy Dr B35 22 A2
Croydon Cl CV3 77 F3
Crummock Cl CV6 49 E2
Crutchley Way CV31 110 A1
Cryersoak Cl 7 B90 71 D4
Cryfield Grange Rd CV4 76 B1
Cubbington CE Comb Sch CV32 106 C3

Cubbington Rd
Coventry CV6 50 A1
Royal Leamington Spa CV32 106 A2
Cuckoo La CV1 151 C3
Culey Wlk B37 33 E1
Culpepper Cl CV10 28 C2
Culverley Cres B93 71 F3
Culworth Cl
Royal Leamington Spa CV31 109 F3
Rugby CV21 83 F4
Culworth Ct CV6 61 F4
Culworth Row CV6 61 F4
Cumberland Cres CV32 106 B2
Cumberland Dr CV10 28 C2
Cumberland Wlk B75 13 D3
Cumbernauld Wlk 7 CV2 63 D4
Cumbria Cl CV1 61 D2
Cumming St 6 CV31 110 A4
Cumsey The CV35 114 A5
Cundall Cl CV31 110 A3
Cunningham Way N CV22 82 B1
Cunningham Way S CV22 82 B1
Cup & Saucer OX17 134 C1
Curdworth La B76 23 D4
Curdworth Prim Sch B76 23 E3
Curie Cl CV21 83 E2
Curlew B77 10 A4
Curlew Cl
Stratford-u-A CV37 144 B2
Warton B79 5 F2
Curlieu Cl CV35 108 A4
Curlieu La CV35 114 C2
Curran Cl CV31 110 A2
Curriers Cl CV4 75 E4
Curtis Rd CV2 62 B3
Curzon Ave CV6 61 F4
Curzon Cl LE10 31 F4
Curzon Gr CV31 110 B3
Cut Throat La B94 87 E4
Cuttle Mill La B76 14 B2
Cuttle Pool La B93 72 C2
Cutworth Cl B76 13 D2
Cymbeline Way CV22 99 E3
Cypress Croft CV3 78 C4
Cypress La CV31 110 A1
Cyprus Ave B96 102 B1

D'Aubeny Rd CV4 76 B4
Dace B77 9 E4
Dadglow Rd CV33 124 B4
Daffern Ave CV7 37 D4
Daffern Rd CV7 39 D1
Dagtail La B97 102 B2
Dahlia Cl LE10 31 F3
Daimler Ave OX16 139 F4
Daimler Cl B36 22 C1
Daimler Rd CV6 61 E3
Daintree Croft CV3 77 E4
Dairyground The OX15 139 A3
Dalby Cl CV3 78 C4
Dale Ave CV37 145 E1
Dale Cl
10 Bishops Tachbrook CV33 122 F8
Long Itchington CV23 115 C4
Warwick CV34 109 D4
Dale End CV10 28 C3
Dale End Cl LE10 31 D4
Dale Meadow Cl CV7 74 A3
Dale St
Royal Leamington Spa CV32 109 F4
Rugby CV21 83 D2
Dale The B95 113 B2
Dalehouse La CV8 93 E4
Dales Cty Jun & Inf Schs The B77 10 A4
Daleway Rd CV3 77 D2
Dalkeith Ave CV22 99 E4
Dallington Rd CV6 60 C3
Dalmahoy Cl CV11 40 B4
Dalmeny Rd CV4 75 E4
Dalton Cl CV23 81 D3
Dalton Gdns CV2 62 C2
Dalton Rd Bedworth CV12 39 D1
Coventry CV5 61 D1
Dalwood Way CV6 50 A2
Daly Ave CV35 114 F3
Dama Rd B78 8 C4
Dame Agnes Gr CV6 62 A4
Damson Cl B97 102 B3
Damson Ct LE10 31 D4
Damson Rd CV35 114 F3
Danbury Cl B76 13 D1
Dane Rd CV2 62 A2
Danesbury Cres CV31 110 B3
Daneswood Rd CV3 79 F4
Daniel Ave CV10 28 B2
Daniel Rd CV9 18 C4
Danvers Cl OX15 139 E1
Danvers Rd OX15 139 E1
Danzey Cl B98 103 D3
Danzey Green La B94 112 E8
Danzey Green Rd B36 22 A1
Danzey Sta B94 112 E8
Daphne Cl CV2 50 B2
Darfield Ct CV8 95 E3
Dark La Astwood Bank B96 102 B1
Bedworth CV12 38 B1
Birchmoor B78 10 C4
Braunston NN11 117 E5
Coventry CV1 151 B4
Hollywood B47 69 D4
Tiddington CV37 145 F2
Wroxton OX15 139 D4
Darley Green Rd B93 72 A1
Darley Rd LE10 31 F3
Darlingscott Rd CV36 149 E2
Darnbrook B77 4 B1
Darnford Cl CV2 62 C4
Darrach Cl CV2 50 C1
Dart B77 10 A3
Dart Cl LE10 31 D4
Dartmouth Rd CV2 62 B3
Dartmouth Sch CV2 62 B3
Darwell Pk B77 4 A1
Darwin Cl CV2 63 D3
Dassett CE Prim Sch The CV33 133 D7
Dassett Rd B93 71 F2
Datchet Cl CV5 60 B2
Davenport Dr B35 22 B2
Davenport Rd CV5 77 D4
Davenport Terr LE10 31 F4
Daventry Rd Barby CV23 101 E1
Coventry CV3 77 E4
Rugby CV22, CV23 99 F1
Southam CV33 147 E2
Staverton NN11 126 D8
Staverton NN11 126 E8
Daventry St CV33 147 D2
David Rd Bedworth CV7 49 F4
Coventry CV1 61 F1
Rugby CV22 99 E4
Davidson Ave CV31 110 A4
Davies Rd Bedworth CV7 49 F4
Moreton-in-M GL56 140 B3
Davis Cl CV32 105 E1
Dawes Cl CV2 62 A2
Dawley Cres B37 33 D1
Dawley Wlk 9 CV2 63 D4
Dawlish Cl CV11 29 F3
Dawlish Dr CV3 77 E3
Dawson Cl Redditch B97 102 B3
Whitnash CV31 110 A1
Dawson Rd CV3 62 A1
Day's La CV2 61 F2
Days Cl CV1 61 F2
Daytona Dr CV5 59 D4
De Mohun Cres CV36 141 F5
De Montfort Rd CV8 92 C3
De Montfort Way CV4 76 B3
De-Compton Cl CV7 49 D4
De-La-Bere Cres LE10 32 A3
Deacon Cl CV22 83 E1
Deacon St CV11 29 E2
Dean St CV2 62 A2
Deanbrook Cl B90 71 D3
Deane Par CV21 101 D4
Deane Rd CV21 101 D4
Deans Way CV7 49 E3
Deanston Croft CV2 50 C1
Deansway CV34 104 C1
Debden Cl Dorridge B93 71 F1
Wellesbourne CV35 146 B1
Dee Wlk Birmingham B36 33 D4
Daventry NN11 117 F1
Deedmore Rd CV2 50 B1
Deedmore Sch CV2 62 B4
Deegan Cl CV2 62 A3
Deeley B77 4 A1
Deep La B46 24 C3
Deepdale B77 4 B1
Deepmore Rd CV22 99 E4
Deer Leap The CV8 93 D3
Deerdale Way CV3 78 C4
Deerhill B77 4 B1
Deerhurst Cl GL56 140 F1
Deerhurst Mews CV22 99 E2
Deerhurst Rd CV6 49 D1
Deerings Rd CV21 101 D4
Deerpark Dr CV34 108 C4
Delage Cl CV6 50 A2
Delamere Cl B36 22 B1
Delamere Rd CV12 38 C1
Delamere Way CV32 106 B2
Delancey Keep B75 13 D3
Delaware Rd CV3 77 E3
Delhi Ave CV6 49 E1
Delius St CV4 59 F2
Dell Cl CV3 78 B3
Dell Ct B95 113 B5
Dell Farm Cl B93 72 A3
Delmore Way B76 22 A3
Delphi Cl CV34 109 F2
Deltic B77 4 A1
Delves Cres CV9 10 B1
Dempster Rd CV12 39 D2
Denbigh Cl OX16 139 F2
Denbigh Cnr B46 45 D3
Denbigh Rd CV6 60 C3
Denby Cl CV32 106 B2
Denby Croft B90 71 D3
Dencer Dr CV8 93 E2
Dene Cl CV35 132 B5
Denegate Cl B76 22 A3
Denehurst Way CV10 28 C2
Denewood Way CV8 93 E3
Denham Ave CV5 60 B2
Denham Ct CV9 18 C4
Denis Rd LE10 31 E3
Denne Cl CV37 145 D3
Dennett Cl CV34 104 C1
Dennis Rd CV2 62 A3
Denshaw Croft CV2 63 D4
Denton Cl CV8 92 B3
Denton Croft B93 71 E2
Denville Rd CV32 106 A2
Deppers Bridge CV33 124 B6
Derby Dr B37 33 D1
Derby La CV9 18 B4
Dereham Ct CV32 106 A1
Derek Ave B78 11 D3
Dering Cl CV2 62 B4
Deronda Cl CV12 39 D2
Derry Cl CV8 80 A2
Dersingham Dr CV6 50 A1
Derwent Cl Coventry CV5 59 F2
Royal Leamington Spa CV32 105 E1
Rugby CV21 83 E3
Derwent Rd Bedworth CV12 39 D1
Coventry CV6 49 D1
Derwent Way CV11 29 F3
Despard Rd CV5 59 E2
Devereux Cl CV4 59 E1
Devitts Cl B90 70 C4
Devon Cl CV10 28 C2
Devon Gr CV2 62 A3
Devon Ox Rd CV23 101 F1
Devonish Cl B49 143 E3
Devoran Cl CV7 50 A4
Dew Cl CV22 99 E2
Dewar Gr CV21 83 F1
Dewsbury Ave CV3 77 D3
Dexter La CV9 16 B2
Dexter Way B78 10 C4
Dial House La CV5 59 F2
Diana Dr CV2 50 C1
Dickens Cl CV10 28 A2
Dickens Heath Rd B90 70 A3
Dickens Rd Coventry CV6 61 D4
Harbury CV33 123 E6
Rugby CV22 99 F3
Dickins Rd CV34 105 D1
Dickinson Ct CV22 83 D1
Didcot Cl B97 102 B3
Didcot Way DE12 3 F4
Diddington La B92, CV7 45 E1
Didgley Gr B37 33 D3
Didsbury Rd CV7 39 D1
Digbey Cl CV5 60 A3
Digby Cres B46 23 D2
Digby Dr B37 44 A3
Digby Pl CV7 46 B1
Digby Rd B46 33 F3
Dighton Cl CV37 129 F7
Dilcock Way CV4 75 F4
Dillam Cl CV6 50 A2
Dillotford Ave CV3 77 E3
Dingle Cl CV6 61 D3
Dingle La Appleby Magna CV9 3 E3
Nether Whitacre B46 24 C3
Dingle The
Cheswick Green B90 70 B3
Nuneaton CV10 28 C3
Dingles Way CV37 145 D3
Dingleside Mid Sch B98 103 D4
Dingley Rd CV12 40 A1
Discovery Way CV3 79 D4
Ditchford Cl B97 102 B2
Ditton Cl CV22 82 B1
Dixon Cl B35 22 A1
Dobbie Rd CV37 129 D1
Dobson La CV31 110 A2
Dockers Cl CV7 74 B4
Doctors La B95 113 B5
Dodd Ave CV34 109 E4
Dodwells Bridge Ind Est LE10 30 C4
Dodwells Rd LE10 30 C4
Doe Bank La CV1 61 D2
Dog Kennel La B90 70 B4
Dog La Fenny Compton CV33 133 D7
Napton CV23 125 C8
Nether Whitacre B46 25 D4
Tamworth B77 4 A3
Dogberry Cl CV3 78 B3
Doglands The CV31 110 A2
Doily Cl OX15 142 D4
Doll Mus CV34 108 C3
Doncaster Cl CV2 62 B4
Done Cerce Cl CV22 99 E2
Donegal Cl CV4 76 A4
Dongan Rd CV34 108 C4
Donibristle Croft B35 22 A2
Donnington Ave CV6 60 C3
Donnington Rd CV36 149 F4
Donnithorne Ave CV10, CV11 29 E1
Doone Cl CV2 62 C3
Dorado B77 9 E3
Dorcas Cl CV11 40 B4
Dorchester Ave CV35 114 F3
Dorchester Gr OX16 139 F2
Dorchester Rd LE10 32 A4
Dorchester Way
Coventry CV2 63 D2
Nuneaton CV11 30 A4
Dordon Prim Sch B78 11 D3
Dordon Rd B78 10 C4
Doris Rd B46 33 F4
Dorlecote Pl CV10 39 E4
Dorlecote Rd CV10 39 E4
Dormer Harris Ave CV4 59 F1
Dormer Pl CV32 109 F4
Dormston Cl B91 71 E4
Dorney Cl CV5 76 C4
Dorothy Powell Way CV2 50 C1
Dorridge Croft B93 71 F1
Dorridge Jun & Inf Schs B93 72 A2
Dorridge Rd B93 72 A1
Dorridge Sta B93 71 F1
Dorset Cl CV10 28 C2
Dorset Rd CV1 61 E3
Dorsington Rd CV37 128 E2
Dosthill Rd (Two Gates) B77 9 E4
Dosthill Sch B77 9 E3
Douglas Rd Hollywood B47 69 D4
Rugby CV21 83 E3
Doulton Cl CV2 50 C1
Dove Cl Bedworth CV12 38 C2
Hinckley LE10 31 D4
Dovecote Cl CV6 60 B3
Dovedale CV21 83 E4
Dovedale Ave CV6 49 F1
Dovehouse Dr CV35 146 B1
Dover Ave OX16 139 F3
Dover Farm Cl B77 10 A4
Dover St CV1 151 A3
Doverdale Cl B98 103 D4
Doverhouse La CV33 123 F7
Dovestone B77 4 B1
Dovey Dr B76 22 A4
Dowler's Hill Cres B98 103 D4
Dowley Croft CV3 63 D1
Down End OX15 142 D4
Downderry Way CV6 62 A3
Downing Cl B93 72 A2
Downing Cres CV12 39 E2
Downton Cl CV2 63 D4
Dowty Ave CV12 38 B1
Doyle Dr CV6 49 F2
Dr Phillips Sh Ctr The CV2 50 B1
Drake St CV6 61 E4
Drakes Cl B97 102 B3
Drakes Cross B47 69 D3
Draper Cl CV8 93 E2
Draper's Fields CV1 151 B4
Drawbridge Rd B90 69 F4
Draycote Water Ctry Pk CV23 116 C8
Draycott Rd CV2 62 B4
Drayton Ave CV37 144 B2
Drayton Cl Bidford-on-A B50 148 B3
Fenny Drayton CV13 19 F3
Hartshill CV10 28 A4
Redditch B98 103 E4
Stratford-u-A CV37 144 B2
Drayton Cres CV5 59 E3
Drayton Ct CV34 104 C1
Drayton Fields Ind Est NN11 117 F2
Drayton La Drayton Bassett B78 8 B3
Fenny Drayton CV13 19 F3
Drayton Leys CV22 100 A4
Drayton Manor Dr
Fazeley B78 8 C4
Stratford-u-A CV37 120 C2
Drayton Manor Pk B78 8 C4
Drayton Rd Bedworth CV12 39 E1
Solihull B90 70 C4
Drayton Sch OX16 139 F4
Drayton Way Daventry NN11 117 F2
Nuneaton CV10 28 B4
Drem Croft B35 22 A1
Drew Cres CV8 93 D2
Dreyer Cl CV22 82 B1
Driftway The CV36 149 F3
Drinkwater Cl CV33 123 F6
Drive The Coleshill B46 34 A3
Coventry CV2 62 C2
Dunchurch CV22 99 F2
Drivers La GL56 141 A1
Dronfield Rd CV2 62 A2
Drovers Way CV33 147 E2
Droylsdon Park Rd CV3 77 D2
Druid Rd CV2 62 A2
Drummond Cl CV6 60 C4
Drummond Way B37 33 E1
Drury La CV21 83 D2
Drybrooks Cl CV7 74 A3
Dryden Cl Kenilworth CV8 92 C2
Nuneaton CV10 27 F3
Dryden Pl CV22 82 C2
Dryden Wlk CV22 82 C2
Drymen Rd CV35 132 D3
Duck La CV37 129 B7
Duck Lake DE12 3 F4
Dudley Gn CV32 106 A1
Dudley Rd CV8 92 C1
Dudley Rise LE10 31 E3
Dudley St Atherstone CV9 18 B4
Coventry CV6 50 A1
Duffy Pl CV21 101 D4
Dugard Pl CV35 122 B7
Dugdale Ave
Bidford-on-A B50 148 B3
Stratford-u-A CV37 145 D3
Dugdale Rd CV6 61 D3
Dugdale St CV11 29 E2
Duggins La CV4, CV7 75 D4
Duke Barn Field CV2 62 A3
Duke St Coventry CV5 60 C1
Nuneaton CV11 29 D2
Royal Leamington Spa CV32 106 A1
Rugby CV21 83 D2
Dukes Jetty CV21 83 D2
Dukes Rd B78 11 D3
Dulverton Ave CV5 60 B2
Dulverton Pl GL56 140 B3
Dumble Pit La B48 85 F4
Dumphouse La B48 85 E2
Dunblane Dr CV32 106 B3
Duncan Dr CV22 99 E3
Dunchurch Boughton CE Mid Sch CV22 99 E2
Dunchurch Cl CV7 74 A4
Dunchurch Cty Fst Sch CV22 99 E2
Dunchurch Hall CV22 99 E2
Dunchurch Highway CV5 60 A2
Dunchurch Rd CV22 99 F3
Dunchurch Trad Est CV23 98 B2
Duncombe Gn 7 B46 33 F4
Duncroft Ave CV6 60 C4
Duncumb Rd B75 13 D3
Dunedin B77 4 A1
Dunhill Ave CV4 59 F2
Dunley Croft B90 70 C3
Dunlop Rd B97 102 B3
Dunn's La B78 11 D3
Dunnerdale CV21 83 E4
Dunnington CE Prim Sch B49 127 E8
Dunnose Cl CV6 61 F4
Dunrose Cl CV2 62 C1
Dunsmore Ave Coventry CV3 78 B3
Rugby CV22 100 C4
Dunsmore Heath CV22 99 E2
Dunstall Cres 2 CV33 122 E8
Dunstan Croft B90 70 B4
Dunster B77 9 E4
Dunster Pl CV6 49 E2
Dunster Rd B37 33 E1
Dunsville Dr CV2 62 C4
Dunton Hall Rd B90 70 A4
Dunton La B76 14 B1
Dunvegan Cl Coventry CV3 63 D1
Kenilworth CV8 93 E2
Duport Rd LE10 31 F4
Durbar Ave CV6 61 E4
Durham Cl CV7 48 C2
Durham Cres CV5 60 A4
Durham Croft B37 33 D1
Durlston Cl B77 4 A3
Dursley La B98 112 A6
Dutton Rd CV2 50 B2
Duttons Cl CV37 121 B7
Duxford Cl Redditch B97 102 A4
Wellesbourne CV35 146 B1
Dwarris Wlk CV34 104 C1
Dyas Rd B47 69 D4
Dyce Cl B35 22 A2
Dyer's La
Chipping Campden GL55 135 A2
Wolston CV8 80 A2
Dyers La B94 87 E4
Dyers Rd CV11 40 C3
Dymond Rd CV6 49 E2
Dysart Cl CV1 61 F2
Dyson Cl CV21 83 F1
Dyson St CV4 59 F2

Eacott Cl CV6 49 D2
Eadie St CV10 28 B2
Eagle Cl CV11 40 A4
Eagle Dr B77 4 B2
Eagle Gr B36 33 D4
Eagle Ho CV1 61 E3
Eagle La CV8 92 C2
Eagle St Coventry CV1 61 E3
Royal Leamington Spa CV31 110 A3
Eagle St E CV1 61 E3
Ealingham B77 4 A1
Earl St Bedworth CV12 39 E1
Coventry CV1 151 C2
Royal Leamington Spa CV32 106 A1
Rugby CV21 83 D2
Earl's Croft The CV3 77 E4
Earl's Wlk CV3 79 E4
Earles Cl CV23 147 F4
Earls Rd CV11 29 D3
Earlsdon Ave N CV5 60 C1
Earlsdon Ave S CV5 77 D4
Earlsdon Bsns Ctr CV5 76 C4
Earlsdon Prim Sch CV5 61 D1
Earlsdon St CV5 76 C4
Earlsmere B94 70 A1
Earlswood Comm B94 87 D3
Earlswood Rd B93 71 E1
Earlswood Sta B94 69 E1
Earlswood Trad Est B94 86 B3
Easedale Cl Coventry CV3 77 D3
Nuneaton CV11 30 A3
Easenhall Cl B93 72 A2
Easenhall Rd CV23 66 A1
Easingwold Rd CV35 132 D4
East Ave Bedworth CV12 39 E1
Coventry CV2 62 A1
East Car Park Rd B40 44 C2
East Cl LE10 31 E4
East Dene CV32 106 A1
East End OX15 142 D4
East Gr CV31 110 A3
East Green Dr CV37 144 B2
East House Dr CV9 16 B2
East Side WR11 128 A2
East St Coventry CV1 61 F2
Long Compton CV36 141 C3
Moreton-in-M GL56 140 A3
Rugby CV21 83 E2
Tamworth B77 9 E3
East Union St CV22 83 D1
East Way B92 45 D2
Eastboro Way CV11 29 F1
Eastbourne Cl CV6 60 C3
Eastcote La B92 56 C2
Eastcotes CV4 60 A1
Eastern Green Jun Sch CV5 59 E3
Eastern Green Rd CV5 59 F2
Eastern Hill B96 102 C1
Eastfield Cl CV37 144 C3
Eastfield Pl CV21 83 D2
Eastfield Rd Nuneaton CV10 29 E3
Royal Leamington Spa CV32 110 A4
Eastgate OX15 139 B8
Eastlands Cty Prim Sch CV21 83 E1
Eastlands Gr CV5 60 C2
Eastlands Pl CV21 83 E2
Eastlands Rd CV21 83 E2
Eastlang Rd CV7 36 C2
Eastleigh Ave CV5 76 C4
Eastleigh Croft B76 22 A4
Eastley Cres CV34 108 A4
Eastnor Gr CV31 110 A4

Easton Gr B47 69 D4
Eastway B40 44 C2
Eastwood Cl 9 CV31 110 B3
Eastwood Gr CV21 101 E4
Easy La CV21 82 C2
Eathorpe Cl Coventry CV2 50 B1
Redditch B98 103 F4
Eaton Cl CV32 105 E1
Eaton Rd CV1 151 B1
Eaves Green La CV7 46 C1
Ebbw Vale Terr CV3 77 E4
Eborall Cl CV34 104 C1
Ebourne Cl CV8 93 D2
Ebrington Dr CV35 114 F5
Ebrington & St James CE Prim Sch GL55 135 B1
Ebro Cres CV3 62 C1
Eburne Prim Sch CV2 50 B1
Eburne Rd CV2 50 B2
Eccles Cl CV2 62 B4
Eckington Cl B98 103 D4
Eclipse Rd B49 143 D2
Eclipse Trad Est B49 143 D2
Ecton Leys CV22 100 A4
Edale B77 4 A1
Edale Gn LE10 31 F3
Edale Way CV6 62 A4
Eddenswood Cl B78 8 C3
Eden Cl B80 103 E2
Eden Croft CV8 93 D2
Eden Gr B37 33 E1
Eden Rd Coventry CV2 63 D4
Rugby CV21 83 F1
Eden St CV6 61 F4
Edge Hill CV9 10 A1
Edge La B95 113 C5
Edgecote Cl CV21 83 F1
Edgefield Rd CV2 63 D4
Edgehill Ctry Pk OX17 133 B3
Edgehill Pl CV4 59 E1
Edgehill Rd CV35 123 C2
Edgewick Com Prim Sch CV6 61 F4
Edgioake La B96 118 C7
Edgwick Park Ind Est CV6 61 F4
Edgwick Rd CV6 61 F4
Edinburgh Cl OX16 139 F4
Edinburgh Cres CV31 109 F3
Edinburgh Rd Hurley CV9 16 B3
Nuneaton CV10 28 B3
Edinburgh Way
Banbury OX16 139 F3
Long Lawford CV23 82 A3
Edingale Rd CV2 62 C4
Edison Rd B76 24 A2
Edmondes Cl CV34 104 C1
Edmonds Cl CV37 129 D1
Edmondscote Rd CV32 109 E4
Edmondson Cl CV22 99 E2
Edmund Rd CV1 61 E3
Edmunds Rd
Banbury OX16 139 F3
Wroxton OX15 139 D4
Edstone Cl B93 71 F2
Edward Bailey Cl CV3 78 C4
Edward Rd Bedworth CV12 39 E2
Coventry CV6 49 D2
Water Orton B46 23 E2
Edward St Coventry CV6 61 F3
Nuneaton CV11 29 E2
3 Royal Leamington Spa CV32 105 E1
Rugby CV21 82 C2
Warwick CV34 108 B4
Edward Tyler Rd CV7 39 D1
Edwards Gr CV8 93 E3
Edyth Rd CV2 62 C2
Edyvean Cl CV22 99 F3
Egerton Cl CV21 82 C3
Eileen Gdns B37 33 D2
Elan Cl CV32 106 B2
Elborow St CV21 83 D2
Elbury Croft B93 71 F3
Eld Rd CV6 61 F4
Elder Cl Kingsbury B78 15 E4
Rugby CV22 82 A1
Elderberry Way CV2 62 A3
Eldersfield Gr B91 71 D4
Eldorado Cl B80 103 E2
Elford Gr B37 33 D1
Elgar Cl CV11 40 A4
Elgar Rd CV6 62 A4
Eliot Cl CV34 104 C1
Eliot Ct CV22 82 C2
Elizabeth Ave B78 5 D1
Elizabeth Ct CV34 109 D3
Elizabeth Rd CV31 109 F3
Elizabeth Way
Kenilworth CV8 92 C3
Long Lawford CV23 82 A3
Elkington Croft 8 B90 71 D3
Elkington La CV23 101 D1
Elkington St CV6 61 F4
Ell La CV23 64 C2
Ellacombe Rd CV2 62 B4
Ellen Badger Com Hospl CV36 137 A4
Ellerbeck B77 4 A1
Ellerdene Cl B98 102 B4
Ellesmere Rd CV12 39 D1
Ellice Dr B36 33 D4
Elliot Cl B50 148 B3
Elliot Dr CV35 146 B2
Elliot's Field Ret Pk CV21 83 D3
Elliotts Orch CV35 122 A7
Elliston Gr CV31 110 B3
Ellys Rd CV1 61 E3
Elm Bank Cl CV32 106 A2
Elm Cl Binley Woods CV3 79 E4
Ilmington CV36 136 B6
Pebworth CV37 128 F1
Southam CV33 147 D2
Elm Dr B49 143 E2
Elm Gr Arley CV7 26 C1
Balsall Common CV7 74 B3
Ebrington GL55 135 F3
Hurley CV9 16 B2
Elm Rd
Royal Leamington Spa CV32 106 A2
Stratford-u-A CV37 144 C3
Elm Row CV23 115 F3
Elm Tree Ave CV4 60 A1
Elm Tree Cl B78 15 E3
Elm Tree Dr LE10 31 F4
Elm Tree Rd CV12 40 B1
Elm Tree Rise B92 57 D3
Elmbank CV33 147 D2
Elmbank Rd CV8 92 C3
Elmbridge Dr B90 71 D3
Elmdene Cl Hatton CV35 114 C5
Wolston CV8 80 A2
Elmdene Rd CV8 93 D2
Elmdon Ct B37 44 A4
Elmdon La Birmingham B37 44 A3
Solihull B26 44 A2
Elmdon Rd B37 44 A4
Elmdon Trad Est B37 44 B3
Elmfield Rd CV10 29 E4
Elmhurst Cl B97 102 B2
Elmhurst Rd CV6 50 A2
Elmore Cl CV3 78 B4
Elmore Rd CV22 82 C1
Elms Ct CV9 3 D1
Elms Dr Austrey CV9 3 D1
Rugby CV22 100 C4
Elms Paddock The CV23 83 F3
Elms The Bedworth CV12 38 C1
Leek Wootton CV35 104 C3
Stratford-u-A CV37 145 D2
Elmsdale Ave CV6 49 F1
Elmstone Cl B97 102 B3
Elmwood Ave CV6 60 C3
Elmwood Cl CV7 74 A3
Elmwood Gr B47 69 D3
Elphin Cl CV6 49 D2
Elsee Rd CV21 83 D2
Elter Cl CV21 83 E4
Eltham Rd CV3 77 F4
Elton Cl CV32 106 B1
Elton Croft B93 71 F2
Elva Croft B36 22 C1
Elvers Green La B93 72 C4
Elwy Circ CV7 49 E3
Ely Cl Birmingham B37 33 D1
Coventry CV2 63 D3
Ely St CV37 145 D1
Embassy Wlk CV2 62 B4
Emerald Way CV31 109 F3
Emerson Rd CV2 62 B2
Emery Cl CV2 62 C4
Emmott Dr CV31 110 A3
Emperor Way CV21 82 C4
Empire Rd CV4 59 F1
Emscote Cty Fst Sch CV34 109 D4
Emscote Lawn Prep Sch CV34 109 D4
Emscote Rd Coventry CV3 62 B1
Warwick CV34 109 D4
Ena Rd CV1 61 E3
End The OX7 142 A2
Endemere Rd CV6 61 E4
Endsleigh Gdns CV31 110 A3
Enfield Rd Coventry CV2 62 A2
Redditch B97 102 B3
Engine La B77 4 A1
England Cres CV31 109 F4
Engleton Rd CV6 61 D3
English Martyrs RC Prim Sch CV21 101 D4
Ennerdale CV21 83 E4
Ennerdale Cl CV32 105 E1
Ennerdale Cres CV11 29 F3
Ennerdale La CV2 62 C2
Ennersdale Bglws B46 23 F1
Ennersdale Cl B46 23 F1
Ennersdale Rd B46 23 F1
Enright Cl CV32 105 F1
Ensign Bsns Ctr CV4 75 F3
Ensign Cl CV4 59 E1
Ensor Cl CV11 30 A3
Ensor Dr B78 4 C1
Epping Way CV32 106 B2
Epsom Cl Bedworth CV12 39 D2
Redditch B97 102 B4
Epsom Rd
Royal Leamington Spa CV32 106 B2
Rugby CV22 82 B1
Epwell Rd Shutford OX15 138 F3
Upper Tysoe CV35 138 B6
Erdington Rd CV9 18 B4
Eric Grey Cl CV2 62 A3
Erica Ave CV12 38 C1
Erica Dr CV31 110 A1
Eringden B77 4 A1
Erithway Rd CV3 77 D2
Ernesford Grange Prim Sch CV3 62 C1
Ernesford Grange Sch & Com Coll CV3 78 B4
Ernest Richards Rd CV12 39 D2
Ernsford Ave CV3 62 A1
Ernsford Cl B93 71 F1
Errington GL56 140 B3
Esher Dr CV3 77 F4
Eskdale CV21 83 E4
Eskdale Rd LE10 31 D4
Eskdale Wlk CV3 78 B4
Essen La CV23 101 F2
Essex Cl Coventry CV5 60 A2
Kenilworth CV8 92 C1
Essex Gn CV33 132 F7
Essex St CV21 83 D2
Esterton Cl CV6 49 E1
Ethelfield Rd CV2 62 A2
Ethelfleda Rd B77 9 F3
Eton Rd CV37 145 E1
Etone Com Sch CV11 29 E3
Ettingley Cl B98 103 D3
Ettington CE Prim Sch CV37 131 B3
Ettington Cl Dorridge B93 71 E1
Wellesbourne CV35 146 B1
Ettington Rd Coventry CV5 60 A2
Wellesbourne CV35 146 B1
Eunal Ct B97 102 C3
Europa Way
Birmingham B26 44 B2
Royal Leamington Spa CV34 109 E3
Eustace Rd CV12 40 B1
Euston Cres CV3 78 B3
Euston Pl CV32 109 F4
Evans Cl Bedworth CV12 39 E2
Stratford-u-A CV37 144 B1
Evans Gr CV31 110 A1
Evans Rd CV22 82 B1
Evelyn Ave CV6 49 F1
Evenlode Cl CV37 145 E1
Evenlode Cres CV6 60 C3
Evenlode Gdns GL56 140 B3
Evenlode Rd GL56 140 B3
Everard Cl CV23 84 A3
Everard Ct CV11 29 F1
Everdon Cl CV22 100 C4
Everdon Rd CV6 49 D1
Everest Rd CV22 99 F4
Everglade Rd CV9 10 B1
Everitt Dr B93 72 A3
Eversleigh Rd CV6 60 C4
Evesham Pl CV37 144 C1
Evesham Rd
Bidford-on-A B50 128 E8
Church Lench WR11 127 A6
Cookhill B49 118 D5
Harvington WR11 127 D4
Littleton WR11 127 F3
Offenham WR11 127 F3
Redditch,Dagtail End B96, B97 102 C2
Redditch,Headless Cross B97 102 B4
Salford Priors WR11 127 F5
Stratford-u-A CV37 144 B1
Evesham St B49 143 D2
Evesham Wlk CV4 76 B3
Evreux Way CV21 83 D2
Exbury Way CV11 39 F4
Exeter Cl CV3 78 B4
Exhall Cl CV37 145 E1
Exhall Fst Sch CV7 49 F4
Exhall Gn CV7 49 F4
Exhall Grange Sch CV7 49 E3
Exhall Rd CV7 49 D3
Exham Cl CV34 104 C1
Exhibition Way B40 44 B2
Exis Ct CV11 29 F1
Exminster Rd CV3 77 F3
Exmoor Dr CV32 106 B2
Exmouth Cl CV2 62 B4
Exton Cl CV7 49 E3
Eydon Cl CV21 83 F3
Eyffler Cl CV34 108 B4

Fabian Cl CV3 78 B4
Fair Cl CV23 97 E1
Fair Isle Dr CV10 28 C1
Fairbanks Cl CV2 63 D4
Fairbourne Way CV6 60 C4
Faircroft CV8 92 C2
Faircroft Rd B36 22 B1
Fairfax Cl CV35 122 A7
Fairfax St CV1 151 C3
Fairfield Ct CV3 78 A4
Fairfield Rise CV7 46 B1
Fairfields Hill B78 10 C4
Fairfields Wlk CV37 144 B2
Fairhurst Dr CV32 105 F2
Fairlands Pk CV4 76 C3
Fairlawn Cl CV32 105 E1
Fairlawns B76 22 A4
Fairmile Cl CV3 78 B4
Fairview Mews 6 B46 33 F4
Fairwater Cres B49 143 E2
Fairway Nuneaton CV11 40 A4
Tamworth B77 9 F3
Fairway Ct B77 4 A2
Fairway Rise CV8 93 E3
Fairway The Banbury OX16 139 F4
Hinckley LE10 31 F4
Fairways Cl CV5 60 A3
Fairways The CV32 105 E1
Falcon B77 10 A3
Falcon Ave CV3 78 C4
Falcon Cl CV11 40 A4
Falcon Cres B50 148 C3
Falcon Lodge Cres B75 13 D3
Falconers Gn LE10 31 F3
Falcons The B75 13 D3
Falkland Cl CV4 75 E4
Falkland Pl CV33 133 A7
Falkland Way B36 33 D3
Falkwood Gr B93 71 F3
Fallow Hill CV31 110 B3
Falmouth Cl CV11 30 A3
Falstaff Ave B47 69 D3
Falstaff Cl Nuneaton CV11 30 A1
Sutton Coldfield B76 22 A4
Falstaff Dr CV22 99 E3
Falstaff Rd CV4 59 F1
Fancott Dr CV8 92 C3
Fant Hill OX15 137 E3
Far Gosford St CV1 61 F1
Far Lash LE10 31 F4
Far Moor La B98 112 A6
Faraday Ave B76 24 A2
Faraday Rd Hinckley LE10 30 C4
Rugby CV22 83 E1
Farber Rd CV2 63 D3
Farcroft Ave CV5 59 E2
Fareham Ave CV22 100 C4
Farley Ave CV33 123 E6
Farley St CV31 110 A4
Farlow Cl CV6 62 A3
Farm Cl Coventry CV6 49 D2
Harbury CV33 123 E6
Shipston-on-S CV36 149 F3
Farm Gr CV22 83 E1
Farm La Easenhall CV23 65 F2
Grendon CV9 11 F3
Littleton WR11 127 F1
Farm Rd Hinckley LE10 31 F3
Kenilworth CV8 92 C1
Royal Leamington Spa CV32 106 A2
Farm St CV33 123 E6
Farm Stile NN11 134 E8
Farm Wlk 2 CV33 122 F8
Farman Rd CV5 61 D1
Farmcote Cl B97 102 B2
Farmcote Rd CV2 50 A2
Farmer Ward Rd CV8 93 D2
Farmhouse Way B90 71 D4
Farmside CV3 78 B3
Farmstead The CV3 78 A4
Farnborough CE Jun & Inf Sch OX17 133 F4
Farnborough Dr B90 70 C3
Farnborough Hall OX17 133 F4
Farnborough Rd B35 22 A2
Farndale Ave CV6 49 E2
Farndon Ave B37 44 A4
Farndon Cl CV12 40 A2
Farnworth Gr B36 22 C1
Farr Dr CV4 60 A1
Farren Rd CV2 62 C3
Farriers Ct CV23 65 E4
Farriers Way Hinckley LE10 31 F3
Nuneaton CV11 29 F1
Farrington Cl CV35 146 B1
Farrington Ct CV35 146 B1
Farther Sand Cl CV35 121 F4
Farthing La B76 23 E3
Farvale Rd B76 22 B3
Faseman Ave CV4 59 F2
Faulconbridge Ave CV5 59 F2
Faultlands Cl CV11 39 F4
Fawley Cl CV3 78 B3
Fawsley Leys CV22 100 A4
Faygate Cl CV3 62 C2
Featherbed La
Bascote CV33 115 B1
Cherington CV36 141 D7
Coventry CV4 76 A3
Redditch B97 102 B3
Rugby CV21 84 A1
Wilmcote CV37 120 D5
Withybrook CV7 52 C3
Featherston Rd LE10 31 F3
Featherstone Cl CV10 29 E1
Feckenham Rd
Astwood Bank B96 102 C1
Redditch, Headless Cross B97 102 B4
Redditch, Hunt End B97 102 B2
Feilding Cl CV2 63 D3
Feilding Way CV10 28 A3
Feldon Mid Sch CV23 115 E3
Felgate Cl B90 71 D3
Fell Gr CV32 106 B2
Fell Mill La CV36 137 A3
Fell's La CV23 125 C8
Fellmore Gr CV31 110 B4
Fellows Way CV21 100 C4
Felspar Rd B77 4 A2
Felton Cl CV2 50 C1
Fen End Rd CV8 73 F2
Fencote Ave B37 33 D2
Fenn Lanes CV13 20 B4
Fennis Cl B93 71 F2
Fenny Compton Rd OX17 134 B5
Fenside Ave CV3 77 E2
Fentham Cl B92 57 D3
Fentham Gn B92 57 D4
Fentham Rd B92 57 D3
Fenton Rd B47 69 D4
Fenwick Cl B49 143 E3
Fenwick Dr CV21 101 D4
Fern Cl Coventry CV2 50 B1
Salford Priors WR11 127 D6
Fern Dale Rd CV7 73 F3
Fern Hill Way CV11 41 E2
Ferncumbe CE Prim Sch The CV35 114 D6
Ferndale Cl CV11 29 F3
Ferndale Ct B46 34 A3
Ferndale Dr CV8 93 D1
Ferndale Mews B46 34 A3
Ferndale Rd Banbury OX16 139 F4
Binley Woods CV3 79 E4
Ferndown Cl CV4 60 A2
Ferndown Ct CV22 82 C1
Ferndown Rd CV22 82 C1
Ferndown Terr CV22 82 C1
Fernhill Cl CV8 92 C3
Fernhill Dr CV32 106 A1
Fernhill La CV7 73 F3
Fernwood Cl B98 103 D3
Ferrers Cl CV4 59 F1
Ferrieres Cl CV22 99 E2
Ferry La CV37 121 D3
Fetherston Cres CV8 79 D1
Fiddlers Gn B92 57 D4
Field Barn Rd
Hampton Magna CV35 114 F4
Warwick CV35 108 A4
Field Cl Kenilworth CV8 93 D3
Warwick CV34 109 D4
Field Gate La CV33 133 E7
Field Head La CV34 109 D3
Field La B91 56 A3
Field March CV3 78 C3
Field View Braunston NN11 117 E5
Ryton-on-D CV8 79 D1
Field View Cl CV7 50 A4
Field Way B94 88 B3
Fieldfare Croft B36 33 D4
Fieldgate La Kenilworth CV8 92 C3
Whitnash CV31 110 A1
Fieldhouse Cl B95 113 B4
Fielding Cl CV9 12 B1
Fields Ct CV34 108 C4
Fields Park Dr B49 143 E2
Fieldside La CV3 62 C2
Fieldways Cl B47 69 D4
Fife Rd CV5 60 C1
Fife St CV11 29 D2
Fifield Cl CV11 29 E1
Fighting Cl CV35 132 B6
Fillingham Cl B37 33 E1
Fillongley CE Fst Sch CV7 36 C2
Fillongley Rd Maxstoke B46 35 E2
Meriden CV7 46 C2
Filton Croft B35 22 A2
Finch Cl CV6 49 E1
Finch La WR11 127 D3
Findon Cl CV12 40 B2
Fineacre La CV8,CV23 96 B3
Finford Croft CV7 74 A3
Fingal Cl CV3 78 B3
Fingest Cl CV5 60 A2
Finham Cres CV8 93 D3
Finham Gr CV3 77 E2
Finham Green Rd CV3 77 D2
Finham Park Comp Sch CV3 77 D2
Finham Prim Sch CV3 77 D2
Finham Rd CV8 93 D3
Finmere CV21 83 E3
Finnemore Cl CV3 77 D3
Finwood Rd CV35 113 F8
Fir Gr CV4 60 A1
Fir Tree Ave CV4 60 A1
Fir Tree Gr CV11 39 E4
Fircroft B78 15 E4
Fire Service Tech Coll GL56 140 C3
Fire Station Rd B26 44 B3
Firethorn Cres CV31 110 A1
Firleigh Dr CV12 40 B1
Firs Dr CV22 82 C1
Firs The Bedworth CV12 38 C1
Coventry CV5 77 D4
Kingsbury B78 15 E4
Lower Quinton CV37 129 E2
Wroxton OX15 139 D4
First Ave
Birmingham, Tyburn B76 22 A3
Coventry CV3 62 B1
First Exhibition Ave B40 44 B2
Firth Ave GL56 140 C3
Firtree Cl OX16 139 F5
Firtree La CV7 37 D4
Fisher Ave CV22 100 C4
Fisher Rd
Bishops Itchington CV33 124 A4
Coventry CV6 61 F4
Fisher's Ct CV34 108 B2
Fishers Cl CV23 101 F1
Fishers Dr B90 69 F3
Fishponds Rd CV8 92 C2
Fishpool La CV7 45 D3
Fitton St CV11 29 D2
Fitzalan Cl CV23 81 D3
Fitzroy Cl CV2 63 D3
Five Ways CV35 90 C1
Five Ways Rd CV35 114 C7
Fivefield Rd CV7 48 C3
Fladbury Cl B98 103 D4
Flamboro' Cl CV3 78 C4
Flamville Rd LE10 32 A3
Flats La CV9 3 D1
Flaunden Cl CV5 60 A2
Flavel Cres CV31 109 F4
Flavel Ct CV9 3 D1
Flax Cl B47 69 D3
Flaxley Cl B98 112 A6
Flecknoe Cl B36 22 B1
Flecknoe St CV3 78 B3
Fleet Cres CV21 83 F1
Fleet St CV1 151 B3
Fleming Rd LE10 30 C4
Fletchamstead Highway CV5 76 B4
Fletcher Gr B93 72 A2
Fletcher Rd LE10 31 F4
Fletchworth Gate CV5 76 B4
Flint Cl CV9 12 C1
Florence Cl Atherstone CV9 12 B1
Bedworth CV12 49 F4

Flower Rd CV37 144 C3
Flowerdale Dr CV2 62 A3
Flude Rd CV7 49 E3
Flying Fields Rd CV33 147 E2
Flynt Ave CV5 60 A3
Foldyard Cl B76 22 A4
Foleshill CE Prim Sch CV6 50 A1
Foleshill Rd CV1, CV6 61 E3
Folkland Gn CV6 61 D4
Folly Ct OX15 142 E8
Folly La Baddesley Ensor CV9 17 E4
Napton CV23 125 B7
Fontmell Cl CV2 63 D2
Ford Cotts CV33 106 C1
Ford La CV37 113 F1
Ford St Coventry CV1 151 C3
Nuneaton CV10 28 C2
Fordbridge Inf Sch B37 33 D3
Fordbridge Rd B37 33 D3
Forde Hall La B94,B95 112 D7
Fordham Ave CV37 145 D2
Fordrift The B37 44 A3
Fordrough The B90 69 E4
Fords Rd B90 69 F4
Fordwell Cl CV5 60 C2
Foredraught B80 103 F2
Foregate St B96 102 C1
Foreland Way CV6 49 D2
Forest Oak Specl Sch B36 22 C1
Forest Rd Dorridge B93 71 F2
Hinckley LE10 31 F4
Forest View B97 102 C3
Forest Way Hollywood B47 69 D3
Nuneaton CV10 28 C1
Forester's Rd CV3 77 F3
Foresters Pl CV21 101 D4
Forfield Pl CV31 110 A4
Forfield Rd CV6 60 C3
Forge Croft B76 22 A3
Forge La B76 22 A3
Forge Rd Kenilworth CV8 93 D3
Shustoke B46 25 D1
Forge Way CV6 49 E2
Forknell Ave CV2 62 B3
Fornside Cl CV21 83 E4
Forrest Rd CV8 92 C2
Forresters Cl LE10 31 F3
Forresters Rd LE10 31 F3
Forryan Rd LE10 31 F4
Forshaw Heath La B94 86 A4
Forshaw Heath Rd B94 69 E1
Forth Dr B37 33 D2
Forties B77 9 F4
Forum Dr CV21 83 E3
Forum Rd B40 44 C2
Forward Rd B26 44 A2
Fosberry Cl CV34 109 D4
Fossdale Rd B77 10 A4
Fosse Cres CV23 96 C2
Fosse Way Chesterton CV33 123 C6
Ettington CV35, CV37 131 C5
Moreton Morrell CV35 123 A3
Shipston-on-S CV36 149 D3
Stretton u F CV23 65 D4
Tredington CV36 136 F6
Ufton CV31,CV33 111 E3
Wolvey CV23 42 C1
Fosseway Ave GL56 140 A2
Fosseway Cl GL56 140 A2
Fosseway Cres CV36 136 F6
Fosseway Dr GL56 140 A2
Fosseway Gdns LE17 43 F3
Fosseway Rd CV3 77 D2
Foster Ave B80 103 F2
Foster Rd CV6 61 D4
Fosterd Rd CV21 82 C3
Founder Cl CV4 76 A4
Fountain Gdns CV35 146 B2
Fountain Way CV37 145 D1
Four Ashes Rd B93 71 F2
Four Oaks Cl B98 102 B4
Four Pounds Ave CV5 60 C2
Fourfields Way CV7 37 D4
Fourways CV9 18 C4
Fowey Cl B76 22 A4
Fowler Rd Coventry CV6 61 D2
Sutton Coldfield B75 13 E3
Fox Ave CV10 29 E4
Fox Cl Harbury CV33 123 F6
Rugby CV21 84 A1
Fox Hill Rd B75 7 D1
Fox Hollies Rd B76 13 D1
Fox's Covert CV13 19 F3
Foxbury Dr B93 72 A2
Foxcote Cl B90 70 B4
Foxcote Dr B90 70 B4
Foxcote Hill CV36 136 B6
Foxcovert La CV13 21 D4
Foxdale Wlk 16 CV31 110 B3
Foxes La CV37 120 C5
Foxes Mdw B76 22 A4
Foxes Way
Balsall Common CV7 74 A3
Warwick CV34 108 B2
Foxfield CV23 66 A4
Foxford Cl B36 22 B1
Foxford Cres CV2 50 A2
Foxford Sch CV6 50 A3
Foxglove B77 4 A2
Foxglove Cl Coventry CV6 49 E1
Rugby CV23 83 F4
Foxhills Cl CV11 30 B1
Foxholes La B97 102 A3
Foxland Cl Birmingham B37 33 E1
Cheswick Green B90 70 B2
Foxon's Barn Rd CV21 83 E3
Foxtail Cl CV37 144 B3
Foxton Rd CV3 62 C1
Foxwood Rd
Birchmoor B78 10 C4
Polesworth B78 4 C1
Framlingham Gr CV8 93 E3
Frampton Cl B37 33 E2
Frampton Wlk CV2 62 C2
Frances Ave CV34 109 D4
Frances Cres CV12 39 D2
Frances Rd Baginton CV8 77 F2
Harbury CV33 123 F6
Francis Cl B78 5 D1
Francis St CV6 61 F4
Franciscan Rd CV3 77 E4
Frank St CV11 29 D2
Frank Whittle Prim Sch
CV2 62 C4
Frankholmes Dr B90 71 D3
Frankland Rd CV6 50 A1
Franklin Gr CV4 59 F1
Franklin Rd Nuneaton CV11 29 E1
Whitnash CV31 110 A2
Frankpledge Rd CV3 77 F4
Frankton Ave CV3 77 E3
Frankton Cl B98 103 F4
Frankton La CV23 97 D3
Frankton Rd CV23 97 F1
Frankwell Dr CV2 50 C1
Fraser Cl CV10 28 A3
Fraser Rd CV6 49 D1
Frasers Way CV37 129 B6
Fred Lee Gr CV3 77 E2
Frederick Bird Prim Sch
CV1 61 F3
Frederick Neal Ave CV5 59 E2
Frederick Press Way 5
CV21 82 C2
Frederick Rd CV7 37 D4
Frederick St CV21 82 C2
Freeboard La CV23 96 C4
Freeburn Cswy CV4 76 B4
Freehold St CV1 61 F2
Freeman Cl CV10 28 B2
Freeman St CV6 61 F3
Freeman's La LE10 32 A3
Freemans Cl CV32 105 F1
Freemantle Rd CV22 82 B1
Freer St CV11 29 F1
Freesland Rise CV10 28 A3
Frensham Cl B37 33 E1
Frensham Dr CV10 28 A3
Freshfield Cl CV5 48 B1
Freshwater Gr 2 CV31 110 B3
Fretton Cl CV6 61 F4
Frevill Rd CV6 62 A4
Friar's Gate CV9 18 B4
Friars Cl CV3 79 F4
Friars La OX15 137 F2
Friars' Rd CV1 151 B2
Friars St CV34 108 B3
Friars Wlk B37 33 E1
Friary Ave B90 71 D3
Friary Cl CV35 114 F3
Friary Rd CV9 12 B1
Friary St CV11 29 D3
Friday Cl B50 148 B3
Friday La B92 56 B2
Friday St
Lower Quinton CV37 129 E2
Pebworth CV37 128 F1
Frilsham Way CV5 60 A2
Frisby Ct CV11 29 F1
Frisby Rd CV4 59 F1
Friswell Dr CV6 61 F4
Friz Hill CV35 131 D8
Frobisher Rd Coventry CV3 77 E3
Rugby CV22 82 B1
Frog La
Balsall Common CV7 74 A3
Ilmington CV36 136 A6
Upper Boddington NN11 134 E8
Welford on A CV37 129 B6
Froglands La WR11 128 A4
Frogmere Cl CV5 60 B3
Frogmore La CV8 73 F1
Frogmore Rd CV37 121 B6
Frolesworth La LE17 43 F4
Front St Ilmington CV36 136 B6
Pebworth CV37 128 E1
Froxmere Cl B91 71 E4
Fryer Ave CV32 105 F2
Frythe Cl CV8 93 E3
Fulbrook La CV35 121 F8
Fulbrook Rd CV2 50 B1
Fulford Dr B76 22 A3
Fulford Hall Rd B94 69 E2
Fullbrook Cl B90 71 D3
Fuller Pl CV35 122 F3
Fullers Cl CV6 60 C4
Fullwood Cl CV2 50 C1
Furlong Mdw CV36 149 F2
Furnace Rd CV12 39 E2
Furndale Rd B46 34 A3
Furness Cl CV21 83 E4
Furrows The CV33 147 E3
Furze Hill Rd CV36 149 F2
Furze La
Chipping Campden GL55 135 C4
Redditch B98 112 A6
Fynford Rd CV6 61 D3
Gables Cl CV22 99 E4
Gables The B78 5 D1
Gadsby St CV11 29 F2
Gadshill CV31 109 F2
Gainford Rise CV3 63 D2
Gainsborough Cres
Knowle B93 72 A3
Rugby CV21 84 A1
Gainsborough Dr
Bedworth CV12 39 D2
Mile Oak B78 8 A4
Royal Leamington Spa CV31 110 B3
Gainsborough Rd CV37 144 B1
Gainsborough Trad Est
CV33 147 D2
Galey's Rd CV3 77 E4
Gallagher Bsns Pk CV6 49 F3
Gallagher Rd CV12 39 D1
Galley Common Fst Sch
CV10 27 F3
Galliards The CV4 76 B2
Gallows Hill CV34 109 D2
Galmington Dr CV3 77 D3
Gannaway Rd CV35 114 B3
Garden Cl Hinckley LE10 31 E3
Knowle B93 71 F3
Mickleton GL55 135 B6
Garden Ct 11 CV34 108 C4
Garden Gr CV12 49 F4
Gardenia Dr CV5 60 A3
Gardens The Kenilworth CV8 93 D2
Radford Semele CV31 110 C3
Rugby CV22 99 E4
Thurlaston CV23 98 C2
Garlick Dr CV8 93 E3
Garnette Cl CV10 28 A3
Garrard Cl WR11 127 F6
Garratt Cl CV23 82 A3
Garrett St CV11 29 F1
Garrick Cl CV5 59 E2
Garrick Way CV37 144 C1
Garrigill B77 4 A1
Garth Cres CV3 78 B4
Garway Cl CV32 105 F2
Garyth Williams Cl CV22 99 F4
Gas House La B49 143 E2
Gas St
Royal Leamington Spa CV31 109 F4
Rugby CV21 83 D2
Gate Farm Dr CV23 53 F2
Gate La Dorridge B93 71 E2
Nether Whitacre B46 24 C3
Gatehouse Cl CV21 101 D4
Gatehouse La CV12 39 D1
Gateley Cl B98 112 A6
Gateside Rd CV6 49 F1
Gatwick Rd B35 22 A2
Gaulby Wlk CV3 63 D1
Gaveston Cl 7 CV34 108 C4
Gaveston Rd Coventry CV6 60 C3
Royal Leamington Spa CV32 105 F1
Gaydon Cl CV6 62 A4
Gaydon Cty Prim Sch
CV35 123 D2
Gaydon Rd CV33 124 A3
Gayer St CV6 50 A1
Gayhurst Cl CV3 78 C4
Gayle B77 4 A1
Gaza Cl CV4 60 A1
Gazelle Cl CV1 151 D3
Geeson Cl B35 22 A2
Gentian Way CV23 83 F4
Gentlemans La B94 112 E7
Geoffery Cl CV2 62 A3
Geoffrey Cl B76 22 A4
George Bach Cl CV23 64 C2
George Eliot Ave CV12 39 E1
George Eliot Hospl CV10 29 D1
George Eliot Rd CV1 61 E3
George Eliot Sch
Nuneaton CV11 29 E1
Nuneaton CV11 39 E4
George Eliot St CV11 29 E1
George Fentham Prim Sch
B92 57 D3
George Fox La CV13 20 A3
George Hodgkinson Cl CV4 59 F2
George La GL55 135 B1
George Marston Rd CV3 62 C1
George Park Cl Ansty CV7 51 E2
Coventry CV2 50 B1
George Rd Warwick CV34 109 D4
Water Orton B46 23 E2
George Robertson Cl CV3 78 C4
George St Arley CV7 37 D4
Coventry CV1 61 F3
Hinckley LE10 31 E4
Nuneaton CV11 29 F1
Royal Leamington Spa CV31 110 A4
Rugby CV21 82 C2
Stockton CV23 115 F3
George Street Ringway
CV12 39 D2
George's Elm La B50 148 C4
Georgian Cl B49 143 D2
Gerard Ave CV4 76 A4
Gerard Rd B49 143 E2
Gerrard St 4 CV34 108 C3
Gerrards Rd CV36 149 F3
Gibbet Hill Rd CV4 76 A2
Gibbet La LE17 68 A3
Gibbons Cl CV4 59 F1
Gibbs Cl CV2 63 D3
Gibbs La WR11 127 D1
Gibson Cres CV12 39 D1
Gibson Dr CV21 84 A1
Gielgud Way CV2 63 D4
Giffard Way CV34 104 C1
Gifford Rd CV35 123 D3
Gifford Wlk CV37 144 B2
Gigg La B76 14 A2
Gilberry Cl B93 72 A2
Gilbert Ave CV22 82 B1
Gilbert Cl 7 Coventry CV1 61 F2
Stratford-u-A CV37 144 C3
Gilberts Rugby Football
Mus CV21 83 D2
Giles Cl CV6 49 E1
Gilfil Rd CV10 29 D1
Gilkes La CV35 137 F8
Gillet Cl CV11 29 D2
Gillett's La OX15 137 E2
Gillians Wlk CV2 63 D4
Gillows Croft B90 71 D4
Gilson Dr B46 33 E4
Gilson Rd B46 33 F4
Gilson Way B37 33 D3
Gingko Wlk CV31 109 F3
Gipsy Cl CV7 74 A3
Gipsy La Balsall Common CV7 74 B3
Nuneaton CV10, CV11 39 E4
Girdlers Cl CV3 77 D3
Girtin Cl CV12 39 D2
Girvan Gr CV32 106 B3
Gisburn Cl CV34 104 C1
Glade The CV5 59 F2
Gladiator Way CV21 82 C4
Gladstone Rd B93 72 A1
Gladstone St CV21 82 C2
Gladstone Terr LE10 31 F4
Glaisdale Ave CV6 49 F2
Glamis Pl OX16 139 F3
Glamorgan Cl CV3 78 B3
Glarmara Cl CV21 83 E4
Glascote Heath Prim Sch
B77 4 A1
Glascote La B77 9 F4
Glascote Rd B77 4 A1
Glasshouse La
Kenilworth CV8 93 E2
Lapworth B94 88 C3
Gleave Rd CV31 110 A2
Glebe Ave CV12 38 C1
Glebe Cl Bidford-on-A B50 148 B2
Coventry CV4 76 A4
Stockton CV23 147 F4
Glebe Cres Kenilworth CV8 93 D2
Rugby CV21 82 C2
Glebe Est CV37 120 B5
Glebe Farm Ind Est CV21 82 C4
Glebe Farm (Mus) CV37 120 C5
Glebe Farm Rd CV21 82 C4
Glebe Fields B76 23 D3
Glebe La Nuneaton CV11 29 F3
Staverton NN11 126 E8
Glebe Pl CV31 110 A4
Glebe Rd Claverdon CV35 113 F3
Hinckley LE10 31 F4
Nuneaton CV11 29 E2
Southam CV33 147 D3
Stratford-u-A CV37 144 B2
Glebe Rise CV9 3 D1
Glebe The Corley CV7 48 B4
Hook Norton OX15 142 D4
Wootton Wawen B95 113 B2
Glebe Way CV7 74 A4
Glebefarm Gr CV3 62 C2
Gleeson Dr CV34 104 C1
Glen Cl CV36 149 F3
Glenbarr Cl LE10 31 D4
Glenbarr Dr LE10 31 D4
Glencoe Rd CV3 62 A1
Glendale Ave CV8 93 D3
Glendale Fst Sch CV10 28 C1
Glendon Gdns CV12 40 B2
Glendon Way B93 71 F2
Glendower Ave CV5 60 B2
Gleneagles B77 4 A3
Gleneagles Cl CV11 30 B1
Gleneagles Rd CV2 62 C3
Glenfield Ave CV10 29 E4
Glenfield Cl Redditch B97 102 B3
2 Solihull B91 71 E4
Glenhurst Rd B95 113 A4
Glenmore Dr CV6 49 F3
Glenmount Ave CV6 49 F3
Glenn St CV6 49 E2
Glenridding Cl CV6 49 F3
Glenrosa Wlk CV4 76 A4
Glenroy Cl CV2 62 C3
Glentworth Ave CV6 49 D1
Glentworth Dr B76 13 D1
Glenville Ave CV9 10 B1
Glenwood Dr B90 70 B2
Glenwood Gdns CV12 39 D3
Gloster Dr CV8 92 C3
Gloster Gdns CV35 146 A4
Gloucester Cl CV11 30 A4
Gloucester La GL55 135 B6
Gloucester St
Coventry CV1 61 D2
1 Royal Leamington Spa
CV31 110 A4
Gloucester Way B37 33 D1
Glover Cl CV34 108 A2
Glover Rd B75 13 D3
Glover St CV3 77 E4
Glover's Cl CV9 18 C4
Glovers Cl CV7 46 B1
Godfrey Cl CV31 110 C3
Godiva Pl CV1 151 D3
Godiva Trad Est CV6 61 F4
Godsons La CV23 125 C8
Gofton B77 10 A4
Gold Cl CV11 39 F4
Goldcrest B77 10 A3
Goldcrest Croft B36 33 D4
Golden Acres La CV3 78 C4
Golden End Dr B93 72 B3
Goldicote Rd CV35 130 F7
Goldsborough B77 4 A1
Goldsmith Ave Rugby CV22 99 F3
Warwick CV34 108 B3
Goldthorn Cl CV5 59 E2
Golf Dr CV11 30 A1
Golf La CV31 110 A1
Good Shepherd Prim Sch
CV6 49 F1
Goodacre Cl CV23 84 A3
Goode Croft CV4 59 F1
Goodere Ave B78 11 D4
Goodere Dr B78 5 D1
Goodeve Wlk B75 13 D3
Goodfellow St CV32 105 E1
Goodman Way CV4 59 E1
Goodyers End Fst &
Mid Schs CV12 49 F4
Goodyers End La CV12 49 E4
Goose La CV37 129 D1
Goosehills Rd LE10 31 F3
Gorcott Hill B98 112 B7
Gordon Cl CV12 39 E2
Gordon St Coventry CV1 61 D1
Royal Leamington Spa CV31 110 A4
Goring Rd CV2 62 A2
Gorse Cl CV22 82 C1
Gorse Farm Rd CV11 40 A4
Gorse La B95 113 A2
Gorse Lea CV33 147 D3
Gorseway CV5 60 B2
Gorsey Cl B96 118 C8
Gorsey La Coleshill B46 23 F1
Wythall B47 69 D2
Gorsey Way B46 23 F1
Gorsy Bank Rd B77 9 F3
Gorsy Way CV10 28 B3
Gosford Ind Est CV1 61 F1
Gosford Park Prim Sch
CV1 61 F1
Gosford St CV1 151 D2
Gospel Oak La CV37 120 F5
Gospel Oak Rd CV6 49 D2
Gosport Rd CV6 61 F4
Gould Cl NN11 117 D5
Gould Rd CV35 108 A4
Grace Rd CV5 59 D4
Grafton Cl B98 103 D4
Grafton La B50 148 C3
Grafton Rd B50 128 C8
Grafton St CV1 61 F1
Graham Cl CV6 50 A1
Graham Rd CV21 83 E2
Graham St CV11 29 E3
Granborough Cl CV3 78 C4
Granbrook La GL55 135 C7
Granby Cl LE10 31 E4
Granby Rd Hinckley LE10 31 E4
Honington CV36 137 A5
Nuneaton CV10 28 C2
Grand Depot Rd CV11 40 C3
Grange Ave
Coventry, Binley CV3 78 C4
Coventry, Finham CV3 77 E2
Kenilworth CV8 92 C4
Grange Cl Nuneaton CV10 28 B4
Ratley OX15 132 F2
Southam CV33 147 D3
Tamworth B77 9 E4
Warwick CV34 109 E4
Grange Dr LE10 31 F3
Grange Farm Prim Sch
CV3 77 D3
Grange Gdns CV35 146 B2
Grange La Harvington WR11 127 D3
Sibford Ferris OX15 142 E8
Grange Pk CV37 145 D2
Grange Rd
Balsall Common CV7 73 F4
Bearley CV37 120 E7
Bidford-on-A B50 148 C2
Coventry CV6 50 A3
Dorridge B93 71 F1
Hartshill CV10 19 E1
Lapworth B94 89 D4
Royal Leamington Spa CV32 106 A2
Rugby CV21 82 C3
Grange The
Cubbington CV32 106 C3
Royal Leamington Spa CV32 106 A1
Grangehurst Prim Sch
CV6 50 A2
Grangemouth Rd CV6 61 D4
Grangers La B98 102 C3
Granhill Cl B98 103 D4
Granoe Cl CV3 78 C4
Grant Rd Bedworth CV7 39 D1
Coventry CV3 62 A1
Grantham St CV2 61 F2
Grantley Dr B37 33 D2
Grants Cl CV33 133 D7
Granvile Rd CV35 146 B2
Granville Gdns LE10 31 E4
Granville Rd Dorridge B93 72 A1
Hinckley LE10 31 E4
Granville St CV32 106 A1
Grapes Cl CV6 61 D3
Grasmere Ave CV3 76 C3
Grasmere Cl CV21 83 E3
Grasmere Cres CV11 29 F4
Grasmere Rd CV12 39 D1
Grasscroft Dr CV3 77 F3
Grassholme B77 10 A4
Grassington Ave CV34 104 C1
Grassington Dr CV11 30 A1
Gratton Ct CV3 76 C3
Gravel Hill CV4 59 F1
Gravel The B76 14 A1
Gray's La GL56 140 A3
Graylands The CV3 77 E2

Grayling B77 .... 9 E3
Grayling Wlk B37 .... 33 E2
Grays Orch CV23 .... 98 C1
Grayswood Ave CV5 .... 60 B2
Great Alne Sch B49 .... 119 D6
Great Balance CV23 .... 64 C2
Great Borne CV21 .... 83 E4
Great Central Way CV21 .... 83 E3
Great Rollright CE
Prim Sch OX7 .... 142 A2
Great William St CV37 .... 145 D2
Greatheed Rd CV32 .... 105 F1
Greaves Cl CV34 .... 109 E4
Greaves Way The CV33 .... 124 B4
Green Cl Long Lawford CV23 .. 81 F2
Studley B80 .... 103 F2
Whitnash CV31 .... 110 A2
Wythall B47 .... 69 D2
Green End CV23 .... 115 D4
Green Farm End CV35 .... 132 B6
Green Field The CV3 .... 78 A4
Green Gables B47 .... 69 D4
Green Gates B95 .... 113 B5
Green La Arley CV10 .... 26 C4
Balsall Common CV7 .... 74 A4
Brinklow CV23 .... 64 B2
Church Lawford CV23 .... 81 E3
Corley CV7 .... 47 E3
Coventry CV3 .... 77 D2
Grendon CV9 .... 11 F2
Middleton B78 .... 14 A3
Nuneaton CV10 .... 28 B4
Oxhill CV35 .... 137 F8
Redditch B97 .... 102 A4
Shipston-on-S CV36 .... 149 F3
Shrewley CV35 .... 114 C6
Shutford OX15 .... 139 A1
Studley B80 .... 103 D3
Swalcliffe OX15 .... 139 A1
Tamworth B78 .... 10 B4
Warwick CV34 .... 108 C4
Wibtoft CV23,LE17 .... 43 D2
Wolvey LE10 .... 42 B3
Green Lane Cl CV36 .... 149 F3
Green Lanes Prim Sch B36 33 D4
Green Lea B77 .... 10 A4
Green The Austrey CV9 .... 3 D1
Barby CV23 .... 101 E1
Chipping Campden GL55 .... 135 B1
Cleeve Prior WR11 .... 128 A4
G Wolford CV36 .... 140 E5
Great Rollright OX7 .... 142 A2
Hook Norton OX15 .... 142 D4
Hornton OX15 .... 139 B7
Kineton CV35 .... 132 F3
Kingsbury B78 .... 15 E3
Lighthorne CV35 .... 123 B2
Long Itchington CV23 .... 115 D4
Nuneaton CV11 .... 29 F1
Orton-on-t-H CV9 .... 6 B2
Priors Marston CV23 .... 125 E4
Rugby CV22 .... 99 E4
Shawell LE17 .... 68 B3
Shrewley CV35 .... 114 D6
Shustoke B46 .... 24 C1
Stoke Golding CV13 .... 21 F4
Stoneleigh CV8 .... 94 B3
Swalcliffe OX15 .... 142 F8
Tamworth B77 .... 4 A3
Wood End B78 .... 10 B2
Greenacre Cl B77 .... 4 A3
Greenacres B76 .... 22 A4
Greenacres Prim Sch B77 .... 4 A3
Greenbank Rd CV7 .... 73 F3
Greendale Cl CV9 .... 18 C4
Greendale Rd Atherstone CV9 18 C4
Coventry CV5 .... 60 B2
Greenfield Ave CV7 .... 74 A4
Greenfields Cl CV36 .... 149 F3
Greenfinch Cl B36 .... 33 D4
Greenfinch Rd B36 .... 33 D4
Greenhart B77 .... 4 A2
Greenhill Cl B77 .... 9 E3
Greenhill Rd Rugby CV22 .... 82 C1
Stoke Golding CV13 .... 21 E4
Whitnash CV31 .... 110 A2
Greenhill St CV37 .... 144 C2
Greenland Ave CV5 .... 59 F3
Greenland Ct CV5 .... 59 F3
Greenlands Dr B98 .... 102 C4
Greenlands Rd B37 .... 33 E1
Greenleaf Cl CV5 .... 60 A2
Greenmoor Rd Hinckley LE10 31 E3
Nuneaton CV10 .... 29 D2
Greenodd Dr CV6 .... 49 F3
Greens Rd CV6 .... 49 D1
Greenside B90 .... 70 B2
Greenside Cl CV11 .... 30 B1
Greensleeves Cl CV6 .... 49 D1
Greensward Cl CV8 .... 93 D3
Greensward The
Coventry CV3 .... 63 D1
Wardington OX17 .... 134 F1
Greenswood CV37 .... 120 E7
Greenway Braunston NN11 . 117 D5
Nuneaton CV11 .... 40 A4
Polesworth B78 .... 5 D2
Warwick CV34 .... 104 C1
Greenway Cl CV36 .... 149 F3
Greenway Nature Trail The
CV37 .... 129 C5
Greenway Rd CV36 .... 149 F3
Greenway The B37 .... 44 A3
Greenways The CV32 .... 106 A2
Greenwood Cl CV23 .... 82 A3
Greenwood Ct CV11 .... 29 F2
Greenwood Rd CV13 .... 21 F4
Greenwood Sq 4 B37 .... 33 D1
Greenwood Way B37 .... 33 D1
Gregory Ave CV3 .... 77 D3
Gregory Hood Rd CV3 .... 77 F2
Grenden Hall Rd CV35 .... 132 D3
Grendon Cl CV4 .... 59 E1
Grendon Dr CV21 .... 83 F4
Grendon Rd B78 .... 11 D4
Grenfell Cl 7 CV31 .... 110 B3
Grenville Ave CV2 .... 62 A2
Grenville Cl CV22 .... 82 B1
Gresham Ave CV32 .... 106 A1
Gresham Pl 7 CV32 .... 106 A1
Gresham Rd CV10 .... 39 D4
Gresham St CV2 .... 62 A1
Gresley Rd CV2 .... 62 B4
Greswold Cl CV4 .... 59 F1
Greswoldes The CV31 .... 110 C3
Gretna Rd CV3 .... 76 C2
Grevel La GL55 .... 135 B2
Greville Rd Alcester B49 .... 143 D3
Kenilworth CV8 .... 92 C2
Warwick CV34 .... 105 D1
Greville Smith Ave CV31 .... 110 A2
Grewcock Cl LE17 .... 43 F3
Grey Mill Cl B90 .... 70 C3
Grey Tree Cres B93 .... 71 F2
Grey's Rd B80 .... 103 F2
Greycoat Rd CV6 .... 49 D1
Greyfriars La CV1 .... 151 B2
Greyfriars Rd CV1 .... 151 B2
Greygoose La GL56 .... 150 A3
Greyhurst Croft 5 B91 .... 71 D4
Greyrick Ct GL55 .... 135 B6
Greys Cl OX16 .... 139 F3
Griff La CV10 .... 38 C3
Griffin Rd CV34 .... 109 E4
Griggs Cl GL55 .... 135 B2
Grimston Cl CV3 .... 63 D1
Grindle Rd CV6 .... 49 F2
Grindsbrook B77 .... 10 A4
Grizebeck Dr CV5 .... 60 A3
Grizedale CV21 .... 83 E4
Grosvenor Cres LE10 .... 31 D4
Grosvenor Rd Coventry CV1 151 A1
Royal Leamington Spa CV31 110 A3
Rugby CV21 .... 83 E2
Grouse Cl CV37 .... 144 B3
Grove Croft CV35 .... 114 F3
Grove Fields CV10 .... 29 E4
Grove La Keresley CV7 .... 48 C4
Lapworth B94 .... 88 C2
Wishaw B76 .... 13 F1
Grove Pk
Hampton Magna CV35 .... 114 F3
Hinckley LE10 .... 32 A3
Grove Pl Nuneaton CV10 .... 28 B2
1 Royal Leamington Spa
CV31 .... 110 A3
Grove Rd Ansty CV7 .... 51 E2
Atherstone CV9 .... 18 B4
Dorridge B93 .... 72 A2
Hinckley LE10 .... 32 A3
Nuneaton CV10 .... 28 B2
Stratford-u-A CV37 .... 144 C1
Grove St Coventry CV1 .... 151 C3
Royal Leamington Spa CV32 . 109 F4
Grove The Bedworth CV12 .... 39 E2
Coleshill B46 .... 33 F2
Hampton in A B92 .... 45 D1
Hinckley LE10 .... 31 E4
Studley B80 .... 103 E2
Grovelands Ind Est CV7 .... 50 A3
Grump St CV36 .... 136 B6
Guardhouse Rd CV6 .... 61 D4
Guernsey Dr B36 .... 33 D3
Guild Rd Aston Cantlow B95 . 119 F6
Coventry CV6 .... 61 E4
Guild St CV37 .... 145 D2
Guilsborough Rd CV3 .... 78 C4
Guinness Cl B98 .... 102 B4
Gulistan Rd CV32 .... 105 F1
Gullet The B78 .... 4 C1
Gullicote La OX17 .... 139 F6
Gulliver's Cl OX15 .... 139 D6
Gulson Hospl CV1 .... 151 D2
Gulson Rd CV1 .... 61 F1
Gun Hill CV7 .... 37 D4
Gun Hill Fst Sch CV7 .... 37 D4
Gun La CV2 .... 62 A3
Gundry Cl CV31 .... 110 A4
Gunn Ct B49 .... 119 E6
Gunn End CV36 .... 149 F4
Gunners La B80 .... 103 F2
Gunnery Terr 5 CV32 .... 105 E1
Gunnings Rd B49 .... 143 E2
Gunton Ave CV3 .... 78 B3
Guphill Ave CV5 .... 60 B1
Guphill La CV5 .... 60 B2
Gurnard B77 .... 9 E3
Gurney Cl CV4 .... 59 F2
Gutteridge Ave CV6 .... 49 D1
Guy Pl E 10 CV32 .... 105 F1
Guy Pl W 9 CV32 .... 105 F1
Guy Rd CV8 .... 92 C1
Guy St
Royal Leamington Spa CV32 . 105 F1
Warwick CV34 .... 108 C4
Guy's Cl CV34 .... 109 D4
Guy's Cliffe Ave CV32 .... 105 E1
Guy's Cliffe Rd CV32 .... 109 F4
Guy's Cliffe Terr CV34 .... 108 C4
Guy's Cross Park Rd CV34 108 C4
Gypsy La Atherstone CV9 .... 12 B1
Dordon B78 .... 11 D2
Kenilworth CV8 .... 92 C1
Water Orton B46 .... 23 E1
Hack La CV36 .... 141 C5
Hackwell St CV23 .... 125 C8
Haddon End CV3 .... 77 F3
Haddon Rd CV32 .... 106 A1
Haddon St CV6 .... 62 A4
Hadfield Cl CV23 .... 84 A3
Hadleigh Croft B76 .... 22 A3
Hadleigh Rd CV3 .... 77 E2
Hadley Cl B47 .... 69 D3
Hadrian Cl CV32 .... 106 A2
Hadrian Dr B46 .... 23 F1
Hadrians Cl B77 .... 9 E4
Hadrians Wlk CV21 .... 82 C4
Hadrians Wlk B49 .... 143 D2
Halberd Cl LE10 .... 31 E3
Hales Cl CV37 .... 121 B7
Hales Park Ind Est CV6 .... 49 F2
Hales St CV1 .... 151 C3
Halford La CV6 .... 49 D1
Halford Rd Ettington CV37 .. 131 A3
Stratford-u-A CV37 .... 144 C1
Whatcote CV36 .... 137 C7
Halfpenny Field Wlk B35 .... 22 A2
Halfway La CV22 .... 99 D2
Halifax Cl Allesley CV5 .... 60 A4
Wellesbourne CV35 .... 146 A1
Hall Brook Rd CV6 .... 49 D2
Hall Cl CV8 .... 94 A3
Hall Cl The CV22 .... 99 E1
Hall Dr Baginton CV8 .... 77 F2
Birmingham B37 .... 44 A4
Stoke Golding CV13 .... 21 F4
Hall End CV11 .... 29 E1
Hall End Pl CV11 .... 29 E1
Hall Gr CV23 .... 64 C2
Hall Green Rd CV6 .... 50 A1
Hall La Coventry CV2 .... 62 C3
Harbury CV33 .... 123 F7
Witherley CV9 .... 19 D4
Wolvey LE10 .... 41 E2
Hall Rd Hinckley LE10 .... 31 E3
Royal Leamington Spa CV32 . 105 F1
Wolvey LE10 .... 41 E2
Hall Wlk B46 .... 33 F2
Hall's Cl CV31 .... 110 A2
Hallam Rd CV6 .... 49 D1
Hallcroft Way B93 .... 72 A3
Hallfields CV31 .... 110 C3
Hallway Dr CV7 .... 51 F3
Halstead Gr B91 .... 71 D4
Halston Green Rd B90 .... 69 F4
Haltonlea B77 .... 10 A4
Hamar Way B37 .... 33 D1
Hambridge Rd CV33 .... 124 C3
Hames La B79 .... 2 B2
Hamilton Cl CV12 .... 38 B1
Hamilton Ct CV10 .... 28 B2
Hamilton Dr B80 .... 103 E2
Hamilton Rd Coventry CV2 .... 62 A2
Radford Semele CV31 .... 110 C3
Redditch B97 .... 102 B4
Tiddington CV37 .... 145 F2
Hamilton Terr CV32 .... 109 F4
Hamlet Cl Nuneaton CV11 .... 30 A1
Rugby CV22 .... 99 E3
Hamlet The CV35 .... 105 D4
Hammersley St CV12 .... 38 C1
Hammerton Way CV35 .... 146 B1
Hammond Bsns Ctr CV11 .... 29 F2
Hammond Cl CV11 .... 29 F2
Hammond Rd CV2 .... 61 F2
Hampden Cl OX16 .... 139 F3
Hampden Ct CV33 .... 133 A7
Hampden Way CV22 .... 99 E4
Hampdon Way CV35 .... 146 B1
Hampshire Cl CV3 .... 78 C4
Hampstead Norreys Rd
CV35 .... 132 D4
Hampton Ave CV10 .... 28 A2
Hampton Cl Coventry CV6 .... 61 F3
Redditch B98 .... 103 D4
Hampton Croft CV35 .... 114 F2
Hampton in Arden Sta B92 . 57 D4
Hampton La Meriden CV7 .... 57 F4
Solihull B91 .... 56 A3
Hampton Lucy CE Prim Sch
CV35 .... 121 F4
Hampton Rd Coventry CV6 .... 61 F3
Knowle B93 .... 72 B4
Warwick CV34 .... 108 A3
Hampton St CV34 .... 108 B3
Hams La Curdworth B76 .... 23 F3
Lea Marston B76 .... 24 A4
Hanbury Cl CV35 .... 132 B6
Hanbury Rd Bedworth CV12 .. 39 E2
Dorridge B93 .... 71 F2
Hancock Gn CV4 .... 75 F4
Hancox Cl CV33 .... 107 E4
Handcross Gr CV3 .... 77 D3
Handley Gr CV34 .... 104 B1
Handley's Cl CV8 .... 79 D1
Hands Paddock CV37 .... 130 E1
Handsworth Cres CV5 .... 59 F2
Hanford Cl CV6 .... 61 F3
Hanger Rd B26 .... 44 A2
Hangmans La B79 .... 2 A1
Hanlith B77 .... 10 A4
Hanover Ct Hinckley LE10 .... 31 F3
Redditch B98 .... 102 B4
Hans Cl CV2 .... 61 F2
Hansell Dr B93 .... 71 F1
Hanson Ave CV36 .... 149 F3
Hanwell Cl B76 .... 22 A4
Hanwell Ct OX17 .... 139 F6
Hanwood Cl CV5 .... 59 E2
Hanworth Cl CV32 .... 106 B1
Hanworth Rd CV34 .... 108 B4
Harbet Dr B40 .... 44 C2
Harborough Dr B36 .... 22 B1
Harborough Rd
Coventry CV6 .... 49 D1
Long Lawford CV21 .... 82 B4
Harbour Cl B50 .... 148 B2
Harbury CE Sch CV33 .... 123 F6
Harbury Cl B76 .... 22 A3
Harbury La
Bishops Tachbrook CV33 .... 123 B7
Royal Leamington Spa
CV33, CV34 .... 109 F1
Harbury Rd CV33 .... 124 C6
Harcourt CV3 .... 78 C3
Harcourt Gdns CV11 .... 29 E2
Hardwick Cl CV5 .... 60 A2
Hardwick La B80 .... 112 B3
Hardwick Pk OX16 .... 139 F5
Hardwick Rd CV23 .... 125 E4
Hardwyn Cl CV3 .... 63 D1
Hardy Cl Nuneaton CV10 .... 28 A2
Rugby CV22 .... 82 B1
Hardy Rd CV6 .... 61 D4
Hare & Hounds La CV10 .... 29 D1
Harebell B77 .... 4 A2
Harebell Way CV23 .... 83 E4
Harebell Wlk 1 B37 .... 33 E1
Harefield La CV12 .... 38 C4
Harefield Rd Coventry CV2 .... 62 A2
Nuneaton CV11 .... 29 E2
Hareway La CV35 .... 122 C7
Harewood Rd CV5 .... 60 B1
Harger Ct CV8 .... 92 C2
Hargrave Cl Coventry CV3 .... 63 D1
Water Orton B46 .... 23 D2
Harington Rd CV6 .... 61 D3
Harlech Cl Banbury OX16 .... 139 F3
Kenilworth CV8 .... 93 E3
Harley St CV2 .... 62 A2
Harlow Wlk 8 CV2 .... 63 D4
Harmar Cl CV34 .... 104 B1
Harmer Cl CV2 .... 63 D4
Harnall Cl B90 .... 70 C4
Harnall Ind Est CV1 .... 151 C4
Harnall La CV1 .... 151 C4
Harnall La E CV1 .... 61 F2
Harnall La W CV1 .... 151 C4
Harnall Row Coventry CV1 .... 61 F2
Coventry CV1 .... 61 F2
Harold Cox Pl CV22 .... 99 F3
Harold Rd CV2 .... 62 B1
Harold St CV11 .... 29 E2
Harpenden Dr CV5 .... 60 A3
Harper Rd CV1 .... 61 F1
Harpers La CV9 .... 19 D4
Harriott Dr CV34 .... 109 E2
Harris CE High Sch CV22 .... 82 C1
Harris Cl B95 .... 113 B4
Harris Dr CV22 .... 99 F4
Harris Mews B95 .... 113 B4
Harris Rd Coventry CV3 .... 62 A1
Warwick CV34 .... 108 B4
Harrison Cl CV21 .... 101 D4
Harrison Cres CV12 .... 39 D1
Harrison Rd B97 .... 102 B4
Harrow La CV37 .... 144 C1
Harrow Rd CV31 .... 110 A2
Harrowbrook Ind Est LE10 .. 30 C4
Harrowbrook Rd LE10 .... 30 C4
Harry Rose Rd CV2 .... 62 B4
Harry Taylor Fst Sch B97 . 102 C3
Harry Truslove Cl CV6 .... 61 D4
Harry Weston Rd CV3 .... 63 D1
Hart Cl CV21 .... 83 E1
Hartington Cl B93 .... 71 F2
Hartington Cres CV5 .... 60 C1
Hartington Gn LE10 .... 31 F3
Hartland Ave CV2 .... 62 A3
Hartlebury Cl B93 .... 71 F2
Hartlepool Rd CV1 .... 151 D4
Hartleyburn B77 .... 10 A4
Hartridge Wlk CV5 .... 60 A2
Hartshill Hayes Ctry Pk
CV10 .... 18 C1
Hartshill Hayes Visitors Ctr
CV10 .... 18 C1
Hartshill Sch CV10 .... 28 A4
Harvard Cl CV35 .... 146 B1
Harvest Hill Cl 15 CV31 .... 110 B3
Harvest Hill La CV5, CV7 .... 47 E2
Harvesters Cl CV3 .... 63 D1
Harvey Cl CV5 .... 60 A4
Harvington CE Fst Sch
WR11 .... 127 D4
Harvington Dr B90 .... 71 D3
Harvington Way B76 .... 22 A4
Harwood Gr B90 .... 70 B4
Haselbech Rd CV3 .... 62 C1
Haseley Bsns Ctr CV35 .... 114 D7
Haseley Cl CV31 .... 110 A3
Haseley Rd CV2 .... 50 B1
Haselor Cl B49 .... 143 E2
Haselor Jun & Inf Sch
B49 .... 119 D4
Hasilwood Sq CV3 .... 62 A1
Haslucks Green Rd B90 .... 69 F4
Hassall Cl 9 CV33 .... 122 F8
Hastings Cl Banbury OX16 .... 139 F3
Tamworth B77 .... 9 F3
Hastings High Sch LE10 .... 31 F4
Hastings Rd Banbury OX16 .. 139 F4
Coventry CV2 .... 62 A2
Wellesbourne CV35 .... 146 B2
Haswell Cl CV22 .... 83 E1
Hatchford Wlk B37 .... 33 D1
Hathaway Cl
Balsall Common CV7 .... 74 A4
Littleton WR11 .... 127 F1
Hathaway Dr Nuneaton CV11 30 A1
Warwick CV34 .... 104 C1
Hathaway Green La CV37 . 144 C3
Hathaway Hamlet CV37 .... 144 B1
Hathaway La CV37 .... 144 B1
Hathaway Rd CV4 .... 59 E1
Hatherden Dr B76 .... 13 D1
Hatherell Rd CV31 .... 110 C3
Hatters Dr CV9 .... 12 B1
Hatton Bank La CV37 .... 121 D5
Hatton Cl CV35 .... 114 F5
Hatton Ctry World
CV35 .... 114 D5
Hatton Sta CV35 .... 114 C5
Hatton Terr CV35 .... 114 F5
Haunch La B76 .... 24 A4
Haunchwood Rd CV10 .... 28 B2
Havendale Cl CV6 .... 61 D3
Hawbridge Cl B90 .... 71 D3
Hawfinch B77 .... 10 A3
Hawk Cl CV11 .... 40 A4
Hawke's La OX15 .... 142 E8
Hawkes Dr CV34 .... 109 E2
Hawkes Mill La CV5 .... 48 A1
Hawkesbury Fields Sch
CV2 .... 50 B2
Hawkesbury La CV2 .... 50 B3
Hawkeshead CV21 .... 83 E4
Hawkeswell La B46 .... 34 A2
Hawkesworth Dr CV8 .... 93 D3
Hawkinge Dr B35 .... 22 A2
Hawkins Cl CV22 .... 82 C1
Hawkins Rd CV5 .... 61 D1
Hawkshead Dr B93 .... 71 F3
Hawkside B77 .... 10 A4
Hawkswood Dr CV7 .... 74 A4
Hawksworth Dr 6 CV1 .... 61 D2
Hawlands CV21 .... 83 E3
Hawley Rd LE10 .... 31 E4
Hawnby Gr B76 .... 13 D1
Hawthorn Ave CV9 .... 16 B3
Hawthorn Cl B49 .... 143 D3
Hawthorn Cres LE10 .... 31 F2
Hawthorn La CV4 .... 59 F1
Hawthorn Rd CV31 .... 109 F3
Hawthorn Way
Hartshill CV10 .... 28 A4
Rugby CV22 .... 82 A1
Hawthorne Ave CV7 .... 37 D4
Hawthorne Cl CV8 .... 80 A2
Hawthorne Dr B47 .... 69 D3
Hawthorne Terr CV10 .... 28 C3
Hawthorns The B78 .... 15 E4
Hay La Coventry CV1 .... 151 C2
Solihull B90 .... 71 D3
Hay Meadow CV36 .... 149 F3
Hay Pool OX17 .... 133 F5
Hay Wood La B93, CV35 .... 90 A2
Haybarn The B76 .... 22 A4
Haydock Cl Coventry CV6 .... 50 A2
Stratford-u-A CV37 .... 144 C1
Haydon Cl B93 .... 71 F1
Haydon Way B49 .... 118 F8
Haydons Cl GL55 .... 135 B2
Haye La B80 .... 112 A5
Hayes Cl CV21 .... 83 E4
Hayes Green Rd CV12 .... 49 F4
Hayes La CV7 .... 50 A4
Hayes Rd CV10 .... 28 A4
Hayle Ave CV34 .... 104 C1
Hayle Cl CV11 .... 30 A3
Haynes Way CV21 .... 82 C4
Haynestone Rd CV6 .... 60 C3
Hays La LE10 .... 31 D4
Haysum's Cl GL55 .... 135 B1
Hayton Gn CV4 .... 75 F4
Haytor Rise CV2 .... 62 B4
Hayward Cl CV35 .... 114 F3
Hayward's Gn CV6 .... 61 D4
Hayway La CV23 .... 116 B4
Hazel Cl Hartshill CV10 .... 28 A4
Royal Leamington Spa CV32 106 A1
Hazel Croft
Birmingham, Chelmsley Wood
B37 .... 33 D1
Braunston NN11 .... 117 E5
Hazel Dr B47 .... 69 D3
Hazel Gr Bedworth CV12 .... 39 E2
Hockley Heath B94 .... 88 B3
Hazel Rd Coventry CV6 .... 50 A1
Nuneaton CV10 .... 28 B3
Hazelcroft B78 .... 15 E4
Hazelgarth B77 .... 10 A4
Hazelhead St Georges
(Ind Est) CV1 .... 61 F1
Hazell Way CV10 .... 29 D1
Hazeltree Gr B93 .... 71 F2
Hazelwood Cl CV22 .... 99 D2
Hazlemere Cl CV5 .... 60 A2
Headborough Rd CV2 .... 62 A3
Headington Ave CV6 .... 49 D1
Headland Cl CV37 .... 129 A6
Headland Rd CV37 .... 129 A6
Headland Rise CV37 .... 129 A6
Headlands The CV5 .... 60 B2
Healey Cl CV21 .... 83 E4
Health Centre Rd CV8 .... 76 B2
Heanley La CV9 .... 16 B3
Hearsall Com Prim Sch
CV5 .... 60 C1
Hearsall Comm CV5 .... 60 C1
Hearsall Golf Course CV5 .... 76 C4
Hearsall La CV5 .... 60 C1
Heart of England Sch CV7 .. 74 B3
Heart of England Way
CV11 .... 29 F2
Heath Ave CV12 .... 38 C1

Heath Cres CV2 62 A3
Heath End La CV37 121 D7
Heath End Rd CV10 28 C1
Heath Farm La CV35 123 C3
Heath La CV23 64 C1
Heath Rd Bedworth CV12 38 C1
Coventry CV2 62 A2
Hollywood B47 69 D4
Heath Terr CV32 105 F1
Heath The CV22 99 E2
Heath Way CV22 100 B4
Heathcote Ind Est CV34 109 E3
Heathcote La
Royal Leamington Spa CV34 109 E2
Warwick CV34 109 D3
Heathcote Rd CV31 110 A2
Heathcote St CV6 61 D4
Heathcote Way CV34 109 E2
Heather Cl Birmingham B36 33 D4
Nuneaton CV10 28 C2
Rugby CV22 82 C1
Southam CV33 147 D3
Stratford-u-A CV37 144 B2
Heather Dr CV12 38 C1
Heather Rd Binley Woods CV3 79 E4
Coventry CV2 50 B1
Heathfield Cl B93 72 A3
Heathfield Rd Coventry CV5 60 B1
Norton WR11 127 B2
Heathfields Cty Inf Sch B77 9 F3
Heathgreen Cl B37 33 E2
Heathley La B78 8 C3
Hebden B77 10 A4
Hebden Ave CV34 104 C1
Hebden Way CV11 30 A1
Heber Dr CV33 123 E6
Heckley Rd CV7 50 A4
Heddle Gr CV6 62 A4
Hedgerow Wlk CV6 49 D2
Hedgerows The CV10 28 C3
Hedges Cl CV33 124 D6
Hedgetree Croft B37 33 E1
Hedging La B77 9 F3
Hedging Lane Ind Est B77 9 F3
Hedingham Gr B37 33 E1
Hedley Croft B35 22 A2
Heemstede La CV32 106 A1
Heera Cl CV6 61 E4
Hele Rd CV3 77 E3
Helen St CV6 61 F3
Helena Cl CV10 28 C2
Hellidon Cl 4 CV32 106 A1
Hellidon Rd CV23 125 F4
Helmdon Cl CV21 83 E3
Helmsdale Rd CV32 106 A3
Helmswood Dr B37 44 B4
Helston Cl CV11 30 A3
Helvellyn Way CV21 83 E4
Hemdale CV11 30 A2
Heming Rd B98 103 F4
Hemingford Rd CV2 63 D4
Hemlingford Croft B37 44 A4
Hemlingford Rd
Kingsbury B78 15 E2
Sutton Coldfield B76 22 A3
Hemmings Cl CV31 110 C3
Hemmings Mill CV35 122 A7
Hemsby Cl CV4 76 A4
Hemsworth Dr CV12 40 A1
Hen La CV6 49 E2
Henbrook La OX15 137 E2
Hendre Cl CV5 60 B1
Henley Cl CV11 29 F4
Henley Coll CV2 62 B4
Henley Mill La CV2 62 B4
Henley Park Ind Est CV2 62 C4
Henley Rd Claverdon CV35 113 E4
Coventry CV2 62 B4
Lowsonford B95 113 D6
Norton Lindsey CV35 114 D3
Royal Leamington Spa CV31 110 A3
Henley St Alcester B49 143 E2
Stratford-u-A CV37 145 D2
Henley-in-Arden High Sch
B95 113 B4
Henley-in-Arden Prim Sch
B95 113 B4
Henley-in-Arden Sta B95 113 A4
Henrietta St CV6 61 F3
Henry Bellairs CE Mid Sch
CV12 39 E2
Henry Boteler Rd CV4 76 A4
Henry Hinde Fst Sch CV22 82 B1
Henry Hinde Mid Sch CV22 82 A1
Henry St Coventry CV1 151 B3
Kenilworth CV8 93 D3
Nuneaton CV11 29 E1
Rugby CV21 83 D2
Henson Rd CV12 38 C1
Henwood La B91 56 A2
Hepworth Rd CV3 63 D1
Herald Bsns Pk CV3 78 C4
Herald Way Coventry CV3 79 D4
Hinckley LE10 31 E2
Herbert Art Gall & Mus
CV1 151 C2
Herbert Fowler Mid Sch
CV10 26 C1
Herbert St CV10 28 C2
Herbert's La CV8 93 D3
Herdwycke Cl CV33 147 E2
Hereford Rd CV11 40 C3
Hereward Coll of FE CV4 59 F1
Herford Way LE10 31 F3
Heritage Ct CV4 76 B2
Heritage Motor Ctr CV35 123 D1
Hermes Cl CV34 109 F3
Hermes Cres CV2 62 C3
Hermit's Croft CV3 77 E4
Hermitage Dr B76 13 D2
Hermitage La B78 4 C1
Hermitage Rd CV2 62 B2
Hermitage Way CV8 93 D2
Heron Cl Alcester B49 143 D3
Cheswick Green B90 70 B2
Heron La CV37 144 B3
Herrick Rd CV2 62 B2
Hertford Cl CV10 28 C2
Hertford Pl CV1 151 A2
Hertford Rd Alcester B49 143 E3
Stratford-u-A CV37 144 C1
Hertford St CV1 151 B2
Hertford Way B93 72 A2
Hesleden B77 10 A4
Heslop Cl CV3 78 C4
Hetton Cl 8 CV34 104 C1
Hewitt Ave CV6 61 D2
Hexby Cl CV2 63 D3
Hexworthy Ave CV3 77 D3
Heybrook Cl CV2 62 B4
Heycroft CV4 76 B2
Heydons Terr OX17 133 F4
Heyford Gr B91 71 E4
Heyford Leys CV22 99 F3
Heyford Way B35 22 A3
Heyville Croft CV8 93 E2
Heywood Cl CV6 62 A4
Hibberd Ct CV8 92 C2
Hibbert Cl CV22 83 D1
Hickman Rd CV10 27 F3
Hicks Cl CV34 104 C1
Hidcote Ave B76 22 A4
Hidcote Cl Nuneaton CV11 39 F4
28 Royal Leamington Spa
CV31 110 B3
Hidcote Gr B37 44 A4
Hidcote Manor Garden
GL55 135 D5
Hidcote Rd Ebrington GL55 135 D3
Kenilworth CV8 93 E3
High Ash Cl CV7 49 F4
High Beech CV5 60 A3
High Brink Rd B46 33 F4
High Cross La
Claybrooke Magna LE17 43 E3
Lowsonford CV35 113 F6
High La OX15 137 E2
High Mdw OX15 138 D1
High Meadow Fst Sch B46 33 F4
High Park Cl CV5 59 F2
High St Alcester B49 143 D2
Astwood Bank B96 102 C1
Barford CV35 122 B8
Bedworth CV12 39 D1
Bidford-on-A B50 148 C2
Bidford-on-A,Broom B50 148 A4
Bishops Itchington CV33 124 A4
Braunston NN11 117 D5
Charwelton NN11 126 D2
Chipping Campden GL55 135 B2
Coleshill B46 34 A3
Coventry CV1 151 C2
Coventry, Keresley CV6 48 C1
Cropredy OX17 134 C1
Cubbington CV32 106 C3
Fenny Compton CV33 133 D7
Great Rollright OX7 142 A2
Hampton in A B92 57 D4
Harbury CV33 123 F6
Henley-in-A B95 113 B5
Hook Norton OX15 142 D4
Hurley CV9 16 B3
Kenilworth CV8 92 C3
Knowle B93 72 B3
Lower Brailes OX15 137 F2
Marton CV23 115 C7
Mickleton GL55 135 C6
Moreton-in-M GL56 140 A3
Napton CV23 125 C7
Nuneaton CV11 29 D2
Polesworth B78 5 D1
Ratley OX15 133 A2
Royal Leamington Spa CV31 110 A4
Rugby CV21 83 D2
Rugby,Hillmorton CV21 101 D4
Ryton-on-D CV8 79 D1
Shipston-on-S CV36 149 F3
Shutford OX15 139 A3
Southam CV33 147 D2
Stockton CV23 147 F4
Stoke Golding CV13 21 E4
Stratford-u-A CV37 145 D1
Studley B80 103 F2
Tamworth B77 9 E2
Warwick CV34 108 C3
Welford on A CV37 129 A7
High Trees Cl B98 102 C4
High Trees Rd B93 72 A4
High View Dr CV7 49 E4
High View Rd CV32 106 B3
Higham La Nuneaton CV11 29 F4
Stoke Golding CV13 21 E3
Stoke Golding,Wykin LE10 21 F2
Higham Lane Sch CV10 29 E3
Higham on the Hill
CE Prim Sch CV13 21 D2
Higham Way LE10 31 F4
Highbury Gn CV10 28 B4
Highclere Gdns OX16 139 F3
Highcliffe Rd B77 9 E4
Highcroft CV35 113 F3
Highcroft Cres CV32 105 E1
Highdown Cres 3 B90 71 D3
Highdown Rd CV31 110 A3
Highfield CV7 46 B1
Highfield Ave Redditch B97 102 B4
Tamworth B77 4 A3
Highfield Cl Kenilworth CV8 92 C2
Snitterfield CV37 121 B7
Highfield Rd Coventry CV2 61 F2
Nuneaton CV11 29 F1
Redditch B97 102 B4
Stratford-u-A CV37 144 C3
Studley B80 103 E2
Highfield Terr CV32 105 E1
Highgrove Coventry CV4 75 F3
Rugby CV22 99 E4
Highland Rd Coventry CV5 60 C1
Kenilworth CV8 93 E4
Royal Leamington Spa CV32 106 A2
Highland Way B98 103 D4
Highlands OX16 139 F5
Highlands Cl CV34 109 D4
Highlands Rd B90 70 C4
Highview CV9 16 B2
Highwaymans Croft CV4 76 B3
Hiker Gr 3 B37 33 E1
Hilary Bevins Cl CV13 20 C2
Hilary Dr B76 13 D3
Hilary Rd Coventry CV4 76 C3
Nuneaton CV10 28 C3
Hill Cl Northend CV33 133 B7
Royal Leamington Spa CV32 106 A2
Hill Cres CV23 96 C3
Hill Crest CV32 106 C3
Hill Crest Hospl B98 103 E3
Hill Farm Ave CV11 30 A1
Hill Farm Prim Sch CV6 61 D4
Hill Fray Dr CV3 78 A3
Hill La Middleton B75 7 D1
Upper Brailes OX15 137 E3
Upper Quinton CV37 129 D1
Hill Rd Grandborough CV23 116 E6
Keresley CV7 48 C3
Lower Boddington NN11 134 E7
Hill Rise OX7 142 A2
Hill Row NN11 117 E4
Hill Side Coventry CV2 62 A3
Kingsbury B78 15 E2
Hill St Bedworth CV12 39 D3
Coventry CV1 151 B3
Hinckley LE10 31 F4
Nuneaton CV10 28 B2
Royal Leamington Spa CV32 106 A1
Rugby CV21 83 D2
Warwick CV34 109 D4
Hill Top Baddesley Ensor CV9 11 D1
Coventry CV1 151 C3
Hill Top Ave CV9 11 D1
Hill View CV33 124 A4
Hill View Rd B50 148 C3
Hill Wootton Rd CV35 105 E3
Hillary Rd CV22 99 F4
Hillborough La B50 128 E7
Hillcrest Rd Nuneaton CV10 28 C3
Polesworth B78 11 D4
Hillfield Mews 3 B91 71 D4
Hillfield Rd CV22 82 B1
Hillhurst Gr B36 22 B1
Hilliard Cl CV12 39 D2
Hillman Gr B36 22 C1
Hillmorton La
Clifton u D CV23 84 A2
Lilbourne CV23 84 C3
Hillmorton Prim Sch CV21 101 D4
Hillmorton Rd Coventry CV2 50 B1
Knowle B93 72 A3
Rugby CV22 83 E1
Hillrise LE10 31 F4
Hillside Appleby Magna DE12 3 F4
Hartshill CV10 28 A4
Napton CV23 125 C8
Hillside Dr CV10 28 B4
Hillside N CV2 62 A3
Hillside Rd Hinckley LE10 31 E3
Stratford-u-A CV37 144 B2
Hilltop Cl Honiley CV8 90 C4
Southam CV33 147 D3
Hillwood Ave B90 71 D3
Hillyard Rd CV33 147 D3
Hilmore Way B77 9 F4
Hilton Ave CV10 28 A3
Himbleton Croft 1 B90 71 D3
Himley Rd CV12 38 B1
Hinckley Bsns Pk LE10 30 C4
Hinckley CE Jun & Inf Sch
LE10 31 E4
Hinckley & District Hospl
LE10 31 E4
Hinckley La CV13 21 E2
Hinckley Rd Ansty CV2, CV7 51 E1
Aston Flamville LE10 32 B4
Burton Hastings LE10 31 F1
Burton Hastings LE10 41 E4
Coventry CV2 63 D4
Hinckley LE10 32 A3
Nuneaton CV11 29 F3
Stoke Golding CV13 21 F4
Hinckley Sta LE10 31 E4
Hind Cl CV34 104 C1
Hinde Cl CV21 83 E4
Hindlip Cl B98 112 A6
Hintons Coppice B93 71 F3
Hipsley Cl B36 22 B1
Hipsley La CV9 16 C3
Hipswell Highway CV2 62 B2
Hipton Hill WR11 127 B3
Hiron Croft CV3 77 E4
Hiron The CV3 77 E4
Hiron Way CV34 108 A4
Hirst Cl CV23 82 A3
Hitchman Mews CV31 110 A3
Hitchman Rd CV31 110 A3
Hithersand Cl CV35 121 F4
Hoarestone Ave CV11 40 A4
Hob La Balsall Common CV7 74 C2
Burton Green CV8 75 D2
Knowle B92 73 D4
Hob Lane CE Fst Sch CV12 39 E2
Hobbins The CV36 149 F3
Hobley Cl CV22 99 E4
Hockett St CV3 77 E4
Hocking Rd CV2 62 C2
Hockley Cl CV23 116 F5
Hockley Heath Prim Sch
B94 88 B3
Hockley La Coventry CV5 59 E3
Ettington CV37 131 B3
Hockley Rd Shrewley CV35 114 C6
Tamworth B77 9 F3
Hoden La WR11 128 B3
Hodge La B77 4 A3
Hodgett's La Berkswell CV7 74 C4
Coventry CV7 75 D3
Hodgson Rd CV37 144 C3
Hodnell Cl B36 22 B1
Hodnell Dr CV33 147 E2
Hodnet Cl CV8 93 D3
Hogarth Cl CV12 39 D2
Hogarth Rd CV37 144 B1
Hogg End OX17 134 F3
Hoggrills End La B46 25 D2
Holbeche Cres CV7 36 C2
Holbeche Rd Knowle B93 72 A4
Sutton Coldfield B75 13 D3
Holbein Cl CV12 39 D2
Holborn Ave CV6 49 E1
Holbrook Ave CV21 83 D2
Holbrook La CV6 49 E1
Holbrook Park Est CV6 61 E4
Holbrook Prim Sch CV6 49 F1
Holbrook Rd
Long Lawford CV23 82 A3
Stratford-u-A CV37 144 B2
Holbrook Way CV6 49 E1
Holcot Leys CV22 100 A4
Holder Cl B50 148 B3
Hole House La B94 88 C1
Holioak Dr CV34 109 D3
Holland Ave B93 72 A4
Holland Cl B50 148 B2
Holland Rd CV6 61 D3
Hollberry Cl B98 112 A6
Hollick Cres CV7 37 D4
Hollicombe Terr CV2 62 B4
Hollies Inf Sch The CV10 28 C3
Hollies Rd B78 11 D4
Hollies The CV23 67 F1
Hollin Brow Cl B93 72 A2
Hollings Gr B91 71 D4
Hollington Way B90 71 E4
Hollinwell Cl CV11 40 B4
Hollis La CV8 92 C4
Hollis Rd CV3 62 A1
Hollow Cres CV6 61 D3
Hollow Way CV23 125 C8
Holloway Field CV6 61 D3
Holloway Hill OX15 138 A1
Holloway La OX15 138 A1
Holloway The
Mollington OX17 134 A2
Priors Marston CV23 125 E4
Warwick CV34 108 B3
Hollowell Way CV21 83 E4
Holly Bank Est CV9 3 D1
Holly Cl LE10 31 F3
Holly Dr Hollywood B47 69 D4
Hurley CV9 16 B2
Holly Farm Bsns Pk CV8 91 D4
Holly Gr
Church Lawford CV23 81 D3
Coventry CV4 60 A1
Holly La Atherstone CV9 12 B1
Balsall Common CV7 74 A2
Portway B48 85 F3
Wishaw B76 13 E2
Holly Lane Ind Est CV9 12 B1
Holly Lodge CV35 146 B2
Holly St CV32 106 A1
Holly Stitches Rd CV10 28 C3
Holly Tree Wlk LE17 43 F3
Holly Wlk Baginton CV8 77 F1
Nuneaton CV11 29 F1
Royal Leamington Spa CV32 106 A1
Stratford-u-A CV37 144 B2
Hollyberry Ave B91 71 D4
Hollybush La Coventry CV6 50 A2
Priors Marston CV23 125 E4
Hollybush Rd OX15 142 D4
Hollyfast La CV7 48 B2
Hollyfast Prim Sch CV6 60 C4
Hollyfast Rd CV6 60 C3
Hollyhurst B46 23 E1
Hollyland B46 24 C1
Hollywell Rd B93 72 A3
Hollywood La B47 69 D4
Holman Way CV11 29 E2
Holmcroft CV2 62 C4
Holme Cl CV21 83 E3
Holme Way CV23 101 E1
Holmes Dr CV5 59 E3
Holmes Rd CV31 110 A2
Holmewood Cl CV8 93 D3
Holmfield Rd CV2 62 A2
Holmsdale Rd CV6 61 F4
Holsworthy Cl CV11 29 F3
Holt Ave CV33 122 E8
Holt Gdns B80 103 F1
Holt Leys CV33 147 E2
Holt Rd Hinckley LE10 31 F3
Studley B80 103 F1
Holt The Mollington OX17 133 F2
Royal Leamington Spa CV32 106 A2
Holte Rd CV9 18 B4
Holtom St CV37 144 C1
Holwick B77 10 A4
Holy Cross RC Jun &
Inf Sch B76 13 D2
Holy Family RC Prim Sch
CV6 49 D2
Holyhead Rd CV5 60 C3
Holyoak Cl Bedworth CV12 38 C1
Rugby CV22 99 E4
Holywell Cl CV4 59 E1
Holywell Rd CV33 147 D2
Home Cl Bubbenhall CV8 95 E3
Staverton NN11 126 E8
Home Farm CV35 104 C3
Home Farm Cl CV9 19 D4
Home Farm Cres CV31 110 A2
Home Furlong CV35 146 B1
Home Mdw CV35 113 F3
Home Park Rd CV11 29 E2
Homefield La CV22 99 F2
Homefield Sch CV22 99 F2
Homeward Way CV3 63 D1
Honeybourne Cl CV5 60 A2
Honeybourne Rd B50 148 C2
Honeyfield Rd CV1 61 E3
Honeysuckle Cl CV23 83 E4
Honeysuckle Dr CV2 50 A1
Honiley Rd Honiley CV8 91 D3
Meer End CV8 74 A1
Honiley Way CV2 50 B1
Honington Hall CV36 137 A5
Honiton Rd CV2 62 B3
Honiwell Cl CV33 123 E6
Hoo La GL55 135 A2
Hood St CV1 61 F2
Hood's Way CV22 82 B1
Hook Norton CE Sch
OX15 142 D4
Hook Norton Rd OX15 142 D8
Hoopers La B96 102 C1
Hope Cl CV7 49 D4
Hope St CV1 61 D1
Hopedale Cl CV2 62 C2
Hopkins Field CV37 129 B3
Hopkins Prec The B49 143 E2
Hopkins Rd CV6 61 D2
Hopper's La CV35 146 B2
Hopton Cl CV5 60 A2
Hopton Crofts CV32 105 E1
Horley Path Rd OX15 139 D5
Hornbeam B77 4 A2
Hornbeam Dr CV4 59 E1
Hornbeam Gr CV31 110 B3
Hornchurch Cl CV1 151 B1
Horndean Cl CV6 61 F4
Horne Cl CV21 101 D4
Horninghold Cl CV3 78 C4
Hornsey Cl CV2 62 C4
Horse Shoe Rd CV6 50 A2
Horsefair CV36 149 F3
Horsefair The 4 LE10 31 E4
Horsepool LE10 32 A3
Horsewell CV33 147 D2
Horsfall Rd B75 13 D3
Horsford Rd CV3 77 F3
Horsham Cl OX16 139 F5
Horton Cl B49 143 E3
Horton Cres CV22 83 D1
Horton Gr B90 71 D3
Hosiery St CV12 39 E1
Hoskyn Cl CV21 100 C4
Hospital La CV12 38 A1
Hospital of St Cross CV22 83 D1
Hospl Rd (West St) GL56 140 A3
Hotchkiss Cl CV35 146 B1
Hotchkiss Way CV3 79 D4
Hothorpe Cl CV3 62 C1
Houldsworth Cres CV6 49 E2
Houndsfield Cl B47 69 E3
Houndsfield Gr B47 69 D3
Houndsfield La B47 69 E3
Houston Rd CV21 83 E3
Houting B77 9 E3
Hove Ave CV5 59 F2
Hovelands Cl CV2 62 B4
Howard Cl Bidford-on-A B50 148 B2
Coventry CV5 59 F2
Dunchurch CV22 99 E2
Howard Rd Nuneaton CV10 29 D2
Redditch B98 103 E4
Howard St CV1 151 C4
Howard Wlk CV31 109 E4
Howat Rd CV7 48 C4
Howcombe La CV23 125 C7
Howcotte Gn CV4 75 F4
Howe Green La CV7 37 E2
Howells Cl CV12 38 B1
Howes Croft B35 22 A1
Howes La CV3 77 E2
Howes Prim Sch CV3 77 F3
Howkins Rd CV21 83 E3
Howlette Rd CV4 59 F1
Hoylake B77 4 A2
Hoylake Cl CV11 30 A1
Huckson Rd CV33 124 B4
Huddisdon Cl 12 CV34 104 C1
Hudson Ave B46 33 F3
Hudson Rd CV22 82 C1
Hugh Rd CV3 62 A1
Hughes Cl Harvington WR11 127 D4
Warwick CV34 104 B1
Whitnash CV31 110 A1
Hughes Hill CV35 114 B6

Hughes La WR11 ... 127 D4
Hulme Cl CV3 ... 63 D1
Humber Ave Coventry CV1 ... 61 F1
Sutton Coldfield B76 ... 22 A4
Humber Cl NN11 ... 117 F2
Humber Gr B36 ... 22 C1
Humber Rd CV3 ... 78 A4
Humber Wlk OX16 ... 139 F4
Humberstone Rd 3 CV6 ... 61 D3
Humphrey Burton's Rd CV3 77 E4
Humphrey-Davy Rd CV12 ... 49 E4
Humphris St CV34 ... 109 D4
Hungerfield Rd B36 ... 22 B1
Hunningham Gr 6 B91 ... 71 D4
Hunscote La CV35 ... 121 F1
Hunt Cl CV35 ... 114 F3
Hunt End La B97 ... 102 B3
Hunt Hall La CV37 ... 129 A6
Hunt La CV9 ... 19 D4
Hunt Paddocks CV8 ... 92 C1
Hunt Terr CV4 ... 76 A4
Hunter Bvd LE17 ... 55 D3
Hunter St CV21 ... 83 E2
Hunter Terr CV5 ... 76 B4
Hunters Cl CV3 ... 63 D1
Hunters La
Fenny Drayton CV13 ... 20 A3
Rugby CV21 ... 83 D3
Hunters Lane Ind Est CV21 . 83 D3
Hunters Pk CV9 ... 11 E1
Hunters Wlk CV9 ... 19 D4
Huntingdon Rd CV5 ... 77 D4
Huntingdon Way CV10 ... 28 C2
Hunts Rd CV37 ... 145 E1
Hurdlers La CV37 ... 121 B6
Hurlbutt Rd CV34 ... 109 E2
Hurley Cl CV32 ... 106 A1
Hurley Comm CV9 ... 16 B3
Hurley La B46 ... 25 F3
Hurley Prim Sch CV9 ... 16 B2
Hurn Way CV6 ... 50 A2
Hurst Green Rd
Bentley Heath B93 ... 71 F2
Minworth B76 ... 22 B3
Hurst Rd Bedworth CV12 ... 39 D2
Coventry CV6 ... 50 A2
Hinckley LE10 ... 31 E4
Southam CV33 ... 147 D2
Hurst The B47 ... 69 D3
Husbandmans Cl CV36 ... 149 F3
Hyacinth Way LE10 ... 31 E3
Hyde Pl CV32 ... 109 F4
Hyde Rd Coventry CV2 ... 62 C2
Kenilworth CV8 ... 93 D3
Hydes La LE10 ... 30 C2

Ibex Cl CV3 ... 62 C1
Ibstock Rd CV6 ... 50 A3
Icknield Cl B50 ... 148 C2
Icknield Ct B50 ... 148 C2
Icknield Row B49 ... 143 D2
Icknield St
Bidford-on-A B50 ... 148 C2
Portway B48 ... 85 D3
Icknield Street Dr B98 ... 103 E4
Iden Rd CV1 ... 61 F2
Idlicote Rd CV36 ... 137 B8
Ilam Pk CV8 ... 93 E3
Ilex Ct CV34 ... 109 D4
Ilford Cl CV12 ... 39 D2
Ilford Dr CV3 ... 77 D3
Ilfracombe Gr CV3 ... 77 D3
Illshaw Cl B98 ... 112 A6
Illshaw Heath Rd B94 ... 70 B1
Ilmer Cl CV21 ... 83 F4
Ilmington Cl CV3 ... 77 D3
Ilmington Prim Sch CV36 . 136 A6
Ilmington Rd
Ilmington CV36 ... 136 D7
Tredington CV36 ... 136 E6
Ilminster Cl LE10 ... 32 A4
Imperial Rise B46 ... 23 F1
Inca Cl CV3 ... 78 C4
Inchbrook Rd CV8 ... 93 E4
Inchford Ave CV34 ... 104 C1
Inchford Cl CV11 ... 29 F1
Ingleton Cl CV11 ... 30 A1
Inglewood Cl CV32 ... 106 A2
Ingon La CV37 ... 121 B5
Ingram Pit La B77 ... 4 A3
Ingram Rd CV5 ... 76 B4
Innace Park Small Ind Units
CV9 ... 12 B1
Innage Cl CV31 ... 110 A4
Innage Terr CV9 ... 18 B4
Innage The B47 ... 69 D3
Innis Rd CV5 ... 76 C4
Innisfree House Sch B47 ... 69 E2
Innsworth Dr B35 ... 22 A2
Instone Rd CV6 ... 49 D1
International Dr B26 ... 44 B2
Inveraray Cl CV8 ... 93 E2
Inverlea Ct GL55 ... 135 B6
Inverness Cl CV5 ... 60 A2
Invicta Rd CV3 ... 78 C4
Ipsley Fst Sch B98 ... 102 C4
Ipswich Wlk B37 ... 33 D1
Irelands La B95 ... 113 D7
Ireton Cl CV4 ... 59 E1
Iris Cl LE10 ... 31 F3
Ironmonger Row CV1 ... 151 B3
Ironstone Hollow OX15 ... 142 E4
Irving Rd CV1 ... 61 F1
Isis Gr B36 ... 33 D4
Islington Cres CV9 ... 10 B1
Ivanhoe Ave CV11 ... 29 F1
Ivor Rd Atherstone CV9 ... 18 C4
Coventry CV6 ... 49 F1
Ivy Cl CV13 ... 21 E4
Ivy Farm La CV4 ... 76 B3
Ivy La Ettington CV37 ... 131 A3
Harbury CV33 ... 123 F6
Mollington OX17 ... 134 A2
Ivy Lodge Cl B37 ... 44 A4
Ivybridge Rd CV3 ... 77 E3
Ivycroft Rd B79 ... 5 F2
Ivyhouse Wlk B77 ... 9 F3
Izod's Cl GL55 ... 135 A1

Jack O'Watton Bsns Pk
B46 ... 23 E2
Jack Thomson Croft WR11 127 F6
Jackdaw Dr B36 ... 33 D4
Jacker's Rd CV2 ... 50 A2
Jacklin Dr CV3 ... 77 E2
Jacknell Rd LE10 ... 30 B4
Jackson Cl
Hampton Magna CV35 ... 114 F3
Keresley CV7 ... 49 D4
Jackson Rd Coventry CV6 ... 49 E1
Rugby CV21 ... 84 A1
Jackson Wlk B35 ... 22 A1
Jacobean La B93 ... 56 A1
Jacox Cres CV8 ... 93 E3
Jade Cl CV1 ... 151 D4
James Dawson Dr CV5 ... 59 D4
James Galloway Cl CV3 ... 78 C4
James Green Rd CV4 ... 59 F1
James Rd B46 ... 33 F4
James St Arley CV7 ... 37 D4
Nuneaton CV11 ... 29 D3
Rugby CV21 ... 83 D2
James Watt Cl NN11 ... 117 F2
Jamescroft CV3 ... 78 C3
Jaques Cl B46 ... 23 D1
Jardine Cres CV4 ... 59 F1
Jasmine Gr Coventry CV3 ... 78 B4
Royal Leamington Spa CV32 106 A1
Jasmine Rd B77 ... 4 A2
Jays Cl B98 ... 112 A6
Jean St CV9 ... 11 E1
Jedburgh Gr CV3 ... 77 D2
Jeff's Cl OX15 ... 137 F2
Jeffrey Cl CV12 ... 49 E4
Jeliff St CV4 ... 59 F1
Jenkins Ave CV5 ... 59 F2
Jenkins Rd CV21 ... 84 A1
Jenner St CV1 ... 151 C4
Jenton Rd CV31 ... 110 A3
Jephcott Cl B49 ... 143 D2
Jersey Croft B36 ... 33 D3
Jervis Rd B77 ... 9 F3
Jesmond Rd CV1 ... 61 F2
Jesson Rd B75 ... 13 D3
Jill La B96 ... 103 D1
Jim Forrest Cl 4 CV3 ... 78 C4
Joan Ward St CV3 ... 77 E4
Joan's Cl 20 CV31 ... 110 B3
Joanna Dr CV3 ... 77 E2
Job's La CV4 ... 60 A1
Jodrell St CV11 ... 29 D3
Joe Williams Cl 7 CV3 ... 78 C4
John Grace St CV3 ... 77 E4
John Gulson Prim Sch CV1 61 E3
John Knight Rd CV12 ... 39 D3
John McGuire Cres CV3 ... 78 C4
John Nash Sq CV8 ... 92 C2
John Nichols St LE10 ... 31 D4
John O'Gaunt Rd CV8 ... 92 C2
John Rous Ave CV4 ... 76 A4
John Shelton Prim Sch
CV6 ... 49 E2
John Simpson Cl CV8 ... 80 A2
John St Bedworth CV12 ... 39 D1
Nuneaton, Coton CV11 ... 29 E1
Nuneaton, Stockingford CV10 . 28 C2
Royal Leamington Spa CV32 . 109 F4
Stratford-u-A CV37 ... 145 D2
John Taylor Way CV35 ... 122 E3
John Thwaites Cl CV22 ... 83 D1
John's Cl LE10 ... 31 E3
Johndory B77 ... 9 E3
Johns Cl B80 ... 103 E2
Johnson Ave CV22 ... 82 C1
Johnson Pl B95 ... 113 B5
Johnson Rd Bedworth CV12 .. 39 E2
Coventry CV6 ... 62 A4
Johnson St CV9 ... 10 B1
Jolyffe Park Rd CV37 ... 145 D2
Jon Baker Ct LE10 ... 31 F4
Jonathan Rd CV2 ... 62 C4
Jones Rd CV7 ... 39 D1
Jones Wood Cl B76 ... 22 A4
Jonkel Ave B77 ... 10 A3
Jordan Cl CV8 ... 93 D1
Jordan Well CV1 ... 151 C2
Jordans Cl B97 ... 102 B3
Jordans The CV5 ... 60 B2
Joseph Cash Prim Sch
CV6 ... 61 E4
Joseph Creighton Cl CV3 ... 78 C4
Joseph Luckman Rd CV12 ... 39 D2
Joseph Way CV37 ... 144 C3
Joyce Pool 15 CV34 ... 108 C4
Jubilee Ave
Lower Shuckburgh NN11 ... 116 E1
Redditch B97 ... 102 B4
Jubilee Cl B50 ... 148 C3
Jubilee Cres CV6 ... 61 D4
Jubilee Ct B78 ... 15 E3
Jubilee St CV21 ... 82 C2
Jubilee Terr CV12 ... 39 D2
Judd Cl CV12 ... 38 C2
Judds La CV6 ... 49 F2
Judge Cl CV23 ... 82 A3
Juggins La B94 ... 86 A4
Julian Cl CV2 ... 62 C4
Juliet Cl CV11 ... 30 A1
Juliet Dr CV22 ... 99 E3
Julius Dr B46 ... 23 F1
Junction St CV1 ... 151 A2
Junewood Cl CV21 ... 83 E4
Juniper B77 ... 4 A2
Juniper Dr Coventry CV5 ... 59 F3
Sutton Coldfield B76 ... 22 A4
Jury St CV34 ... 108 C3
Justins Ave CV37 ... 144 C3

Kanzan Rd CV2 ... 50 A2
Kareen Gr CV3 ... 79 E4
Karen Cl CV10 ... 28 C4
Karlingford Cl CV5 ... 76 B4
Kathleen Ave CV12 ... 38 C1
Kay Cl CV21 ... 83 E4
Kaysbrook Dr CV23 ... 97 D3
Keats Cl CV10 ... 28 A2
Keats Rd Coventry CV2 ... 62 B1
Stratford-u-A CV37 ... 145 D1
Keble Rd GL56 ... 140 A2
Kebull Gn CV4 ... 75 F4
Keeling Rd CV8 ... 93 D3
Keenan Dr CV12 ... 38 B1
Keepers Cl B46 ... 34 A2
Keepers Wlk CV12 ... 38 B1
Keetley Cl CV36 ... 149 F2
Kegworth Cl CV6 ... 50 A2
Keir Cl CV32 ... 106 A1
Keith Rd CV32 ... 106 A2
Kele Rd CV4 ... 76 A4
Kelmscote Rd CV6 ... 60 C4
Kelsey Cl CV11 ... 29 F2
Kelsey La CV7 ... 74 B3
Kelsey's Cl CV8 ... 79 F2
Kelsull Croft B37 ... 33 D1
Kelvin Ave CV2 ... 62 B3
Kelvin Rd CV32 ... 106 B3
Kelway CV3 ... 63 D1
Kem St CV11 ... 29 F1
Kemble Dr B35 ... 22 A2
Kemerton Way B90 ... 70 C3
Kemp Cl CV34 ... 109 D4
Kempley Ave CV2 ... 62 B1
Kemps Green Rd
Balsall Common CV7 ... 74 A3
Tanworth-in-A B94 ... 88 A1
Kempsey Cl B98 ... 103 D4
Kempsford Cl B98 ... 102 C3
Kempton Cres CV32 ... 106 B2
Kendal Ave Coleshill B46 ... 33 F4
Royal Leamington Spa CV32 . 105 E1
Kendal Cl Nuneaton CV11 ... 30 A3
Redditch B98 ... 112 A6
Kendal Rise CV5 ... 60 B2
Kendall Ave CV37 ... 145 D2
Kendon Ave CV6 ... 60 C3
Kendrick Cl CV6 ... 50 A2
Kenhill Rd OX15 ... 138 F5
Kenilworth Castle CV8 ... 92 B3
Kenilworth Cl B97 ... 102 B3
Kenilworth Ct CV3 ... 77 E4
Kenilworth Dr CV11 ... 29 D2
Kenilworth Rd
Balsall Common CV7, CV8 ... 74 B2
Coventry CV3 ... 76 C2
Cubbington CV32 ... 106 B3
Hampton in A B92 ... 57 F3
Kenilworth CV8 ... 93 E4
Knowle B93 ... 72 C3
Lighthorne Heath CV35 ... 123 D2
Meriden CV7 ... 45 E1
Royal Leamington Spa CV32 . 105 F3
Kenilworth Sch CV8 ... 93 E3
Kenilworth Sch Castle
Sixth Form Ctr CV8 ... 92 C1
Kenilworth St 12 CV32 ... 105 F1
Kenilworth Way OX16 ... 139 F3
Kennan Ave CV31 ... 109 F3
Kennedy Dr CV22 ... 82 B1
Kennedy Sq 11 CV32 ... 106 A1
Kennel La CV9 ... 19 D4
Kennet Cl CV2 ... 62 B4
Kenning Cl CV23 ... 115 C4
Kenpas Highway CV3 ... 77 D3
Kensington Rd CV5 ... 61 D1
Kent Cl CV3 ... 77 F3
Kent Rd CV33 ... 132 F5
Kent The CV21 ... 84 A1
Kenthurst Cl CV5 ... 59 E2
Kentmere Cl CV2 ... 50 C1
Kents La CV37 ... 131 A4
Kenway B47 ... 69 D4
Kenwyn Gdns CV7 ... 50 A4
Keppel Cl CV22 ... 82 B1
Keppel St CV1 ... 61 F3
Keresley Brook Rd CV6 ... 49 D1
Keresley Cl CV6 ... 49 D1
Keresley Grange Prim Sch
CV6 ... 48 C1
Keresley Green Rd CV6 ... 48 C1
Keresley Newland
Comb Sch CV7 ... 48 C4
Keresley Rd CV6 ... 61 D4
Kerns Terr CV37 ... 145 D2
Kerr Way GL56 ... 140 C3
Kerria Ctr B77 ... 4 A2
Kerria Rd B77 ... 4 A2
Kerrils Way CV3 ... 63 D1
Kerswell Dr B90 ... 71 D3
Kestrel B77 ... 10 A3
Kestrel Cl Hinckley LE10 ... 31 F3
Stratford-u-A CV37 ... 145 D3
Kestrel Croft 2 CV3 ... 78 C4
Keswick Cl CV11 ... 30 A3
Keswick Dr CV21 ... 83 E4
Keswick Gn CV32 ... 105 E1
Keswick Wlk CV2 ... 62 C2
Kettlebrook Rd B90 ... 71 E3
Kettlewell Cl CV34 ... 104 C1
Keviliok St CV3 ... 77 E3
Kew Cl CV8 ... 93 E3
Kew Rd CV21 ... 83 D2
Keys Dr CV22 ... 82 B1
Keys Hill CV9 ... 11 E1
Keys La CV23 ... 125 F4
Keyte Rd CV36 ... 136 B6
Keyte's La CV35 ... 122 B7
Keytes Acre GL55 ... 135 E3
Kiblers La CV35 ... 131 D2
Kielder Dr CV10 ... 28 C1
Kiftsgate Court Gardens
GL55 ... 135 C6
Kilburn Dr CV5 ... 60 C2
Kilby Gn LE10 ... 31 F3
Kilby Gr CV31 ... 110 B3
Kilbye Cl B77 ... 9 F3
Kildale Cl CV1 ... 151 D3
Kildwick Way 5 CV34 ... 104 C1
Killworth Rd CV21 ... 101 D4
Kiln Cl
Royal Leamington Spa CV32 106 A1
Studley B80 ... 103 E2
Kiln Way Polesworth B78 ... 4 C1
Shilton CV12 ... 51 F4
Kilnsey Gr CV34 ... 104 C1
Kilsby Gr B91 ... 71 E4
Kilsby La CV21 ... 101 E4
Kilsby Rd CV23 ... 101 E1
Kimbell Cl CV33 ... 124 B1
Kimberley B77 ... 9 F4
Kimberley Cl CV5 ... 59 F2
Kimberley Rd Baginton CV8 .. 77 F1
Bedworth CV12 ... 39 E2
Rugby CV21 ... 83 D2
Kimberley Wlk B76 ... 22 B3
Kimble Cl CV5 ... 60 A2
Kinchford Cl B91 ... 71 D4
Kineton CE Jun & Inf Sch
CV35 ... 132 B6
Kineton High Sch CV35 ... 132 C6
Kineton La B94 ... 71 D1
Kineton Rd Coventry CV2 ... 62 B3
Kenilworth CV8 ... 93 E2
Southam CV33 ... 147 D2
Wellesbourne CV35 ... 146 C1
Kineton Road Ind Est
CV33 ... 147 D2
King Edward Rd
Coventry CV1 ... 61 F2
Nuneaton CV11 ... 29 E2
Rugby CV21 ... 83 D2
King Edward VI Coll CV11 ... 29 E2
King Edward VI Gram Sch
CV37 ... 145 D1
King George's Ave
Bedworth CV12 ... 39 D3
Coventry CV6 ... 49 F1
King George's Ct CV23 ... 82 A3
King George's Way LE10 ... 31 D4
King Henry VIII Sch CV1 ... 151 A1
King John's La CV35 ... 132 E2
King John's Rd CV35 ... 132 B6
King Richard St CV2 ... 61 F2
King St Bedworth CV12 ... 39 E1
Royal Leamington Spa CV32 106 A1
Rugby CV21 ... 83 D2
King William St CV1 ... 61 F2
King's Hill La CV8 ... 77 D1
King's La Broom B50 ... 148 A3
Newton Regis B79 ... 2 B2
Norton WR11 ... 127 B2
Snitterfield CV37 ... 121 B6
Stratford-u-A CV37 ... 144 C4
Kingcomb La GL55 ... 135 A2
Kingfield Rd CV1, CV6 ... 61 E4
Kingfisher B77 ... 10 A3
Kingfisher Ave CV10 ... 28 B3
Kingfisher Dr B36 ... 33 D4
Kingfisher Way B49 ... 143 D3
Kingham Cl B98 ... 112 A6
Kingham Hill Sch OX7 ... 150 A1
Kingland Dr CV32 ... 105 E1
Kingley Ave B49 ... 143 E3
Kings Ave CV9 ... 18 C4
Kings Coughton La B49 ... 143 D3
Kings Gdns CV12 ... 39 E1
Kings Gr CV2 ... 62 A2
Kings High Sch for Girls
CV34 ... 108 C4
Kings Newnham La CV23 ... 80 C4
Kings Newnham Rd CV23 ... 81 D3
Kingsbridge Rd CV10 ... 29 E3
Kingsbrook Dr B91 ... 71 D4
Kingsbury Bsns Pk B76 ... 22 C3
Kingsbury Cl B76 ... 22 B3
Kingsbury Fst Sch B78 ... 15 E3
Kingsbury Mid Sch B78 ... 15 E3
Kingsbury Rd Coventry CV6 ... 60 C3
Curdworth B76 ... 23 D4
Minworth B76 ... 22 B3
Sutton Coldfield B35, B76 ... 22 A3
Kingsbury Sch B78 ... 15 E3
Kingsbury Water Park B76 . 15 D3
Kingscote Gr CV3 ... 77 D2
Kingscote Rd B93 ... 71 F1
Kingsfield Ind Est CV1 ... 61 E3
Kingsford Cl B36 ... 22 B1
Kingshurst CV31 ... 110 C3
Kingshurst Inf Sch B37 ... 33 D3
Kingshurst Jun Sch B37 ... 33 D3
Kingsland Ave CV5 ... 60 C1
Kingsland Dr B93 ... 71 F2
Kingsley Ave CV21 ... 83 F1
Kingsley Cres CV12 ... 40 A2
Kingsley Orch CV21 ... 83 F1
Kingsley Prep Sch B93 ... 72 A2
Kingsley Rd 12 CV33 ... 122 F8
Kingsley Sch The CV32 ... 105 F1
Kingsley Terr CV2 ... 62 C4
Kingsley Wlk CV2 ... 62 C4
Kingston La CV35 ... 113 E3
Kingston Mews CV31 ... 110 B3
Kingston Rd CV5 ... 60 C1
Kingsway Coventry CV2 ... 62 A2
Kingsbury B78 ... 15 E3
Lighthorne Heath CV35 ... 123 D2
Nuneaton CV11 ... 29 D2
Royal Leamington Spa CV31 . 109 F3
Rugby CV22 ... 83 D1
Kingswood Ave CV7 ... 48 A4
Kingswood Cl Coventry CV6 .. 49 E1
Lapworth B94 ... 89 F3
Kingswood Rd CV10 ... 28 A2
Kington Rise CV35 ... 113 E2
Kinman Way CV21 ... 83 E3
Kinross Cl CV10 ... 28 C1
Kinross Rd CV32 ... 106 A2
Kinsall Gn B77 ... 10 B3
Kinsham Dr B91 ... 71 D4
Kintyre The CV2 ... 63 D4
Kinver Cl CV2 ... 50 C1
Kinver Croft B76 ... 22 A4
Kinwalsey La CV7 ... 46 C3
Kinwarton Dovecote B49 .. 143 F3
Kinwarton Farm Rd B49 ... 143 E3
Kinwarton Rd B49 ... 143 E2
Kinwarton Workshops
B49 ... 143 E3
Kipling Ave CV34 ... 108 B2
Kipling Cl CV10 ... 28 A3
Kipling Rd Coventry CV6 ... 61 D4
Stratford-u-A CV37 ... 130 A8
Kirby Ave CV34 ... 104 C1
Kirby Cl Brandon CV8 ... 79 F3
Coventry CV1 ... 61 E3
Kirby Cnr CV4 ... 76 A3
Kirby Corner Rd CV4 ... 76 A3
Kirby Rd Coventry CV5 ... 60 C1
Rugby CV21 ... 83 F1
Kirigushi Rd CV35 ... 132 E5
Kirkby Cl CV21 ... 83 F3
Kirkdale Ave CV6 ... 49 E2
Kirkland Way B78 ... 8 A4
Kirkstone CV21 ... 83 E4
Kirkstone Rd CV12 ... 39 D1
Kirkstone Wlk CV11 ... 30 A3
Kirkwall CV33 ... 147 D2
Kirtland Cl CV9 ... 3 D1
Kirton Cl Coventry CV6 ... 48 C1
Whitnash CV31 ... 110 A2
Kissing Tree La CV37 ... 121 D3
Kitchener Rd CV6 ... 61 F4
Kitebrook Cl 9 B90 ... 71 D4
Kites Cl CV34 ... 104 C1
Kites Nest La CV35 ... 114 E8
Kittermaster Rd CV7 ... 46 B1
Kitwood Ave B78 ... 10 C3
Kixley La B93 ... 72 B3
Klevedon Cl CV11 ... 30 A1
Knebley Cres CV10 ... 29 E1
Knibbs Sh Ctr The 13
CV34 ... 108 C4
Knight Ave CV1 ... 61 F1
Knightcote Dr
Royal Leamington Spa CV32 . 109 F4
Solihull B91 ... 71 D4
Knightley Cl CV32 ... 106 C3
Knightlow Ave CV3 ... 78 B3
Knightlow CE Mid Sch
CV23 ... 96 C4
Knightlow Cl CV8 ... 93 E2
Knightlow Way CV33 ... 123 F6
Knights Cl LE10 ... 31 E2
Knights Ct LE10 ... 30 C4
Knights La CV37 ... 145 F2
Knightsbridge Ave CV12 ... 39 E2
Knob Hill CV23 ... 96 C3
Knoll Croft
Cheswick Green B90 ... 70 B2
Coventry CV3 ... 77 E3
Knoll Dr Coventry CV3 ... 77 E3
Warwick CV34 ... 104 C1
Knottesford Cl B80 ... 103 E2
Knowlands Rd B90 ... 71 D4
Knowle CE Jun & Inf Sch
B93 ... 72 B3
Knowle Hill Hurley CV9 ... 16 B2
Kenilworth CV8 ... 93 E3
Knowle Rd B92 ... 56 C1
Knowle Wood Rd B93 ... 72 A2
Knowles Ave CV10 ... 28 B2
Knox Cres CV11 ... 29 F4
Kranji Rd CV33 ... 132 F5
Kurtus B77 ... 9 E3
Kyetts Cnr OX17 ... 134 C1
Kynner Way CV3 ... 79 D4
Kyter La B35 ... 22 A1

Laburnum Ave
Coventry CV6 ... 60 C3
Kenilworth CV8 ... 93 D2
Laburnum Cl
Bedworth CV12 ... 38 C1
Hollywood B47 ... 69 D3
Kingsbury B78 ... 15 E3
Laburnum Dr
Sutton Coldfield B76 ... 13 D2
Whitnash CV31 ... 110 A2

Laburnum Gr
Nuneaton CV10 28 B3
Rugby CV22 99 F4
Warwick CV34 105 D1
Lacell Cl CV34 104 C1
Ladbroke By – Pass CV33 124 D5
Ladbroke Pk CV34 104 C1
Ladbroke Rd CV33 124 B4
Ladbrook Cl B98 102 C4
Ladbrook Rd CV5 60 A2
Lady Byron La Knowle B93 71 F4
Knowle,Copt Heath B93 56 A1
Lady Katherine Leveson CE Prim Sch B93 73 D3
Lady La Coventry CV6 49 F2
Earlswood B90, B94 70 A2
Lady Warwick Ave CV12 39 E1
Ladycroft CV32 106 C3
Ladyfields Way CV6 49 D2
Ladygrove Cl B98 103 D4
Ladymead Dr CV6 49 D1
Lair The B78 10 C4
Lake View Rd CV5 60 C2
Lakeland Dr B77 10 A4
Lakes Sta The B94 86 C4
Lakeside CV12 39 D1
Lakeside Dr B90 70 C4
Lakin Ct CV34 108 C4
Lakin Dr CV33 124 A4
Lamb St CV1 151 B3
Lambert Cl B50 148 B3
Lambert Specl Sch CV37 145 D3
Lambeth Cl Birmingham B37 33 D2
Coventry CV2 62 C4
Lambourn Cres CV31 110 B3
Lambourne Cl CV5 60 A2
Lamerton Cl CV2 62 B3
Lamintone Dr CV32 105 E1
Lammas Croft CV31 110 A2
Lammas Ct CV8 80 A2
Lammas Rd CV6 60 C2
Lammas Wlk CV34 108 B4
Lamorna Cl CV11 29 F2
Lamp La CV7 36 C3
Lampitts Gn OX15 139 D4
Lamprey B77 9 E3
Lancaster Cl Atherstone CV9 12 C1
Wellesbourne CV35 146 B1
Lancaster Pl CV8 92 C1
Lancaster Rd Hinckley LE10 31 E4
Rugby CV21 83 D2
Lance Cl LE10 31 E3
Lanchester Dr OX16 139 F4
Lanchester Rd CV6 61 D3
Lanchester Way
Birmingham B36 22 C1
Daventry NN11 117 F2
Lancia Cl CV6 50 A2
Lancing Rd CV12 40 B1
Land La B37 44 A4
Landor Rd Knowle B93 72 A3
Redditch B98 103 D4
Warwick CV34 108 B4
Whitnash CV31 110 A2
Landrail Wlk B36 33 D4
Landsdowne Pl CV21 83 E1
Landseer Cl CV21 84 A1
Lane Cl OX15 139 D6
Lane Croft B76 22 A4
Lane The Burmington CV36 137 A1
Little Compton CV36 141 A6
Laneside CV3 78 C3
Langbank Ave CV3 78 B4
Langcliffe Ave CV34 104 C1
Langcomb Rd B90 70 A4
Langdale Ave CV6 49 E2
Langdale Cl
Royal Leamington Spa CV32 106 B2
Rugby CV21 83 E4
Langdale Dr CV11 30 A3
Langdale Rd LE10 31 D4
Langfield Rd B93 72 A4
Langlands The CV35 121 F4
Langley Croft CV4 60 A1
Langley Dr B35 22 A1
Langley Hall Dr B75 13 D3
Langley Hall Rd B75 13 D3
Langley Heath Dr B76 13 D2
Langley Rd Claverdon CV35 113 E3
Whitnash CV31 110 A2
Langley Sch B75 13 D3
Langley Wlk B37 33 E1
Langlodge Rd CV6 49 D1
Langnor Rd CV2 62 B3
Langton Cl CV3 78 C4
Langton Rd CV21 83 F1
Langwood Cl CV4 76 A4
Lankett The CV33 133 D7
Lansbury Cl CV2 62 C4
Lansdowne Cir CV32 106 A1
Lansdowne Cl CV12 39 D2
Lansdowne Cres
13 Royal Leamington Spa CV32 106 A1
Studley B80 103 E2
Tamworth B77 9 E4
Lansdowne Rd 10
Royal Leamington Spa CV32 106 A1
Studley B80 103 E2
Lansdowne St Coventry CV2 61 F2
Royal Leamington Spa CV32 106 A1
Lant Cl CV7 75 D4
Lapwing B77 10 A3
Lapwing Dr B92 57 D4
Lapworth CE Jun & Inf Sch B94 89 E2
Lapworth Cl B98 102 C4
Lapworth Oaks B94 89 E2
Lapworth Rd CV2 50 B1
Lapworth St B94 89 D1
Lapworth Sta B94 89 E2
Larch Cl Alcester B49 143 D3
Rugby CV22 82 A1
Stratford-u-A CV37 145 D2
Larch Croft B37 33 D1
Larch Gr CV34 105 D1
Larch Tree Ave CV4 60 A1
Larches The Bedworth CV7 50 A4
Kingsbury B78 15 E4
Larchfields CV8 80 A2
Larchwood Rd CV7 39 D1
Larkfield Way CV5 60 A3
Larkin Cl CV12 40 A2
Larkspur Rugby CV23 83 E4
Tamworth B77 9 E2
Latham Rd CV5 61 D1
Latimer Cl CV8 92 C1
Latymer Cl B76 22 A4
Lauderdale Ave CV6 49 E2
Lauderdale Cl CV23 82 A2
Launceston Dr CV11 29 F2
Laurel Ave B78 11 D4
Laurel Cl CV2 50 C1
Laurel Dr Hartshill CV10 28 A4
Rugby CV22 82 A1
Stockton CV23 147 F4
Laurel Gdns CV22 99 F4
Laurels Cres CV7 74 B3
Laurels The Bedworth CV12 38 C1
Kingsbury B78 15 E4
Lavender Ave CV6 60 C3
Lavender Cl CV23 83 F4
Lavender Hall La CV7 58 B1
Lavenham Cl CV11 40 B4
Lawford Cl CV3 62 C1
Lawford Heath Ind Est CV23 98 B4
Lawford Heath La CV23 98 B3
Lawford La CV22 82 A1
Lawford Rd
Royal Leamington Spa CV31 110 A3
Rugby CV21 82 B2
Lawley Cl CV4 60 A1
Lawns The Bedworth CV12 38 B1
Hinckley LE10 31 F4
Lawnsdale Cl B46 33 F4
Lawnswood Hinckley LE10 31 D4
Sutton Coldfield B76 22 A4
Lawrence Dr B76 22 B3
Lawrence Gdns CV8 93 D3
Lawrence Mackie Gdns CV35 146 C2
Lawrence Rd Bedworth CV7 50 A4
Rugby CV21 83 E2
Lawrence Saunders Rd CV6 61 D3
Lawrence Sheriff Sch CV21 83 D2
Lawrence Sherriff St CV22 83 D1
Lawson Ave CV37 145 F2
Lawton Cl LE10 30 C4
Lay Gdns CV31 110 C3
Le Hanche Cl CV7 49 D4
Lea Cl Alcester B49 143 E3
Stratford-u-A CV37 144 A2
Lea Cres CV21 82 B3
Lea Croft Rd B97 102 B3
Lea Green La B47 69 E3
Leacrest Rd CV6 49 D1
Leaf La Coventry CV3 77 E5
Coventry CV3 77 F3
Leafield Cl CV2 62 C4
Leagh Cl CV8 93 D4
Leam Cl CV11 29 F1
Leam Gn CV4 76 B3
Leam Rd
Lighthorne Heath CV35 123 D2
Royal Leamington Spa CV31 109 E4
Leam St CV31 110 A4
Leam Terr CV31 110 A4
Leam The NN11 117 F1
Leamington Hastings CE Inf Sch CV23 116 B6
Leamington Rd Coventry CV3 77 E3
Kenilworth CV8 93 D1
Long Itchington CV23 115 C4
Princethorpe CV23 96 B1
Ryton-on-D CV23 96 A4
Southam CV33 124 C8
Leamington Spa Sta CV31 109 F4
Lear Gr CV34 109 F2
Leas Cl CV12 39 D2
Leasowe's Ave CV3 76 C2
Leasowes Children's Farm The B94 87 E1
Leather St CV23 115 D4
Leathermill La CV10 19 E2
Leaward Cl CV10 28 C1
Ledbrook Rd CV32 106 C3
Ledbury Rd CV31 110 B3
Ledbury Way B76 22 A4
Lee Cl CV34 104 C1
Lee Rd Hollywood B47 69 D4
Royal Leamington Spa CV31 109 F3
Lee The CV5 60 B2
Leeder Cl CV6 49 E1
Leek Wootton CE Fst Sch CV35 105 D3
Leeming Cl CV4 76 B3
Leicester Cswy CV1 61 E3
Leicester Ct CV12 40 B1
Leicester La Cubbington CV32 94 C1
Royal Leamington Spa CV32 106 B3
Leicester Rd Atherstone CV9 12 C1
Bedworth CV12 39 D2
Nuneaton CV11 29 E3
Rugby CV21 83 D4
Shilton CV7 51 F3
Leicester Row CV1 151 B4
Leicester St Bedworth CV12 39 D2
Bulkington CV12 40 B1
Royal Leamington Spa CV32 106 A1
Leigh Ave CV3 77 E2
Leigh CE Prim Sch CV4 75 E4
Leigh Cres CV23 115 D3
Leigh Rd Rugby CV21 82 C4
Sutton Coldfield B75 13 D3
Leigh St 3 CV1 61 F2
Leighton Cl Coventry CV4 76 B1
Royal Leamington Spa CV32 106 B2
Leisure Wlk B77 9 F3
Lennon Cl CV21 101 E4
Lennox Cl CV3 78 C3
Lenton's La CV2 50 C2
Leofric St CV6 61 D3
Leopold Rd CV1 61 F2
Lesingham Dr CV4 59 F1
Lestock Cl CV22 82 B1
Letchlade Cl CV2 62 B4
Level The OX15 138 F5
Leven Cl LE10 31 D4
Leven Croft B76 22 A4
Leven Way CV2 63 D4
Lever Rd CV21 84 A1
Leveson Cres CV7 74 A3
Levett Rd B77 4 A3
Levy Cl CV21 82 C2
Lewis Ct CV9 18 C3
Lewis Rd Coventry CV1 61 E3
Radford Semele CV31 110 C3
Leyburn Cl Coventry CV6 49 F1
Nuneaton CV11 30 A1
10 Warwick CV34 104 C1
Leycester Pl CV34 108 C3
Leycester Rd CV8 93 D1
Leyes La CV8 93 E3
Leyes The CV23 68 A1
Leyfields Cres CV34 108 B2
Leyland Rd Bulkington CV12 40 A1
Coventry CV5 60 B2
Nuneaton CV11 29 F1
Leyland Specl Sch CV11 29 F1
Leymere Cl CV7 46 B1
Leys Cl Northend CV33 133 B7
Wroxton OX15 139 D4
Leys High Sch The B98 103 E3
Leys La CV7 46 B1
Leys Rd Harvington WR11 127 B5
Rugby CV21 101 E4
Leys The Bidford-on-A B50 148 C3
Halford CV36 137 A8
Salford OX7 150 C3
Upper Boddington NN11 134 E8
Leysbourne GL55 135 B2
Leysfield WR11 127 C4
Leyside CV3 78 C3
Libbards Gate 4 B91 71 E4
Libbards Way B91 71 D4
Liberty Rd B77 9 F3
Liberty Way CV11 29 F2
Library Cl LE10 32 A3
Lichen Gn CV4 76 B3
Lichfield Cl Arley CV7 37 D4
Nuneaton CV11 30 A4
Lichfield Rd Coventry CV3 77 E4
Water Orton B46, B76 23 E2
Wishaw B76 14 A2
Lichfield St B78 9 D4
Liecester Rd LE10 41 F3
Lifford Way CV3 79 D4
Light Hall Sch B90 70 A4
Light La CV1 151 B4
Lighthorne Rd CV35 132 B6
Lightoak Cl B97 102 B3
Lightwood Cl B93 72 A4
Lilac Ave CV6 60 C3
Lilac Cl LE10 31 F3
Lilac Dr CV22 82 A1
Lilac Gr CV34 105 D1
Lilac Rd CV12 39 E3
Lilbourne Rd CV23 84 B3
Lilley Cl CV6 49 E1
Lilley Green Rd B48 85 E3
Lillington Ave CV32 105 F1
Lillington CE Fst Sch CV32 106 A2
Lillington Cl
Royal Leamington Spa CV32 106 A2
Sutton Coldfield B75 13 D2
Lillington Prim Sch CV32 106 A2
Lillington Rd Coventry CV2 50 B1
Royal Leamington Spa CV32 106 A2
Solihull B90 70 A4
Limbrick Ave CV4 60 A1
Limbrick Wood Prim Sch CV4 59 F2
Lime Ave CV32 106 A2
Lime Cl B47 69 D3
Lime Gr
Birmingham, Chemsley Wood B37 33 D1
Coventry CV4 60 A1
Hurley CV9 16 B2
Kenilworth CV8 93 D2
Nuneaton CV10 28 C3
Lime Kiln B78 11 D4
Lime Rd CV33 147 D3
Lime Tree Ave Coventry CV4 60 A1
Rugby CV22 99 D4
Limekiln La B94 70 B1
Limes Ave CV37 144 B1
Limes Coppice CV10 27 F4
Limes The CV12 38 C1
Limestone Hall La CV23 81 D2
Linaker Rd CV3 78 B3
Lincoln Ave CV10 28 A4
Lincoln Cl Warwick CV34 104 C1
Wellesbourne CV35 146 B1
Lincoln Gr B37 33 D1
Lincoln St CV1 151 C4
Lincroft Cres CV5 60 C2
Lindale CV21 83 E4
Linden Ave CV35 146 C2
Linden Cl CV34 104 C1
Linden Lea CV12 39 D2
Lindera B77 4 A2
Lindfield The CV3 78 B4
Lindhurst Dr B94 88 B3
Lindisfarne Dr CV8 93 E2
Lindley Rd Bedworth CV12 38 B1
Coventry CV3 62 A1
Lindridge Cl B98 112 A6
Lindridge Dr B76 22 B3
Lindridge Jun Sch B75 13 D3
Lindridge Rd B75 13 D3
Lindsay Wlk CV33 132 F7
Lindsey Cres CV8 93 D1
Lineholt Cl B98 103 D3
Linen St CV34 108 B3
Linford Wlk CV2 50 C1
Lingard Rd B75 13 D3
Lingwood Dr CV10 28 C2
Links Rd CV6 61 D4
Linkway CV31 109 F3
Linley Rd CV33 147 D3
Linnell Rd CV21 83 F1
Linnet Cl CV3 78 B3
Linstock Way CV6 50 A2
Linthouse Wlk B77 9 F3
Lintly B77 4 A1
Linwood Dr CV2 50 C1
Lion Fields Ave CV5 60 A3
Liskeard Cl CV11 30 A3
Liskeard Rd CV35 132 D3
Lisle Gdns 4 CV35 122 F8
Lister Cres CV9 12 C1
Lister St CV11 29 E2
Little Acre B97 102 B3
Little Brom CV9 11 E1
Little Church St
Coventry CV1 151 C4
Rugby CV21 83 D2
Little Duke St CV11 29 D2
Little Elborow St CV21 83 D2
Little Farm CV3 78 B3
Little Field CV2 62 A3
Little Forge Rd B98 103 E4
Little Gr CV22 83 E1
Little Heath Ind Est CV6 50 A1
Little Lawford La CV21 82 A4
Little London La CV23 68 A1
Little Park St CV1 151 C2
Little Pennington St 3 CV21 82 C2
Little Pittern CV35 132 B6
Little Pk CV33 147 D2
Little South St CV1 61 F2
Little Woods B97 102 C3
Littlemead Rd B90 69 F4
Littleshaw Croft B47 69 E2
Littleshaw La B47 69 E2
Littlethorpe CV3 78 B3
Littleton CE Fst Sch WR11 127 F1
Littleton Cl Kenilworth CV8 93 D4
Sutton Coldfield B76 13 D1
Littleton Croft 6 B91 71 E4
Littlewood Cl 2 B91 71 D4
Littlewood Gn B80 103 E2
Littleworth
Chipping Campden GL55 135 A2
Henley-in-A B95 113 B4
Litton B77 4 B1
Liveridge Cl B93 71 F3
Liveridge Hill B95 113 B7
Livery St CV32 109 F4
Livingstone Ave CV23 81 F2
Livingstone Rd CV6 61 F4
Liza Ct CV21 83 E4
Llewellyn Rd CV31 110 A3
Lloyd Cl
Hampton Magna CV35 114 F3
Norton WR11 127 C2
Nuneaton CV11 29 E1
Lloyd Cres CV2 62 C2
Lloyd Rd CV21 83 E3
Loach Dr CV2 50 A2
Lobelia Cl LE10 31 F3
Lochmore Cl LE10 31 D4
Lochmore Dr LE10 31 D4
Lochmore Way LE10 31 D4
Lock Cl CV37 145 D2
Lock La CV34 108 B4
Locke Cl CV6 49 D1
Lockhart Cl CV8 93 D2
Lockheed Cl CV31 109 F3
Lockhurst La CV6 61 E4
Locking Croft B35 22 A2
Locks The CV21 84 A1
Loder Cl CV4 59 F2
Lodge Cl Atherstone CV9 19 D3
Hinckley LE10 32 A3
Lodge Cres CV34 108 B2
Lodge Croft B93 72 A3
Lodge Green La CV7 46 C1
Lodge Green La N CV7 46 C2
Lodge Rd Coventry CV3 62 A1
Knowle B93 72 A3
Rugby CV21 83 D2
Stratford-u-A CV37 144 C2
Logan Rd CV2 62 C4
Lollard Croft CV3 77 E4
Lomita Cres B77 9 E4
Lomond Cl LE10 31 D4
London End NN11 134 E8
London Rd
Coventry, Cheylesmore CV3 77 F4
Coventry, Willenhall CV3 78 A3
Hinckley LE10 31 F4
Middleton B75, B78 13 E4
Moreton-in-M GL56 140 B3
Ryton-on-D CV8 79 D1
Shipston-on-S CV36 149 F2
Stretton on D CV23 96 C4
Sutton Coldfield B75 7 D2
Willoughby CV23 117 C6
Long Brook La CV7 73 F3
Long Close Ave CV5 60 A3
Long Close Wlk B35 22 A2
Long Furlong CV22 100 A4
Long Hyde Rd WR11 127 F1
Long Itchington CE Prim Sch CV23 115 D4
Long La CV5, CV7 48 B1
Long Lawson Comb Sch CV23 82 A3
Long Marston Rd
Mickleton CV37 135 B8
Pebworth CV37 128 F2
Welford on A CV37 129 B5
Long Shoot The CV11 30 B3
Long St Atherstone CV9 18 B4
Bulkington CV12 40 B1
Dordon B78 11 D3
Longborough Cl B97 102 A3
Longcroft Cl B35 22 A1
Longdon Cl B98 103 D4
Longdon Rd B93 72 A3
Longdown La CV23 117 D7
Longfellow Ave CV34 108 B2
Longfellow Cl B97 102 B4
Longfellow Rd CV2 62 B2
Longfield Rd CV31 110 A3
Longford Cl
Bidford-on-A B50 148 C3
Dorridge B93 72 A2
Longford Park Prim Sch CV6 50 A2
Longford Rd Bedworth CV7 50 A3
Coventry CV6 50 A2
Longford Sq CV6 50 A2
Longhope Cl B98 112 A6
Longleat Dr B90 70 C3
Longleat Gr 25 CV31 110 B3
Longley Ave B76 22 B3
Longrood Rd CV22 99 E3
Longstone Cl B90 71 D3
Longwood Cl CV4 75 F3
Lonscale Dr CV3 77 D3
Lonsdale Rd CV32 106 A2
Lord Lytton Ave CV2 62 B1
Lord St CV5 60 C1
Lords La B80 103 F1
Lorenzo Cl CV3 78 B3
Lothersdale B77 10 B4
Loudon Ave CV6 61 D3
Loughshaw B77 4 B1
Louisa Ward Cl CV23 115 C7
Love La LE10 32 A3
Love Lyne B97 102 A3
Loveday Cl Atherstone CV9 12 B1
Royal Leamington Spa CV32 105 F1
Lovelace Ave B91 71 E4
Lovell Cl CV7 50 A4
Lovell Rd CV12 39 D2
Loverock Cres CV21 83 F1
Lovetts Cl LE10 30 C4
Low Rd WR11 127 A6
Lowbrook La B90 69 E2
Lowdham B77 4 B1
Lowe Rd CV6 49 D1
Lower Ave CV31 109 F4
Lower Cape CV34 108 B4
Lower Cladswell La B49 118 C5
Lower Eastern Green La CV5 59 F2
Lower End Bubbenhall CV8 95 E3
Salford OX7 150 C2
Shutford OX15 139 A3
Lower Farm La OX17 133 F2
Lower Ford St CV1 151 D3
Lower Grinsty La B97 102 A4
Lower High St GL55 135 A2
Lower Hillmorton Rd CV21 83 E1
Lower Holyhead Rd CV1 151 A3
Lower House La CV9 11 D2
Lower Ladyes Hills CV8 93 D3
Lower Leam St CV31 110 A4
Lower Prec CV1 151 B3
Lower Rd CV7 51 E3
Lower St Rugby CV21 101 D4
Willoughby CV23 117 B6
Lower Villiers St 9 CV32 106 A1
Lowes Ave CV34 104 C1
Lowes La CV35 146 B1
Loweswater Cl CV11 30 A3
Loweswater Rd CV3 62 C1
Lowforce B77 10 B4
Lowry Cl CV12 39 D2
Lowther St CV2 61 F2
Loxley CE Prim Sch CV35 130 F7
Loxley Cl Coventry CV2 50 B1
Wellesbourne CV35 146 B2

Loxley Rd Alveston CV37 ..... 121 D1
Stratford-u-A CV37 ..... 145 E1
Wellesbourne CV35 ..... 146 B1
Loxley Way CV32 ..... 106 A1
Lucas Rd LE10 ..... 31 E3
Luce Cl B35 ..... 22 A2
Lucian Cl CV2 ..... 63 D4
Luddington Rd CV37 ..... 129 E8
Ludford Cl Ansley CV10 ..... 27 D2
Stratford-u-A CV37 ..... 144 B2
Ludford Rd CV10 ..... 28 B3
Ludgate Ct B77 ..... 4 A3
Ludlow Cl B37 ..... 33 E1
Ludlow Rd CV5 ..... 61 D1
Ludlow's La CV35 ..... 114 C7
Luff Cl CV3 ..... 78 A4
Lugtrout La B91 ..... 56 A3
Lulworth Pk CV8 ..... 93 E3
Lumley Gr B37 ..... 33 E1
Lumsden Cl CV2 ..... 62 C4
Lunar Cl CV4 ..... 76 B3
Lundy View B36 ..... 33 D3
Lunn Ave CV8 ..... 92 C2
Lupin Cl LE10 ..... 31 E3
Lupton Ave CV3 ..... 77 E4
Luscombe Rd CV2 ..... 62 C4
Luther Way CV5 ..... 59 F2
Lutterworth Rd
Brinklow CV23 ..... 64 C2
Churchover CV23 ..... 67 E3
Coventry CV2 ..... 62 B3
Hinckley LE10 ..... 32 B2
Nuneaton CV11 ..... 40 B4
Pailton CV23 ..... 54 B1
Shawell LE17 ..... 68 B3
Wolvey LE10 ..... 41 F3
Lutterworth Road Commercial Est LE10 ..... 32 A3
Luxor La CV5 ..... 59 D4
Lychgate Cl LE10 ..... 32 A3
Lychgate La LE10 ..... 32 B3
Lydd Croft B35 ..... 22 A2
Lydford Cl CV2 ..... 62 B4
Lydgate Rd CV6 ..... 61 D3
Lydstep Gr CV31 ..... 110 B4
Lye Green Rd CV35 ..... 113 F4
Lyecroft Ave B37 ..... 33 E1
Lymesy St CV3 ..... 77 E4
Lymington Cl CV6 ..... 61 E4
Lymore Croft CV2 ..... 63 D4
Lynbrook Cl B47 ..... 69 D4
Lynbrook Rd CV5 ..... 76 B4
Lynch The Nuneaton CV11 ..... 29 E1
Polesworth B78 ..... 4 C1
Lynchgate Rd CV4 ..... 76 B3
Lyndale B77 ..... 9 F3
Lyndale Rd CV5 ..... 60 B2
Lyndhurst Cl LE10 ..... 32 A4
Lyndhurst Croft CV5 ..... 59 E2
Lyndhurst Rd CV21 ..... 83 F1
Lyndon Croft B37 ..... 44 A4
Lyneham Gdns B76 ..... 22 A3
Lyng Cl CV5 ..... 60 A2
Lyng Hall Sch CV2 ..... 62 B3
Lynmouth Cl CV11 ..... 29 F3
Lynmouth Rd CV2 ..... 62 C4
Lynton Cl CV34 ..... 104 C1
Lynton Rd CV6 ..... 49 F1
Lynwood Wlk 18 CV31 ..... 110 B3
Lysander Cl CV35 ..... 146 B1
Lysander Ct CV37 ..... 145 D1
Lysander St CV3 ..... 78 B3
Lyster Cl CV34 ..... 108 A4
Lythall Cl CV31 ..... 110 C3
Lythalls La CV6 ..... 49 F1
Lythalls Lane Ind Est CV6 ..... 49 F1
Lytham B77 ..... 4 B3
Lytham Cl B76 ..... 22 A3
Lytham Rd CV22 ..... 82 C1
Lyttelton Rd CV34 ..... 108 C4
Lyttleton Cl CV3 ..... 63 D1

M40 Distribution Pk CV35 ..... 146 A1
Macaulay Rd Coventry CV2 ..... 62 B2
Rugby CV22 ..... 99 F4
Macbeth App CV34 ..... 109 E2
Macbeth Cl CV22 ..... 99 F3
Macdonald Rd CV2 ..... 62 B2
Macefield Cl CV2 ..... 50 B1
Mackenzie Cl CV5 ..... 60 A4
Mackley Way CV33 ..... 123 E6
Madam's Hill Rd B90 ..... 70 B4
Madden Pl CV22 ..... 82 B1
Madeira Croft CV5 ..... 60 C1
Madrona B77 ..... 4 A2
Magdalen Cl CV37 ..... 129 D2
Magdalen Rd CV23 ..... 117 C6
Magna Park LE17 ..... 55 E3
Magnet La CV22 ..... 99 E4
Magnolia B77 ..... 4 A2
Magnolia Cl CV3 ..... 77 D3
Magnus B77 ..... 9 F3
Magpie La CV7 ..... 73 F3
Maguire Ind Est CV4 ..... 75 F4
Magyar Cres CV11 ..... 40 A4
Maidavale Cres CV3 ..... 77 E2
Maidenhair Dr CV23 ..... 83 E4
Maidenhead Cl CV37 ..... 145 D2
Maidenhead Rd CV37 ..... 145 D2
Maidwell Dr B90 ..... 70 C4
Main Ave B26 ..... 44 B2
Main Rd Ansty CV7 ..... 51 E2
Austrey CV9 ..... 3 D1
Baxterley CV9 ..... 17 D4
Binton CV37 ..... 120 A1
Broughton OX15 ..... 139 E1
Claybrooke Magna LE17 ..... 43 F3
Kilsby CV23 ..... 101 F2
Main Rd continued
Lower Quinton CV37 ..... 129 E2
Meriden CV7 ..... 58 B4
Newton Regis B79 ..... 2 B2
Main St Aston le W NN11 ..... 134 F5
Badby NN11 ..... 126 F5
Birdingbury CV23 ..... 115 F7
Burmington CV36 ..... 141 A8
Church Lench WR11 ..... 127 A6
Cleeve Prior WR11 ..... 128 A4
Clifton u D CV23 ..... 83 F3
Easenhall CV23 ..... 65 F2
Frankton CV23 ..... 97 E1
Grandborough CV23 ..... 116 F6
Hanwell OX17 ..... 139 F6
Harborough Magna CV23 ..... 66 A2
Higham-on-t-H CV13 ..... 21 D2
Littleton WR11 ..... 127 F1
Long Lawford CV21 ..... 82 A3
Long Lawford,Newbold on A CV21 ..... 82 B4
Mollington OX17 ..... 134 A2
Monks Kirby CV23 ..... 53 F2
Newton LE17 ..... 68 A1
North Newington OX15 ..... 139 D2
Offenham WR11 ..... 127 D1
Orton-on-t-H CV9 ..... 6 B2
Rugby CV22 ..... 99 E4
Shawell LE17 ..... 68 B3
Sibford Gower OX15 ..... 142 D8
Stoke Golding CV13 ..... 21 E4
Stretton u F CV23 ..... 65 D4
Thurlaston CV23 ..... 98 C2
Tiddington CV37 ..... 145 F2
Tysoe CV35 ..... 138 B7
Willey CV23 ..... 54 C3
Willoughby CV23 ..... 117 C6
Withybrook CV7 ..... 52 C3
Wolston CV8 ..... 80 A2
Wroxton OX15 ..... 139 D4
Makepeace Ave CV34 ..... 104 C1
Malam Cl CV4 ..... 60 A1
Maldale B77 ..... 4 B1
Maldens The CV36 ..... 149 F3
Malham Cl CV11 ..... 30 A1
Malham Rd Tamworth B77 ..... 10 B4
Warwick CV34 ..... 104 C1
Malins The CV34 ..... 109 D3
Mallaby Cl B90 ..... 70 A4
Mallard Ave CV10 ..... 28 B3
Mallard Cl CV37 ..... 144 B3
Mallard Rd B80 ..... 103 F2
Mallender Dr B93 ..... 71 F3
Mallerin Croft CV10 ..... 28 A3
Mallory Dr CV34 ..... 108 B4
Mallory Rd
Bishops Tachbrook CV33 ..... 122 F8
Lighthorne Heath CV35 ..... 123 D2
Mallory Way CV6 ..... 49 F2
Mallow Way CV23 ..... 83 E4
Malmesbury Rd CV6 ..... 49 D2
Malt House Cl CV33 ..... 133 B7
Malt House La WR11 ..... 127 A6
Malthouse Cl Ansley CV10 ..... 27 D2
Harvington WR11 ..... 127 D3
Malthouse La Earlswood B94 ..... 86 C4
Kenilworth CV8 ..... 92 C3
Long Compton CV36 ..... 141 C3
Shutford OX15 ..... 139 A3
Malthouse Row B37 ..... 44 A4
Maltings The Nuneaton CV11 ..... 29 F3
Royal Leamington Spa CV32 ..... 105 F1
Studley B80 ..... 103 E2
Maltmill La B49 ..... 143 E2
Malvern Ave Nuneaton CV10 ..... 28 A2
Rugby CV22 ..... 83 E1
Malvern Dr B76 ..... 22 A4
Malvern Rd
Balsall Common CV7 ..... 74 B3
Coventry CV5 ..... 60 C2
Redditch B97 ..... 102 B4
Manby Rd B35 ..... 22 A2
Mancetter Rd Atherstone CV9 ..... 19 D3
Nuneaton CV10 ..... 28 B4
Mander Gr CV34 ..... 108 B2
Manderley Cl CV5 ..... 59 E3
Manfield Ave CV2 ..... 63 D4
Mann's Cl CV8 ..... 96 A4
Manning Wlk CV21 ..... 83 D2
Mannings Cl OX15 ..... 142 D8
Manor Barns CV36 ..... 136 B6
Manor Cl Charwelton NN11 ..... 126 D2
Hinckley LE10 ..... 31 E3
Manor Court Ave CV11 ..... 29 D3
Manor Court Rd CV11 ..... 29 D3
Manor Ct Cleeve Prior WR11 ..... 128 A4
Ettington CV37 ..... 131 A3
Fenny Compton CV33 ..... 133 D7
Manor Cty Prim Sch B78 ..... 8 C3
Manor Dr Stretton on D CV23 ..... 96 C3
Ullenhall B80 ..... 112 D4
Wilmcote CV37 ..... 120 C4
Manor Est CV8 ..... 79 F2
Manor Farm Cl CV23 ..... 101 E1
Manor Farm Rd CV36 ..... 136 F6
Manor Gn CV37 ..... 145 E1
Manor Ho B96 ..... 102 C2
Manor House Cl
Aston Flamville LE10 ..... 32 C3
Rugby CV21 ..... 82 B4
Manor House Dr CV1 ..... 151 B2
Manor House La B46 ..... 23 D2
Manor La Claverdon CV35 ..... 114 A4
Clifton u D CV23 ..... 84 A3
Ettington CV37 ..... 131 A3
Honiley CV8 ..... 91 D3
Kineton CV35 ..... 132 B5
Manor La continued
Shipston-on-S CV36 ..... 149 F3
Wroxall CV35 ..... 90 C2
Manor Mews B80 ..... 103 F2
Manor Orch Harbury CV33 ..... 123 E6
Horley OX15 ..... 139 D6
Manor Park OX17 ..... 134 B4
Manor Park Jun & Inf Sch CV3 ..... 77 E4
Manor Park Rd CV11 ..... 29 D3
Manor Park Sch CV11 ..... 29 D3
Manor Pk WR11 ..... 127 D3
Manor Rd Atherstone CV9 ..... 18 C3
Bishops Itchington CV33 ..... 124 A4
Claybrooke Magna LE17 ..... 43 E3
Coventry CV1 ..... 151 B1
Dorridge B93 ..... 71 F2
Harbury CV33 ..... 123 F6
Kenilworth CV8 ..... 92 C3
Littleton WR11 ..... 127 F1
Loxley CV35 ..... 130 F7
Royal Leamington Spa CV32 ..... 106 A2
Rugby CV21 ..... 83 D2
Staverton NN11 ..... 126 D8
Stockton CV23 ..... 147 F4
Stratford-u-A CV37 ..... 145 E1
Studley B80 ..... 103 F2
Wythall B47 ..... 69 D2
Manor Rd Ind Est CV9 ..... 18 C4
Manor Way LE10 ..... 31 E3
Mansard Ct B46 ..... 34 A4
Manse Cl CV7 ..... 39 D1
Mansel St CV6 ..... 61 F4
Mansell Rd B97 ..... 102 B4
Mansell St CV37 ..... 144 C2
Mansion St 1 LE10 ..... 31 E4
Mansions Cl CV33 ..... 124 A4
Mansley Bsns Ctr The CV37 ..... 144 B2
Manson's Bridge Rd B35 ..... 22 A2
Manston Dr CV35 ..... 146 B1
Manta Rd B77 ..... 9 E3
Mantilla Dr CV3 ..... 77 D3
Manton Croft B93 ..... 71 F2
Maple Ave CV7 ..... 39 D1
Maple Cl LE10 ..... 31 F3
Maple Dr B78 ..... 15 E4
Maple Gr Rugby CV21 ..... 83 D2
Stratford-u-A CV37 ..... 144 C3
Warwick CV34 ..... 105 D1
Maple Leaf Dr B37 ..... 44 B4
Maple Rd Nuneaton CV10 ..... 28 C3
Royal Leamington Spa CV31 ..... 109 F3
Maple Rise B77 ..... 4 A2
Maple Wlk 3 B37 ..... 33 D1
Maplebeck Cl CV5 ..... 61 D2
Maples The CV12 ..... 38 C1
Mapleton Rd CV6 ..... 60 C4
Maplewood B76 ..... 22 A4
Mapperley Cl CV2 ..... 63 D4
Mappleborough Green Jun & Inf Sch B98 ..... 112 A5
Marble Alley B80 ..... 103 F2
March Rd OX17 ..... 133 E2
March Way CV3 ..... 78 B4
Marchant Rd LE10 ..... 31 E4
Marchfont Cl CV11 ..... 30 A1
Marcos Dr B36 ..... 22 C1
Marcroft Pl CV31 ..... 110 B3
Mardol Cl CV2 ..... 62 B4
Marfield Cl B76 ..... 22 A3
Margaret Ave CV12 ..... 39 D2
Margaret Cl CV33 ..... 123 F6
Margaret Rd CV9 ..... 18 C4
Margeson Cl CV2 ..... 62 C1
Margetts Cl CV8 ..... 92 C2
Marie Brock Cl CV4 ..... 60 A1
Marie Cl CV9 ..... 19 D4
Marie Corelli Sch CV37 ..... 144 B2
Marigold Dr LE10 ..... 31 F3
Marina Cl CV4 ..... 75 F4
Marion Rd CV6 ..... 61 E4
Mark Antony Dr CV34 ..... 109 E2
Market End Cl CV12 ..... 38 B1
Market Hill CV33 ..... 147 D2
Market Mall CV21 ..... 83 D2
Market Pl Alcester B49 ..... 143 D2
Hinckley LE10 ..... 31 E4
Nuneaton CV11 ..... 29 E2
Rugby CV21 ..... 83 D2
Shipston-on-S CV36 ..... 149 F3
2 Warwick CV34 ..... 108 C3
Market Sq CV35 ..... 132 B6
Market St Atherstone CV9 ..... 18 B4
Polesworth B78 ..... 5 D1
Rugby CV21 ..... 83 D2
Warwick CV34 ..... 108 B3
Market Way CV1 ..... 151 B2
Markham Dr CV31 ..... 110 A2
Marlborough Cl LE10 ..... 32 A4
Marlborough Dr CV31 ..... 110 B3
Marlborough Rd
Coventry CV2 ..... 62 A2
Nuneaton CV11 ..... 29 D2
Rugby CV22 ..... 99 F4
Marlborough Way B77 ..... 9 F4
Marlcroft CV3 ..... 78 C3
Marleigh Rd B50 ..... 148 B3
Marlene Croft B37 ..... 33 E1
Marler Rd CV4 ..... 75 F4
Marlin B77 ..... 9 E3
Marlissa Dr CV6 ..... 49 F1
Marloes Wlk CV31 ..... 110 B3
Marlow Cl CV5 ..... 60 A2
Marlow Rd CV9 ..... 16 B3
Marlowe Cl Banbury OX16 ..... 139 F3
Nuneaton CV10 ..... 27 F3
Marlston Wlk CV5 ..... 60 A2
Marlwood Cl CV6 ..... 49 F2
Marner Cres CV6 ..... 61 D3
Marner Rd Bedworth CV12 ..... 39 D2
Nuneaton CV10 ..... 29 D1
Marnhull Cl CV2 ..... 62 C2
Marrick B77 ..... 4 B1
Marriners La CV5 ..... 60 A3
Marriott Rd Bedworth CV12 ..... 38 B1
Coventry CV2 ..... 61 D2
Marsdale Dr CV10 ..... 28 C2
Marsett B77 ..... 10 B4
Marsh La
Bradnock's Marsh B92 ..... 57 E3
Curdworth B76 ..... 23 E3
Hampton in A B92 ..... 57 D3
Water Orton B46 ..... 23 E2
Marsh Rd CV37 ..... 120 B5
Marshall Ave CV36 ..... 149 F3
Marshall Lake Rd B90 ..... 70 B4
Marshall Rd CV7 ..... 49 F4
Marshalls Cl OX15 ..... 138 F5
Marsham Cl CV34 ..... 109 D4
Marshbrook Cl CV2 ..... 50 C2
Marshdale Ave CV6 ..... 49 F2
Marshfield Dr CV4 ..... 76 B1
Marston Ave CV35 ..... 123 D2
Marston Cl 8 CV32 ..... 106 A1
Marston Dr B37 ..... 33 D3
Marston Green Jun & Inf Sch B37 ..... 44 A4
Marston La Bedworth CV12 ..... 39 E3
Nuneaton CV11 ..... 39 F4
Wishaw B76 ..... 14 C1
Marten Cl CV35 ..... 108 A4
Martin Cl Coventry CV5 ..... 59 F2
Stratford-u-A CV37 ..... 145 D3
Martin La CV22 ..... 99 E4
Martindale Rd CV7 ..... 50 B4
Martins Dr CV9 ..... 12 C1
Martins Rd CV12 ..... 38 C1
Martlesham Sq B35 ..... 22 A2
Martley Cl B98 ..... 103 D4
Martley Croft B91 ..... 71 D4
Marton Rd Birdingbury CV23 ..... 115 E7
Long Itchington CV23 ..... 115 D5
Martyrs' Cl The CV3 ..... 77 E4
Mary Arden's House CV37 ..... 120 D5
Mary Herbert St CV3 ..... 77 E4
Mary Slessor St CV3 ..... 78 B4
Marystow Cl CV5 ..... 60 A4
Masefield Ave CV34 ..... 108 B2
Masefield Rd CV37 ..... 145 D1
Maseley Ct CV37 ..... 129 D2
Mason Ave CV32 ..... 106 B2
Mason Cl Bidford-on-A B50 ..... 148 C3
Redditch B97 ..... 102 B4
Mason Croft The Shakespeare Inst (Univ of Birmingham) CV37 ..... 144 C1
Mason Ct LE10 ..... 31 D4
Mason La B94 ..... 69 F1
Mason Rd Coventry CV6 ..... 49 F1
Redditch B97 ..... 102 B4
Masons Rd CV37 ..... 144 B2
Masons Way CV37 ..... 144 B2
Masser Rd CV6 ..... 49 E2
Massey Shan Ave GL56 ..... 140 C3
Master's Yd CV23 ..... 115 F7
Masters Rd CV31 ..... 110 A2
Mathe Croft CV31 ..... 110 B3
Matlock Cl CV21 ..... 83 E4
Matlock Rd CV1 ..... 61 E3
Matterson Rd CV6 ..... 61 D3
Matthews Cl CV37 ..... 145 D2
Maud Rd B46 ..... 23 E2
Maudslay Rd CV5 ..... 60 C1
Maureen Cl CV4 ..... 59 E1
Mavor Dr CV12 ..... 38 B1
Mawby's La DE12 ..... 3 F4
Mawnan Cl CV7 ..... 50 A4
Max Rd CV6 ..... 60 C3
Maxstoke Cl Meriden CV7 ..... 46 A1
Tamworth B77 ..... 9 E2
Maxstoke Croft B90 ..... 70 B4
Maxstoke La Coleshill B46 ..... 34 A3
Meriden CV7 ..... 46 A1
May Farm Cl B47 ..... 69 D3
May La Ebrington GL55 ..... 135 E2
Hollywood B47 ..... 69 D4
Rugby CV22 ..... 82 B1
May St CV6 ..... 61 F4
May's Hill B95 ..... 113 A4
Mayama Rd B78 ..... 8 C4
Maybird Ctr CV37 ..... 144 C2
Maybridge Dr B91 ..... 71 D4
Maybrook Ind Est CV37 ..... 144 C2
Maybrook Rd
Stratford-u-A CV37 ..... 144 C2
Sutton Coldfield B76 ..... 22 A3
Maycock Rd CV6 ..... 61 E4
Mayfair Dr CV10 ..... 27 F2
Mayfield B77 ..... 10 B4
Mayfield Ave CV37 ..... 145 D2
Mayfield Cl Bedworth CV12 ..... 39 D2
17 Royal Leamington Spa CV31 ..... 110 B3
Mayfield Ct CV37 ..... 145 D2
Mayfield Dr Henley-in-A B95 ..... 113 A5
Kenilworth CV8 ..... 93 E2
Mayfield Rd Coventry CV5 ..... 61 D1
Nuneaton CV11 ..... 29 F1
Southam CV33 ..... 147 D3
Mayflower Dr CV2 ..... 62 C1
Mayhurst Cl B47 ..... 69 E3
Mayhurst Rd B47 ..... 69 D3
Maynard Ave Bedworth CV12 ..... 49 E4
Warwick CV34 ..... 109 D4
Mayne Cl CV35 ..... 114 F3
Mayo Rd CV36 ..... 149 F4
Mayor's Croft CV4 ..... 76 A4
Maypole La CV9 ..... 11 E1
Maypole Rd B79 ..... 5 F2
Mayswood Rd B95 ..... 113 A3
Maythorn Ave B76 ..... 22 A3
Maythorn Gr 4 B91 ..... 71 D4
Maytree Cl B37 ..... 33 D1
Mc Kinnell Cres CV21 ..... 83 F2
McDonnell Dr CV6 ..... 49 F3
McMahon Rd CV12 ..... 49 F4
Mead The OX17 ..... 133 F2
Meadfoot Rd CV3 ..... 78 C3
Meadow Cl Ansty CV7 ..... 51 E2
Hockley Heath B94 ..... 88 B3
Kingsbury B78 ..... 15 E3
Royal Leamington Spa CV32 ..... 106 B2
Stratford-u-A CV37 ..... 144 B2
Stretton on D CV23 ..... 97 D3
Wolvey LE10 ..... 41 E2
Meadow Croft Arley CV7 ..... 26 C1
Wythall B47 ..... 69 D2
Meadow Crofts CV33 ..... 124 B5
Meadow Ct CV11 ..... 29 D2
Meadow Dr Hampton in A B92 ..... 57 D4
Hinckley LE10 ..... 32 A4
Meadow Gdns CV9 ..... 17 E4
Meadow Green Prim Sch B47 ..... 69 D2
Meadow La B94 ..... 89 E2
Meadow Rd Alcester B49 ..... 143 D3
Coventry CV6 ..... 49 D2
Hartshill CV10 ..... 28 A4
Henley-in-A B95 ..... 113 B4
Hurley CV9 ..... 16 B3
Rugby CV21 ..... 82 C3
Southam CV33 ..... 147 D3
Warwick CV34 ..... 109 D4
Wolston CV8 ..... 80 A2
Wythall B47 ..... 69 D2
Meadow Rise B95 ..... 112 E6
Meadow St Atherstone CV9 ..... 18 B4
Coventry CV1 ..... 151 A2
Nuneaton CV11 ..... 29 D3
Meadow Sweet Rd CV37 ..... 144 C3
Meadow Way
Fenny Compton CV33 ..... 133 E7
Harborough Magna CV23 ..... 66 A2
Meadows Sch CV4 ..... 59 F2
Meadows The
Bidford-on-A B50 ..... 148 B3
Hinckley LE10 ..... 32 A4
Leek Wootton CV35 ..... 105 D4
Meadowside CV11 ..... 40 A4
Meadowsweet CV23 ..... 83 E4
Meadway CV2 ..... 62 A3
Meadway N CV2 ..... 62 A3
Meadway The Hinckley LE10 ..... 31 F4
Redditch B97 ..... 102 B4
Mearse La WR7 ..... 118 B5
Medhurst Cl CV22 ..... 99 E2
Medina Rd CV6 ..... 49 F1
Medland Ave CV3 ..... 76 C3
Meer End Rd CV8 ..... 74 B1
Meer St CV37 ..... 145 D2
Meerhill Ave B90 ..... 71 D3
Meeting House La CV7 ..... 74 B3
Meeting La B49 ..... 143 E2
Meir Rd B98 ..... 103 E4
Melbourne Cl CV11 ..... 39 F4
Melbourne Rd CV5 ..... 61 D1
Meldrum Ct CV33 ..... 132 F7
Meldrum Rd CV10 ..... 28 B2
Melfort Cl CV3 ..... 62 C1
Melksham Sq B35 ..... 22 A2
Mellish Ct CV22 ..... 82 C1
Mellish Rd CV22 ..... 82 C1
Mellor Rd CV21 ..... 101 D4
Mellowdew Rd CV2 ..... 62 B2
Mellowship Rd CV5 ..... 59 E3
Mellwaters B77 ..... 10 B4
Melmerby B77 ..... 10 B4
Melrose Ave CV12 ..... 49 E4
Melrose Cl LE10 ..... 31 D4
Melton Rd CV32 ..... 106 A2
Melville Cl Bedworth CV7 ..... 50 A4
Rugby CV22 ..... 82 C1
Melville Rd CV1 ..... 61 D2
Memorial Rd CV33 ..... 133 D7
Menai Wlk B37 ..... 33 D2
Mendip Dr CV10 ..... 28 A2
Mendip Way B77 ..... 4 B1
Meon Cl CV37 ..... 129 D1
Meon Rd GL55 ..... 135 C7
Mercer Ave Coventry CV2 ..... 62 A3
Water Orton B46 ..... 23 D2
Mercia Ave CV8 ..... 92 C2
Mercia Bsns Village CV4 ..... 75 F3
Mercia Way CV34 ..... 109 D4
Mercian Pk B77 ..... 4 A2
Mercian Way B77 ..... 4 A2
Mercot Cl B98 ..... 103 D3
Mercury Ct B77 ..... 4 A2
Mere Ave B35 ..... 22 A2
Mere La LE10 ..... 42 B2
Meredith Rd CV2 ..... 62 B1
Merevale Ave Hinckley LE10 ..... 31 E4
Nuneaton CV11 ..... 29 D2
Merevale Cl Hinckley LE10 ..... 31 E4
Redditch B98 ..... 103 E4
Merevale La CV9 ..... 17 F4
Merevale Rd CV9 ..... 12 B1
Merevale View CV9 ..... 18 B4

Merganser B77 10 A3
Meriden CE Prim Sch CV7 46 B1
Meriden Cl B98 112 A6
Meriden Dr B37 33 D3
Meriden Hill CV7 58 C4
Meriden Rd Berkswell CV7 58 B2
Fillongley CV7 36 B1
Hampton in A B92 57 D4
Meriden St CV1 61 D2
Merlin Ave CV10 28 A3
Merlin Cl B77 10 A3
Merrifield Gdns LE10 31 F3
Merrington Cl 5 B91 71 E4
Merrivale Rd CV5 60 C2
Merryfields Way CV2 50 C1
Mersey Rd CV12 40 A2
Merstone Sch B37 33 D1
Merttens Dr CV22 82 C1
Merynton Ave CV4 76 C3
Meschines St CV3 77 E3
Metalloys Ind Est B76 22 A3
Metcalfe Cl OX15 139 E4
Metchley Croft B90 70 C3
Mews Rd CV32 109 E4
Mews The Atherstone CV9 18 B4
Bedworth CV12 39 D1
Kenilworth CV8 92 C2
Rugby CV21 84 A1
Mica Cl B77 4 A1
Michael Blanning Gdns
B93 71 F2
Michael Drayton Mid Sch
CV10 28 A4
Michaelmas Rd CV3 151 B1
Michell Cl CV3 78 A4
Mickle Mdw B46 23 D2
Micklehill Dr B90 70 A4
Mickleton Cl B98 102 C4
Mickleton Cty Prim Sch
GL55 135 B6
Mickleton Dr CV35 114 F5
Mickleton Rd Coventry CV5 77 D4
Ilmington CV36 136 A7
Middelburg Cl CV11 30 A1
Middle Bickenhill La B92 45 D2
Middle Hill OX15 142 D4
Middle La
Nether Whitacre B46 24 C3
Shotteswell OX17 139 E8
Wroxton OX15 139 B4
Middle Lock La CV35 114 E5
Middle Rd CV33 123 D7
Middle Ride CV3 78 C3
Middle St Ilmington CV36 136 B6
Tredington CV37 136 E7
Middleborough Rd CV1 151 A4
Middlecotes CV4 60 A1
Middlefield Ave B93 72 A2
Middlefield Dr CV3 63 D1
Middlefield La CV37 130 E1
Middlefleld Dr CV3 63 D1
Middlemarch Bsns Pk
CV3 78 B1
Middlemarch Mid Sch
CV10 29 D1
Middlemarch Rd
Coventry CV6 61 E4
Nuneaton CV10 29 E1
Middlemore Cl B80 103 E2
Middlesmoor B77 10 B4
Middleton Cl CV35 138 B6
Middleton Hall B78 8 C1
Middleton La B78 13 F3
Middletown
Moreton Morrell CV35 122 F3
Studley B80 103 E1
Middletown La B96 103 E1
Midland Air Mus CV3 78 A2
Midland Oak Trad Est CV6 49 F1
Midland Rd Coventry CV6 61 F3
Nuneaton CV11 29 D3
Midland Trad Est CV21 83 D3
Midpoint Park Ind Est
B76 22 B3
Milburn B77 10 B4
Milburn Hill Rd CV4 76 A3
Milby Dr CV11 30 A4
Milby Fst & Mid Sch CV11 29 F4
Milcote Cl B98 103 D4
Milcote Rd CV37 129 C6
Mildmay Cl CV37 144 C1
Mile La CV1 151 C1
Mile Tree La CV2 50 C4
Milebush Ave B36 22 B1
Miles Mdw CV6 50 A1
Milestone Dr CV22 99 F4
Milestone Rd CV37 130 B8
Milford Cl Allesley CV5 60 A3
Redditch B97 102 B3
Milford Gr B90 71 E4
Milford St CV10 29 D1
Mill Bank B46 25 E2
Mill Bank Mews CV8 93 D3
Mill Cl Braunston NN11 117 D5
Broom B50 148 A4
Coventry CV2 50 A2
Hollywood B47 69 D4
Norton Lindsey CV35 114 C2
Nuneaton CV11 29 F1
Southam CV33 147 D3
Mill Cres Kineton CV35 132 B6
Kingsbury B78 15 E2
Southam CV33 147 D3
Mill Ct CV36 149 F3
Mill End CV8 93 D3
Mill Farm Cl CV22 99 E2
Mill Hill CV8 77 E2
Mill House Cl CV32 109 E4
Mill House Dr CV32 109 E4
Mill House Terr CV32 109 E4
Mill La Alcester B49 143 D1
Aston Cantlow B95 119 F6
Barford CV35 122 A7
Bentley Heath B93 71 F2
Bramcote CV11 40 C4
Broom B50 148 A4
Bulkington CV12 40 A2
Chipping Warden OX17 134 F3
Cleeve Prior WR11 128 A4
Clifton u D CV23 83 F3
Coventry CV3 62 C1
Cubbington CV32 106 C3
Drayton OX15 139 E4
Earlswood B94 86 A4
Fazeley B78 9 D4
Fenny Compton CV33 133 D7
Fillongley CV7 36 B3
Halford CV36 136 F8
Harbury CV33 123 F7
Kineton CV35 132 B6
Lapworth B94 89 E2
Lowsonford,Finwood CV35 113 E7
Lowsonford,Turner's Green
CV35 113 F8
Mickleton GL55 135 B6
Newbold-on-S CV37 130 F1
Shrewley CV35 114 C6
Stratford-u-A CV37 145 D1
Tredington CV36 136 F6
Welford on A CV37 129 A7
Witherley CV9 19 D3
Wolvey LE10 41 F3
Wythall B47 69 D1
Mill Pleck B80 103 F2
Mill Pool La B93 89 D4
Mill Race La CV6 50 A2
Mill Race View CV9 12 B1
Mill Rd
Royal Leamington Spa CV31 110 A4
Rugby CV21 83 E3
Southam CV33 147 D3
Mill Row LE10 41 F3
Mill St Bedworth CV12 39 D2
Coventry CV1 151 A3
Harbury CV33 123 E7
Kineton CV35 132 B6
Nuneaton CV11 29 E2
Royal Leamington Spa CV31 110 A4
Shipston-on-S CV36 149 F3
Warwick CV34 108 C3
Mill Terr CV12 39 D3
Mill Wlk CV11 29 E2
Millais Cl CV12 39 D2
Millbank CV34 105 D1
Millbeck CV21 83 E4
Miller's Bank B50 148 A4
Millers Cl Dunchurch CV22 99 D2
Lower Boddington NN11 134 E6
Welford on A CV37 129 B6
Millers Dale Cl CV21 83 E4
Millers Gn LE10 31 F3
Millers La Hornton OX15 139 B8
Monks Kirby CV23 53 E2
Millers Rd CV34 108 C4
Millfield Prim Sch B78 9 D4
Millfields Ave CV21 100 C4
Millholme Cl CV33 147 E2
Millhouse Ct CV6 61 F4
Milliners Ct CV9 18 B4
Millison Gr B90 71 D4
Mills La OX15 139 D4
Millway Dr 1 CV33 122 F8
Milner Cl CV12 40 B1
Milner Cres CV2 50 C1
Milner Dr B79 4 C4
Milrose Way CV4 75 F4
Milton Ave CV34 108 B3
Milton Cl Bedworth CV12 39 E1
Bentley Heath B93 71 F2
Redditch B97 102 B4
Milton Rd B93 71 F2
Milton St CV2 62 A2
Milverton Comb Sch
CV32 105 F1
Milverton Cres 1 CV32 105 F1
Milverton Cres W 2
CV32 105 F1
Milverton Hill CV32 109 F4
Milverton House Prep Sch
CV11 29 E2
Milverton Rd Coventry CV2 50 B1
Knowle B93 72 B3
Milverton Terr CV32 109 F4
Miners Wlk B78 4 C1
Minions Cl CV9 18 B4
Miniva Dr B76 13 D1
Minster Cl
Hampton Magna CV35 114 F3
Knowle B93 72 A4
Minster Rd CV1 61 D2
Minton Rd CV2 50 C1
Minworth Ind Pk B76 22 A3
Minworth Jun & Inf Sch
B76 22 B3
Minworth Rd B46 23 D2
Mira Dr CV10 20 B2
Miranda Cl CV3 78 B4
Mistral Cl LE10 31 F4
Mitcheldean Cl B98 102 C4
Mitchell Ave CV4 76 A4
Mitchell Rd CV12 39 E1
Mitchison Cl CV23 117 E8
Moat Ave CV3 76 C3
Moat Cl Bubbenhall CV8 95 E3
Thurlaston CV23 98 C1
Moat Croft Birmingham B37 33 D1
Sutton Coldfield B76 22 A4
Moat Dr B78 8 C3
Moat Farm Dr
Bedworth CV12 49 E4
Rugby CV21 101 D4
Moat Farm La B95 112 E6
Moat Gn CV35 108 A1
Moat House Ct B80 103 F4
Moat House La Coventry
CV4 76 B4
Shustoke B46 25 D1
Moat La LE10 41 F3
Mobbs La OX15 142 D4
Mockley Wood Rd B93 72 A4
Modbury Cl CV3 77 E3
Model Village The CV23 115 D3
Molesworth Ave CV3 62 A1
Mollington La OX17 133 D2
Mollington Prim Sch
OX17 133 F2
Mollington Rd CV31 110 A2
Momus Bvd CV2 62 B1
Moncrieff Dr CV31 110 B3
Monk's Croft The CV3 77 E4
Monks Dr B80 103 E2
Monks Kirby La CV23 53 F3
Monks Rd Binley Woods CV3 79 E4
Coventry CV1 61 F1
Monks Way CV34 108 B3
Monkspath B90 71 D3
Monkspath Bsns Pk B90 70 C4
Monkspath Cl B90 70 B4
Monkspath Hall Rd B90 71 D4
Monkspath Jun & Inf Sch
B90 71 D3
Monkswood Cres CV2 62 B4
Monmouth Cl Coventry CV5 60 A2
Kenilworth CV8 92 C3
Monmouth Gdns CV10 28 C2
Montague Rd Rugby CV22 99 E3
Warwick CV34 109 D4
Montague's Cnr CV37 129 A6
Montalt Rd CV3 77 F4
Montana Wlk CV10 28 C2
Montfort Rd B46 33 F3
Montgomery Ave CV35 114 F3
Montgomery Cl Coventry
CV3 78 B2
Stratford-u-A CV37 144 C1
Montgomery Dr CV22 82 B1
Montilo La CV23 66 B3
Montjoy Cl CV3 78 B4
Montley B77 10 B4
Montpellier Cl CV3 77 E3
Montrose Ave CV32 106 A3
Montrose Dr Birmingham
B35 22 A2
Nuneaton CV10 28 C2
Montrose Rd CV22 83 D1
Montsford Cl B93 71 F3
Monument Way CV37 145 D3
Monwode Lea La B46 26 A2
Moor Burgess Activity Ctr
B77 4 A1
Moor Farm Cl CV23 96 C3
Moor Fields B49 143 E2
Moor La
Tamworth, Amington B77 4 A3
Willoughby CV23 117 B6
Moor Rd CV10 28 A4
Moor St CV5 60 C1
Moor The B76 22 A4
Moor Wood Farm CV10 18 C1
Moorcroft Cl Nuneaton
CV11 30 A1
Redditch B97 102 A3
Moore Cl Appleby Magna
DE12 3 F4
Warwick CV34 104 C1
Moore Wlk CV34 109 E4
Moorend Ave B37 33 D1
Moorfield Ave B93 71 F3
Moorfield Rd B49 143 D2
Moorfield The CV3 78 A4
Moorhill Rd CV31 110 A2
Moorhills Croft B90 70 A4
Moorlands Ave CV8 92 C2
Moorpark Cl CV11 40 B4
Moorwood Cres CV10 28 A4
Moorwood La Hartshill CV10 28 A4
Nuneaton CV10 27 F4
Morar Cl B35 22 B2
Moray Cl LE10 31 D4
Mordaunt Rd CV35 146 C2
Moreall Mdws CV4 76 B2
Moreland Croft B76 22 A3
Moreton Cl CV37 145 E1
Moreton Hall Ag Coll
CV35 122 E2
Moreton Morrell La CV35 123 B2
Moreton-in-Marsh
District Hospl GL56 140 A3
Moreton-in-Marsh Sta
GL56 140 A3
Morgan Cl Arley CV7 36 C4
Banbury OX16 139 F4
Norton Lindsey CV35 114 C2
Studley B80 103 F1
Morgan Gr B36 22 C1
Morgans Rd CV5 59 E2
Morgrove Ave B93 71 F3
Morland Cl CV12 40 B1
Morland Rd CV6 49 E1
Morningside CV5 77 D4
Mornington Ct B46 34 A4
Morpeth B77 9 E4
Morrell St CV32 105 F1
Morris Ave CV2 62 B2
Morris Cl CV21 82 C3
Morris Croft B36 22 C1
Morris Dr Banbury OX16 139 F4
Nuneaton CV11 29 E1
Whitnash CV31 110 A1
Morris Hill B78 11 D4
Morris Rd NN11 117 F2
Morse Rd CV31 110 A2
Morson Cres CV21 83 F1
Morston B77 9 E2
Mortimer Rd CV8 92 C1
Morton Cl CV6 49 D1
Morton Gdns CV21 83 E1
Morton La B97 102 A4
Morton Morrell CE
Prim Sch CV35 122 F2
Morton St CV32 105 F1
Morville Cl B93 71 E2
Mosedale
Moreton-in-M GL56 140 B3
Rugby CV21 83 E4
Moseley Ave CV6 61 D2
Moseley Prim Sch CV6 61 D2
Moseley Rd CV8 93 D2
Moss Cl CV22 82 C1
Moss La Beoley B98 112 A8
Newbold-on-S CV37 130 E1
Moss St 8 CV31 110 A4
Mossdale B77 10 B4
Mossdale Cl CV6 61 D3
Mossdale Cres CV10 28 C1
Mosspaul Cl CV32 105 E1
Mottistone Cl CV3 77 E3
Moultrie Rd CV22 83 D1
Mount Cres CV37 144 B2
Mount Dr CV12 39 D2
Mount Nod Prim Sch CV5 60 A2
Mount Nod Way CV5 60 A2
Mount Pleasant
Bishops Itchington CV33 124 A4
Stockton CV23 147 F4
Stratford-u-A CV37 144 B2
Tamworth B77 9 E4
Mount Pleasant Cl CV23 147 F4
Mount Pleasant La B95 112 E6
Mount Pleasant Rd CV12 39 D2
Mount Pleasant Terr CV10 28 C3
Mount Rd Henley-In-A B95 113 B4
Hinckley LE10 31 E4
Mount St Coventry CV5 60 C1
Nuneaton CV11 29 D2
Mount Street Pas CV11 29 D2
Mount The Coventry CV3 77 F4
Curdworth B76 23 E3
Mountbatten Ave CV8 93 E2
Mountbatten Cl CV37 144 B1
Mountford Cl CV35 146 C2
Mountford Rise CV35 123 B2
Mowbray St CV2 61 F2
Mowe Croft B37 44 A4
Mows Hill Rd B94 113 A8
Moxhull Rd B37 33 D3
Moyeady Ave CV22 100 C4
Moyle Cres CV5 59 E2
Much Park St CV1 151 C2
Muirfield B77 4 A3
Muirfield Cl CV11 40 B4
Mulberry Cl CV32 106 A1
Mulberry Ctr The CV37 145 D2
Mulberry Dr 5 CV34 108 C4
Mulberry Rd Coventry CV6 62 A4
Rugby CV22 82 A1
Mulberry St CV37 145 D2
Mull Croft B36 33 D4
Mullard Dr CV31 110 A2
Mullensgrove Rd B37 33 D3
Mulliner St CV6 61 F3
Mulliners Cl 2 B37 33 E1
Muntz Cres B94 88 B3
Murcott Rd CV31 110 A2
Murcott Rd E CV31 110 A2
Murray Rd Coventry CV6 61 D4
Rugby CV21 83 D2
Murrayian Cl CV21 83 D2
Murton B77 10 B4
Musborough Cl B36 22 B1
Myatt Rd WR11 127 D1
Myatt's Field WR11 127 D4
Myers Rd CV21 101 E4
Mylgrove CV3 77 E2
Mynors Cres B47 69 D3
Myrtle Gr CV5 60 C1
Mythe La CV9 19 D4
Mythe View CV9 12 C1
Myton Cres CV34 109 E3
Myton Crofts CV31 109 E4
Myton Gdns CV34 109 D3
Myton La CV34 109 E3
Myton Rd CV31, CV34 109 D3
Myton Sch CV34 109 D3
Mytton Rd B46 22 C2

Nailcote Ave CV4 75 E4
Nailcote La CV7 75 D4
Nailsworth Rd B93 71 E1
Nairn Cl CV10 29 D1
Napier St CV1 61 F2
Naples Rd CV35 132 F5
Napton Dr CV32 106 A1
Napton Gn CV5 60 A2
Napton Rd CV23 147 F4
Napton Rise CV33 147 E2
Narberth Way CV2 62 C4
Nares Cl CV22 82 C1
Narrow La B95 113 F6
Narrows The LE10 31 F4
Naseby Cl CV3 78 C4
Naseby Rd CV22 83 E1
Nash's La GL55 135 E3
Nashes The CV37 129 F7
Nathaniel Newton Fst Sch
CV10 28 A4
National Ag Ctr CV8 94 A2
National Ex Ctr B40 44 C2
National Motorcycle
Mus The B92 45 D1
Navigation Way CV6 62 A4
Neal Ct CV2 63 D4
Neale Ave CV5 60 A3
Neale Cl CV12 40 B1
Neale's Cl CV33 123 F7
Nebsworth La CV36 135 F5
Needhill Cl B93 71 F3
Needle Cl B80 103 F2
Needlers End La CV7 74 A4
Neilston St CV31 110 A4
Nellands Cl CV36 136 B6
Nelson Ave CV34 109 D4
Nelson Cl CV37 131 A4
Nelson La CV34 109 D4
Nelson St 5 CV1 61 F2
Nelson Way CV22 82 B1
Nemesia B77 4 A2
Nene Cl CV3 78 B4
Nene Side Cl NN11 126 F6
Nene Wlk NN11 117 F1
Nesfield Gr B92 57 D4
Nesscliffe Rd CV33 132 F5
Netherfield B98 103 D4
Nethermill Rd 1 CV6 61 D3
Nethersole Sch The B78 5 D1
Nethersole St B78 5 D1
Netherwood La B93 90 A4
Netting St OX15 142 D4
Nevada Way B37 33 E1
Nevill Cl CV31 109 F3
Neville Gr CV34 104 C1
Neville Rd
Birmingham, Castle Bromwich
B36 22 C1
Hollywood B90 69 F4
Neville Wlk B35 22 A1
New Ash Dr CV5 59 F3
New Bldgs CV1 151 C3
New Broad St CV37 144 C1
New Brook St 2 CV32 109 F4
New Century Pk CV3 62 B1
New Century Way CV11 29 D2
New Cl CV35 114 F3
New End Rd B46 35 D2
New Inn La WR11 127 D5
New Leasow B76 22 A4
New Mill La B78 9 D4
New Park Cotts OX15 137 F2
New Rd Alderminster CV37 130 D3
Appleby Magna DE12 3 F4
Ash Green CV7 49 D3
Astwood Bank B96 118 C8
Bedworth CV12 38 A2
Coventry CV6 48 C1
Ebrington GL55 135 E3
Henley-in-A B95 113 A4
Hinckley LE10 32 A3
Hollywood B47 69 D4
Kineton CV33 132 F6
Lowsonford CV35 113 E6
Norton Lindsey CV35 114 C2
Pebworth CV37 128 F1
Ratley OX15 133 A2
Shotteswell OX17 139 E8
Shuttington B79 1 B1
Studley B80 103 F2
Tamworth B77 9 F4
Temple Grafton B49 119 E1
Temple Herdewyke CV33 133 A6
Water Orton B46 23 D2
New Row B78 8 C3
New St Baddesley Ensor CV9 11 E1
Bedworth CV12 39 E1
Birchmoor B78 10 C4
Bulkington CV12 40 B1
Cubbington CV32 106 C3
Dordon CV9 11 D3
Fazeley B78 9 D4
Kenilworth CV8 92 C3
Napton CV23 125 C7
Royal Leamington Spa CV31 110 A4
Rugby CV22 82 C2
Shipston-on-S CV36 149 F3
Stratford-u-A CV37 144 C1
Tiddington CV37 145 F2
Warwick CV34 108 C3
New Union St CV1 151 B2
Newall Cl CV23 83 F3
Newbold Avon Mid Sch
CV21 82 C3
Newbold Cl
Bentley Heath B93 71 F3
Coventry CV3 62 C1
Newbold Comyn Pk CV32 110 B4
Newbold Pl
Royal Leamington Spa CV32 110 A4
Wellesbourne CV35 146 C2
Newbold Rd Rugby CV21 82 C3
Wellesbourne CV35 146 C3
Newbold St CV32 110 A4
Newbold Terr CV32 110 A4
Newbold Terr E CV32 110 A4
Newbold & Tredington
CE Prim Sch Newbold-on-S
CV37 130 E1
Tredington CV36 136 F6
Newborough Cl CV9 3 D1

Newburgh Cres CV34 108 C4
Newburgh Prim Sch CV34 108 B2
Newbury Cl 12 CV31 110 B3
Newby Cl CV3 77 F3
Newby Gr B37 33 D2
Newcastle Croft B35 22 B2
Newcombe Cl CV22 99 E2
Newcombe Rd CV5 61 D1
Newcomen Cl CV12 49 E4
Newcomen Rd CV12 38 B1
Newdegate Pl CV11 29 E2
Newdegate Rd CV12 39 D2
Newdegate St CV11 29 E2
Newdigate CV31 110 B3
Newdigate Cty Fst & Mid Sch,CV12 38 B1
Newdigate Rd Coventry CV6 61 F3
Sutton Coldfield B75 13 D3
Newent Cl B98 112 A6
Newey Ave CV12 49 E4
Newey Rd CV2 62 B2
Newfield Ave CV8 93 D2
Newfield Rd CV1 61 E3
Newgale Wlk CV31 110 B4
Newhall Rd CV2 62 B4
Newham Gn CV10 28 B4
Newhaven Cl CV6 60 C3
Newhouse Croft CV7 74 A3
Newington Cl CV6 60 B3
Newington Rd B37 44 A4
Newland Cl B98 103 D4
Newland La CV7 49 D4
Newland Rd Coventry CV1 61 E3
Royal Leamington Spa CV32 106 B2
Newland St CV22 82 C2
Newlands La B37 44 A3
Newlands Rd
Baddesley Ensor CV9 11 E1
Bentley Heath B93 71 F2
Newlands The B80 103 E2
Newlyn Cl CV11 29 F2
Newman Cl CV12 39 D2
Newmarket Cl CV6 50 A2
Newmarsh Rd B76 22 A3
Newnham La B95 120 C7
Newnham Rd Coventry CV1 61 F3
Royal Leamington Spa CV32 106 A2
Newport Cl B97 102 A3
Newport Dr B49 143 D2
Newport Rd CV6 49 E1
Newquay Cl CV11 29 F3
Newscut La OX17 134 C1
Newsholme Cl 1 CV34 104 C1
Newstead Ave LE10 31 E2
Newstead Cl CV11 29 F1
Newstead Dr CV33 147 D2
Newstead Way CV3 63 D1
Newton Cl Coventry CV2 62 C4
Hartshill CV10 19 D1
Redditch B98 103 D3
Newton La Newton CV23 68 A2
Newton Regis B79 2 A2
Newton Regis B79 2 C1
Newton Manor La CV21 83 F4
Newton Rd Hinckley LE10 30 C4
Knowle B93 72 A4
Newton CV23 84 A4
Newton Regis CE Prim Sch B79 2 B2
Newtown Rd Bedworth CV12 39 D1
Nuneaton CV11 29 E3
Nibbits La NN11 117 E5
Nicholas Chamberlaine Comp Sch CV12 39 E2
Nicholls St CV2 61 F2
Nicholson Cl CV34 104 C1
Nickson Rd CV4 59 F1
Nightingale B77 10 A3
Nightingale Ave B36 33 D4
Nightingale Cl
Atherstone CV9 12 C1
Great Alne B49 119 D6
Nightingale La
Cleeve Prior WR11 128 A4
Coventry CV5 76 C4
Nimbus B77 9 E2
Nine Days La B98 103 D3
Nineacres Dr B37 33 D2
Ninefoot La B77 9 F4
Ninian Pk B77 9 E3
Ninian Way B77 9 F3
Niton Rd CV10 29 E3
Niven Cl CV5 60 A3
No Man's Heath La CV9 3 D2
Noble Cl CV34 108 B3
Nod Rise CV5 60 A2
Node Hill Cl B80 103 E2
Nolans Cl CV6 49 E2
Nook The CV11 29 F1
Norcombe Gr B90 71 D3
Nordic Drift CV2 63 D3
Norfolk Cl LE10 31 E2
Norfolk Cres CV10 28 C2
Norfolk St Coventry CV1 61 D2
Royal Leamington Spa CV32 106 A1
Norfolk Terr CV4 76 A4
Norluck Ct CV36 149 F3
Norman Ashman Coppice CV3 79 E4
Norman Ave Coventry CV2 50 C1
Nuneaton CV11 29 D2
Norman Place Rd CV6 60 C4
Norman Rd CV21 82 C3
Normanby Mdws CV31 110 A1
Normandy Cl CV35 108 A4
North Ave Bedworth CV12 39 E1
Birmingham B40 44 C3
Coventry CV2 62 A2
North Brook Rd CV5 60 B4
North Cl Braunston NN11 117 E5
Cubbington CV32 106 C3
Hinckley LE10 31 F3
North Leamington Sch CV32 105 F2
North Leamington Sch (Binswood Hall) CV32 105 F1
North Rd CV23 83 F3
North St Atherstone CV9 18 C4
Coventry CV2 62 A3
Kilsby CV23 101 F2
Marton CV23 115 C7
Nuneaton CV10 28 C2
Rugby CV21 83 D2
North View CV7 51 D1
North Villiers St CV32 106 A1
North Warwickshire & Hinkley Coll Hinckley LE10 31 F4
Nuneaton CV11 29 F3
Northampton La CV22 99 E2
Northcote Rd CV21 82 C1
Northcote St 12 CV31 110 A4
Northcote Wlk CV9 12 B1
Northend Rd CV33 133 C7
Northey Rd CV6 61 E4
Northfield Rd Coventry CV1 61 F1
Hinckley LE10 31 E4
Southam CV33 147 D2
Northgate St CV34 108 C4
Northlands Cty Prim Sch CV21 83 D2
Northolt Dr B35 22 A2
Northside Cl B98 102 C4
Northumberland Ave CV10 28 C2
Northumberland Rd
Coventry CV1 61 D2
Royal Leamington Spa CV32 105 F1
Northvale Cl CV8 93 D3
Northway Birmingham B40 44 C3
Royal Leamington Spa CV31 110 A3
Rugby CV21 83 D2
Norton Curlieu La CV35 114 C3
Norton Dr CV34 104 C1
Norton Green La B93 72 B1
Norton Hill CV9 3 E1
Norton Hill Dr CV2 62 C3
Norton La B47, B94 69 F2
Norton Lea CV35 114 C2
Norton Leys CV22 99 F3
Norton Rd B46 33 F4
Norton View GL55 135 B6
Nortons Cl CV33 133 B7
Norwich Cl CV11 30 A4
Norwich Dr CV3 77 D3
Norwood Gr CV2 50 C1
Nova Croft CV5 59 E2
Novotel Way B26 44 B2
Nuffield Rd Coventry CV6 62 A4
Hinckley LE10 30 C4
Nugent Gr B90 70 B2
Nuneaton La CV13 20 C1
Nuneaton Rd Bedworth CV12 39 D2
Bulkington CV12 40 A2
Fillongley CV7 36 C2
Furnace End B46,CV10 26 B3
Hartshill CV10 19 D1
Nuneaton Trent Valley Sta CV11 29 E3
Nunts La CV6 49 D2
Nunts Park Ave CV6 49 D2
Nunwood La CV23 96 A1
Nursery Cl Mickleton GL55 135 C7
Moreton-in-M GL56 140 A4
Nursery Hill Fst Sch CV10 27 F4
Nursery La CV31 110 A3
Nursery Rd Ansley CV10 27 F4
Atherstone CV9 18 C4
Nutbrook Ave CV4 59 F1
Nuthurst B75 13 D2
Nuthurst Cres CV10 27 E2
Nuthurst Gr B93 72 A2
Nuthurst Grange Rd B94 88 B2
Nuthurst La CV10 27 E1
Nuthurst Rd B94 113 B8
Nutt's La LE10 31 D4
Nymet B77 9 F4

Oak Avenue Woodside CV7 26 C1
Oak Cl Baginton CV8 77 F1
Bedworth CV12 39 E2
Hinckley LE10 31 F3
Oak Ct CV34 109 F1
Oak Farm Cl B76 22 A4
Oak La Allesley CV5 47 F1
Barston B92 57 D1
Oak Leigh CV35 123 D2
Oak Rd CV37 145 F2
Oak Rise B46 33 F3
Oak St CV22 83 D1
Oak Tree Ave CV3 77 D3
Oak Tree Cl
Bentley Heath B93 71 F2
Royal Leamington Spa CV32 106 A1
Oak Tree La Cookhill B49 118 D5
Hollywood B47 69 D3
Sambourne B96 103 D1
Oak Tree Rd Coventry CV3 79 D4
Harvington WR11 127 C4
Oak Way CV4 59 E1
Oakdale Rd CV3 79 E4
Oakdene Cl CV35 113 F3
Oakdene Cres Hatton CV35 114 C5
Nuneaton CV10 29 E4
Oakenhayes Cres B76 22 B3
Oakey Cl CV6 49 F2
Oakfield Gdns CV9 18 C4
Oakfield Jun Sch CV9 18 C4
Oakfield Rd Coventry CV6 60 C3
Rugby CV22 82 C1
Oakfields Way B91 56 A3
Oakford Dr CV5 59 F3
Oakhall Dr B93 71 F2
Oakham Cl B98 103 D3
Oakham Cres CV12 40 B1
Oakham La NN11 126 D8
Oakham Rd GL56 141 A1
Oaklands B76 23 D3
Oaklands Croft B76 22 A4
Oaklands The
Birmingham B37 44 A4
Coventry CV4 60 A1
Oakleigh Rd CV37 144 C3
Oakley CV8 73 F1
Oakley Wood Rd CV33 122 F7
Oakmoor Rd CV6 50 A2
Oakridge Rd CV32 106 B2
Oakroyd Cres CV10 28 B4
Oaks Pl CV6 50 A2
Oaks Rd CV8 92 C1
Oaks The CV12 38 C1
Oakthorpe Dr B37 33 D3
Oaktree Cl Bearley CV37 120 D7
Kingsbury B78 15 E3
Moreton Morrell CV35 122 E3
Oaktree Farm Mobile Homes Pk B94 86 A4
Oakwood Cl CV9 11 E1
Oakwood Gr CV34 105 D1
Oakwood Rd B47 69 D3
Oakworth Cl CV2 62 C4
Oaston Rd CV11 29 E2
Oban Dr CV10 29 D1
Oban Rd Coventry CV6 49 F3
Hinckley LE10 31 D4
Oberon Cl Nuneaton CV11 30 A1
Royal Leamington Spa CV34 109 F2
Rugby CV22 99 E3
Occupation Rd CV2 62 B2
Oddicombe Croft CV3 77 E3
Odingsel Dr CV23 115 C4
Odstone Dr LE10 30 C4
Offa Dr CV8 93 D2
Offa Rd CV31 110 A3
Offchurch La CV31 110 C3
Offchurch Rd CV32 106 C2
Offenham CE Fst Sch WR11 127 D1
Ogley Dr B75 13 D3
Okehampton Rd CV3 77 F3
Okement Gr CV23 82 A3
Oken Rd CV34 108 B4
Olaf Pl CV2 63 D4
Old Brewery Cl CV36 137 A4
Old Budbrooke Rd
Hampton Magna CV35 114 F4
Warwick CV35 108 A4
Old Church Rd Coventry CV6 50 A1
Water Orton B46 23 D2
Old Crown Mews CV2 50 B3
Old Damson La B92 44 A1
Old Farm La B46 25 D3
Old Farm Rd CV9 18 C3
Old Ford Ave CV33 147 D3
Old Forge Dr B98 103 E4
Old Forge Rd
Fenny Drayton CV13 20 A3
Great Rollright OX7 142 A2
Old Green La CV8 73 E1
Old Hedging La B77 9 E3
Old Hinckley Rd CV10 29 E3
Old House La CV7 48 A4
Old Kingsbury Rd B76 22 B3
Old La B48 85 E2
Old Leicester Rd CV21 83 D4
Old Manor Cl B78 8 C3
Old Meeting Yd CV12 39 D2
Old Mill Ave CV4 76 B3
Old Mill Rd B46 33 F4
Old Milverton La CV32 105 F3
Old Milverton Rd CV32 105 E1
Old Orchard The GL55 135 E3
Old Rd
Bishops Itchington CV33 124 B4
Braunston NN11 117 E4
Meriden CV7 46 C1
Ratley OX15 132 F2
Shipston-on-S CV36 149 F3
Southam CV33 147 D2
Old Rectory Cl CV23 67 E3
Old Rectory Gdn B49 143 D2
Old Red Lion Ct CV37 145 D1
Old School Cl WR11 127 D1
Old School End OX15 142 D4
Old School La
Hampton Magna CV35 114 F3
Lighthorne CV35 123 C2
Wilmcote CV37 120 C4
Old School Mews CV32 106 A2
Old Snitterfield Rd CV37 120 E7
Old Sq 1 CV34 108 C3
Old Station Rd B92 57 D4
Old Town CV37 145 D1
Old Town Mews CV37 144 C1
Old Tramway Wlk CV37 145 D1
Old Tree La CV35 138 B6
Old Warwick Rd
Lapworth B94, CV35 89 E2
Rowington CV35 114 A7
Royal Leamington Spa CV31 109 F4
Old Winnings Rd CV7 48 C3
Oldany Way CV10 28 C1
Oldberrow Cl 4 B90 71 D3
Oldbury Rd CV10 18 C1
Oldbury View CV10 19 D1
Oldbutt Rd CV36 149 F3
Oldfield Rd CV5 60 C2
Oldham Ave CV2 62 C2
Oldham Way CV23 82 A2
Oldington Gr B91 71 D4
Oldwich La E Honiley CV8 90 C4
Knowle CV8 73 E1
Oldwich La W B93 90 B4
Olive Ave CV2 62 B3
Oliver St Coventry CV6 61 F3
Rugby CV21 82 C2
Olivier Way CV2 63 D4
Olney Rd CV35 132 D3
Olton Ave CV5 59 F2
Olton Cl CV11 41 D4
Olton Pl CV11 28 C2
Olympus Ave CV34 109 E3
Olympus Cl CV5 59 D4
Omar Rd CV2 62 B1
Ombersley Cl B98 103 E4
Omega Pl CV21 83 D2
Onley La CV22 100 B3
Onley Terr CV4 76 B4
Onslow Croft CV32 105 F1
Openfield Croft B46 23 E1
Oratory Dr CV3 78 B3
Orchard Cl Austrey CV9 3 D1
Badby NN11 126 F6
Bidford-on-A B50 148 B2
Bishops Itchington CV33 124 B4
Bubbenhall CV8 95 E3
Coleshill B46 33 F4
Curdworth B76 23 D4
Hartshill CV10 28 A4
Hinckley LE10 32 A3
Hurley CV9 16 B2
Lower Brailes OX15 137 F2
Mickleton GL55 135 C7
Polesworth B78 5 D2
Salford OX7 150 C2
Shipston-on-S CV36 149 F3
Tamworth B77 9 E3
Welford on A CV37 129 B6
Witherley CV9 19 D4
Wolvey LE10 41 E2
Orchard Cres CV3 77 E4
Orchard Ct Atherstone CV9 18 B4
Coventry CV3 63 D1
Orchard Dr Alcester B49 143 D2
Coventry CV5 59 E2
Orchard Gr
Astwood Bank B96 118 C8
Stockton CV23 147 F4
Orchard Meadow Wlk B35 22 A2
Orchard Piece OX17 134 A2
Orchard Pl
Harvington WR11 127 D4
Redditch B80 103 F4
Orchard Rd
Hockley Heath B94 88 B3
Hook Norton OX15 142 D4
Orchard Rise CV9 11 E1
Orchard St Bedworth CV12 39 D2
Hinckley LE10 31 F4
Nuneaton CV11 29 E2
Orchard The Baxterley CV9 17 E4
Lower Quinton CV37 129 D2
Marton CV23 115 C7
Staverton NN11 126 D8
Whatcote CV36 137 E7
Orchard View OX17 134 C1
Orchard Way Hollywood B47 69 D4
Long Itchington CV23 115 C4
Nuneaton CV10 28 B3
Rugby CV22 99 E4
Southam CV33 147 D3
Stratford-u-A CV37 144 C1
Stretton on D CV23 96 C3
Studley B80 103 F1
Orchards The
Cheswick Green B90 70 B2
Hollywood B47 69 D4
Newton CV23 68 A1
Orchid Way CV23 83 E4
Ordnance Rd CV6 61 F3
Orford Cl CV35 146 C2
Orford Rise CV10 27 F2
Oriel Gr GL56 140 A2
Orion Cres CV2 50 C1
Orkney Cl CV10 29 D1
Orkney Croft B36 33 D4
Orlando Cl CV22 99 E3
Orlescote Rd CV4 76 C3
Orpington Dr CV6 49 E2
Orrian Cl CV37 144 C3
Orson Leys CV22 99 F4
Orton Ave B76 22 A3
Orton Cl B46 23 D2
Orton Hill CV9 6 C4
Orton La Austrey CV9 6 B3
Orton-on-t-H CV9 6 C1
Twycross CV9 3 F1
Orton Rd Coventry CV6 49 E2
Warton B79 5 F2
Orton Way B35 22 A1
Orwell Cl Clifton u D CV23 84 A3
Nuneaton CV10 28 A3
Orwell Rd CV1 61 F1
Osbaston Cl CV5 59 F2
Osborne Ct CV31 110 A2
Osborne Rd CV5 77 D4
Osbourne Croft B90 70 B3
Oslo Gdns CV2 63 D4
Osney Cl OX15 142 D4
Osprey B77 10 A3
Osprey Cl Coventry CV2 63 D3
Nuneaton CV11 40 A4
Ossetts Hole La CV35 113 E4
Oswald Rd CV32 109 E4
Oswald Way CV22 82 B2
Oswestry Cl B97 102 B4
Oswin Gr CV2 62 B2
Othello Cl CV22 99 E3
Ottery B77 10 A3
Our Lady of the Angels RC Fst Sch CV11 29 E2
Our Lady of the Assumption RC Prim Sch CV4 59 F1
Our Lady Of the Wayside RC Prim Sch B90 70 B4
Our Lady & St Teresa's RC Comb Sch CV32 106 B3
Our Lady's RC Prim Sch
Alcester B49 143 D3
Princethorpe CV23 96 B1
Ousterne La CV7 36 B2
Outermarch Rd CV6 61 E4
Outwood Cl B98 102 C4
Outwoods Cl CV9 18 B4
Oval Rd CV22 100 B4
Over St CV6 62 A4
Overbare Cl B94 87 D1
Overberry Cl CV2 50 B1
Overberry Orch 5 CV33 122 E8
Overdale B96 102 C1
Overdale Rd CV5 60 B2
Overell Gr CV32 105 E1
Overslade Cres CV6 60 C4
Overslade Manor Dr CV22 99 F4
Oversley Rd B76 22 A3
Overstone Rd CV7 52 C3
Overton Dr B46 23 E2
Overtons Cl CV31 110 C3
Overwoods Rd B77 10 A2
Owen Sq CV9 18 B4
Owen St CV9 18 B4
Owenford Rd CV6 61 E4
Owl End La NN11 134 E7
Owl End Way NN11 134 E7
Ox Cl CV2 62 A3
Ox Leys Rd B75, B76 13 E2
Oxendon Way CV3 78 C4
Oxford Cl CV11 29 F4
Oxford Rd Marton CV23 115 C8
Marton CV23 115 D7
Princethorpe CV8,CV23 96 B2
Oxford Row 11 CV32 105 F1
Oxford St Coventry CV1 61 F2
Moreton-in-M GL56 140 A3
Royal Leamington Spa CV32 105 F1
Rugby CV21 83 E2
Southam CV33 147 D2
Oxford Way CV35 146 A1
Oxhayes Cl CV7 74 B3
Oxhey Hill OX17 134 B2
Oxhill Bridle Rd CV35 131 E3
Oxhill Rd CV35 138 B6
Oxley Dr CV3 77 E2
Oxstall Cl B76 22 B3
Oxway Cl CV36 149 F3

Packington Ave CV5 60 A3
Packington La Coleshill B46 34 A1
Little Packington CV7 45 E3
Maxstoke B46 35 D1
White Stitch CV7 46 A2
Packington Pl 4 CV31 110 A4
Packmore St CV34 108 C4
Packsaddle Hill CV37 145 F4
Packwood Ave CV21 101 E4
Packwood Cl
Bentley Heath B93 71 F2
26 Royal Leamington Spa CV31 110 B3
Packwood Cotts B93 71 F1
Packwood Gn CV5 60 A2
Packwood House B94 89 D3
Packwood La B94 89 D2
Packwood Rd B94 89 D4
Paddiford Pl CV10 28 B2
Paddock Cl CV23 125 C8
Paddock Dr B93 72 A1
Paddock La Redditch B98 102 C4
Stratford-u-A CV37 144 C1
Paddock The
Lower Boddington NN11 134 E7
Newton CV23 68 A1
Paddocks Cl Polesworth B78 4 C1
Wolston CV8 80 A2
Paddocks The
Bulkington CV12 40 A2
Mollington OX17 133 F2
Norton WR11 127 B2
Stretton on D CV23 96 C3
Warwick CV34 108 C4
Paddox Cl CV22 100 C4
Paddox Mid Sch CV22 100 B4
Paddox Prim Sch CV22 100 C4
Padgate Cl B35 22 A2
Padmore Ct CV31 110 A3
Padstow Cl CV11 29 F3
Padstow Rd CV4 75 F4
Page Rd CV4 75 F4
Pages La OX15 139 B7
Paget Ct CV2 50 A2
Paget's La CV8 95 E3
Pailton Cl CV2 50 B1
Pailton Rd CV23 66 A2
Painswick Cl B98 102 C3
Pake's Croft 2 CV6 61 D3
Palefield Rd B90 70 C3
Palermo Ave CV3 77 F3

Pallett Dr CV11 29 F4
Palm Tree Ave CV2 50 B1
Palmer La CV1 151 B3
Palmer Rd CV31 110 A2
Palmer's Cl CV21 101 D4
Palmerston Rd CV5 76 C4
Pampas Cl CV37 144 C3
Pancras Cl CV2 50 C1
Pandora Rd CV2 62 C4
Pangbourne Cl CV11 29 F4
Pangbourne Rd CV2 62 B4
Pangfield Pk CV5 60 B2
Pantolf Pl CV21 82 C4
Papenham Gn CV4 76 A4
Parade CV32 109 F4
Parade The Birmingham B37 . 33 D3
Nuneaton CV11 29 E2
Paradise St Coventry CV1 ... 151 C1
Rugby CV21 83 E2
Warwick CV34 108 C4
Paradise Way CV7 51 D1
Paragon Way CV7 50 A4
Parbrook Cl CV4 75 F4
Parbury B77 9 E3
Park Ave Coleshill B46 33 F3
Coventry CV6 49 E2
Nuneaton CV11 29 F2
Polesworth B78 11 D4
Studley B80 103 F2
Park Cl Avon Dassett CV33 .. 133 C4
Claverdon CV35 113 F3
Hanwell OX17 139 F6
Hook Norton OX15 142 D3
Kenilworth CV8 93 D3
Park Croft B47 69 D3
Park Ct CV37 144 C2
Park Dr Claverdon CV35 113 F3
Royal Leamington Spa CV31 . 109 F4
Park Farm Ind Est B98 103 E4
Park Gr B46 23 E1
Park Hall WR11 127 E6
Park Hall Cres B36 22 B1
Park Hall Mews WR11 127 E6
Park Hall Sch B36 22 C1
Park Hill Hook Norton OX15 142 D4
Kenilworth CV8 93 D3
Lower Shuckburgh NN11 116 F1
Park Hill Cty Mid Sch CV8 .. 93 E3
Park Hill La Allesley CV5 60 A3
Coventry CV5 60 A3
Park Hill Prim Sch CV5 60 A2
Park La Astley CV10 37 E3
Berkswell CV7 58 A1
Birmingham B26 44 B2
Birmingham, Castle Vale B35 . 22 B2
Great Alne B49 119 D6
Harbury CV33 123 F6
Ilmington CV36 135 F7
Lower Shuckburgh NN11 116 F1
North Newington OX15 139 E2
Nuneaton CV10 27 F2
Snitterfield CV37 121 C6
Southam CV33 147 D2
Swalcliffe OX15 142 F8
Park Paling The CV3 77 F4
Park Piece CV35 132 B6
Park Rd Baddesley Ensor B78 . 11 D1
Bedworth CV12 39 D1
Chipping Campden GL55 135 A1
Coleshill B46 33 F3
Coventry CV1 151 B1
Hinckley LE10 31 F4
Hook Norton OX15 142 D4
Kenilworth CV8 93 D3
Polesworth B78 11 D4
Royal Leamington Spa CV32 106 A2
Rugby CV21 83 D2
Stratford-u-A CV37 144 C2
Tamworth B77 9 E3
Park Sq B37 44 B4
Park St Coventry CV6 61 F4
Nuneaton CV11 29 E2
Royal Leamington Spa CV32 . 105 F1
Park Street Ind Est CV6 61 E4
Park The OX15 137 F3
Park View Cookhill B96 118 F3
Hockley Heath B94 88 B3
Park View Cl CV7 50 A4
Park Wood La CV4 75 E4
Parkend CV21 83 E4
Parkers La GL56 140 A3
Parkes St CV34 108 B4
Parkfield Cl B77 9 E4
Parkfield Cres B77 9 E4
Parkfield Dr Birmingham B36 22 B1
Kenilworth CV8 93 D3
Parkfield Prim Sch B77 9 E4
Parkfield Rd Coleshill B46 33 F3
Keresley CV7 49 D3
Rugby CV21 82 C3
Parkfields CV33 147 D2
Parkgate Prim Sch CV6 49 D2
Parkgate Rd CV6 49 E2
Parkhill Dr CV5 60 A3
Parkinson Dr CV9 12 C1
Parkland Cl CV6 49 E2
Parklands Ave CV32 106 B2
Parkside CV1 151 C2
Parkstone Rd CV6 49 F1
Parkville Cl CV6 49 E2
Parkville Highway CV6 49 D2
Parkway CV2 63 D4
Parmington Cl B97 102 A3
Parnell Cl CV21 82 C2
Parr Cl CV34 109 E3
Parrotts Gr CV2 50 B3
Parry Rd CV2 62 B4
Parson St B77 9 F4
Parson's La LE10 31 F4
Parson's Nook CV2 62 A3
Parsonage Cl 13 CV33 122 F8
Parsons Cl CV36 149 F3
Partridge Cl B37 33 E2
Partridge Croft CV6 50 A1
Partridge La B97 102 A4
Partridge Rd CV37 144 B2
Patch La B98 102 C3
Patrcia Cl CV4 59 E1
Pattens Rd CV34 105 D1
Patterdale CV21 83 E4
Patterton Dr B76 22 A4
Pattison Coll CV3 62 A1
Pauline Ave CV6 50 A1
Pavilion Way CV5 60 C2
Paxmead Cl CV6 49 D1
Paxton Rd CV6 61 D2
Paybody Hospl CV5 60 B3
Payne Cl CV32 106 A1
Payne's La CV1 61 F2
Paynell Cl CV6 49 D1
Paynes La CV21 82 B2
Payton St CV37 145 D2
Peace Wlk B37 33 D1
Peacock Ave CV2 50 C1
Peacock Ct CV35 146 B2
Peacock La CV35 138 C7
Peacocks The CV34 108 A1
Peake Ave CV11 29 F4
Pear Tree Ave Kingsbury B78 15 E3
Nuneaton CV10 28 C3
Pear Tree Cl
Chipping Campden GL55 135 B1
Shuttington B79 4 C4
Pear Tree Way CV22 82 A1
Pearl Hyde Prim Sch CV2 .. 63 D3
Pearmans Croft B47 69 D3
Pears Cl CV8 92 C3
Pearson Ave CV6 50 A1
Peat Cl CV22 82 C1
Pebble Cl B77 4 A2
Pebworth Ave B90 71 D3
Pebworth Cl CV5 60 A2
Pebworth Cty Fst Sch CV37 128 F1
Peddimore La B76 22 B4
Pedmore Cl B98 103 D4
Peel Cl Coventry CV6 61 F3
Drayton Bassett B78 8 C3
Hampton in A B92 57 D3
Peel La CV6 61 F3
Peel Rd CV34 108 C4
Peel St CV6 61 F3
Pegasus Jun & Inf Sch B35 22 A2
Pegmill Cl CV3 77 F4
Pelham La B49 119 D5
Pembridge Rd B93 71 F2
Pembroke Cl Bedworth CV12 38 B1
1 Warwick CV34 108 C4
Pembroke Gdns CV35 146 B1
Pembroke Way CV11 29 E2
Pembrook Rd CV6 49 E1
Pembury Ave CV6 50 A2
Penarth Gr CV3 78 C4
Pencraig Cl CV8 93 E3
Pendenis Cl CV6 62 A4
Pendicke St CV33 147 D2
Pendigo Way B40 44 C2
Pendred Rd CV22 82 C2
Pendrell Cl B37 33 D2
Penelope Cl CV33 123 F6
Penfold Cl 3 CV33 122 F8
Penmire Cl CV9 11 E2
Penn La Tanworth-in-A B94 86 B2
Wibtoft LE17 43 E1
Pennant Rd LE10 31 E3
Pennine Way Nuneaton CV10 28 A2
Tamworth B77 10 A4
Pennington Mews 4 CV21 . 82 C2
Pennington St 1 CV21 82 C2
Pennington Way CV6 61 F4
Penns Cl CV32 106 C3
Penns La B46 33 F4
Penny Park La CV6 49 D2
Pennyford La B95 113 B1
Pennymoor Rd B77 10 A4
Pennystone Cl CV31 110 B3
Penrhyn Cl OX16 139 F4
Penrith Cl Coventry CV6 49 E1
Royal Leamington Spa CV32 . 105 F1
Penrith Gr B37 33 E1
Penrose Cl CV4 76 A4
Penryhn Cl CV8 93 E3
Penryn Cl CV11 30 A2
Pensham Croft B90 71 D3
Penshurst Way CV11 39 F4
Pensilva Way 2 CV1 61 F2
Pentire Cl CV11 29 F3
Penzance Way CV11 30 A3
Pepper La CV1 151 B2
Pepys Cnr CV4 59 F2
Perch Ave B37 33 D2
Percival Dr CV33 123 F6
Percival Rd CV22 100 B4
Percy Cres CV8 92 C1
Percy Rd Kenilworth CV8 92 C1
Warwick CV34 108 C4
Percy St Coventry CV1 151 A3
Stratford-u-A CV37 145 D2
Percy Terr 7 CV32 105 E1
Peregrine Dr CV5 60 A3
Perimeter Rd
Birmingham B40 44 B2
Birmingham B40 44 C2
Perkins Cl Hornton OX15 139 B8
Salford Priors WR11 127 E6
Perkins Gr CV21 83 F1
Permian Cl CV21 83 E3
Perry Mill La B95 112 E6
Perryfields Cl B98 102 C3
Perryford Dr B91 71 E4
Perryman Dr B78 15 F4
Perrymill La B96 103 D1
Pershore Pl CV4 76 C3
Perth Rise CV5 60 A2
Peter Hall La
Brinklow CV7,CV23 64 A3
Coventry CV7 63 F3
Peterbrook Cl B98 102 C4
Peterbrook Rd B90 69 F4
Peterlee Wlk 6 CV2 63 D4
Petitor Cres CV2 50 B1
Pettiford La B95 113 C3
Pettiver Cres CV21 83 F1
Pettyfields Cl B93 72 A3
Peveril Dr CV3 77 D3
Peyto Cl CV6 49 E1
Pheasant Cl Bedworth CV12 .. 38 C4
Stratford-u-A CV37 144 B2
Pheasant Croft B36 33 D4
Pheasant La B98 102 C4
Phillippes Rd 13 CV34 104 C1
Phipps Ave CV21 83 F1
Phoenix Bsns Pk LE10 30 C4
Phoenix Way CV6 49 F2
Piccadilly B78 9 F1
Piccadilly Cl B37 33 E1
Piccadilly Cres B78 9 F1
Pickard Cl CV21 83 F4
Pickard St CV34 109 D4
Pickford Cl CV11 30 A1
Pickford Grange La CV5 59 E4
Pickford Green La CV5 59 E4
Pickford Way CV5 60 A3
Picton Croft 4 B37 33 E1
Piers Cl CV34 108 C4
Pike Cl LE10 31 E3
Pike Dr B37 33 E2
Pikehorne Croft B36 22 B1
Pikers La CV7 48 A2
Pilgrims Gate LE10 32 A3
Pilgrims La CV23 67 F1
Pilkington Rd CV5 76 B4
Pill La GL56 140 F1
Pilling Cl CV2 62 C4
Pimlico La CV37 121 D2
Pinbury Croft B37 33 D1
Pinchester Cl GL56 141 A1
Pinders La CV21 83 D2
Pine Cl Stoke Golding CV13 21 F4
Stratford-u-A CV37 144 B1
Pine Ct CV32 106 A2
Pine Gr CV21 84 A1
Pine Sq B37 33 D1
Pine Tree Ave CV4 60 A1
Pine Tree Rd CV12 39 E2
Pine Trees Cres CV33 147 E3
Pineham Ave CV33 123 F6
Pinehurst CV32 106 C3
Pines The Bedworth CV12 38 C1
Cheswick Green B90 70 B3
Coventry CV4 75 E4
Pinewood Ave CV9 10 B1
Pinewood Dr CV3 79 E4
Pinewood Gr CV5 77 D4
Pinfold Gn NN11 126 F6
Pinfold St CV21 82 C2
Pingle Ct CV11 29 E1
Pink Green La B98 112 A8
Pinley Fields CV3 78 A4
Pinner's Croft CV2 62 A3
Pinnock Pl CV4 59 F1
Pinwall La CV9 12 C2
Pioneer Units CV11 29 F2
Pipe La CV9 6 B2
Piper's End LE10 41 E2
Piper's La CV8 93 D3
Pipers La CV10 27 E4
Pipers Rd B98 103 E4
Pipewell Cl CV22 82 B1
Pirie Cl CV33 123 F6
Pit Hill CV8 95 E3
Pitt La B92 44 B1
Pittons La CV23 101 E1
Pittway Ave CV36 149 F3
Pixhall Wlk B35 22 A2
Plain Rd The OX15 139 A3
Plane Gr B37 33 D1
Plank La B46 23 D1
Plantagenet Dr CV22 99 F3
Plantation The OX17 134 C1
Plants Brook Rd B76 22 A4
Plants Hill Cres CV4 59 F1
Pleasant Way CV32 106 A1
Pleck The B50 148 B2
Plexfield Rd CV22 82 B1
Pleydell Cl CV3 78 B3
Plomer Cl CV22 99 E4
Plot Rd OX15 139 A3
Plott La CV23 96 C3
Plough Hill Rd CV10 28 A3
Plough La CV33 124 A4
Ploughmans Holt CV33 147 D3
Plover Cl Alcester B49 143 D3
Stratford-u-A CV37 144 B3
Plowden Cl NN11 134 F5
Plowman St CV21 82 C2
Plymouth Cl CV2 62 B4
Plymouth Pl CV31 110 A4
Poitiers Rd CV3 77 E3
Polesworth High Sch B78 .. 10 C4
Polesworth Sta B78 5 D2
Polperro Dr CV5 60 A3
Pomeroy Cl CV4 75 E4
Pondthorpe CV3 78 C3
Pontrilas Rd CV35 132 D4
Pontypool Ave CV3 78 C3
Pool Bank St CV11 29 D2
Pool Cl Little Compton GL56 .. 140 F1
Rugby CV22 99 E4
Welford on A CV37 129 B6
Pool Close Cotts GL56 140 F1
Pool End Cl B93 71 F3
Pool Mdw B76 22 A4
Pool Rd Nuneaton CV10 28 C3
Studley B80 103 F2
Poole Rd CV6 61 D3
Pooley La B78 4 C1
Pooley Veiw B78 5 D1
Poolgate CV35 138 B6
Poolhead La Earlswood B94 .. 86 B4
Tanworth-in-A B94 86 C3
Poolside Gdns CV3 77 D3
Pope St CV22 82 C2
Popes La B96 102 C1
Poplar Ave Bedworth CV12 39 E1
Birmingham, Coleshill Heath B37 44 B4
Poplar Cl Alcester B49 143 E2
Knightcote CV33 124 B1
Poplar Gr CV21 83 D2
Poplar Rd
Bishops Itchington CV33 124 B4
Coventry CV5 60 C1
Dorridge B93 71 F2
Napton CV23 125 C8
Poplars Cl GL55 135 A1
Poplars La B96 102 A1
Poplars The CV10 28 B2
Poplars Trad Est B80 103 E3
Poppy Dr CV23 83 F4
Poppyfield Ct CV4 76 B2
Porchester Cl CV3 63 D1
Porlock Cl CV3 77 F3
Porter Cl CV4 75 F4
Portia Cl CV11 30 A1
Portland Dr CV10 28 B2
Portland Pl
6 Royal Leamington Spa CV32 109 F4
Rugby CV21 83 E1
Portland Pl E 5 CV32 109 F4
Portland Pl W 4 CV32 109 F4
Portland Rd CV21 83 E1
Portland St CV32 109 F4
Portleys La B78 8 B2
Portree Ave CV3 62 C1
Portsea Cl CV3 77 E3
Portway Cl Coventry CV4 75 F4
Royal Leamington Spa CV31 . 110 B3
Portwrinkle Ave CV6 62 A3
Post House Gdns CV23 66 A4
Post Office La
Lighthorne CV35 123 B2
Stockton CV23 147 F4
Witherley CV9 19 D4
Post Office Rd CV9 11 E1
Post Office Wlk B96 102 C1
Post Office Yd CV23 64 C2
Postbridge Rd CV3 77 E3
Postle Cl CV23 101 F1
Potters Cl CV23 64 C2
Potters Green Prim Sch CV2 50 C1
Potters Green Rd CV2 50 C1
Potters La Darlingscott CV36 136 D5
Polesworth B78 11 D4
Potters Rd CV12 38 C1
Potton Cl CV3 78 C3
Potts Cl CV8 93 E2
Poultney Rd CV6 61 D3
Pound Cl Berkswell CV7 58 B2
Lapworth B94 89 D2
Shipston-on-S CV36 149 F3
Pound House La
Tanworth-in-A B94 87 F2
Tanworth-in-A B94 88 A2
Pound La Badby NN11 126 F6
Coleshill B46 34 A2
Furnace End B46 25 E2
Mickleton GL55 135 B6
Royal Leamington Spa CV32 106 A2
Sibford Gower OX15 138 D1
Pound The OX15 139 D2
Powell Rd CV2 62 A2
Powell Way CV11 29 E2
Powis Gr CV8 93 E3
Powys Gr OX16 139 F4
Poyser Rd CV10 39 E4
Pratts La B80 112 A4
Prebend The CV33 133 B7
Precinct The CV1 151 B3
Precision Way B49 143 E3
Prescelly Cl CV10 28 A2
Prescott Ave OX16 139 F3
President Kennedy Sch & Com Coll CV6 49 D2
Prestbury Cl B98 112 A6
Preston Cl CV4 75 F4
Preston Fields La B95 113 D6
Preston La CV37 130 A4
Prestwick Rd B35 22 A2
Pretorian Way CV21 83 D4
Price Rd CV32 106 C3
Pridmore Rd CV6 61 E4
Priest Meadow Cl B96 102 B1
Priestfield Rd B97 102 C3
Priesthills Rd LE10 31 E4
Primley Ave B77 9 F3
Primrose Cl CV23 83 F4
Primrose Ct GL56 140 A3
Primrose Dr LE10 31 F3
Primrose Hill CV34 104 C1
Primrose Hill St CV1 151 C4
Primrose La B49 143 E1
Primsland Cl B90 71 E4
Prince Harry Rd B95 113 B4
Prince Of Wales Rd CV5 60 C2
Prince William Cl CV6 60 C3
Prince's Ave CV11 29 D2
Prince's Dr CV31 109 E4
Prince's Rd B78 5 D1
Prince's St Nuneaton CV11 29 E2
Royal Leamington Spa CV32 106 A1
Princes Cl CV3 78 A4
Princes Dr CV8 93 D4
Princes Rd CV9 16 B3
Princes St CV21 83 D2
Princess Rd Atherstone CV9 .. 18 C4
Hinckley LE10 31 F4
Princess St CV6 61 F4
Princethorpe Coll CV23 96 B2
Princethorpe Way CV3 78 C4
Prior Deram Wlk CV4 76 B4
Priors Cl CV7 74 A3
Priors Field Comb Sch CV8 92 B4
Priors Harnall CV1 151 D4
Priors Mdw CV33 147 E2
Priors The CV12 39 E1
Priorsfield Rd
4 Coventry CV6 61 D2
Kenilworth CV8 92 B3
Priorsfield Rd N 3 CV6 61 D2
Priorsfield Rd S CV6 61 D2
Priory Cl Coleshill B46 34 A3
Lapworth B94 89 E3
Priory Croft CV8 93 D2
Priory Ct B80 103 F3
Priory La CV35 131 D2
Priory Mews CV34 108 C4
Priory Rd Alcester B49 143 D2
Kenilworth CV8 93 D2
Warwick CV34 108 C4
Wolston CV8 80 A2
Priory Row CV1 151 C3
Priory St Coventry CV1 151 C3
Nuneaton CV10 28 B2
Royal Leamington Spa CV31 . 109 F3
Priory Terr CV31 110 A4
Priory Wlk CV9 18 C3
Privet Rd CV2 50 A1
Proffitt Ave CV6 50 A1
Progress Cl CV3 79 D4
Progress Way CV3 79 D4
Prospect Rd CV31 110 A3
Prospect Way
Daventry NN11 117 F2
Rugby CV21 83 E3
Prossers Wlk B46 33 F4
Providence St CV5 76 C4
Provost Williams CE Prim Sch CV8 79 D1
Provost Williams CE Prim Sch (annexe) CV8 95 E3
Ptarmigan Pl CV11 29 F2
Puckering's La 3 CV34 108 C3
Pudding Bag La CV23 98 C1
Pudlicott La GL55 135 E1
Pughe's Cl LE10 32 A3
Pullman Cl B77 4 A1
Pump La CV7 36 B2
Purbrook B77 9 F4
Purcell Ave CV11 40 A4
Purcell Cl CV32 110 A4
Purcell Rd CV6 62 A4
Purefoy Rd CV3 77 E4
Purley Chace La CV9 18 B2
Purley Way CV9 18 C3
Purlieu La CV8 92 B3
Purnells Way B93 72 A3
Purser Dr CV34 108 A2
Purton Cl B49 143 E1
Purton Mews CV31 110 B3
Putney Wlk B37 33 D2
Pyeharps Rd LE10 31 F3
Pyt Pk CV5 60 B2
Pytchley Rd CV22 83 E1
Pytman Dr B76 22 A4

Quadrant The Coventry CV1 151 B2
Nuneaton CV11 29 F2
Quail La CV37 144 B2
Quaker Cl CV13 20 A3
Quantock Dr CV10 28 A2
Quarry Cl
Leek Wootton CV35 104 C4
Rugby CV21 82 C3
Quarry Fields CV35 104 C4
Quarry La Atherstone CV9 19 D3
Chadwick End CV35 90 B1
Cleeve Prior WR11 128 A4
Nuneaton CV11 29 F1
Quarry Rd CV8 92 C3
Quarry St CV32 109 E4
Quarry Yd CV10 28 B2
Quarryfield La CV1 151 C1
Quarrywood Gr CV2 62 A2
Queen Eleanors Dr B93 72 A4
Queen Elizabeth Rd CV10 28 B3
Queen Elizabeth Sch CV9 18 C4
Queen Isabel's Ave CV3 77 E4
Queen Margaret's Rd CV4 .. 76 B4

Queen Mary's Rd
Bedworth CV12 .... 39 E3
Coventry CV6 .... 61 F4
Queen Philippa St CV3 .... 77 E3
Queen St Astwood Bank B96 102 C1
Bedworth CV12 .... 39 E1
Coventry CV1 .... 151 C4
Cubbington CV32 .... 106 C3
Hook Norton OX15 .... 142 D4
Royal Leamington Spa CV32 106 A1
Rugby CV21 .... 83 D2
Queen Victoria Rd CV1 .... 151 B2
Queen Victoria St CV21 .... 83 E2
Queen's Cl CV8 .... 92 C2
Queen's Cres OX15 .... 139 E4
Queen's Dr CV35 .... 114 A8
Queen's Rd Atherstone CV9 ... 18 C4
Coventry CV1 .... 151 A2
Hinckley LE10 .... 31 F4
Kenilworth CV8 .... 92 C2
Nuneaton CV11 .... 29 D2
Queen's Sq CV34 .... 108 B3
Queens Arc CV11 .... 29 E2
Queens Ave CV36 .... 149 F3
Queens CE Mid Sch CV11 .... 29 D2
Queens Cl Harbury CV33 .... 123 F6
Shipston-on-S CV36 .... 149 F3
Queens Rd Bretford CV23 .... 80 C4
Tredington CV36 .... 136 F6
Queens St CV36 .... 136 F8
Queens Way Dordon B78 .... 10 C3
Hurley CV9 .... 16 B2
Queensferry Cl CV22 .... 99 E4
Queensland Ave CV5 .... 60 C1
Queenspark CV31 .... 109 F3
Queensway
Bidford-on-A B50 .... 148 B3
Nuneaton CV10 .... 29 E3
Royal Leamington Spa CV31 . 109 F3
Queensway Trad Est CV31 109 F3
Quilletts Cl CV6 .... 50 A1
Quince B77 .... 4 A2
Quince Tree Specl Sch
B77 .... 4 A2
Quiney's Leys CV37 .... 129 A7
Quiney's Rd CV37 .... 144 B1
Quinn Cl CV3 .... 78 A4
Quinney's Ct B50 .... 148 B2
Quinney's La B50 .... 148 C3
Quinneys La B98 .... 103 D3
Quinton Par CV3 .... 77 E4
Quinton Pk CV3 .... 77 E4
Quinton Prim Sch CV37 .... 129 D2
Quinton Rd CV1 .... 151 C1
Quorn Way CV3 .... 78 C4

Race Leys Fst Sch CV12 .... 39 D2
Race Leys Mid Sch CV12 .... 39 D2
Racemeadow Prim Sch
CV9 .... 12 C1
Racemeadow Rd CV9 .... 12 C1
Radbourn La CV33 .... 124 E5
Radbourne Cl CV33 .... 147 E2
Radbrook Way CV31 .... 110 B3
Radcliffe Rd CV5 .... 76 C4
Radford Circ 5 CV6 .... 61 D2
Radford Cl CV9 .... 12 C1
Radford Prim Sch CV6 .... 61 D3
Radford Rd Coventry CV1 .... 61 D3
Royal Leamington Spa CV31 . 110 B4
Radford Semele
CE Prim Sch CV31 .... 110 C3
Radley Dr CV10 .... 29 D1
Radnor Dr CV10 .... 28 C1
Radnor Wlk CV2 .... 62 C4
Radway Rd B90 .... 70 C4
Raglan Cl CV11 .... 29 E2
Raglan Gr CV8 .... 93 D3
Raglan St CV1 .... 151 D3
Raglan Way B37 .... 33 E1
Ragley Cl B93 .... 72 A4
Ragley Hall B96 .... 118 F2
Ragley Mill La B49 .... 143 D2
Ragley Rd WR11 .... 127 D4
Ragley Way CV11 .... 29 F1
Railway St CV23 .... 82 A2
Railway Terr Atherstone CV9 18 B4
Rugby CV21 .... 83 D2
Rainsbrook Ave CV22 .... 100 C4
Rainsbrook Cl CV33 .... 147 E2
Rainsbrook Dr
Nuneaton CV11 .... 30 A1
Solihull B90 .... 70 C3
Rainsbrook Valley Rly
CV22 .... 100 B3
Rainscar B77 .... 10 A4
Rainsford Cl CV37 .... 129 F7
Raison Ave CV11 .... 29 F4
Raleigh Rd CV2 .... 62 A1
Ralph Cres B78 .... 15 E3
Ralph Rd CV6 .... 60 C3
Ramp Rd B26 .... 44 B3
Ramsay Cres CV5 .... 60 A4
Ramsden Ave CV10 .... 28 B3
Ramsden Rd CV9 .... 19 D4
Ramsey Rd CV31 .... 110 A4
Ramshill La B94 .... 112 E7
Ran-tan The B97 .... 102 C3
Ranby Rd CV2 .... 61 F2
Rance Way B78 .... 15 E3
Randall Rd CV8 .... 92 C2
Randle Rd CV10 .... 28 B2
Randle St CV6 .... 61 D3
Randolph Cl CV31 .... 110 B3
Ranelagh St CV31 .... 110 A3
Ranelagh Terr CV31 .... 109 F3
Range Meadow Cl CV32 .... 105 E2
Rangemoor CV3 .... 78 B3
Rangeworthy Cl B97 .... 102 B4
Rankine Cl CV21 .... 82 B4
Rannoch Cl LE10 .... 31 D4
Rannock Cl CV3 .... 62 C1
Ransom Rd CV6 .... 61 F4
Ransome Rd CV7 .... 37 D4
Ranulf Croft CV3 .... 77 E4
Ranulf St CV3 .... 77 E4
Raphael Cl CV5 .... 60 B2
Ratcliffe La CV9 .... 12 C2
Ratcliffe Rd Atherstone CV9 .. 12 C1
Hinckley LE10 .... 31 F3
Ratcliffe St CV9 .... 18 B4
Rathbone Cl Keresley CV7 .... 49 D3
Rugby CV21 .... 101 D4
Rathlin Croft B36 .... 33 D3
Ratliffe Rd CV22 .... 99 F4
Rattlecombe Rd OX15 .... 138 E5
Raveloe Dr CV11 .... 29 F1
Raven Cragg Rd CV5 .... 76 C4
Raven Way CV11 .... 29 F1
Ravenglass CV21 .... 83 E4
Ravensdale Ave CV32 .... 105 E1
Ravensdale Prim Sch CV2 ... 62 B2
Ravensdale Rd CV2 .... 62 B2
Ravenshaw La B91 .... 56 A2
Ravenshaw Way B91 .... 56 A2
Ravensthorpe Cl CV3 .... 78 C4
Ravenstone B77 .... 10 A4
Ravenswood Hill B46 .... 33 F4
Rawlins Croft B35 .... 22 B2
Rawlinson Rd CV32 .... 106 A1
Rawn View CV9 .... 18 C3
Rawnsley Dr CV8 .... 93 E3
Raygill B77 .... 10 A4
Raymond Cl CV6 .... 49 F3
Raynor Cres CV12 .... 38 B1
Raynsford Wlk CV34 .... 104 B1
Raywoods The CV10 .... 28 C2
Read St CV1 .... 61 F2
Reading Ave CV11 .... 29 F4
Reading Cl CV2 .... 50 A2
Readings The CV33 .... 133 E7
Reardon Ct CV34 .... 104 C1
Recreation Rd CV6 .... 50 A2
Rectory Cl Allesley CV5 .... 60 B3
Barby CV23 .... 101 E1
Bedworth CV7 .... 39 D1
Drayton Bassett B78 .... 8 C3
Harvington WR11 .... 127 D3
Stockton CV23 .... 147 F4
Warmington OX17 .... 133 D2
Whitnash CV31 .... 110 A2
Rectory Dr CV7 .... 39 D1
Rectory Gdns OX15 .... 139 E4
Rectory La Allesley CV5 .... 60 B3
Barby CV23 .... 101 E1
Lower Brailes OX15 .... 137 F2
Rectory Rd Arley CV7 .... 26 C1
Hook Norton OX15 .... 142 D4
Sutton Coldfield B75 .... 13 D3
Red Deeps CV11 .... 39 E4
Red Deeps Specl Sch CV10 39 D4
Red Hill CV35 .... 131 B8
Red Hill Cl B80 .... 103 F3
Red La Astley CV10 .... 37 F4
Burton Green CV8 .... 75 E1
Coventry CV6 .... 61 F3
Kenilworth CV8 .... 92 B4
Red Lion Cl CV33 .... 147 D3
Red Lion St OX17 .... 134 C1
Red Lodge Dr CV22 .... 99 F4
Red Rd CV35 .... 132 B5
Red Wing Wlk B36 .... 33 D4
Redcap Croft CV6 .... 49 E2
Redcar Cl CV32 .... 106 B2
Redcar Rd CV1 .... 61 F3
Reddicap Heath Rd B75 .... 13 D2
Reddings La B46 .... 25 D3
Reddings The B47 .... 69 D3
Redditch Rd B80 .... 103 E3
Redditch Wlk 4 CV2 .... 63 D4
Redesdale Ave CV6 .... 60 C3
Redesdale Pl GL56 .... 140 A2
Redfern Ave CV8 .... 93 D3
Redhill Bank CV37 .... 130 B3
Redhill Cl CV35 .... 146 B1
Redhouse Cl B93 .... 71 F2
Redlake B77 .... 9 F4
Redland Cl CV2 .... 50 C1
Redland Rd CV31 .... 110 A3
Redlands Cres CV37 .... 144 B2
Redliff Ave B36 .... 22 B1
Redmoor Way B76 .... 22 B3
Redruth Cl Coventry CV6 .... 62 A4
Nuneaton CV11 .... 30 A2
Redwing B77 .... 10 A3
Redwing Cl CV37 .... 144 B3
Redwood Croft CV10 .... 29 D1
Redwood Dr B78 .... 15 E4
Reed Sq B35 .... 22 A2
Reeds Pk CV33 .... 111 F1
Rees Dr CV3 .... 77 E2
Reeve Dr CV8 .... 93 D2
Reeves Rd LE10 .... 31 F3
Regal Ct CV9 .... 18 C4
Regal Rd CV37 .... 144 C2
Regal Road Trad Est
CV37 .... 144 C2
Regency Cl Henley-in-A
B95 .... 113 B4
Nuneaton CV10 .... 29 E3
Regency Ct CV5 .... 76 C4
Regency Dr Alcester B49 .... 143 D3
Coventry CV3 .... 76 C3
Kenilworth CV8 .... 92 C2
Regency Ho CV32 .... 110 A4
Regent Gr CV32 .... 109 F4
Regent Pl
2 Royal Leamington Spa
CV31 .... 110 A4
Rugby CV21 .... 83 D2
Regent St Bedworth CV12 .... 39 E2
Coventry CV1 .... 151 A2
Hinckley LE10 .... 31 E4
Nuneaton CV11 .... 29 E3
Royal Leamington Spa
CV32 .... 109 F4
Rugby CV21 .... 83 D2
Regina Cres CV2 .... 63 D4
Regis Wlk CV2 .... 62 C4
Reindeer Rd B78 .... 8 C4
Relay Dr B77 .... 10 B4
Relton Mews CV6 .... 61 F3
Rembrandt Cl CV5 .... 60 B2
Remburn Gdns CV34 .... 108 C4
Remembrance Rd CV3 .... 78 B3
Renfrew Sq B35 .... 22 A2
Renfrew Wlk CV4 .... 76 A4
Renison Rd CV12 .... 38 C1
Repington Ave CV9 .... 12 B1
Repington Rd N B77 .... 4 A3
Repington Rd S B77 .... 4 A3
Repington Way B75 .... 13 D3
Repton Dr CV6 .... 50 A1
Reservoir Dr B46 .... 24 C1
Reservoir Rd CV21 .... 83 E3
Retreat St B96 .... 102 C1
Revel CE Prim Sch The
CV23 .... 53 F1
Rex Cl CV4 .... 75 E4
Reynolds Cl CV21 .... 84 A1
Reynolds Rd CV12 .... 39 D2
Rhoose Croft B35 .... 22 A2
Rhyl Rd CV11 .... 40 C3
Ribble Cl CV12 .... 40 A1
Ribble Rd CV3 .... 61 F1
Ribblesdale B77 .... 10 A4
Ribbonfields CV11 .... 29 E2
Rich Cl CV34 .... 109 D4
Richard Joy Cl CV6 .... 49 E1
Richard Lee Prim Sch CV2 . 62 C2
Richards Cl CV8 .... 92 C3
Richardson Cl CV34 .... 104 C1
Richman Gdns OX16 .... 139 F4
Richmond Rd Atherstone
CV9 .... 18 B4
Hollywood B47 .... 69 E4
Nuneaton CV11 .... 29 D2
Rugby CV21 .... 83 E1
Richmond St CV2 .... 62 A2
Richmond Way 2 B37 .... 33 E2
Rickard Cl B93 .... 71 F3
Riddell Cl B49 .... 143 E2
Riddings Gdns B78 .... 11 D4
Riddings La CV9 .... 11 E2
Riddings The Coventry CV5 ... 76 C4
Grendon CV9 .... 11 E1
Sutton Coldfield B76 .... 22 A4
Riddon Dr LE10 .... 31 D4
Ridge Ct CV5 .... 60 A3
Ridge La CV10 .... 18 A1
Ridgeley Cl CV34 .... 104 C1
Ridgethorpe CV3 .... 78 C3
Ridgeway Ave CV3 .... 77 E3
Ridgeway Cl B80 .... 103 F1
Ridgeway Mid Sch B96 .... 118 C8
Ridgeway Specl Sch CV34 105 D1
Ridgeway The
Astwood Bank B96 .... 118 D6
Barby CV23 .... 117 F8
Hinckley LE10 .... 31 E3
Warwick CV34 .... 105 D1
Ridgewood Cl CV32 .... 105 E1
Ridgewood Rise B77 .... 4 A3
Ridgley Rd CV4 .... 75 F4
Ridgway The CV37 .... 120 C3
Ridley La B46 .... 25 D3
Ridsdale Cl WR11 .... 127 F6
Rigby Cl CV34 .... 109 E2
Rigdale Cl CV2 .... 62 C1
Riley Cl Daventry NN11 .... 117 F2
Kenilworth CV8 .... 93 E2
Riley Dr Banbury OX16 .... 139 F4
Birmingham B36 .... 23 D1
Riley Sq CV2 .... 50 A1
Rimell Cl CV37 .... 130 E1
Ringway Hill Cross CV1 .... 151 A3
Ringway Queens CV1 .... 151 A2
Ringway Rudge CV1 .... 151 A2
Ringway St Johns CV1 .... 151 C2
Ringway St Nicholas CV1 .. 151 B3
Ringway St Patricks CV1 .. 151 B1
Ringway Swanswell CV1 .. 151 C3
Ringway Whitefriars CV1 . 151 C3
Ringwood Highway CV2 .... 50 C1
Rinhill Gr 8 CV31 .... 110 B3
Riplingham 13 CV32 .... 105 F1
Ripon Cl CV5 .... 60 A4
Risborough Cl CV5 .... 60 B2
Risdale Cl CV32 .... 105 E1
Rise The B37 .... 44 A4
Rising La Chadwick End B93 ... 90 A3
Lapworth B94 .... 89 F3
Rising Rd B94 .... 89 E3
River Cl Bedworth CV12 .... 38 C1
Royal Leamington Spa CV32 . 109 E4
River Dr CV9 .... 12 B1
River House Specl Sch
B95 .... 113 B4
River Way CV36 .... 137 A3
River Wlk CV2 .... 50 B1
Riverford Croft CV4 .... 76 B2
Rivermead CV11 .... 29 D2
Rivermead Dr CV37 .... 145 F2
Riversdale Rd CV9 .... 19 D4
Riverside Alcester B49 .... 143 E2
Studley B80 .... 103 F2
Witherley CV9 .... 19 D4
Riverside Cl CV3 .... 78 A4
Riverside Ct 1 B46 .... 33 F4
Riverside Gdns B95 .... 113 B4
Riverside Ind Est B78 .... 9 D4
Riversleigh Rd CV32 .... 105 E1
Riversley Rd CV11 .... 29 E2
Ro-Oak Rd CV6 .... 60 C3
Roach B77 .... 9 E3
Roach Cl B37 .... 33 E2
Roanne Ringway CV11 .... 29 D2
Robert Cl CV3 .... 78 B2
Robert Cramb Ave CV4 .... 75 F4
Robert Hill Cl CV21 .... 84 A1
Robert Rd CV7 .... 49 F4
Roberts Cl CV23 .... 96 C3
Roberts La WR11 .... 127 F1
Robertson Cl CV23 .... 84 A3
Robey's La B78 .... 4 B2
Robin Cl B36 .... 33 D4
Robin Hood Rd CV3 .... 78 B3
Robinia Cl CV32 .... 106 A1
Robins Cl OX7 .... 142 A2
Robins Gr CV34 .... 108 B2
Robins Way CV10 .... 28 A2
Robinson Rd CV12 .... 49 E4
Robinson Way LE10 .... 31 F2
Robinson's End Mid Sch
CV10 .... 28 A2
Robinson's Way B76 .... 22 B3
Robotham Cl CV21 .... 82 C3
Rocheberie Way CV22 .... 99 F4
Rochester Cl CV11 .... 29 D2
Rochester Rd CV5 .... 76 C4
Rochford Cl B76 .... 22 A4
Rochford Ct B90 .... 71 D3
Rock Cl Coventry CV6 .... 50 A1
Nuneaton CV10 .... 27 F2
Rock La CV7 .... 48 B4
Rock Mill La CV32 .... 109 E4
Rocken End CV6 .... 61 E4
Rockford Cl B98 .... 102 C3
Rockingham Cl B93 .... 71 E1
Rocky La CV8 .... 93 E1
Rodborough Rd B93 .... 71 F2
Rodhouse Cl CV4 .... 59 E1
Rodney Cl CV22 .... 82 B1
Rodway Dr CV5 .... 59 E2
Roe Cl CV34 .... 108 C4
Roebuck Pk B49 .... 143 D3
Rogers La CV37 .... 131 A3
Rogers Way CV34 .... 108 A2
Rokeby County Inf Sch
CV22 .... 100 A4
Rokeby Ct CV22 .... 99 F4
Rokeby Jun Sch CV22 .... 100 A4
Rokeby St CV21 .... 83 E2
Rolan Dr B90 .... 69 F4
Roland Ave CV6 .... 49 E2
Roland Mount CV6 .... 49 E2
Rollason Cl CV6 .... 61 E4
Rollason Rd CV6 .... 61 D4
Rolling Stones GL55 .... 135 B2
Rollright Stones OX7 .... 141 D1
Roman Cl LE17 .... 43 F3
Roman Ct B77 .... 9 F4
Roman Rd CV2 .... 62 A2
Roman Row CV36 .... 141 F5
Roman Way Alcester B49 .... 143 D2
Coleshill B46 .... 23 F1
Coventry CV3 .... 77 E2
Dordon B78 .... 11 D3
Halford CV36 .... 136 F8
Rugby CV21 .... 83 D4
Southam CV33 .... 147 E2
Romford Rd CV6 .... 49 D1
Romilly Cl B76 .... 13 D2
Romney B77 .... 9 F4
Romney Rd OX16 .... 139 F5
Romsey Ave CV10 .... 29 E4
Ronald Gr B36 .... 22 B1
Rookery Cl CV13 .... 20 A4
Rookery La Coventry CV6 .... 49 D2
Ettington CV37 .... 131 A3
Newbold-on-S CV37 .... 130 E1
Preston Bagot B95 .... 113 E5
Rookery The
Birchley Heath CV10 .... 17 F1
Nuneaton CV10 .... 27 F3
Rooks Nest CV23 .... 64 C2
Roosevelt Dr CV4 .... 59 F1
Rope Way OX15 .... 142 D3
Roper Cl CV21 .... 101 D4
Ropewalk B49 .... 143 D2
Rosaville Cres CV5 .... 60 A3
Rose Ave Coventry CV6 .... 60 C3
Henley-in-A B95 .... 113 B5
Rose Croft CV8 .... 92 C3
Rose Hill CV9 .... 18 C4
Rose La Napton CV23 .... 125 C7
Nuneaton CV11 .... 29 E2
Rose Rd B46 .... 33 F4
Roseberry Ave CV2 .... 50 B1
Rosebery Rd B77 .... 9 E2
Rosefield Pl 10 CV32 .... 109 F4
Rosefield St CV32 .... 110 A4
Rosefield Wlk 9 CV32 .... 109 F4
Rosegreen Cl CV3 .... 77 F3
Rosehall Cl B98 .... 102 C3
Rosehip Dr CV2 .... 62 A3
Roseland Rd CV8 .... 92 C2
Roselands Ave CV2 .... 62 B4
Rosemary Cl CV4 .... 59 F2
Rosemary Hill CV8 .... 92 C3
Rosemary Way LE10 .... 31 D4
Rosemount Cl CV2 .... 62 C4
Rosemullion Cl CV7 .... 50 A4
Roses La OX7 .... 150 C3
Roseway CV13 .... 21 E4
Rosewood CV11 .... 29 F1
Rosewood Ave CV22 .... 100 A4
Rosewood Cl LE10 .... 31 F3
Rosewood Cres CV32 .... 106 A1
Ross Cl CV5 .... 60 A3
Ross Way CV11 .... 40 A4
Rossendale Way CV10 .... 28 C1
Rosslyn Ave CV6 .... 60 C3
Roston Dr LE10 .... 31 D4
Rothay B77 .... 9 F4
Rother Rd OX16 .... 139 F5
Rother St CV37 .... 144 C1
Rotherby Gr B37 .... 44 A4
Rotherfield Cl CV31 .... 110 A4
Rotherham Rd CV6 .... 49 E1
Rotherhams Oak La B94 .... 87 F4
Rothermans Hill CV9 .... 17 E4
Rothesay Ave CV4 .... 60 A1
Rothesay Cl CV10 .... 29 D1
Rothley Dr CV21 .... 83 F4
Rothwell Rd CV34 .... 104 B1
Rough Coppice Wlk B35 .... 22 A1
Rough Hill Dr B98 .... 102 C3
Rough The B97 .... 102 B4
Roughknowles Rd CV4 .... 75 E3
Rouncil La CV8 .... 104 B4
Round Ave CV23 .... 82 A3
Round Close Rd OX15 .... 142 D4
Round House Rd CV3 .... 78 A4
Round Moor Wlk B35 .... 22 A2
Round Oak Specl Sch
CV32 .... 106 A2
Round St 2 CV21 .... 82 C2
Roundhill Rd OX17 .... 134 A2
Rounds Gdns CV21 .... 82 C2
Rounds Hill CV8 .... 92 C1
Rouse La CV35 .... 137 F8
Rover Dr B36 .... 22 C1
Rover Rd CV1 .... 151 B2
Row The CV7 .... 51 E2
Rowan Cl Binley Woods CV3 ... 79 E4
Hollywood B47 .... 69 D3
Kingsbury B78 .... 15 E3
Stratford-u-A CV37 .... 144 C3
Rowan Dr Rugby CV22 .... 82 A1
6 Warwick CV34 .... 108 C4
Rowan Gr CV2 .... 50 C1
Rowan Rd CV10 .... 28 B3
Rowan Way B37 .... 33 E1
Rowans The Bedworth CV12 . 38 C1
Harvington WR11 .... 127 D4
Rowborough Cl CV35 .... 114 F5
Rowbrook Cl B90 .... 69 F4
Rowcroft Rd CV2 .... 63 D3
Rowington Cl CV6 .... 60 B3
Rowington Gn CV35 .... 89 F1
Rowland Ave Polesworth B78 . 5 D2
Studley B80 .... 103 F2
Rowland Ct CV7 .... 26 C1
Rowland St CV21 .... 82 C2
Rowland Way CV9 .... 12 B1
Rowley Cres CV37 .... 145 D2
Rowley Dr CV3 .... 78 A2
Rowley La CV3 .... 78 A2
Rowley Rd Coventry CV3, CV8 78 A2
Whitnash CV31 .... 110 A1
Rowley's Green La CV6 .... 49 F2
Rowleys Green Lane
Ind Est CV6 .... 49 F2
Rowse Cl CV21 .... 83 E4
Rowthorn Dr B90 .... 71 D3
Roxburgh Croft CV32 .... 106 B3
Roxburgh Rd CV11 .... 29 F1
Royal Cres CV3 .... 78 B3
Royal Ct LE10 .... 31 E4
Royal Leamington Spa
Rehabilitation Hospl
CV34 .... 109 F2
Royal Oak Ind Est NN11 .... 117 F2
Royal Oak La CV12 .... 49 E4
Royal Oak Way N NN11 .... 117 F2
Royal Oak Way S NN11 .... 117 F2
Royal Oak Yd CV12 .... 39 D2
Royal Shakespeare
Theatre CV37 .... 145 D1
Royston Cl CV3 .... 63 D2
Rubens Cl CV5 .... 60 B2
Rudge Rd CV1 .... 151 A2
Rufford Cl Alcester B49 .... 143 E3
Hinckley LE10 .... 31 E2
Rugby Coll CV21 .... 83 E1
Rugby High Sch CV22 .... 99 E3
Rugby La CV23 .... 97 D3
Rugby Midland Sta CV21 .... 83 E2
Rugby Rd Barby CV23 .... 101 E1
Binley Woods CV3 .... 79 E4
Brandon CV8 .... 80 A3
Brinklow CV23 .... 64 C2
Bulkington CV12 .... 40 B1
Church Lawford CV23 .... 81 E3
Clifton u D CV23 .... 83 F3
Dunchurch CV22 .... 99 E2
Easenhall CV23 .... 65 F2
Harborough Magna CV23 .... 66 A1
Hinckley LE10 .... 31 E3
Kilsby CV21,CV23 .... 101 F3
Lilbourne CV23 .... 84 C3
Long Lawford CV23 .... 82 A2
Pailton CV23 .... 66 A4
Princethorpe CV23 .... 96 C1
Royal Leamington Spa CV32 . 105 E1
Shawell LE17 .... 68 A4

Rugby Sch CV22 83 D1
Ruislip Cl B35 22 A2
Rumbush La B94 69 F2
Rumer Cl CV37 129 B4
Runcorn Cl Birmingham B37 33 E2
Redditch B98 102 C4
Runcorn Wlk 10 CV2 63 D4
Runneymede Gdns CV10 28 C2
Runnymede Dr CV7 74 B3
Rupert Brooke Rd CV22 99 F4
Rupert Kettle Dr CV33 124 B4
Rupert Rd CV6 61 D4
Rush La B77 9 D4
Rushbrook La B94 86 B2
Rushbrook Rd CV37 145 E1
Rushford Cl B90 71 D4
Rushleigh Rd B90 69 F4
Rushmoor Dr CV5 60 C2
Rushmore St CV31 110 A4
Rushmore Terr 13 CV31 110 A4
Rushock Cl B98 103 E4
Rushton Cl CV7 74 B4
Rushwick Gr B90 71 D3
Ruskin Cl Coventry CV6 60 B3
Nuneaton CV10 28 A3
Rugby CV22 99 F3
Russell Ave CV22 99 E2
Russell Cl CV23 115 D4
Russell St Coventry CV1 151 C4
Royal Leamington Spa CV32 105 F1
Russell St N CV1 151 C4
Russell Terr CV31 110 A4
Russelsheim Way CV22 83 D1
Rutherford Glen CV11 29 F1
Rutherglen Ave CV3 78 A3
Rutland Ave Hinckley LE10 31 E4
Nuneaton CV10 28 C2
Rutland Croft 3 CV3 78 C4
Rydal B77 10 A4
Rydal Ave CV11 30 A3
Rydal Cl Allesley CV5 60 A4
Hinckley LE10 30 C4
Rugby CV21 83 E3
Ryde Ave CV10 29 E4
Ryder Cl CV35 114 F3
Ryder Row CV7 37 D4
Ryders Hill Cres CV10 28 B4
Rye Cl Banbury OX16 139 F5
Stratford-u-A CV37 144 C3
Rye Croft B47 69 D3
Rye Fields 1 CV33 122 E8
Rye Grass Wlk B35 22 A2
Rye Hill CV5 60 A3
Rye Piece Ringway CV12 39 E2
Ryeclose Croft B37 33 E2
Ryefield La B76 14 A1
Ryegrass La B97 102 B3
Ryelands The CV23 98 B4
Ryhope Cl CV12 38 B1
Ryknild St B49 143 D3
Ryland Cl CV31 110 B3
Ryland Rd CV35 122 B8
Ryland St CV37 144 C1
Rylston Ave CV6 49 D1
Rylstone Way 4 CV34 104 C1
Ryon Hill CV37 145 F4
Ryton B77 9 F4
Ryton Cl CV4 76 A4
Ryton Gardens CV8 79 F1

Sabin Cl CV23 115 C4
Sabin Dr CV33 107 E4
Sackville Cl Hanwell OX17 139 F6
Stratford-u-A CV37 144 B2
Sacred Heart RC Prim Sch CV2 62 A2
Saddington Rd CV3 78 C4
Saddlebow La CV35 114 B2
Saddlers Cl LE10 31 F3
Saddleton St CV35 138 C7
Sadler Cl CV37 144 C3
Sadler Rd CV6 61 D4
Sadlers Ave CV36 149 F3
Sadlers Cl CV36 149 F3
Sadlerswell La B94 88 A3
Saffron B77 4 A2
Saffron Cl CV23 83 F4
Saffron Mdw CV37 144 C1
Saffron Wlk CV37 144 C1
Saintbury Cl CV37 145 E1
Saintbury Dr B91 71 E4
Saints Way CV10 29 E3
SS Peter & Paul RC Prim Sch CV2 62 C4
St Agatha's Rd CV2 62 A2
St Agnes Cl B80 103 E2
St Agnes La CV1 151 B3
St Agnes Way CV11 29 F2
St Albans Cl CV32 105 E1
St Andrew's CE Inf Sch CV5 59 E3
St Andrew's Cres CV37 144 C1
St Andrew's Rd Coventry CV5 76 C4
Royal Leamington Spa CV32 106 A3
St Andrews B77 4 A2
St Andrews Benn CE Fst Sch CV21 83 E2
St Andrews Benn CE Prim Sch CV21 83 E2
St Andrews Cres CV22 100 A4
St Andrews Dr CV11 30 A1
St Ann's Cl CV31 110 B4
St Ann's Rd CV2 62 A2
St Anne's RC Prim Sch Birmingham B37 33 D1
Coventry CV3 78 B3
Nuneaton CV10 28 B4
St Anne's Rd CV22 82 C1
St Annes Gr B93 72 A3
St Anthony's RC Comb Sch CV31 110 B4
St Antony's RC Prim Sch B37 33 D3
St Asaphs Ave B80 103 E2
St Athan Croft B35 22 A2
St Augustine's RC Comb Sch CV8 92 C4
St Augustine's RC Prim Sch CV6 61 D4
St Augustine's RC Sch B97 102 B3
St Augustine's Wlk CV6 61 D4
St Austell Cl CV11 30 A3
St Austell Rd CV2 62 C2
St Bartholemews Cl CV3 63 D1
St Bartholomew's CE Prim Sch CV3 78 C4
St Benedict's RC High Sch B49 143 E2
St Benedict's RC Prim Sch Atherstone CV9 18 C4
Coventry CV1 61 F2
St Benedicts Cl CV9 18 B4
St Bernards Wlk CV3 78 B3
St Blaise Ave B46 23 E1
St Bride's Cl 3 CV31 110 B3
St Catherine's LE10 31 F4
St Catherine's Cl CV3 78 A4
St Catherine's Cres CV31 109 F2
St Catherine's RC Prim Sch GL55 135 A2
St Chads Rd
3 Bishops Tachbrook CV33 122 E8
Studley B80 103 E2
St Christian's Croft CV3 77 F4
St Christian's Rd CV3 77 F4
St Christopher Prim Sch CV5 60 B2
St Christopher's Cl CV34 108 B4
St Columba's Cl CV1 151 B4
St David's Cl CV31 110 B4
St David's Prim Sch GL56 140 A3
St Davids Orch CV3 78 C4
St Davids Way CV10 39 D3
St Edith's Cl CV23 53 F2
St Edith's Gn 1 CV34 109 D4
St Editha's Ct B78 5 D1
St Edithas Rd B78 11 D4
St Edmonds Rd CV9 16 B3
St Edward's RC Prim Sch B46 34 A3
St Edwin's Cl WR11 127 B2
St Elizabeth's RC Prim Sch CV6 61 F4
St Elizabeth's Rd CV6 61 F4
St Faith's CE Jun Sch B49 143 E2
St Faith's Rd B49 143 E3
St Francis RC Comb Sch CV12 39 E2
St George & St Teresa RC Sch B93 72 A2
St George's Cl
Moreton-in-M GL56 140 A3
Stratford-u-A CV37 144 B2
St George's Rd
Atherstone CV9 12 C1
Coventry CV1 61 F1
Royal Leamington Spa CV31 109 F3
Solihull B90 70 B4
St Georges Ave CV22 99 F4
St Georges Way CV10 39 D4
St Gerard's (Warwickshire) Orthopaedic Hospl B46 34 A3
St Gerards RC Jun & Inf Sch B35 22 A2
St Giles Cty Mid Sch CV7 49 F4
St Giles Rd Coventry CV7 49 E3
Gaydon CV35 132 E8
St Govan's Cl 4 CV31 110 B3
St Gregory's RC Prim Sch Coventry CV2 62 C2
Stratford-u-A CV37 145 E3
St Gregory's Rd CV37 145 D2
St Helen's Rd CV31 110 A3
St Helen's Way CV5 60 A4
St Helena Rd B78 11 D4
St Ives Rd CV2 62 C2
St Ives Way CV11 29 F3
St James' Ave CV35 146 C2
St James CE Fst Sch CV33 147 D3
St James CE Mid Sch CV12 40 B1
St James Cl WR11 127 D3
St James Cres CV33 147 D3
St James Ct GL56 140 A2
St James Gdns CV12 40 B1
St James' La CV3 78 B3
St James Meadow Rd CV32 105 E1
St James Rd CV33 147 D3
St James's Cl LE10 31 E3
St John Fisher RC Prim Sch CV2 62 B3
St John St CV21 83 D2
St John the Baptist CE Fst Sch CV31 109 F4
St John the Baptist RC Prim Sch B36 33 D4
St John the Divine CE Prim Sch CV3 78 B3
St John Vianney RC Prim Sch CV5 60 A2
St John's Ave CV8 93 D2
St John's CE Prim Sch CV5 60 B2
St John's Cl
Cherington CV36 141 D7
Henley-in-A B95 113 A4
St John's Ct 9 CV34 108 C4
St John's La CV23 82 A3
St John's Rd
Cherington CV36 141 D7
Royal Leamington Spa CV31 110 A3
St John's St Coventry CV1 151 C2
Kenilworth CV8 93 D2
St Johns CV34 108 C4
St Johns Ave CV22 100 C4
St Johns Cl Knowle B93 72 A3
Stratford-u-A CV37 144 C1
St Johns Mid Sch CV8 92 C1
St Johns Rd CV10 27 F4
St Joseph's RC Comb Sch CV31 110 A2
St Joseph's RC Mid Sch CV11 29 E2
St Joseph's RC Prim Sch OX16 139 F3
St Joseph's RC Sch CV23 53 F2
St Joseph's Sch CV8 93 D4
St Jude's Cres CV3 78 B4
St Judes Ave B80 103 E2
St Laurence Ave CV34 108 B3
St Laurence Cl CV35 114 A8
St Lawrence CE Prim Sch CV23 125 C7
St Lawrence Cl Knowle B93 72 A3
Napton CV23 125 C8
St Lawrence Rd CV10 27 D2
St Lawrence's Rd CV6 49 F1
St Leonard's Wlk CV8 79 D1
St Leonards Cl
Birmingham B37 44 A4
Dordon B78 11 D3
St Leonards View B78 10 C4
St Luke's Rd CV6 49 E2
St Margaret Rd Coventry CV1 61 F1
Stoke Golding CV13 21 F4
St Margaret's CE Mid Sch CV31 110 A2
St Margaret's CE Prim Sch CV8 80 A2
St Margaret's Rd CV31 110 A3
St Margaret's Specl Sch CV12 39 D2
St Margarets CE Prim Sch CV13 21 E4
St Marie's RC Inf Sch CV22 83 D1
St Marie's RC Mid Sch CV22 82 C1
St Mark's Annexe (Coventry & Warwickshire Hospl) CV1 151 C4
St Mark's Ave CV22 99 E4
St Mark's Cl Gaydon CV35 132 E8
Ullenhall B95 112 E6
St Mark's Mews CV32 105 F1
St Mark's Rd CV32 105 E1
St Martin's LE10 31 F3
St Martin's Catholic High Sch CV13 21 F4
St Martin's Cl CV37 144 C1
St Martin's Rd CV8 77 E1
St Martins Ave B80 103 E2
St Mary St CV1 151 C2
St Mary's CE Jun Sch B80 103 F2
St Mary's Cl
Priors Hardwick CV23 125 D3
Southam CV33 147 E3
Ullenhall B95 112 E6
Warwick CV34 108 B4
St Mary's Cres CV31 110 A4
St Mary's La OX7 142 F2
St Mary's RC Comb Sch CV33 147 E2
St Mary's RC Jun & Inf Sch B80 103 F2
St Mary's RC Prim Sch Aston le W NN11 134 F5
Coventry CV1 61 F2
St Mary's Rd Alcester B49 143 E2
Atherstone CV9 18 C4
Fillongley CV7 36 C2
Hinckley LE10 31 E4
Nuneaton CV11 29 D3
Royal Leamington Spa CV31 110 A4
Stratford-u-A CV37 145 D2
St Mary's Terr CV31 110 A4
St Marys Acre CV37 120 E7
St Marys Gr B79 2 B2
St Matthews Cl WR11 127 E6
St Matthews St CV21 83 D2
St Mawgen Cl B35 22 B2
St Michael's Cl Arley CV7 37 D4
Bishops Itchington CV33 124 A4
Claverdon CV35 113 F3
Weston u W CV33 107 E4
Wood End CV9 10 B1
St Michael's Cres CV23 147 F4
St Michael's Dr DE12 3 F4
St Michael's Hospl CV34 108 C4
St Michael's Rd
Claverdon CV35 113 F3
Coventry CV2 62 A2
Warwick CV34 108 B4
St Michael's Way CV10 28 B2
St Michaels Cl CV9 12 C1
St Michales Cl CV33 111 F1
St Milburgh Cl WR11 127 D1
St Nicholas Ave CV8 92 C2
St Nicholas CE Comb Sch CV8 92 C3
St Nicholas Church St CV34 108 C4
St Nicholas Cl Alcester B49 143 E2
Austrey CV9 3 D1
Coventry CV1 61 E3
St Nicholas Est CV9 11 E1
St Nicholas Rd
Henley-in-A B95 113 B4
Radford Semele CV31 110 C3
St Nicholas St CV1 151 B4
St Nicholas Wlk B76 23 D3
St Nicolas CE Fst Sch CV11 29 F3
St Nicolas Park Dr CV11 29 F4
St Nicolas Rd CV11 29 E3
St Osburg's RC Prim Sch CV1 151 A3
St Osburg's Rd CV2 62 A2
St Oswalds CE First Sch CV21 82 B2
St Patrick's CE Prim Sch B94 70 B1
St Patrick's RC Prim Sch Birmingham B37 33 E1
Coventry CV2 50 B1
St Patrick's Rd CV1 151 B1
St Patricks RC Comb Sch CV31 109 F3
St Paul's CE Comb Sch CV32 106 A1
St Paul's CE Comb Sch (Annexe) CV32 106 A1
St Paul's CE Fst Sch CV10 28 B2
St Paul's Cl CV34 108 B3
St Paul's Cres 3 B46 33 F4
St Paul's Ct B77 9 E2
St Paul's Rd Coventry CV6 61 F3
Nuneaton CV10 28 B2
St Paul's Sq 12 CV32 106 A1
St Paul's Terr CV34 108 B3
St Peter's Ave CV9 19 D4
St Peter's CE Prim Sch CV35 122 B7
St Peter's Cl Redditch B97 102 C3
Water Orton B46 23 D1
Witherley CV9 19 D4
St Peter's Ct CV1 151 D4
St Peter's Dr CV10 27 F2
St Peter's Rd
7 Royal Leamington Spa CV32 109 F4
Rugby CV21 83 E2
Wellesbourne CV35 146 B2
St Peters La B92 44 B1
St Peters Rd Atherstone CV9 19 D4
Kineton CV35 132 B6
St Swithin's Dr CV37 129 D2
St Thomas More RC Fst Sch B98 103 D4
St Thomas More RC Prim Sch CV3 77 E3
St Thomas More Sch CV10 29 D2
St Thomas' Rd CV6 50 A2
St Thomas's Ct CV1 61 D1
St Wulstan Way CV33 147 E3
Salcombe Cl Coventry CV3 78 B3
Nuneaton CV11 29 F3
Salem Rd LE10 31 F3
Salford Cl Coventry CV2 62 A3
Redditch B98 103 D3
Salford Priors CE Prim Sch WR11 127 F6
Salford Rd B50 148 B2
Salisbury Ave CV3 77 E3
Salisbury Dr Nuneaton CV10 28 A4
Water Orton B46 23 E2
Salisbury Rd LE10 32 A4
Salt La CV1 151 B2
Salt Way B96 118 B7
Salt Way La OX15 137 F2
Salter St B94 70 B1
Salters La B95 120 C7
Saltisford CV34 108 B4
Saltisford Gdns CV34 108 B4
Salts La B78 8 C2
Sam Gault Cl CV3 78 C4
Sambourne La
Astwood Bank B96 102 C1
Coughton B49 118 E7
Sambourne B96 103 D1
Sambourne Park La B96 118 D8
Sammons Way CV4 59 E1
Sampson Cl CV2 62 B4
Sanby Cl CV12 39 D2
Sanctus Dr CV37 144 C1
Sanctus Rd CV37 144 C1
Sanctus St CV37 144 C1
Sand Barn La CV37 121 D6
Sanda Croft B36 33 D3
Sandbarn Cl B90 70 C3
Sandel Cl CV37 144 C2
Sanders Cl Atherstone CV9 12 C1
Braunston NN11 117 D5
Sanders Rd Bedworth CV6 50 A3
Salford Priors WR11 127 F6
Sandfield Cl B90 70 A4
Sandfield Rd CV37 144 C1
Sandfine Rd OX15 139 D1
Sandford Cl CV2 50 C2
Sandford Gn OX16 139 F4
Sandford Way CV22 99 E2
Sandgate Cres CV2 62 C1
Sandhills Cres B91 71 D4
Sandhurst Gr CV6 61 D3
Sandilands Cl CV2 62 C2
Sandon Rd CV11 29 D3
Sandown Ave CV6 49 F1
Sandown Cl CV32 106 B2
Sandown Rd CV21 83 E2
Sandpiper B77 10 A3
Sandpiper Cl CV37 144 B3
Sandpiper Rd CV2 50 A2
Sandpits Cl Curdworth B76 23 D3
Tysoe CV35 138 B6
Sandpits La CV6 48 C1
Sandpits Rd CV35 138 B7
Sandpits The CV12 40 B1
Sandwick Cl CV3 78 C4
Sandy La Blackdown CV32 105 F3
Coventry CV1 61 E3
Furnace End B46 25 F2
Marton CV23 115 D7
Monks Kirby CV23 53 F2
Newton Regis B79 2 B3
Royal Leamington Spa CV32 105 E2
Rugby CV21 82 C2
Sandy Lane Bsns Pk CV1 61 E3
Sandy Way Barford CV35 122 B7
Tamworth B77 4 A2
Sandy Way La B78 11 E4
Sandythorpe CV3 78 C3
Sankey Gr GL56 140 A2
Santos Cl CV3 78 C4
Sapcote Rd LE10 32 A4
Saplings The B76 22 A4
Sapphire Dr CV31 109 F3
Sapphire Gate CV2 62 B1
Saracen Dr CV7 73 F3
Sargeaunt St CV31 109 F4
Sark Dr B36 33 D3
Satchwell Wlk 8 CV32 109 F4
Saumur Way CV34 109 E3
Saunders Ave CV12 39 D1
Saunton Cl CV5 60 A4
Saunton Rd CV22 82 C1
Savages Cl CV33 122 F8
Savernake Rd CV35 132 C4
Saville Gr CV8 93 E3
Sawbridge Rd CV23 116 F5
Saxon Cl Binley Woods CV3 79 E4
Polesworth B78 4 C1
Stratford-u-A CV37 145 E1
Studley B80 103 F3
Tamworth B77 9 F3
Saxon Mdws CV32 105 E1
Saxon Rd CV2 62 A2
Saxon Wood Rd B90 70 B3
Saxonfields B50 148 B2
Scafell CV21 83 E4
Scafell Cl CV5 60 A2
Scammerton B77 10 A4
Scar Bank CV34 104 C1
Scarborough Way CV4 75 F4
Schofield Rd B37 33 D3
Scholars La CV37 144 C1
Scholfield Rd CV7 49 D3
School Ave WR11 127 F6
School Cl Birmingham B37 33 D3
Braunston NN11 117 E5
Coventry CV3 61 F1
Great Alne B49 119 D6
Hinckley LE10 32 A3
Long Compton CV36 141 C3
School Dr B47 69 D2
School Gdns CV21 84 A1
School Hill Hartshill CV10 28 A4
Mollington OX17 133 F2
Napton CV23 125 C8
Offchurch CV33 111 D4
School House La CV2 63 D3
School La Badby NN11 126 F6
Bearley CV37 120 E7
Bedworth CV7 49 F4
Kenilworth CV8 92 C3
Ladbroke CV33 124 D5
Lea Marston B76 24 A4
Littleton WR11 127 F1
Lower Brailes OX15 137 F2
North Newington OX15 139 E2
Nuneaton CV10 27 F3
Priors Marston CV23 125 E4
Radford Semele CV31 110 C3
Shuttington B79 4 C4
Stretton on D CV23 96 C3
Tamworth B77 9 E3
Tiddington CV37 145 F2
Warmington OX17 133 D2
Wolvey LE10 41 F2
Wroxall CV35 90 C2
School Rd Alcester B49 143 D2
Bulkington CV12 40 B1
Great Alne B49 119 D6
Henley-in-A B95 113 B4
Hockley Heath B94 88 A4
Pebworth CV37 128 F1
Salford Priors WR11 127 F6
Snitterfield CV37 121 B6
Wellesbourne CV35 146 C2
School St
Church Lawford CV23 81 D3
Churchover CV23 67 E3
Dunchurch CV22 99 E2
Long Lawford CV23 82 A2
Rugby CV21 84 A1
Southam CV33 147 E2
Stockton CV23 147 F4
Wolston CV8 80 A2
School Wlk CV11 29 F1
Scotchill The CV6 49 D1
Scotland End OX15 142 D4
Scots Cl CV22 99 E4
Scots La CV6 60 C3
Scott Ave CV10 29 E4

Scott Cl B50 148 B3
Scott Rd Kenilworth CV8 92 C1
Redditch B97 102 B4
Royal Leamington Spa CV31 110 A3
Seabroke Ave CV22 82 C2
Seafield La B48 85 F2
Seaford Cl CV6 50 A2
Seagrave Rd CV1 151 D1
Sealand Dr CV12 39 D2
Sear Hills Cl CV7 74 A3
Seathwaite CV21 83 E4
Seaton B77 9 F4
Seaton Cl Hinckley LE10 32 A4
Nuneaton CV11 29 F3
Sebastian Cl CV3 78 A3
Seckington La B79 2 B2
Second Ave CV3 62 B1
Second Exhibition Ave B40 44 B2
Sedgemere Gr CV7 74 B3
Sedgemoor Rd CV3 78 A3
Sedlescombe Pk CV22 99 F4
Seed Field Croft CV3 77 F4
Seekings The CV31 110 A2
Seeney La B76 15 D1
Seeswood Cl CV10 28 B1
Sefton Rd Coventry CV4 76 C3
Tamworth B77 9 E2
Seggs La B49 143 D2
Segrave Cl CV35 132 B6
Selborne Rd CV22 99 E4
Selby Way CV10 28 A3
Selsdon Cl B47 69 E3
Selsey Cl CV3 78 B2
Selside CV21 83 E4
Selworthy Rd CV6 49 F2
Semele Cl CV31 110 C3
Seneschal Rd CV3 77 F4
Sennen Cl CV11 30 A3
Seven Acre Cl 4 CV33 122 E8
Seven Meadows Rd CV37 144 C1
Severn Ave LE10 31 D4
Severn Cl CV32 106 B2
Severn Rd Bulkington CV12 40 A2
Coventry CV1 61 F1
Severn Stars Ind Est CV3 78 A4
Sevincott Cl CV37 144 B2
Sevington Cl B91 71 E4
Sewall Highway CV2 62 A3
Seymour Cl Coventry CV3 78 B3
Hampton Magna CV35 114 F3
Seymour Gate GL55 135 B2
Seymour Gr CV34 109 E3
Seymour Rd Alcester B49 143 E3
Nuneaton CV11 29 E2
Rugby CV21 83 E3
Stratford-u-A CV37 144 B1
Shackleton Way LE17 55 E3
Shadow Brook La B92 56 C4
Shadowbrook Rd CV6 61 D3
Shaft La CV7 47 D2
Shaftesbury Ave CV7 49 D4
Shaftesbury Rd CV5 76 C4
Shakers La CV23 115 C5
Shakesfield Cl CV36 136 F6
Shakespeare Ave
Bedworth CV12 39 E1
Warwick CV34 108 B2
Shakespeare Ctr Mus The
CV37 145 D2
Shakespeare Dr CV11 30 A1
Shakespeare Gdns CV22 99 F4
Shakespeare La WR11 127 D3
Shakespeare Rd B90 70 B4
Shakespeare St
Coventry CV2 62 A2
Stratford-u-A CV37 145 D2
Shakespeares Birthplace
Mus CV37 145 D2
Shakleton Rd CV5 61 D1
Shanes Castle Rd CV35 132 D3
Shanklin Dr CV10 29 E3
Shanklin Rd CV3 78 A2
Shannon B77 9 F4
Shap Fell CV21 83 E4
Sharnford Rd LE10 32 C3
Sharp Cl CV6 49 E1
Sharpe Cl CV34 108 C4
Sharpe St B77 4 A3
Sharpless Rd LE10 31 F4
Sharpley Ct CV2 63 D4
Sharratt Rd CV12 39 D1
Shaw's La CV35 114 C8
Shawberry Ave B35 22 A2
Shawbury La B46 35 E4
Shawbury Village B46 35 F3
Shawe Ave CV10 29 E4
Shawell Rd LE17 68 B4
Shawfield B47 69 D3
Shawhurst Croft B47 69 D4
Shawhurst La B47 69 D3
Shearings The OX15 142 D4
Sheep Dip La CV23 96 C1
Sheep St
Chipping Campden GL55 135 A1
Rugby CV21 83 D2
Shipston-on-S CV36 149 F3
Stratford-u-A CV37 145 D1
Sheepclose Dr B37 33 D2
Sheepcote Cl CV32 106 A1
Sheepy La CV9 6 C2
Sheepy Rd Atherstone CV9 12 B1
Sheepy Magna CV9 12 C3
Shefford Rd CV35 132 D3
Shelbourne Rd CV37 144 A2
Sheldon Gr 6 CV34 104 C1
Sheldon Rd B98 103 D4
Shelfield Cl CV5 60 A2
Shelley Ave CV34 108 B2
Shelley Cl Bedworth CV12 39 E1
Redditch B97 102 B4
Shelley Rd Coventry CV2 62 B2
Stratford-u-A CV37 145 D1
Shellon Cl CV3 78 C4
Shelly Cres B90 71 D3
Shelly La B90 71 D3
Shelton Sq CV1 151 B2
Shelton St B77 9 F4
Shelwick Gr B93 71 F2
Shenington CE Prim Sch
OX15 138 F5
Shenstone Ave CV22 83 F1
Shenstone Dr CV7 74 A3
Shenton Cl CV13 21 F4
Sheperds Hill CV33 147 E2
Shepherd Cl CV4 59 F2
Shepherd Pl CV35 132 B5
Shepherd St CV23 115 C7
Shepherds Cl CV23 115 D3
Shepperton Bsns Pk CV11 29 E1
Shepperton St CV11 29 E1
Sheppey Dr B36 33 D3
Sherard Croft B36 33 D3
Sherborne Cl B46 34 A2
Sherborne Rd LE10 32 A4
Sherbourne Ave CV10 28 A2
Sherbourne Cres CV5 60 C2
Sherbourne Fields Sch CV6 60 B3
Sherbourne St CV1 61 D1
Sherbrooke Ave B77 9 F3
Sherdmore Croft B90 70 C3
Sheridan Cl CV22 99 F4
Sheridan Dr CV10 27 F3
Sheridan Wlk B35 22 A2
Sheriff Ave CV4 76 A4
Sheriff Rd CV21 83 E2
Sheriffs Orch CV1 151 B2
Sheringham Cl CV11 29 F1
Sherington Ave CV5 60 B2
Sherlock Rd CV5 60 B2
Sherwell Dr B49 143 D2
Sherwood Cl CV9 10 B1
Sherwood Jones Cl CV6 61 D3
Sherwood Rd CV13 21 F4
Sherwood Wlk CV32 106 B2
Shetland Cl CV5 60 A2
Shetland Dr CV10 29 D1
Shetland Wlk B36 33 D3
Shevlock Way CV6 62 A3
Shillingstone Cl CV2 63 D2
Shilton & Ansty Fst Sch
CV7 51 F3
Shilton Cl B90 70 C3
Shilton Ind Est CV7 51 F4
Shilton La Barnacle CV2, CV7 51 D2
Bulkington CV12 40 B1
Coventry CV2 50 C2
Shilton CV7, CV12 51 E4
Shinehill La WR11 128 A1
Shipston Rd
Alderminster CV37 130 B5
Coventry CV2 62 B3
Long Compton CV36 141 C4
Upper Tysoe CV35 138 B6
Shipton-on-Stour
Prim Sch CV36 149 F3
Shire Cl CV6 50 A1
Shirebrook Cl CV2 50 B1
Shires Gate Ret Pk CV31 109 F3
Shires Ret Pk CV34 109 E3
Shires The CV23 81 D3
Shirlett Cl CV2 50 A2
Shirley La CV7 59 D3
Shirley Rd CV2 63 D4
Shirrall Dr B78 7 F2
Shopping Ctr The CV31 110 A3
Shopping Prec The CV34 105 D1
Shorncliffe Rd CV6 60 C3
Short Acres CV35 132 C6
Short La CV23 115 C4
Short St Coventry CV1 151 C2
Nuneaton CV10 28 B2
Shortland Cl B93 72 A4
Shortlands CV7 49 E3
Shortley Rd CV3 77 F4
Shortwoods The B78 11 D3
Shottery CV37 144 B1
Shottery CE Prim Sch
CV37 144 B1
Shottery Cl CV5 60 A2
Shottery Rd CV37 144 C1
Shotteswell Rd B90 70 A4
Shoulderway La CV36 149 F1
Showell La CV7 47 D1
Shrewley Comm CV35 114 B6
Shrubberies The CV4 76 C2
Shrubland St CV31 110 A3
Shrubland Street
Com Prim Sch CV31 110 A3
Shuckburgh Cres
Bourton on D CV23 97 F1
Rugby CV22 100 B4
Shuckburgh Gr 3 CV32 106 A1
Shuckburgh Rd
Napton CV23 125 C8
Priors Marston CV23 125 E4
Shulman's Wlk CV2 62 B4
Shultern La CV4 76 B3
Shuna Croft CV2 63 D4
Shustoke CE Prim Sch
B46 25 D1
Shutford Rd
North Newington OX15 139 D2
Shutford OX15 139 B1
Shutt La B94 70 A1
Shuttington Rd B79 4 A3
Shuttle St CV6 62 A4
Shuttleworth Rd CV23 83 F3
Sibford Gower Rrim Sch
OX15 142 D8
Sibford Rd
Hook Norton OX15 142 D4
Shutford OX15 138 F2
Sibford Sch OX15 142 D8
Sibree Rd CV3 78 A2
Sibton Cl CV2 50 B1
Sidbury Gr B93 71 F2
Siddeley Ave Coventry CV3 62 A1
Kenilworth CV8 92 C2
Siddeley Way NN11 117 F2
Sidelands Rd CV37 144 B2
Sidenhill Cl B90 70 A4
Sidmouth Cl Coventry CV2 62 B4
Nuneaton CV11 29 F3
Sidney Rd CV22 100 B4
Sidney Stringer
Com Tech Coll CV1 151 C3
Signal Hayes Rd B76 13 D1
Signal Wlk B77 4 A1
Silica Rd B77 4 A1
Silksby St CV3 77 E4
Silver Birch Ave CV12 38 C1
Silver Birch Dr B47 69 D3
Silver Birch Gr CV31 109 F3
Silver Link Rd B77 4 A1
Silver St Coventry CV1 151 B3
Newton CV23 68 A1
Wroxton OX15 139 D4
Silver Trees Dr CV12 40 A2
Silver Wlk CV10 28 C2
Silverbirch Cl CV10 28 A4
Silverdale Cl CV2 50 A2
Silverstone Dr CV6 49 F3
Silverton Rd CV6 61 F4
Simmonds Way CV9 12 B1
Simmons Cl B78 8 A1
Simmons Ct CV35 146 B2
Simms La B47 69 D3
Simon Cl CV11 29 E1
Simon Rd B47 69 D4
Simon Stone St CV6 61 F4
Simpkins Cl CV33 107 E4
Simpson Rd CV36 149 F3
Sinclair Ave OX16 139 F4
Singer Cl CV6 62 A4
Singer Croft B36 22 C1
Sir Henry Parkes Prim Sch
CV4 76 B4
Sir Henry Parkes Rd CV5 76 B4
Sir John Moore CE Sch
DE12 3 F4
Sir Thomas White's Rd
CV5 60 C1
Sir William Lyons Rd CV4 76 B3
Sir Winston Churchill Pl
CV3 79 E4
Siskin Dr CV3 78 B2
Siskin Parkway E CV3 78 B1
Siskin Parkway W CV3 78 B1
Sitwell Ave CV23 115 D3
Sixteen Acres La B50 148 C1
Skelwith Rise CV11 30 A3
Sketchley Hall Gdns LE10 31 E3
Sketchley Hill Cty Prim Sch
LE10 31 F3
Sketchley La LE10 31 E3
Sketchley La Ind Est LE10 31 D3
Sketchley Manor La LE10 31 E3
Sketchley Mdws LE10 31 E3
Sketchley Meadows
Bsns Pk LE10 31 E2
Sketchley Old Village LE10 31 E3
Sketchley Rd LE10 31 F3
Skiddaw CV21 83 E4
Skidmore Ave B77 9 E3
Skilts Sch B98 112 B6
Skipton Gdns CV2 62 A3
Skipwith Cl CV23 64 B2
Skipworth Rd CV3 63 D1
Sky Blue Way CV1 61 F2
Skye Cl Birmingham B36 33 D3
Nuneaton CV10 28 C1
Slack's Ave CV9 18 B4
Slade Cl CV11 40 B4
Slade Gr B93 71 F3
Slade Hill CV35 114 F4
Slade La Sutton Coldfield
B75 7 D2
Tamworth B77 9 E2
Slade Mdw CV31 110 C3
Slade Rd CV21 83 E1
Slade The CV33 133 E6
Slateley Cres B90 70 C3
Slater Rd B93 71 F2
Sleath's Yd CV12 39 D2
Sledmere Cl CV2 50 A2
Sleets Yd CV12 39 D1
Slimbridge Cl Redditch
B97 102 C3
2 Solihull B90 71 D3
Slingates Rd CV37 145 D2
Slingsby B77 9 E4
Slingsby Cl CV11 29 F1
Slough The B97 103 D2
Slowley Hill CV7 26 A1
Small Brook Bsns Ctr
B50 148 C3
Small Ho OX15 142 D8
Small La B94 86 C3
Smalley Pl CV8 92 C2
Smarts La CV35 138 B6
Smarts Rd CV12 38 C1
Smeaton La CV23 64 C3
Smercote Cl CV12 38 B1
Smite Cl CV23 53 F2
Smith St Bedworth CV12 38 C1
Coventry CV6 61 F3
13 Royal Leamington Spa
CV31 109 F4
Warwick CV34 108 C4
Wood End CV9 10 B1
Smith's La CV37 121 B6
Smith's Way B49 143 E3
Smithford Way CV1 151 B3
Smiths La B93 71 F4
Smiths Way B46 23 D2
Smiths Wood Sch B36 33 D3
Smithy La Aston Flamville LE9 32 B4
Church Lawford CV23 81 E3
Tamworth B77 9 F4
Smithy Rd CV9 17 E3
Smockington La LE10 42 A4
Smorrall La CV12 38 B1
Smythe Gr CV34 104 C1
Snape Rd CV2 62 C3
Snarestone Rd DE12 3 F4
Sniterfield La CV37 121 C7
Snitterfield La CV37 114 C1
Snitterfield Prim Sch
CV37 121 B6
Snitterfield Rd CV37 120 E7
Snitterfield St CV35 121 F4
Snowdon Cl CV10 28 A2
Snowford Hill CV33 115 A5
Snows Drive Hill B90 70 B3
Snowshill Cl CV11 39 F4
Snuff La OX17 139 E8
Soar Way LE10 31 D4
Soden Cl CV3 78 B3
Soden's Ave CV8 79 D1
Solent Dr CV2 50 C1
Solihull Coll
Chelmsley Campus B37 33 E2
Solihull Parkway B37 44 C4
Solihull Rd B92 56 C3
Solway Cl CV31 110 B3
Somerby Dr B91 71 D4
Somerly Cl CV3 78 C4
Somers Pl 8 CV32 109 F4
Somers Rd Keresley CV7 49 D3
Meriden CV7 45 F1
Rugby CV22 82 B2
Somerset Dr CV10 28 C2
Somerset Rd CV1 61 E3
Somerton Dr B37 44 A4
Sommerville Rd CV2 62 B2
Soot La OX17 133 D2
Sopwith Croft B35 22 A1
Sorbus B77 4 A2
Sorrel B77 4 A3
Sorrel Cl CV4 75 F4
Sorrel Dr Kingsbury B78 15 E4
Rugby CV23 83 E4
Sorrell Rd CV10 39 E4
South Ave CV2 62 A1
South Car Park Rd B40 44 C2
South Cl NN11 117 E5
South Dr B46 33 F3
South End OX7 142 A2
South Green Dr CV37 144 B2
South Par CV33 123 F6
South Rd CV23 84 A3
South Ridge CV5 60 A2
South St Atherstone CV9 18 B4
Coventry CV1 61 F2
Rugby CV21 83 E2
South Terr CV31 110 A2
South View B78 15 E2
South View Rd
Long Lawford CV23 81 F2
Royal Leamington Spa CV32 106 B3
South Way B40 44 C2
Southam Cl CV4 75 F4
Southam Cres CV35 123 D2
Southam Dr CV33 147 D1
Southam Prim Sch CV33 147 D3
Southam Rd Cropredy OX17 134 A2
Dunchurch CV22 99 D1
Kineton CV35 132 B6
Ladbroke CV33 124 D6
Long Itchington CV23 115 D3
Mollington OX17 134 A2
Priors Marston CV23 125 E4
Southam CV33 124 B8
Ufton CV33 111 E2
Ufton CV33 115 A1
Southam Sch CV33 147 D3
Southam St CV35 132 B6
Southbank Rd Coventry CV6 60 C3
Kenilworth CV8 92 C2
Southbrook Rd CV22 83 D1
Southcott Way CV2 50 C1
Southern La CV37 145 D1
Southey Cl B91 71 D4
Southey Rd CV22 99 F4
Southfield Cl CV10 29 E3
Southfield Dr CV8 93 D3
Southfield Rd Hinckley LE10 31 F4
Rugby CV22 83 E1
Southam CV33 147 D1
Southfields Cl B46 34 A2
Southlands Atherstone CV9 18 C4
11 Royal Leamington Spa
CV31 110 A4
Southlea Ave CV31 109 F3
Southlea Cl CV31 109 F3
Southleigh Ave CV5 76 C4
Southlynn Gdns CV36 149 F3
Southmead Gdns B80 103 F2
Southport Cl CV3 78 A3
Southrop Rd OX15 142 D3
Southway CV31 110 A3
Sovereign Cl CV8 92 C1
Sovereign Rd CV5 61 D1
Sovereign Row CV1 61 D1
Sowe Valley Prim Sch CV3 78 B4
Spa View CV31 110 A2
Sparkbrook St CV1 61 F2
Sparrow Cock La B93 73 E1
Sparrowdale Specl Sch
CV9 11 E2
Sparta Cl CV21 83 D3
Spartan Cl CV34 109 F2
Speedway La CV8 79 F4
Speedwell Dr CV7 74 A3
Speedwell La CV9 11 D1
Speedwll Cl CV23 83 F4
Spencer Ave CV5 61 D1
Spencer Rd CV5 151 A1
Spencer St CV31 109 F4
Spencer Yd CV31 109 F4
Spencer's La CV7 58 C1
Spernal Ash B49 103 F1
Spernal La Great Alne B80 119 C7
Studley B80 112 A1
Spetchley Cl B97 102 B3
Sphinx Dr CV3 62 A1
Spicer Pl CV22 82 B1
Spiers Cl B93 72 A3
Spilsbury Cl CV32 105 F1
Spilsbury Croft B91 71 D4
Spindle St CV1 61 E3
Spindles The LE10 31 F3
Spinney Cl Arley CV7 36 C4
Binley Woods CV3 79 F4
Birchmoor B78 10 C4
Spinney Dr B90 70 B2
Spinney Hill
Braunston NN11 117 E5
Warwick CV34 105 D1
Spinney La CV10 28 B2
Spinney Rd LE10 31 E3
Spinney The Atherstone CV9 19 D4
Bishops Itchington CV33 124 B4
Coventry CV4 76 B2
Long Lawford CV23 82 A3
Royal Leamington Spa CV32 105 E1
Wythall B47 69 D2
Spire Bank CV33 147 D2
Spires The CV10 28 B2
Spon End CV1, CV5 61 D2
Spon Gate Prim Sch CV1 61 D2
Spon La CV9 11 F3
Spon St CV1 151 A3
Spring Cl 10 Coventry CV1 61 F2
Ettington CV37 131 A3
Spring Coppice Dr B93 72 A2
Spring Ct CV8 95 E3
Spring Hill Arley CV7 36 C4
Bubbenhall CV8 95 E3
Combrook CV35 131 F7
Spring Hill Rd CV10 28 B3
Spring La Combrook CV35 131 E6
Lapworth B94 88 B2
Radford Semele CV31 110 C3
Tanworth-in-A B94 88 A3
Spring Pool CV34 108 C4
Spring Rd Barnacle CV7 51 D3
Coventry CV6 49 F1
Spring St CV21 83 D2
Springbrook Cl B36 22 B1
Springbrook La B94 87 D4
Springfield OX17 139 F6
Springfield Cl CV36 149 F3
Springfield Cres
Bedworth CV12 39 D1
Sutton Coldfield B76 13 D2
Springfield Gr CV33 147 D3
Springfield House
Specl Sch B93 73 D3
Springfield Pl CV1 151 C4
Springfield Rd
Coventry CV1 151 C4
Hinckley LE10 31 E4
Nuneaton CV11 29 F1
Shipston-on-S CV36 149 F2
Sutton Coldfield B76 13 D2
Tamworth B77 9 E4
Springfields B46 33 F3
Springfields Rd B49 143 D3
Springhill CV10 28 A4
Springs Cres CV33 147 D3
Springside B98 103 E4
Springwell Rd 6 CV31 110 B3
Spruce B77 4 A2
Spruce Gr CV31 109 F3
Squadron Cl B35 22 B2
Square La CV7 37 D1
Square The Dunchurch CV22 99 E2
Ettington CV37 131 A3
Fazeley B78 9 D4
Kenilworth CV8 92 C2
Nuneaton CV11 29 F1
Stockton CV33 147 F4
Swalcliffe OX15 142 F8
Tysoe CV35 138 B7
Wolvey LE10 41 E2
Wootton Wawen B95 113 A3
Squire Pl CV33 133 D7
Squires Croft Coventry CV2 50 C1
Sutton Coldfield B76 13 D1
Squires Gate Wlk B35 22 A2
Squires Gn LE10 31 F3
Squires Rd CV23 96 C3
Squires Way CV4 76 B3
Squirrel Hollow B76 13 D1
Spring La CV8 93 D3
Stable Wlk CV11 29 F1

Stableford Cl B97 102 B4
Stacey Ct CV22 99 E3
Stadium Cl CV6 49 E1
Stafford Cl CV12 40 B1
Stafford St CV9 18 C4
Staines Cl CV11 29 F4
Stainforth Cl CV11 30 A1
Stainsby Croft B90 71 D3
Staircase La CV5 60 B4
Stamford Ave CV3 77 E3
Stamford Gdns CV32 105 F1
Stanbrook Rd B90 71 D3
Stand St CV34 108 B3
Standard Ave CV4 60 A1
Standedge B77 10 A4
Standish Cl CV2 62 C1
Standlake Mews 23 CV31 110 B3
Stanford Cl B97 102 A3
Stanier Ave CV1 61 D2
Stanley Ct CV31 110 B4
Stanley Rd Atherstone CV9 18 B4
Coventry CV5 76 C4
Nuneaton CV11 29 D3
Rugby CV21 83 F1
Stannells Cl CV37 129 E8
Stansfield Gr CV8 93 E2
Stanton Bridge Prim Sch CV6 61 F3
Stanton Rd 13 CV31 110 B3
Stanton Wlk CV34 104 B1
Stanway Rd CV5 77 D4
Stapenhall Rd B90 71 D3
Stapledon Gn CV33 132 F7
Staples Cl CV12 40 B2
Stapleton Cl Studley B80 103 E2
Sutton Coldfield B76 22 A3
Stapleton Dr B37 33 D2
Stapleton La CV13 21 F4
Stapleton Rd B80 103 E2
Star Cnr CV23 101 E1
Star Ind Pk CV2 62 C3
Star La CV35 114 A4
Starbold Cres B93 72 A3
Starbold Rd CV33 124 A4
Starcross Cl CV2 62 B4
Stare Gn CV4 76 B3
Stareton Cl CV4 76 C3
Starkey Croft B37 33 E1
Starley Pk CV7 50 A4
Starley Rd CV1 151 A2
Starley Way B37 44 B3
Starmer Pl CV35 114 D6
Startin Cl CV7 49 F4
Station App Dorridge B93 71 F1
Royal Leamington Spa CV31 109 F4
Station Ave Coventry CV4 75 E4
Warwick CV34 108 C4
Station Dr B94 69 E1
Station La B94 89 E2
Station Rd Alcester B49 143 D2
Arley CV7 36 B4
Balsall Common CV7 74 A4
Birmingham B37 44 A4
Bishops Itchington CV33 124 A4
Chipping Campden GL55 135 C2
Claverdon CV35 114 A3
Clifton u D CV23 83 F3
Coleshill B46 23 F1
Cropredy OX17 134 C1
Fenny Compton CV33 133 E7
Hampton in A B92 57 D4
Harvington WR11 127 D3
Hatton CV35 114 C5
Henley-in-A B95 113 A5
Higham-on-t-H CV13 20 C2
Hinckley LE10 31 E4
Hook Norton OX15 142 E4
Kenilworth CV8 92 C2
Knowle B93 72 A2
Lapworth B94 89 E2
Long Marston CV37 129 C2
Moreton-in-M GL56 140 A3
Polesworth B78 5 D1
Salford Priors WR11 127 F6
Shipston-on-S CV36 149 F3
Shustoke B46 24 B2
Stockton CV23 116 A3
Stoke Golding CV13 21 E4
Stratford-u-A CV37 144 C2
Studley B80 103 E2
Warwick CV34 108 C4
Wilmcote CV37 120 C5
Wythall B47 69 D2
Station Sq CV1 151 B1
Station St CV9 18 B4
Station St E CV6 61 F4
Station St W CV6 61 F4
Staunton Way B26 44 B2
Staunton Rd CV31 110 A3
Staveley Way CV21 83 E3
Staverton CE Prim Sch NN11 126 E8
Staverton Cl CV5 60 A2
Staverton Leys CV22 100 A4
Staverton Rd NN11 126 F8
Staverton Sports Ctr NN11 117 F1
Steele St CV22 82 C2
Steels La CV36 141 D7
Steeping Rd CV23 82 A3
Steeplefield Rd CV6 61 D3
Steeples The CV23 116 F5
Stefen Way NN11 126 F8
Stella Croft B37 33 E1
Stennels Cl CV6 60 C4
Stephen St CV21 82 C2
Stephens Rd B76 13 D2
Stephenson Cl
Daventry NN11 117 F2
Royal Leamington Spa CV32 105 E1
Tamworth B77 4 A1
Stephenson Dr B37 33 D1
Stephenson Rd
Bedworth CV7 50 B4
Hinckley LE10 30 C4
Stepney Rd CV2 62 A2
Steppes Piece B50 148 B3
Stepping Stones Rd CV5 60 C2
Sterling Way CV11 39 F4
Stevenage Wlk 2 CV2 63 D4
Stevenson Rd CV6 61 D4
Stewart Cl CV4 60 B1
Stewart St CV11 29 E2
Stidfall Gr CV31 110 B3
Stileman Cl CV37 129 D2
Stiper's Hill B78 5 D1
Stirling Ave CV32 106 A3
Stirling Cl CV3 78 C4
Stirling Ct OX16 139 F3
Stirling Rd B90 70 C4
Stivichall Croft CV3 77 D3
Stivichall Prim Sch CV3 77 D3
Stocking La OX15 138 E5
Stocking Mdw CV23 53 F2
Stockingford Fst & Mid Sch CV10 28 B2
Stocks La CV23 98 C2
Stockton Cl Birmingham B76 22 B3
Knowle B93 72 A2
Stockton Gr 1 CV32 106 A1
Stockton Prim Sch CV23 147 F4
Stockton Rd Coventry CV1 151 D4
Long Itchington CV23 115 E3
Stockwells GL56 140 A3
Stoke Gn CV3 62 A1
Stoke Heath Prim Sch CV2 62 A3
Stoke La LE10 21 F4
Stoke Park Sch & Com Coll CV2 62 A2
Stoke Prim Sch CV2 62 A2
Stoke Rd Fenny Drayton CV13 20 C4
Stoke Golding CV13 21 F3
Stoke Row CV2 62 A2
Stokesay Cl CV11 29 D2
Stone Ave B75 13 D3
Stone Bridge GL56 140 D7
Stone Cross B46 23 D2
Stone Ct OX7 142 A2
Stone Pits Mdw CV37 120 C5
Stonebow Ave B91 71 D4
Stonebridge Highway CV3 77 F2
Stonebridge Rd Coleshill B46 33 F3
Lighthorne Heath CV35 123 C3
Little Packington B46 45 D4
Long Itchington CV23 115 B4
Stonebridge Trad Est CV3 78 A2
Stonebrook Way CV6 49 F2
Stonebury Ave CV5 59 F2
Stonefield Cl CV2 63 D4
Stonehaven Dr CV3 77 E2
Stonehill Croft B90 70 C3
Stonehill Wlk B77 9 F3
Stonehills CV21 83 E4
Stonehouse Cl CV32 106 B3
Stonehouse La CV3 78 B2
Stoneleigh Ave CV8 93 D3
Stoneleigh Cl Hartshill CV10 19 D1
Redditch B98 102 C3
Stoneleigh CV8 94 B3
Stoneleigh Rd
Blackdown CV32 106 A4
Coventry CV4 76 C1
Kenilworth CV8 93 D3
Stoneleigh CV8 94 A2
Stonely Rd CV13 20 C2
Stonepits La B97 102 B2
Stoneton Cl CV33 147 E2
Stoneton Cres CV7 74 A3
Stoneway NN11 126 F5
Stoneway Gr 11 CV31 110 B3
Stonewell Cres CV11 40 A4
Stoney Ct CV3 79 D4
Stoney La CV35 114 C6
Stoney Rd Coventry CV1 151 B1
Nuneaton CV10, CV11 29 D3
Stoney Stanton Rd CV1, CV6 61 F3
Stoneydelph Inf Sch B77 4 A1
Stoneydelph Jun Sch B77 4 A1
Stoneymoor Dr B36 22 B1
Stoneywood Rd CV2 62 C4
Stonleigh Ave CV5 76 C4
Stonydelph La B77 10 A4
Stornoway Rd B35 22 A2
Storrage La B48 85 D2
Stour B77 10 A3
Stour Ct CV36 149 F3
Stour Valley Com Sch CV36 149 F3
Stour View CV36 137 A8
Stourton Cl B93 72 A4
Stow Rd GL56 140 A3
Stowe Dr CV33 147 D2
Stowe Pl CV4 59 E1
Strachey Ave CV32 105 F1
Straight Mile CV23 98 A2
Stratford Ave CV9 18 B4
Stratford Cty Prim Sch CV37 144 C1
Stratford Rd Alcester B49 143 E2
Bidford-on-A B50 128 D7
Stratford Rd continued
Dorridge B94 71 D2
Drayton OX15 139 F4
Hampton Lucy CV35 121 E4
Hampton Lucy CV35 121 F2
Henley-in-A B95 113 A3
Hockley Heath B94 88 B3
Ilmington CV36 136 B7
Lighthorne Heath CV35 123 D2
Loxley CV35 130 F8
Mickleton GL55 135 B7
Newbold-on-S CV37 130 E1
Shenington OX15 138 F7
Shipston-on-S CV36 149 F3
Solihull B90 70 B4
Temple Grafton B49 119 E3
Warwick CV34 108 B2
Wellesbourne CV35 146 A2
Wroxton OX15 139 C4
Stratford St Coventry CV2 62 A2
Nuneaton CV11 29 E2
Stratford-upon-Avon Coll CV37 144 C2
Stratford-upon-Avon Gram Sch For Girls CV37 144 B1
Stratford-upon-Avon High Sch CV37 144 C2
Stratford-upon-Avon Hospl CV37 144 C2
Stratford-upon-Avon Racecourse CV37 129 E8
Stratford-upon-Avon Sta CV37 144 C2
Strathearn Rd CV32 105 F1
Strathmore Ave CV1 61 F1
Strathmore Rd LE10 31 D4
Strawberry Fields CV7 46 A1
Strawberry Wlk CV2 50 B1
Streamside Cl CV5 60 A4
Stretton Ave CV3 78 B3
Stretton Cl LE10 31 E3
Stretton Cres CV31 110 A3
Stretton Ct Hinckley LE10 31 E2
Rugby CV21 83 E4
Stretton Rd Nuneaton CV10 29 D2
Solihull B90 70 A4
Wolston CV8 80 A1
Stroma Way CV10 28 C1
Strutt Rd LE10 32 A3
Stuart Cl CV34 108 B3
Stuart Ct CV6 62 A4
Stuart Gdns CV33 132 F7
Stubbs Cl CV12 39 D2
Stubbs Gr CV2 62 A3
Studland Ave CV21 83 F1
Studland Gn CV2 63 D2
Studley Cty Inf Sch B80 103 F2
Studley High Sch B80 103 F2
Studley Rd B98 103 D4
Sturley Cl CV8 93 D3
Sturminster Cl CV2 63 D2
Styles Cl CV31 110 A4
Styvechale Ave CV5 77 D4
Sudbury Cl CV32 106 B2
Sudeley B77 9 E4
Sudeley Cl B36 22 A1
Sudeley Rd CV10 39 E4
Suffolk Cl Bedworth CV12 39 D2
Coventry CV5 60 A2
Nuneaton CV10 28 C2
Suffolk St CV32 106 A1
Sugarswell La OX15 138 D7
Sulgrave Cl CV2 62 C4
Sullivan Rd CV6 62 A4
Sumburgh Croft B35 22 A2
Summer La B76 22 B3
Summerhouse Cl B97 102 A3
Summerton Rd CV31 110 A2
Sumner Cl CV35 114 F3
Sumner Rd B46 34 A3
Sun Rising Hill OX15 132 D1
Sun St CV21 83 E2
Sunbeam Cl B36 22 C1
Sunbury Rd CV3 78 B3
Suncliffe Dr CV8 93 D1
Sunderland Pl CV35 146 B1
Sundew St CV2 50 B1
Sundorne Cl CV5 60 A2
Sunningdale B77 4 B3
Sunningdale Ave
Coventry CV6 49 E1
Kenilworth CV8 93 D2
Sunningdale Cl CV11 30 A1
Sunnybank Ave CV3 78 A3
Sunnydale Cres LE10 31 D4
Sunnydale Rd LE10 30 C4
Sunnyhill LE10 31 F4
Sunnyhill S LE10 31 F3
Sunnyside B95 119 F7
Sunnyside Cl
Balsall Common CV7 74 B4
Coventry CV5 60 C2
Sunnyside La CV7 74 B4
Sunset Cl B78 11 D4
Sunshine Cl CV8 93 D1
Sunway Gr CV3 77 D3
Surrey Cl Hinckley LE10 31 F2
Nuneaton CV10 28 C2
Sussex Cl CV10 28 C2
Sussex Rd CV5 60 C2
Sutcliffe Ave CV37 130 D3
Sutcliffe Dr CV33 123 E6
Sutherland Ave CV5 60 A2
Sutherland Cl CV34 104 C1
Sutherland Dr CV12 39 D2
Sutton Ave CV5 59 F2
Sutton Cl NN11 134 F6
Sutton La OX15 137 E1
Sutton Rd B78 8 A4
Sutton Sq B76 22 C3
Sutton Stop CV6 50 A3
Swadling St CV31 109 F3
Swain Crofts CV31 110 A3
Swains Gn LE10 31 F3
Swalcliffe Sch OX15 142 F8
Swale Rd B76 13 D1
Swallow Ave B36 33 D4
Swallow Cl CV37 145 D3
Swallow Rd CV6 49 E1
Swallowdean Rd CV6 60 C4
Swallows' Mdw B90 70 B4
Swan Cl GL56 140 A3
Swan Ct CV37 145 D1
Swan La CV2 61 F2
Swan St Alcester B49 143 D2
Royal Leamington Spa CV32 106 A1
Warwick CV34 108 C3
Swan's Nest CV37 145 D1
Swanage Gn CV2 63 D2
Swancroft B95 113 A5
Swancroft Rd CV2 62 A3
Swanfold CV37 120 C5
Swans Cl CV37 120 C5
Swanswell St CV1 151 C4
Swanswood Gr 8 B37 33 E2
Swerford Rd OX15 142 D3
Swift Cl B36 33 D4
Swift Rd CV37 145 D3
Swift Valley Ind Est CV21 82 C4
Swift's Cnr CV3 77 F4
Swillington Rd CV6 61 D3
Swinburne Ave CV2 62 B1
Swinburne Cl CV10 28 A3
Swinburne Rd B97 102 B4
Swindale B77 10 A4
Swindale Croft CV3 78 C4
Swinford Gr B93 71 F2
Swinford Rd
Lutterworth LE17 68 C4
Shawell LE17 68 B3
Swinnerton Mid Sch CV11 29 E1
Swiss Lodge Dr B78 8 C4
Sycamore B77 9 F4
Sycamore Ave B78 11 D4
Sycamore Cl Hinckley LE10 31 F3
Sibford Gower OX15 142 D8
Stockton CV23 147 F4
Stratford-u-A CV37 144 C3
Wellesbourne CV35 146 C2
Sycamore Cres Arley CV7 37 D4
Birmingham B37 44 A4
Sycamore Dr B47 69 D3
Sycamore Gr Rugby CV21 83 D2
Southam CV33 147 D3
Warwick CV34 105 D1
Sycamore Rd Coventry CV2 50 A1
Kingsbury B78 15 E3
Nuneaton CV10 28 B3
Sycamores The CV12 38 C1
Sydenham Dr CV31 110 A3
Sydenham Ind Est CV31 110 A3
Sydenham Prim Sch CV31 110 B3
Sydnall Fields CV6 49 F2
Sydnall Rd CV6 49 F2
Sykesmoor B77 10 A4
Sylvan Dr CV3 76 C3
Synkere Cl CV7 49 D3
Sywell Leys CV22 99 F3

Table Oak La CV8 74 A1
Tachbrook Cl CV2 50 B1
Tachbrook Park Dr CV34 109 F3
Tachbrook Rd CV31 109 F2
Tachbrook St CV31 110 A3
Tackford Cl B36 22 B1
Tackford Rd CV6 62 A4
Tackley Cl B90 70 A4
Tailor's La CV37 129 D1
Tainters Hill CV8 93 D3
Talbot Cl OX16 139 F4
Talbot Rd CV37 145 D2
Talisman Cl CV8 92 C2
Talisman Sq CV8 92 C2
Talland Ave CV6 62 A3
Tallants Cl CV6 62 A4
Tallants Rd CV6 62 A4
Talton Cl B90 71 D3
Tamar Cl CV23 82 A3
Tamar Dr B76 22 A4
Tamar Rd Bulkington CV12 40 A1
Tamworth B77 10 A3
Tame Bank B78 15 E3
Tame Valley Bsns Ctr B77 9 F3
Tame Valley Ind Est B77 9 F4
Tame Way LE10 31 D4
Tameside Dr B35 22 A1
Tamworth Bsns Ctr B77 4 A2
Tamworth Bsns Pk B77 4 A2
Tamworth Rd Cliff B78 9 E1
Corley CV7 37 D1
Fillongley CV7 36 B3
Keresley CV6, CV7 48 B3
Kingsbury B78 15 E4
Polesworth B78 4 C1
Sutton Coldfield B75 7 D1
Tamworth B77 9 E4
Tamworth Rd (Dosthill) B77 9 E3
Tangmere Dr B35 22 A2
Tanhill B77 10 A4
Tankards Hill GL56 136 B1
Tanners Green La B47 69 D1
Tanners' La CV4, CV7 59 D1
Tannery Cl CV9 18 C4
Tansley Cl B93 71 F2
Tanwood Cl Redditch B97 102 A3
Solihull B91 71 D4
Tanworth La
Henley-in-A B95 113 A7
Redditch B98 112 B8
Solihull B90 70 B3
Tanworth-in-Arden CE Sch B94 87 D1
Tanyard Cl CV4 59 E1
Tapcon Way CV2 62 C3
Tappinger Gr CV8 93 E3
Tapster La B94 88 C1
Tarlington Rd CV6 60 C3
Tarn Cl CV12 39 D1
Tarquin Cl CV3 78 B4
Tarragon Cl CV2 50 B1
Tarrant B77 9 F4
Tarrant Wlk CV2 63 D3
Tatnall Gr CV34 108 C4
Tattle Bank CV33 147 D2
Taunton Way CV6 49 D1
Tavern La CV37 144 B1
Taverners La CV9 18 B4
Tavistock St CV32 105 F1
Tavistock Way CV11 29 F3
Tavistock Wlk CV2 62 B4
Tay Croft B37 33 E2
Tay Rd CV6 61 D3
Taylor Ave CV32 106 A1
Taylor Cl CV8 93 D3
Tea Gdn The CV12 49 F4
Teachers Cl CV6 61 D3
Teal Bsns Ctr LE10 30 B4
Teal Cl CV37 144 B3
Teal Rd B80 103 F2
Teasel Cl CV23 83 E4
Ted Pitts La CV5 48 A1
Teign B77 10 A3
Telegraph St CV36 149 F3
Telephone Rd CV3 62 B1
Telfer Rd CV6 61 D4
Telford Ave CV32 106 A3
Telford Cty Fst & Mid Sch CV32 106 B3
Telford Rd CV7 50 B4
Templar Ave CV4 60 A1
Templars' Fields CV4 76 A4
Templars Prim Sch CV4 60 A1
Templars The CV34 108 C3
Temple Ave CV7 73 F3
Temple End CV33 123 E6
Temple Gr CV34 108 B3
Temple Grafton CE Prim Sch B49 119 E1
Temple Hill LE10 41 F3
Temple La B93 73 D2
Temple Rd B93 72 A2
Temple St CV21 83 E1
Temple Way B46 23 F1
Templeton Cl B93 72 A2
Ten Acres B49 143 E2
Tenby Cl CV12 38 B1
Teneriffe Rd CV6 49 F1
Tenlons Rd CV10 28 C1
Tennant St CV11 29 F2
Tennyson Ave Rugby CV22 99 F4
Warwick CV34 108 B2
Tennyson Cl CV8 93 E2
Tennyson Rd Coventry CV2 62 B2
Redditch B97 102 B4
Stratford-u-A CV37 130 A8
Terrace Rd CV9 18 B4
Terrett Ct CV37 145 D1
Terry Ave CV32 105 E1
Terry Rd CV1 61 F1
Tewkesbury Dr CV12 39 E2
Thackeray Cl
Lower Quinton CV37 129 D2
Nuneaton CV10 28 A2
Rugby CV22 99 F4
Thackhall St CV2 61 F2
Thames Cl CV12 40 A2
Thames Rd NN11 117 F1
Thamley Rd CV6 61 D2
Thatchers Cl OX15 138 D3
Theatre St CV34 108 B4
Thebes Cl CV5 59 D4
Theddingworth Cl CV3 78 C4
Thickthorn Cl CV8 93 D1
Thickthorn Orchs CV8 93 D1
Thimble End Rd B76 13 D1
Thimbler Rd CV4 76 B4
Third Exhibition Ave B40 44 B2
Thirlestane Cl CV8 93 E3
Thirlmere CV21 83 E4
Thirlmere Ave CV11 29 F3
Thirlmere Cl CV4 59 F2
Thirlmere Rd Bedworth CV12 39 D1
Hinckley LE10 31 D4
Thirsk Rd CV3 77 E3
Thistle Way CV23 83 E4
Thistlewood Gr B93 90 A3
Thistley Field E CV6 61 D4
Thistley Field N CV6 61 D4
Thistley Field S CV6 60 C3
Thistley Field W CV6 60 C4
Thomas Jolyffe Cty Prim Sch CV37 145 D3
Thomas Landsdail St CV3 77 E4
Thomas Lane St CV6 50 A1
Thomas Naul Croft CV4 59 F2
Thomas Sharp St CV4 76 A4
Thomas St Bedworth CV12 39 D1
Royal Leamington Spa CV32 106 A1
Thomas Way CV23 82 A3
Thomas Wlk B35 22 A2
Thompson's Rd CV7 48 C3

Thomson Cl CV21 83 D3
Thorn Cl CV21 83 E3
Thorn Stile Cl CV32 106 C3
Thorn Way CV23 115 D4
Thornby Ave Kenilworth
CV8 93 D2
Tamworth B77 9 F4
Thorncliffe Cl B97 102 A3
Thorncliffe Way CV10 27 F4
Thorney Rd CV2 62 A3
Thornfield Ave CV13 21 F4
Thornfield Way LE10 31 F4
Thorngrove Ave 7 B91 71 E4
Thornhill Dr CV11 40 B4
Thornhill Rd CV1 61 E3
Thornley Cl CV31 110 C3
Thornley Gr B76 22 B3
Thorns Cty Fst Sch CV8 93 D2
Thornton Cl Coventry CV5 59 E2
Warwick CV34 104 C1
Thornton Rd B90 70 C3
Thorntons La CV23 125 C7
Thorntons Way CV10 28 A2
Thornycroft Rd LE10 31 F4
Thorpe Rd OX17 134 F1
Threadneedle St CV1 61 E3
Three Cocks La WR11 127 D1
Three Corner Cl B90 69 F4
Three Cornered Cl CV32 106 C3
Three Oaks Rd B47 69 D2
Three Pots Rd LE10 31 F2
Three Shires Jct CV6 49 F1
Three Spires Ave CV6 61 D3
Three Spires Ind Est CV6 50 A3
Three Spires Sch CV5 60 B3
Throckmorton Rd
Alcester B49 143 E2
Redditch B98 103 D4
Thurlestone Rd CV6 60 C4
Thurlow Cl CV9 12 B1
Thurne B77 9 F4
Thurnmill Rd CV23 82 B2
Thursfield Rd CV32 106 A2
Tibberton Cl B91 71 D4
Tibbetts Cl B49 143 E2
Tiber Cl CV5 59 F2
Tiber Way CV21 82 C4
Tiberius Cl B46 23 F1
Tidbury Cl B97 102 B3
Tidbury Green Jun &
Inf Sch B90 69 F2
Tiddington Cl B36 22 A1
Tiddington Rd CV37 145 E2
Tideswell Cl CV3 63 D1
Tidmarsh Cl CV7 74 A3
Tidmarsh Rd CV35 105 D4
Tidmington Cl CV35 114 F5
Tile Gr B37 33 D3
Tile Hill Coll of FE CV4 59 F1
Tile Hill La
Coventry, Allesley CV4, CV5 60 B1
Coventry, Tile Hill CV4 60 A1
Tile Hill Sta CV4 75 E4
Tile Hill Wood Sch CV4 59 E1
Tile Hurst Dr CV4 59 E1
Tilehouse Green La B93 71 F3
Tilehouse La B90 69 F3
Tilemans La CV36 149 F4
Tilesford Cl B90 71 D3
Tilewood Ave CV5 59 F2
Tilia Rd B77 4 A3
Tilton Rd LE10 31 F3
Timberlake Cl 10 B90 71 D3
Timothy Gr CV4 60 A1
Timothy's Bridge Rd CV37 144 B2
Timsa Rd CV35 132 E5
Tink-A-Tank CV34 108 C4
Tinkers Green Rd B77 9 F3
Tinkers La Earlswood B94 87 F4
Lapworth B94 88 C1
Mollington OX17 133 F2
Tintagel Cl CV3 78 B3
Tintagel Gr CV8 93 D2
Tintagel Way CV11 30 A3
Tintern Way CV12 39 E2
Tipper's Hill La CV7 36 C3
Tippett Cl CV11 40 A4
Tipping's Hill B97 102 B3
Tisdale Rise CV8 93 D3
Tite La OX15 142 D4
Tithe Barn Cl CV35 114 F4
Tithe Barn La B94 87 E3
Tithe Cl CV13 21 E3
Tithe Ct WR11 127 F2
Titheway WR11 127 F2
Tithings The OX15 142 F8
Tiverton Dr CV11 29 F3
Tiverton Gr CV2 62 B3
Tiverton Rd CV2 62 B3
Tiverton Sch CV6 60 B3
Tiveycourt Rd CV6 50 A2
Tocil Croft CV4 76 B2
Toft Hill CV23 99 D1
Tokchong Rd CV35 132 E5
Toler Rd CV11 29 D3
Toll Gate Cl CV37 144 A2
Toll Gate Rd CV33 147 D3
Tollard Cl CV2 62 C3
Tolson Ave B78 9 D4
Tolson Cl B77 9 E3
Tom Brown St CV21 83 E2
Tom Henderson Cl CV3 78 C4
Tom Hill B94 87 D2
Tom Ward Cl CV3 78 C4
Tomkinson Rd CV10 28 C2
Tomlinson Rd B36 22 B1
Tommy's Turn La OX15 137 E1
Tompson Cl NN11 117 E5
Toms Town La B80 103 F2
Tomson Ave CV6 61 D2
Tomwell Cl CV33 147 D3
Tonbridge Rd CV3 78 A3
Top Rd CV7 51 D4
Top St DE12 3 F4
Topcliffe Jun & Inf Sch
B35 22 A2
Topp's Dr CV12 38 C1
Topp's Heath CV12 38 C1
Torbay Rd CV5 60 B2
Torcastle Cl CV6 61 F4
Torcross Ave CV2 62 B3
Torpoint Cl CV2 62 B4
Torrance Rd CV21 82 C2
Torridge B77 10 A3
Torrington Ave CV4 75 F4
Torside B77 10 A4
Torwood Cl CV4 75 F3
Totnes Cl CV2 62 B4
Tove Ct CV23 82 A3
Towbury Cl B98 102 C3
Tower Cl Bidford-on-A B50 148 C3
Stratford-u-A CV37 145 D3
Tower Croft
Bidford-on-A B50 148 C3
Birmingham B37 33 D2
Tower Hill B50 148 C3
Tower Rd Bedworth CV12 39 D1
Rugby CV22 83 E1
Tower St Coventry CV1 151 B3
5 Royal Leamington Spa
CV31 110 A4
Tower View Cres CV10 28 A2
Towers Cl CV8 92 C1
Town Feilds Cl CV5 60 A4
Town Ground CV35 131 F5
Town Yd CV23 64 C2
Townesend Cl CV34 104 C1
Townhill OX15 133 A2
Townsend Cl B79 2 B2
Townsend Croft CV3 77 E4
Townsend Dr CV11 29 F2
Townsend La
Long Lawford CV23 82 A2
Upper Boddington NN11 134 E8
Townsend Rd Coventry CV3 77 E4
Rugby CV21 83 E2
Tiddington CV37 145 F2
Townsends Cl CV11 31 D1
Trafalgar Ct B50 148 B2
Trafford Cl CV9 12 B1
Trafford Dr CV10 28 B3
Traitor's Ford La OX15 142 B6
Trajan Hill B46 23 F1
Travellers Way B37 33 E2
Tredington Cl B98 103 D4
Tredington Rd CV5 59 F2
Treedale Cl CV4 75 E4
Trefoil B77 4 A3
Treforest Rd CV3 78 B4
Tregorrick Rd CV7 50 A4
Tregullan Rd CV7 50 A4
Trehern Cl B93 72 A3
Treherne Rd CV6 61 D4
Trelawney Rd CV7 50 A4
Tremelline Way CV7 36 C4
Trenance Rd CV7 50 A4
Trench La B49 143 F2
Treneere Rd CV7 50 A4
Trensale Ave CV6 60 C2
Trent Rd Bulkington CV12 40 A1
Hinckley LE10 31 D4
Nuneaton CV11 29 E3
Trent Wlk NN11 117 F1
Trentham Cl CV11 39 F4
Trentham Gdns CV8 93 E3
Trentham Rd Coventry CV1 61 F2
Hartshill CV10 19 D1
Tresillian Rd CV7 50 A4
Trevelyan Cl Claverdon
CV35 113 F3
Stratford-u-A CV37 144 B2
Trevelyan Cres CV37 144 B2
Treviscoe Cl CV7 50 A4
Trevor Cl CV4 75 E4
Trevor White Dr CV22 83 D1
Trevose Ave CV7 50 A4
Trewint Cl CV7 50 A4
Triangle The CV5 60 A2
Tribune Trad Est CV21 83 D3
Trident Bsns Pk CV11 29 E2
Trimpley Cl B93 71 F2
Trinity Cl Banbury OX16 139 F4
Stratford-u-A CV37 145 D1
Warton B79 5 F2
Trinity La CV1 151 B3
Trinity RC Sch The
Royal Leamington Spa CV32 105 E1
Warwick CV34 109 E3
Trinity Rd Kingsbury B78 15 F4
Wood End B78 10 A2
Trinity St Coventry CV1 151 B3
Royal Leamington Spa CV32 105 F1
Stratford-u-A CV37 145 D1
Trinity Vicarage Rd LE10 31 E4
Trinity Wlk CV11 29 F2
Triton Pk CV21 82 C4
Triumph Cl CV2 62 C2
Triumph Wlk B36 23 D1
Trojan Bsns Ctr CV34 109 F2
Troon B77 4 B2
Trossachs Rd CV5 59 F2
Troubridge Wlk CV22 82 B1
Troughton Cres CV6 61 D3
Troutbeck Ave CV32 105 E1
Troutbeck Rd CV5 59 F2
Troy Ind Est B96 103 D2
Troyes Cl CV3 77 F4
Trueman Cl CV34 108 C4
Truemans Heath La B47 69 E4
Truggist La CV7 74 C4
Truro Cl CV11 29 F3
Truro Wlk B37 33 D1
Trust Cotts B49 118 D8
Tryan Rd CV10 28 C2
Tuckwell Cl CV23 147 F4
Tudman Cl B76 22 A4
Tudor Ave CV5 59 F2
Tudor Cl CV7 74 A3
Tudor Cres CV9 12 B1
Tudor Ct Coventry CV7 49 F4
Warwick CV34 108 B3
Tudor La CV33 147 D2
Tudor Rd CV10 28 B3
Tuer The WR11 127 A6
Tulip Tree Ave CV8 93 D3
Tulip Wlk B37 44 B4
Tulliver Cl CV12 39 D2
Tulliver Rd CV10 29 E1
Tulliver St CV6 61 D3
Tunnel Rd CV10 27 E2
Turchill Dr B76 22 A4
Turlands Cl CV2 63 D4
Turnberry B77 4 B3
Turnberry Dr CV11 40 B4
Turner Cl Bedworth CV12 39 D2
Rugby CV21 101 D4
Warwick CV34 108 A2
Turner Rd CV5 60 B2
Turnhouse Rd B35 22 A2
Turnpike Dr B46 23 E1
Turpin Ct CV31 109 F3
Turton Way CV8 93 E2
Tutbury B77 9 E4
Tutbury Ave CV4 76 C3
Tutehill B77 10 A4
Tuttle Hill CV10 28 C3
Tuttle Hill Ind Est CV10 28 C4
Twenty One Oaks CV9 17 F3
Twycross La CV9 6 C3
Twycross Rd LE10 31 F3
Twycross Wlk CV34 104 B1
Twycross Zoo CV9 3 F1
Twyford Ctry Ctr WR11 127 C1
Tybalt Cl Coventry CV3 78 B3
Royal Leamington Spa CV34 109 E2
Tyler St CV37 145 D2
Tylers Gr B90 70 C3
Tylney Cl CV3 63 D1
Tyne Cl B37 33 E2
Tyne Rd NN11 126 F8
Tynemouth Cl CV2 50 B3
Tyntesfield Specl Sch
CV22 99 F4
Tynward Cl CV3 77 D3
Tysoe CE Prim Sch CV35 138 C7
Tysoe Cl B94 88 B3
Tysoe Croft CV3 78 C4
Tysoe Rd CV35 132 B4
Tythebarn La B90 69 F3
Tything Rd B49 143 E3

Ufton Croft CV5 60 A2
Ufton Fields CV33 123 F8
Ufton Hill CV33 111 F1
Ullapool Cl B97 102 B3
Ullenhall La B95 112 D6
Ullenhall Rd Knowle B93 72 A3
Ullenhall B95 112 E6
Ullenhall St B95 112 E6
Ullswater B77 10 A4
Ullswater Ave Nuneaton
CV11 29 F3
Royal Leamington Spa CV32 105 E1
Ullswater Rd Bedworth
CV12 39 D1
Coventry CV3 62 C1
Ulverscroft Rd CV3 77 E4
Ulverston CV21 83 E4
Umberslade Rd
Earlswood B94 87 E4
Tanworth-in-A B94 87 F2
Underhill Cl Coventry CV3 77 E2
Redditch B98 102 C3
Underpass The B40 44 C2
Underwood Cl B97 102 A4
Unicorn Ave CV5 59 F2
Unicorn La CV5 59 F2
Union Pl CV6 49 F2
Union Rd CV32 105 F1
Union St Rugby CV22 83 D1
Stratford-u-A CV37 145 D2
Univ of Warwick CV5 76 B2
Univ of Warwick
Science Pk CV4 76 A3
Univ of Warwick
(Westwood) CV4 76 A3
Upavon Cl B35 22 A2
Uplands CV2 62 A3
Upleadon Cl B97 102 A3
Upper Abbey St CV11 29 D3
Upper Crossgate Rd B98 103 E4
Upper Eastern Green La
CV5 59 F3
Upper Grove St 3 CV32 105 F1
Upper Hill St CV1 151 A3
Upper Holly Wlk CV32 106 A1
Upper Pk CV3 78 B3
Upper Ride CV3 78 B3
Upper Rosemary Hill CV8 92 C3
Upper Spon St CV1 61 D2
Upper Spring La CV8 92 C4
Upper Well St CV1 151 B3
Upper York St CV1 61 D1
Upperfield Way CV3 63 D1
Upton House OX15 138 E8
Upton La CV13 21 D4
Upton Rd CV22 82 B2
Utrillo Cl CV5 60 B2
Uxbridge Ave CV3 62 B1

Valanders La CV36 136 B6
Vale Cl CV21 101 D4
Vale The CV3 78 B4
Vale View CV10 28 C2
Valencia Croft B35 22 A2
Valentine Cl CV37 129 F8
Vallet Ave B49 143 D3
Valletta Way CV35 146 B1
Valley Cl B97 102 A3
Valley La Lapworth B94 89 F4
Tamworth B77 9 F4
Valley Rd Coventry CV2 62 A3
Earlswood B94 70 A1
Nuneaton CV10 27 F2
Radford Semele CV31 110 C2
Royal Leamington Spa CV32 106 B2
Valley The CV31 110 C2
Van Dyke Cl CV5 60 B2
Vanguard B77 9 E3
Vardon Dr CV3 77 E2
Vauxhall Cl 8 CV1 61 F2
Vauxhall Cres B36 22 C1
Vauxhall St CV1 61 F2
Vaynor Dr B97 102 B4
Vaynor Fst Sch The B97 102 B4
Veasey Cl CV11 29 F2
Vecqueray St CV1 61 F1
Ventnor Cl CV2 62 C2
Ventnor St CV10 29 E3
Venture Ct LE10 30 C4
Verden Ave CV34 108 A2
Verdon Cl CV35 122 B8
Verdun Cl CV31 110 A1
Vere Rd CV21 83 F1
Vermont Gr CV31 110 B3
Verney Cl
Butlers Marston CV35 131 F4
Lighthorne CV35 123 B2
Verney Dr CV37 144 C3
Verney Gdns CV37 144 C3
Verney Rd CV35 123 C3
Vernon Ave CV22 100 C4
Vernon Cl 9 Coventry CV1 61 F2
Royal Leamington Spa
CV32 105 F2
Vernons La CV10, CV11 28 C2
Verona Cl CV11 30 A1
Vesey Cl B46 23 D1
Vicarage Cl Atherstone CV9 18 C4
Dordon B78 10 C3
Vicarage Field CV34 109 D4
Vicarage Gdns OX17 134 C1
Vicarage Hill Badby NN11 126 F5
Clifton u D CV23 83 F3
Middleton B78 14 A4
Tanworth-in-A B94 86 C2
Vicarage La Coventry CV7 49 E4
Dunchurch CV22 99 E2
Harbury CV33 123 F6
Long Compton CV36 141 C3
Priors Marston CV23 125 F4
Warwick CV35 108 A1
Water Orton B46 23 D1
Vicarage Rd
Cheswick Green B94 70 B2
Dorridge B94 88 C4
Flecknoe CV23 117 B2
Napton CV23 125 C8
Royal Leamington Spa
CV32 106 A2
Rugby CV22 82 C2
Stoneleigh CV8 94 A3
Vicarage Rise 8 CV33 122 F8
Vicarage St CV11 29 E2
Victoria Ave CV21 82 C2
Victoria Bsns Ctr 10 CV31 110 A4
Victoria Dr B78 9 D4
Victoria Mews CV34 108 B4
Victoria Rd Atherstone CV9 18 C3
Bidford-on-A B50 148 B3
Hartshill CV10 28 A4
Hinckley LE10 31 F3
Royal Leamington Spa
CV31 109 F4
Victoria St Coventry CV1 151 D4
Nuneaton CV11 29 E2
Royal Leamington Spa
CV31 109 F4
Rugby CV21 82 C2
Warwick CV34 108 B4
Victoria Terr 11 CV31 109 F4
Victoria Way B50 148 B3
Victory Rd CV6 49 F1
Vilia Cl LE10 31 F2
Villa Cl CV12 40 B1
Villa Cres CV12 40 B1
Villa Rd CV6 61 D3
Village Hall Yd CV23 115 D4
Village Mews CV22 99 E4
Village St WR11 127 D4
Villiers Rd CV8 93 D3
Villiers St Coventry CV2 62 A2
Nuneaton CV11 29 D2
Royal Leamington Spa CV32 106 A1
Vincent Ave CV37 145 D2
Vincent St Coventry CV1 61 D1
Royal Leamington Spa
CV32 106 A1
Vine La CV34 108 C4
Vine St CV1 151 C3
Vinecote Rd CV6 49 F2
Vineyard The LE17 43 F3
Violet Cl Coventry CV2 50 B2
Rugby CV23 83 F4
Virginia Pl CV10 28 C2
Virginia Rd CV1 61 F2
Viscount Cl Birmingham
B35 22 A1
Royal Leamington Spa CV31 109 F3
Vittle Dr CV34 108 B4
Vogue Cl CV1 151 D3
Vulcan Way LE17 55 E4

Wackrill Dr CV32 106 B2
Wade Ave CV3 77 D3
Wade Gr CV34 104 C1
Wade La CV35 123 D2
Wadebridge Dr CV11 29 F3
Waggoner's La B78 7 F4
Waggoners Cl CV8 95 E3
Wagstaffe Cl CV33 123 E6
Wain Cl B49 143 E3
Wainbody Ave N CV3 77 D3
Wainbody Ave S CV3 76 C3
Wainbody Wood Sch CV5 76 B1
Wainrigg B77 10 A4
Wake Gr CV34 108 A3
Wakefield Cl Coventry CV3 78 C4
Hurley CV9 16 B2
Wakefield Gr B46 23 D2
Wakeford Rd CV10 18 A2
Wakehurst Cl CV11 39 F4
Wakelin Rd B90 70 A4
Walcot Gn B93 72 A1
Walcote Cl LE10 30 C4
Walford Gr CV34 104 C1
Walford Pl CV22 100 C4
Walkers Orch CV8 94 A3
Walkers Rd CV37 145 D3
Walkers Way Bedworth
CV12 38 C1
Coleshill B46 34 A3
Walkwood CE Mid Sch
B97 102 B4
Walkwood Cres B97 102 B3
Walkwood Rd B97 102 B3
Wall Ave B46 33 F3
Wall Hill Rd CV5, CV7 48 A2
Wallace Rd CV6 61 D4
Waller Cl CV35 104 C4
Waller St CV32 106 A1
Wallingford Ave CV11 29 F4
Wallsgrove Cl CV32 106 A2
Walmer Way B37 33 E2
Walmley Ash La B76 22 B3
Walmley Ash Rd B76 22 A4
Walmley Jun & Inf Schs
B76 22 A4
Walnut Cl Birmingham B37 33 D1
Braunston NN11 117 E5
Hartshill CV10 28 A4
Harvington WR11 127 D3
Nuneaton CV10 28 C3
Walnut Croft CV9 17 E4
Walnut Dr CV32 106 A2
Walnut Paddocks CV35 138 B6
Walnut St CV2 50 A1
Walnut Tree Cl CV8 93 D2
Walnut Way CV22 82 A1
Walsal End La B92 56 C2
Walsall St CV4 76 A4
Walsgrave CE Prim Sch
CV3 63 D3
Walsgrave Gdns 5 CV2 63 D4
Walsgrave Rd CV2 62 A2
Walsh La CV7 46 C1
Walsingham Dr CV10 39 D4
Walter Scott Rd CV12 39 E1
Waltham Cres CV10 28 A3
Walton Cl Coventry CV3 78 C4
Nuneaton CV11 40 A4
Walton Rd
Hampton Lucy CV35 121 F4
Wellesbourne CV35 146 C1
Walton W ay CV35 146 B1
Wandsbeck B77 9 F4
Wanley Rd CV3 77 E3
Wansfell Cl CV4 76 A4
Wantage Rd B46 23 F1
Wappenbury Cl CV2 50 B1
Wappenbury Rd CV2 50 B1
Wapping La B98 112 A7
Ward Gr CV34 109 E4
Warden Rd CV6 61 D3
Wardens Ave The CV5 60 A3
Wardens The CV8 93 E3
Wardour Dr B37 33 E1
Ware Orch CV23 101 E1
Ware Rd CV23 101 E1
Wareham Gn CV2 63 D3
Waring Way CV22 99 E2
Warings Green Rd B94 70 B1
Warkworth Cl OX16 139 F4
Warmington Cl CV3 78 C4
Warmington Gr CV34 108 A4
Warmington Rd B47 69 D3
Warmwell Cl CV2 62 C2
Warneford Pl GL56 140 A3
Warner Cl CV34 104 B1
Warner Row CV6 61 F4
Warren Cl CV32 106 A2
Warren Dr B93 72 A2
Warren Field CV8 79 D1
Warren Gn CV4 75 F4
Warren Rd CV22 83 E1
Warrington Cl B76 13 D1
Warton Cl CV8 93 E2

Warton La Austrey CV9 3 D1
Orton-on-t-H CV9 6 B2
Warton B79 5 F4
Warton Nethersole CE Fst Sch B79 5 F2
Warwick Ave CV5 77 D4
Warwick By-Pass
Warwick, Hampton Magna CV35 108 A3
Warwick, Heathcote CV34 109 D1
Warwick Castle CV34 108 C3
Warwick Cl B80 103 E2
Warwick Cres CV37 145 D2
Warwick Ct CV37 145 D2
Warwick Dr CV9 12 B1
Warwick Gdns CV10 28 C2
Warwick Gn CV12 40 B1
Warwick Highway
Redditch B98 102 C4
Redditch B80 112 A5
Warwick Hospl CV34 108 C4
Warwick La CV1 151 B2
Warwick Mus CV34 108 C4
Warwick New Rd CV32 109 E4
Warwick Pl
Royal Leamington Spa CV32 105 F1
Shipston-on-S CV36 149 F3
Southam CV33 147 D2
Warwick Rd
Chadwick End B93 90 A4
Coventry CV3 151 B1
Ettington CV37 131 A4
Hanwell OX17 139 F5
Henley-in-A B95 113 C4
Kenilworth CV8 93 D1
Kineton CV35 132 B6
Knowle B93 72 B2
Leek Wootton CV35 104 C4
Norton Lindsey CV35 114 C2
Sherbourne CV35 121 E7
Snitterfield CV37 121 C5
Southam CV33 147 D2
Stratford-u-A CV37 145 E3
Upper Boddington NN11 134 E8
Wellesbourne CV35 146 B2
Wolston CV8 80 A2
Warwick Row CV1 151 B2
Warwick Sch CV34 109 D3
Warwick St Coventry CV5 60 C1
Royal Leamington Spa CV32 105 F1
Southam CV33 147 D2
Warwick St Mary's RC Prim Sch CV34 108 C4
Warwick Sta CV34 108 C4
Warwick Tech Pk CV34 109 D3
Warwick Terr CV32 105 F1
Warwicks The CV35 114 F3
Warwickshire Coll CV32 109 E4
Warwickshire Coll of Ag CV11 29 F3
Warwickshire Mus CV34 108 C3
Warwickshire Nuffield Hospl The CV32 105 F3
Wasdale Cl CV32 105 E1
Washbourne Rd CV31 110 A1
Washbrook La CV5 48 A1
Washbrook Pl CV36 136 B6
Washford Dr B98 103 E4
Washford Ind Est B98 103 F4
Washford La B98 103 E4
Wasperton Cl 6 CV3 78 C4
Wasperton La CV35 122 C7
Waste La Baddesley Ensor CV9 11 F1
Balsall Common CV7 74 C3
Coventry CV6 48 C1
Watch Cl CV1 151 A3
Watchbury Cl B36 22 B1
Watchmaker Ct CV1 151 A2
Watcombe Rd CV2 62 C4
Water La CV35 131 E3
Water Orton La B76 22 C2
Water Orton Prim Sch B46 23 D1
Water Orton Rd B36 22 C1
Water Orton Sta B46 23 D2
Water Tower La CV8 92 C3
Watercall Ave CV3 77 E3
Waterdale B90 70 B3
Waterfall Cl CV7 46 B1
Waterfield Gdns CV31 110 B4
Waterfield Way LE10 31 E3
Watergall Cl CV33 147 E2
Waterloo Ave B37 33 D2
Waterloo Cl
Stratford-u-A CV37 130 B8
Wellesbourne CV35 146 B1
Waterloo Cres B50 148 C3
Waterloo Ct CV34 109 D4
Waterloo Dr CV37 145 E1
Waterloo Ind Est
Bidford-on-A B50 148 C3
Birmingham B37 33 D3
Waterloo Pk B50 148 C3
Waterloo Pl 5 CV32 105 F1
Waterloo Rd
Bidford-on-A B50 148 C3
Hinckley LE10 31 E4
Waterloo St 6 Coventry CV1 61 F2
Royal Leamington Spa CV31 110 A4
Waterman Rd CV6 61 F3
Watersbridge Gdns CV10 29 E1
Waterside Polesworth B78 5 D1
Stratford-u-A CV37 145 D1
Waterside Cl B24 22 A3
Waterside Ct CV31 110 A3
Watersmeet Gr CV2 62 A3
Watersmeet Rd CV2 62 A3
Waterson Croft B37 33 E2
Watery La
Cheswick Green B90 70 B2
Corley CV7 47 E3
Coventry CV6 49 D2
Hook Norton OX15 142 D4
Keresley CV7 48 C2
Knowle B93 72 C2
Portway B48 85 E4
Shipston-on-S CV36 149 F3
Shustoke B46 24 B1
Ullenhall B95 112 E6
Warwick CV35 108 A1
Wathen Rd
Royal Leamington Spa CV32 106 A1
Warwick CV34 108 C4
Watling Cl LE10 31 E2
Watling Cres CV23 68 B1
Watling Ct CV11 29 F2
Watling Dr LE10 31 E2
Watling Rd CV8 93 D3
Watling St Atherstone CV9 19 D4
Dordon B78 10 B3
Hinckley CV11, LE10 30 B4
Tamworth B77 9 E4
Watson Cl 3 CV34 104 C1
Watson Rd CV5 60 B1
Wattisham Sq B35 22 A2
Watton Gn B35 22 A2
Watton La B46 23 E1
Watts La CV21 101 D4
Watts Rd B80 103 F1
Waugh Cl B37 33 D1
Wavebeck Ct CV23 82 A3
Waveley Rd CV1 61 D2
Wavendon Cl CV2 50 C1
Waveney B77 9 F4
Waveney Cl LE10 31 D4
Waverley Ave CV11 29 F1
Waverley Rd Kenilworth CV8 93 D2
Royal Leamington Spa CV31 110 A3
Rugby CV21 84 A1
Waverley Sq CV11 29 F1
Waverton Ave B79 5 F2
Waverton Mews 24 CV31 110 B3
Wavytree Cl CV34 108 B4
Wawensmere Rd B95 113 A2
Wayside B37 44 A4
Weale Gr 7 CV34 104 C1
Weatheroak Rd B49 143 E2
Weaver Ave B76 13 D1
Weaver Dr CV21 82 B2
Weavers Cl CV36 149 F3
Weavers Hill B97 102 B2
Weavers Row OX15 139 A3
Weavers Wlk CV6 62 A4
Webb Dr CV21 83 E4
Webb Ellis Rd CV22 82 C1
Webb St CV10 28 B2
Webster Ave CV8 93 D3
Webster Steet CV6 61 F4
Webster Way B76 22 A4
Weddington Fst Sch CV10 29 E4
Weddington La CV10 20 A2
Weddington Rd CV10 29 E4
Weddington Terr CV10 29 E3
Wedgnock Gn CV34 108 B4
Wedgnock Ind Est CV34 104 B1
Wedgnock La CV34 104 B1
Wedon Cl CV4 75 F4
Weford Aviation Mus GL56 140 A3
Weigh Bridge Ct GL55 135 B2
Welbeck Ave LE10 31 E2
Welcombe Hills Ctry Pk CV37 145 D4
Welcombe Rd CV37 145 D2
Welcome St CV9 18 C4
Welford Cl B98 102 C3
Welford Pl CV6 61 E4
Welford Rd
Bidford-on-A B50 128 D6
Long Marston CV37 129 B4
Rugby CV21 83 E2
Tamworth B77 9 E3
Welford-on-Avon Cty Prim Sch CV37 129 A6
Welgarth Ave CV6 60 C3
Welham Croft B90 71 D3
Well Bank OX15 142 D4
Well Cl B97 102 C3
Well La Shenington OX15 138 F5
Staverton NN11 126 D8
Tanworth-in-A B94 87 D1
Well Spring Cl CV9 18 C4
Well St CV1 151 B3
Welland Cl
Long Lawford CV23 82 B3
Water Orton B46 23 D1
Welland Rd CV1 61 F1
Welland Way B76 22 A4
Wellesbourne CE Prim Sch CV35 146 C2
Wellesbourne Gr CV37 144 C1
Wellesbourne Rd
Alveston CV37 121 D3
Barford CV35 122 B7
Coventry CV5 60 A2
Lighthorne CV35 123 B2
Loxley CV35 130 F8
Wellington Cl CV35 146 B1
Wellington Parkway LE17 55 E3
Wellington Rd
Moreton-in-M GL56 140 B3
Royal Leamington Spa CV32 106 B1
Wellington St CV1 151 D4
Wells Cl CV10 27 F2
Wells St CV21 83 D2
Wells Wlk B37 33 D1
Welsh Cl CV34 104 C1
Welsh Rd Aston le W NN11 134 F6
Bascote CV33 115 B2
Coventry CV2 62 A2
Lower Boddington NN11 134 E7
Napton CV33 125 C5
Offchurch CV33 107 D1
Offchurch CV33 111 F4
Welsh Rd E CV33 147 E1
Welsh Rd W CV33 147 D3
Welton Cl B76 13 D1
Welton Pl CV22 100 B4
Welton Rd Braunston NN11 117 E5
Warwick CV34 104 B1
Wembrook Cl CV11 29 E1
Wendiburgh St CV4 76 A4
Wendover Rise CV5 60 B2
Wenlock Way CV10 28 A2
Wensum Cl LE10 31 D4
Wentworth Dr CV11 30 A1
Wentworth Rd
10 Royal Leamington Spa CV31 110 B3
Rugby CV22 82 C1
Wesley Rd CV21 101 D4
Wessenden B77 10 A4
Wessex Cl CV12 39 D2
Wessons Rd B50 148 C3
West Ave Bedworth CV12 39 E1
Coventry CV2 62 A1
West Cl LE10 31 E4
West End Cleeve Prior WR11 128 A4
Hornton OX15 139 B7
West Green Dr CV37 144 A2
West Leyes CV21 83 D2
West of St Laurence CV35 114 A8
West Orchards Sh Ctr CV1 151 B3
West Ridge CV5 60 A3
West Rock CV34 108 B4
West Side WR11 128 A2
West Side Bsns Ctr CV4 75 F4
West St Coventry CV1 61 F2
Long Lawford CV23 82 A2
Royal Leamington Spa CV31 110 A4
Shipston-on-S CV36 149 F3
Shutford OX15 139 A3
Stratford-u-A CV37 144 C1
Warwick CV34 108 B3
West View Rd
Royal Leamington Spa CV32 106 B3
Rugby CV22 82 C1
Westbourne Gr CV22 82 C1
Westbury Rd Coventry CV5 60 B3
Nuneaton CV10 28 B2
Westcliff Dr CV34 104 C1
Westcliffe Dr CV3 77 D3
Westcotes CV4 60 A1
Westerham Cl B93 71 F3
Western Dr LE17 43 F3
Western Hill Cl B96 102 C1
Western Rd CV37 144 C2
Western Road Ind Est CV37 144 C2
Westfield Cl Dorridge B93 71 F1
Nuneaton CV10 29 E3
Stratford-u-A CV37 144 C3
Westfield Cres CV35 146 B2
Westfield Cty Fst Sch CV22 82 C1
Westfield Cty Jun & Inf Schs LE10 31 D4
Westfield Rd Hinckley LE10 31 D4
Rugby CV22 82 C1
Southam CV33 147 D2
Westgate Cl CV34 108 B3
Westgate Cty Prim Sch CV34 108 B3
Westgate Rd CV21 83 F1
Westgrove Ave 6 B90 71 D3
Westham La CV35 122 A7
Westhill Rd Blackdown CV32 106 A3
Coventry CV6 60 C3
Westholme Rd B50 148 B3
Westlea Rd CV31 109 F3
Westleigh Ave CV5 76 C4
Westmead Ave B80 103 F2
Westminster Dr
Hinckley LE10 31 F2
Nuneaton CV10 28 A4
Westminster Rd CV1 151 A1
Westmorland Ave CV10 28 C2
Westmorland Rd CV2 62 C2
Weston Cl Dorridge B93 72 A1
Dunchurch CV22 99 E2
Royal Leamington Spa CV31 110 B3
Warwick CV34 108 C4
Weston Ct CV36 141 D3
Weston La Bubbenhall CV8 95 D2
Bulkington CV12 40 A2
Weston St CV1 151 C4
Westonbirt Cl CV8 93 E3
Westway CV21 83 D2
Westwood Bsns Pk CV4 75 F3
Westwood Cres CV9 18 B4
Westwood Heath Rd CV4 75 F3
Westwood Rd
Atherstone CV9 18 B4
Coventry CV5 61 D1
Rugby CV22 100 C4
Westwood Way CV4 76 A3
Wetherell Way CV21 83 E4
Wexford Rd CV2 50 B1
Weymouth Cl CV3 78 B3
Whaley's Croft CV6 61 D4
Wharf Ind Est The CV23 65 D4
Wharf La B94 88 B2
Wharf Rd Coventry CV6 61 F3
Stratford-u-A CV37 144 C2
Wharf St CV34 109 D4
Wharf The CV37 120 C5
Wharrage Rd B49 143 E2
Wharrington Cl B98 103 D4
Wharrington Hill B98 103 D4
Whatcote Rd CV35 137 F8
Whateley Hall Cl B93 72 B4
Whateley Hall Rd B93 72 A4
Whateley La B78 9 F2
Whateley's Dr CV8 93 D3
Wheat St CV11 29 E2
Wheatcroft Dr B37 33 E1
Wheate Croft CV4 59 F1
Wheaten Cl B37 33 E2
Wheatfield Cl B36 33 D4
Wheatfield Ct GL55 135 B6
Wheatfield Rd CV22 82 B1
Wheathill Cl CV32 105 F1
Wheatley Grange B46 33 F3
Wheatsheaf La B94 113 C8
Wheelbarrow La CV35 114 A3
Wheeler Cl B93 90 A4
Wheeley Moor Rd B37 33 D3
Wheelwright La CV6 49 E2
Wheelwright Lane Comb Sch CV7 49 E3
Wheler Rd CV3 78 A4
Whernside CV21 83 E4
Whetstone Dr CV21 83 F4
Whichcote Ave CV7 46 B1
Whiley Cl CV23 83 F3
Whitacre Rd Knowle B93 72 A4
Nuneaton CV11 29 F2
2 Royal Leamington Spa CV32 106 A1
Whitacre Rd Ind Est CV11 29 F2
Whitaker Rd CV5 60 B2
Whitburn Rd CV12 38 B1
Whitchurch Cl B98 102 C3
Whitchurch Way CV4 75 F4
White Beam Rd B37 44 B4
White Friars La CV1 151 C2
White Friars St CV1 151 C2
White Hart La CV33 111 F1
White Horse Hill CV37 121 B6
White House Hill B95 120 B7
White St CV1 151 C3
Whitebeam Cl CV4 59 E1
Whitefield Cl CV4 75 E3
Whitehall Cl CV10 19 D1
Whitehall Rd CV22 83 D1
Whitehead Dr Kenilworth CV8 93 E4
Minworth B76 22 B3
Whitehorn Dr CV32 106 A1
Whitehorse Cl CV6 50 A3
Whitehouse Cres CV10 28 B2
Whitehouse Rd B78 11 D3
Whitelaw Cres CV5 60 B3
Whitemoor Dr B90 71 D4
Whitemoor Hill Rd B96 118 D8
Whitemoor Rd CV8 93 D3
Whitemoors Cl CV13 21 F4
Whitemoors Rd CV13 21 F4
Whitepits La B48 85 F2
Whitepump La B95 112 E7
Whites Row CV8 93 D2
Whiteside Cl CV3 78 C4
Whiteslade Cl B93 72 A4
Whitestitch La CV7 46 B2
Whitestone Fst Sch CV11 40 A4
Whitestone Rd CV11 40 A4
Whiteway OX17 133 F2
Whitfield Cl CV37 145 F2
Whitford Dr B90 71 E4
Whiting B77 9 E4
Whitley Abbey Comp Sch CV3 77 F3
Whitley Abbey Prim Sch CV3 78 A3
Whitley Ct CV3 77 F4
Whitley Rd B95 113 B4
Whitley Village CV3 77 F4
Whitlock's End Halt B90 69 F4
Whitmore Park Prim Sch CV6 49 D1
Whitmore Park Rd CV6 49 E2
Whitmore Rd CV31 110 A2
Whitnash Cl CV7 74 A3
Whitnash Cty Comb Sch CV31 110 A2
Whitnash Gr CV2 62 B3
Whitnash Rd CV31 110 A2
Whittington Cl CV34 109 D4
Whittington La CV9 12 A1
Whittle Cl Coventry CV3 78 C4
Daventry NN11 117 F3
Rugby CV22 99 E4
Whittle Rd LE10 30 C4
Whittleford Gr B36 22 B1
Whittleford Rd CV10 28 B2
Whittons Cl OX15 142 D4
Whitwell Dr B90 71 D3
Whitworth Ave CV3 62 A1
Whitworth Cl CV35 146 B1
Whoberley Ave CV5 60 B1
Whoberley Hall Prim Sch CV5 60 B2
Wickham Cl CV6 48 C1
Wickham Rd B80 103 F2
Wiclif Way CV10 28 A2
Widdecombe Cl CV2 62 B4
Widdrington Rd CV1 61 E3
Widney Cl B93 71 F3
Widney La B91 71 D4
Widney Manor Rd B91 71 E4
Widney Manor Sta B91 71 E4
Widney Rd B93 71 F3
Wigford Rd B77 9 E3
Wiggins Hill Rd B76 22 C4
Wight Croft B36 33 D3
Wigston Hill CV9 17 E3
Wigston Rd Coventry CV2 50 C1
Rugby CV21 84 A1
Wike La B96 118 E8
Wilcox Cl CV33 124 A4
Wild Goose La B98 103 E4
Wildcroft Rd CV5 60 B2
Wildey Rd CV12 38 B1
Wildmoor Cl CV2 50 A2
Wilford Gr B76 22 A3
Wilkes Way B50 148 B3
Wilkins Cl CV35 122 A7
Wilkinson Way B46 25 D1
Willday Dr CV9 12 B1
Willenhall La CV3 78 C4
Willenhall Wood Prim Sch CV3 78 B3
Willes Rd CV31, CV32 110 A4
Willes Terr CV31 110 A4
Willett Gdns CV35 146 B2
William Arnold Cl CV2 62 A2
William Beesley Cres CV11 40 C3
William Bree Rd CV5 59 E3
William Bristow Rd CV3 77 F4
William Cl OX16 139 F4
William Groubb Cl CV3 78 B4
William Iliffe St LE10 31 D4
William McKee Cl CV3 78 C4
William Morris Cty Prim Sch OX16 139 F4
William St Bedworth CV12 39 E1
Nuneaton CV11 29 F2
Royal Leamington Spa CV32 110 A4
Rugby CV21 83 D2
William Tarver Cl CV34 109 D4
Williams Rd CV31 110 C2
Willington St CV11 29 D3
Willis Gr CV12 39 E2
Willoughby Ave CV8 92 C2
Willoughby Cl Alcester B49 143 D3
Coventry CV3 78 C4
Willoughby Pl CV22 100 B4
Willow Bank CV37 129 A7
Willow Bank Rd B93 71 F3
Willow Brook Rd CV8 80 A2
Willow Cl Alcester B49 143 D1
Bedworth CV12 39 D3
Hinckley LE10 31 F3
Kingsbury B78 15 E4
Nuneaton CV10 28 A4
Willow Ctyd CV2 62 B4
Willow Dr
Cheswick Green B90 70 B2
Wellesbourne CV35 146 C2
Willow End GL56 141 A1
Willow Gr CV4 60 A1
Willow Meer CV8 93 D3
Willow Park Ind Est CV13 21 E4
Willow Rd CV10 28 C3
Willow Sheets Mdw CV32 106 C3
Willow Tree Gdns CV21 101 D4
Willow Way B37 33 D1
Willowbank Rd LE10 31 E4
Willowdale LE10 31 D4
Willowfields Rd CV11 30 A1
Willowherb Cl 5 CV3 78 C4
Willows CE Prim Sch The CV37 144 C1
Willows Dr N CV37 144 C2
Willows The Atherstone CV9 12 C1
Bedworth CV12 38 C1
Hollywood B47 69 D3
Stratford-u-A CV37 144 C1
Wilmcote CE Prim Sch CV37 120 C4
Wilmcote Gn CV5 60 A2
Wilmcote La B95 120 A5
Wilmot Ave B46 33 F3
Wilnecote Gr CV31 110 A3
Wilnecote High Sch B77 9 F3
Wilnecote Jun Sch B77 9 F4
Wilnecote Sta B77 9 E4
Wilson Cl CV22 82 B1
Wilson Dr B75 13 D3
Wilson Gn CV3 62 C1
Wilson Gr CV8 93 E2
Wilson's La CV6 49 F3
Wilsons La CV7 50 A3
Wilsons Rd B93 72 B3
Wilton Rd CV7 74 A3
Wiltshire Cl Bedworth CV12 39 D2
Coventry CV5 60 A2
Wimborne Dr CV2 63 D2
Wimbourne Cl CV10 28 A3
Wimbourne Rd B76 13 D2
Wimpstone La CV37 130 B4
Winceby Pl CV4 59 E1
Winchat Cl CV3 62 C1
Winchcombe Rd B49 143 E2
Winchelsea Cl OX16 139 F5

Winchester Ave CV10 29 E4
Winchester Dr
Birmingham B37 33 D1
Hinckley LE10 32 A4
Winchester St CV1 61 F2
Wincott Cl CV37 145 E1
Windermere B77 10 A4
Windermere Ave
Coventry, Binley CV3 62 C1
Coventry, Upper Eastern Green CV5 59 F2
Nuneaton CV11 29 F3
Windermere Cl CV21 83 E4
Windermere Dr CV32 105 E1
Windmill Ave [2] B46 33 F4
Windmill Cl Kenilworth CV8 93 D3
Warton B79 5 F2
Windmill Dr B97 102 B3
Windmill Gdns NN11 126 E8
Windmill Hill
Bidford-on-A B50 128 E8
Royal Leamington Spa CV32 106 B3
Windmill Hill The CV5 60 A4
Windmill Ind Est CV5 59 F4
Windmill La Astley CV10 37 F3
Austrey CV9 3 D1
Balsall Common CV7 74 B2
Baxterley CV9 17 E3
Corley CV7 47 E3
Dorridge B94 89 D4
Dunchurch CV22 99 D2
Ladbroke CV33 124 E5
Staverton NN11 126 E8
Windmill Rd Atherstone CV9 12 B1
Bedworth CV7 50 A4
Coventry CV6 50 A2
Nuneaton CV10 28 B4
Royal Leamington Spa CV31 109 F3
Windmill Way
Southam CV33 147 D3
Tysoe CV35 138 B6
Windridge Cl CV3 78 B3
Windrush Cl B97 102 B3
Windrush Dr LE10 31 D4
Windrush Rd B47 69 D4
Windrush Way CV23 82 A3
Windsor Ct LE10 32 A3
Windsor Pl [7] CV32 105 F1
Windsor Rd B78 5 D2
Windsor St Coventry CV1 61 D1
Hinckley LE10 32 A3
Nuneaton CV11 29 D2
Royal Leamington Spa CV32 109 F4
Rugby CV21 83 E2
Stratford-u-A CV37 144 C2
Windward Way B36 33 D3
Windy Arbor Prim Sch B37 33 E1
Windy Arbour CV8 93 D2
Windyridge Rd B76 22 A3
Winfield Rd CV11 29 D3
Winfield St CV21 83 E2
Wingfield Rd B46 33 F3
Wingfield Way CV6 49 D1
Wingrave Cl CV5 60 A3
Winifred Ave CV5 61 D1
Winnallthorpe CV3 78 C3
Winsford Ave CV5 60 A2
Winsford Cl CV7 74 A3
Winsham Wlk CV3 77 E2
Winslow Cl Coventry CV5 60 A2
[4] Royal Leamington Spa CV32 105 E1
Winspear Cl CV7 46 A1
Winster Ave B93 71 F2
Winster Cl CV7 49 D4
Winston Ave CV2 62 B4
Winston Cl Coventry CV2 62 B4
Stratford-u-A CV37 144 B1
Winterton Rd CV12 40 B1
Winthorpe Dr B91 71 E4
Winton Gr B76 22 A3
Winwick Pl CV22 99 E4
Winyates Rd CV35 123 D2
Wise Gr Rugby CV21 83 F1
Warwick CV34 104 C1
Wise St CV31 109 F4
Wise Terr CV31 109 F4
Wishaw Cl B98 103 D4
Wishaw La Curdworth B76 23 D4
Middleton B78 14 B3
Minworth B76 22 C4
Wisley Gr CV8 93 E3
Wistaria Cl CV2 50 A1
Witham The NN11 117 F1
Witherley CE Prim Sch CV9 19 D4
Witherley Rd Atherstone CV9 18 C4
Witherley CV9 19 D3
Withington Gr B93 71 F2
Withum Cl B76 13 D1
Withy Hill Rd B75 13 D4
Withybrook La CV7 51 F3
Withybrook Rd
Bulkington CV12 40 B1
Solihull B90 70 A4
Withycombe Dr OX16 139 F3
Woburn Cl CV31 110 B3
Woburn Dr CV10 29 D1
Wolds End Cl GL55 135 B2
Wolds La LE10 41 F2
Wolfe Rd CV4 75 F4
Wolford Rd GL56 140 D6
Wolfstan Dr CV23 115 D4
Wolseley Cl B36 23 D1
Wolsey Rd CV22 99 E3
Wolsey St CV3 78 B3
Wolston Bsns Pk CV8 80 A2
Wolston La CV8 79 F1
Wolverton Prim Sch CV35 114 B2
Wolverton Rd
Birmingham, Marston Green B37 44 A4
Coventry CV5 60 A2
Norton Lindsey CV35 114 C2
Snitterfield CV37 121 B7
Wolvey CE Prim Sch LE10 41 E2
Wolvey Rd Bulkington CV12 40 C1
Hinckley LE10 31 F2
Wood Cl B46 33 F4
Wood Croft B47 69 D3
Wood End Fst Sch CV9 10 B1
Wood End Jun Sch CV2 50 B1
Wood End La Fillongley CV7 37 D2
Tanworth-in-A B94 86 C3
Wood End Sta B94 86 C2
Wood Hill Rise CV6 49 E1
Wood La Arley CV7 26 B1
Aston Cantlow B95 119 F5
Astwood Bank B96 118 C6
Birmingham, Marston Green B37 44 A4
Cherington CV36 141 D7
Earlswood B94 69 F1
Hampton in A B92 56 C1
Hartshill CV10 28 A4
Higham-on-t-H CV13 20 C2
Shilton CV7 51 E3
Wood St Bedworth CV12 39 D3
Nuneaton CV10 28 C2
Royal Leamington Spa CV32 110 A4
Rugby CV21 83 D2
Southam CV33 147 D2
Stratford-u-A CV37 145 D1
Wood End CV9 10 B1
Wood Terr B96 118 D8
Woodbank LE10 32 A4
Woodberrow La B97 102 B3
Woodberry Dr B76 13 D1
Woodbine St [1] CV32 109 F4
Woodbine Wlk B37 33 E1
Woodburn Cl CV5 60 A2
Woodbury Cl B97 102 A3
Woodby La LE17 55 F4
Woodchester Rd B93 71 F1
Woodclose Ave CV6 60 C3
Woodclose Rd B37 33 D2
Woodcock Cl B94 86 C2
Woodcot Park Dr CV37 120 B5
Woodcote Ave
Kenilworth CV8 92 B3
Nuneaton CV11 29 F4
Woodcote Dr Dorridge B93 72 A1
Leek Wootton CV35 104 C4
Woodcote La CV35 104 C4
Woodcote Rd
Royal Leamington Spa CV32 105 F2
Warwick CV34 108 C4
Woodcraft Cl CV4 60 A1
Woodend Croft CV4 75 F4
Woodfield Rd Coventry CV5 76 C4
Hinckley LE10 31 E3
Woodford Cl Ash Green CV7 49 E3
Nuneaton CV10 28 B2
Woodford La CV10 19 E2
Woodgate Rd LE10 32 A4
Woodgreen Cl B97 102 A4
Woodhall Cl CV11 30 A1
Woodhams Rd CV3 78 B2
Woodhouse Cl CV3 78 C4
Woodhouse High Sch B77 4 A2
Woodhouse La B77 4 A3
Woodhouse St CV34 108 B3
Woodington Fst Sch B75 13 D3
Woodington Rd B75 13 D3
Woodland Ave
Claybrooke Magna LE17 43 F3
Coventry CV5 76 C4
Hinckley LE10 32 A4
Woodland Rd Kenilworth CV8 93 D4
Tamworth B77 4 A2
Woodland Way B78 10 C4
Woodlands Ave B46 23 D1
Woodlands Cl B78 11 D3
Woodlands Inf Sch B90 70 A4
Woodlands Jun & Inf Sch B36 33 D3
Woodlands La
Bedworth CV12 38 C2
Solihull B90 70 A4
Woodlands Rd
Bedworth CV12 38 C2
Binley Woods CV3 79 E4
Stratford-u-A CV37 144 C3
Woodlands Sch The CV4 59 E2
Woodlands The
Hartshill CV10 28 A4
Staverton NN11 126 D8
Wood End CV9 10 B1
Woodlands Way B37 33 E2
Woodloes Ave N CV34 104 C1
Woodloes Ave S CV34 104 C1
Woodloes Fst Sch CV34 104 C1
Woodloes La CV34 104 C1
Woodloes Mid Sch CV34 104 C1
Woodloes Rd B90 70 A4
Woodman Ct CV37 144 C2
Woodpecker Gr B36 33 D4
Woodridge Ave CV5 60 A3
Woodrow Cres B93 72 A3
Woodrow Ctr B98 103 D4
Woodrow Dr B98 103 D3
Woodrow Fst Sch B98 103 D4
Woodrow N B98 103 D4
Woodrow S B98 103 D4
Woodrow Wlk B98 103 D4
Woodrush Dr B47 69 D3
Woodrush High Sch The B47 69 D3
Woodshires Rd CV6 49 F3
Woodsia Cl CV23 83 E4
Woodside Arley CV7 26 B1
Grendon CV9 11 E1
Woodside Ave N CV3 76 C3
Woodside Ave S CV3 76 C3
Woodside Bsns Pk CV21 83 D2
Woodside Cl CV9 10 B1
Woodside Cres B93 72 A2
Woodside Pk CV21 83 D3
Woodstock Cl LE10 32 A3
Woodstock Cres B93 71 F2
Woodstock Rd Coventry CV3 77 E4
Nuneaton CV11 29 F1
Woodston Gr B91 71 E4
Woodville Rd CV34 108 C4
Woodward Cl CV31 110 A1
Woodward Ct CV37 121 B6
Woodway CV35 114 F3
Woodway Ave CV35 114 F3
Woodway Cl CV2 62 C4
Woodway La
Claybrooke Parva LE17 43 E2
Coventry CV2 50 C1
Woodway Park Sch & Com Coll CV2 50 C1
Woodway Rd OX15 142 D8
Woodway Wlk CV2 62 C4
Woolaston Rd B98 103 E4
Woolgrove St CV6 50 A2
Wooll St CV21 83 D2
Woolpack Way CV9 18 B4
Woolwich Rd CV11 40 C3
Wootton Cl CV37 145 E1
Wootton Ct CV2 62 B4
Wootton Green La CV7 74 A4
Wootton La B92 57 F1
Wootton St CV12 39 E2
Wootton Wawen Jun & Inf Sch B95 113 A2
Wootton Wawen Sta B95 113 A2
Worcester Cl CV5 60 A4
Worcester Pl CV36 149 F3
Worcester Rd CV8 93 D2
Worcester St CV21 83 D2
Worcester Wlk B37 33 D1
Wordsworth Ave
Redditch B97 102 B4
Warwick CV34 108 B3
Wordsworth Dr CV8 93 E2
Wordsworth Rd
Bedworth CV12 39 E1
Coventry CV2 62 B2
Rugby CV22 99 F3
Workhouse La LE10 32 A2
Works Rd B26 44 A2
Worsdell Cl CV1 61 D2
Worsfold Cl CV5 60 A4
Worthy Down Wlk B35 22 A2
Wren Cl DE12 3 F4
Wren St CV2 61 F2
Wrenbury Dr CV6 50 A2
Wright Cl B78 15 E3
Wright St CV1 61 F2
Wrigsham St CV3 77 E4
Wroxall Abbey (Sch) CV35 90 C1
Wroxall CE Jun & Inf Sch CV35 90 C2
Wroxall Dr CV3 78 B3
Wroxton CE Prim Sch OX15 139 D4
Wroxton Coll OX15 139 D4
Wroxton Ct OX15 139 D4
Wyatt Rd B75 13 D3
Wyatts Ct CV12 39 D2
Wych Elm Dr CV31 109 F3
Wych-Elm Cl CV22 82 A1
Wychbold Cl B97 102 A3
Wychbury B76 13 D1
Wychwood Ave Coventry CV3 77 E2
Knowle B93 72 A4
Wychwood Cl [14] CV33 122 F8
Wychwood Dr B97 102 B3
Wycliffe Gr CV2 62 A3
Wycliffe Rd W CV2 62 B3
Wye Cl Bulkington CV12 40 A1
Hinckley LE10 31 D4
Royal Leamington Spa CV32 106 B2
Sutton Coldfield B76 22 A4
Wyke Rd CV2 62 B2
Wykeley Rd CV2 62 B2
Wyken Ave CV2 62 B3
Wyken Cl B93 71 F1
Wyken Croft CV2 62 B3
Wyken Croft Prim Sch CV2 62 C3
Wyken Grange Rd CV2 62 B3
Wyken Way CV2 62 A3
Wykham La OX15 139 F1
Wyld Ct CV5 60 A3
Wyley Rd CV6 61 D3
Wynbrook Gr B90 71 D3
Wyncote Cl CV8 93 D2
Wyndshiels B46 34 A3
Wynter Rd CV22 82 B2
Wyre La CV37 129 B3
Wythall Sta B47 69 E2
Wythburn Way CV21 83 E4
Wythwood Gr B47 69 E3
Wythwood Rd B47 69 E3
Wyver Cres CV2 62 B2
Wyvern Cl CV35 146 B1

Yardley Chase Rd CV35 132 D4
Yardley Cl CV34 104 C1
Yardley St CV1 61 F2
Yarmouth Gn CV4 75 F4
Yarn Cl B47 69 D3
Yarningale Cl B98 102 C3
Yarningale La CV35 113 E5
Yarningale Rd CV3 78 B3
Yarranton Cl CV37 144 C3
Yarrow Cl CV23 83 E4
Yates Ave CV21 82 C3
Yatesbury Ave B35 22 A2
Yelverton Rd CV6 61 E4
Yeomanry Cl [10] CV34 108 C4
Yew Cl CV3 62 B1
Yew Tree Cl B94 89 E2
Yew Tree Ct CV9 3 D1
Yew Tree Gdns B95 113 A4
Yew Tree Hill CV23 64 C2
Yew Tree La B94 113 D8
Yew Trees The B95 113 B4
Yew Wlk B37 33 D1
Yewdale Cres CV2 50 C1
Yews The CV12 38 C1
York Ave Atherstone CV9 12 C1
Bedworth CV12 39 E1
York Cl Coventry CV3 78 B3
Studley B80 103 E2
York Rd CV31 109 F4
York St Coventry CV1 61 D1
Nuneaton CV11 29 D2
Rugby CV21 82 C2
Yorkminster Dr B37 33 E2
Yorksand Rd B78 8 C4
Young Cl CV34 108 A3
Yule Rd CV2 62 B3
Yvonne Rd B97 102 B4

Zorrina Cl CV10 28 A3

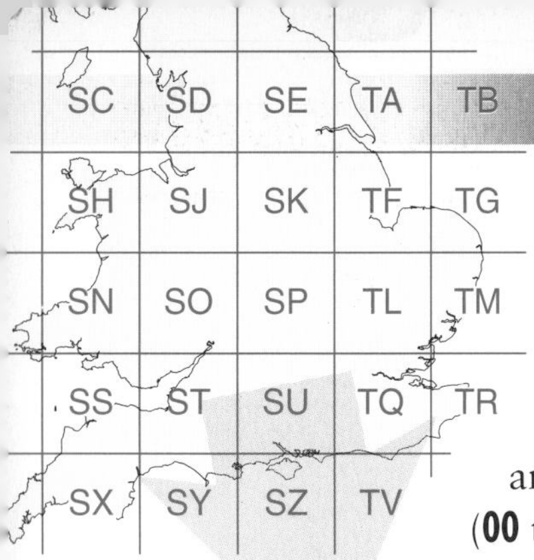

Any feature in this atlas can be given a unique reference to help you find the same feature on other Ordnance Survey maps of the area, or to help someone else locate you if they do not have a Street Atlas.

The grid squares in this atlas match the Ordnance Survey National Grid and are at 500 metre intervals. The small figures at the bottom and sides of every other grid line are the National Grid kilometre values (**00** to **99** km) and are repeated across the country every 100 km (see left).

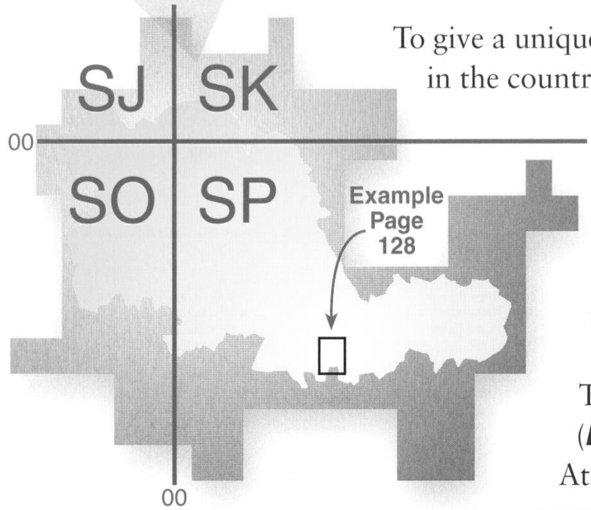

To give a unique National Grid reference you need to locate where in the country you are. The country is divided into 100 km squares with each square given a unique two-letter reference. The atlas in this example falls across the junction of four such squares. Start by working out on which two-letter square the page falls. The Key map and Administrative map are useful for this.

The bold letters and numbers between each grid line (**A** to **F**, **1** to **8**) are for use within a specific Street Atlas only, and when used with the page number, are a convenient way of referencing these grid squares.

Example *The railway bridge over DARLEY GREEN RD in grid square B1 on page 128*

Step 1: Identify the two-letter reference, in this case page 128 is in **SP**

Step 2: Identify the 1 km square in which the railway bridge falls. Use the figures in the southwest corner of this square: Eastings **17**, Northings **74**. This gives a unique reference: **SP 17 74**, accurate to 1 km.

Step 3: To give a more precise reference accurate to 100 m you need to estimate how many tenths along and how many tenths up this 1 km square the feature is (to help with this the 1 km square is divided into four 500 m squares). This makes the bridge about **8** tenths along and about **1** tenth up from the southwest corner.

This gives a unique reference: **SP 178 741**, accurate to 100 m.

Eastings (read from left to right along the bottom) come before Northings (read from bottom to top). If you have trouble remembering say to yourself "Along the hall, THEN up the stairs"!

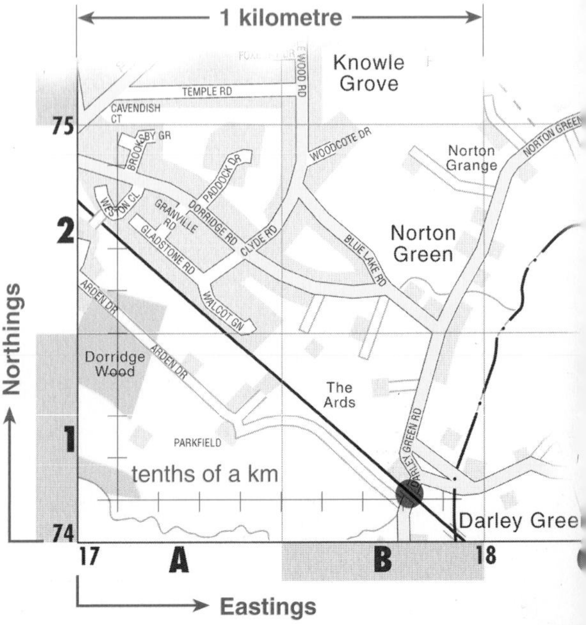

Name and Address	Telephone	Page	Grid Reference

Addresses

Name and Address	Telephone	Page	Grid Reference

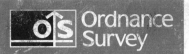

Ordnance Survey

STREET ATLASES ORDER FORM

PHILIP'S

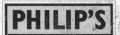

The Street Atlases are available from all good bookshops or by mail order direct from the publisher. Orders can be made in the following ways. **By phone** Ring our special Credit Card Hotline on **01933 443863** during office hours (9am to 5pm) or leave a message on the answering machine, quoting your full credit card number plus expiry date and your full name and address. **By post or fax** Fill out the order form below (you may photocopy it) and post it to: **Philip's Direct, 27 Sanders Road, Wellingborough, Northants NN8 4NL** or fax it to: **01933 443849**. Before placing an order by post, by fax or on the answering machine, please telephone to check availability and prices.

COLOUR LOCAL ATLASES

	PAPERBACK	
	Quantity @ £3.50 each	£ Total
CANNOCK, LICHFIELD, RUGELEY	☐ 0 540 07625 2	➤ ☐
DERBY AND BELPER	☐ 0 540 07608 2	➤ ☐
NORTHWICH, WINSFORD, MIDDLEWICH	☐ 0 540 07589 2	➤ ☐
PEAK DISTRICT TOWNS	☐ 0 540 07609 0	➤ ☐
STAFFORD, STONE, UTTOXETER	☐ 0 540 07626 0	➤ ☐
WARRINGTON, WIDNES, RUNCORN	☐ 0 540 07588 4	➤ ☐

COLOUR REGIONAL ATLASES

	HARDBACK	SPIRAL	POCKET	
	Quantity @ £10.99 each	Quantity @ £8.99 each	Quantity @ £5.99 each	£ Total
BERKSHIRE	☐ 0 540 06170 0	☐ 0 540 06172 7	☐ 0 540 06173 5	➤ ☐
	Quantity @ £10.99 each	Quantity @ £8.99 each	Quantity @ £4.99 each	£ Total
MERSEYSIDE	☐ 0 540 06480 7	☐ 0 540 06481 5	☐ 0 540 06482 3	➤ ☐
	Quantity @ £12.99 each	Quantity @ £9.99 each	Quantity @ £4.99 each	£ Total
DURHAM	☐ 0 540 06365 7	☐ 0 540 06366 5	☐ 0 540 06367 3	➤ ☐
HERTFORDSHIRE	☐ 0 540 06174 3	☐ 0 540 06175 1	☐ 0 540 06176 X	➤ ☐
EAST KENT	☐ 0 540 07483 7	☐ 0 540 07276 1	☐ 0 540 07287 7	➤ ☐
WEST KENT	☐ 0 540 07366 0	☐ 0 540 07367 9	☐ 0 540 07369 5	➤ ☐
EAST SUSSEX	☐ 0 540 07306 7	☐ 0 540 07307 5	☐ 0 540 07312 1	➤ ☐
WEST SUSSEX	☐ 0 540 07319 9	☐ 0 540 07323 7	☐ 0 540 07327 X	➤ ☐
SOUTH YORKSHIRE	☐ 0 540 06330 4	☐ 0 540 06331 2	☐ 0 540 06332 0	➤ ☐
SURREY	☐ 0 540 06435 1	☐ 0 540 06436 X	☐ 0 540 06438 6	➤ ☐
	Quantity @ £12.99 each	Quantity @ £9.99 each	Quantity @ £5.50 each	£ Total
GREATER MANCHESTER	☐ 0 540 06485 8	☐ 0 540 06486 6	☐ 0 540 06487 4	➤ ☐
TYNE AND WEAR	☐ 0 540 06370 3	☐ 0 540 06371 1	☐ 0 540 06372 X	➤ ☐
	Quantity @ £12.99 each	Quantity @ £9.99 each	Quantity @ £5.99 each	£ Total
BIRMINGHAM & WEST MIDLANDS	☐ 0 540 07603 1	☐ 0 540 07604 X	☐ 0 540 07605 8	➤ ☐
BUCKINGHAMSHIRE	☐ 0 540 07466 7	☐ 0 540 07467 5	☐ 0 540 07468 3	➤ ☐

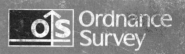

Ordnance Survey

STREET ATLASES ORDER FORM

COLOUR REGIONAL ATLASES

	HARDBACK	SPIRAL	POCKET	
	Quantity @ £12.99 each	Quantity @ £9.99 each	Quantity @ £5.99 each	£ Total
CHESHIRE	☐ 0 540 07507 8	☐ 0 540 07508 6	☐ 0 540 07509 4	➤ ☐
DERBYSHIRE	☐ 0 540 07531 0	☐ 0 540 07532 9	☐ 0 540 07533 7	➤ ☐
SOUTH HAMPSHIRE	☐ 0 540 07476 4	☐ 0 540 07477 2	☐ 0 540 07478 0	➤ ☐
NORTH HAMPSHIRE	☐ 0 540 07471 3	☐ 0 540 07472 1	☐ 0 540 07473 X	➤ ☐
OXFORDSHIRE	☐ 0 540 07512 4	☐ 0 540 07513 2	☐ 0 540 07514 0	➤ ☐
WARWICKSHIRE	☐ 0 540 07560 4	☐ 0 540 07561 2	☐ 0 540 07562 0	➤ ☐
WEST YORKSHIRE	☐ 0 540 06329 0	☐ 0 540 06327 4	☐ 0 540 06328 2	➤ ☐
	Quantity @ £14.99 each	Quantity @ £9.99 each	Quantity @ £5.99 each	£ Total
LANCASHIRE	☐ 0 540 06440 8	☐ 0 540 06441 6	☐ 0 540 06443 2	➤ ☐
STAFFORDSHIRE	☐ 0 540 07549 3	☐ 0 540 07550 7	☐ 0 540 07551 5	➤ ☐

BLACK AND WHITE REGIONAL ATLASES

	HARDBACK	SOFTBACK	POCKET	
	Quantity @ £11.99 each	Quantity @ £8.99 each	Quantity @ £3.99 each	£ Total
BRISTOL AND AVON	☐ 0 540 06140 9	☐ 0 540 06141 7	☐ 0 540 06142 5	➤ ☐
	Quantity @ £12.99 each	Quantity @ £9.99 each	Quantity @ £4.99 each	£ Total
CARDIFF, SWANSEA & GLAMORGAN	☐ 0 540 06186 7	☐ 0 540 06187 5	☐ 0 540 06207 3	➤ ☐
EDINBURGH & East Central Scotland	—	☐ 0 540 06181 6	☐ 0 540 06182 4	➤ ☐
EAST ESSEX	☐ 0 540 05848 3	☐ 0 540 05866 1	☐ 0 540 05850 5	➤ ☐
WEST ESSEX	☐ 0 540 05849 1	☐ 0 540 05867 X	☐ 0 540 05851 3	➤ ☐
NOTTINGHAMSHIRE	—	☐ 0 540 05859 9	☐ 0 540 05860 2	➤ ☐
	Quantity @ £12.99 each	Quantity @ £9.99 each	Quantity @ £5.99 each	£ Total
GLASGOW & West Central Scotland	☐ 0 540 06183 2	☐ 0 540 06184 0	☐ 0 540 06185 9	➤ ☐

Post to: Philip's Direct, 27 Sanders Road, Wellingborough, Northants NN8 4NL

- ◆ Free postage and packing
- ◆ All available titles will normally be dispatched within 5 working days of receipt of order but please allow up to 28 days for delivery

☐ Please tick this box if you do not wish your name to be used by other carefully selected organisations that may wish to send you information about other products and services

Registered Office: Michelin House, 81 Fulham Road, London SW3 6RB

Registered in England number: 3597451

I enclose a cheque / postal order, for a **total** of ☐

made payable to *Octopus Publishing Group Ltd*, or please debit my

☐ Access ☐ American Express ☐ Visa ☐ Diners

account by ☐

Account no ☐☐☐☐ ☐☐☐☐ ☐☐☐☐ ☐☐☐☐

Expiry date ☐☐ ☐☐

Signature...

Name...

Address...

....

....

....POSTCODE

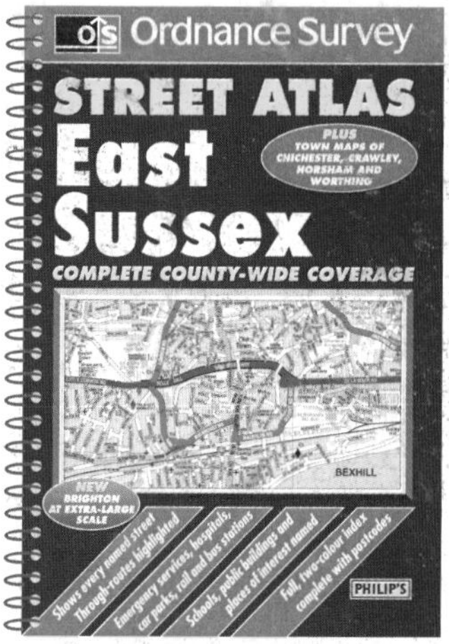

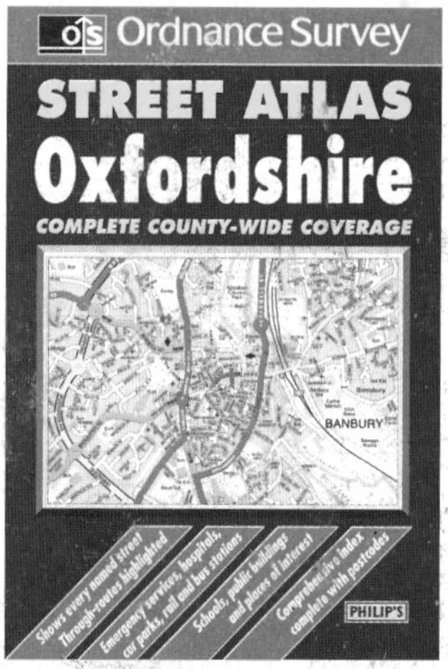

PHILIP'S

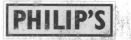